Public Vision, Private Lives

Public Vision, Private Lives

Rousseau, Religion, and 21st-Century Democracy

With a new essay by the author

MARK S. CLADIS

Columbia University Press
New York

Columbia University Press
Publishers Since 1893
New York, Chichester, West Sussex
Copyright © 2003 Mark S. Cladis
Preface, acknowledgments, and "Religion, Democracy, and Modernity: The Case
for Progressive Spiritual Democracy" copyright © 2007 Columbia University Press

Library of Congress Cataloging-in-Publication Data

Cladis, Mark Sydney.
Public vision, private lives : Rousseau, religion, and 21st-century democracy /
Mark S. Cladis ; With a new essay by the author.
p. cm.
Includes bibliographical references and index.
ISBN 0-231-13969-1 (pbk. : alk. paper)
1. Rousseau, Jean-Jacques, 1712–1778.   2. Democracy.   3. Privacy.   4. Public
interest.   5. Religion and politics.   I. Title.
JC179.R9C53 2007
322'.1–dc22   2006029195

Casebound editions of Columbia University Press books are printed on permanent
and durable acid-free paper.
Printed in the United States of America

p 10 9 8 7 6 5 4 3 2 1

In memory of two whom I called teacher, colleague, and friend, *Robert S. Michaelson (1919–2000)* and *Victor S. Preller (1931–2001)*

That our affections kill us not, nor dye.
                                              —Donne

Contents

Preface

I can tell you the conclusion to this book. The commitments, hopes, and loves of the public and private life often conflict, causing pain and loss. Yet we should resolve to maintain both of them despite potential friction and grief. It is better to cope with the inevitable conflict than to eliminate one for the sake of the other.

By beginning with the end I have not given too much away, as I might if this book were a mystery novel. Rather, like most journeys, the destination draws its meaning and significance from the process of arriving. And what is the journey? An exploration of the tension between our public and private lives—between our obligations to others and our care for ourselves—and the partial remedies that cope with that tension, bringing a measure of human happiness.

I wrote this book on 18th-century Rousseau to gain perspective on 21st-century America. Reflection on the nature of the public and private life in modernity is closely related to reflection on the nature of religion in modernity. And both these topics bear on salient issues confronting the United States today. The nature and place of the public and private in democratic life, the nature and place of religion in modernity—these twin themes mark the broad parameters of my questions in *Public Vision, Private Lives*.[1] Not coincidentally, they also mark salient questions of our age. This book is an attempt to understand better these fundamental questions. If we learn how to ask the central questions, we may learn how and where to look for some help in our efforts to move forward wisely and courageously.

In this Columbia University Press edition of *Public Vision, Private Lives* I have added the new and substantive introduction, "Religion, Democracy, and Modernity." Writing this new introduction gave me the opportunity to reflect on the fundamental issues that led me to write this book. Why Rousseau? Why religion? Why the public and private? I attempted to make explicit how the topics in this book contribute to our understanding of the relationship between religion, democracy, and modernity. This, in turn, led me to reflect on the place of religion in the American public and political landscape.

I don't remember when I first became interested in the relationship between public and private. About twenty years ago, as a young graduate student, I wrote a paper for Richard Rorty on Hegel's and Kierkegaard's depictions of the individual in society. The paper was, above all, long—it was a lengthy trek for me (and no doubt for Rorty as well). Writing this preface occasioned my going through boxes and finding the paper. With chagrin, I discovered that I am still wrestling with very much the same set of issues. Evidently, some journeys take much time—perhaps a lifetime.

My interest in things public and private led to the paper for Rorty. Before graduate school, I lived for some time in Angoon, Alaska, a town of about five hundred Tlingit Indians and the only settlement on Admiralty Island. There was much to love about Angoon, especially its natural beauty and kind people. It offered an unencumbered existence in which one could encounter the fundamentals of life: birth and death, food and shelter, society and solitude. The oscillation between public and private often matched the rhythmic cycles of summer and winter, low tide and high, fishing season and net-repairing season. I could tell stories of what might be called a Tlingit way of life: To listen is to participate, and to participate is to understand; life is shared, and an aspect of the shared life is the privilege and even duty to seek one's own vision. There was much diversity of opinion and vision, and even friction between contested views. However, this diversity was held within a shared framework—a common history, a mutual future, and joint commitments to community, children, and health. I was a young man when I lived in Angoon. I suspect my experience there placed me on a path to the writing of this book. Angoon, like Rousseau, made me think and wonder about life together, life alone, and the relationship between the two. And I began to ask whether we—those outside the Tlingit community—could do better.

I can go back still further. I was raised as a Greek American. My parents fed me on the daily Greek bread of community, tradition, and family. However, that bread was made from the bittersweet recipe so common among first-generation families. It included the direction, "Go out and make something of yourself." These words of love and hope are biting. To make something of one's self, one must leave home, exit the community, perhaps even forsake the tradition, and find one's own place of achievement. That individual achievement is not meant to be self-serving. On the contrary, however private or lonesome the manner of production, the achievement is expected somehow to contribute to a greater good. The relationship and conflict between individual aspiration, family, local community, and the larger common good marked my inner landscape at an early age.

Chekhov once said that it is in the beginnings and endings of stories that we are most tempted to lie. If I had written a different book, would I now be narrating a story about a different graduate paper, some other summer or childhood experience? But to pretend that I could have written a different book may be the greater deception. I chose some of my history, but mostly I found myself in it. And that history is shared. My personal circumstances shape how I see and experience the social webs on which I move. But I am not alone in those webs; they bear many. So although my life and work for some time now have been occupied with the subject of this book, this is not a personal or idiosyncratic book. The relationships between public and private and between religion and modernity are questions for our time. Community and privacy, the common good and individual rights, religion and modernity—these are more than textbook entries. These so-called polarities define much of our daily, moral life and often the conflict we encounter as we navigate that life. They represent clusters of palpable hopes and beliefs, institutions and practices that we esteem and sometimes distrust.

To offer an account of the relationship between public and private in modern democracies is not unlike attempting to portray the liberal, human condition.[2] The topic is fundamental, at least for democratic societies. While a democracy enables citizens to pursue private concerns, it also calls on citizens to think and act on behalf of the public good at both local and national levels. A democracy is not only a political arrangement; it is also a cultural achievement sustained by the distinctive beliefs and practices of its citizens. And citizens are not abstract, lifeless political actors. They are particular human beings with abiding hopes, pressing needs, painful fears, strong attachments, and deep-seated beliefs about how to achieve well-being. Duty to self and to others, love of things public and private often intertwine; sometimes they compete, sometimes one enhances the other. My goal is to explore how we conceive and experience the public and private life and to probe the complexities and ambiguities that cling to that very distinction. Central to this exploration is an account of the relationship between religion and modernity, as I argue in the new introduction to this Columbia University Press edition.

As we begin the 21st century, it is becoming urgent that we gain clarity on and appreciation of the things we call public and private. We will find it more difficult to solve such pressing social problems as poverty, racism, and environmental degradation if we fail to see ourselves as a public body with a shared history and future, and if we lack the private resources—such as courage, resolve, attentiveness, and discerning perspective—that enable us to morally engage one another. My fear is that our public and private lives are becoming increasingly impoverished. As our public life turns dispirited, impersonal, and bureaucratic, the private life becomes a self-absorbed shelter, promising—if not delivering—warmth, repose, and meaning. Like a pendulum, our lives swing between an extreme private domain and the other extreme, the domain of work, marketplace, and government. In their extreme forms, these domains are not likely to provide personal or public fulfillment, but rather loneliness and alienation, even in the company of others. The public and private depend on each other. One can enrich or, conversely, threaten the other.

The public and private are not fixed concepts but vary depending on time, place, and circumstance. When I drive through the low-income housing outside Baltimore and I see African Americans outside on their porches and steps, engaging in easy sociability with neighbors, talking, laughing, arguing, and even a few watching a television—planted there on the public sidewalk—I know that in this community, the public and private are not neatly separated. Recently I experienced something similar when traveling in rural Italy. Everywhere I saw the colorful sight of private laundry, displayed in public, hanging out to dry on lines that linked private home to private home. I also walked the Italian footpaths that crisscross countryside and village, the *strada pubblica* and *strada privata* that mingle and merge in such a way that one is seldom sure where the public road ends and the private one begins. And earlier in my life I used to walk the one dirt street of Angoon, the Tlingit Indian village I once called home. In the temperate months, household activities were conducted on that public, muddy street. Day care, that is, sixteen-year-olds looking after twelve-year-olds, twelve-year-olds watching eight-year-olds, and so on, took place in full view. So did cooking, skinning, sewing, reading, domestic quarreling, and much else. In the winter, however, all returned behind closed doors, as if the cold drew a line in the snow between public and private.

The main sight in the street in winter was the trace of snow walkers—footprints of children and a few adults leading to or from the school.

The public and private are understood and lived variously. Most of my friends and colleagues do not display in public their wet, clean laundry or watch television on the sidewalk. The boundaries between most middle-class American homes, and between public and private property, are clearly marked. Streets and sidewalks are for brisk travel, not leisurely conversation. Laundry is not in plain view, although a president's sex life could be. Different cultures, different classes, different notions of public and private. Even within one society, such as my own, the terrain of the public and private is large and diverse.

On our tour of this perplexing terrain, we cannot explore every region. This study is directed primarily at North Atlantic democracies and their largely middle-class populations. I suspect that the very distinction between public and private is especially located in middle- and upper-class quarters. But not exclusively so. The public–private distinction touches and shapes all our lives to some extent. To call it a middle-class invention would be to dismiss too much diverse human experience, too many varieties of hopes, fears, beliefs, and practices. In this study, although we must limit our exploration, we will still range widely, noting what we see, acknowledging what is puzzling, registering what seems to enhance or diminish our public and private lives.

When one is exploring such a large terrain, a travel companion is helpful. Jean-Jacques Rousseau, his thought and life, will be our companion. Although he has traveled this territory extensively, I would rather not call him our guide. Guides tend to take the shortest route to the destination, and their commentaries usually are accurate, systematic, and succinct. In contrast, Rousseau wanders, and his thought, though always illuminating, is rarely systematic and often wrong. To my mind, Rousseau simply does not have the authority of a guide. And yet, though not always being reliable, he makes me think and wonder and pay close attention to the way ahead—to the maze of footpaths that crisscross the uneven topography of our public and private lives. On this journey I have entered into a conversation with Rousseau, or have brought him into one with us, so as to understand better our institutions and convictions, our hopes and fears, about life alone and life together.

To that end, I have offered an account that reads something like a dramatic narrative, with myriad plots and subplots, leading the reader here and there on a rewarding but winding path—as opposed to providing a single, systematic argument that delivers the reader directly to a solitary, indubitable conclusion. Some may call this approach circuitous. I would prefer to say that, in good Wittgensteinian fashion, I explore my subject from a variety of perspectives, achieving a clarity that comes from learning to see from many angles. The winding path does entail more risk; the steps on the way are less certain. Yet good philosophy and scholarship, like life itself, often entail risk.

We will accompany Rousseau into the varied terrain of public and private and of religion and modernity. The tension between the hopes and desires of the individual and the requirements of a shared public life are at the heart, or the knot, of Rousseau's thought and life. He wrestled with the various conflicting claims that the public and private life issue: prerogatives and obligations to self, friends, family, vocation, civic life, and humanity. He wrestled with these and found ways to mitigate the tension between them. His challenge was to discover forms of life that sustain both a replete private and a robust public life. His ideal was the self-possessed, civic-minded individual whose fulfillment springs from commitment to the common good and enjoyment of personal independence. Working at the juncture of diverse French individualist and absolutist traditions, Rousseau forged a new vision: human happiness found not strictly in the private life (as Montaigne had held) or exclusively in the public life (as Montesquieu finally maintained) but in a complex combination of the two.

However, Rousseau did not perfectly unite the private and public, the individual and society. Ultimately, he understood that friction between genuine selfhood and social cooperation cannot be entirely effaced. In his characteristically unsystematic fashion, and in such texts as *The Social Contract, Emile, The New Eloise,* and *Reveries of the Solitary Walker,* Rousseau depicted aspects of this friction: self-assertion versus renunciation, private perfection versus public compromise, fidelity to a universal deity versus loyalty to a provincial civil religion, and private contentment versus public felicity. Rousseau recognized this tension and explored strategies to eliminate it, yet ultimately he refused to surrender the goods of either side of the conflict, preferring to keep them together, precariously. In the end, this refusal to evade the tension may be his greatest contribution to modern social thought. The determination to wrestle with such tension, without denying or eliminating it, is an indispensable lesson for citizens of democracies.

I wish I could say that Rousseau provided a way to reconcile harmoniously the public and private in democratic society. Still, he did illuminate this modern drama of the contingent yet inevitable storms that bluster as we attempt to find public and private meaning and contentment. Few writers have portrayed more poignantly the strain of loneliness in a hollow private life or the weight of alienation in a barren public life; few writers have depicted more movingly the peace and satisfaction of an ample private life or the sense of belonging and purpose of a lively public life.

In this study, I have listened closely to the religious pitch in Rousseau's voice. When attempting to portray the most characteristic aspects of the public and private, including their potential reconciliation and inevitable conflict, Rousseau reached for a religious vocabulary. Inward spiritual longing versus civil theology, inner wholeness versus social solidarity, private morality versus a common faith, the universal claims of humanity versus the particular claims of citizenship—these contrasting sets of goods are profoundly expressed by Rousseau's religious vocabulary, a vocabulary that illuminates the conflicting, legitimate claims of the public and private domains. The theological traditions with which Rousseau worked enabled him to articulate a model that supports commitment to both shared projects and private pursuits.

One could never mention religious themes while discussing such "secular" topics as the general will or individual rights, of course. The implicit religious dimensions usually can be described as something other than religious. Yet as a philosopher trained in the academic study of religion, I have learned that much can be gained by attending to the religious background and assumptions that are implicit in so-called secular discourse. By asking the neglected question, that is, the question that pertains to the religious heritage of secular philosophical debate and discourse, we are likely to hear something new. Moreover, Rousseau's explicit discussion of religion in its public and private manifestations help us as we consider the relationship between religion, democracy, and modernity.

Endeavoring to fashion a democratic republic in which the private life is supported and protected and the public life is inclusive, lively, and just is a worthy challenge. We will often fail. No golden mean, no perfect harmony will be achieved. Still, the endeavor is the way forward. Honoring both love of self and love of that which is larger than the self—these twin poles, with all the tension between them—marks Rousseau's work, his vision, his challenge. And this captures the challenge of democracy in the 21st century.

Immanuel Kant, a man of dynamic thought yet fixed routines, was so famously exact in his habits that the people of Königsberg are said to have set their clocks by his daily afternoon walk. One day the punctual philosopher was not seen. Fearing the worst, some peered in his window. Heart attack? Stroke? No. That morning Kant had received his copy of Rousseau's *Emile*, and he couldn't put it down. Try as I might, I, too, have not been able to put Rousseau down.

Acknowledgments

For this Columbia University Press paperback edition of *Public Vision, Private Lives*, I have the profound pleasure of offering additional acknowledgments. Wendy Lochner, senior executive editor at Columbia, greeted the idea of this new edition with much enthusiasm, and she ushered this book through each stage of production with expert skill, goodwill, and cheerfulness. The new, substantive introduction to the paperback edition—"Religion, Democracy, and Modernity: The Case for Progressive Spiritual Democracy"—was written at my new home institution, Brown University. At Brown, I am grateful for much. Colleagues in the Department of Religious Studies have welcomed me with warmth and provided much in the way of intellectual community. I am especially grateful to Matthew Bagger, John Reeder, and, in the Department of Philosophy, Bernard Reginster for their detailed comments on a draft of the new introduction. My students at Brown are bright, adventuresome, and good-hearted, and each day they remind me of the significance, responsibility, and joy of my vocation. I am especially grateful to the students in my graduate seminar, "The Emergence of Modern Liberal and Communitarian Thought," who helped me think through many of the themes in the new introduction.

My life has been surprised by joy in the past, but never so completely as by my wife, Mina Cladis. Smart, graceful, lovely, and supportive—these are her ways. If I wake eager each morning to greet and hold a piece of the day, it is because Mina will be there, in this day, in this life. And each day she reads and critiques what I write, and for this I am a better author.

We may write in private, but writing is never a private act. Influences abound from every conceivable direction. I don't pretend to know all the influences that informed this work, but I'm delighted to tell you the ones I know and appreciate.

There is a towering secondary literature on Rousseau, for which I am mostly grateful. I read it, learned from it, and have indicated specific debts in the notes. Four scholars in particular deserve mention here. Judith Shklar's political philosophy, moral psychology, and fierce commitment to liberal democracy challenged and inspired me, even when I was most likely to disagree. Nannerl Keohane's rich historical accounts of French political thought and moral theology in the 17th and 18th centuries helped me to grasp the significance of how much Rousseau's world was like and unlike our own. Bernard

Gagnebin and Marcel Raymond, the general editors of the Pléiade edition of Rousseau's complete works, have produced the single most important aid for students of Rousseau. I am deeply indebted to them.

Numerous friends, colleagues, and students have commented on one or more chapters: Arnold Eisen, John Ferejohn, Henry Levinson, Gordon (Mike) Michalson, Wayne Proudfoot, Mary Shanley, Jeffrey Stout, James Wetzel, and Diane Yeager; Darlene Despeignes, Lauri Friedman, Tara Knowland, Michelle Larsen, Sarabinh Levy-Brightman, Emily Lydgate, and Lauren Reber. A singular note of gratitude goes to Jeffrey Stout, an exceptionally supportive colleague and friend, who has taught me much about honorable work and working honorably. My colleagues in the Department of Religion at Vassar College are a community of scholars, bright and congenial, who have helped my work and often my life. Within that community, special thanks goes to Deborah Dash Moore, who read everything I sent her way and offered keen observations and much encouragement; and to Lawrence Mamiya, who taught me much about the sociology of religion and who introduced me to the Green Haven maximum security prison, where I learned about forms of public and private at their best and worst. For the original Oxford University Press cloth edition of this book (2003), I am grateful to Cynthia Read, a supportive editor, and to Cornelia B. Wright, a careful copyeditor. And for this new Columbia University Press edition, Carol Anne Peschke provided additional, skillful editing.

I have benefited from generous institutional support. Vassar College provided sabbatical support and research funds. A Fulbright Senior Research Award and a Summer Stipend from the National Endowment of the Humanities allowed me to spend the academic year 1992–93 in Paris, where I first conceived the main arguments of this book. During that time, I was a research fellow at the Centre de Recherche en Epistémologie Appliquée (CREA) of the École Polytechnique. I have profited greatly from the faculty at CREA, and especially from its director, Jean-Pierre Dupuy, whose collegiality and friendship have enriched my work. I have also benefited from conversations and meals with my Parisian colleagues Alain Caillé, Richard Clement, Lucien Scubla, and Laurent Thevenot. In the last ten years, I have spent much time in Paris, where I have been graciously housed by the Maison Suger, for which I thank its director, Jean-Luc Lory, of the Maison des Sciences de l'Homme. And I am grateful to all my colleagues at the CREA for providing me with an intellectual home in Paris. The able staff at the Bibliothéque d'Études Rousseauistes, just outside Paris in Montmorency, has been of great assistance, and for my privileges there I am grateful to its director, Robert Thiery.

In 1995, for the Hilary and Trinity terms, I was a fellow at Wolfson College, Oxford University, and a visiting scholar at the University's Institute of Social and Cultural Anthropology. The college and the institute provided many opportunities to test and refine my arguments. While in Oxford, I was also a member of the lively British Centre for Durkheimian Studies. I am particularly grateful to W.S.F. Pickering, Nick Allen, and Willie Watts Miller for their collegial support. In 1998, I was a fellow at the Rockefeller Foundation's Bellagio Study Center. The society and solitude of my residency at Bellagio endowed the chapter on the private life and provided me with a broad vista—physical and intellectual—from which to write the original introduction to this study.

Earlier drafts of portions of this book appeared as the following essays: "Redeeming Love: Rousseau and Eighteenth-Century Moral Philosophy," *Journal of Religious Ethics* 28 (2000): 221–51; "Lessons from the Garden: Rousseau's Solitaires and the Limits of Liberalism," *Interpretation* 24 (1997): 183–200; "What Can We Hope For? Rousseau and Durkheim on Human Nature," *Journal of the History of the Behavioral Sciences* 32 (1996): 456–72; "Rousseau's Soteriology: Deliverance at the Crossroads," *Religious Studies* (Cambridge University Press) 32 (1996): 79–91; "Tragedy and Theodicy: A Meditation on Rousseau and Moral Evil," *Journal of Religion* 75 (1995): 181–99. I am grateful to the editors and publishers for permission to include in this book revised versions of these articles.

Over the years I have received intellectual and moral sustenance from fellows of the Center for Speculative Inquiry, especially its director, Paul Kane. His thoughtfulness and friendship have graced my work and once saved my life. After many years of sharing lunch with Paul once a week, I continue to draw renewal from that deep well of friendship. I am also grateful to another fellow, Erin Edmison, who suggested the title of this study, *Public Vision, Private Lives*. The Walker family have taught me much about chickens, children, and community and have furnished a living model for how to integrate things public and private without conflating them. Jeff Walker has been a source of inspiration, wisdom, and joy for me and for many others. John and Jenny Cladis, bakers of that bittersweet Greek bread, continue to shine as models of excellence in the art of living—lives of generosity, grace, wisdom, and warmth. Above all, I am grateful for their steadfast love—for each other and for their children. Mina and I hold this same gratitude for her parents, Hae-Pung and Sang-Sun Kim, and we can only hope that our children will honor us as we seek to honor them.

I dedicate this book to the memory of Robert S. Michaelson and Victor S. Preller. Bob Michaelson was an exemplary teacher and human being, known for his discerning judgment, integrity, and gentle manner. In pioneering work, he retold American religious history in a way that includes perspectives of Native Americans, and he thereby taught us much about the privileges, dangers, and responsibilities of writing history. On Fridays for fifteen months, Vic Preller lovingly and brilliantly escorted me through the work of Wittgenstein. In the hands of Vic, Wittgenstein persuaded me that on a fundamental, epistemological, and moral level, we live not as discrete but as connected individuals.

Religion, Democracy, and Modernity: The Case for Progressive Spiritual Democracy

Looking Back to Look Forward

Thinking about the nature of the public and private life in modernity is closely related to thinking about the nature of religion in modernity. *Public, private, religion, modernity:* this book explores and wrestles with these broad and salient concepts. It invites the reader to reconsider the nature of modernity—its political, cultural, and legal forms—in relation to religion by reflecting on the birth of modernity. Jean-Jacques Rousseau, I argue, is probably the single most useful thinker to reflect on for this purpose. His vision and contradictions have become our own. His depiction of religion, in its public and private manifestations, and his depiction of individuals, in their public and private lives, have informed the moral and political terrain in which we find ourselves today. Recognizing this becomes especially significant and useful as we wrestle with what otherwise seem to be the most intractable issues of the day—issues pertaining to the relationship between religion, democracy, and modernity.[1]

"Preparing for the Journey," the original introduction to this book (which follows), is what you might expect from an introduction to a book on Rousseau, religion, and the public and private life. There I rehearse my main questions, topics, and interpretations of Rousseau; I give much attention to delineating the very categories *public* and *private*; and I describe my approaches or methods in this study. In contrast, "Religion, Democracy, and Modernity," this new introduction to the Columbia paperback edition, is a reflection on the fundamental issues that led me to write this book. I have attempted to make explicit how the topics in this book contribute to our understanding of the relationship between religion, democracy, and modernity. And this task has led me to consider further the place of religion in the American public and political landscape. I challenge the manner in which Rousseau, Rawls, and Rorty, each in his own way, attempt to render religion safe in democracies by relegating religious belief to the private sphere. To this end, I later propose four models to help us think about religion in the public and political landscape, and I champion one of them: "Public Landscape as Varied Topography."

Within this model operates what I call spiritual democracy: a dynamic, lively, culturally specific and culturally contested, progressive democracy. Spiritual democracy is embodied democracy, embodied because it refers not only to a society's legal codes and principles but also to its democratic culture and symbols, its daily practices and institutions. I call it spiritual because of its broad scope, encompassing the nation's character and institutions, the peoples' diverse identities, and a distinctively democratic exchange between the two—between the nation's public vision and the citizens' complex, private lives. *Public Vision, Private Lives*—a title of a book, a democratic equation, and a challenge at the heart of spiritual democracy. Rousseau helps me articulate this challenge, offering lessons both positive and negative.

As you read this introduction, you may find helpful the following map of my central argument. I refer to two types or forms of religion that are found in the United States and elsewhere. First, there is what I call a civil public religion or a common faith. This Rousseauean (and Durkheimian) concept of religion pertains to clusters of beliefs, practices, and symbols that contribute to a shared moral perspective. Rousseau, I argue, endeavored to articulate and promote a distinctively democratic, embodied common faith. What I call American spiritual democracy is a specific instance of this embodied, common faith. The second form of religion that I use is historical religions. This refers to what most people usually associate with the notion of religion, namely such religions as Hinduism, Buddhism, Judaism, Christianity, Islam, Gaia, or Wicca. These specific religious traditions, along with civil public religion, are invoked when I provide four models of the place of religion in American public life. One of these models, "Public Landscape as Varied Topography," maintains that all voices, including religious ones, should be welcomed in political and public deliberation. And it is under this model, I argue, that American spiritual democracy is most at home. Throughout my argument it is important to note that I do not hold civil public religion and historical religion to be necessarily mutually exclusive. Part of my task is to narrate the tangled ways in which their relationship to one another is complex and varied.

Spiritual democracy, I should make clear, is a distinctively progressive political stance, and I proselytize for it. "Public Landscape as Varied Topography," in contrast, is a normative, legal model that includes both progressive and conservative perspectives. Spiritual democracy, as I describe it, acknowledges the legitimate inclusiveness of this model and is happy to work within it.

Religion, Identity, and Progressive Democracy

It would be naive, and probably dangerous, to fail to attend to the religious aspects of life together and life alone. The manner and language of religion—so familiar in society, so alien in the academy—are gaining critical consideration. Scholars in the social sciences and in political and legal theory are turning their attention to the relationship between religion, law, and politics. If our attention was once diverted from this triad, it was in part because of what are now largely discredited theories about the inevitable march of secularization. There was an assumption that the world would increasingly abandon religion, that the actual state of the world would come to match an ideal of the European Enlightenment, namely an enlightened age free of strife, free of religion.

The assumption was doubly flawed. First, it was based on an erroneous interpretation of the Enlightenment as a monolithic force that discounted religion (e.g., as opposed to the Enlightenment itself having religious origins and objectives). And second, it was based on the view that modernity would necessarily usher in secularism, that is, an age in which religion had no significant standing. Yet sociologists and religious studies scholars, among others, have come to realize that religion as an intellectual, cultural, and political force is not waning on the globe. Today, this realization should be clear to anyone even vaguely familiar with current events. Among the majority of the planet's inhabitants, including those in North America, religion is thriving.[2]

In order to reassess the present state of affairs, we ought to spend some time reflecting on the past. It is difficult to know where we stand without some distance to provide helpful perspective. By looking back to our past, we gain a place to stand in order to look forward to the present. More specifically, in order to reconsider the nature of modernity in relation to religion, we should turn to the birth of modernity. With this end in mind, looking back at Jean-Jacques Rousseau is especially useful.

This act of looking back is not a naive gaze, an unfocused look of curiosity to see what we may happen to find. It is more intentional than that. It is an act of focused, deliberate observation that is attentive to the very questions, issues, and assumptions that shape the interpretive lenses we use—that we inevitably must use. So we look back to better understand where we stand, yet this very act of looking back implies that we already have some sense of our present location. Otherwise, we would not have any idea how to look back—where to look, what to look for, or even that we are looking. Approaching the past, then, entails some orientation in the present, yet orientation in the present entails some familiarity with the past. This dialectical dance between past and present, between the far away and the close to home, marks the pages in the following narrative, an account of the bearing Rousseau's thought has on our lives, especially as we consider the public and private in relation to religion.

Rousseau understood that religion, of some form, would persist. His challenge was to formulate a model of the state that articulated and promoted the rights and dignity of the individual within a moral idiom of social traditions and commitment to a common good. In order to accomplish this profound challenge, he reached for a religious vocabulary to express the deepest aspects of the public life, the private life, and the potential harmony and conflict between the two. He was one of the first to recognize what may seem like a contradiction: A democratic nation that supports human rights requires some form of common faith, and by "common faith" I mean common beliefs and practices that contribute to a shared—even if limited—moral perspective. In the parlance of contemporary political theory, Rousseau attempted to formulate a progressive communitarian defense of liberalism.[3]

This defense does not envision liberalism as a strictly political system based on procedural justice. Procedural justice—that is, the protection of individuals from unjust harm by means of the rule of law—captures but one aspect of Rousseau's social contract. Indeed, the social contract both depends on and creates a morally robust, liberal form of life that embodies distinctive notions of human flourishing. How else are we to make sense, for example, of Rousseau's attempts to inculcate tolerance as a liberal *virtue*—as a *dogma* of civil religion?

I understand that the very idea of a civil religion or common faith gives us pause today, and for good reason. We imagine a muscular state attempting to create a fiercely nationalistic solidarity by means of civic symbols, myths, and creeds. Rousseau, too,

shared this fear, at least most of the time. There was an occasion, the case of the relatively defenseless Poland attempting to survive its bellicose neighbors, when Rousseau
advocated the development of precisely the kind of nationalistic, civil religion that alarms
us. In the case of Poland, it was meant to ensure the identity and survival of its citizens,
even should they experience invasion and loss of home land.[4] Barring this extreme case,
Rousseau usually feared and opposed civil religion as a means to achieve intensely nationalistic aims. In his view, such a fervent public religion threatens to submerge the
private entirely into public, attempting to cast the individual's soul into the collective
soul of the *corps politique*, the political body.

Rousseau's hope in what I am calling a common faith sought the opposite outcome:
the furthering not of a totalitarian regime but rather of a democratic republic. In the
position I have constructed and called Rousseau's middle way, his fundamental normative stance, a common faith serves as a means to preserve and cultivate dynamic social
traditions and ideals—beliefs, practices, symbols, institutions, and customs—that embody
and further such social democratic ideals as justice, equality, liberty, and tolerance. In
this social democratic endeavor lies my chief interest in Rousseau, religion, and in the
birth of modernity.

For some time now, I have been interested in models and defenses of democratic
institutions that do not rely exclusively on either appeals to rational choice or market
efficiency models, often purportedly derived from principles of universal, deliberative
human rationality; or political arguments based on natural reason or any other anchors
in a transcendent, ahistorical moral reality. My interest, rather, is in exploring models
that describe democratic society as a social, cultural achievement and recognize that its
protection and development entail attention to its social, cultural basis.

This should not imply that I am not deeply committed to principled approaches that
generate arguments about how to achieve a progressive, flourishing society. I would be
greatly dismayed if my focus on the sociohistorical nature of our political and moral
beliefs and practices were to suggest that I am discounting principled arguments. I am
not attempting to reduce political theory to sociology, moral deliberation to historical
inquiry, or social criticism to social manipulation. Rather, I am bringing attention to
the sociohistorical character of our democratic beliefs, practices, and institutions and of
the normative principles that we commonly bring to debates and conversations about
how best to establish a just, flourishing society.

To my mind, when we acknowledge the sociohistorical nature of such democratic
achievements as human rights, rule of law, consent of the people, and celebration of
diversity, we acknowledge the fragility of these achievements. These achievements are
not written and secured in a foundation of transcendent stone. Sociocultural forces erected
them and can just as easily bring them down. Even the most basic liberal achievements
cannot be taken for granted. This should make us vigilant, especially if we hold that
there are some things that no one, anywhere, at any time, should need to worry about
happening to them. This stance, which is stated most powerfully by Judith Shklar, is
fundamental to my work and plays a profound, normative role in this book.[5] And, alas,
this stance will always be timely. For example, I had once assumed that the United
States had unequivocally forsworn the use of torture and was a world leader in efforts
to eradicate torture everywhere. However, torture has made a comeback, despite laws
that prohibit it. So has spying on U.S. citizens and imprisoning them without charges

brought against them and without access to legal counsel. In the absence of a socio-cultural base to support just laws, laws can be interpreted, amended, or ignored in unjust ways. This is exactly what Rousseau had in mind when he claimed that the law alone cannot bring justice. If a society—its beliefs and practices, traditions and cultures—does not support a normative principle, or supports it ambivalently, the principle is vulnerable.

To bring attention to the sociocultural nature of democratic beliefs, practices, and institutions, then, is to bring warning but also hope. For that which has been made can also be remade, enhanced, and fortified. By acknowledging sociohistorical, liberal forms of life that support democratic institutions, we can purposefully attend to and cultivate this dynamic material—socially embedded beliefs and practices, ideals, and customs—in order to strengthen and further such achievements as human rights and social justice.

Again, then, let me state what this project is *not*: It is not a venture in discovering a single national, moral identity, and then working to sustain it. No such monolithic identity exists in the United States or in other North Atlantic, liberal democracies. And even if one did exist, we as citizens would want to question it, explore it, evaluate it, reform it, and not simply reproduce it. Rather, this project—what I will soon describe as the cultivation of a spiritual democracy—is a venture in recognizing the ways democratic beliefs, practices, and institutions are embedded in sociocultural ways of life and in how that recognition can assist us in strengthening and extending a robust, progressive democracy.

So when Rousseau invokes civil religion or a common faith as a means to buttress democracies, I take note. Not because I maintain that the United States or other democracies would be well served by civic professions of faith or by nationalistic iconic symbols. Nothing could be further from my view. It is rather because I take Rousseau's political interest in religion to acknowledge that democratic ideals, beliefs, and practices are embedded in sociohistorical traditions that entail some manner of social mainte-nance and critique. A religious vocabulary enabled Rousseau to highlight the need to be attentive to social matter—traditions, beliefs, customs, ideals, symbols, and rituals—for the sake of establishing and sustaining a vibrant, progressive democratic society.

But there's more. Religion in the modern West often goes to the core of one's iden-tity as a public and private person, and therefore religion was especially useful to Rousseau—and is useful to us—for thinking about democratic identity: the identity of citizens both as public agents who work on shared projects and as private individuals who are protected in their pursuit of diverse aims, desires, and goals. Religion in the West has been instrumental in shaping our notions of public space (e.g., the dedicated community of the like-minded), of private space (e.g., an interior, cultivated spirituality), and of the relationship between the two (e.g., tension between public, civil theology and private, spiritual authenticity). Thinking about religion, I will argue, helps us think about the very nature of what we call the public life, the private life, and the transactional—and often tense—relationship between the two.

One could argue that the genealogy of liberal and communitarian thought, both of which inform democratic institutions, is largely a story about religion in the modern West. We could cast Martin Luther and John Calvin, for example, as two early, leading figures in this narrative. When Luther severed the political realm from the spiritual realm and then went on to privatize that spiritual realm, we have the birth of a model of society in which a premium is placed on individuals' pursuit of their own private vision of the good, of what matters most. For Luther, the chief role of the civil order is not to encourage a shared vision of the good or the practice of civic virtues. Rather, its fundamental purpose is to impose an external peace—a stable social order—for the sake of protecting one's conscience from coercion and one's body and property from harm. Negative justice is the fundamental aim of government, then, and this view has greatly informed a variety of liberal principles and institutions.

In contrast, Calvin expected more from the political sphere. Governments are not simply to impose a negative justice, keeping citizens from robbing and killing each other; rather, governments are charged with establishing a holy commonwealth. This means that the government is involved with leading its citizens toward civic virtue. In the well-run, orderly society, individuals are transformed into members of a common good, sharing in collective beliefs, practices, and ideals that pertain to all spheres of life.

This allusion to Luther and Calvin is just one example of how one could argue that religion has contributed to our culturally specific notions—however plural—of the public life, the private life, and the relationship between them. And religion has influenced how scholars have theorized about political institutions and about how those institutions are to accommodate notions of the public and private. For these reasons, among others, reflecting on religion—from a sociohistorical and philosophical point of view— illuminates many of our deepest concerns about democracy in the 21st century. Such concerns include the following:

- Do liberal democracies need to cultivate a shared, public discourse and even something like a common good in order to pursue such joint projects as social justice, gender equality, and human rights?
- Do the discovery and articulation of principles of justice entail deliberation by a people who possess something like a democratic character, however dynamic and plural such a character might be construed?
- Is a liberal, democratic society best understood as a collection of individuals, protected by legal rights, who may or may not be interested in civic community and a common good? Or as members of a large civic community, committed to a common good, who maintain that shared, common interests take precedence over private interests? Must we choose between these models? Are there other models? Is there a middle way?
- Which aspects of gemeinschaft—community and tradition—remain appropriate in a liberal democracy and in which spheres of our public and private lives?
- How can democratic society experience renewal? Can a protected and nurtured private life provide distinctive resources—such as courage, resolve, attentiveness, and discerning perspective—that contribute to a lively, inclusive, renewed democracy? And can a robust public life enhance a rich, private life?
- Is human happiness found in the public life, in the private life, or in a complex combination of the two?

I suppose I can explore many of these issues central to contemporary democratic society without referring to religion or using a religious vocabulary. I can imagine some friendly critics asking, "Why do you insist on referring to religion? Why do you insist on a democratic common faith? Why not simply refer to democratic culture?" My response is this: Religion has powerfully informed our public visions and private lives. It has shaped shared, public identities as well as intimate, private expressions of self and meaning. The ways of religion lead us to reflect critically on the ways of identity, character, and culture. Thinking about religion also highlights a central aspect of democracies, namely the intricate relationship between private and public, between self-regard and regard for that which is greater than the self yet embraces it.

Thinking about religion, then, leads us to think about fundamental issues that go to the heart of democratic society. And Rousseau understood as much. When he attempted to portray the most characteristic aspects of the public and private and the relationship between the two, he reached for a religious vocabulary. Honoring both love of self and love of that which is larger than the self—these twin poles, with all the tension between them—mark Rousseau's work, vision, and challenge, the challenge of 21st-century democracy.

Rousseau, Religion, and Democracy

Rousseau's relationship to religious paradigms is practically unexplored territory.[6] He is usually characterized as an Enlightenment philosopher—even if a rather romantic one—who is thoroughly secular. It is commonly assumed, then, that Rousseau can be well understood without reference to religious thought or thought about religion. In fact, however, when we ask of Rousseau the neglected question, when we listen to the religious pitch in his thought, which has shaped his thought, bright light is cast on central themes in his work, including the nature and place of the public and private in democratic life. And this theme, I have noted, is inexorably connected to the nature and place of religion in modernity.

Rousseau associated the deepest aspects of the public and private with religion. The tension between the hopes and desires of the individual and the requirements of a shared public life was at the heart of his life and thought. To explore religion in his work is to explore the conflicting claims with which he wrestled: prerogatives and obligations to self, friends, family, vocation, civic life, and humanity. He grappled with these, and he found ways to mitigate the tension between them. At the juncture of diverse theological and secular traditions, Rousseau forged a conception—a rich account—of human happiness found not exclusively in the public life, nor exclusively in the private life, but in a complex relationship between them.

Interpretively, I have placed Rousseau at the crossroads of Enlightenment optimism and Augustinian pessimism because at that tense, interpretive juncture, we begin to grasp his uncomfortable double vision. In one direction, he beheld humans able to transform their societies humanely; in the other direction, he perceived humans destined for immense suffering unless they dodge social involvement. At this awkward juncture of religious and secular traditions, Rousseau sought to remind us both of our responsibility to morally transform ourselves and our society and, at the same time, of our powerlessness to radically transform either the self or society.

All seem to agree that Rousseau spurned any notion of, anything resembling, original sin or innate corruption and that he, along with most Enlightenment philosophers, blamed corrupt, irrational social institutions for the majority of our miseries. Yet if we have eyes to see the religious contours of his thought, we see that, contrary to this standard interpretation of Rousseau, he worked with a notion similar to original sin.[7] This brings to light a current in his thought that otherwise would go unnoticed: Every time he offers a public or private remedy—a cure for some lamentable social or personal condition—he punctures it a bit, shrinks it, noting its limits. Rousseau is constantly reminding us of our responsibility to improve our public and private lives yet warning us that such efforts will always be marred, will never be sufficient, that humility is needed even concerning our highest achievements, because our achievements are always only ambiguously good, never entirely good. This Augustinian aspect of Rousseau's thought comes through as we ask the neglected question, the question about religion.

Rousseau might not have solved the problem of how to establish a harmonious balance between the various public and private claims that mark modernity. But he did brightly illuminate the modern drama of the contingent yet inevitable storms that bluster as we attempt to find public and private meaning, contentment, and justice in an age marked by both individualistic and associational ways of life. Rousseau explored the trials and promises of public visions and private lives by speaking a language set at the intersection of religion and modernity.

I locate Rousseau in the diverse traditions of 18th-century French philosophy and theology. These French traditions depicted variously the relationship between love of self and love of God (or love of things outside the self, "things public"), and they thereby produced intricate models of the relationship between the public and private. Rousseau wrestled with these complex, competing traditions, and he produced what some think of as a confusing—and confused—mass of writing. But we can see coherence—even if we don't always like what we see—by constructing a conceptual framework that takes into account the specifics of when and to whom he was writing, on one hand, and his overall normative vision, on the other. In this book, this framework takes the form of what I call his paths to partial redemption—roughly, for our purposes here, the private path, the public path, and the tense (and often unhappy) middle way between them.[8]

Think of these as soteriological paths or strategies that range from the most public to the most private. That is, they are strategies that range from an engineered, totalized, public existence in something like an authoritarian society to, on the other extreme, an escape into a radically asocial, solitary existence. In this introduction to the paperback edition, I want to briefly highlight the path that attempts to reconcile the public and private rather than pose them as alternatives. This path is what I am calling the precarious middle way.

For Rousseau, as for Kant and Freud, there is an eternal struggle between concern for the self and obligation to others. Religion enabled Rousseau to express this struggle, and religion—on what I have constructed as the middle way—allowed him to mitigate it. On this middle way, equipped with a religious vocabulary, Rousseau struggled both to protect and to reconcile the public and private, for he understood this endeavor to be at the heart of a democratic republic. Yet the success of the middle way, I have said, is doubtful. Of all paths to redemption, the middle path is the most risky. Yet it is also, I later argue, the most promising. It may be a tense way. It may not manage to dodge all the conflict Rousseau would have us avoid. Still, it best captures the ideals, hopes, and aspirations that we have come to associate with a wide variety of public and private projects and spaces. This is not to say that the other paths—the extreme public path and the radical private path, for example—are not worthy of our attention. They are. They teach us much about the satisfactions, requirements, and limits of the public life alone, the private life alone, and, ultimately, the need to seek wise ways to pursue aspects of both.

Religious Dimensions of the Middle Way

As Rousseau wrestled with the relationship between religion, law, and the state, he encountered the limits of each: Religion alone could not provide a social contract, the law alone could not provide justice, and the state alone could not provide human flourishing. When Rousseau spoke in the mode of Enlightenment optimism, he held that some combination of religion, law, and the state could bring about public and private well-being. However, when he spoke in the mode of Augustinian pessimism—his more habitual voice—he held that, ultimately, no sociopolitical arrangement could provide for human flourishing.[9]

Rousseau grasped a central challenge to modern, democratic society, namely how to maintain commitment both to the pluralism that respect for human dignity and autonomy entails and to the commonality that a lively republic entails. Rousseau articulated this worthy challenge in the idiom of religion. He had become convinced of two things. First, he was convinced that a civil religion or common faith of some sort is necessary to cultivate in citizens an affection for and a commitment to something like a shared, common good (however minimally defined). The law, with only the force of the law, is not enough, he argued, to sustain a just and flourishing society. However, he had also become convinced that freedom of religion, and a robust civic protection of such freedom, is necessary for individuals to flourish as human beings. In Rousseau's view, individuals, stripped of their freedom to pursue religious or philosophical comprehensive views, will wither inwardly—morally and spiritually. They will experience something like moral or spiritual alienation. Moreover, as public citizens they will be unable to bring to society the imaginative, autonomous reflection needed for democratic, political deliberation.

Rousseau's challenge—and a chief challenge of democracies today—was to formulate a social model that could incorporate public and private aspects of religion, broadly defined. In this book *public religion* and *private religion* should not be construed narrowly. What I'm calling public religion or a common faith can encompass any set of beliefs and practices that contributes to a shared, even if limited, moral perspective. We find aspects of a common faith, then, in a shared democratic culture—the kind of culture that responds with indignation when someone's rights are trampled on, for example. Likewise, private religion need not be restricted to personal religious devotion as traditionally understood. Rather, private religion can refer to any array of deep, abiding personal beliefs that help individuals make sense of the moral and natural universe in which they find themselves.

Rousseau, in what I am calling his middle way model of democratic society, attempted to use aspects of both public and private religion, even though he was fully aware of the tension between them and the dangers that adhere to each if divorced from the other. Of a society allowing the private to be utterly subsumed under the public, Rousseau feared a fiercely nationalistic, patriotic religion, and we can all see contemporary examples of this in the United States and elsewhere. Of a society allowing the public to dissolve into the private, he feared a narcissistic, self-absorbed spiritual life that, among other things, would be willing to remain naive and unconcerned about dangerous social, economic, and political trends. The middle way model, in contrast, attempts to engender a democratic common faith while safeguarding personal belief.

A basic question for us today is, Why did Rousseau maintain that there is a need for something like a democratic common faith, that is, for beliefs and practices that contribute to shared, even if not comprehensive, moral and political democratic perspectives? Unlike in Montesquieu's or Locke's models of society, where coordinated self-interest provides the fundamental social cohesion, in Rousseau's model social cohesion and cooperation require more. Among other things, these require a shared understanding—a common faith—that unites individuals in collective projects and institutions, values, and goals. Such commonality need not entail broad agreement on every issue. But societies, including liberal ones, need some shared beliefs and practices, some common faith, lest they waste away as citizens battle against one another in a chronic, low-grade war of all against all with such weapons as callousness, business brutality, and exploitation of the poor and marginalized.

When Rousseau attempted to express the strength and nature of the beliefs and practices that bring together otherwise disparate modern individuals, he was compelled to adopt a religious vocabulary. It was the strongest vocabulary available, he felt, for articulating the level of commitment and affection needed to sustain liberal, democratic institutions.[10] Yet he was determined to promote not only a public religion or a common faith. Rousseau was also convinced that if individuals were not allowed to pursue *personal* religious belief, then their well-being, virtue, and capacity for autonomous reflection—including reflection on significant public matters—would be impeded. This point will receive further elaboration.[11] Suffice to say for now that Rousseau linked inwardness, autonomy, and deliberation in such a novel and compelling way that Kant and a long line of Romantics thereby inherited an altered conceptual, moral universe. And today we move about in this Rousseauean universe, a realm populated by individuals who, in private, search "their hearts"—listening to the voice of conscience (Rousseau), to the good will (Kant), to Intuition and not tuitions (Emerson)—listening inwardly for the sake of both private perfection and public concord, for the achievement of a flourishing, self-conscious community of individuals.

There is an additional, pragmatic reason Rousseau favored the protection of personal religion. In his view, freedom of personal religious belief would serve the social function of reducing religious strife, thereby promoting peace. The liberal premise here is that people are less likely to fight over religion if they are allowed to pursue their own religion freely.

Protecting personal religious belief can be interpreted broadly here. Rousseau's avocation of religious tolerance in the 18th century is equivalent, in our time, to championing the protection of all kinds of beliefs and practices that some would deem mistaken, offensive, even immoral. Unlike, say, John Calvin, Rousseau restricted the reach of the civil, common faith. Or put more accurately, Rousseau's common faith put the protection of private belief and practice at the center of the shared, public good. Tolerance becomes a salient, normative feature in his rather minimalist civil profession of faith.

Rousseau, then, offered a seemingly paradoxical vision: A public religion serves to join people in a shared, democratic perspective, and a chief feature of this shared perspective is respect for private belief and practice. By permitting religious diversity, Rousseau honored what he considered to be the liberty needed for personhood and citizenship.

Religion Made Safe in Democracy: Rousseau, Rawls, and Rorty

By relegating personal religious diversity to the private sphere, Rousseau made religion safe for the republic. Rousseau would have sided here with John Rawls in his overall stance that personal religious arguments—or arguments based in personal religion—have no or little place in political deliberation on essential public matters. France, Rousseau's step-home, has followed Rousseau's lead in this, and hence the French to this day would prefer to see no personal religion in public. A recent example of this is France's banning of the Islamic headscarf in public schools. Although this is a complicated issue, one could argue that France continues to enforce a public, civil religion—what is called *laïcité*, or neutrality, but what in fact is the sanctity of *French* public culture (as opposed to the culture of its immigrant populations, e.g., Italian, Jewish, or, more recently, Islamic).

Rousseau's sociopolitical model, for all its complexity, refuses here on this point to wrestle with an ongoing, central democratic challenge: how to accommodate and respect—but not privilege—religious diversity in public space and in political deliberation. For in Rousseau's model, individual religious convictions are safely tucked away in the private sphere. Public religion—the minimalist yet mutual beliefs and practices that support a democratic common faith and shared moral perspectives—sustains public and political deliberation. Private or personal religion, in contrast, is deemed contentious and divisive unless it is rendered safe by being consigned to the private sphere—the sphere of the local voluntary group, the family, or the individual. It must not be brought into the larger public sphere, either as a resource for moral and political deliberation or as a sign of identity, because its partisan nature has great potential to introduce division and therefore conflict into the public life of the state. And for Rousseau, conflict is the worst thing.[12]

Sequestering religious belief to the private sphere is, I take it, the view that most Rawlsian liberals, including Richard Rorty, hold today. The idea is to keep religion out of public, political debate, because in this view religion is based on beliefs not subject to public reasoning, and religion is therefore divisive. But freedom of religion—a cardinal right in liberal democracies, in the Bill of Rights in the U.S. Constitution—should entitle individuals and communities to bring religious convictions to their political stances. Or at least this is how I interpret the significance of the right to the free exercise of religion. If religious beliefs are central to some citizens' identities—to their deepest sense of self and moral orientation—then to ask citizens to bracket (to exorcise) religious belief for the sake of political deliberation is to ask them to become someone else when faced with many of the most significant issues that citizens are asked to consider. It is to demand that one become alienated from oneself.

I realize this is a complex issue and that it is not easy to summarize the stances of those I have called Rawlsian liberals. Some such liberals are suspicious of religion in any public or political debate, and this is where I would usually place Rorty. Rorty is a champion of what he calls the "happy, Jeffersonian compromise," a means to privatizing religion and keeping it out of the public square.[13] What exactly is the compromise here, and who is making it? The compromise is between the Enlightenment and the religious, and it consists of this: The religious may keep their religious belief, but only on the condition that they are willing to privatize their belief, that is, keep it out of public life. Ponder this compromise for a little while, and it soon becomes clear that it is offering the following: You may hold all the religious beliefs you want as long as they remain irrelevant to many things that matter most, for example, to public discussion and policy on laws, schools, the environment, energy, war, and social services.

Rorty justifies his position on religion and the public life by claiming that "the main reason religion needs to be privatized is that, in political discussion with those outside the relevant religious community, it is a conversation-stopper."[14] This is not the appropriate place for me to offer a full response to Rorty's claim, but I do want to note that there are many ways to stop a conversation, and the U.S. Constitution—as Rorty knows—does not bar them from public life and debate on public policy. Some forms of speech, such as hate speech, perhaps may be barred. But by *conversation-stopper* Rorty means a person making a statement in political discussion to which others have *no* response, presumably because the statement—or the moral grounds that support the statement—is not shared by them. In such a situation, perhaps the person who uttered the conversation-stopper should have known better, spoken differently, offered a statement that was more conducive to discussion, and so on. Perhaps. But we do not always know in advance what will stop a conversation. Moreover, conversation-stopping, as Rorty himself recognizes, is a legally permissible, even if not always socially acceptable, activity.

We may for good reason want public interlocutors to exhibit a wide range of virtues, including attentiveness, discretion, and sensitivity to audience as well as courage, honesty, and judgment. But these virtues and their corresponding vices do not run along religious versus nonreligious lines. In my view, Rorty could better advance his aims by describing in detail the kind and quality of conversation he would like to see on public issues rather than by attempting to rally "we atheists" to "enforce Jefferson's compromise."[15]

It is not clear to me, then, why Rorty needs to single out the religious. Sometimes it seems as if, for Rorty, religious people with progressive views have such views despite their religion, whereas religious people with reactionary views have such views because of their religion. Perhaps this is why Rorty said to a large group of scholars at the American Academy of Religion that religious people, for the most part, do not make good citizens.[16] I share many of Rorty's progressive political views. And I, too, fear political reactionaries, including those belonging to what is called the religious right. Unlike Rorty, however, I hold that religious and nonreligious interlocutors can and often do engage in political conversations of significance in which comprehensive views are admissible. When I enter debate on a wide range of political issues, I want that debate to be inclusive and lively, even if that means talking and listening to people with whom I have strong disagreements. I can hope that virtues associated with civility, fairness, and cooperation are present.[17] But I cannot enforce such virtues, especially by stating in advance that all reference to religion be excluded.

Earlier in his career, Rawls seemed to share Rorty's wish that religion stay out of public life. But later, in *Political Liberalism*, Rawls prohibited the public exchange of religious arguments only when addressing "constitutional essentials and questions of basic justice."[18] Nonetheless, in either the more or the less restrictive case, citizens whose outlooks are informed by religion are still being required to refrain from making reference to this profound aspect of their identity when engaging in significant political deliberation and debate.

Psychologically, it is not clear to me that people can so neatly uncouple aspects of their identity. Politically, it is not clear to me that we want some citizens to repress the *real* reasons that tacitly support the only kind of (supposedly neutral) public expression of reasons that Rawls will permit. Juridically, it is not clear to me that we can draw a pragmatically useful and meaningful line between "questions of basic justice" and all the other (lesser yet related) issues that pertain to questions of justice and the nature and arrangement of our public institutions. And finally, epistemologically, it is not clear to me that what Rawls calls "public reason" can in fact be defended as "the reason of citizens," that is, as an inclusive style of deliberation that can be said to be acceptable to all reasonable people.

In my view, this epistemological doubt is intensified, not weakened, when Rawls, in the "Introduction to the Paperback Edition" of *Political Liberalism*, permits comprehensive religious doctrines to enter in public reason, provided that "in due course public reasons . . . are presented sufficient to support whatever the comprehensive doctrines are introduced to support."[19] This new concession is essentially saying, "An argument wearing the cloth of religion may be permitted provided that at some point the religious vestments are removed, thus allowing naked public reason to appear." In other words, the only religious argument that can be permitted and trusted is one that could initially have been stated in other terms, namely the terms of public reason. And yet this very idea of translation between "private reason" and "public reason" is precisely what gives me pause.

After all, public reason is not a flexible, native language like German that can freely and without restriction incorporate concepts from outside itself. This is why Donald Davidson's argument about translatability does not apply here to the attempt to translate between expressions of public and private reason. This is because public reason, by definition, is restrictive. It intentionally keeps out what Rawls calls the "background culture with its many forms of nonpublic reason."[20] But are there not interesting and helpful perspectives embedded in "nonpublic reason" that, in Rawls's model, would never be allowed to have a bearing on essential and basic matters of justice? Can a line be reasonably drawn between public and nonpublic (private) reason? How is the line to be drawn? We cannot look to public reason itself as the arbiter, because it is the scope and nature of public reason that are under consideration. Rawls seems to think the public itself—that is, reasonable citizens—will acknowledge the reasonableness of his project and the validity of his distinction between public and nonpublic reason.

There is an assumption here that all reasonable views about justice can be—or should be able to be—stated in such a way that all reasonable citizens could be expected to accept them. But this once-lofty hope—reaching back as it does to the admirable motives of the Enlightenment thinkers who sought to eliminate religious conflict and to establish a lasting social peace based on citizens' compliance to reason—is now, in my view, an intrusion on a democratic polity that places a premium on the perspectives of a diverse citizenry, despite potential conflict, and that constitutionally protects the expression of such perspectives. The noble Enlightenment hope in public reason should be reformulated, not as Rawls's hope in public over nonpublic reason but as a democratic hope in a lively, rough-and-tumble political process of free and open exchange. This process of exchange is not limited in advance by what all "might reasonably be expected to reasonably endorse."[21] Rather, this process acknowledges that what is reasonable to endorse is itself debatable and that some voices in the debate will not always be deemed reasonable by others in the debate. This unkempt process goes to the heart of a democracy that honors diversity. The test of the democratic process is not, ultimately, that it produce "the reasonable" but rather that it foster an inclusive, lively, and open exchange.

I have said, then, that I am committed to a democratic process that is dynamic and inclusive of religious and other voices that Rawlsians would deem nonpublic and therefore would exclude. Moreover, I have claimed that this inclusive process pertains to issues of basic justice, among other issues. In light of my commitment to inclusivity, which presumably entails much diversity, why, then, am I also committed to giving attention to the need for what I have been calling a democratic common faith or a shared, democratic understanding? Why would I sanction diversity while also arguing for the importance of shared perspectives?

It is precisely because of my commitment to inclusivity that I am arguing for the cultivation of a democratic common faith—of shared beliefs and practices that can sustain such institutions as the Bill of Rights and such ideals as equality. If I have focused on religion, it is because the language of religion is one way to capture both the public engagement and the private wherewithal that robust democratic commitment entails—*public*, because this commitment entails pulling together for the sake of shared projects of significance, and *private*, because this commitment entails such personal virtues as resolve, restraint, openness, humility, respect, and affection. I criticized Rousseau's democratic model for excluding personal religious belief from the political realm (Rousseau would have been uneasy with my own emphasis on lively and potentially discordant political debate). Nonetheless, he did grasp what most Rawlsian liberals have not: as John Dewey put it, that "unless democratic habits of thought and action are part of the fiber of a people, political democracy is insecure. It cannot stand in isolation."[22]

Democratic "habits of thought and action" are what I am attempting to capture by using Rousseau's notion of a public religion and what I am calling a democratic common faith. And "the fiber of a people" is what I mean by a democratic culture—a culture that includes a cluster of various democratic virtues and character traits. *Culture, virtue, character*—these concepts bring to mind the interwoven public and private dimensions of religion, and religion, I have said, has shaped many of our collective notions of the public and private life that are negotiated, debated, and reinterpreted daily in democratic society.

Like Rousseau, then, I use a religious vocabulary to help understand the public and private dimensions of modern democratic society. Yet I do not insist on the name *religion* to refer to the intricate, transactional relationship between the public and private that mark democratic society. Religion is not the one and only interpretive key that allows us to study critically the public and private spheres of democratic life. Yet the concept of religion, given its historical association with community and public identity on one hand and with the interior life and individual character on the other, allows me to make many of the claims I most want to make.

American Spiritual Democracy

Culture, virtue, character, and religion are four central concepts in my argument, four central concepts that prompted my initial interest in Rousseau, and four central terms in the vocabulary of today's religio-political conservatives. Later in this introduction I will reflect on the contemporary political situation in the United States in light of my arguments about religion, modernity, and democracy. For now, I want to allude to what I will call a North American tradition of progressive, spiritual democracy. This will enable me to show that culture, virtue, character, and religion need not be associated with conservative politics. Indeed, these four concepts, central to my argument, are at the core of a vital tradition of North American progressive democracy.

By *spiritual democracy* I refer to what I earlier called a dynamic, lively, culturally specific and culturally contested, embodied democracy. I do not mean a mystical, nationalistic political body. Nor do I mean a democracy based on supposed transcendent or immutable ideals. As I am using it here, *spiritual* does not refer to anything ahistorical, disembodied, or even "free-standing" in a Rawlsian sense (i.e., it does not refer to a separate or modular realm of values). I use the term *spiritual democracy* to refer to a democracy that is not exclusively or primarily understood as a set of democratic procedures or legal codes. It is not bereft of procedural justice, legal codes, or of such democratic principles as "one person, one vote." But its scope is not limited to elections and procedures, for it includes the manners and character of a nation and its citizens. *Spiritual democracy*, then, refers to a society's democratic culture and laws, its ideals and institutions, working together to enhance each other. Indeed, I call it spiritual because of its extensive scope, encompassing the nation's character, its citizens' diverse identities, and a distinctively democratic transactional relationship between the two—between the nation's public vision and its citizens' multifarious, private lives.

Many figures could fit into a genealogy of what I am calling a progressive, American spiritual democracy. Walt Whitman, who specifically wrote of "a sublime and serious Religious Democracy," could be interpreted as belonging to it.[23] In many ways, he is Rousseau's American counterpart. Both Rousseau and Whitman articulated a democracy that pertained to the manners and traditions of a people and not only to formal institutional arrangements. Both Rousseau and Whitman emphasized the necessity of a strong public commitment to shared democratic projects, the protection of private pursuits, and the need to relate the public and private without conflating them. Both argued for the cultivation of a vital, shared sense of democratic public identity on one hand and a vibrant, commodious interiority that animates private lives on the other. Finally, both customarily celebrated the public and private hopes, achievements, and victories of the common person under ordinary, daily circumstances rather than the extraordinary deeds of the powerful individual or eccentric genius. For these reasons, among others, it makes sense to reflect briefly on Whitman as Rousseau's spiritual heir in North America, promulgating a spiritual democracy.

When Whitman wrote of "a sublime and serious Religious Democracy," he was referring to what he called the third stage in the development of American democracy.[24] The first stage is the establishment of democratic, legal rights, as expressed in the Constitution, for example. The second stage is the material basis for daily living, as exhibited by railways, cotton production, schools, and monetary currency, for example. The third stage is the development of what Whitman called "Religious Democracy" and of what I am calling the spiritual basis of democracy, namely the many and diverse sociocultural threads that form a complex, democratic social fabric. This intricate weave is composed of poetry and pottery, literature and carpentry, opera and folk songs, theology and masonry, women and men, old and young. We can think of spiritual democracy as a vast assortment of cultural practices and productions that both expresses and shapes a people's democratic aspirations and identity in daily life.

I hope it is clear that *culture*, as I am using the term, should not be understood as being monolithic, unchanging, or high (as in refined manners and taste). Whitman's hope was in plural, dynamic, democratic forms of life, inclusive of a wide variety of human expression and practice. Although he never slighted the significance of achieving "equal franchise" or "an elected government" (the ongoing work of the first stage), he maintained that there is a "deeper, higher progress," one that reaches deep into the manners and character of a nation as well as into the interior life of the solitary individual. Hence Whitman declared, "Did you, too, O friend, suppose democracy was only for elections, for politics, and for a party name? I say democracy is only of use there that it may pass on and come to its flower and fruits in manners, in the highest forms of interaction between men and their beliefs . . . *democracy in all public and private life*."[25]

Each member of society is called on to contribute uniquely to the complex weave of the emerging spiritual democracy. Some will offer their poetry, as in Whitman's case, others will offer skills in making furniture or teaching children. Whatever one's contribution, all are part of the unending task of building a spiritual democracy—a nation governed by democratic laws and principles, supported by democratic practices and culture. This public engagement in building a spiritual democracy does not bring the diminishment of individuality but rather its flourishing. Here, again, Whitman and Rousseau sounded the same note, maintaining that individuals are most likely to flourish when they are connected to an inclusive and lively public life that fosters common interests and that protects and nurtures private lives. Whitman traveled on what I call Rousseau's middle way when he expressed his hope that American individualism and American love of country can "mutually profit and brace each other, and that from them *a greater product, a third, will arise*."[26]

The exact shape and nature of this "third" is difficult to discern, but Whitman's *Leaves of Grass* can be interpreted as a poetic expression of this "greater product." The first two lines of this distinctively North American masterpiece establish the tone and scope of the work:

> One's-Self I sing, a simple separate person,
> Yet utter the word Democratic, the word En-Masse.[27]

The emergent third way or mode of being affirms the independence and agency of the self and the self's interdependence and coming together with others to create joint public achievements in a democratic fashion. *Leaves of Grass* celebrates this distinctive arrangement of individuals and families in relation to community and society. The diverse poems attempt to capture the rich content of lived lives—lives in solitude and in society; lives lived with friends, lovers, and family and with co-workers, shopkeepers, and strangers; lives lived in spheres of personal hopes, ideals, and fears and also in work, associations, and politics; lives embedded in sociopolitical arrangements that honor both public and private ventures and yet ultimately lives whose continuous movement between various realms challenges any absolute lines drawn between public and private.

The very title of this collection of poems, *Leaves of Grass*, invokes the notion of honoring both distinct individuality (private paths, each blade of grass) and the ensemble (public paths, the weave intact). This movement toward relating, yet not conflating, these two modes of existence—the blade and the weave, the private and the public—is the poetic expression of "the third," the movement Whitman hopes will increasingly become embodied in the everyday, material existence of an American spiritual democracy. The weave needs the blades, the blades need the weave. In spiritual democracy, the dialectical relationship between weave and blade is embedded in both law and everyday practice and culture.

Leaves of Grass, then, is a poetic vision of diversity woven together to form a spiritual democracy. The weave is not elegant, seamless, or in any way immaculate. It is stitched together this way and that, tousled and scruffy. Yet it does possess a beauty of sorts—a rich and textured tangle that comes "out of hopeful green stuff woven."[28] This is the tangle of lives intersecting here and there, arguing and debating, working and praying, gathering and separating, yet in the main moving together toward generosity and justice, openness and civility, moving toward a lively and living spiritual democracy.

It is this movement toward something—something more humane, more just, more equitable—that gives a self and a society a moral identity. Whitman saw himself and his nation moving in a particular, democratic direction, even as he attempted to move himself and his nation in that direction. We can name others who belong in a genealogy of North American spiritual democracy (and Rousseau could have a place in it as one who inspired much democratic reflection among Americans). Thomas Paine, Sojourner Truth, Ralph Waldo Emerson, Abraham Lincoln, Frederick Douglass, Elizabeth Cady Stanton, Susan B. Anthony, Booker T. Washington, John Dewey, Jane Addams, Rosa Parks, Martin Luther King Jr., Wendell Berry, and Terry Tempest Williams—this is a short list of likely candidates. There are others—those who wrote little or nothing at all, for example. My grandmother, Mary Cladis, a Greek immigrant who arrived in the States with no money and no knowledge of English and who strove all her life to join and forge a democratic society committed to generosity, acceptance of diversity, justice, and economic equity—she, too, belongs on the list, as do countless others. We can argue about who exactly belongs on this list—we *should* argue about it and all that it means, what it stands for—but we need a list, a genealogy, a collection of stories about where we have been and where we are heading. How else are we going to discover and shape who we are? Again, the list and its meaning—past agents and their complex narratives—is contestable. It is plural, it is fluid, it is contradictory. We will argue about the telling of these North American stories and even about who is the "we" that tells the stories. But we must tell them. We must tell stories about a progressive American democracy, and we must add our own lines—our own lives—to them and thereby become characters and agents in them.

Sometimes we meet a person and we think, "Now, here in front of me is a *person*, a distinct character, someone who stands for something, is grounded in something, hopes and strives for something." It is the same with a nation. Nations, too, have characters, even pluralistic ones. What is America's character? What does it stand for? What are its stories? Where has it been, and where is it heading? These are questions worth asking. And if you are a member of the United States, then these questions are not only about the society in which you live but about you yourself. For it is difficult to know one's own identity if one does not know the identity of the society into which one has been thrown—in which one was raised, in which one works and votes, in which one raises children, works for community, cares for the elderly, grows old, and is eventually buried. Self-knowledge and self-identity are intimately bound up with societal knowledge and societal identity.[29]

Again, none of this is to suggest that a pluralistic society such as our own does not contain multiple sociolinguistic, cultural, and ethnic groups that contribute importantly to the complex identity of individuals or to the complex identity of the nation. It is not to suggest that a person's or the nation's identity is simple, homogeneous, or fixed. It is to suggest that our rich identities, fed by diverse streams, can also be fed by a vision of who we can become as a people, a people who are capable of bringing diverse backgrounds and perspectives to enrich the most admirable democratic stories that we know and tell. A public vision that can link our diverse lives in significant, shared projects— this is a goal worthy of our consideration.

Rousseau understood as much. He endeavored to articulate a social model that connected political institutions and laws with what I have called a democratic common faith, that is, with democratic virtues and beliefs, symbols and ideals. This did not entail nationalistic efforts to have every aspect of the self dedicated to the state. Far from it. The citizen's highest dedication is to democratic ideals and principles that guide and judge the state. Moreover, one's identity is not solely as citizen. Citizenship is only one aspect of one's identity. For example, in Rousseau's account of the general will, one's deliberation on and identification with the common good represents an interval in one's life, not its totality. Still, Rousseau's democratic social model did acknowledge, as I describe in chapters 7 and 10, the need for public rituals, creeds, customs, and common stories in order to inform a shared democratic identity among citizens. The specific shape of these 18th-century rituals and stories will not be ours in the 21st century, but we nonetheless stand to learn much from Rousseau's efforts to sustain democratic laws and institutions by means of democratic culture and identity.

Our task is both simpler and more complex than Rousseau's. It is simpler because, unlike Rousseau, we do not need to invent public democratic rituals, customs, and stories (as he did in *The Social Contract*). We share a common, complex history—regardless of when our own diverse individual histories arrived in the United States—that informs a common future. And, unlike in Rousseau's 18th-century French society, in the United States today such democratic features as the rights and protection of the individual are widely shared tenets, already embedded in law and to some degree in cultural practices. Symbolically, we possess a vast repertoire of such powerful symbols as the Declaration of Independence and the Bill of Rights, the images of Sojourner Truth and Martin Luther King Jr., the Lincoln Memorial and the Women's Rights National Historic Park. Compared with Rousseau's time and place, our history and our present are better stocked with democratic beliefs, practices, and institutions.

Yet our task is also more complex than Rousseau's, precisely because of our longer democratic history. On one hand, we have taken democracy for granted and perhaps are no longer as inspired to work and struggle for the achievement of a more extensive and robust democracy. We often assume it is already here to stay, and therefore we are naive about its actual fragility and about the need to enhance it. On the other hand, we have become cynical about what we can achieve together. This is in part because our history as a democracy is in fact laden with antidemocratic events and deeds, with brutality and exploitation. This is seen most explicitly in the near extermination of Native Americans and in the slavery of people of African descent. In light of our checkered and tainted history, questions loom: Whose history is to be told? Do we all belong to a shared history and, if we do, whose version of it? Who gets to tell it? Which victories, which losses, are recounted? These questions, to my mind, are not to be asked and answered once but are part of an ongoing struggle and commitment to narrate our past and to work toward a more humane future.

Without a sense of our history, without narrating stories that lead to where and who we are—moral achievements, shameful deeds, and lives and events in between—our efforts to move forward will be hindered. Without an ample supply of stories and rituals, practices and symbols that represent democratic struggle, we as a people may eventually resign ourselves to such antidemocratic practices as economic injustice, racism, or state-sponsored torture and spying on citizens. With no sense of a shared identity—a democratic common faith—our democracy is vulnerable.

I worry that as long as liberal political theorists remain naive about the need for and significance of democratic culture, virtue, and character, they will offer few resources for tackling some of the greatest challenges to democracy in the 21st century. We need to attend to the forms of life that sustain and extend democratic laws and principles. These forms of life—what I am calling spiritual democracy—would be replete with stories, symbols, practices, and other means of identity and character formation. The vocabulary and practice of religion invoke and bring together many of the public and private resources needed to support just such a spiritual democracy.

Religion and Culture: For Better, for Worse

This reference to religion may make us nervous, and for good reason. We often associate intolerance, irrationality, and fanaticism with religion. But religion can also bring to mind generosity of spirit, informed moral judgment, and peacemaking. Religion can be put to different ends. In any case, in this book I am not advocating religion per se. Rather, I am looking at how Rousseau used religious categories to cast light on the human drama of life together, life alone, and how best to support these two interrelated modes of existence. Rousseau understood that religion powerfully exhibits and shapes human identity. It provides a response to such fundamental questions as Who am I? and Where am I heading? Moreover, in providing a response to these questions, it separates and distinguishes ways of life. Religion seldom trades in neutrality.

This is another lesson that we stand to learn from Rousseau's use of a religious vocabulary. Liberal political theory often purports to speak in the universal, innocuous voice of neutrality. Yet liberal theories, like religion itself, rarely function neutrally. We can no more afford to be neutral about democratic law, principles, and theories of justice than we can about democratic culture, virtue, and character. So although I happen to agree with many of the material conclusions of, say, John Rawls's democratic liberal theory, I maintain that his positions, despite his statements to the contrary, rely on and convey a particular, substantive moral orientation. They express a distinct moral identity. And to be heard and interpreted appropriately, they must be embedded in distinct sociolinguistic cultures—distinct democratic forms of life.

As I argued earlier, a salient aspect of these democratic forms of life is the premium placed on human dignity and autonomy. This is central to the identity of democratic character, and it is expressed variously, both in law and in cultural practice. Its most significant legal expression may be the First Amendment of the U.S. Constitution.[30] The right to freedom of religion, speech, press, assembly, and to petition the government for redress of grievances—these freedoms pertain to a wide range of activities that exemplify human dignity and autonomy in our public and private lives. In our private lives, these freedoms allow individuals to pursue activities that, though not necessarily having special public significance, are deemed to be worthwhile, meaningful, edifying, or pleasant. In our public lives, these freedoms ensure that individuals can gather, speak, publish, and petition in their efforts to shape a shared social environment that reflects their views on issues that pertain to the commonwealth. Government is forbidden to obstruct or restrict freedom of religion and expression because it is understood that these freedoms allow individuals to exercise agency—to work on the structure, shape, and character of their public and private lives.

This premium placed on human dignity and autonomy, as expressed in the First Amendment, is a salient feature of what I am calling spiritual democracy, for it marks both democratic culture and law, in ideal and actual forms. We endeavor to embody more fully the ideal in the actual, that is, to express the evolving ideal of human dignity and autonomy in the everyday lives and activities of individuals and communities, markets and schools, hospitals and prisons, courts and legislative assemblies. As I argue in chapter 10, Rousseau placed human dignity and autonomy at the heart of democracy by envisioning a social and political order that enabled individuals to consider and to shape their public and private lives. When Rousseau spoke in his most normative voice, he articulated a way of life that permits individuals to pursue their lawful private lives without government interference while also allowing individuals to see their will—their autonomy and moral imagination—in the political and social order in which they dwell.

Rousseau's implicit religious vocabulary for communicating the significance of human autonomy in both our private and public lives—the *particular will* and the *general will*—allowed him to express perfectly the creative yet tense relationship between what it is to shape a private life and what it is to shape a public life. In both cases, autonomy is honored, perhaps especially when there is conflict between the two. In the private life alone, there is not necessarily a direct and explicit relationship between my choices and the choices of those around me. Presumably, I could simply ask myself, "What is the best course to pursue for my private life?"[31] whereas in the shaping of the public life the general will is determined by the autonomous reflection of many individuals asking themselves the same question: "What is the best course to pursue for our shared life together, for the common political body?" In negotiating the potential tension between public and private paths, the self exercises much autonomy. As both Montaigne and Rousseau understood, we often have more control in fashioning the exact shape of our private lives. But according to Rousseau, this observation in no way diminishes the fact that in a democracy, self-autonomy participates fully in collective autonomy, even though the precise shape of the collective is outside the control of the single individual. Permitting and encouraging the expression of one's autonomy in public and private spheres, and acknowledging the potential conflict between them, is central to the moral orientation that marks democratic forms of life.

In Rousseau's view, the ongoing process of determining the general will is a rather discrete, if not exactly private, affair. One deliberates on the public good in private, not in town meetings or in other public forums.[32] To my mind, this is an unfortunate and limited view. Note, however, that Rousseau placed no restriction on what reasons one might draw on when deliberating on the general will, as long as one is asking oneself about what is good for the common good and not for one's own private interest. One brings one's full identity to bear on public issues, and as long as the democratic process is honored in the discovery—or the creation—of the general will, one experiences the general will as one's own. If limits are placed on the types of reasons one could use, as Rawls would have it, one could cease to experience the general will as one's own. Autonomous reflection, a central feature in democratic character and identity, could be vitiated. And for Rousseau, this outcome amounts to one of the most painful forms of alienation: to no longer see oneself in the greater life that encompasses one.

In sum, I have been arguing that we identify in our past and cultivate in our present what I have called a spiritual democracy, where law, critical reflection, and culture work together to promote progressive democracy. Following Rousseau and Whitman, this approach highlights the identity, character, and moral orientation that animate and nourish members of a robust, progressive democracy. In particular, the language of religion and culture allow me to draw attention to the beliefs and practices of a democratic common faith and to the necessity of such a shared, democratic understanding for the sake of sustaining and extending democratic legal codes, principles, and institutions. Religion and culture are useful categories insofar as they remind us how democratic identities, in public and private spheres, are fashioned and rooted in the sociolinguistic material of history, institutions, and everyday practice.

I understand that my chosen vocabulary—that of religion and culture—may give some pause. I have attempted to defend my use of religion and clarify how I am and how I am not using it. But what of culture? *Culture* has become a term that is almost as problematic and contested as religion. There has been a tendency to essentialize culture, that is, to assume that cultures are discrete, homogeneous entities. In this view, modern European culture, for example, is a clearly identifiable culture with distinct boundaries around it. It is also common to identify culture with the manners, customs, and artistic and intellectual achievements of an upper class, as expressed in the term *high culture*. Along with Seyla Benhabib and Kathryn Tanner, among others, I consider such views of culture to be inadequate. I mostly agree with Benhabib when she writes, "I do not believe in the purity of cultures, or even in the possibility of identifying them as meaningfully discrete wholes. I think of cultures as complex human practices of signification and representation, of organization and attribution, which are internally riven by conflicting narratives."[33]

In good pragmatist fashion, however, I also argue that the very term *culture* should not be essentialized. In that spirit, I suggest that it is useful to think of one of its meanings as a flexible, dynamic, thin cluster of beliefs, customs, and practices that diverse individuals can inhabit even as, or especially as, they contest its content and significance. American spiritual democracy relies on the cultivation of just such a thin yet pervasive and profound democratic culture. An aspect of this culture is the beliefs and practices associated with the First Amendment, and therefore contestation in the public sphere is an inevitable feature of what I am calling the culture of American spiritual democracy. Moreover, "thin" democratic culture is compatible with such potentially "thick" cultural identities as Puerto Rican, Greek, or Korean.

In *Situating the Self*, Benhabib states that a central premise in her work is that "the crucial insights of the universalist tradition in practical philosophy can be reformulated today without committing oneself to the metaphysical illusions of the Enlightenment. These are the illusions of a self-transparent and self-grounding reason [and] the illusion of a disembedded and disembodied subject."[34] I applaud this statement and I am committed to a similar project of critical retrieval. Moreover, I want to note that my use of the term *democratic thin culture* has much in common with Benhabib's use of *the universalist tradition*. As Benhabib uses the term *tradition* to refer to a broad set of beliefs and principles—"crucial insights" broad enough evidently for Benhabib to maintain the term *universalist*—I use the term *democratic culture* to refer to broad clusters of beliefs and practices with which diverse individuals—some with thick or at least complex cultural identities—can identify. In light of Benhabib's commitment to the embedded and the embodied, how could we expect aspects of what she is calling the universalist tradition to be achieved if not embedded and embodied in belief and practice, that is, in cultural practices of some sort?

Again, my bringing attention to the significance of what I am calling democratic culture and a democratic common faith is not to discount the necessity of critical, normative inquiry. To underscore the importance of embedded and embodied democratic principles is not to advocate social engineering. Although I am arguing that normative principles and arguments and such legal institutions as the Constitution need to be embedded in sociolinguistic, cultural ways of life—they wouldn't make sense free standing—this is not to reduce their status to cultural agreement or consensus. Normative principles and arguments are formed and operate in a variety of ways. One of their functions is to act as regulative ideals, reminding a people of some of their own highest ideals. This is not the place to offer a discourse on normativity. However, I do want to emphasize that I am not suggesting that we and our tribe cultivate a democratic identity in the absence of critical reflection. Spiritual democracy brings together normativity—including legal codes and critical reflection—and cultural embeddedness. And this relationship between the critical and the cultural is one area about which Rousseau has much to teach us.

When we think of the attainments of democratic polities, we often think of human rights. The establishment and enforcement of rights has been one of the chief accomplishments of democratic societies. However, democracy should not be reduced to rights, even though they should always remain a salient feature. It is useful to think of sustainable democracy as a bridge. It does not enforce uniformity; rather, it spans diversity. The length of the span is measured by its encouragement and protection of social and political engagement. In the absence of dynamic engagement, democracy threatens to become a set of lifeless principles and procedures. Democracy, then, is a bridge, and the bridge is sustained by robust engagement. And engagement is a cultural practice. The path and destination of this normative model, the bridge, is what I have called spiritual democracy.

The Span of Spiritual Democracy in the United States Today:
A Practical Reflection

I wrote this book on Rousseau to better understand my own country, the United States. The topic of the public and private life in the modern West is closely related to that of religion in modernity, and both these topics pertain to significant issues confronting the United States today. Or at least this is what I have tried to argue so far. Now I want to reflect specifically on the place of religion in the American public and political land-scape. If we try to describe this landscape without reference to religion, we risk generat-ing a distorted map. We risk getting lost—of not knowing where we stand or where we are heading. This is because by almost any measure, the United States is a deeply and diversely religious country. Those of us who are scholars in social and political theory need to acknowledge this fact, and then we need to address this pressing question: How can our immense religious diversity become a distinct source of strength in the United States? Some would maintain that a more basic and realistic question is, How can we contain religion in order to solve the problem of conflict caused by religious diversity? This, too, is a worthy question and endeavor, and it has become a leading paradigm or approach at least since seventeenth-century Europe sought to escape the brutality of religiously inspired wars. My fear is that if we start by attempting to *solve* the issue of religious diversity, especially by containment, then diversity will begin and end in our conversations as a *problem*. I would rather begin with the view that diversity is a distinct source of hope in America's democratic experiment.

When I speak of religious diversity, I refer both to religious perspectives and to per-spectives on religion, including Richard Rorty's "antireligious" perspective that America should hope for organized religion to "wither away."[35] I want to ask, along with Nicho-las Wolsterstorff in his exchange with Rorty, "How can persons who embrace such profoundly different comprehensive perspectives as do Rorty and I on reality, human life, and the good, nonetheless live together as equals in a just, stable, and peaceful society?"[36] I suggest that our hope for such an outcome is that diversity itself contribute to the establishment of a "just, stable, and peaceful society"—a society that embraces Wolsterstorff and Rorty, theist and atheist, and those in between as well as outside these well-known camps. I suggest that welcoming religious diversity in public debate and forums is the way forward, the way in which difference becomes a potential strength and not a liability. My comments here cannot be more than programmatic. Substantive arguments will be supplied at a later time, in a different publication.

Here is my understanding of the contemporary context for these reflections on religion in the U.S. public and political landscape. Religions appear to have made an unexpected, some might say volcanic, public entry. After decades of predictions about the death of religion, *religions* at least are still very much alive and well. Whether they were ever in decline is still an open question. Nonetheless, much has changed. We once believed that religion in the modern West was destined to be relegated to the individual's private life; we are now keenly aware of the various roles religion plays on the national and interna-tional public stage. We also held that modernity was replacing community and tradition with individualism and self-creation. Now, however, we recognize that gemeinschaft is not a thing of the past and that radical autonomy and ahistorical reason were the dreams of some well-meaning yet often naive enlightenment philosophers.

There are other germane changes. In the last fifty years, the First Amendment has been used by the courts to address such issues as prayer in public schools, the display of religious symbols in public spaces, and the teaching of creationism or intelligent design. Most of these rulings have attempted to remove religion—its symbols, teachings, or rituals—from government, public space. Some see this trend as contributing to the privatization of religion and, more generally, see privatized religion as a direct result of the First Amendment.[37] However, this view is belied by the large amount of public religiosity in the United States, especially when compared to European countries with state-sponsored religions. More plausibly, the separation of church and state as articulated in the First Amendment has augmented the public vitality of religion in America.

Religion appearing in public, then, is not a novel development in recent U.S. history. But the shape of the current debate *about* religion in public is something new. This debate has been inspired in part by the emergence of what is commonly known as the religious right, a loose alliance of a variety of conservative religious groups and the Republican party. Although "the" religious right was to some extent fostered by Republican party officials who sought to create a large conservative voting bloc, this alliance often is a tense one. The religious right's push for anti-abortion legislation, for example, often is at odds with the positions of Republican congressional representatives, and the Republican representatives' push to wage war and cut social services occasionally is at odds with the positions of the religious right. But the religious right seems willing to make compromises as long as the Republican party is willing to promote (what is called) conservative religious values. The religious right suspects that if conservative religion is kept out of politics, then a different kind of religion will take its place: the philosophy and politics of secular humanism. In this view, secular humanism, if not checked, would permit gay marriage and late-term abortions and forbid the teaching of intelligent design, banning God from the classroom. If not checked, the moral character of the country could collapse. The stakes, then, seem high.

But as I noted, this alliance is a tense one, and the religious right is not a monolithic group. Nor is the left that opposes it. The political left, mainly Democrats, fear that if the religious right is not checked, then the political and judicial direction of the country will be unduly shaped by conservative religious values. Some on the left, such as Rorty, would like to see religion disappear altogether. Yet if atheists such as Rorty are truly committed to advancing progressive politics in the United States, then they cannot afford to divide the religious from the nonreligious. I say this because the left is as dependent on the Democratic party as is the right on the Republican, and therefore people such as Rorty need to learn to work with Democrats who hold religious beliefs—beliefs that often inform many of their public, political positions. The following recently appeared in the *Atlantic Monthly*:

> As you may already know, one of American's two political parties is extremely religious. Sixty-one percent of this party's voters say they pray daily or more often. An astounding 92 percent of them believe in life after death. And there's a hardcore subgroup in this party of super-religious Christian zealots. . . . Half of the members of this subgroup believe Bush uses too little religious rhetoric.[38]

The political party? The Democrats. The subgroup? African American Democrats. Like the Republican party, Democrats are diverse and are religious.

Moreover, religious diversity in this country goes well beyond liberal and conservative Jews and Christians. Muslims, Hindus, and Buddhists live in every region in the country. Today there are more Muslims in the United States than there are Episcopalians, Jews, or Presbyterians. And this is just to name what we used to call the "world religions." In addition to Judaism, Christianity, Islam, Hinduism, and Buddhism, there are hundreds of other religious affiliations in America: Native American, Afro-Caribbean, Baha'i, Jain, Shinto, Taoist, Zoroastrian, and such pagan and new age religious groups as Gaia and Wiccan communities.

One could argue that there is a connection between such rich religious diversity and the First Amendment. As the First Amendment kept any one religion from becoming a national religion, it opened the way for a plurality of religions to take root in this country. In the face of this immense religious diversity, positions such as Rorty's facile public–private distinction as applied to religion—positions that would keep religion at home and out of public view—seem abstract and hollow. What would it mean to tell a member of the Navajo Nation or Gaia community, "If you insist on being religious, at least have the courtesy to keep it private. Religion should have no bearing on such issues as global warming or on what lands nuclear reactors are placed"? The context for serious discussion of religion in the American public and political landscape is acknowledgment of the depth, breadth, and diversity of America's religious landscape.

I propose four models of religion in the public and political landscape. No abstract theory of religion or of democracy can help us move forward as we as a nation grapple with the place of religion in public. Concrete models are a pragmatic way to offer both provisional descriptions of our situation and normative suggestions for how to achieve a more flourishing, if not perfect, union. The four models I propose are "Religion over the Public Landscape," "Religion Banned from the Public Landscape," "Public Landscape as Religious Space," and "Public Landscape as Varied Topography."

Religion over the Public Landscape

According to this model, religion is necessary for the health of the public and political life in the United States. By *religion* I mean here what we traditionally call religion (organized, historical religions such as Judaism or Christianity) as opposed to a Rousseauean civil religion or to a broad Durkheimian notion of religion. In this model, religion is necessary to inculcate virtues that sustain a vital citizenry. Such virtues might include justice, moral reasoning, and courage. Although these virtues may be fostered primarily in such private settings as homes and voluntary associations, they are exercised in public for the sake of the public. If religion and its concomitant virtues were excluded from public life, the moral health of the country would deteriorate.

This model is commonly associated with traditional, conservative religion. Members of the "moral majority" or the "religious right" easily come to mind, as do those who would like to see a constitutional amendment declaring the United States a "Judeo-Christian" nation. But forms of politically progressive religion also belong to this model. Some argue that a robust democracy in the United States relies on the beliefs and practices of progressive forms of Christianity, Judaism, and now Islam. It is not uncommon to hear political liberals arguing that peace, freedom, and justice in our land require the kind of moral vision that accompanies the religion of such figures as Abraham Lincoln,

Walter Rauschenbusch, Reinhold Niebuhr, Dorothy Day, Abraham Heschel, Martin Buber, and Martin Luther King Jr. If we do not support progressive religion in our republic, then human rights, the protection of the marginalized, the protection of the environment, and the eradication of racism will not even be expressed as national aspirations, much less as future achievements. In sum, liberalism unaided by religion is bereft of the resources necessary to generate significant moral community, meaning, and action.[39]

I appreciate that this model, "Religion over the Public Landscape," acknowledges the importance of religiosity in American's past and present and does not attempt to relegate religion to the private realm but rather welcomes it into the public and political landscape. Yet its placement of religion *over* the public is problematic. By *over* I mean its insistence that America can reach its most significant moral and political goals only if religion "watches over it"—as in "cares for it"—providing vast, unique, and indispensable moral resources. It may be empirically true that, given where and how most Americans are morally educated, to keep religion out of the public life would be to deprive the republic of a significant moral resource. But that is a contingent fact that could be disputed and, in any case, is subject to change. I do not reject the idea that religion can inculcate virtues that sustain a vital citizenry; I reject the idea that a vital citizenry or national moral achievements *require* religious belief. Again, this is not to say religion does not contribute to such progress or even that, for contingent reasons, it is not pragmatically useful for the nation to avail itself of the moral resources associated with religion. But should the citizenry drift away from religious belief, this should not imply that the nation would necessarily drift away from its moral obligations and the likelihood of moral progress. Religion, whether conservative or progressive, is not a timeless, essentialistic feature of the moral life.

Religion Banned from the Public Landscape

According to this model, religion should be kept out of the political and even much of the public life in the United States. For the sake of simplicity, I have in this model subsumed the political under the public. Nonetheless, the political should be understood as a subcategory of the broader category, the public. Some, such as Rawls in his latest publications, want to prohibit the exchange of arguments based on religion only when addressing "constitutional essentials and questions of basic justice." Here religion is banned only from a segment of the political realm. In contrast, Richard Rorty would like to see religion consigned entirely to the private life and removed from the nation's political and public life.

Rawls's and Rorty's positions are not unique to them but represent broad schools of thought. What they share is the belief that the separation of church and state not only should prohibit the establishment of a national religion or the public funding for religion but also should place additional constraints on religion in our public or political landscapes. What they share, though often with different justifications, is some version of Kant's idea of public reason. This is the view that citizens in public debate are not to speak the language—the ideals, dogmas, and beliefs—of such restrictive or private groups as religious associations. When addressing the public, one is to offer public reasons—

that is, reasons that transcend, or at least that are not bound by, the local, private reasons of lesser, particular organizations.

I have already suggested why I have grave doubts about the success of strategies that attempt to divide neatly a person's store of beliefs and reasons into the public and private (Rorty) or into the political and public (Rawls). My qualms are based on psychological, political, juridical, and epistemological considerations. I do agree with Kant that when addressing the public one should be aware of both the diversity of the (universal, that is, broad) audience and the commonality of the topics of concern. This awareness should inform how one speaks, how one presents one's arguments. But we probably don't need Kant to teach us that. And those who do lack tact and skill in public debate are not likely to improve their behavior by reading analytic philosophy or political theory.

Moreover, we should not attempt to pass laws, interpret the Constitution, or offer political principles that would prohibit poor form or bad taste in public. If the category of hate speech is interpreted too broadly (as Rorty seems willing to do by including under it those who on religious grounds oppose same-sex marriage), then we will empty that category of its meaning and power, and we will open the possibility of imprisoning those who, like me, find our current military undertaking in Iraq hateful.[40] Rorty does not maintain that it should be illegal to oppose same-sex marriage on religious grounds. But by putting those who oppose same-sex marriage in the category of those engaging in "hate speech" and "incitement to violence," he fails to exhibit the virtues that Kant wanted of us when we address the public. Rorty is either weakening the category of "hate speech" or applying it irresponsibly. In my view, it is precisely on issues such as same-sex marriage that we should hear all the arguments in public so that those of us who support same-sex marriage can champion it meaningfully and engage those who oppose our view.

Rorty wants religion to be kept private, and this means that churches, synagogues, and mosques should not educate their members about public or political issues.[41] Rather, religion should restrict itself to helping "individuals find meaning in their lives" and serving "as a help to individuals in their times of trouble."[42] However, it is not at all clear how religious communities are to assist individuals with issues of meaning or in times of trouble and yet, at the same time, not address public and political issues. Are religious communities to be mute on such issues as war, social security, and environmental policies? May not such issues connect profoundly with issues of meaning, especially during times of trouble? Rorty's arguments rely greatly on a facile distinction between public and private. I wrote this book, in part, to explore the ambiguities and complexities that cling to that very distinction, a distinction that is carrying much weight in a variety of contemporary debates, both within and outside academia.

Before moving to the next model, I want to note that we should not associate this model, "Religion Banned from the Public Landscape," exclusively with secularists or nonbelievers. There are today religious sectarians who are content to withdraw their religious perspectives and communities from public and political involvement. Such sectarians belong to this model, insofar as they want to retreat from society at large, preserve their traditions, protect their communities from a society gone wild, and allow religion to be banned from a public landscape that they themselves would rather not enter.

The Public Landscape as Religious Space

According to this model, the health of the republic depends on a pervasive, shared civil religion. The paradigmatic case for this model is Rousseau's civil religion, namely an explicit profession of faith that declares sacred the (legitimate) laws of the land. I do not know anyone advocating this model in its most pristine form. I doubt whether even Rousseau ever meant for us to take Rousseauean civil religion literally (see chapter 10). Proposing civil religion may have been his way of reminding his generation and ours of the indispensability of some shared beliefs and practices for a vibrant, democratic republic, especially if that republic counts tolerance as one of its chief virtues. A republic that places a premium on tolerance, and hence diversity, must be attentive to building shared perspectives that support diversity and democratic law and principles.

If civil religion is understood not as an explicit profession of faith but rather as an implicit set of shared civic beliefs, practices, and symbols, then "Public Landscape as Religious Space" becomes a recognizable position. No one and no state agency declared the Lincoln Memorial or the Bill of Rights as a sacred site or symbol. These became sacred (in a Durkheimian sense) as they accrued public significance and figured importantly in the public formation of moral identity and commonality. Such symbols, principles, or monuments can be said to create an implicit, civil religion.

This is not the place to offer a full-blown account of civil religion. Robert Bellah and others have done much good work on it. However, I need to mention the "Public Landscape as Religious Space" model because it pertains directly to our reflection on the place of religion in public. If the model has any plausibility at all, then it suggests that religion, as understood in this model in a Durkheimian fashion, will always have a place in the public and political landscape. This model brings a specific and useful complexity to the topic of religion and the public life. Those for and those against religion in public life often speak of religion as a clearly defined set of beliefs and practices. Boundaries between "secular" and "religious" seem plain and unambiguous. In my view, however, a merit of this model is its refusal to accept this all-too-tidy borderline. Moreover, the model can easily acknowledge the various religious aspects of how, say, Martin Luther King Jr. can seamlessly—and within the very same sentence—evoke the sacredness of human rights (conjuring civil religion) and the dignity of all humans as creatures of God (conjuring traditional theology). In other words, this model not only questions facile distinctions between a "secular public" and a "private religious" sphere but also brings attention to different types of public expressions of religious commitment.

The model is not without problems. Conceptually, it relies on a broad definition of religion, so broad that almost any significant public symbol, ritual, or principle could be considered religious. Politically, a different set of problems arise. Whereas some see civil religion as a form of healthy, national moral solidarity and declare it compatible with a wide variety of religious traditions, others fear that it is a form of national idolatry or a way to sanction, by sanctifying, nationalistic ideologies and aspirations.

In my view, the model can do helpful conceptual work in the hands of scholars of religion. It can generate useful accounts of various social, public phenomena that—in form and function—resemble what we often associate with religion. On the separate and different issue of civil religion and nationalism, it strikes me that civil religion in the United States is not a homogeneous set of symbols and doctrines but is rather an assorted collection of conflicting elements subject to multiple interpretations and serving multiple purposes. For my purposes, "Public Landscape as Religious Space" adds some useful complexity to an otherwise simplistic discussion of the nature of religion in modernity and, more specifically, of religion in the democratic public arena.

Public Landscape as Varied Topography

This is the model I champion. Unlike in the other three models, note that the word *religion* is not in the title of this model. This is not to suggest, as in the second model, that religion should be excluded from the public. Rather, it is to suggest that in this model religion is not initially treated as a special case.

I realize this may sound like a dodge, addressing the issue of *religion* in *public* by eliminating the first of the two terms. But at least as a starting point, this model begins by treating religion (as traditionally understood, i.e., religions such as Judaism or Jainism, Buddhism or Baha'i) just like any other more or less comprehensive world view, such as Marxism, American pragmatism, secular humanism, or hedonism. In this model, one does not decide in advance who may speak, or what kind of arguments one may offer, in public and political debate—even debate on "constitutional essentials and questions of basic justice." In the "Public Landscape as Varied Topography" model, all voices are welcome. Moreover, a working assumption in this model is that the voices usually are varied in form and content. Some voices may be explicitly religious; others may be explicitly nonreligious. In some cases it may not be clear because the language is mixed or because some interpret the voice as religious and others do not. Some voices may be explicitly moral or moralistic; others may be explicitly managerial or amoral. But these distinctions do not matter, according to this model, because no voice is treated as a special case. Or, to say the same thing differently, liberty of conscience and freedom of speech deem that each voice is a special case worthy of a hearing.

This model makes no predictions about whether allowing a varied public topography is likely to produce more conflict or more harmony. In some instances it may lead to divisiveness, in others to accord. But in any case, harmony, often a worthy aim, is not usually the most salient issue. More salient is attention to an open and inclusive conversation and debate. According to "Public Landscape as Varied Topography," if we as individuals and political camps cannot always celebrate the outcome of the debate and the vote, we can at least celebrate the process. Unlike Rousseau, then, we should not deem social disagreement and conflict as the worst thing. Besides, when the religious voice is treated like any other voice, we may see that it is no more or no less likely to create debilitating conflict.

After having noted in what ways religion should not be treated as a special case, "Public Landscape as Varied Topography" goes on to acknowledge that, in some sense, religion is a special subject. Or, more accurately, religion in the United States is *treated* as a special subject. For example, it is a phenomenon addressed by the U.S. Constitution. I have noted that the establishment clause in the First Amendment prohibits the federal government from establishing—officially funding or otherwise sponsoring—religion, and in the very same clause it guarantees the free exercise of religion. In short, government can neither espouse religion nor prohibit citizens' religious activity.

Of course, if the legal standing of religion in the United States were as clear and tidy as I just expressed it, we would not have the constant procession of cases brought to the Supreme Court, cases that routinely split the judges and the country. Happily, for my purposes here, I do not need to address the various and often contradictory interpretations of the First Amendment and how they have been applied to state governments by way of the Fourteenth Amendment. It is enough to note that religion is a special topic in our society.

Given our history of religion, which includes religious persecutions on one hand and religious revivals on the other, we as a people tend to be both religious and wary of religion. There are highly charged issues that pertain to religion in the United States that would not merit consideration in other societies. Different societies, different histories, different concerns. In our society, if a belief or practice is associated with religion, that may be enough for it to become controversial if it enters the public space of government or education, in part because from our history of religion we have learned some lessons of caution.

Adherents to each of the models I have proposed wrestle in one way or another with the issue of religion and conflict. Some appeal to a civil religion in the hope that it will bring national unity (the third model), others appeal to a neutral public space in the hope that it will render religion private and thereby safe for democracy (the second model), and still others appeal to religion as a widely held treasury of virtue that, if not thwarted by government or other secular forces, will fund the country with morality and unity (the first model). And although each model has its merits, each also tends to make doubtful assumptions about how to defuse possible conflict associated with religion: The third model (in some versions) assumes the existence of a pervasive and comprehensive national world view, the second model assumes the viability of stripping away citizens' religious identities in public and political debate, and the first model assumes that traditional religion in the United States, if given free rein, will ensure the moral flourishing of the nation.

Although the fourth model, "Public Landscape as Varied Topography," certainly does not seek to introduce unnecessary conflict and strives to contribute to accord where needful, it focuses more on honoring the First Amendment than on reducing social discord. It seeks to uphold *both sides* of the First Amendment: to prohibit government from officially sponsoring religion and to guarantee the free exercise of religion. This entails allowing religious voices in public and political debate while disallowing state funding and action that promote a particular religion. This model would largely support U.S. Supreme Court decisions since the 1960s that, on one hand, have prohibited state-sponsored religious practice such as school prayer and, on the other hand, have allowed public schools to teach *about* religion—that is, to study religion as an academic subject.[43] This distinction is crucial and reflects the spirit of the fourth model: It prevents the state from promoting a particular religion while authorizing the state to host the study of, and thereby provide a forum on, religious diversity. Indeed, both acts—

forbidding school-sponsored prayer and educating about diverse religious traditions—work in concert as a powerful educational lesson to teach students about living, working, playing, and arguing in a pluralistic society. Respecting diversity in this fashion may be our best course to social accord in the United States on matters where accord is needful.

There are many potential adherents to this model. Noah Feldman, for example, has recently argued for the following "Church–State Solution": "Offer greater latitude for religious speech and symbols in public debate, but also impose a stricter ban on state financing of religious institutions and activities." Although I tend to think of the fourth model not as a solution to a problem but rather as a helpful model for thinking about how to cope variously with an ongoing difficulty, I am inclined to agree with Feldman when he writes, "Ultimately, the nation may have more success generating loyalty from religiously diverse citizens by allowing inclusive governmental manifestation of religion than by banning them."[44] Again, reduction of conflict is not the chief goal of the fourth model. Still, I can't help but hope and even believe that acknowledging and honoring our differences in public and political arenas will lead to a more cooperative society. Welcoming all voices not only is the right thing to do—legally and morally—but may also be the most strategic way to draw on a powerful yet still latent source of strength in the United States: the vitality of its diversity.

A Place for Spiritual Democracy

What I have described as spiritual democracy works well within the fourth model, "Public Landscape as Varied Topography." Spiritual democracy is not identical to it, however. It is one of many possible stances within the model. Spiritual democracy is a distinctively progressive political stance that recognizes the need to attend to both the legal and cultural aspects of a democracy. In contrast to this particular stance, "Public Landscape as Varied Topography" includes both progressive and conservative perspectives. Spiritual democracy, in turn, acknowledges the legitimate inclusiveness of the fourth model and is happy to work within it.

By promulgating progressive spiritual democracy, I am attempting to garner support. I am proselytizing. I want to bring in converts. Perhaps I can convince some that the progressive way is a deeply American way. Or perhaps I can convince those who are already committed to progressive democracy but who, in my view, have not sufficiently grasped the relationship between democracy, religion, and culture. Needless to say, many will not be convinced. Still, if you are like me, someone who sides with progressive politics, then you will want to work hard to make public arguments, to galvanize progressive solidarity, to embed progressive democracy more fully in our institutions and cultures, and all the while to admit—and not attempt to shut down—the right of your challengers to promote their positions. To do otherwise is to risk eroding some of the very ideals that motivate us.

I do not mean to sound sanguine about this. I worry greatly about the rise of conservative politics in the United States. But if we are to be committed to the good work of spiritual democracy, we need to begin and end with tools we believe in: courage, moral wisdom, and justice *for all*. Here, justice entails, among other things, giving each his or her own vote and voice. And, beyond honoring this process, there are grounds for hope. Like a pendulum, politics swings. There are signs that it may soon drift leftward. I would say that politics swings like Hegel's dialectic, but that dialectic ultimately swings upward, and evidence for that kind of hope is mixed at best.

We all need to recognize human fallibility. Take strong stands, but realize that they are provisional and that if we are to achieve something good and lasting, we need to work with each other. I suppose I am hopeful—some may say naive—in my belief that cooperation amid diversity is a source of strength. But the other options—despair, or the attempt to segregate or suppress diversity—seem less helpful or plausible. There are times when hope in something good and right is the most rational option, despite heavy odds against it. But hope requires other virtues. As Lincoln said during an earlier time of division in this country, we are called to act "with malice toward none; with charity for all."

Religion, Democracy, and Modernity: The Way Forward

In Rousseau's work, we gain perspective on the nascent modern era wrestling with its relationship to religion. Rousseau and his peers were too close to their own epoch to see clearly where they stood; we, on our side of modernity, are too close to our epoch to see clearly where we stand. But by looking back at them, we do gain some perspective, some clarity for our own time. What do we see? We see religion. We see religion in many forms when we look back at the outset of what we call modernity and of the movement we call secularization. And we see a variety of approaches that sought to reconcile religion with modernity and modernity with religion. These approaches were various. Some included strategies designed to honor religious diversity or to render such diversity safe, one way or another, for the life of the state, and some worked to cultivate a form of common faith, or shared perspectives that sought to promote a variety of democratic virtues. At the beginning of the secular age we see not the absence of religion but its abundance—and an abundance of sociopolitical approaches for how to accommodate religion, even while those very approaches were being informed by religion.

This should tell us something significant about ourselves, about contemporary liberal society. Modernity—for all its multiplicity—has for the most part engaged with, wrestled with, and been informed by religion, in one form or another. Modernity has never been a monolithic intellectual, cultural force antithetical to religious belief and practice. Yes, some strands of modernity have been hostile toward religion, especially toward traditional religion (we can think of Baron d'Holbach and David Hume, or Karl Marx and Nietzsche, to name four who have greatly influenced my thought).[45] Yet to the same or even greater degree, it could be said that modernity is the outcome of religious influence and that modernity continues to support, and even rely on, religion in a wide array of forms. To this day, religion continues to shape the identity of individuals in their public and their private lives, and therefore it is not much of a stretch to claim that religion continues to shape modernity.

What lessons, then, can we learn from Rousseau about the relationship between religion, democracy, and modernity? A positive lesson from Rousseau is his understanding that a democratic society, even a liberal one, needs some kind of democratic common faith. Indeed, the lesson from Rousseau is that liberal democratic societies that safeguard diversity are *especially* in need of a common faith, that is, of shared democratic beliefs and practices. This common faith will entail commitment to the protection of a wide range of beliefs and practices, including those associated with religion. This is a profound positive lesson to be learned from Rousseau.

However, we should not follow Rousseau in his attempt to shield civil society from division and conflict by keeping religion out of public sight. In the same way that Rousseau held that women in public were dangerous, he also held that (except for the civil religion sanctioned by the state) religion in public was a menace and hence should not be allowed to venture outside the private, domestic life.[46] This is where Rousseau, Rawls, and Rorty work together to define and defend a prominent position on religion and modernity, a position that I have opposed. I have tried to indicate that, although I appreciate why many are wary of religion in public, the risk of allowing religion in public and political exchange is not as great as the promise of inviting it in. This, in my mind, goes to the heart of the promise of a liberal democracy in which diversity of perspective is brought to bear on common projects.

Yet if diversity is to be brought to bear on common projects, it will require of us constant attention to the question of what we do share and should share as a nation. If diversity is to do good work, it will require attention to the issue of some common, albeit shifting ground. It will require something like the cultivation of a democratic common faith. This, I believe, is the way forward to achieving a more genuine and progressive democratic republic.

Most of the time, Rousseau is better at diagnosing our problems than offering solutions. Or, to put it differently, his solutions highlight the nature of our dilemmas. The constant dialectic in his thought between life together and life alone, between the politics of the common good and the politics of rights, is the most distinctive mark of his work, and this, I believe, has made it an enduring source for our reflection. His ultimate hope or vision is a form of life in which individuality is protected and public life encouraged. And although he was, to my mind, overly cautious about religion in public, his middle way remains a promising way, with all its precariousness, rich diversity, and potential friction. For the capacity of a society to embrace diversity—including religious diversity—without denying or attempting to abolish it is the mark of a mature democracy. Achieving this capacity will be one of the greatest challenges of new and old democratic institutions in the 21st century.

Notes

1. There was once much debate about when modernity began. Now most of the debate is about when it ended, or about whether it has ended. In this book, I use the term *modernity* to refer to intellectual, cultural, and political developments that began roughly in the seventeenth century and are still very much with us today. The rise of the nation-state; notions of individualism, liberty, and equality; the distinction between public and private; the invention of the social contract; urbanization, industrialization, and compulsory education—these are some features I associate with modernity (although many of these have premodern antecedents). This is not to deny more recent developments that are often referred to as postmodern (e.g., suspicion of ahistorical reason and radical autonomy, or the rise of globalization and the digital revolution). Are we too close to our own age to see when modernity ended and when the postmodern

began? There are good arguments on either side of this issue. But I do not need to weigh in on this. In this book, modernity includes what is now commonly called postmodern.

2. I have no prediction about the future of religion, that is, about the prevalence of religion in the next one to two hundred years (and I certainly have no theory about humans being naturally religious). However, I would like to note that predictions about the future of religion are inextricably linked to how one defines religion. For example, Émile Durkheim's early work embraced the idea that religion was destined to disappear in modernity. His later work argued the opposite, however, namely that religion permeates the modern world as much as it had the premodern one. But his *notion* of religion also changed: It became more flexible and inclusive of a variety of human beliefs and practices. As one who is wary of essentialist definitions of religion, I also tend to be wary of the main evidence that is often used to support secularization theories: participation in organized religion (e.g., church or temple attendance). Of course, even this evidence suggests that religion today is robust.

3. The work of Émile Durkheim, which offers some of the finest critical interpretations of Rousseau, was greatly informed by what I am calling Rousseau's communitarian defense of liberalism. See Cladis, *A Communitarian Defense of Liberalism: Emile Durkheim and Contemporary Social Theory* (Stanford, Calif.: Stanford University Press, 1992), pp. 11–28.

4. See chapter 7, pp. 127–43.

5. Judith Shklar, *Ordinary Vices* (Cambridge: Harvard University Press, 1984).

6. Some have ventured into this territory, such as Pierre-Maurice Masson, *La religion de Jean-Jacques Rousseau* (Paris: Librairie Hachette, 1916); Pierre Burgelin, *Jean-Jacques Rousseau et la religion de Genève* (Geneva: Éditions Labor et Fides Genève, 1962); Ronald Grimsely, *Rousseau's Religious Thought* (Oxford: Oxford University Press, 1970); and Helena Rosenblatt, *Rousseau and Geneva* (Cambridge: Cambridge University Press, 1997).

7. See chapter 6, pp. 100–4.

8. In fact, I develop five paths; see chapters 7–10.

9. I use "Enlightenment optimism" and "Augustinian pessimism" more as ideal types than as the historically rich and diverse traditions of thought that each could include. By Enlightenment optimism, I generally refer to the belief that humans are naturally good and can deliver themselves from evil and oppression. In contrast, Augustinian pessimism is the belief that humans cannot cure themselves, that no measure of enlightenment can rid humans of a deep-seated proclivity to beget disordered lives that injure them and those around them.

10. Clearly, a religious vocabulary was not the only vocabulary he used for this purpose. He also used, for example, Greek and Roman virtue language (which, of course, contains its own religious roots and dimensions).

11. See chapter 10, pp. 189–97.

12. Remember, I am describing the role of religion in what I have called Rousseau's remedy, the middle way. In his contrary remedies, the extreme public path, there is no personal religion, and on the extreme private path, there is no public religion.

13. Richard Rorty, *Philosophy and Social Hope* (New York: Penguin, 1999), p. 169.

14. Ibid., p. 171.

15. Ibid., p. 169.

16. The Annual Meeting of the American Academy of Religion, November 2003.

17. See Jeffrey Stout's *Democracy and Tradition* (Princeton: Princeton University Press, 2004), pp. 85–86, for a discussion on democratic virtues in public speech.

18. John Rawls, *Political Liberalism* (New York: Columbia University Press, 1996), p. 215.

19. Ibid., pp. li–lii. For a fuller—and, in my view, the most helpful—treatment of Rawls on religion and public reason, see Stout, *Democracy and Tradition*, pp. 65–77.

20. John Rawls, *Collected Papers* (Cambridge: Harvard University Press, 1999), p. 576.

21. Rawls, *Political Liberalism*, p. 1.

22. John Dewey, "Democracy in the Schools," in *The Philosophy of John Dewey*, ed. Joseph Ratner (New York: Random House, 1939), pp. 720–21.

23. Walt Whitman, "Democratic Vistas," in *Whitman: Poetry and Prose* (New York: Library of America, 1982), p. 977.

24. I think of these not as rigid historical stages but rather as aspects of a democracy that develop and reinforce each other.

25. Whitman, "Democratic Vistas," p. 956 (italics added).

26. Ibid., p. 941 (italics added).

27. Walt Whitman, *Leaves of Grass*, in *Whitman: Poetry and Prose* (New York: Library of America, 1982), p. 165.

28. Ibid., p. 193.

29. For a full treatment of the relationship between self-identity and society identity, see Charles Taylor's *Sources of the Self* (Cambridge: Harvard University Press, 1989), pp. 25–52.

30. See Robert Post's forthcoming book, *Democracy and Equality*, in which he argues that democracy is best understood not as particular decision-making procedures such as popular sovereignty but rather as a normative idea that refers to such substantive political values as those expressed in the First Amendment.

31. This is not to suggest that one can ever, even in solitude, live outside sociolinguistic frameworks. Within sociolinguistic scaffoldings we all must always live. I develop this point in the original introduction that follows.

32. For a fuller treatment of this, see chapter 10, p. 206.

33. Seyla Benhabib, *The Claims of Culture* (Princeton: Princeton University Press, 2002), p. ix.

34. Seyla Benhabib, *Situating the Self* (New York: Routledge, 1992), p. 4.

35. Richard Rorty, "Religion in the Public Square: A Reconsideration," *Journal of Religious Ethics* 31:1 (2003): 142.

36. Nicholas Wolsterstorff, "An Engagement with Rorty," *Journal of Religious Ethics* 31:1 (2003): 130.

37. See Ronald White Jr., "The Trajectory of Disestablishment," in *An Unsettled Arena: Religion and the Bill of Rights*, ed. Ronald White Jr. and Albright Zimmerman (Grand Rapids, Mich.: Eerdmans, 1990), p. 51. For the opposite view, see Jean Bethke Elshtain, "Faith of Our Fathers and Mothers: Religious Belief and American Democracy," in *Religion in American Public Life*, eds. Azizah Y. al-Hibri, Jean Bethke Elshtain, and Charles Hayes (New York: Norton, 2001), p. 44.

38. Steven Waldman in the online magazine *Slate*, cited by Paul Bloom in "Is God an Accident," *Atlantic Monthly* (December 2005): 106.

39. See Robert Booth Fowler, *Unconventional Partners* (Grand Rapids: Eerdmans, 1989), pp. 157–59.

40. Rorty, "Religion in the Public Square: A Reconsideration," p. 143.

41. Ibid., p. 148.

42. Ibid., p. 142.

43. Whether a moment of silence in public schools would be permissible is a complicated issue that I cannot address here.

44. Noah Feldman, "A Church–State Solution," in the *New York Times Magazine* (July 3, 2005): 32 and 50. Also found in Feldman, *Divided by God* (New York: Farrar, Straus and Giroux, 2005), pp. 237 and 243.

45. Some would object to my placing even these four figures in a nonreligious or antireligious strand of modernity. Some argue that Hume was a deist advancing a humanistic religion, that Marx developed a religious teleology, and that Nietzsche offered a religious world view in the gospel of Zarathustra. And what of the French materialist, d'Holbach? One could claim that

his work is inspired by a religious naturalism. Take, for example, his ode to nature, *Système de la Nature*:

> O thou [Nature cries to us], denounce those empty theories which are usurpers of my privileges. . . . It is in my empire alone that true liberty reigns. . . . Return, then, my child to thy fostering mother's arms! Deserter, trace back thy wandering steps to Nature. She will console thee for thine evils; she will drive from thy heart those appalling fears which overwhelm thee. Return to nature, to humanity, to thyself. (Baron d'Holbach, *Système de la nature*, vol. 2, chapter 12, cited in James Livingston, *Modern Christian Thought* [Englewood Cliffs, N.J.: Prentice Hall, 1997], p. 8)

46. I treat the topic of Rousseau and women throughout the book, but in particular, see "Preparing for the Journey," pp. 23–31.

Public Vision, Private Lives

Preparing for the Journey

An Introduction

Fellow Travelers

Let me begin with a word about how I have written this book, and for whom. In these pages when I speak of "we or "us," I refer to members of democratic societies, or at least to those familiar with them. I am not writing from everywhere, or from nowhere; I write from the perspective of a liberal democracy, specifically the United States. Within these bounds, however, I have written with many in mind, as did Rousseau himself. Rousseau has presented us with many faces: the social theorist, ethicist, political and religious philosopher, pedagogue, novelist, literary critic, psychologist, musician, and botanist. These faces we will meet, and these disciplines we must cross. Additionally, not only Rousseau, but our topic—the relation between public and private—cuts across many diverse fields and issues: women's studies, democratic theory, modern European history, social theory, philosophy of religion, reproductive rights, social justice, privacy laws, solitude, and community, to name a few. Our topic has become pressing and even grave in various regions in the world. When presenting my work to colleagues from the Middle East or Eastern Europe, for example, I learn much as they translate my concerns and proposals into their local contexts—contexts where the lines between public and private, and between politics and religion, are often formed and reformed with bullets. Although the conflict that I discuss in these pages is less lethal, its scope is wide and potentially quite injurious. And I do not neglect—nor did Rousseau—to reflect on the tremendous human suffering that can occur when political powers brutally impose ideologies and fail to recognize any distinction between its citizens' public and private lives. I have, then, written this book for many. My principal audience, however, are members of liberal democracies with interests in social theory, political philosophy, and philosophy of religion. Rousseauean specialists, I hope, will profit from my study. I have certainly gained much from their work. However, given that my aim is to bring Rousseau into conversation with a broad audience, I often do not explicitly address the interesting and sundry issues embedded in the voluminous secondary literature on Rousseau—literature written largely by and for fellow specialists.

A few years ago, I gave a lecture on some material that is used here in chapter 8, "Evading the City: The Private Path." After the lecture a friend and colleague, Pasquale Pasquino, asked me, "What, as a political philosopher, am I to do with categories like solitude and the private life?" His candid comment made me realize that part of my challenge is to introduce uncommon categories into our ethical and political deliberations. Individual rights already figure importantly in our discussions. Rights allow the individual, among other things, to create a private space, a world, if you will, in which the individual is safe and at ease. Yet the relation between that private world and the public is usually examined abstractly in terms of formal rights. We fail to study, for example, the often dramatic, public consequences that flow from the private choices and meditations of individuals as they wrestle with issues about lifestyle, religion, family, finances, the environment, and other significant moral, practical, or philosophical issues. Revolutions are dreamed of and nurtured not only in factories and in the streets, but in the company of close friends, and even in solitude.

We never know in advance the relation between the goings-on in our protected private space and public discourse and action. In my backyard, I watch my chickens eagerly scratch the soil, and I contrast their diverse daily routines to that of a chicken that spends its entire life inside a small cage in a huge coop, never to experience sunlight or wind. I grow determined to buy free-range eggs and I begin to think about, and even write about, public policy and the treatment of farm animals.[1] And it doesn't stop there. I also begin to consider the controlled, oppressive environment in which many laborers work. Like chickens in mechanized coops, migrant and other workers have little freedom to fashion their practices in ways that bring satisfaction. Their relation to the land, animals, and work is bent to maximize profits, not human flourishing. Revising Marx, such workers see neither themselves, nor the animals, in their work; with supervisor watching, they see with constricted assembly-line vision a parade of disjointed commodities. A private activity like owning a few chickens, then, can lead one to ask and wonder about little things, like grubs, but also about big things, like the dark face in the field or factory. And the more we wonder, the more we live and see differently.

Privately cultivated interests and dispositions of the individual, then, bear on the public life, just as the public life—collective dispositions, goals, and values—reaches into the private life. Attention to this transactional relation is at the heart of this study and Rousseau's own approach. "Society," he insisted, "must be studied in the individual and the individual in society. Those who want to treat politics and morals separately will never understand anything of either of them."[2]

Mapping the Terrain

I have much to map: Rousseau, religion, the public and private, and the controversies that surround these issues. My approach to Rousseau and these issues is consistent with my field of expertise—social theory and ethics as they relate to religion in society. My main contribution to social theory and religious studies has been my investigations of the religious nature and origins of democratic society. Social theory, ethics, and religious studies—these are my fields of inquiry, and at their intersection stand my publications. This is certainly the position of this study.

I locate Rousseau in the diverse traditions of eighteenth-century French moral philosophy and theological ethics. These French traditions depicted variously the relation between love of self and love of God (or love of things outside the self) and thereby produced intricate models of the relation between public and private. Rousseau, perhaps more than any other figure in the eighteenth century, wrestled with these complex, competing traditions. I place Rousseau at the crossroads of Enlightenment optimism and Augustinian pessimism, and I show that this awkward spiritual location enabled him to probe and articulate the tension and harmony between our concern for ourselves and our obligation to others.[3] My placement of Rousseau at these crossroads will be a dominant theme in this study. In the *Confessions*, Rousseau claimed that his early reading, especially of the writings of Port-Royal and the Oratory, had made him "half a Jansenist."[4] My argument will be that Rousseau never entirely extricated himself from Jansenist, Augustinian pessimism. From the tangled French traditions of human goodness and fallenness, from a maze of beliefs about our ability and inability to care for ourselves and others, at the intersection of Enlightenment optimism and Augustinian pessimism, Rousseau formulated what I will call his paths to partial redemption—the private path, the public path, and the tense middle way between them.

My focus on the religious nature of Rousseau's thought has informed many of my arguments, including their presentation. For example, I have fashioned the opening chapters in the shape of that famous myth, central to Western thought, that speaks of a fall from a lovely garden and the various attempts to survive and even flourish outside the garden. This narrative, in this book, is not about a distant past but about present possibilities of joy and sorrow in solitude and community. I argue that the Garden—if not God's, then Nature's—allowed Rousseau to portray humans in radical isolation. Social life creeps onto the stage with a fall that unfolds in several phases. Each step away from the Garden—a hypothetical state of isolation, the state of nature—takes us further into the psychological and sociological complexity of the tension and conflict between life alone and life together. And with each step we sink deeper into the labyrinths of moral evil and modern misery on the one hand, and ambiguous moral progress and precarious social happiness on the other. In contrast to most interpreters of Rousseau, I argue that if we identify categorically the natural with the good and the social with evil, we fail to do justice to Rousseau's provocative account of the passage from the amoral Garden to the equivocally moral City.

The book begins by focusing on life in the Garden, because its inhabitants—Rousseau's Solitaires—have as much to tell us about association as about solitude.[5] Rousseau attributed liberal characteristics to the Solitaires, specifically the freedom from inflicting and receiving unnecessary harm. Yet in the Garden there is neither humanity nor virtue, only simple Solitaires and the natural maxim, "*Do good to yourself with as little harm as possible to others.*"[6] In spite of Rousseau's allegiance to the natural maxim, he wanted more: public and private virtue and joy must risk at least as much vice and pain. To move from the simple maxim to the virtues, from the Solitaires to humanity, from the Garden to society, is to be willing to love things outside the self, and to be vulnerable to such loves. Rousseau, then, came to realize that alone, as radical solitaires, although we are protected from much pain, we can be neither truly happy nor moral. In the company of others, however, even as we seek to do good, we risk inflicting harm. Rousseau's response to this dilemma illuminates a salient feature of modern liberal society:

the more we seek to do good, the more we risk doing evil; or, conversely, the more we avoid such risk, the more we dodge our moral obligations.

By the time we have traveled with Rousseau to the end of a rather dismal journey into social life (part I), we ask whether there is a way to improve our condition (part II). This question, the question of restoration or redemption, dominated much of Rousseau's thought. He posed two different, even contrary, remedies: a public path and a private path. The public path reflects, if only dimly, the Enlightenment hope that human fallenness can be overcome by reforming society; the private path reflects the Augustinian conviction that humans, due to their inward fallen condition, cannot cure themselves of sin or evil. The one recommends that individuals ensconce themselves snugly within the enlightened, educative community; the other recommends that individuals cultivate a spiritual interior life and extricate themselves from commitments and other social entanglements that exacerbate the human propensity to inflict harm.

At the crossroads, Rousseau, like Janus, gazed in two directions at the same time, or at least in rapid succession. In one direction, he beheld humans able to transform their societies humanely; in the other, he perceived humans destined for immense suffering unless they dodge social involvement. Rousseau never cast off this uncomfortable double vision. Ultimately, he recognized the necessity of both the public and private life even as he detailed the inevitable conflict between them.

One way to account for Rousseau's double vision is to locate him at the crossroads of Augustinian pessimism and Enlightenment optimism. Whether he was aware of his awkward position is difficult to say. Perhaps his proximity to these two traditions obstructed his perception of how he was tangled up in them. There is a chance, however, that greater awareness of his historical locality would not have significantly altered his tensive position. Whether dwelling in his age or in ours, perhaps Rousseau would still seek to inhabit some juncture, some crossway, from which he could remind us of both our responsibility for ourselves and our powerlessness to radically transform ourselves.

After Rousseau produced his perhaps clearest expression of the Augustinian fallen condition ("I sense myself enslaved and free at the same time; I see the good, I love it, and I do the bad"), he wrote, "If to prefer oneself above all else is an inclination natural to man, and if, however, the first sentiment of justice is innate in the human heart, let those who say man is a simple being remove these contradictions."[7] For Rousseau, as for Kant and Freud, there is an eternal struggle between our concern for ourselves and our obligation to others. However, a close reading of the role of religion in Rousseau's work suggests a path that enables us to reconcile, at least partially, the previous two paths rather than pose them as alternatives. On this reading, Rousseau described the Flourishing City as composed of members who have undergone a conversion to the religion of the heart. This conversion enables individuals to trade private willfulness and egoism for social cooperation and genuine selfhood. It requires as much solitude as social support; one consults the heart—the convictions of conscience—as one participates in the general will. The religion of the heart, in sum, brings together personal inwardness and social commitment, private perfection and social usefulness, love of self and love of things public. This third path—the middle way of mixed loves—we find in Rousseau's most famous works, The Social Contract and Emile. To unlock these pivotal works, the middle way provides a novel and useful interpretive key.

In chapter 10, I highlight the religious dimensions of Rousseau's thought on the middle way. Rousseau associated the deepest aspects of the public and private life with religion, and he employed a religious vocabulary when he articulated their potential reconciliation and conflict. He maintained that freedom, equality, and individual rights require support not only from law, but from common, shared traditions and commitments—from something like a common, secular faith. Moreover, he held that freedom of religious belief is necessary for individuals to flourish as human beings and as citizens. A cultivated interior life can bring personal fulfillment, and it can enable a person to become "self-possessed," that is, capable of autonomous deliberation in private and public domains. Rousseau's middle way sought to capture both the public and private aspects of religion: to champion a unifying, common faith as well as to protect private projects.

Public and private religion, we will see, need not be narrowly defined. Public religion can encompass any set of shared beliefs and practices that contributes to moral solidarity. We find aspects of public religion in shared democratic culture—the kind of culture, for example, that responds with righteous indignation when someone's rights are trampled on, as if a sacrilege had been committed. Likewise, private religion need not be restricted to personal religious devotion as traditionally understood. Rather, private religion can refer to any deep, abiding personal beliefs that help individuals make sense of the moral and natural universe in which they find themselves. Rousseau's commitment to both public and private religion pertains to the heart to this book—the relation between the public and private in liberal, democratic society. On the middle way, Rousseau struggled to reconcile the public and private.

In Rousseau's view, however, the success of the middle way is doubtful. Of the three paths to redemption, the middle path winds the most precariously between public and private. It is not, then, the proverbial happy middle way. At best, it is the way of a worthy challenge: the challenge to society to maintain commitment to both the public and private spheres, in spite of their conflict. Rousseau's implicit admission of its difficulties can be heard especially in his later writings, when the tired, aged, often paranoid Rousseau offered the more cautious, even if less fully human, extreme public and private paths. While Rousseau's own life usually shunned the risk of tension and division, such risk is in fact a strength of the third path. To tolerate this friction is a central, moral attribute of liberal, democratic societies. Liberalism would cease to be genuinely human if, like the Solitaires, the safety of the individual were to become not a primary but the sole goal. Conversely, it would cease to be liberal if it put society first in every case. For liberalism to continue as a promising social order, it must hazard the risks of commitment to a shared, public life; it must remain awkwardly wed to a politics of the common good.

There is still another path—the way of Clarens, or the Mountain Village. In chapter 9, I discuss this path that integrates solitude, family, work, community, and love. In the Mountain Village, self-sufficient families enjoy community life, agreeable work, and natural beauty. In many ways, this was Rousseau's personal ideal. Clarens has much to teach us about what we may hope for from family and friends, from local community, and from those intermediate spheres where the lines between public and private are not stark, where individuals can gather and share their different yet related lives. Yet the way of Clarens has no political life. It has neither a government nor a cultural tradition of safeguarding individual rights. Hence we should fear anything resembling a national Clarens. Any all-encompassing, national communitarian aspirations should give us pause. Clarens, like Rousseau's other paths, remains partial, incomplete, and provisional.

Can we achieve a lively and just common life and also support thriving private lives? I have put this question to Rousseau, and I offered his various responses as the four paths: the extreme public path of "Poland" (chapter 7); the extreme private path of the Solitaire (chapter 8); Clarens's way of work, family, and community (chapter 9); and the middle way of the Flourishing City (chapter 10). Although none of these paths is entirely satisfying, Rousseau remains a lively and brilliant companion in the exploration of the relation between the public and private in democratic societies. Most of the time he is better at diagnosing our problems than offering solutions. Or to put it differently, his solutions highlight the nature of our dilemmas. The constant dialectic in his thought between life together and life alone, between the politics of the common good and the politics of rights, is the most distinctive mark of his work, and this has made it an enduring source for our reflection. His ultimate hope or vision is a form of life in which individuals are both at ease in their private lives and at home in community—where individuality is protected and public life is encouraged.

Judith Shklar, perhaps our finest student of Rousseau, concluded that Rousseau called on his readers to make a choice between being "men" (independent moral beings) or "citizens" (dependent social beings).[8] My conclusion is that Rousseau ultimately called us to become both, yet this requires our willingness to endure inevitable conflict between the public and private. Such conflict is not a sign of desperate division, but of moral struggle—the lot of humans outside the Garden.

Walking Styles

I have described this book as a journey or conversation with Rousseau. This characterizes my approach or method. Unfortunately, "conversation" is often a mild term conjuring such placid images as fireside chats. It connotes, however, other meanings as well, and these capture much of what I have done. Without entering the sundry debates of contemporary hermeneutics, conversing with Rousseau, in this book, means to pose certain questions to his texts, to listen carefully to the responses, and to attempt to learn something helpful, though not always something true. For example, when Rousseau consigns women to the private sphere and appeals to "Nature herself" as an accomplice, we learn much about Rousseau as an architect of, and conduit for, eighteenth-century trends that pertain to women, subjugation, and social stratification. We do not learn something true about the ontological nature of women (as if there were one). Rather, we grasp something helpful for understanding a portion of an effective history that infuses our present: women prevented from obtaining such visible, public positions as CEO or high, elected official, or the more subtle, daily subjugation of women.

"Conversation" is an appropriate metaphor for still another reason. It suggests an engagement that leads to discovery as much as to invention. I have brought to Rousseau's texts as much as I have taken from them. I have made as much as I have found. For example, the narrative framework in part I—the Solitaire's fall or tumble from Nature's Garden to urban sociability—is one I have both discovered in Rousseau's writings and have constructed imaginatively to illuminate those writings. The same could be said of what, in part II, I call the paths to redemption. I constructed these paths as heuristic tools that both creatively enter the texts and natively emerge from them. "Conversation," I am suggesting, captures something of this interpretive dance between reader and text, between myself and Rousseau. That dance will vary from reader to reader, and from generation to generation. There is no final reading. In the flow of life, our perspectives change and the meaning of texts shifts, each generation addressed anew.

I have attempted to render and measure Rousseau for my generation. This has entailed, among other things, recognizing the friction—dissimilarity grating against similarity—between his time and our own, and the lessons to be learned in that friction. I have not developed thick, historical accounts of Rousseau's ideas and the history that led up to them; nor, however, have I neglected to use the past to view ourselves in a new light. If pushed to identify the one principle or bridge that I built to link Rousseau's thought to our own, I would point to the normative issues that drive this book: *Justice and well-being, in light of the problems and promises posed by the public and private in modern democracies.* When I read Rousseau, the question behind all my other questions is: How does this contribute to the art of living well, to living with integrity and joy? Due to his character, and his location in time and space—in prevailing sociohistorical currents and the singular circumstances of his life—Rousseau was one of the first to recognize and describe the mounting strains of modern existence. His genealogy of modern alienation and misery, while not always reliable and rarely systematic, has much to offer us. In this study I am more interested in learning from his offerings than in producing a comprehensive critique of his work. I do not ignore his limits and errors, for these, too, have much to teach us. But my focus is not Rousseau himself, but rather an employment of Rousseau to help us think about the nature of the public and private.

In my effort both to bring light to and draw lessons from Rousseau, I have approached his work more systematically than he ever did. We should not complain that Rousseau did not follow a systematic philosophical method; few humans, or philosophers for that matter, ever do. We may complain that his arguments were not more linear, or wish they were less embedded in rhetorical embellishment or in the circumstances that occasioned his writing. This, however, is more a judgment of style than of competence. Like many reformers, Rousseau claimed that he was "not interested in reforming people, but simply telling them the truth." In fact, he crafted his truth to disturb us, to make us aware of our frenzied, anxious existence, in the hope that with such awareness we might be able to ameliorate our condition.

Some have claimed that the truth Rousseau would speak to us is marked by paradox. Proust noted that today's paradox is tomorrow's prejudice, and this ironically accords with an original meaning of the Greek *paradoxos*, namely, that which goes against common sense. I suppose that, given this definition, Rousseau was a paradoxical thinker, for he often challenged much that was considered common sense; meanwhile, much of our common sense—about repose in solitude, fellowship in community, beauty in nature—has become Rousseauean. There are others, however, who would prefer to call paradox a mysteriously useful, wise, or perceptive incongruity that is often mistaken by the uninitiate as a useless, sloppy, or ridiculous contradiction. I do not ascribe to Rousseau many paradoxes of this sort, because I want to avoid associating their almost mystical quality with Rousseau, seldom a particularly mystical thinker.

Still, I am more sympathetic with those who see enigmatic paradox in Rousseau's work than with those who see only careless contradiction. Both camps, I believe, have identified in some of Rousseau's stances what the French call an *indécisibilité*: two credible positions that contradict each other and between which we can't decide. What could help us decide is some sort of criterion. Those who celebrate paradoxes are often attracted to complex subjects that permit or even seem to demand a multiplicity of criteria, whereas those whose profession is to eliminate contradictions prefer uncluttered subjects measured by precise gauges. This latter group, which interprets "undecidability" as indecision at best or obtuseness at worst, has voiced the by-now familiar complaint that Rousseau's message to us is riddled with contradictions and ambiguities.

The charge is not entirely misplaced, and I am grateful to those who have exposed specific, unseemly contradictions in Rousseau's work. The force of the general complaint, however, attenuates when we realize that it often carries the erroneous assumption that Rousseau wanted but failed to offer a single message in a systematic discourse. Rousseau was never capable of or interested in those carefully marshaled, limited arguments that we nowadays associate with caricatures of analytic philosophy. When clarity and consistency become not merely the means but the goal of our research, our subject matter narrows in scope and complexity.

Rousseau, in contrast, pursued untidy, complex topics that compelled him to navigate a maze of themes and criteria. If his various claims are severed from their context, and are placed side by side, divorced from the challenging terrain he explored, then the charge of contradictory thought appears convincing. The charge seems less impressive, however, when we evaluate Rousseau's various messages in their native environment—a sundry of challenging issues that emerge from the larger questions that preoccupied his thought. If we situate his claims in the balance between his particular arguments and his general stances and inquiries, then we are less likely to take a qualification for a contradiction, or to take an inherent ambiguity in subject matter for sloppy reasoning.

To this end, I have placed Rousseau's thought in a narrative not alien to it. The narrative structure has enabled me to embed Rousseau's arguments in specific contexts which themselves, in turn, form the parts of a larger whole. Working among these plots and subplots offers a decisive advantage, permitting us to move felicitously between the parts and the whole of Rousseau's thought. To be sure, some interpretive dance of this sort is required of all profitable readings. But the narrative approach, while not appropriate for all or even most subjects, seems especially suitable when faced with the windings and turnings of Rousseau's life and thought.[9] With such an approach, the richness of Rousseau's arguments is more apparent, and the so-called contradictions look more like nuanced descriptions of complex social and psychological events and circumstances. This is not to deny that Rousseau's thought—and life—on occasion lacked integral consistency and coherence. More often, however, the inconsistency and incoherence belong to the human behavior that Rousseau perspicuously portrayed without worrying whether the sketches permitted exact judgments. Actually, he did sometimes worry about this, but not enough to cause him to work his troublesome wooden blocks with more harmony or balance than he himself saw in the subjects before, and within, him.

A narrative approach is often more useful as a supplement, not a substitute, to a more systematic examination. Hence, without forsaking the narrative I present in the first four chapters, I explore more systematically, in the remaining chapters of part I, issues that the narrative introduced: the very idea of the state of nature, the inevitability of the Fall, the nature and origin of evil, and the prospect of restoration. In part II, continuing with the more analytic approach, I investigate Rousseau's proposed public and private remedies, and the tension between them. I have, then, constructed a frame to host an array of images—ideas and stances, hopes and fears—that Rousseau created on different occasions, giving birth to diverse visions. To display this work, illuminating it anew yet without distortion, has been my task.

Public and Private Canvassed

There is no single, essentialist definition of public or private that captures all the dimensions of either concept. This observation applies to most substantial concepts, and especially to concepts that mutually define each other, as is the case of public and private. Think of public and private as two poles of a continuum. Activities that belong near the poles—writing in one's private diary, at one end, giving a public speech, at the other— are fairly straightforward cases. Yet as we travel away from each pole, it becomes difficult to define the activities of the middle region as definitively public or private. Most daily events and practices belong to this between space, appearing public from one point of view, private from another, depending on circumstances.

Here is still another complication in the attempt to define public and private. There is not one, but many useful and appropriate continuums on which to place the public and private. The activities and practices that we associate with the public and private straddle different sets of polarities. Take, for example, "the private sector." It belongs to a continuum whose poles are private businesses operating under no government regulation or state intervention, on the one hand, and government agencies or state-run operations, on the other. On such a continuum, where are we to place the activity of a solitary walk, a street party, or a demonstration? For these activities, we need a different public-private continuum, perhaps one ranging from the solitary to the social. On some occasions, we can utilize a broad, general public-private continuum on which a wide range of heterogeneous activities are placed. Usually, however, such imprecise scales provide little help.

In this study, the meaning of the terms *public* and *private* will usually be disclosed by the various contexts in which I use them. Provisional definitions can be helpful, however, and that is what I now wish to provide. Think of these as impressionistic canvases of the varied public-private terrain that we will explore more carefully in the following chapters.

The private life is as diverse a notion as the public life. It brings to mind the individual and her solitary moments, her hidden fantasies, her contemplative moments, her unspoken hopes and fears. Also we think of the individual in relation to others— lovers, family members, close friends. These relationships are marked by intimacy, trust, and vulnerability—as opposed to reserve, caution, or contracts. Sometimes we extend the idea of the private to include a community, an organization, or a local establishment, especially those we are tempted to characterize as one big happy—or not-so-happy— "family." Although in this study I do not usually include such social life under the heading of the private, I appreciate why some would. In these social spaces—a religious congregation, for example, or a neighborhood coffee shop—we feel at home. Familiarity, ease, and comfort—these characterize the private life, and also some local bars. For this very reason, out-of-town travelers often feel uncomfortable when entering a local establishment. Opening the door, impaled by the stare of onlookers, they hesitate at the threshold between outside and inside, as if they have accidentally entered a stranger's home. Again, we find that public and private are relative terms that mutually define each other. In the same bar that appeared too local, too domestic to the outsider, a local couple is secluded in a corner, privately discussing their troubled child, mindful that none should overhear them in such a public setting. We can go further still: one parent, say, the father, is haunted by images from his childhood that are too painful, too buried, too private to bring to the light of conversation. The meaning of public and private emerges from our interpretation of the details of a context. In this book, I will mainly explore the private life in terms of individuals alone with themselves, or else in spheres of intimacy.

Under the rubric of private, I will not usually include what we call the financial "private sector." I will include the activity of individuals pursuing self-interest, but that activity cannot be limited to the private sector. The private sector is private insofar as it is contrasted to state ownership, agencies, and administration. Yet, as a domain, the private sector refers more to an economic, public arrangement than to a domain of solitude, intimacy, friendship, or even community. Besides, although the private sector contains local bars and coffee shops (insofar as these are not state owned operations), increasingly the private sector is dominated by national or multinational business operations that provide a homogeneous experience for the customer. Most anyone can walk into a shopping mall and feel "at home" even if far from home. This has its own set of advantages and disadvantages, and both sets spring from the impersonal, "universal" character of the shopping mall. The private sector receives everyone, at least in theory, with the same greeting. And to be open to all is to be personal to none, because the personal always entails some exclusion. The private sector, then, is often public. Some businesses do operate like a family or circle of friends for which personal history is as or more important than financial goals or business credentials. More and more, however, business is defined by bureaucracy, impersonal procedures, and the feverish pursuit of bottom-line targets. Indeed, when CEOs or deans act otherwise, they may be accused of nepotism, incompetence, or worse. In this study, the private life has little to do with the financial private sector as a domain, except this: the very nature and importance of the private life is largely in response, and even in opposition, to the impersonal, hectic, and bureaucratic existence that increasingly characterizes the so-called private sector.

What, then, typifies the private life? To bring to mind the private life, imagine that you are alone, walking in the woods, either for pleasure or on a necessary journey. We could place your walk on a city street and in the company of others. However, we want to start this journey on what the clock maker's son, Rousseau, considered to be the private path's most pristine segment: the woods, and alone.[10]

Without quotidian worries and hectic amusements, you are free to attend to the changing path in front of you, and to your relation to that path. At last, you have some time and space to consider your life, not in its crushing details, but as a whole—as if from a gentle distance. And though you may ponder some troubling features of your life—glaring limits, repetitive failures, unrealized goals, ruined faith, and so forth—the expanse of the woods and the view it affords eases your mind and lends hope, placing problems and fears in helpful perspective. In repose and peace, you can think and ponder with clarity and focus and with that spirit of generosity that seems to issue from the beauty of the woods.

Many of us, I suspect, are lured on occasion to the image of, if not the reality of, this private path, or a least to some of its many offerings. For us, today, the solitary walker is an inviting image. Yet eighteenth-century readers were surprised and some were offended by Rousseau's book, *Reveries of the Solitary Walker*, even by its very title. It struck many as odd, indulgent, and antisocial if not misanthropic. Why must Rousseau stand outside society? Why must he shun us and haunt our countryside as a dark, secretive phantom? Today, in contrast, we regard the phantom with respect, sometimes with envy. We have this regard because we are the beneficiaries of a romantic tradition, with Rousseau at its font, that celebrates the image of the solitaire. But there is more. We inhabit a world that is increasingly marked by instrumental reasoning, on the one hand, and frantic lifestyles, on the other. As each minute of our day becomes scheduled, and each act calculated for maximum yield—even our vacations and leisure must deliver us ready for productivity—we sink into the swift yet exact currents of contemporary public existence. In our exhaustion and perhaps despondency, we may long for the private path, provided we have time and sight to catch a glimpse of it.

Rousseau created the private path, one of the four ways to redemption, in the wake of a dismal and painful public life. He was one of the first to recognize and describe the mounting strains of modern existence. In part I, I rehearse Rousseau's genealogy of modern alienation and misery; we need not preview that here. For now, it is enough to note that Rousseau's private path was his response, or protest, to what he perceived as an increasingly heartless world: a hollow, barren public existence born by a mass of anxious, covetous, private selves. Rousseau suffered in such a world, dreamt of fleeing it, and attempted an escape. That attempt I am calling the private path. And while most of us value private *retreats*, Rousseau explored the private path as *a way of life*. In the following pages we will ask, without a robust public life, can there be a replete private life? Does the joy of solitude become bitter grief when solitude ceases to be a temporary refuge but becomes an abiding form of life?

These thoughts are but broad strokes that portray the terrain of the private life and the path that Rousseau cleared on it. What of the public life? It, too, is a complex concept. It brings to mind those activities and events that we associate with the marketplace, vocations, government agencies, civic participation, public leadership, and a host of social events and community organizations. Government agencies, the market, and the workplace are often marked by reserve, bureaucracy, and contracts. Yet public space is not marked only by these characteristics, especially when it includes community activities, organizations, and local establishments. As I noted before, in a religious congregation, a neighborhood coffee shop, or bar, we can feel at home. Familiarity, ease, and comfort—these, too, often characterize such public realms. Yet in them we are not entirely "at home." We are not, for example, likely to talk, or even dress, as if we were in our private, domestic space. In public, we are aware that we are not alone: we are in the presence of others, and to speak, or dress, too freely could give offense, or at least make people ill at ease. There are social conventions that operate in public, not in the home. Usually, the more impersonal the public space, the more abundant the social conventions. For this reason, many out-of-town travelers feel comfortable when entering such an impersonal, public establishment as a national restaurant franchise, say, a Howard Johnson's. Opening the door, the travelers are ignored by all and do not feel the least bit conspicuous, for they have entered an anonymous public space. Again, however, we find that public and private are relative terms that mutually define each other. Within this same establishment that appears to some travelers to be public, safe, and impersonal, an interracial couple is ushered to a secluded table, lest their particularity should appear too conspicuous, even repugnant, in a conventionally homogeneous, white public space. We can go further still: one partner, feeling discomfort even in the corner of the restaurant, longs for a larger public arena, perhaps the canyons of New York City, where diversity abounds, while the other partner, dreading all public space, longs for the safety of home. The meaning of public and private, again, emerge from our interpretation of the details—details of a context, details of a life, details that a culture celebrates, ignores, or loathes.

To bring to mind the public life, we begin with a fictitious case to illustrate some notable aspects of this broad terrain. Imagine that you have emerged from your walk in the woods—of, say, a city park. You cross a busy boulevard as you make your way to the neighborhood coffee shop—Stacey's, we'll call it. Upon entering, you make your way to the only unoccupied table, acknowledging some familiar faces on the way. Greg, who's at the register, announces with a subtle grin on an otherwise straight face that "the famous philosopher" has arrived, while Stacey, who is in the back baking bread, flashes a smile at Greg and shouts a rushed greeting to you. As you wait for your lunch partner, you might enter easy conversation with fellow lunchers at nearby tables. If you know them well, you might discuss the upcoming elections; if not so well, the weather or coffee-of-the-day. You sip your coffee, enjoy the background music, and delight in this place that is neither home nor foreign, but comfortably familiar; a place where you are surrounded not by family, but by acquaintances and strangers. Presently Paul, "the famous poet" in Greg's parlance, arrives, and your lunch conversation begins. After eight years of this lunch routine, the conversation begins quickly but not predictably; it is relaxed, but not superfluous. Although myriad subjects emerge, so do such common themes as how to integrate the various aspects of one's existence—solitude, family, friends, work, social commitments—into a coherent, graceful way of life. Talking about the integration of things public and private seems to help. Also, the ethos of the coffee shop—a familiar yet public setting—enhances the conversation.

You leave Stacey's refreshed, much as the woods had restored you. Perspective, again, has visited your life, and has brought some relief. Next, you walk down the block to pick up your prescription from Roy at the local pharmacy, and then to a small bookstore to visit Walter, the owner, and see if a book has arrived. During the rest of the day, at work, you carry with you a sense of belonging to a specific place, and this somehow adds significance to your work. In the afternoon, you use your office phone to make some personal local calls about an upcoming election that you and some of your friends are involved in. You worry about the propriety of using the office phone for such "personal" calls, but the calls need to be made, and you cannot make them this evening, because today is Thursday. Thursday evenings you visit a local establishment different from Stacey's—a maximum security prison where you participate in various prisoner-run discussion groups. After ten years of this Thursday evening prison routine, the conversation there, like at Stacey's, begins quickly but not predictably; it is relaxed, but not superfluous. Here, at the prison, your exchange with the inmates encompasses the whole human drama—life and death, wealth and poverty, forgiveness and bitterness, solitude and solitary confinement, community and the prison industrial-complex, friends and antagonists, family visits and family tragedies. Although myriad subjects emerge, so do such common themes as how to integrate the various aspects of one's existence—solitude, family, friends, work, social commitments—into a tolerable way of life within the context of a maximum security prison. You leave the prison both emotionally exhausted and yet, somehow, renewed, much as the woods and Stacey's had restored you. Again, having encountered a palpable reality outside your own narrow worries and concerns, you have gained helpful perspective. Somehow the prison, like beauty itself, allowed you to become preoccupied, effortlessly, with things other than cramped self-interest. On Thursdays you return home late, exhausted, and hungry. There is much still to be done—make dinner and bathe children, for example. Still, even as you complain of fatigue, you accept and perhaps even welcome the familiar tasks in this domain of intimacy.

This fictitious case illustrates aspects of the public life, but also suggests difficulties in our attempts to define it. My examples of public and private no doubt reflect my background and identity. Bookstores and lunch partners—these are largely middle-class phenomena; and the very notion of solitude may be gendered in a society where women, encumbered with employment and domestic responsibilities, have little time to think about solitude, even when they are alone, as they work on or ponder the tasks before them. Still, in spite of the limitations of my examples, I am convinced that in this study basic issues pertaining to the public and private manifest themselves, albeit differently, in diverse social and economic circumstances.

Many of us, from various backgrounds, long for a public life that is rich, diverse, and meaningful. A satisfying public life contains civic activities such as involvement in local and national elections as well as informal social activities such as lunch at the local coffee shop or easy sociability among neighbors on the front porch. Public space includes not only the courthouse but also the public park; not only City Hall but also the neighborhood bar or grocery. Dances, protests, festivals, quilting circles, cooperative work, public storytelling, get-out-the-vote campaigns, public lectures, farmers' markets, PTA meetings, vigils—these are public activities that occur in such public places as streets and houses of worship, schools and colleges, parks and farms, town halls and, at designated times, private living rooms. Usually, the more one engages in these communal, social activities, the more one becomes dedicated to establishing and maintaining a flourishing public life. Shared aims and loves are cultivated among active public participants as they work together on common projects. Consensus or homogeneity does not necessarily emerge; however, the activity of shared work often enables a diverse group to work together harmoniously for the sake of building a humane way of life. Moreover, working together for a public, shared good—a good that is more than a mere aggregate of private goods—imparts a shared joy that cannot be achieved alone.

However, studies conducted by Robert Putnam and Robert Wuthnow, among others, suggest that a vibrant, meaningful public life is becoming scarce.[11] Increasingly, our public existence is marked not by civic or community activities, but by the impersonal transactions of the marketplace, the bureaucratic labyrinths of work and government offices, and the programmed greetings from uninspired McDonald's employees and AT&T solicitors. Both formal and informal social participation has declined, from participation in national elections to visiting with neighbors. Retreat from civic, national participation is matched at the local level. There are fewer and fewer local establishments, groups, and events in which community members can gather informally to share observations, work on common ventures, and note the changes that have improved and disfigured their communities. As a shared history becomes forgotten—few care to hear it, fewer still can tell it—a shared future is neglected as well. Community is reduced to a place to work, on the one hand, and a vicinity in which to rent an apartment or own a home, on the other. Between work and home, there is little life. No longer a place to greet and chat with people, the street has become exclusively a means of transportation, usually by car. From point *a* to point *b* (whether these be locations or tasks), we quickly move, resenting any interruption or delay, for our rationalized, highly organized lives permit no unaccounted-for minute.

Traditional sites of public gatherings, such as the Town Hall, have become bureaus for politicians and administrators and for those in need of permits, extensions, and other types of bureaucratic assistance. Schools and colleges serve exclusively their own student bodies, not the surrounding community. Farms are more likely to produce goods for other states than for local residents, providing residents little reason to visit farms, much less care about their fate. Even our private time has become increasingly exclusive and scheduled. Public parks now often attract not social gatherings but private families wishing that limited "quality time" not be interrupted by others. No longer hosting community gatherings, the domestic living room has become for family use only. Yet even this common space is used less, as each family member, pursuing a hectic schedule, requires intense, individualized recreation, usually in the privacy of his or her bedroom via a television or computer monitor.

In sum, as the public life becomes cold, impersonal, and bureaucratic, the private life becomes focused on itself, severed from social relations other than those of family members. As the public and private become increasingly differentiated, each becomes more extreme: the public becomes more impersonal, the private more cloistered—even solitary. As a result, the public life—such as it is—is not nourished by a replete private life, and the private life—such as it is—is not fed by a robust public life.

The story I am telling here I first read in Rousseau. He complained of an increasingly barren public life in which shared public places, loves, and activities were waning. He noted that we now pay others to entertain us instead of gathering publicly to entertain ourselves. We work more hours and receive less satisfaction, because as the division of labor increases, job satisfaction decreases. We may have more material possessions yet we have less time and joy, because our anomic desires make us eternally dissatisfied, leading us to work harder to gain what is sure to disappoint us. Even those who would like to pursue a simple life, Rousseau noted, must labor under a heavy tax burden, so that governments can fund wars and expansion. Above all, Rousseau highlighted the correlation between a society that promotes the pursuit of narrow self-interest, on the one hand, and the deterioration of its members' public and private lives, on the other.

One of the first to document the onslaught of unhappy modern trends, Rousseau also offered ways to reverse those trends. The extreme public path is one of those ways, best exemplified by his work, *The Government of Poland*. The type of society on the extreme public path is marked by the public and private having become one. More precisely, the private life is subsumed under the public. A species of extreme patriotism, it seeks to cast the individual's soul into the collective soul of *le corps politique*, the political body. On this path there is no distinction between virtue and patriotism, between morality and politics, between society and the state. The fervor of individual *amour-propre* (all-consuming, narrow self-interest) is conducted away from the self and directed to the group. Indeed, all individual loves and commitments are directed to the largest association, the political body, to curb the destructive force of *amour-propre*—anomic, rapacious self-interest.[12]

Later we will investigate why Rousseau offered such an extreme remedy. For now, it is enough to note that Rousseau was old and exhausted when he wrote *Poland*. While he himself was following the private path as an attempt to dodge the grief and pain that he had experienced in the grip of an oppressive public life, he imagined a different kind of public life for the Poles—an all-encompassing, supportive one. A completely public existence, like an utterly private one, can control disillusionment and strife by focusing one's existence on well-defined aims with assured outcomes. Rousseau, having himself experienced much loss, sought to establish a kingdom for the Poles that was not subject to loss. We will need to examine the advantages of Rousseau's extreme public path as well as the grave costs. We will ask, among other things, without a replete private life, can there be a robust public life? Does the joy of public participation become oppressive when such participation ceases to be an aspect of life, but defines the entirety of life?

For each of Rousseau's paths to restoration and healing, we will note what it has to offer, what are its limits, and what light it casts on the public and private in democratic society. Rousseau's ultimate vision, I have suggested, is found on the middle path, in which a fulfilling public and private life are integrated yet not merged without distinction. Yet as Rousseau became aged and alienated, having suffered much from personal loss and political exile, he increasingly doubted the possibility of the middle way.

Public and Private Delineated

I have been attempting to portray, with broad strokes, the terrain of the public and private that we will explore in this study. I now wish to inspect these concepts in a somewhat more analytical fashion.[13] Analytic precision, however, should not imply our subject is tidy. As we have seen, the public and private define each other mutually and variously. An event can therefore be interpreted as private from one perspective, public from another. A women's reading group that meets in its members' homes could be construed as private, insofar as its membership is restricted and confidentiality is protected. Yet it also could be considered public, insofar as its members are from the community and are wrestling with public issues. Complexity abounds because the meaning of the public and private is not fixed: the distinction between the two has been understood variously by different peoples at different times.

Nonetheless, among the different usages of these terms, there are rough family resemblances. These resemblances are what allow us to speak of multiple meanings of public and private. Even if a single thread, to change the metaphor, does not connect all the meanings of public or private, the connotations connect here and there, resulting in a quilt of meanings. Throughout this study, I inspect various squares, patches drawn from diverse situations. For each square I provide a context, and the context circumscribes the meaning. However, I spend more time with some squares than with others. I can offer here, then, provisional, pragmatic definitions that will help the reader to understand how I will usually employ the terms *public* and *private*.

The private will mainly refer to the life of the individual as it exists outside public obligations and commitments, while the public will refer to life among such involvements. Yet the private need not be equated with the solitary, and the public need not be equated with a society's common good. The private life, in this study, does not refer to a space that is epistemologically sealed off from a society's sociolinguistic frameworks— a society's languages, beliefs, ideals, practices, and institutions. Even private reflection is rooted in a society's language and institutions. I can enter a room alone to think, but my thought draws from a public resource—a linguistic and cultural treasure of socially constructed meanings, symbols, and images. My thought may be private insofar as I have not shared it with others. It may even be relatively novel or unique. Still, it is fashioned from a social medium, and it can be shared in that medium. There is a dark side to this epistemological connection between public and private. Pervasive, oppressive social constructions can haunt us even when we are alone. A private gaze in the mirror, for example, can torment us, especially women living in a society dominated by insidious social images of the perfect, disciplined body.

The private, then, does not occur outside social conventions, but occupies a set of conventions that constitute a somewhat distinctive realm. That realm, the private life, includes intimacy, confidentiality, sexuality, family, friendship, and trust. While we are not free from social conventions in private, we are free from public view. We can talk and act without fear of public misunderstanding or censure. If our private comments are made public without consent, we experience betrayal; therein lies the importance of trust in the private life. In private, we do speak of public matters. Yet we also speak of goals, hopes, beliefs, and activities that do not pertain to public or political matters. Indeed, the private is sometimes a refuge from such matters. Many think of the home as a safe haven from an exhausting public existence, yet the private life should not be equated with the domestic. The private may include domesticity, but it also entails solitary moments, intimate conversations, and unspoken thoughts, even in the most public places.

In contrast to this intimate, often concealed life that is protected from unwanted observation, the public life includes such accessible spheres as markets, government offices, political organizations, and the informal sociability of streets, coffee shops, and beauty salons. These spheres might not be as open to all as we would like, thereby giving us grounds for complaint, because we expect public realms to be accessible. Nonetheless, our public lives, including public obligations and commitments, usually operate in a realm less exclusive than that of intimate, close relationships. Again, I would not want to be dogmatic about where we draw the line between public and private. Churches and synagogues, temples and mosques, for example, are public from one point of view, private from another; so are visiting hours at a maximum security prison. The point of view is determined by the character of the group, the individual's relation to the group, and the question being asked of each. Still, in this study, the public life usually refers to our relation to social groups, organizations, and agencies, or else to the open realm of public streets and parks.

It is often helpful to define something by looking at a pristine or extreme instance of it. For the public life, Rousseau has provided such an instance. On the extreme public path that he prescribed for Poland, there is no separation between public and private: all aspects of one's life are dedicated to the political body. Here, the line between public and private is easy to draw, because there are no personal obligations, no private hopes and aspirations, and no protection from public display. The line is drawn easily because there is nothing to separate: the public consumes the private.

Another approach to defining the public and private is to note the polarities that we associate with them. In economics, we juxtapose socialism (a public, nationalized economy) with laissez-faire capitalism (a private-sector economy). Most Western democracies pursue a mixed economy, that is, an economy that falls somewhere between the socialist and capitalist poles. This polarity inspires different conceptions of the individual's relation to the public. Socialists usually depict the individual as working *directly* for the commonweal, insofar as the individual is employed by the state and is producing goods for fellow citizens. Capitalists, in contrast, depict the individual as contributing *indirectly* to the commonweal, insofar as the pursuit of self-interest generates national prosperity as individuals enter mutually advantageous exchanges.

If we turn to a different public-private continuum, we find the economy and government, together, occupying one pole, and the home the other. The poles on this continuum are the impersonal and the personal, and between them is that spontaneous social life that characterizes the local coffee shop or mall, the neighborhood market or barber shop. On this continuum, it is difficult to draw the line between public and private when we reach that broad space between the polar extremes. Turning to still another continuum, we can juxtapose the individual's private life, including her economic self-interest, with her political commitments and civic virtue. Here, the public life pertains to the shared ideals and goals of the political community as opposed to personal ideals and goals of the individual as she pursues her career and family life, or her sexual, religious, and aesthetic preferences. Again, between these poles the public and private become intertwined and difficult to separate. Career choices, for example, can reflect both personal inclination and political commitment.

Some public-private polarities are, by definition, morally charged, that is, they necessarily exalt one pole and condemn the other. For example, when Rousseau championed the public path, he often juxtaposed private pettiness to public virtue. The virtuous self, in this view, subordinates self-interests for the sake of the general good. The private is held in suspect, while the public is deemed good. However, when championing the private path, Rousseau juxtaposed the morally self-possessed individual with the crowd that blindly follows public opinion. Indeed, when advocating the private path, Rousseau held that there is a moral order higher than society's general good, and that the way to discover it is to withdraw from society—retreating to oneself, then embracing the universal. From this point of view, there is always something parochial about society's common good, and commitment to the group or nation is often at odds with commitment to a universal moral order. Here, then, the nation is considered private when compared to the universal.

Finally, there is a polarity that juxtaposes humankind to nature—nature being a term, a place-holder, that refers to the totality of all things. Like the universal, nature relativizes our most public ventures and institutions. In Rousseau's vocabulary, nature is a category even larger than the universal, for it not only contains a moral order, but beauty as well. In the *Reveries of the Solitary Walker*, for example, Rousseau reflected on the joy of contemplating the beauty of nature: "A profound and sweet reverie seizes one's senses, and one is lost, with a blissful self-abandonment, in the immensity of this beautiful order, with which one feels at one. . . . One sees and feels nothing but the whole."[14] Here we have reached the limit of our topic, the relation between things public and private. Nature, encompassing all life forms, subsumes human endeavors public and private, and may render our very topic, like all things human, small and insignificant.

I mention this final polarity—humankind's particularity compared to nature's generality—because Rousseau often evoked the grandeur of nature to tame human audacity and arrogance. He was especially concerned about self-righteous religious fanatics, on the one hand, and disdainful indifferent philosophers, on the other. The former tormented the masses while the latter neglected them; both justified their positions with decrees that, they claimed, issued from God or Reason, whereas Rousseau claimed they issued in fact from their own personal vanity. I also mention the human-nature polarity because Rousseau was convinced that much human unhappiness springs from our attempts to thwart nature. When conflict occurs between our plans and nature's necessity, nature wins. To recognize as much, Rousseau held, would spare us much unnecessary grief.

Public and Private in Conflict

I have thus far provided intuitive portraits and analytic accounts of the public-private distinction. I now wish to illustrate the *conflict* that occurs between the public and private. Predictably, such conflict is as various as are the definitions of public and private.

In the Michael Ondaatje novel *The English Patient*, and the movie based on it, we encounter in dramatic form what each of us experiences in our own lives: multiple and often conflicting commitments. The Englishman had commitments to his work, his government, his friends, and to his lover—his friend's wife. When the husband learns of the affair between his wife and the Englishman, he attempts a suicide-murder to kill all three of them by way of a plane crash in a remote region in north Africa. The husband dies instantly, his wife is injured, and the Englishman, unharmed, carries her to a cave to protect her from intense desert heat. Leaving her with some provisions, he promises to return. This promise leads to a conflict as acute as the original conflict between his devotion to his lover and his friendship with her husband. When the British government prevents him from returning to the cave, the Englishman trades strategic maps to the Germans (who are at war with the British) for assistance that allows him to keep his promise. He returns to the cave and finds his lover, dead. Given his delayed return, her death does not surprise him. Yet he had a promise to keep, and he risked his life keeping it, in spite of the outcome.

The English Patient vividly illustrates conflicts that arise within an individual due to a variety of public and private commitments. Within the private realm, the Englishman suffered from conflict between his relationship to his lover and to her husband, his friend; equally striking, he later underwent conflict between a private promise (to return to the cave) and a public obligation (to assist the Allies, not the Germans). Both forms of conflict are seemingly ineluctable. That is, as long as humans have diverse loyalties, public and private, such conflict will emerge. And both forms of conflict—no doubt due to their pervasive, elemental nature—have been immortalized in literature and legend. Sophocles, for example, depicts Antigone's torn soul as she wrestles with her private obligation to provide a proper burial for her brother, Polynices, and her public obligation to obey the law of Creon that prohibits her brother's burial.

Perhaps more complicated still is the tangle of commitments that snares the characters of Arthurian legend. King Arthur, Guinevere, and Lancelot love each other; they also love the public ideals associated with the Round Table. Lancelot is torn between his public commitment to the Round Table and his private love of Guinevere. Moreover, in the private realm he is divided between his friendship to Arthur and his affair with Guinevere. Arthur is trapped within the same set of conflicts. Once he learns of the affair, he must decide whether to uphold the public law of the Round Table, which would demand the death of his friends, or else disregard the law, which would assert the primacy of the private over the public, thereby vitiating the law of the land.

Ironically, it is Lancelot—the utopian perfectionist—who breaks the law, and it is Arthur—the liberal realist who expects people to fail and hence places importance on the rule of law—who must sorrowfully struggle over what to do in light of Lancelot and Guinevere's betrayal. Such struggle and sadness, we will see in later chapters, Rousseau well understood. They arise, he held, from conflicts among our loves and commitments. He also knew a partial remedy: evade conflict by retreating to an extreme private life, in which one has duties only to oneself, or else embrace an extreme public life, in which all duties are directed toward a well-ordered public, national existence. Both these paths, he knew, demand a heavy toll: the loss of those things that we cherish in a public, or else in a private, life. As much as he hated conflict, he could not bring himself to recommend wholeheartedly these extreme paths that evaded conflict. Not to travel these paths, however, would bring conflict—the struggle and sadness that cling to humans who attempt to have vital public and private lives, both. For most of us, then, conflict and tragedy seem inevitable.

Inevitable, because it is natural for humans to have multiple obligations that circumstances place in conflict. Even the best moral theories cannot exempt one from such conflict. A Kantian is as likely to suffer from it as is a consequentialist: incompatible duties are as likely as incomparable outcomes. One *can* make better or worse life choices, and one can recognize avoidable conflict (for example, don't fall in love with your friend's spouse, or at least don't have an affair). Unavoidable conflict, however, will remain (choosing whether to attend your child's concert or speak at the town meeting on new zoning laws, for instance). And with unavoidable moral conflict follows inescapable moral loss.

I am particularly interested in the conflict and loss that result from incompatibilities between public and private commitments. In the private realm, our moral behavior and vision are often heavily informed by particular relationships to people and familiar institutions (a friend or a local establishment). In the public realm, our moral outlook is often informed not by personal relationships, but by more impersonal considerations or even by universalist stances such as deontology (do the right thing, in spite of consequences) or consequentialism (the right thing to do is that which brings the greatest good). I do not wish here to embark on a discussion of grand moral theories. I only point out that our duty to friends, family, and lovers often entails a different set of moral considerations than our duty to town, nation, and globe. Even if one were a Kantian deontologist or a strict consequentialist in every realm of life, conflict between, say, keeping a promise to a loved one and a promise to a distant organization would still involve a distinctive form of loss that emerges from our inhabiting both public and private realms.

Sometimes conflict between public and private is only apparent. Montaigne presents us with such a case in his essay, "Of Friendship." After the Roman consuls condemned Gracchus for treason, the state prosecutor, Laelius, put on trial Gracchus's best friend, Blossius. Asked how much he would have been willing to do for Gracchus, Blossius replied, "Everything."

> "What, everything?" pursued Laelius. "And what if he had commanded you to set fire to our temples?" "He would never have commanded me to do that," responded Blossius. "But what if he had?" Laelius insisted. "I would have obeyed," he replied.[15]

In his commentary on this case, Montaigne seems equally disappointed with Blossius's final, bold confession—"I would have obeyed"—and with Laelius calling the confession seditious. The confession, in Montaigne's view, is gratuitous, because Blossius, knowing his friend as his own soul, is confident that Gracchus would never ask that he commit treason. The question put to him should have been rejected, and the prosecutor never should have asked it. Laelius failed to realize that virtuous friendships do not lead friends astray. Hence even if Gracchus and Blossius were "friends more than citizens," their private friendship would not lead to criminal acts against the public.

Unlike this idealized case, however, conflict between public and private is not usually so easily dissolved. Many in democratic societies, for example, cherish both freedom and equality, yet these two values often create tension between the public and private. We may be torn between the desire to exercise our freedom by sending our children to the closest public school, and the desire to establish greater educational equality by having our children bused across town. Here, freedom supports our private desire to keep our children close to home, while equality bolsters our public commitment to busing. Either option entails some sacrifice of value and aspiration.

One last example. Penetrating the core of self and group identity, religion has often been the occasion for dramatic and intractable instances of conflict between public and private. Historically, members of minority religious communities have often had to choose, for example, between pursuing personal religious beliefs and seeking public office. During the last two centuries, the successful emergence of liberal democracies is in large part due to their having managed religious strife by fostering tolerance. Indeed, religious tolerance has become something of a symbol of democratic virtue and a central tenet of democratic states. Yet even this public virtue, tolerance, can conflict with individual religious belief and practice. The French government, for example, prohibits young Islamic women from veiling themselves in public schools, maintaining that veiling violates the neutral, public space of the classroom. This public endorsement of neutrality—neutrality being the French method of rendering tolerance—conflicts with the "private" religious beliefs of many French Muslims. Again, loss cannot be avoided.[16]

Public and Private in Controversy: Women, Politics, and Epistemology

I have been discussing varieties of conflict between public and private. I now wish to address a different type of conflict—the conflict and controversy that surrounds the very idea of the public-private distinction. Many feminists, including myself, claim that the distinction between public-private is often gendered, relegating women to the domestic sphere and excluding them from political and economic spheres. Communitarians, for their part, are suspicious of a distinction that carves out a space for private, discrete selves, while libertarians and some liberals distrust a distinction that seems to insist on a shared public life. And socialists complain that the public-private distinction is based on an uncritical acceptance of the necessity of private property. Lastly, some philosophers complain that the distinction rests on the unsupportable epistemological view that humans can retreat to a private space divorced from all sociolinguistic frameworks. There is, then, much controversy and debate surrounding the topic of this book. Rousseau is implicated in these controversies and also sheds helpful light on them.

Regarding the epistemological controversy, I work with the assumption that humans are inescapably social creatures, that is, we are shaped by and rooted in language, institutions, customs, and traditions. The private, as much as the public, is grounded in sociolinguistic terrains—terrains into which we are thrown, but also that we can shape. The distinctions that we associate with the public-private are written in and by society, not nature. A private walk in the woods, for example, is not a radically asocial, uninterpreted event. Different societies provide different interpretive resources for considering and evaluating what I call a private walk. Likewise, I can think a private thought—a thought unshared; the thought remains, however, intimately connected to a particular sociolinguistic form of life.

Rousseau often encouraged the individual to escape an artificial, social life in order to embrace a natural, flourishing existence. These exhortations were moral, not epistemological. Marriages based on social status, frivolous behavior for the sake of social acceptance and gain, and taxation that crushed the poor were some social practices that he considered artificial and destructive. As a social critic, he had many complaints against society. However, his remedies did not entail the epistemological recommendation that individuals divorce themselves from all sociolinguistic mediums. When he contrasted the natural to the artificial, for example, he was measuring a morally bankrupt social existence, such as that of the Parisians, by a wholesome social existence, such as that found among the inhabitants of the high Valais. This is not to deny that Rousseau often accorded nature a normative role. With the honorific title, "natural," he anointed and sanctified many of his own points of view—a practice that he vigorously criticized in others! In such cases, we can critically engage his substantive positions while noting and exposing his eighteenth-century appeal to laws of nature.

The distinction between public and private is contested by various stripes of socialists. These scholars often maintain that the public-private distinction is rooted in an uncritical acceptance of private property. In this view, governments of liberal nations secure individual rights primarily to protect private property. I would suggest, however, that even if historically privacy and private property were often intertwined, we need not continue to reduce the former to the later. Privacy, which includes control over one's body, the protection from state surveillance, and the freedom to pursue such personal matters as religion and lifestyles, is surely a concept that can be unfettered from private property. We even have such historical examples as Montaigne, for whom privacy was not coupled to property, but to introspection and friendship. Liberalism, the politics of rights, is not necessarily tied to any particular economic arrangement. Even if liberalism emerged in capitalistic societies, it has traveled elsewhere. The Netherlands and Sweden, for example, are liberal societies with socialist economies. Liberalism, in the pages of this book, is principally a pledge that there are some things that humans should not have to worry about, for example, a night of torture, an unwarranted search and seizure inside one's home, a painful and frivolous arrest, or harassment due to one's religion or sexual orientation.

The public-private distinction has also proved to be controversial between liberals and communitarians, that is, between those committed to the politics of rights, on the one hand, and those to the politics of the common good, on the other. The liberal model of society usually conceives society as a group of discrete citizens, protected by rights, who may or may not share common values, beliefs, or goals; the communitarian model, in contrast, conceives society as a group of members who are committed to shared values, beliefs, and goals. Communitarians are suspicious of the public-private distinction, for they fear it fosters a domain that encourages individuality. They maintain that as individuals pursue their liberal rights, they reside within an increasingly constricted private space, sharing less and less in common with one another; hence society's common good becomes thin and unable to generate agreement on public goods, values, and ends. Liberal and communitarian positions are usually depicted as being radically opposed to each other. Yet there need not be radical conflict between them. Elsewhere I have argued that individual rights are the product of particular, shared, moral traditions, and that individual rights have become a salient feature of the common good of liberal societies.[17] In other words, rights are not merely private; rather, they manifest our commitment to the protection of the individual and define much of who we are as a people.

I am, then, a defender of liberal, democratic society, and often my support of it is communitarian in character. Liberal society, with its insistence on individual rights, has made tremendous moral gains. Among those gains is the protection of minorities against heartless majoritarianism. Liberal society, in other words, has served to protect communities. In this country, for example, associational liberty—the right to associate with whom one chooses—has often been defended by the Supreme Court by appealing to the right to privacy. This same constitutional right has been the most successful defense of a citizen's control over such personal concerns as one's body, as in, for example, the case of abortion. And as we begin the twenty-first century and the danger of government and corporate technological surveillance increases, we will no doubt discover again the wide implications of individual rights.

Yet liberalism cannot remain a viable social order if it is dedicated to the protection of individual rights alone. It must embrace commitment to a common good; it must remain tensely linked to something like communitarianism. Flourishing democracies require a public space in which diverse individuals and groups can debate and pursue shared projects and goals. Democracies, then, require the protection and support of both public and private spheres.

Protection and support, however, do not necessitate a strict line separating the public and private in every case. Much good has come from the recent emergence of identity politics in the United States, although some forms of this politics can threaten both the public and private. Identity politics has successfully reminded us that so-called personal features, for example, gender, race, and sexuality, have implicit and explicit political ramifications. An example of identity politics is the refrain, "the personal is political." To completely identify the personal with the political, the private with the public, however, is to imperil democratic society. An exclusive focus on a particular, even an oppressed group jeopardizes a public space that is both plural and shared. Moreover, by radically politicizing personal matters, identity politics threatens to exploit one's private space.[18] A healthy democratic society can afford neither to collapse nor to radically separate the public and private. Rather, it needs to recognize a complex interrelation and a qualified separation between them. This is because our public and private lives, while closely related, frequently have distinctive needs and goals.

The final controversy I wish to address pertains to women and the public-private distinction. Carole Pateman is not alone when she claims that "the dichotomy between the private and the public is central to almost two centuries of feminist writing and political struggle; it is, ultimately, what the feminist movement is about."[19] Dismantling the dichotomy is imperative, in this view, because it sequesters women, confining them to a private, domestic space and excluding them from the workplace and from the political realm. Gender is not a private issue or personal attribute, because to be born a woman is to enter a culturally defined, legally bolstered framework that keeps a woman in her (subservient) place. Additionally, the domestic realm—protected and sealed-off—is hidden from public inquiry, thereby obstructing law enforcement from intervening in cases of violence against women.

Much of the feminist complaint against the public-private distinction springs from its identifying the private life with one version of the domestic life. The private and the domestic become one, as the private life is reduced to a concept of domesticity that emerged to a great extent in the eighteenth century. Earlier, domesticity had often referred to the daily household activity of men and women. I am not suggesting that it was egalitarian, but it was a realm that included both men and women and that was concerned with both economics and morality. Due to a variety of socioeconomic changes, the domestic sphere—especially for the middle and upper classes—became increasingly separated from economic activity, and women were assigned a new role and unique place in it.[20] It became a refuge within which women provided moral and emotional nourishment to weary men returning from the cruel public realm of economics and politics. It also became a sequestered sphere in which children received a moral education couched in maternal love.

This new doctrine of domesticity emerged in the wake of widespread anomie caused by rapid urban growth and industrialization in Western Europe. Work increasingly became identified with a workplace outside the home, and competition for jobs increased. As men strived in the heartless city, women were to maintain the moral hearth in the warm home. To retain her special gifts, woman must not be sullied by the foolishness of city salons or by the callousness of city politics and commerce. This, of course, was not the whole story. There were other countertrends, and women could never be systematically confined within this new, narrow form of domesticity. Nonetheless, this account does accurately depict social trends that were especially pervasive among the middle class. And Rousseau's contribution to these social developments, while complex, is unquestionable.

Rousseau believed that European societies were on a downward path leading to gross material inequality, anomic acquisitiveness, and social callousness. Women, in Rousseau's view, were part of the remedy to heal an increasingly insensitive and unhappy society. If women would take their place in the home, providing their children and men with maternal love and moral strength, men could enter public life and become honorable citizens, putting the common good above self-serving gain. Believing that women held much power over men, Rousseau attempted to direct that power for the good of society. Women were one of the few forces strong enough to counteract other forces that were harming men and all those around them—especially that destructive psychological force, *amour-propre*, in the perilous social context of an early division of labor and industrialization. One of Rousseau's responses to the new economic division of labor, then, was to imagine a new moral division of labor: the private domestic life separate yet equal to the public economic life, as the morally superior woman is separate yet equal to the intellectually and physically superior man. With woman's help, man could overcome his selfish (*amour-propre*-driven) self. He might just become a decent citizen. A corrupt public life would thereby be purged by an immaculate, domestic life; and a redeemed public life would, in turn, support a domestic life otherwise subject to threats. This is illustrated by the Jacobins' "Republic of Virtue," which, inspired by Rousseau, sought to ensure that women were not deterred from their sacred duty of raising citizens, that is, virtuous men.

Rousseau, the "prophet of breast-feeding" and the eighteenth century's educational sage, did as much as anyone to articulate and propagate a vision of the virtuous woman who serves her family and country by reigning supreme in a private empire that sustains her men and children with emotional warmth and moral sustenance. To my knowledge, Rousseau never acknowledged or recognized that this gendered moral division of labor unjustly assigns women to a narrow domestic role. Although Rousseau believed that women's and men's roles were separate in function but equal in importance (indeed, he held that, with respect to morals, women play the more important role), he never extended to women the powerful and life-enhancing vision that he offered to men. Political equality, freedom from unjust dependency and glaring economic inequality, the right to participate in the discovery of the general will—these features of Rousseau's dream are not envisioned for women. Joan Landes states the case well: "Woman's duty consists of subordinating her independent aims and interests to a higher goal, the ethical life of the community. But unlike her male companion, of whom Rousseau also demands the sublimation of particular interests on behalf of a desire for the public good, woman is barred completely from active participation in the very sphere that gives purpose to her actions."[21] Rousseau's prescription for women is intended to heal the political body. The unintended yet certain consequence is women's alienation from the very public life they helped to restore.

It is indisputable that Rousseau propagated a form of domesticity that was demeaning and harmful to women. His ideas and attitudes concerning women, however, were far from consistent or unambiguous. He was neither a misogynist nor a proto-feminist, as some have labeled him. Yet in the ample area between these extremes, he ranged widely. This range can be gauged by two of his literary characters, Sophie and Julie. In his famous educational treatise, *Emile*, Rousseau described the education appropriate for Emile's future wife, Sophie. At the close of the book, Emile's tutor announces, "Dear Emile, a man needs counsel and guidance throughout his life. . . . I abdicate today the authority you confided to me, and here, in Sophie, is your governor from now on."[22] If Sophie is to replace Emile's God-like tutor, this seems to imply that Sophie's education would need to be divine as well. And indeed, Sophie is to study the arts and sciences, and especially ethics. Still, Sophie's education is far from divine or inspired. It is also far from Emile's. Emile is raised to become an independent thinker who pursues what is good rather than pursing social opinion so that he merely appear good. Sophie, in contrast, is raised to be dependent—dependent on both her future husband and on social opinion. Even Sophie's religion is to come from her husband, which stands in stark contrast to Emile's religious education, which essentially begins and ends with, "Consult your own heart." Remarkably, Rousseau, who feared dependency perhaps more than death itself, assigned Sophie to a life of it. It is as if Rousseau balanced, ounce for ounce, Emile's autonomy with Sophie's subservience.

I do not wish to be unfair to Rousseau, for the long section in *Emile* on Sophie's education does not consistently demean women. Yet if there is one theme that stands out among the rest, it is this: "In the union of the sexes each contributes equally to the common aim, but not in the same fashion. . . . One should be active and strong, the other passive and weak."[23] That Rousseau assumed his readers would know which attributes went with which sex is a sad commentary on both him and his audience. Yet if Sophie is passive and weak, Rousseau's more famous woman, Julie, is active and strong.

Rousseau's best-selling epistolary novel, *Julie; or, The New Eloise*, enjoyed seventy-two editions between 1761 and 1800. In page after page, Rousseau gave a profound voice to the powerful and independent Julie. While Sophie's religion derives from her husband, Julie's religion springs from her own heart. Such decisional autonomy over religion is significant because, in Rousseau's view, religion penetrates and shapes the depths of personal identity and public character. Julie's identity is her own. She also is quick to unmask male pretention. When St. Preux, her former lover, accuses her of being unduly preoccupied with appearances and therefore of "having been a woman for once in her life," Julie reproaches him for his "air of masculine superiority" and articulately defends herself. Julie has little patience for male antics and macho posturing. For example, with wit and skill she forcefully argues against dueling, which she calls "avenging yourself on a man who insults you by having him kill you."[24] She has perhaps even less patience for men who engage in verbose philosophical dueling that produces more chatter than wisdom.[25] On this and other issues, and more than any other character in the novel, Julie represents Rousseau's own voice and heart.

Especially his heart. If Rousseau is famous for exploring his interior life and making that life public for the sake of edification, Julie is a literary incarnation of that effort. With profundity and honesty, Julie dives deep into herself to ask questions of worth, motives, ethics, and love. Each time St. Preux exhibits even the slightest sign of self-deception, Julie checks it. Having examined closely her own soul, she is in a position to help others detect self-deceit. As a lover, friend, wife, and mother, Julie investigates and honors her interior life, and in doing so she lent dignity and significance to the lives of countless eighteenth-century women who devoured *Julie*—women who were disenfranchised in most every way.

Julie, then, is a very different woman than Sophie; this is because Rousseau placed them on different paths. On the public path, Rousseau needed women to support their men in "the City," that arena of potential chaos and corruption. Mutually interdependent, women provide moral sustenance, men provide economic and political sustenance. Rousseau never disapproved of women working in fields or pastures or at useful crafts; he condemned women engaged in gossipy chatter in city salons—the very chatter and salons that he himself shunned. Men and women require protection from the degeneracy—the selfishness, materialism, and artificiality—that is practically endemic to modern European city life, Paris being Rousseau's favorite example. In the salons of the City, women and men concentrate on appearances, caring more about how they are perceived for the sake of social gain than about such substantive matters as character, the plight of the poor, or the common good. Women are saved from such corruption by being sequestered to the home, and men, in turn, are redeemed by their virtuous women. This is the context for which Rousseau created Sophie: private women enabling men on a public city path.

On the extreme private path, in contrast, there are no citizens, and no men or women to please: one lives for oneself, not for how one appears to others. There is no mutual dependency, no moral division of labor. Living a self-possessed way of life, any form of dependency looms as a threat. Women embody that threat to men. Neither Julie nor Sophie is found on the extreme private path—a path that permits no company. Rousseau did not specifically exclude women from what I am calling the private path, yet he did suggest on occasion that women are not capable of the independence that this extreme path requires. Men desire women, while women desire *and* need men; men would survive more easily without women than women would without men.[26] Women, in this view, might attempt to detract men from the private path, and Sophie and Julie would be equally dangerous to the radically independent man. Julie does have a rich private life, and she enjoys private retreats in solitude. But she does not, and perhaps in Rousseau's view cannot, travel the extreme private path on which solitude is not a temporary retreat, but an enduring way of life.

Where is Julie's place, then? On which path is she? In the Swiss mountains, in a village, on a course between the extreme public and private paths. In chapter 9, where I discuss this in-between terrain, the way of Clarens, we discover not only Rousseau's personal ideal path to redemption, but also Rousseau's ideal woman. In the Mountain Village, the division of labor between men and women is not greatly pronounced. Here Rousseau's woman sets aside frivolous city amusements and instead picks up "the fishing line, bird snares, the haying rake, and the harvester's basket."[27] On this path, Rousseau reintroduced an older notion of domesticity: the integrated life of a family, in which work and pleasure, utility and aesthetics, public and private, men and women, are not sharply distinguished. Unlike in the City, work is not pushed out of the home and confined to a special workplace; rather it stays home, encompassing such household activities as cultivating useful gardens, baking bread, and keeping bees. Pleasure is found in such daily activities and in special gatherings and fêtes. Julie's work is, to be sure, differentiated somewhat from her husband's, yet the household contains the labor of both as well as the shared pleasures. Julie is not a submissive, dependent wife, but an independent, thinking spouse. Julie is not Sophie. On the path that goes between the extreme public and private paths, women's lives are not radically relegated to the private, because the very distinction between public and private is not severe. Sophie must inhabit and sustain a space restricted to the domestic as an antidote to the potentially corrupting public space of the City. In contrast, Julie's Clarens, surrounded by whole-some mountain folk and natural beauty, has permeable walls, for the outside is not threatening.

Even with respect to Julie, Rousseau is not a proto-feminist. Although Julie is not weak and passive, her roles are primarily those of wife and mother. Nonetheless, Julie is a strong, dynamic woman, especially compared to Sophie. Perhaps for this reason, few readers thought much about Sophie. Julie, in contrast, due to her vivid personality and moral fiber, became famous overnight, and remains so. Without challenging the lot of dispossessed women—those with few political or economic rights—Rousseau did, in his own way, attempt to empower women by dignifying their roles as friend, wife, mother, social critic, and as introspector—especially as introspector, thereby exemplify-ing what he considered to be his own special talent. With the publication of *Julie*, the private lives of women were anointed with public significance. Women were perhaps still to remain quiet in public; few could now doubt, however, the richness of their thoughts and emotions. Women were perhaps still to remain near home; none would now doubt, however, the significance of their roles as moral educators and sustainers of the political body. This may be why many of the most progressive and politically active women of Rousseau's time became "fervent admirers and defenders of [Rousseau's] character and writings."[28] Rousseau addressed women as moral agents and as tacit political agents. Writing to women, and not just to men about women, Rousseau attributed to women much agency. As vehicles of social moral regeneration, women were to stay close to home and exercise their superior gifts in the moral and interior life.[29]

Rousseau's attitudes and ideas about women, I have said, are deeply problematic, complex, and often ambiguous. This introduction is not the place to sort out such a tangled web. Also, not wanting to relegate the topic of Rousseau and women to one chapter, I have woven it throughout the book. This has enabled me to situate the sub-ject concretely in the context of Rousseau's specific arguments about the public and private. Still, at the outset of this study, I wanted to begin to address some of these issues and indicate my position.

We can and should complain that Rousseau was not a more progressive thinker on the topic of women. There were conceptual resources, even in the eighteenth century, from which he could have drawn and fashioned progressive and normative views about women. Although these views would not have been widely accepted, many of Rousseau's positions belonged to that category—to the progressive and therefore the unacceptable. His support of egalitarianism, the education he prescribed for Emile, his condemnation of capital—these are views that Rousseau held, and held largely alone. He was forced into exile, alone, due to the radical nature of his thought. His own social and political thought, then, could have served him as a resource to envision women empowered in every sphere of life. Instead, Rousseau sowed seeds for men's social and political em-powerment—seeds that women would later claim for themselves, in ways that Rousseau himself, sadly, never imagined.

Given the era in which Rousseau wrote, some would recommend that I look the other way when I stumble on Rousseau's demeaning statements about women. Others, in contrast, would insist that, due to his eighteenth-century prejudices, Rousseau can have nothing to say to us about the relation between the public and private, or about any other substantive issue. For my part, I have chosen neither to ignore the offensive passages nor to dismiss the entirety of Rousseau's work. The more difficult and promising course, I believe, is to discover in Rousseau's authorship what is edifying, what is harmful, and to what extent the harmful aspects poison the edifying aspects. Rousseau helped to fashion a social construct of women that is troubling and disparaging; I want to understand that construct better, not overlook it. His work also contributes powerfully to our normative understanding of the public and private and the conflict between them. I want to profit from that good work. One of my goals is to redescribe Rousseau's edifying work in light of my feminist commitments, in part by erasing the gendered lines between public and private. Ultimately, I want to articulate and advance the salutary aspects of the public and private life, for all to enjoy.

We *can* redefine the public and private because these are not essentialistic notions written in nature below or heaven above. They are substantial yet flexible social constructs. Reflecting on the sociohistorical nature of our institutions and practices, Michel Foucault noted that "since these things have been made, they can be unmade, as long as we know how it was that they were made."[30] By investigating the public and private, we gain a chance to reshape both. Feminist scholarship has disclosed the ways that the public-private has often really meant the domestic-public dichotomy, a distinction that has served to keep women at home and out of the workplace. From such scholarship I have learned much. Yet we need not reduce the private life to a narrow view of domesticity that entraps women. The private life, for men, is often associated with friendship, contemplation, and the moral regeneration that comes from temporary retreats. Can we not capture these goods for women? Must the right to privacy, which has greatly advanced women's empowerment, be tied to a narrow view of domesticity? If we resist the temptation to reduce the private to the domestic, we can redescribe it to enhance, not oppress, the lives of women.

In sum, rather than simply identifying public-private with man-woman, I have explored the rich and complex nuances of the public and private. Rousseau has helped me do this. He has helped me to think about how a robust public life and replete private life contribute to flourishing democracies. He has clarified for me the importance of a public sphere committed to common projects, including the common endeavor to protect a diverse citizenry, and the necessity of a private sphere where identity is freely pursued, protected from harassment, and where love of self does not turn to destructive narcissism and narrow egoism. These are some lessons I have gathered from Rousseau.

In this section I have shown that the public-private distinction is a contentious one, spawning much controversy. It remains, however, a conspicuous feature of our everyday vocabulary, institutions, and practices, as well as of theoretical discourse and moral deliberation. Commitment to preserving the public-private distinction—and the various values and goods that it represents—prevents us from becoming either an entirely communitarian or libertarian society. True, we will lose the distinctive goods that these alternatives, in their extreme form, have to offer. Yet we have more to gain, in my view, by investigating and judiciously maintaining a tense, complex distinction between public and private—a distinction that should neither be indelibly drawn nor entirely erased. If we fail to distinguish the different domains of public and private, we impoverish both. A democratic society that acknowledges only a shared public life hazards the loss of a significant public resource, namely, a diverse and autonomous citizenry. Political perspectives and the capacity for autonomy are greatly nurtured in the private realms. Also, without a protected private space, intimacy and identity are threatened by state or majoritarian tyranny. Conversely, a democracy that supports only a private life hazards the loss of shared projects and common goals, for our commonality is greatly fostered by those public realms in which a diverse populace gathers, debates, and moves forward, if only by inches. Moreover, without a maintained public space, we lose a unique deposit of shared happiness and meaning that cannot be mined alone.

Compass and Destination

In this book, my aim is not to blaze a straight trail to a single destination, but to tour, with Rousseau, the rough and varied terrain of public and private. My goals are not only descriptive, however, but also normative. I write not only to describe what is, but to discover how things can be, even how they should be. I write as an edifying philosopher or social critic, as one who is trying to find better ways. This style of writing entails some complaint and protest. I am saddened, for example, by the eclipse of community life in our society, and by the rise of a consumerism that encourages individuals to pursue narrow self-interest over common aims. I am dismayed that our public life is becoming increasingly impersonal, bureaucratic, and contractual, while our private lives are becoming increasing constricted, self-absorbed, and lonely. Can we hope to discover collective solutions to such social problems as poverty, racism, and environmental degradation as long as we fail to perceive ourselves as a people with a shared history and future? And can we hope to sustain a vital public life without those resources that we cultivate in private—courage, resolve, and moral wherewithal, for instance? These are some of my complaints and worries, and these I carry with me as I seek to discover beneficial models of the public and private.

We may well want to ask, Is the current state of affairs really so awful? Are human community and personal happiness in such disrepair? In many ways, our society is in good order. The right to privacy has been widely expanded and enforced by the courts, enabling individuals to pursue private projects free from social harassment. We have laws and cultural practices that allow such groups as the Sierra Club or the National Organization for Women to gather and meet in private, as well as to express their views in public. We have many opportunities to develop flourishing public and private lives. Yet there is also much working against us. We spend long hours at the workplace, leaving us little time for community involvement and national politics, on the one hand, or for home activities and private reflection, on the other.[31] Instead of frequenting a locally owned restaurant or coffee shop, we save time and money at the closest fast-food monopoly. In a consumer society that radically separates work and home, leaving little space between, we never have enough money or time. Desperate for both, we feel that we cannot afford to concern ourselves with pressing social, or often even personal, problems.

In response to an increasingly bureaucratic and loveless public life, the private life has become a safe refuge for intimacy and the nuclear family. Yet are we asking too much of the private life? Can the immediate family provide all the warmth and sociability that was available when the private was less constricted and the public was more sociable? Moreover, as utilitarian goals and instrumental reasoning dominate the public domains, will these characteristics not seep into and erode the private life? Will familial emotional support itself become part of a means-end calculation? Are we far from a time when children sue parents, and parents make contracts with their children? The public and private then mutually cripple each other when public arenas become dominated by narrow private interests, and when private arenas become contractual and narcissistic, unable to nourish or refresh even the individual.

Yet again I ask, is our situation so dreary? I have drawn something of a caricature, I admit. I have exaggerated actual features to highlight more subtle social winds and currents that press against our everyday lives. I offer in this book few explicit remedies to contemporary problems. Instead, I delve deeply into Rousseau's thought as might a diver in search of clues about a past that bears on the present. My hope is that this will bring greater understanding of who we are today and what challenges are before us. Rousseau's hope was to create a place where we are at ease in private, at home in community, and engaged in public. The free-spirited, civic-minded individual was his ideal. It is one of mine as well.

As we explore the various threads and knots of Rousseau's thought, this question will follow us: How can we foster vital public and private lives without absolutizing either? This question, in turn, will lead us to such basic issues as whether humans are naturally social or solitary, whether human greed is inevitable or contingent, and whether there are remedies to check the unnecessary suffering that we inflict on ourselves and on those around us. Yet our principal questions will always be, how are we to achieve both individual autonomy and shared commitments? How are we to maintain the dignity of private persons with diverse loves and the worth of public groups with shared goals? And how are we to cope with the inevitable tension between the aims, goods, and loves of the private life and those of the public? These questions guide this work at every step, as we explore the relation between the public and private in democratic society.

PART I

FROM THE GARDEN TO THE CITY:
THE TRAGIC PASSAGE

1

Nature's Garden

Insofar as there is something we care to call Western consciousness, there is a pattern of thought etched on to it that is seemingly ineluctable. Theologians once called it *Heilsgeschichte*, or sacred history. It is the view that among the various twists and turns of history one can discern a divine trajectory—a sacred drama. It begins with the narrative of our dramatic expulsion from a lovely, peaceful Garden; continues through our various attempts to repair, even if only partially and provisionally, our painful existence outside that Garden; and ends with our perfect reconciliation with nature and the divine.

This narrative furnishes the general principle that history is linear; it is heading somewhere, and somewhere better. In spite of the horrors of the twentieth century we still cling to the idea of progress, the secular rendering of this account. Its durability is evidenced by its having survived the horrors of the eighteenth and nineteenth centuries. Alongside champions of progress, however, there have also been prophets of doom. Theologically, this doom often takes the shape of devastating assessments of humankind that feature pettiness, greed, envy, vanity, derision, and injustice—in a word, human sinfulness. Divine judgment, sooner or later, will visit the people. Secular prophets of doom—think of some of your favorite social critics—offer a similar appraisal of humanity and lament that we are sealing our fate in a human-made hell. Yet even these gloomy prophets often wrestle with the question, what are our chances of liberating ourselves? If we can get out of our entrapment, perhaps we can take some lessons with us. Perhaps we can do better next time. Perhaps we can make a little progress. Thus even secular prophets of doom have not entirely escaped the spell of *Heilsgeschichte*.

Jean-Jacques Rousseau was such a prophet. The narrative of deposed humans attempting to break through the gates of Hell and recapture the Garden was employed by Rousseau even as he sabotaged it. In his account, Paradise was never idyllic, the Fall was not sudden but gradual, and restoration is neither certain nor final. Human history after the Fall is not linear but cyclical: the wheel of life turns from bad to worse to bad to worse. Yet in spite of his ambiguous relation to the drama of decline and ascent, Rousseau could not free himself from it. He eloquently depicted a time of human innocence, detailed its corruption, and imagined redemptive ways of life that, if not as guileless as existence in the Garden, are at least satisfying and not too psychologically exhausting.

In the next six chapters, and indeed throughout this book, I argue that an investigation of Rousseau's preoccupation with the divine drama casts considerable light on his conception of the relation between the public and private life. I narrate Rousseau's account of the Garden and the Fall in chapters 1, 3, and 4. Chapter 1 examines Nature's Garden—the state of nature—and the Solitaires, its gentle inhabitants. Chapter 2 breaks away from the narrative style to pose the question, were the Solitaires moral or happy? Chapters 3 and 4 resume the narrative and chart the stages of the Fall, while chapters 5 and 6 provide a more systematic account of lessons to be learned from the narrative, specifically the function of the state of nature, the inevitability of the Fall, the nature of evil, and the possibility of a harmonious relation between the public and the private life in what I will call the ousted condition. Rousseau's fullest description of the Garden and the Fall is found in his first and second Discours—"Discourse on the Arts and Sciences" (1750) and "Discourse on the Origin of Inequality" (1755).[1] The first Discours depicts our ousted condition, while the second charts the route from Nature's Garden to social tumult. Rousseau hoped that with such a map we could see not only how we left happiness behind, but how we might proceed in search of, if not another garden, at least a way out of some modern sorrow and injustice. Even in these dreary discourses, then, Rousseau sketched routes to some better places.

I have suggested that our examining the Garden-Fall-Restoration saga will illuminate Rousseau's depiction of the public and private life and the tension between them. The approach is useful, but I am not claiming that attention to the saga exposes the essence of Rousseau's thought—some secret center. The drama is implicit in Rousseau's work, but it does not hold the secret key to it. There are, I believe, as many keys to open up Rousseau as there are thieves like me trying to break in. Likewise, my starting at the beginning—in the Garden and with Rousseau's first two major published works—should not imply that the essential Rousseau is to be found there. I have started at the beginning because, given the story I am telling, I have found this entrance helpful.

Some important questions will be postponed until chapter 5. Are we to understand humans in Nature's Garden—the state of nature—as a bygone age, an eternal possibility, or a heuristic device? Can we make any sense of radically asocial humans, that is, of Rousseau's natural Solitaires who lack all social ties? Must we discard this notion as bad epistemology or fallacious metaphysics, or can we learn something from it about the problems and promises of solitude and society? And finally, was the Fall inevitable, and is our ousted condition inescapable? In light of Rousseau's pessimistic account of modern social life, how seriously can we take his paths to deliverance? To these questions, responses must wait until we have lingered a bit in the Garden and have moved through the stages of the Fall. I do not want to evaluate components of the drama until I have presented the whole, because the beginning can be understood only in view of the end, and the end in view of the beginning.

For now, however, think of the next four chapters, moving from the Garden through the stages of the Fall, not as a historical inquiry but as a sociopsychological journey mapping the contours of modern misery and joy. I will argue that Rousseau was more eager to present us with ourselves and our self-inflicted social wounds than with a primitive species and their painless asocial existence. I call it a psychological voyage because the principal actors in the first and second *Discours* are such human powers and proclivities as love, esteem, pity, and the drive for perfection. I call it sociological because social circumstances move these principal players in often predictable, almost scripted, directions. Rousseau described himself as "the historian of the human heart," and this perfectly captures his ability to focus psychological and sociological brilliance on a single point—an illumination of the private life in light of the public, and the public in light of the private.[2]

The Garden's Solitaires

"Learn what God ordered you to be and your place in the human condition."[3] With this quotation from Persius, the Roman satirical poet who celebrated Stoic moral doctrine, Rousseau ushered his readers into a genealogy that recounts how humans managed to lose sight of their place in the divine order. What is the nature of this order? How are we to discover it? We can look to Nature's Garden. "Everything is good leaving the hands of the Author of things, everything degenerates in the hands of man. . . . Man does not want anything as nature made it, not even man himself."[4] This passage reveals a central thread that runs through Rousseau's quilted thought. Humans, unhappy with the way things are, tamper with things and make them worse. The natural order becomes confused and chaotic. To discover the natural order of things and our place in it, it is worthwhile to search for things untouched. Hence the importance of Nature's Garden, the original order and innocence, before, foot "being shod," humans trod on it.[5]

The Garden is a place abundant with wildlife, forests, and streams; a region sparsely populated—not colonized—by primitive humans. These primitives are not barbaric or savage, but simple and uncivilized—"the first embryo of the species."[6] Before we probe the heart—the psychological springs—of this simple creature, let us observe him from afar. "I see him," wrote Rousseau, "sating his hunger under an oak, quenching his thirst at the first stream, finding his bed at the foot of the same tree which furnished his meal, and *voilà*—his needs are satisfied."[7] Well, perhaps not all needs, for elsewhere Rousseau claimed that "the only goods he [the natural man] knows in the universe are food, a female, and rest."[8] On these three, then, food, sleep, and sex, the primitives set their minds. But the lowliest of these is sex.[9]

The essential needs, then, are basic and private: they pertain to the individual alone. Even sex is isolated from any form of relationship. Those involved are detached and disinterested. Such sexual intercourse—"having nothing to do with the heart"—is devoid of any social intercourse. After the act, "The two sexes knew each other no more." Even should a child result from this uncoupled coupling, Rousseau was not willing to introduce a meaningful social tie into his Garden. Once weaned, "The offspring would be nothing to its mother."[10] There are, then, no tethers between these solitary creatures, and therefore no lashes. Their needs are as simple as their language—private grunts. And since they can easily satisfy their needs, they have no need of each other. Nomadic but not homeless, for there are many trees; alone but not lonely, for they have no need of others; speechless but not muffled, for there are none to silence them; propertyless but not poor, for all their needs are satisfied; slothful but not neglectful, for they have no duties: such are the broad strokes of Rousseau's portrait of the Garden's Solitaires.

John Harsanyi, who won the Nobel prize for his pioneering work in game theory, has claimed that "people's behavior can largely be explained in terms of two dominant interests: economic and social acceptance."[11] Rousseau would agree (although he often subsumed the former under the latter). We can think of Rousseau's Solitaire in Nature's Garden, however, as an answer to the question, what would a human look like without either economic or social interests? In the absence of these interests the Solitaire is a stranger to such traits as vanity, jealousy, pride, and envy and to such conflicts as quarrels, property disputes, injustice, and war. There is no jealousy, for example, because there is no love; there are no quarrels, because there is no pride; there is no war, because there is no property.[12] Without financial or social worries, the Solitaire neither laments the past nor dreams of a future. "His imagination paints nothing for him; his heart demands nothing of him." There is as little to regret as there is to hope for. Living entirely in the present, not even the thought of death disturbs the Solitaire, for that would entail missing the past and fearing the future.[13]

Such present-mindedness renders impossible common projects that depend on promises in the past and shared goals for the future. Public obligations are as meaningless as private dreams when one lives entirely in the present. The Solitaire, simply put, is incapable of cooperation. Rousseau detected a correlation between reliance on others and preoccupation with the past or future. The dependent creature continually reflects on its history of assurances received and assurances given—its assets and debts—and on how to exploit these in the future. The life of the Solitaire, in contrast, manifests the converse correlation, namely, a correlation between self-sufficiency and present-mindedness. The Solitaire enjoys its nap without worrying whether it ought to be fulfilling an obligation; it eats the entire kill without worrying whether it ought to share it and thereby procure a future favor. The Solitaire needs no favors and hence it has no obligations. Dwelling entirely in the present, it dwells there alone.

Except for such physical trials as occasional hunger or contending with a ferocious animal, Rousseau has systematically excluded from his Garden occasions for gratuitous pain. This is why there can be no social ties; relationships are painful. Moreover, if the Solitaire could imagine wants in addition to its basic needs, that is, conceive of new desires as basic needs, then the Solitaire could abuse itself. It could burden its back with excessive travail and its mind with dissatisfaction. But Rousseau protected his Solitaire from this source of pain by permitting the Solitaire to feel "only his true needs." Minimal needs allow the Solitaire to be self-sufficient, and self-sufficiency, in Rousseau's view, is all-important, for it alone can protect one from association—that cardinal source of injury. Without need of anyone, the Solitaires cannot be hurt. Moreover, immunity to others protects the Solitaire from the desire to injure others, for there are no occasions for it to become angry with or resentful of another. The Solitaire, then, "without need of his fellow kind and without any desire to hurt them," is free from them, and hence free from heartache and grief.[14]

Physical blows, of course, may occasionally fall. Imagine a Solitaire finding a nice hunk of fresh meat near the hands of a fellow Solitaire. The first Solitaire may attempt to seize the meat if it deemed that this course of action would prove easier than downing its own deer. The second, reasoning similarly, would protect its kill unless it deemed it easier to get another. Should a fight begin, it will concern the meat alone. Since pride plays no role, the whole incident would be over after a few blows: "The victor eats, and the vanquished searches elsewhere for fortune, and all is at peace."[15] Should this same series of events repeat itself, the vanquished would no doubt relocate, and peace again would reign. In the absence of pride, the stakes fall dramatically and no grudge or resentment can fester. In the Garden, then, conflict is rare, and when it does occur, it is ephemeral.

As this example illustrates, the Garden is not free of natural inequalities. Some animals are swifter, some are stronger, some are smarter. The same can be said of the Solitaires. Yet because there are so few occasions for making comparisons among them, their inequalities are almost always relative to other animals, not to each other. Rousseau has thereby extracted such stings of inequality as envying the strong or scorning the weak. In the Garden, in the absence of social relations, inequality is not evil.

The Solitaire knows only two evils, hunger and pain.[16] Without belittling these, it should be kept in mind that, all things considered, the Solitaire is a truly excellent "human machine"—"the most advantageously organized of all" the animals. Most of the time, therefore, the Solitaire is capable of protecting itself from the two evils. Its powers match its limited needs, and hence evil remains restricted. There is a relation between minimal needs, sufficient powers, and confined evil. Should the powers diminish, as with age, the Solitaire will experience more physical evil. Should the needs increase, the powers must be augmented if the Solitaire is to avoid evil. Needs can require expanded powers in two ways; minimal needs can become more difficult to meet, or new needs can be added to the original ones. By definition, however, an increase of needs cannot occur in the Garden. The equilibrium between minimal needs and sufficient powers is largely what makes the Garden a garden.[17]

Tragically, this balance must be disturbed if the Solitaire is to become fully human. Rousseau endowed the Solitaire with a faculty for development, or what he called, "the faculty of perfectibility."[18] As this faculty is exercised, new needs are created, sociability becomes required, and new evils are felt. In order to explore these claims, I need to lead us still deeper into the soul of the Solitaire, into the heart of Rousseau's moral psychology.

Tragic Features of the Heart

The second *Discours*, "On the Origin of Inequality," features four human properties: perfectibility, freedom, self-love, and compassion. Perfectibility and freedom are intimately related, and these two faculties distinguish humans from beasts.[19] Unlike the other animals, humans are not determined by instincts but exercise free will. Nature dictates its commands to all animals, including humans, but humans have the liberty to dissent, and they are conscious of this liberty. In the Garden, for example, the voice of nature might command that its residents be afraid of water, but the Solitaire may nonetheless choose to dive into the depths in search of food. The Solitaire will have learned how to swim thanks to the faculty of perfectibility, and this demonstrates how freedom and perfectibility are related. The Solitaires are free to improve themselves variously. In fact, they are, ironically, driven toward self-improvement.

This suggests that a source of conflict is built into the human soul. For instance, in the above example nature supplied both a fear of water and a propensity to develop the ability to swim. The potential conflict between the voice of nature and the faculty of perfectibility becomes more profound when, in his later writings, Rousseau adds the moral pitch, conscience, to the voice of nature.[20] Conscience delivers general moral guidance but not the will or desire to follow such guidance. Perfectibility could inspire one to climb the lofty heights of virtue, or, conversely, to venture into the depths of vice (as did Milton's antihero, Satan). When Rousseau described the moral flexibility of perfectibility—its potential to aid or collide with the voice of nature—he usually highlighted its darker side: "This distinctive and almost unlimited faculty is the source of all the misfortunes of man; it drags man, over the course of time, out of that original condition, in which he would spend tranquil and innocent days; it is this faculty—which cultivates through the ages his insights and his errors, his vices and his virtues—that makes him at length a tyrant over himself and over nature."[21]

At first blush, it may seem odd that an antiprogress theorist like Rousseau would catalog *perfectibilité* as a salient human characteristic. But the oddity looks more like irony once we realize that this faculty leads humans to adopt multifarious and complex ways of life that pave some imaginative avenues to human joy, but more paths to human sorrow.[22] While the Solitaires are free to dissent from nature and to improve themselves innocuously, those outside the Garden, in contrast, are empowered by freedom and perfectibility—diversely and creatively—to injure themselves, others, and nature. It would seem, then, that, contrary to all the standard interpretations of Rousseau, a cause of the Fall is located in the soul of the Solitaire. For Rousseau placed at the heart of his philosophical anthropology a proclivity for expanded powers that are, by Rousseau's lights, the sources of misfortune. Since I will argue that the Fall occurs gradually—a series of slow tumbles that leads to a plunge—I do not want to provide a systematic account of it until we have followed the Solitaires well out of the Garden. For now it is enough to note that with expanded powers come such fonts of misery as imagination, memory, knowledge of good and evil, the making of comparisons, complexity, change, technology, property, inequality, and frivolous wants masquerading as needs.

In spite of this baneful ledger, I will later argue that we interpret the journey out of the Garden as what Christian thinkers like John Milton have called a "blessed fall." Blessed in the theological account, because if humans had not embraced sin, there would have been no occasion for Christ to display his love on the cross and his power in the resurrection. Blessed in Rousseau's account, because had the Solitaires not left the Garden, the world never would have known the warmth and moral achievement of human community. The Fall is the necessary price to unleash the splendor of humanity, brandishing all its virtue and vice, its genius and stupidity, its works of art and war, its gentle sociability and destructive associations.

Outside the Garden, then, perfectibility and freedom, like fire or ice, cannot be simply loved or hated. But in the Garden they function as innocently as the Solitaires themselves are innocent. This is because in the Garden freedom and perfectibility are exercised privately and therefore primitively. Without social relations there is no impetus to perfect one's domination over another. Without envy or competition, needs remain limited, and hence there is no stimulus to misuse nature or to hurt oneself by multiplying one's labors. Freedom and perfectibility remain harmless as long as the Solitaire's gaze is on itself, and not on another. This argument, of course, is largely semantical. Once primitive freedom and perfectibility lead to more complex forms of life, they, by definition, forfeit their simplicity and innocence. Initially benign, both faculties become dangerous, steering the Solitaire out of uncomplicated solitude into tangled associations. Although the chains of society bring a measure of happiness and morality, their weight disfigures the Solitaire's natural frame, even its bent to love itself and its aversion to injure others.

This brings us to the two other elements in Rousseau's moral psychology, namely, self-love (*amour de soi*) and compassion (*pitié*).[23] The former is a prereflective, ardent interest in the self's "welfare and preservation"; the latter is a "natural repugnance at seeing any sentient being, and particularly those similar to us, suffer pain or death."[24] Self-love and compassion, unlike freedom and perfectibility, are unambiguously good. They are "the first and most simple operations of the human soul," and by that Rousseau meant that they come not from moral philosophy or positive law, but "directly from the voice of nature."

From self-love springs our primal duty to self. Avoiding pain and injury, seeking food and shelter: these are some of the ways that we love ourselves. Self-love is the basis of our "*passions primitives*, all of which lead to our happiness . . . and which are entirely sweet and loving in their essence."[25] Whereas the Reformation theologian Martin Luther charged that "we are to hate ourselves, even our own names," because we are essentially disgraceful creatures worthy of hate, Rousseau insisted that we are essentially graceful creatures worthy of love. That we can effectively bury and lose sight of our original loveliness goes without saying. Later I show how love of self becomes hatred of self and of others. In the Garden, however, self-love is the principal mandate in the life of the Solitaire. Principal, but not exclusive, for it is occasionally modified by compassion (*pitié*).

If duty to self emanates from *amour de soi*, then duty to others emanates from *pitié*. Compassion, that "innate repugnance at seeing suffering in a fellow creature," prevents the Solitaire from causing injury to any sentient being, "except in the legitimate case when his own preservation is at stake and he is obliged to give preference to himself."[26] *Pitié* is a "pure impulse of nature," prior to any kind of reflection. It produces anguish in us when we observe suffering in others. Causing us to share—indirectly yet decidedly—the suffering of others, *pitié* connects us to the other. It is, to be sure, a painful tie, one that we would rather not have, yet therein lies its ability to deter us from causing unnecessary harm. For, to inflict gratuitous pain would produce grief within ourselves.

In the Garden, identification occurs through observed suffering. In the sufferer the Solitaire sees itself, or at least an aspect of itself—its own experience of pain. Shared suffering, via *pitié*, is a primitive social phenomenon of wide scope. The scope of identification is as wide as the number of creatures that suffer, because compassion is prompted by identification with sentient beings, not only with rational ones. No doubt, identification—and hence compassion—is proportionate to the number of shared characteristics between the observer and the sufferer; the more lines of identification, the more compassion. Solitaires, then, feel greater *pitié* for other Solitaires than for lower animals. Still, when describing what makes creatures worthy of compassion, Rousseau placed the capacity to suffer above the ability to reason. Although animals "are deprived of intelligence and liberty," Rousseau insisted that they have prerogatives that humans are obliged to recognize. The capacity to suffer, "being common to beast and man, should at least give the beast the right not to be uselessly mistreated by man."[27]

Rousseau's insistence on treating animals decently springs from his minimizing the distinction between animals and humans, or rather, his maximizing the identity between the two. This line of thought reveals not only Rousseau's conception of our moral duties to animals, but of human nature. Insofar as we view ourselves chiefly as suffering creatures rather than rational creatures, we can identify with animals as mutual sufferers. And for Rousseau, suffering is the worst thing. It is to be avoided and hated more than pleasure is to be sought and loved. Suffering in the Garden, therefore, is to be kept to an absolute minimum. A greater premium is placed on the absence of suffering than on the presence of pleasure. To understand as much is to understand much of Rousseau. This lone "social" faculty, *pitié*—which itself is painful—functions not to enhance charitable communion, but to curtail cruel interaction.

Throughout his life, Rousseau held that the human creature is first and foremost a suffering creature. In *Emile*, for example, he claimed, "All are born naked and poor, all are subject to the miseries of life, to griefs, ills, needs, suffering of every kind; finally, all are condemned to death. This is what it truly means to be human, this is what no mortal can escape."[28] No mortal, not even the Solitaire, is exempt from suffering, but the Solitaire is spared from suffering's greatest source—that of associations.

Compassion itself tends to keep the Solitaire private. The scope of compassion, I have said, is broad, but its consequences are limited. It does not, for example, motivate acts of altruism. It merely prevents the Solitaire from inflicting unwarranted harm as it pursues the prompting of *amour de soi*, self-love. It thereby fortifies the Solitaire's isolation, for without the desire to profit from another's misery, the Solitaire is protected from a conspicuous form of social interaction. It is an open question whether *pitié* would direct the Solitaire to assist a fellow creature that it found in need.[29] Outside the Garden, in contrast, the range of compassion's activities tends to increase, while its scope narrows. By this I mean that Rousseau understood compassion as a source of such social virtues as generosity, clemency, benevolence, and friendship, and yet he also held that humans increasingly fail to identify not only with lower animals worthy of compassion, but with fellow humans as well.[30]

Again, this is pure tragedy. In order for compassion to deepen, to become more profound, its scope, it would seem, almost by necessity, narrows. In the Garden, there is an easy "agreement and combination" between *pitié* and self-love which establishes a peaceful environment for the Solitaires to pursue their private existence. To secure such harmony, it is not "necessary to introduce the principle of sociability." On the contrary, sociability would threaten it. Agreement between duty to self and duty to others, then, does not require an innate social faculty or even developed reasoning capabilities.[31] These duties are naturally governed by *pitié* and self-love. Yet the agreement between them and the harmony that they establish are as simple as the Solitaires are primitive. Self-love and compassion, in the Garden, are cautious faculties. *Amour de soi*, for example, ensures that the Solitaire feed itself, but it will not direct the Solitaire, say, to forfeit some meals in order to scale a mountain and enjoy the beauty and grace that it offers. *Pitié* ensures that the Solitaire inflicts no unnecessary harm, but it will not lead the Solitaire, say, to jeopardize its own life in an attempt to save another. If self-love and compassion are to become complex and profound, the Solitaire's simplicity and innocence must be sacrificed.

Rousseau wrote that "self-love [*amour de soi*] is a natural sentiment . . . which, guided in man by reason and modified by *pitié*, creates humanity and virtue."[32] In the Garden, however, there is neither humanity nor virtue, only simple Solitaires and the natural maxim, "*Do good to yourself with as little harm as possible to others.*"[33] This maxim, which perfectly combines self-love and *pitié* and which requires neither education nor virtue won by reason, is less sublime than that maxim of rational justice, "Do to others as you would have them do to you." Yet if the maxim of the Solitaires is "indeed much less perfect . . . it is perhaps more useful." Some might even claim that this primitive maxim of the Solitaires represents the crowning achievement of modern liberalism, namely, societies dedicated to doing minimal harm.

This claim will occupy much of our attention throughout this study of Rousseau. For now, however, I simply want to note that, in spite of Rousseau's allegiance to the natural maxim, he wanted more. He wanted such virtues as courage, wisdom, generosity, and justice. He wanted a robust humanity that understood duty to self to mean more than self-preservation and duty to others to mean more than doing no harm. He wanted more because he knew that flourishing public and private lives take root not in cautious soils or in isolated gardens, but in individuals and communities willing to embrace cooperation and risk. He wanted more, and yet he well understood that this would require the Solitaires to develop capacities and relationships that would rush them out of the Garden, because the development of complex public and private lives invariably corrupt both compassion and self-love. Public and private virtue and joy must risk vice and pain. To move from the simple maxim to the virtues, from the Solitaires to humanity, from the Garden to the City, requires that one is committed to things outside the self, and such commitment necessarily entails jeopardy and vulnerability.

In *Emile* Rousseau wrote, "A truly happy being is a solitaire; God alone enjoys absolute happiness."[34] God alone is perfectly invulnerable to pain, for God is radically alone and absolutely self-sufficient.[35] But humans are not divine, and hence immediately after stating that "God alone enjoys absolute happiness" Rousseau asked, How can we talk of a truly happy human solitaire? "Which of us has any idea what that means? If some imperfect [that is, human] creature could be self-sufficing, what would he have to enjoy? He would be alone, he would be miserable." Here we come to the heart of the tragedy, to the heart of Rousseau's life and thought. Only in solitude can humans be exempt from most pain; only by blocking associations can injustice be checked. Yet this form of life—the simple life in the Garden—is loveless, not because the self isn't worthy of love, but because private love cannot be deemed love proper in the absence of loving things other than the self. Precisely the self-sufficiency of the Solitaire—which protects it from sorrow and makes it like a god—averts it from loving others. For in the absence of dependency, that is, of vulnerability, there can be no love of others. Hence the passage that begins with "A truly happy being is a solitaire," ends with "I do not understand how one who has need of nothing could love anything; I do not understand how he who loves nothing can be happy." This is our passage, too, from the Garden to the City.

2

Revisiting the Garden's Solitaires

Alone, as radical Solitaires, we are sheltered from pain, yet we can be neither truly happy nor moral. Together, in the company of others, we can experience ambiguous moral progress and precarious human joy, yet we hurt each other. These are the twin horns of Rousseau's depiction of our dilemma. This dilemma and Rousseau's response to it highlight a perplexing feature of liberal society: the more we seek to do good, the more we risk inflicting harm; conversely, the more we seek to avoid such risk, the more we dodge our moral commitments. In this chapter I will show that the Garden's Solitaire was not, in fact, genuinely happy or virtuous; I will argue that alone, we cannot be truly happy or moral. Then, in the following two chapters, I will show how our efforts to achieve happiness and virtue inevitably lead to avenues of sorrow and vice. The Fall is not from Paradise but from simple innocence. The ousted condition is not the human inability to throw off the yoke of original sin, but the inevitable risk—risk of pain and corruption—that accompanies the human pursuit of happiness and virtue. The tragic passage from the Garden to the City, I will show, leads from solitary invulnerability to vulnerable sociability.

Are the Solitaires moral or amoral? Can they attain genuine happiness? I would not want to be dogmatic while addressing these questions. Rousseau was dogmatic, but in a contradictory fashion that suggests he held that the truth of these matters lay at polar extremes. For example, he categorically asserted that "man is naturally good" and that "men are wicked."[1] I want to see if we can make sense of the apparent contradiction, and to that end I will examine the Solitaires first as moral, then as amoral, creatures. I am not dedicated to defending Rousseau, but to discovering what light the predicament of the Solitaires may shed on the relation between the public and private life in liberal society. If I thought that Rousseau's reflections on the Solitaires served only as speculation about a bygone era, I would have little interest in it.

Moral Solitaires

Let us begin, then, with the moral status of the Solitaires. Are they moral? We can approach this issue by asking, moral compared to whom? The inhabitants of Rousseau's

Garden certainly look moral when compared to the creatures that populate Thomas Hobbes's Wilderness.[2] Rousseau endowed his Solitaires with gentle *amour de soi* and *pitié* precisely to distinguish them from Hobbes's beastly egoists driven by the anomic pursuit of possession and domination. The Solitaires, while not "timid" and "fearful," *pace* Pufendorf, were not "concerned only with attacking and fighting," *pace* Hobbes.[3] The Garden is not the war against all—it is not nearly social enough.[4] In Rousseau's view, Hobbes had successfully imagined a time and place prior to political society, but not prior to society itself. Hobbes's "state of nature" is in fact a fairly advanced stage in social development. Unwittingly, Hobbes attributed a vicious egoism—an egoism that can emerge only from associations—to supposedly natural humans. Hence Rousseau complained that Hobbes's anachronistic, egoistic ascription had given natural humans a bad name.[5] Rousseau's Garden, in contrast, was meant to depict truly natural creatures, and the result was the discovery—or the invention—of solitary beings enjoying only the most benign egoism, *amour de soi*.

Here, then, is one way to take Rousseau's claim that "man is naturally good": Humans are not naturally rapacious, but pacific. The Solitaire is driven not by innate egoism, but by gentle self-love (*amour de soi*), and this power "is the least prejudicial to that of others." Indeed, self-love promotes peace, because it encourages only the gratification of modest, basic needs, not the "satisfaction of a multitude of passions which are the work of society." Caring for the self does not require the Solitaire to attempt to become the "sole proprietor of the entire universe."[6] I am suggesting, then, that the Solitaire's peaceful existence looks moral when compared to the stormy and violent existence of Hobbes's natural humans.

This negative argument—that the Solitaire is moral insofar as it does no harm—is supported by Rousseau's more general belief that vice does more harm than virtue does good.[7] Rousseau explicitly criticized Hobbes for implying that because one in the state of nature "has no idea of goodness, he is naturally wicked; that he is vicious because he does not know virtue." In contrast, Rousseau argued that "savages are not wicked precisely because they do not know what it is to be good: for it is neither the development of understanding nor the restraint of law, but the peacefulness of the passions and the ignorance of vice that keep them from doing ill."[8] Here, then, is another way to take Rousseau's claim that "man is naturally good": Humans, although not naturally equipped with knowledge of virtue, are naturally ignorant of vice; and, given that vice does more harm than virtue does good, ignorance of vice can be considered a morally advantageous condition.

Although ultimately I want to argue that Rousseau was not satisfied with minimal notions of morality, it is worth noting that when Rousseau surveyed the corruption and human exploitation of his day, minimal decency—embodied in the natural maxim, "Do no unnecessary harm"—looked quite appealing. His Solitaires are remarkably similar to what some would consider the ideal liberal citizenry.[9] Although they do little good, they commit no cruelty. Although they do not meaningfully associate with each other, they do not disturb each other. The peaceful, morally shallow existence of the Solitaires would be destroyed should, let us imagine, a missionary or an emissary from a distant culture attempt to inculcate virtue and shared loves in the Solitaires. The simple emotions associated with self-love and pity—loving survival and hating cruelty—would be replaced by a passion for the morally flourishing community and a hatred of the mediocre citizen.

Freedom (here, the absence of constraints) would have to be exchanged for "virtue," since moral repression—outfitting citizens with a standard moral uniform—is often the cost of moral perfection. Moreover, once a premium was placed on virtue, individuals would have to appear to have achieved it. Such pretense inevitably invites a host of vices, from personal hypocrisy to public tyranny. Both the Solitaire and the liberal citizen, then, must be protected from missionaries of virtue, lest their peaceful, private existence be shattered by fierce public crusades.

In Hobbes's account, the inhabitants of the Wilderness are not natural liberals. On the contrary, these creatures interfere daily with each other's pursuit of happiness. They must be convinced that in order to get much of what they want—not all, but much—they need to sacrifice some liberties in order to pursue others in peace. Those in the Hobbesian state of nature, then, dwell in ignorance, yet unlike Rousseau's Solitaires, they are not ignorant of vice, but of what in fact is in their best interest, or at least the best way to pursue their self-interest. They stand in need of enlightenment. Of course, if an all-powerful dictator is converted to Hobbesianism, then the enlightenment of the people is no longer critical. They will become enlightened liberals or else lose their heads.

Rousseau described a Hobbesian scenario and sequence of events—a war of all against all exchanged for a despotic peace. In Rousseau's account, however, this sequence of events is not the first step out of the state of nature, but what I will call the fifth and sixth. Without getting too far ahead of my argument, I want to make it clear that, in spite of Rousseau's and Hobbes's vastly different accounts of "natural humans," both held that humans are better off when their needs and desires are heavily circumscribed—by a General Will, for example, or by a Leviathan. For both Rousseau and Hobbes, public order and private peace are paramount. How to achieve that peace separates Rousseau and Hobbes, and their different prescriptions for peace rest on, in part, their different conceptions of the natural human. Although some of Rousseau's political writings seem to come close to erecting a Leviathan, I will argue in chapter 10 that Rousseau's devotion to freedom ultimately led him in a different direction than Hobbes's. For now it is enough to note that Rousseau did not put peace first in every case. In *The Social Contract*, for example, after noting that some claim that despotism brings civic peace, Rousseau asked rhetorically, "Tranquility is found also in dungeons, but is that enough to make them desirable places to live in?"[10]

Still, even Rousseau's and Hobbes's divergent prescriptions reveal agreement: both doubted that ignorance of virtue was the chief cause of social disorder. Here is where Christianity, Hobbes, and Rousseau agree to disagree with a Platonic tradition that identifies evil with ignorance. Displacing ignorance with knowledge will not solve our deepest public and private moral dilemmas. This claim will play an important role when I provide a systematic account of Rousseau's conception of evil and compare it to Christian and Platonic conceptions. Here, however, I simply want to note that while Hobbes and Rousseau were both skeptical of counting on virtue to establish harmony, only Rousseau highlighted the moral implications of the ignorance of vice so that he could compare the benefits of amoral creatures who know no virtue to the liabilities of moral creatures who practice vice. The Solitaires' ignorance of vice is what won them the appellation, "naturally good."

Virtue and knowledge, I have said, are not salient features in Hobbes's—unlike the Platonic—prescription for a peaceful society. Yet in Hobbes's remedy there is, in fact, a form of knowledge that plays a prominent role. It is not the Platonic knowledge of original harmony and forms, but the nearly as geometric knowledge of how to organize the political state. Not "the many," however, only "the one"—the almighty despot—requires such knowledge. This form of enlightenment, in a pair of powerful hands, can do much good, although many problems will remain. Leviathan is no cure-all, yet under it, a peace relative to the savage Wilderness will reign. Neither the knowledge of virtue nor the ignorance of vice, on the part of the citizens, is essential as long as they are minimally smart enough to recognize the unfortunate consequences of crossing Leviathan. For Rousseau, on the other hand, an enforced peace would not be nearly as socially valuable as a ubiquitous ignorance of vice among the general citizenry. Whether an enforced peace is a more realistic goal than peaceful ignorance is a question for part II of this study.

For the moment, I want to suggest another way to take Rousseau's claim that "man is naturally good." The Solitaires, naturally ignorant of vice, are free from the "multitude of passions which are the work of society," and hence can "listen to the voice of conscience in the silence of the passions."[11] This account suggests that natural humans are good not only comparatively, that is, relative to modern corruption, but absolutely. The intrinsic goodness of the natural human entails that "sublime science of simple minds" whose principles are "graven on every heart." Natural humans are the true philosophers whose wisdom springs not from theoretical arguments but from the "peacefulness of their passions." Their ignorance of vice—greed, envy, pride, and cruelty—allows them to act naturally; to be natural, in this case, is to be good.[12]

This rhetoric exalting the natural human was not unique to Rousseau. Just as God had looked at nature, the new creation, and declared, "It is good," so did much of the eighteenth century. Diderot and d'Holbach, for example, celebrated nature as our true mentor and mother and sang the praise of those free, happy, innocent, and often naked primitives whose lives apparently followed nature's ways. Rousseau added many new lines of praise. Now, however, I want to argue that the Garden, in spite of all its advantages, was no paradise on earth. All things considered, it was not a suitable place for humans to dwell. To be sure, it wasn't nasty or brutish, *pace* Hobbes, but neither was it ideal or even adequate, for neither genuine happiness nor morality could take root there. Establishing this claim is crucial for the first part of my larger argument, namely, that alone, we can't be truly happy or moral.

Amoral Solitaires

In a gloss on Rousseau, Judith Shklar wrote, "Morality is born only with an awareness of others."[13] Awareness of others, however, is precisely what the Solitaires lack and what gives them their well-deserved name. Are they, then, immoral? Perhaps they are, on some accounts of immorality. The Christian tradition, for example, counts as immoral sins of commission *and* omission. The Solitaires may do little harm, but they also neglect to do good. In the Christian account, then, it might appear that the Solitaires are immoral. This view is not limited to Christianity: other religious and secular traditions condemn moral inactivity, for example, passive acceptance of the practices of the Nazi German state. Yet it is not clear that "sins of omission" applies to the Solitaires, because they have not neglected any obligations—they have none. Hence Rousseau, for good reason, contended that they are fundamentally amoral. The Solitaires, "having between them no kind of moral relation or known obligations, could be neither good nor bad, could have neither vices nor virtues."[14]

Although for the last 200 years Rousseau has been accused of idealizing the Solitaires—those noble savages—he himself was usually careful not to claim that they were lovely _moral_ creatures. Against Hobbes, for example, he argued not that natural humans were good and virtuous, but only that they were not wicked and vicious.[15] The Solitaires were neither mean-spirited egoists nor well-intended altruists. Nor did they occupy some moral location between egoism and altruism. Without advancing a definition of morality, I think we can nevertheless safely assume—as did Rousseau—that morality entails, among other things, some set of duties or obligations. Insofar as the Solitaire did not owe its "neighbor" any moral consideration, the Solitaire cannot be said to have occupied even a marginal moral position. It inhabited no moral position, because the Garden permitted no meaningful "awareness of others." The qualification _meaningful_ is required here because, as I have shown, there are in fact at least two relations in the Garden: first, the Solitaire's relation to itself, which is prompted by self-love (_amour de soi_); and second, the Solitaire's relation to other sentient creatures, which is prompted by pity. The Garden did allow, then, some type of duty to self and duty to others. As we have seen, however, the moral vision of self-love and pity in the Garden are constricted, at least by most standards.[16] They roughly correspond to what might be our moral praise of one who manages to care for him- or herself without causing others gratuitous pain. Most animals would merit such praise.

Outside the Garden—as we will eventually see—self-love and pity become moral dispositions capable of tremendous good. Inside, they direct only a natural, passive amorality. Such a natural amorality should be distinguished from an _unnatural_ amorality. Imagine a serial killer who randomly inflicts harm and apparently lacks what is commonly called a conscience. He is, let us say, ignorant of vice, for his crimes are not motivated by greed, envy, pride, and so on. He is also ignorant of virtue, for he has no sense of good or evil. Although the courts might judge him incapable of making moral decisions and thus a fundamentally amoral agent, he would remain radically unlike the Solitaire because he lacks pity; hence his amorality could not be deemed natural, by Rousseau's measure. This example is meant to help us appreciate the allure of the Solitaires by distinguishing the salutary effects of natural amorality, which is directed by both self-love and pity, from the harmful effects of amorality more generally.

We can appreciate why Rousseau and some modern-day liberals would be tempted to prefer passive amorality to active animosity. The Solitaires embody the vision of a society that places the protection of individual pursuits above all else as long as the individual commits no gratuitous harm. Such a society, of course, is not interested in "sins of omission." The age-old question about our obligation to act as our brother's or sister's "keeper" is addressed in the negative by the extreme liberalism exemplified by Rousseau's Solitaires. If we enforce moral care for our neighbor, if we as a society worry about sins of omission, then we chance persecuting those whose moral vision differs from our own. We risk becoming the wrong kind of keeper, the kind that entraps "the other" and causes needless pain. The line between guardian and warden is fine, and this frail boundary prompts fears that attract liberals to the Solitaires.[17] For this reason,

Rousseau insisted that "the most important lesson of morality . . . is *never to harm any-one*. The very precept of doing good, if it is not subordinated to this one, is dangerous, false, and contradictory."[18] "Dangerous," because, seeking perfection, doing good could lead us to extreme measures that torment the very ones we seek to help; "false" and "contradictory," because, attempting to make of ourselves more than we should, we become less than we could be—creatures who can dodge inflicting great harm, and who can even do some limited good. Even equipped with goodwill, we risk doing great harm in our efforts to do good. Hence Rousseau warned, "If we were kings and beneficent, we would do, without knowing it, a thousand real evils for an apparent good that we believed we were doing."[19]

Still, the Solitaires, in spite of their natural gentleness, do not represent the moral vision Rousseau offers for individuals in modern societies. As I have said, he set his sights higher than minimal decency. The stillness—the passive amorality—of the Solitaire's amoral lives approaches the stillness of death, for in death we escape relationships, obligations, and concerns, moral and otherwise, and we attain the ultimate stillness of the passions: the release from both fear and joy, from disappointment and hope. The Garden is green, but its still life is the portrait of death, because the absence of morality is a mortal wound to genuine human existence.[20] This is why the Garden is not a place for humans to dwell.[21]

Having argued that the Solitaires are fundamentally amoral creatures, what are we to say about my earlier arguments that they *are* moral? I have attempted to show how we can make sense of Rousseau's two apparently contradictory claims. I see no way nor reason to try to form, in good Hegelian fashion, a new thesis from the contradiction. As is often the case when reading Rousseau, more is gained by exploring the tensions and contradictions that punctuate his writings than by attempting to resolve or—worse still—to ignore them. The Solitaires, I have argued, can be construed as moral on some ac-counts and as amoral on others. It is the standard, the measure, that determines the outcome. I don't think Rousseau's measure, in this case, changed or wavered thought-lessly. I would prefer to say that, in good Wittgensteinian fashion, he looked at his Solitaires from this angle and then from that, fleshing out a variety of perspicuous state-ments that appear disturbingly inconsistent only when placed side by side and out of context.

Content Solitaires

Are the Solitaires happy? If happiness is to have all or most of one's needs and desires satiated, then the Solitaires are truly happy. Food, shelter, and sex are readily available in the Garden, and hence the Solitaire is entirely satisfied. Such happiness ought not be construed simply as the satisfaction of physical needs but as the realization of a psycho-logical condition, namely, freedom from anxiety and dread. This is the point of the rhetorical question Rousseau posed, whether we "would not be, on the whole, in a happier situation" if, like the Solitaires, we "had no harm to fear, or good to hope for, from any one?"[22] Earlier a negative argument suggested that the Solitaire is moral insofar as it does no harm. Here a negative argument suggests that the Solitaire is happy insofar as it is free from expanding needs and the disappointment and pain that accompanies dependency on others. View the Solitaire, then, as absolutely happy given its serene psychology, and relatively happy when compared to the increasingly dismal human condition that will be depicted when we examine, in the next two chapters, the stages of the Fall.

What if happiness, however, pertains not only to the satisfaction of needs, but also to the quality or nature of them? What if a tranquil psychology is not even a necessary—much less a sufficient—condition of human happiness? Could one not argue, along roughly Aristotelian lines, that happiness is a retrospective judgment on the virtuous life? Or, if that definition is too stringent and too distant from Rousseau, can we not at least say that the happy life entails some struggle and defeat as one pursues goals, often complex and difficult ones, capable of bringing deep, meaningful satisfaction? "The happiness of the natural man," Rousseau noted in *Emile*, "is as simple as his life; it consists in not suffering; it is constituted by health, liberty, and the necessities of life. The happiness of the moral man is something else."[23] That "something else" includes, among other things, what Rousseau called "the love of virtue." In the *Geneva Manuscript* (the first version of *The Social Contract*), for example, immediately after lamenting that "our needs bring us together to the extent that our passions set us apart," Rousseau went on to claim that if humans had remained Solitaires, "our understanding would not have developed; we would live without feeling anything, we would die without having lived . . . there would be neither kindness in our hearts nor morality in our actions, and we never would have tasted the most delicious sentiment of the soul, which is the love of virtue."[24]

In light of these views, the Solitaire cannot be deemed truly happy. Rousseau did not readily admit as much, and for some good reasons. The Solitaire's happiness, I said, springs from (1) the satisfaction of basic, physical needs and (2) a peaceful psychology. That these are the two conditions is no coincidence, given that Rousseau, as a social critic, descried the tremendous suffering in a world where (1) the basic needs of the poor are not met, and (2) the "necessities" of the well-to-do rotate anomically, that is, insatiably. To Rousseau's sore eyes, these two—very different yet related—modern "deficiencies" made the Solitaire a candidate, albeit by default, for happiness. A simple form of life free of receiving or inflicting unnecessary pain—this may not be a prescription for human bliss, but it may appeal to many, especially those who find themselves crushed by anxiety, rancor, or social injustice.

We can view Rousseau's own life as punctuated by various attempts to capture the Solitaire's simple, tranquil life. That life, however, never entirely satisfied him.[25] His periodic ventures into solitude brought some satisfaction and respite, but ultimately they left him longing for those components of human joy that come with association. During his seasons of outermost retreat, Rousseau was with a pen, reaching for the distant world with his writings, even late in his life when he was convinced that he would be understood only by future generations. His pen and books, however, could not altogether provide him with the gifts of human society. Yet human association entailed vulnerability—a susceptibility to harm's way. Knowing this all too well, he nonetheless could not deny that to live fully is to love, and to love is to be vulnerable. He flatly stated this, we have seen, when he described our frail yet sole chance for happiness.[26]

The simple happiness—contentedness—of the Solitaires cannot and should not satisfy us, because we—including Jean-Jacques, often in spite of his comments to the contrary—

have naturally become social animals, and hence we must incur the risk that attends human association. Happiness, in Rousseau's account, is ultimately a gamble: one must be willing to play and perhaps lose. Yet if happiness is risky outside the Garden, it is impossible inside it. Again, the image of the Garden's lifeless still life comes to mind. I do not mean to say, of course, that ventures into solitude are excursions into death, that is, into the absence of genuine life. Much in the following chapters—especially in chapter 8—can be read as an examination of the goods that attend life alone. For the moment I only mean to say that if solitude should become a way of life—as opposed to a periodic counterpose to life together—its chances for enhancing either the public or private life diminish. Even monasteries have common hours and feast days. Yet there remain some who, greatly fearing and despising the suffering and corruption in the world, would prefer to escape it entirely. An examination of Rousseau's account of that suffering and corruption will put us in a good position to appreciate his frequent eremitic escapes.

From the Garden to the Blessed Country

The Precarious Passage

In the previous chapter I have attempted to support the first part of my claim: alone, we cannot be truly happy or moral. Now I need to establish the second part: together, we suffer and become corrupt. To that end, here and in the next chapter I will chart the course of the Fall from the simple contentment, invulnerability, and innocence of the Garden to the complex gratifications, vulnerability, and corruption of the City. This will be a story of costly progress: the Solitaire must sacrifice itself in order to release its inner potential for development, thereby giving birth to a new creation, the social human. I cast the Fall in seven stages that are based on the second *Discours*, "On the Origin of Inequality." To his credit, Rousseau did not individuate these stages precisely, and I would not be dismayed if some claim to find more or fewer than seven stages of development. My aim is to expose the trajectory of the fall, not to establish definitively the borders between its stages.

A word of caution: with each stage we reach a new level of human sorrow. Even this chapter, which details the Fall from stage one through four and concludes with what may sound hopeful, the Blessed Country, recounts a heartbreaking story of frail, momentary happiness. Should this melancholic narrative seem unduly cheerless, keep in mind that I am, after all, recounting the Fall—never a particularly cheerful subject. Moreover, I am showing fidelity to Rousseau's deep pessimism. Still, be not overly discouraged: helplessness was not Rousseau's principal or at least not sole outlook, as we will see in part II, where I explore the avenues he recommended for our partial redemption.

Nature's Careless Shove

In the *first stage*, the Solitaire took its first step toward making comparisons and differentiating between the species.[1] The Solitaire was pushed in this direction by some natural changes in the Garden and by the Solitaire's innate—and hence natural—ability to cope with those changes. Increased competition for food supplies, the occasional drought and severe winter, and unfortunate encounters with ferocious carnivores obliged the

Solitaire "to apply" itself. New technologies developed. Those living by the sea, for example, invented the hook and line; those in the forest, the bow and arrow. Fire was discovered, and soon the Solitaires were eating cooked meat. With this new culinary habit, it becomes increasingly difficult for us to continue to call these creatures the Garden's Solitaires, for by cooking flesh, by moving from the raw to the cooked, they have imposed the artificial onto the natural, and they have thereby transformed both nature and themselves.

Such new activity produced a "kind of reflection" and belief in superiority of the human species over other animals. "The first time he looked into himself, it produced the first movement of pride in him," and such pride of the species, Rousseau claimed, prepared the way for what would become the primacy of the individual.[2] This first step toward separation, isolating the human species from the rest of nature, will lead to other divisions: first, a multiplicity of partitions between groups of humans, and finally, the individual disconnected from all else—at best in tolerable solitude, at worst estranged from nature, humans, and even itself. Such distinctions and separations, we have seen, tend to truncate compassion's scope, reducing one's ability to identify with other sentient beings. Yet such division is also the only way for public and private spheres to emerge. Without fluid yet palpable boundaries between the self and the group, there can be neither genuine public nor private domains.[3]

While identification with all sentient beings may wane, identification among members of a particular group increases. In some instances, compassion prevails even over self-love (*amour de soi*), as when one is willing to die for the group in order to shield the group from suffering. Identification with the group, an essential element for public life, requires that the group be circumscribed, that is, that there be insiders and outsiders.[4] This same path of division leads, moreover, to the creation of the private life. Jean Bodin correctly held that "nothing can be public, where nothing is private," and I would add, nothing can be private, where nothing is public.[5] The public and private gather meaning as they are juxtaposed to each other. This claim may seem to suggest that the Solitaires cannot cast any light on the private life, since they knew no public life. That, however, is precisely one of the things we *can* learn from the Solitaires: insofar as they shared little in common, they gained little from privacy in the way of retreat, renewal, and contemplative joy. Later I will support this claim, yet I will also argue that, as conceptually precise entities, the Solitaires—ideal types in a Weberian sense—highlight many aspects of life alone. For the moment, however, my point is that the misery we associate with division is often the cost of the delight we achieve in community and even in solitude.

Weak Associations, Unhappy Hares

In the *second stage* of the Fall we find the first simple associations.[6] "Taught by experience that the love of well-being is the sole motive of human actions, he [the early human] found himself in a position to distinguish the rare occasions when common interests should make him count on the assistance of his fellows, and those still rare cases when competition should make him suspect them." In these voluntary, transitory, pragmatic associations, both the benefits and risks to well-being were slight. A robust group depends on its members' commitment to future goals, even as its members depend on the future support and benefits of the group. Suffering results when members, for example, are betrayed by the group, or the group by some of its members. Rousseau, however, has described the primitive association as an "unfettered" one that "obligated no one" and "that endured as long as the transitory occasion that formed it." It could deliver neither happiness nor misery, because the group was as frail as its members' commitment to it. Again, Rousseau makes a connection between future goals and dependency: since "foresight was nothing" to these early humans, they experienced neither the benefits nor risks of trust. "If a deer was to be taken, every one sensed clearly that each must faithfully guard his post. But if a hare happened to come within reach of one of them, there is no need to doubt that he pursued it without scruple, and, having caught his prey, cared very little to have caused his companions to miss theirs."[7]

In the course of time human dependency and trust increased, and with these arrived the emergence of complex language. In a narrative sketching the migration from the Garden to the City, one would expect an account of the origin of language. What is surprising about the second *Discours* is how hesitant Rousseau was to provide such an account (although he eventually would complete an essay dedicated to the subject, as did many other eighteenth-century *philosophes*). Some of his contemporaries, such as Condillac, had assumed that the early inventors of language lived in an already established society. Yet Rousseau, sensibly enough, cast the issue as a which-came-first dilemma: "Which was the more necessary, society already united for the institution of languages, or languages already invented for the establishment of society?"[8]

I, for one, am relieved that Rousseau did not try to solve this dilemma, at least not in the second *Discours*. He did, briefly, narrate the evolution of languages, but that development was tied inextricably to the development of society.[9] The track from "inarticulate cries, plenty of gestures, and some imitative sounds" to conventional speech is a rather utilitarian one. The formation of social ties and language go hand in hand, and, once again, the salient issue for Rousseau pertained to dependency: society and language develop as humans find that they need each other.

The conventions of language and the customs and laws of society serve the needs of dependent humans who increasingly relate to each other in a strictly utilitarian fashion. This interpretation of Rousseau is supported by his later account of the origin of languages.[10] In that work, *Essay on the Origin of Language*, Rousseau recounted the lamentable fall of languages from early musical "chanted" expressions of passion to contemporary "unhappy daughters of utility." On this account, "it was not hunger or thirst, but love, hatred, compassion, and anger that wrung from [early humans] their first voice."[11] This tale of the original languages follows the same trajectory as that of the second *Discours*: as dependency increases, so does the utilitarian character of language. "As needs increase such that human affairs become intertwined . . . language changes its character: it becomes more precise and less passionate; it substitutes ideas for feelings. . . . it becomes more exact and clear, but more drawling, dull, and cold."[12] Finally, it becomes a language of public manipulation and private calculation designed to deliver one message, "give me money."[13] From passionate expressions of the heart to cold acts of utility: such is the procession of language, a result of interdependency.

Private Huts, Personal Fantasies

The path toward dependency—the erosion of the Solitaire's private life—becomes steeper in the *third stage* of the Fall.[14] Rousseau introduced three developments that escalated the need for mutual reliance—the institutions of property, family, and the division of labor between men and women. These three are related. With the introduction of family units, sleeping under "the first tree" is no longer satisfactory, giving rise to the first huts; with the huts appears a distinction between the private domestic space for women and the public hunting grounds for men. Remarkably, in all three cases Rousseau attempted to minimize potential harm by rendering each form of dependency innocuous.

Over the years Rousseau's stance on private property became increasingly equivocal, as he associated it with a servile dependency on possessions on the one hand, and with a self-reliant—often agricultural—lifestyle on the other.[15] In the second *Discours*, however, Rousseau's position was less ambivalent. He began the second part of the *Discours*—his description of the Fall—with the following: "The first one who, having enclosed a piece of ground, thought to say, '*this is mine*' . . . was the real founder of civil society. How many crimes, wars, and murders, how many miseries and horrors would humankind been spared, by one who pulled up the stakes . . . and cried to his fellows . . . 'You are lost if you forget that the fruits belong to all, and the earth to no one.'"[16] Inside the Garden, the land was naturally public and the people naturally private; outside, the land is artificially private and the people artificially public. The early Solitaires satisfied their limited needs on bounteous lands; the modern human herd, in contrast, stampedes and maims to settle on restricted lands—often gorging and choking on the glory and esteem found there. Needing little, the Solitaires were free from much; needing much, the City dwellers bear the heavy "yoke of possessions"—possessions that bring little joy, but the loss of which brings much unhappiness. Dependency on things and dependency on people are themselves interdependent insofar as people are necessary to acquire things, and things are necessary to acquire people—a valuable commodity, indeed.

In the third stage of the Fall, however, Rousseau was willing to mitigate private property's harmful effects. Although he referred to property as "in itself the source of a thousand quarrels and conflicts," he immediately noted why—in this case—such deleterious effects did not follow. These early humans had a natural gift for evading conflict. They preferred to build their own huts than do battle over someone else's. As their needs were still fairly minimal, they had not yet chained themselves to the conquest of property. Conquest might have involved, for example, enlisting some to help overcome others, and such collaboration would entail dependency on, and future obligations to, allies. It was better and easier to build alone than to fight together.

We will have many opportunities in the following chapters to observe Rousseau's often subtle advocacy of this method, *the evasion of conflict*.[17] It becomes, I later argue, one of his chief strategies for reducing the friction between the public and private: dodge those situations that put the two in conflict. If applied systematically, the method would lead one directly back to the Garden—alone, perhaps unhappy, but free from confrontation. Applied systematically, it becomes impossible to engage in most commitments, because, in the absence of the omniscience of God or the Great Legislator in *The Social*

Contract or perhaps Wolmar in *Julie*, one could never know in advance if a commitment would lead to conflict between duty to self and duty to others. In stage three, however, commitments were nonexistent. Life was still rather close to the Garden, and the evasion of conflict helped to keep it that way. The early human, Rousseau noted, had no interest in attempting to capture his neighbor's hut, "not so much because it did not belong to him," but because the ensuing struggle would simply be too great a bother. There was, then, no conflict between an existing obligation to respect property rights (duty to others) and a desire for a fancy mud hut (duty to self). The evasion of such simple conflict protected early humans from more complex ones that would flow from an existence fraught with commitments.

What of the introduction of the family? Does that not introduce commitments, even if only personal ones? Rousseau wrote that "the first expansion of the heart was the effect of a novel situation that brought together, in a common dwelling, husbands and wives, fathers and children."[18] One might have thought that Rousseau would treat the "first expansion of the heart" as a traditional theologian might handle the snake in the Garden—fearfully, if not balefully. After all, the Solitaire's peaceful condition is based on a simple, constricted heart. Its expansion opens the tragic passage to love and jealousy, forgiveness and murder, glory and war. Rousseau must have known this. Nonetheless, he attributed to this new family life "the sweetest feelings known to humanity: conjugal love and paternal love." One need not know much about Rousseau's own life to realize that he was severely hurt by precisely these two affections.[19] In spite of this, or perhaps because of it, the third stage can be read as Rousseau's private fantasy in which "each family became a little society, the more united as reciprocal attachment and liberty were its only bonds." In contrast to these simple natural families, the families of Rousseau's day were complex legal institutions governed by economics, classism, and reputation; marriage was typically an arrangement based on property.[20]

Rousseau rendered familial dependency harmless by basing the primitive family not on law, custom, or obligation, but on pure voluntarism. It was founded on liberty, and hence it remained natural and served as an example of an ideal private society. Presumably, should the nature of its bonds change, the "sweetest feelings known to humanity" would turn bitter. In regard to this ideal family, Rousseau did not allude to any possible disappointment or suffering. Of stage three, we might be tempted to imagine that before the family bonds could turn to irons, the evasion of conflict would take place; the family would separate rather than hurt each other. Rousseau, however, knew all too well the pain that such separation could bring, for it was separation from his father and later from Madame de Warens that had smarted him.[21] How, then, can Rousseau ensure that familial attachments do no harm? There are two ways: design bonds that break painlessly or bonds that simply do not break. In the first case, disengagement is not painful because the voluntary and therefore optional bonds are never very strong. In the second case, the bonds do not break because, given minimal needs, the family member's mutual demands are light and hence not likely to cause estrangement. Either way, however, we run up against what looks like a psychological impossibility: Rousseau's longing for a warm, supportive family that is risk-free. This fantasy, we will see in chapter 8, played an important role in Rousseau's thought when he envisioned the private path to redemption. It inspired Rousseau's desperate and impossible vision of a life rich in love yet free from the possibility of receiving or inflicting pain.

A division of labor between the sexes is the third form of dependency that Rousseau introduced in stage three. In the Garden, where the "manner of life" of women and men "had been the same," each sex existed independently of the other. In the absence of differentiation, there was no complimentary dependency. Even the sexual act itself, you will recall, was a rather disengaged activity. In stage three, in contrast, "The two sexes . . . began to establish different ways of living. The women became more sedentary and accustomed themselves to take care of the hut and the children, while the men went out for search for common subsistence."[22] With this differentiation dependency became ineluctable, yet surprisingly, Rousseau introduced this division of labor between the sexes in a cavalier fashion. The sexually independent Solitaire was transformed, in stage three, into a sexually dependent spouse—apparently with Rousseau's full blessing.

It would seem, then, that Rousseau deemed natural *this* form of differentiation and dependency.[23] In fact, he tacitly sanctified the three cases of dependency as three pillars of a *natural, social* existence: the autonomous, supportive family with the wife and children in the private hut and the husband in the open public lands. Rousseau has quietly introduced here what will become an important and perplexing concept in his work—natural, social creatures. When the shady tree is cut into a wooden hut, when physical intercourse becomes conjugal love, and when undifferentiated male and female become differentiated husband and wife, the natural plays a new normative role, and we catch our first glimpse of Rousseau's vision of social creatures leading natural lives. Apparently, for Rousseau the very idea of a natural social existence was not, contrary to a score of commentators, an oxymoron. We will return to this notion in chapters 5 and 6 when we explore more analytically the Fall and Rousseau's redemptive solutions for fallen humanity. For the moment, however, some reflection on Rousseau's natural yet social women is appropriate.

To those "amiable and virtuous women citizens" of Geneva, Rousseau offered special praise in the dedication to the second *Discours*: "How blessed when your chaste power, exercised solely within the limits of conjugal union, makes itself felt only for the glory of the State and the public good." Rousseau asked, sincerely enough, what Genevan husband could be so barbaric as to "resist the voice of honor and reason from the mouth of a tender wife?" It is the unique role of women—actually, of wives—to employ their "sweetness and wisdom," their "amiable and innocent rule," to protect public "tranquility and good morals" and to perpetuate "love for the laws of the State and harmony among the citizens." Wives, that is, women in their appropriate social roles, are to engineer public peace by exercising from their private empire "the rights of the heart and of nature for the sake of duty and virtue."[24] This is their natural role, and insofar as they perform it, they are nature's gift to social men. In the first *Discours*—"On the Arts and Sciences"—Rousseau had written that "the ascendancy which women have obtained over men" is not "an evil in itself. It is a gift which nature has made them for the good of humankind." He went on to state that women should be given a better education, since "men will always be what women want them to be."[25]

Outside the Garden, then, women come to hold tremendous authority over men, and with it the power for good or evil. As long as women act naturally—housed in their private domain, quietly yet profoundly influencing their men to embrace harmony and virtue—they do good. The ascendancy of women over men, under these conditions, could be "productive of as much good," Rousseau noted, "as it is now of evil." The present danger and evil is a result of women having become *direct* "preceptors of the public." That line is from Rousseau's public letter—a short book, really—to d'Alembert, three years after the publication of the second *Discours*.[26] Again, he asserted that an agreeable and virtuous woman is "nature's most charming object, the most able to touch a sensitive heart and to lead it to the good." Yet this object, like other charms, is dangerous, too; should it escape its sheltered pocket, men would be lured toward impotence as women grew sovereign in all domains.

Rousseau was adamant about this. The presence of women in public is unnatural and brings disastrous results. The balanced dependency between men and women that was delicately achieved in the third stage is eventually upended, with men tangling helplessly and women looming anxiously. "The best woman" is the least seen in public and "the least spoken of." Rousseau admired the Spartan who, "hearing a foreigner magnificently praise a woman of his acquaintance, interrupted him angrily: 'Cease, you,' he said to him, 'to slander a good woman.'" Thus Rousseau condemned his society which, in contrast to the Spartans', held that "the most esteemed woman is the one who is the loudest, about whom the most is said, who is the most often seen in society, at whose home one dines the most . . . who judges, pronounces, decides," and so on.[27] The seen woman with a voice, even in her own salon, is too public to retain her status as nature's gift to society.

It would be convenient to ignore these passages. After all, can we expect twenty-first-century progressive thought from an eighteenth-century thinker? There is, however, too much at stake here to look the other way. This is the first flagrant case of destructive essentialism we have yet encountered in Rousseau's thought. Woman's essential nature, that is, her natural essence, has assigned her to a domestic cage. Later, after we have explored the seven stages of the Fall, we will be in a position to appraise nature's role in and out of the Garden. One of our questions will be, without embracing its awkward metaphysical and essentialist implications, can we learn something good and useful from Rousseau's employment of "the natural"? In front of us now, however, is a clear example of unhelpful and even vicious naturalism, because it asserts that women are essentially different from men and that difference is demeaning to women and limiting to both women and men. In *Emile* Rousseau wrote, "It is necessary to be oneself at all times and not struggle against nature." If we are to shudder appropriately at such statements, we must not direct our glance away from Rousseau's dangerous prejudices.[28]

However, it would be silly and perhaps arrogant to think that, due to his eighteenth-century prejudices, Rousseau has nothing good and interesting to say to us about the relation between the public and private, among other things. It has become easy to dismiss those authors who do not hold all our deep convictions. Yet the more difficult and fruitful work is to discover in their authorship what is edifying, what is harmful, and to what extent the harmful aspects poison the edifying ones.

The Second Garden

The *fourth stage* is perhaps the most difficult to characterize. I call it the Second Garden, although the Blessed Country—a place between the Garden and the City—is probably more accurate.[29] Of this stage Rousseau wrote, "This period of expansion of the human faculties, keeping a just mean between the indolence of the primitive state and the petulant activity of our self-interests, must have been the happiest and most stable of epochs."[30] Tragically, however, the Second Garden also contained new developments that would prove fatal to emerging humankind. If the Fall is, as I have described it, a series of tumbles that leads to a plunge, then think of the Second Garden as the narrow ledge from which the early humans are about to drop.

The Second Garden, stage four, is the result of a happy development from stage three; the solitary family joined or formed with others a neighborhood of self-sufficient families. This society of families was united not by government or law, but by shared character and manners. The families were, to be sure, independent of each other; otherwise Rousseau, given his fear of dependency, could not have called this the happiest stage. There was, however, "some connection between the different families," which marks a significant difference between this and the previous stage. Precisely this cautious sociability marked the happiness of the Second Garden. In the absence of a developed division of labor, families were not dependent on each other, yet there was enough association to engender the "pleasures of mutual and independent intercourse." This fragile balance between private and public—this "independent intercourse"—is exceedingly pertinent for our study, for it suggests that, ultimately, Rousseau's vision of humanity's happiest state is not lodged in either radical solitude or fatalistic social assimilation. The chances of sustaining the delicate balance, however, is another matter.

The inhabitants of the Second Garden—poised between listless Solitaires and anxious contemporaries—enjoyed a qualified solitariness, a limited gregariousness. As the "heart and head were brought into play," "singing and dancing," music and art, beauty and love began to bloom. The inhabitants experienced many of the good things that we associate with community, such as identity, fellowship, even love, but without bearing many of its unfortunate side effects—such as vanity, envy, and hate. They could steady this otherwise teetering position because their needs were still relatively simple.

Yet in this the happiest stage we find the saddest episode of Rousseau's bleak story. Simply put, the inhabitants did not know that they were singing and dancing on a precipice. They did not know they were in danger of falling. But they were, and they did; dancing on the ledge is risky. Hence, from social festivity—one of the very sources of human joy—comes danger and tragedy. And how did they lose their balance? "Each began to look at the others, and to wish to be looked at himself, and public esteem became valued. Whoever sang or danced best, whoever was the handsomest, the strongest, the most dexterous, or the most eloquent, came to be the most highly regarded; and this was the first step toward inequality and at the same time toward vice."[31] Making comparisons begat esteem, public esteem begat inequality, inequality begat envy and contempt, and these begat "men bloody and cruel." This is the genealogy of human misery: one false step off the ledge and down the chute of *amour-propre*.

Depending on the context, *amour-propre*—one of Rousseau's more famous concepts—can be translated variously: self-interest, selfishness, pride, preoccupation with public esteem, or an "anxious awareness of oneself as a social object."[32] It is perhaps best understood in contrast to Rousseau's other famous love, *amour de soi*. In the second *Discours* Rousseau juxtaposed the gentle, natural ways of self-love (*amour de soi*)—which directs the self to the pursuit of well-being relative to the self alone—to the turbulent, rapacious ways of *amour-propre*, "a relative and factitious feeling, born in society, that drives each individual to make more of himself than all others."[33]

Like *amour de soi*, *amour-propre* can be thought of as duty to self, but this time to a different self. The self in the Garden had limited needs, especially insofar as it had no use of the opinion of others. Being liked or feared was not likely to help it find food or shelter. The Solitaire lived within itself, for itself, without regard for others. The self in modern society, in contrast, is restless, especially insofar as it needs—or thinks it needs—public esteem. This self projects itself outside itself, viewing itself as others would view it. The modern self is more concerned with its appearance to others than with its absolute condition—its actual happiness, talents, virtue, and so on.[34] But it is worse than that. While the gap between "being" and "seeming" grows, the distinction between them becomes increasingly insignificant because appearance—how one is regarded—becomes all that matters. The aged Rousseau once put it like this: "All seek their happiness in appearance, no one cares about reality. All place their essence in the illusionary: all, slaves and dupes of *amour-propre*, live not in order to live but to make others believe that they have lived."[35] *Amour-propre* could not overrun the Garden, because there "each regarded himself as the only observer of his actions, the only being in the universe who took any interest in him." This may sound bleak, but that, once again, is the price of tranquility.

Pascal once wrote, "These ropes that attach respect to such and such a person in particular, are imaginary cords." Nannerl Keohane has suggested that this *pensée* was followed by, "Domination founded on opinion and imagination rules sometimes, and this empire is sweet and voluntary; that of force reigns continually, always. Thus opinion is like the queen of the world, but force is its tyrant."[36] In Rousseau's account, however, cords of opinion are chains of enslavement, and its "sweet empire" can be as tyrannical as any dictator. To become bound to opinion is the work of *amour-propre*, and it is this other-oriented aspect of *amour-propre* that exaggerates the importance of "honor" and "offense." Honor, here, refers to appearing illustrious in the eyes of others, while "offense" refers to that honor being publicly offended. In both cases, the opinion of others is the salient concern. The Solitaires cannot offend each other. They can fight each other and thereby hurt each other, physically, but they cannot give offense. Their sight is on that which concerns *amour de soi*—basic needs pertaining to well-being. Unlike the occasional, short-lived, rational battles that spring from *amour de soi*, those of *amour-propre* are frequent, enduring, and often foolish. Foolish because, unlike the pursuit of well-being that is associated with *amour de soi*, *amour-propre* often saddles us with concerns that frustrate well-being.

Too often it is forgotten that Rousseau was discussing Hobbes when, in the second *Discours*, he first introduced the concepts, *amour-propre* and *amour de soi*. Rousseau needed a way, a concept, to distinguish his peaceful, natural Solitaires from Hobbes's fierce, natural brutes. The contrast between the two loves served Rousseau well: the natural self is guided by a serene love that is easily and completely satisfied; the artificial self is driven by a tumultuous love that is insatiable. Hobbes, in Rousseau's view, erroneously attributed the grasping love to natural humans. This should not imply, however, that humans outside the Garden are moved only by the anomic love, *amour-propre*. The situation outside the Garden is more complicated than that; social humans possess both loves and are torn by them. In the good human, however, *amour de soi* is more prevalent than *amour-propre*. Thus in *Emile*, Rousseau held that "the gentle and affectionate passions are born of self-love [*amour de soi*], and the hateful and irascible passions are born of selfishness [*amour-propre*]. What makes a man essentially good is to have few needs and little desire to compare himself with others; what makes him essentially bad is to have many needs and to care much about opinion."[37]

In addition to *amour de soi*, compassion (*pitié*) acts to moderate "the ferociousness of *amour-propre*."[38] If it is dependency on the opinion of others that is characteristic of *amour-propre*, then it is identification with others that marks compassion. The former leads the self to see itself through the eyes of the other, the latter to see the other through the other's eyes. Both *amour-propre* and compassion, then, are outward looking, but the regard of the former is interested, while the latter is disinterested. Compassion can discount the importance of public esteem and opinion by enabling us, temporarily, to forget ourselves and act for the sake of the other. *Amour de soi* can also break the chains of opinion, but by opposite means. It causes us not to forget ourselves, but to live within ourselves without a care or worry for the other. In either case, the self is free from the yoke of opinion, for it abides not by troubling artificial cares but by wholesome natural impulses that, Rousseau would like us to believe, lead to well-being. Thus, on the last page of the first *Discours*, Rousseau asked, "What good is it to search for happiness in the opinion of others, when we can find it in ourselves?"[39]

Rousseau's challenge to the Englishman, Mr. Hobbes, was facilitated by a variety of French theologians. While some have claimed that Rousseau's distinction between *amour de soi* and *amour-propre* is arbitrary, there is in fact a long, tangled history behind it.[40] Rousseau's contrast between the two loves is not from scratch, and *pitié* can be placed in a distinctive French tradition in which Augustine's two loves, love of God and love of self, eventually become three—disinterested love (*charité*), selfish love (*amour-propre*), and neutral or benign self-love (*amour de soi*). In the *City of God*, Augustine described two loves—the love of self (*cupiditas*) and the love of God (*caritas*).[41] The former, which tends toward hatred of God, marks the citizens of the earthly city, whereas the latter, which tends toward hatred of self, marks the citizens of the heavenly city. Debates over the relation between these two loves dominated much French theology and moral philosophy in the seventeenth and early eighteenth centuries. While the most austere Augustinians insisted that love of God and love of self radically oppose each other, there were moderate Augustinians who attempted to soften the distinction. A severe denunciation of self-love was seen as an unhelpful condemnation of much of what it is to be human. After all, the great commandment is to "love your neighbor as *yourself*." While none were interested in conflating love of God and love of self, some sought a love vocabulary that would make a distinction between a benign and a vicious self-love, thus setting in opposition to the love of God the vicious self-love, not the benign one.

Jean-Pierre Camus, the bishop of Belley, made a distinction between a covetous, possessive *amour-propre*, which works against *charité*, and a neutral, harmless *amour de soi*, which does not thwart charity.[42] Here, love of self (*amour de soi*), as a gift of God, does not hinder one's ability to love God or others (*charité*). *Amour-propre*, in contrast, undermines all relationships because it leads the self to use others for purely selfish ends. In fact, *amour-propre* does not even serve the self favorably, for it directs the self to ends that are in contradiction with its true interest.[43] Increasingly in the seventeenth century, a poisonous *amour-propre* was distinguished from an innocuous *amour de soi*, and while both were contrasted to *charité*, *amour de soi* was not seen as standing in opposition to it.

The origin of the loves, according to some theologians, could be traced back to the Garden and the Fall. In these accounts, one love alone was present in the Garden. Only after the Fall did the varieties of love come into being. François Sénault, for example, held that prior to the Fall, there was only the one undifferentiated love, *amour naturel*. After the Fall, this natural love was shattered and gave rise to the opposing loves, *amour-propre* and *charité*.[44] Similarly, Nicolas de Malebranche held that in the Garden humans were governed by that very love which God held for himself—*amour de soi*.[45] Again, *amour-propre* entered the drama as humans were expelled from the Garden.

Charité in the meantime had come to refer not only to love of God, but to all disinterested love directed at such things outside the self as neighbor, country, and stranger. Indeed, the love of God had increasingly become synonymous with, or had been transformed into, the love of public things (*choses publiques*). To love God entailed striving to love as God loves. The king in French monarchical tradition, although not typically deified, was to love his kingdom by willing its common good; preferential treatment was deemed ungodly, because it failed to imitate God's disinterested love. Citizens themselves, in French republican traditions, were called on to love the common good above their own particular interests.[46] Writers as diverse as Sebond, Le Moyne, Descartes, and Pascal argued that by loving God one is freed from isolating self-love. As God loves the whole, so citizens are empowered to join together and love the political community. By the early eighteenth century in France, when theological arguments had begun to lose much of their public voice, a powerful social ideal remained: self-love (*amour-propre*), the opposite of *charité*, divides and weakens the political community, unless it could be transformed or coordinated for the sake of the public good.

The various accounts of the loves are far from unanimous. Yet in these complex debates over types of self-love and their relation to love of God and *choses publiques*, the French theologians had provided material that enriched eighteenth-century moral thought, including that of Rousseau. I am not claiming that Rousseau's love vocabulary—*amour de soi*, *amour-propre*, and *pitié*—perfectly corresponds to the three loves of, say, Jean-Pierre Camus or the others. I am only alluding to the traditions with which Rousseau worked. His critique of *amour-propre* is as harsh as any Augustinian's, his approval of *amour de soi* matches that of any disciple of Camus, and his depiction of *pitié*—disinterested care for beings other than the self—shares a family resemblance with *charité*. Moreover, Rousseau explicitly assigned *amour-propre* to the social human's fallen condition. There are, of course, differences between Rousseau's usage and that of the traditions leading up to him. Rousseau, for example, was practically alone when he fleshed out in detail the moral—as opposed to the strictly social or economic—possibilities that attend to that inoffensive self-love, *amour de soi*. In contrast to the theologians, Rousseau elevated *amour de soi* to new moral heights. His fear of the unnecessary harm that flows from *amour-propre* led him to celebrate the minimal decency of those governed by *amour de soi*: although they do little good, they commit no cruelty. This negative argument—that one is moral insofar as one does no harm—is supported by Rousseau's more general belief that vice does more harm than virtue does good.

The greatest discontinuity between Rousseau's vocabulary of loves and that which he inherited may seem to be between *pitié* and *charité*. But that appearance is misleading. If we compare the limited moral scope of *pitié* in the Garden to that of robust *charité* (in either its theological or secular guise), then, yes, the distance between the two is great. Outside the Garden, however, *pitié* becomes the source of such social virtues as generosity, clemency, and benevolence.[47] Outside the Garden *pitié* looks a lot like disinterested *charité*. Again, I am not arguing that there is a perfect correspondence between Rousseau's concepts and those he was taught. Rousseau, like Freud, would view *charité*'s theological command, "Love your neighbor as yourself," as a prescription for self-deception and social destruction. To satisfy the command, individuals would need to attempt to repress systematically their natural *amour de soi*,; finding that impossible, they would feel compelled to feign selfless love and to justify even the most insufferable acts in the name of *charité*. *Amour-propre*, spurring our anxiety over appearances, sabotages especially our loftiest ideals—even the Christian love commandment—because while our ideals encourage the self to gaze outside itself, *amour-propre* directs the self to have all eyes on itself.

To speak of insufferable acts and sabotaged ideals is to get somewhat ahead of my narrative. I wanted, however, to highlight the intimate connection between the innocent origin of *amour-propre*—a public fête—and its destructive trajectory. "Whoever sang or danced best . . . came to be of most consideration." From such simple social comparisons would flow a host of public and private vices, from economic inequality to personal cruelty. Yet before we explore this hapless chain of events, let us not make the mistake of most commentators; namely, being eager to rush into Rousseau's trenchant critique of modern society, they neglect to notice that, in Rousseau's account, the Fall takes place in stages, and that first four stages of the Fall, in fact, are not a dramatic depiction of a devastating Fall into wickedness and unhappiness. Indeed, the first stages depict a series of rather graceful tumbles onto a pleasant yet cautious social existence. Not surprisingly, the next three stages of the Fall—the Plunge, the Ruse, and the Age of Slavery—will not be nearly as graceful. Thus far we have not discovered a serpent in the Garden; in chapter 5 we will learn that it was there all along. If we could not see it, it was because it was not out in plain view, but was buried deep within us, inseparable from our latent powers, hopes, and aspirations.

4

The Rush to Slavery

I called the fourth stage the Second Garden because it represents Rousseau's vision of happy humans precariously balanced between solitude and community, invulnerability and vulnerability, independence and dependence. The Second Garden bore not only this frail balance but also the latent forces that would capsize it. Chief among these was *amour-propre*—the fetish for, and hence dependency on, public opinion. Related to this were three other dormant sources of sorrow: the discovery of new technologies and the division of labor they occasioned; private property under conditions of inequality; and such psychological developments as the maturation of memory, foresight, and imagination. Together these would topple the achievement of the Second Garden, namely, the enjoyment of human company without needing it. Of this liminal fourth stage Rousseau wrote, "So long as men remained content with their rustic huts . . . adorned themselves with feathers and shells . . . in a word, so long as they applied themselves to tasks that a single individual could accomplish, and to arts that did not require the collaboration of several hands, they lived free, healthy, good, and happy lives."[1] Yet these conditions of well-being would not last forever. Dependency, especially as driven by *amour-propre*, would eventually spoil human happiness. In this final chapter of the narration of the Fall, we will see how the precarious joy and liberty of the Second Garden collapsed and paved the road to the pain and slavery of the corrupt City.

The Plunge

Here is the line that runs between stage four and the plunge, *stage five*: "From the moment one man was in need of the help of another; from the moment it appeared useful to one to have provisions for two, equality disappeared, property was introduced, work became necessary, and vast forests changed into smiling fields that had to be watered by the sweat of men, and where slavery and misery were soon seen to germinate and grow together with the crops."[2] What brought about this revolution? The accidental discovery of iron and the use of corn. This claim, I hope, is surprising, since I have prepared us for an inevitable—not an accidental—plunge from stage four to five. Before examining

Rousseau's claim that "the invention of the two arts, metallurgy and agriculture, pro-duced this great revolution," I want to address this surprise by returning briefly to a curious statement found in the previous period, stage four.

To account for why the happiest humans would relinquish their golden age, Rousseau alluded to "some kind of fatal accident which, for the common good, should never have happened." In the meantime, "all subsequent progress appears to have been so many steps toward the perfection of the individual, but in reality toward the decrepitude of the species."[3] This is not just a bit of rhetoric. It expresses the thrust of Rousseau's broad argument: as individuals advance inexorably, driven by perfectibility and free-dom, their needs become more complex and they become increasingly dependent on each other; this dependency wreaks havoc, pain and corruption. Yet this account sug-gests that the Fall was inevitable—somehow built into the human soul—and hence it stands at odds with the "fatal accident" account. Whether the Fall was inescapable or accidental turns out to be an intricate question, one that I must postpone until we have surveyed the entire Fall.

For the moment, however, I want to note that the two accounts are not radically contradictory. One could argue that the accidental material developments and the in-evitable spiritual developments worked together to perfect the individual and spoil the species. When speculating on the discovery of iron, for example, Rousseau credited "the extraordinary circumstance of some volcano,"[4] spewing molten lava, with giving humans the idea to heat and combine metals. Yet Rousseau immediately added that those who witnessed this timely—though actually inauspicious—explosion must have possessed enough *foresight* to undertake the difficult task of imitating nature's foundry. Foresight also played a decisive role in the discovery of the use of corn, because, however humans may have discovered the principles of agriculture, it is "essential for farming to be re-solved to accept initial loss in order to reap a subsequent gain."[5] I am suggesting, then, that *accidental* technological breakthroughs and *inevitable* psychological maturation jointly shoved humans out of the Second Garden. We can depict this dualistically as the junc-ture of material and spiritual causes. This dualism does not refer to the natural and supernatural, but to sensations and potentialities—to speak in Lockean terms.[6] Rousseau inhabited a Lockean world in which external stimuli and innate psychological mecha-nisms worked together naturally, and in this case disastrously, to hasten the inevitable plunge.

What is the significance of the discovery of iron and use of grain? In short, they forced relatively private lives to mingle as these discoveries advanced a new level of dependency in the form of the specialization of labor. For example, there were now those who mined the minerals, those who produced the iron, those who maintained the kilns, and those who fed these various specialists. From specialization came the multiplication of commodities and complex systems of exchange, and from these came a heightened sense of private property and public justice; it is a short step from rules of justice to conventions of inequality, as we will see in the sixth stage. In the Garden, inequality was not evil; it was simply a reflection of the natural distribution of talents. This all changed when a division of labor placed formerly private humans in the close quarters of public arenas. Those who possessed natural advantages—in wit, beauty, strength, and skill—excelled in the new competitive arenas and were rewarded with wealth. Wealth, in and of itself, is not a menace, but when it becomes an expression of *amour-*

propre, it drives individuals to enhance their social standing at the expense of others by exploiting natural inequalities.

In this original race for wealth, then, the naturally gifted had a head start. Later, however, due to rules of justice that favored the rich and due to unequal payment for different services (although all "labored equally"), there would be only a random relation between natural inequality and what Rousseau called "moral or political" inequality, namely, inequality based on convention.[7] Unlike Voltaire, Rousseau did not embrace the idea that all humans were created equally. He showed, rather, how innocuous natural inequalities were initially transformed into varieties of esteem and humiliation, and how social conventions would eventually ensure that esteem would cleave to the wealthy and powerful and humiliation to the poor and powerless regardless of the distribution of talents.

This, then, is Rousseau's account of how "iron and corn first civilized men and ruined humankind":[8] from iron and grain came property and justice, and from property and justice came inequality and humiliation. This genealogy of sorrow is driven by both psychological and sociological developments, chiefly the progression of *amour-propre* and the division of labor. I want us to pause here to examine the effect of these developments on the private and public life.

Now that "memory and imagination" were "in full play," the psychological conditions were ripe for self-fixation: individuals could now keenly remember how they had viewed others and could imagine how others had viewed them. Offense and grudges could be nurtured, honor and esteem craved. "It soon became necessary to possess or to affect" various skills and merit in order to gain respect; "it was necessary, for one's advantage, to appear other than what one really was."[9] This aspect of *amour-propre* we have already explored. Yet I still need to make clear the irony—and not just sarcasm—of Rousseau's linking the progression of *amour-propre* with the perfection of the individual. He claimed that "it is to this love of being talked about, to this fury to distinguish ourselves which almost always takes us outside ourselves, that we owe the best and the worst things among humans, our virtues and our vices, our science and our errors, our conquerors and our philosophers; that is to say, a multitude of evil things for a small number of good ones."[10]

In mentioning "a small number of good ones," Rousseau was bowing ever so cautiously to a rather popular tradition in France that had been celebrating the pursuit of self-interest for at least a century.[11] With public eyes on the individual—a goal of *amour-propre*—the individual strives harder and longer for personal wealth and glory, and that quest creates genuine public achievements in the political, economic, scientific, and artistic realms. Later, in stage six, more will need to be said of this tradition and Rousseau's response to it. We will see that Rousseau suspected that public conflict—not harmony— is the more likely outcome in a society composed of individuals driven by *amour-propre*. For the moment, however, I want to point to another aspect of Rousseau's opposition to this French "invisible hand" tradition. Insofar as public achievements are realized, they come at a high price to the individual. The cost is the loss of self—of freedom, virtue, and joy. The self living outside itself for others becomes a slave to public opinion. Moreover, since opinion is fleeting, always in flux, the public slave is an exhausted one, constantly calculating what actions (words, deeds, gestures) at what time will have the best effect. This slave—dedicated to self-advancement—has little leisure or desire to contemplate its loss of joy. The voice of *amour de soi*, the call to healthy self-love, is lost in the clamor of *amour-propre*.

This theme—alienation of self—is not limited to Rousseau's early work. It permeates his writings. For example, in his last work, the *Reveries of the Solitary Walker*, Rousseau lamented that even in the gentle science of botany, nature's garden "becomes for us merely a public theater where we seek to gain admirers." The woods in which the self, animated by *amour de soi*, once thrived are displaced by public arenas in which the self withers like "exotic plants in the gardens of the curious."[12] Again, the irony is that the advancing self is in fact a kept self. And again, dependency is depicted as a malignant tumor: it increasingly debilitates as it develops. The advancing self moves ahead by leaving itself, taking stock of how it is viewed, and acting accordingly. This habit of estrangement transforms the self into an object to be handled expertly by the self. In the process, the self becomes a commodity whose ownership remains with the self but whose value is determined by onlookers. Through this process, the freedom of *amour de soi*—living within oneself—is exchanged for the chains of *amour-propre*—acting for others. Rousseau's logic here is meant to mock the celebration of autonomy insofar as it is understood as individuals pursuing ambition and greed under the guise of enlightened self-interest. The more the self is dedicated to autonomy thus defined, the more the self becomes excessively dependent on its audience.

This so-called private self, then, actually exists on an intensely public stage. Yet what kind of a public stage is this? There is a stage that we could roughly call Aristotelian on which the morally wise act and improve each other. Here, it is admirable to acquire a good reputation—the good opinion of others. Living outside public regard is hazardous and selfish, for alone one can neither learn from moral exemplars nor serve as one. On this stage, public perception is a vehicle of moral education, and public judgment—the opinion of the wise—is valued. Moreover, the high regard of others belongs to those whose attainment of excellence contributes to the common good. Virtue serves the public, and the public fosters virtue. When we compare what Rousseau disparagingly called the "public stage" to this idealized classical depiction of a different kind of stage, we realize that the self, when driven by *amour-propre*, not only ceases to have a genuinely private life, insofar as its actions are calculated for public view, but ceases to have a genuinely public life, insofar as there are no common goods, only the shared interest that each individual appear better than his or her fellow.[13]

Amour-propre, then, and the dependency that it breeds, manages to injure both private joy and the public good. Rousseau's arguments for the need to protect the private life from a tyrannous public life are reminiscent of Montaigne's in his years as mayor of Bordeaux. Of himself Montaigne wrote, "The mayor and Montaigne have always been two, with a very clear separation." The reason for this separation is that it is necessary for liberty's sake to keep "a back shop all our own, entirely free, in which to establish our real liberty and our principal retreat and solitude." Liberty is threatened by public life, for in that realm one must "live not so much according to himself as according to others, not according to what he proposes to himself but according to what others propose to him."[14] This opposition between living within and outside oneself is similar to how Rousseau characterized the battle between *amour de soi* and *amour-propre*, indeed, between liberty and slavery. The battle could be described as being waged over the question, "Who am I?" The identity of the self inflamed with *amour-propre* is determined by the crowd, whereas the identity of Aristotle's *phronemos* (the morally wise), or Montaigne's self in the "back-shop," or Rousseau's Wolmar in *Julie* (who, like God, is morally self-sufficing) is determined by the self's own distinctive character.

In the public herd or crowd (Rousseau employed both metaphors) the self loses its most precious treasure, liberty. The herd carries us "far from our real selves": "We no longer exist where we are, we exist outside our place." Only "the wise man can keep his own place."[15] In the crowd, our place is determined by the dynamics of the group. Its conventions—its dress, manners, sentiments, and prejudices—become our own. This socialization, in itself, is not oppressive. It becomes oppressive when the social conventions exclude harmless or beneficial variety and dissent. It becomes oppressive when individuals suffer merely because they do not—or cannot—conform to the ways of the crowd.[16] Finally, it becomes oppressive when individuals slavishly follow the crowd, relinquishing life-enhancing liberty. Surely the wise one who "can keep his own place" is the true antithesis to the crowd.

Some, however, may want to reserve that place for eccentric romantics whose very creativity is defined over and against the crowd.[17] Yet Rousseau's liberalism was not dedicated to releasing the creative genius within each of us. A society of individuals spawning ever-new vocabularies in the name of self-creation was not his aim. In terms of his vision and critique of society, Rousseau is closer to Charles Dickens or Zora Neale Hurston, who portray how simple joys are thwarted by social callousness and injustice, than to Friedrich Nietzsche or Richard Rorty, who depict how imaginative individuality is impeded by superstition and orthodoxy. If Rousseau, like Montaigne, championed a private space for the individual, it was primarily a safe space, not a creative one. In that space, the wise one "keeps his own place," independent of the crowd, with character intact. The wise, who in Rousseau's view are often the simple and uneducated, wear no masks or guises to accommodate the crowd, but don candid hearts and sovereign minds. They value autonomy, that is, being true to themselves in a Kantian sense—self-legislating, not catering systematically to others. To be free from oppressive dependency, then, is the aim of Rousseau's liberalism. Self-sufficiency per se was never the goal, but was envisioned as a protective strategy to shield individuals from the tremendous social forces that work against simple happiness and virtue.[18]

Virtue, like many of Rousseau's key terms, means different things in different contexts. Here, virtue is understood to mean sincerity, autonomy, and inwardness, as opposed to hypocrisy, dependency, and outwardness. "Inward" and "outward" are moral, not epistemological, metaphors in Rousseau's vocabulary. The Solitaire "lives within himself," while the City dweller "lives always outside himself, and only knows how to live in the opinion of others." Consequently, "we have nothing except a deceitful and frivolous appearance, honor without virtue, reason without wisdom, and pleasure without happiness."[19] We can correlate these Rousseauean metaphors—living "within" and "outside" the self—with self-esteem and social esteem, that is, with the healthy love and respect of self that we associated with *amour de soi*, and the anomic love and egoism that we associate with *amour-propre*. Candidness, independent thinking, and sincerity are the dispositions Rousseau threaded together when he challenged the prevailing ethic of "living outside the self."

In his Preface to the second *Discours* Rousseau claimed that the inscription on the Temple of Delphi, "Know thyself," is the most important and difficult precept to grasp.

To live outside ourselves is to "always ask others what we are, and never dare to ask ourselves." To know thyself, in contrast, is the first step toward challenging this prevalent practice, for it demands sincerity and deliberation apart from the crowd. Rousseau was not alone when he juxtaposed living "within" and "outside" the self and the ways of life they represent, for he had inherited this discourse from a French moral tradition that included Montaigne and Pascal. "We wish to live in the minds of others an imaginary life, and in order to do this, we force ourselves to appear other than we are. We work incessantly to embellish and preserve our imaginary being, and neglect the true one."[20] These words of Pascal are the thoughts of Rousseau, for in them we find Rousseau's moral compass that juxtaposes appearance and sincerity, self-deception and self-knowledge.

With Pascal, Rousseau shared another theme as well: the anxious and ambitious crush those who attempt to live innocently within themselves. Rousseau once imagined a wrestling match between a "primitive" Solitaire and a "civilized" contemporary. If both were "naked and unarmed," the Solitaire would easily win the match, for it "always carries itself whole and intact." However, "give civilized man time to gather all his machines around him, and he will no doubt easily overcome the savage."[21] In spite of the Solitaire's strength in nakedness, it will be defeated—every time—in the face of the City Dweller's armory. Sincerity faces enormous obstacles, for a transparent conscience is no match for an insensitive world restlessly pursuing reputation and ambition. If virtue is rare, one reason for it is that vice is well armed.

Earlier I mentioned that even if a "very few good" achievements do spring from *amour-propre*, they come at a high price to the individual, namely, the loss of self—loss of freedom, virtue, and joy. Now I want to discuss the public loss that results from *amour-propre* and related developments. For in this period, stage five, with *amour-propre* in full play, social conflict became rampant as individuals habitually used others as means to attain private goals. Rousseau described Kant's nightmare when he detailed the various methods that were employed to manipulate others as instruments of self-gratification. "All-consuming ambition," especially in the form of increasing fortunes, "less from real need than as from the desire to put oneself above others," conferred "a dark propensity to injure one another, a secret jealousy, which is all the more dangerous, for it dons the mask of benevolence as it strikes its blow in greater security."[22] From the private flames of *amour-propre* arose public grief in the form of treacherous competition, deceit, and conflict of interests. At this point in Rousseau's narrative of the Fall, discussion of inequality, private property, and the division of labor dominate his depiction of social woes.

We have seen that in Rousseau's account natural inequality (inequality of strength, for example) is not an evil in and of itself. It is a natural, benign fact of life. It only becomes evil when, outside the Garden, natural inequality is translated into moral and civic inequality, as, for example, when a person's esteem or access to such civic institutions as the courts are determined by his or her social position. In stage five of the Fall, however, there were no civic institutions, for there still was no government. It is remarkable, then, that inequality plays such a prominent role in this place between the Garden and the City. It points to the severity of Rousseau's pessimistic philosophical anthropology. Even in the absence of corrupt official offices and institutions, degrading inequality appeared "among private persons as soon as they united in a single society and they were forced to compare themselves one with another." In the company of others, in Rousseau's view, humans are *naturally* inclined to make comparisons. Four principal types of inequality can be associated with wealth, social status, power, and natural talents. Although the latter "is the origin of all the others, wealth is the one to which they are in the end all reduced." Here, then, Rousseau made an explicit connection between financial and social inequality.[23]

The essence of Rousseau's dark view of inequality lies in the following claim: "If one sees a handful of the powerful and rich on the pinnacle of grandeur and fortune, while the crowd crawls in obscurity and misery, it is because the former esteem the things they enjoy only insofar as others are deprived of them, and because, without changing their actual condition, they could cease to be happy if the people ceased to be miserable."[24] This view is depressing because it suggests that social inequality is not simply a side effect of the race for material and social goods; rather, inequality itself is a goal of the race. An aim of democratic societies is civic and to some extent economic equality, at least insofar as citizens require housing, education, and perhaps employment to exercise their political rights. Yet it would seem that, in Rousseau's view, aiming for equality is to aim for the impossible because people, stirred by *amour-propre*, do not want equality. They want to outdo their fellows, and no matter how poor or how rich one is, there is always someone above to envy and someone below to disdain.

If inequality was simply a result of the pursuit of scarce goods, we could place hope in the promise of technology and of liberal society to bring a decent standard of living to the masses. This, in fact, is largely what liberal societies have done, at least relative to the standard of living of most past and many contemporary societies. In Rousseau's pessimistic account, however, inequality is not a measure of someone's position relative to an absolute level of material or social goods. It is, rather, a measure of the economic and social distance between individuals. It is people, not goods, that humiliate. Goods are simply an excellent instrument that people can use to inflict humiliation. Earlier I said that "living within oneself" can be interpreted as the possession of a healthy love and respect of self that we associate with *amour de soi*. The individual living within herself, exempt from the passions of *amour-propre*, can pursue such goods as excellence in farming or in law for the sake of those goods themselves. Such a person can flourish, say, without much material wealth or the need to compare her station to another's. In contrast, those habitually living outside themselves (the vast majority of us, in Rousseau's view) pursue goods almost exclusively in arenas of competition and rivalry for the sake of vanity and public esteem.

Inequality is the appropriate context from which to survey Rousseau's equivocal stance on private property. In an equitable society in which the citizen's dignity is not under constant assault, private property could permit individuals to enjoy a measure of self-reliance, which in turn would minimize dependency and those occasions for comparison that foster envy or contempt. Under conditions of social inequality, however, property incarnates the human passion to defeat and surpass one's fellows. Consequently, after Rousseau listed the woes found in the fifth stage, he noted that "all these evils are the first effect of property, and the inseparable train of growing inequality."[25]

I should mention that, even in the absence of private property, Rousseau has endowed these early humans with plenty of means to make their lives painful. Abolishing private property would not abolish the various ways that humans find themselves alienated from themselves, their fellows, and nature. There are other tangible symbols of public esteem, some of which cannot be bought. In academia, to cite a contemporary example, esteem is often measured by such external goods as publications, rank, prestigious grants, influence with the dean, and so on. Property, however, is one of the more direct routes to alienation. It is a palpable symbol of one's social worth. Since it usually can be easily quantified, it permits precise evaluations and comparisons between individuals, allowing them to determine their own worth and the worth of those above and below them.

In stage five, those worth the most eventually considered their status as a kind of right to the possessions of those below them. The alienation of the poor, having been reduced to the status of property, is well understood. Rousseau, however, did not neglect to point out the strife, anxiety, and unhappiness of the wealthy. In the master-slave relation, the masters also experience alienation, for their worth as well is determined by something outside them—their property, or more accurately, the social esteem of which their property is a symbol. Moreover, since the status of a master or of a slave is a relative one, a master can be a slave to some, even as a slave can be a master to others. Both master and slave are therefore entangled in endless contests that permit no decisive victories.

But what of relative victories—don't they count for something? By relative victories I mean, for example, the absolute difference between adequate and inadequate food and housing. To put it differently, even if we accept Rousseau's description of the master-slave relation, which, like Hegel's, relativizes the master's power, are there any of us who would prefer to be the slave? Rousseau's sympathies, in fact, were invariably with the least well off. The last sentence of the second *Discours* denounces that "type of inequality which reigns over all governed people" in which "a handful of people gorge themselves with superfluities, while the starving multitude lacks basic necessities." Such sentiments dot virtually all of Rousseau's writings.[26] If he emphasized the role of relativity in his account of inequality, it is because he was attempting to explain why we seem to desire inequality itself, that is, desire to surpass our fellows, even if—and in some cases, especially if—that entails their humiliation and suffering. Without losing sight of the material deprivations that are associated with inequality, Rousseau also explored inequality's psychological mechanisms and sting. Moreover, Rousseau perceived a connection between those anomic (ever growing and changing) desires that are endemic to the race for public esteem and the lack of basic resources available to the poor. Unlike Voltaire, Rousseau challenged the trickle-down theory that the luxury of the rich raised the living standard of the poor. The rich devoured resources, taxed farmers to support their luxuries and wars, and monopolized and exploited the means of production.[27]

In this account of inequality, *amour-propre* has played a leading role, but so have associations, since *amour-propre* comes into play precisely when humans begin to interact with one another. In chapters 7 and 10, we will examine Rousseau's public plan for restoring aspects of the Garden to the life of the City. His plan attempted, among other things, to curtail the effects of *amour-propre* by a new design—a new covenant—for human society. At this point, however, as we chart the Fall, we need to explore in greater detail the problems attending human association. Stage five culminated in what Rousseau called "a horrible state of war." At first glance, this war looks very much like Hobbes's war of all against all, but on closer inspection important differences come into view. The warriors were not in the Hobbesian state of nature, but in society. The battle, moreover, was not over material goods necessary for survival. That kind of battle, we saw, took place in the Garden on those rare occasions when a Solitaire, prompted by self-love (*amour de soi*), attempted to secure its immediate survival. Because amassing goods for the future, or protecting one's honor, does not bear on immediate survival, conflict in the Garden was restricted and ephemeral. Its duration was as limited as the objects of the contest. The state of war in stage five, in contrast, concerned that which was unattainable—the satisfaction of *amour-propre*.

Rousseau's state of war, then, is more radical than Hobbes's war, because it is rooted in the limitless desire to eclipse one's fellows, not the limited desire to secure survival. Yet one might wonder whether securing survival could not lead to a war of all against all as radical as the one Rousseau described. Hobbes's primitives, after all, unlike Rousseau's Solitaires, possessed memory and imagination. They could remember the pains of hunger and imagine future scenarios in which they would suffer from deprivation. Under these conditions and motivated by *amour de soi*, one could be driven to attempt to surmount all potential obstacles to a painless survival. This could entail, for example, accumulating great wealth and suppressing all possible challengers. Surely here we have the psychological components of an endless battle, especially given the assurances required to mollify human insecurity. Moreover, in addition to this insecure Hobbesian type, can we not also imagine an individual driven by greed and who has little interest in public perception? This one does not care if some have more, some have less, and whether anyone perceives his or her worth. The unique character and sorrow of those motivated by avarice alone was identified by Charles Dickens when he presented us with Mr. Ebenezer Scrooge.

These lines of thought suggest several lessons. The Hobbesian warriors are psychologically more private than those in Rousseau's state of war. They possess memory and imagination, but not outwardly oriented *amour-propre*. This suggests that memory and imagination themselves, apart from *amour-propre*, are problematic. They contribute to human restlessness and conflict, yet without them, unable to form plans for the future in light of the past, one is likely to end up on the jagged shores of the Sirens. The wealthy Ebenezer types, in their turn, are even more private than the Hobbesian warriors. As they are more secure and hence need not worry about remote threats to their survival, they are not the least bit preoccupied with others. The plausibility of the Hobbesian and the Ebenezer types is, I think, undeniable, as is their potential to do tremendous harm. Rousseau, however, never claimed that *amour-propre* alone was responsible for human misery. I have tried to illustrate this by depicting a fall that occurs in several stages, with psychological and sociological complexity increasing accordingly. Moreover, stage five is marked by the presence of both *amour-propre* and the division of labor. This latter sociological condition—the division of labor—makes the self-centered existence of the Hobbesian and Ebenezer types difficult to maintain.

It would not be impossible to maintain, but highly improbable. Herein lies the importance of the division of labor in Rousseau's account. Regardless of one's initial motivations or disposition, in a society marked by the division of labor one must collaborate with others and in the process become dependent on them. In this arena of dependency the deleterious effects of *amour-propre* are nearly inescapable. In stage three we saw what Rousseau considered a benign division of labor between husband

and wife. Although this dependency rendered each spouse weaker separately, together they were stronger than either had been individually. This division of labor did not bring social havoc because it was limited; it engendered an association of two. In stage five, however, a full-blown division of labor placed not only various occupations in need of one another, but also entire classes—the upper, the lower, and the middle classes.[28]

In this context *amour-propre* became fully engaged, leading individuals to make comparisons and to acquire new needs that could only be met with the hands—and the eyes—of others. Here is where all become master and slave, for none are free from envy or contempt. Here all scurry to get ahead of the next, and employ artful means—sometimes flattery, sometimes cruelty—to reach their calculated destination. Sadly, just when *pitié* was most needed, "the cries of natural compassion" were suppressed by this "civil war" in which each was most dependent on those whom one used the most.[29] As a result of the war, in the next stage of the Fall freedom would be surrendered and dependency would deepen.

The Ruse

Think of *stage six* as an account of how the last remnants of freedom were exchanged for a veneer of peace.[30] In the previous stage we saw how the division of labor, private property under conditions of inequality, and such psychological developments as the maturation of memory, foresight, and imagination all contributed to an unpleasant and exhausting war of each against all. To end this war, in stage six, a Hobbesian remedy was offered and accepted: embattled, exhausted humans sacrificed their remaining liberties to a social contract that purported to bring stability and peace. Freedom fell as humans sought protection from the wars they themselves had started.

To call the war and the remedy Hobbesian is not the least bit anachronistic. In Rousseau's day, Hobbes had captured the imagination of the French, and it may be more than a coincidence that Hobbes's own imagination had been roused while in France. Hobbes and Locke were the two English philosophers with whom Rousseau had to reckon, and both figure importantly in the sixth stage.[31] A social contract was offered, but unlike that of Hobbes or Locke, this so-called public contract turned out to be more of a private ruse. I write "private" because Rousseau claimed that it was one class, the rich, who crafted the contract and presented it to the people as a common, public way to achieve peace and justice, although it actually resulted in "new fetters on the poor and gave new powers to the rich."[32] The wealthy had the most to lose in the war against all, since their riches and status were vulnerable to troops of poor bandits and jealous usurpers. Moreover, the wealthy had no legal or moral claim to their riches or titles, for most had acquired them by unjust means. Even those who had gained their riches by honest work could not appeal to the (Lockean) argument, "I built this wall, I earned this land by my industry," for those in need of the same land could respond, "Do you not know that a multitude of your fellows are dying or suffering from need of what you have too much of, and that you must have the express and unanimous consent of humankind to appropriate more of the common subsistence than you need for your own maintenance."[33]

It was at this time of greatest need that the "rich man" conceived "the most artful plan that ever entered the human mind: to employ in his favor the forces of those who attacked him. . . . 'Let us join,' he said, 'to protect the weak from oppression, to restrain the ambitious, and to secure for each the possession of what belongs to him: let us institute rules of justice and peace, to which all will be obliged to conform.'"[34] Regrettably, all accepted the contract, "all ran forward to their chains." This act marked the beginning of political society, which rendered the wealth and power of the rich legitimate and protected them by state forces in the name of justice. This "social" contract, then, in Rousseau's account, is in fact a partisan contract that empowers the rich and imprisons the poor by legitimizing and protecting gross inequalities. The public apparatus of justice began as a servant to the private interests of the wealthy.

We get the idea, then, that Rousseau did not consider the contract that instituted political society to be fair.[35] But fairness is not usually the only consideration when evaluating social contracts, especially if one is trying to understand the allure of a Hobbesian contract. What of peace? Did the contract establish a society in which individuals could pursue many private interests under conditions of relative peace, if not of equality? Moreover, could such conditions of relative peace enable even poor individuals, eventually, to acquire some wealth? Hobbesians and some of the Port-Royal Jansenists had argued that a society of law and order in which individuals were permitted to pursue private interests would generate social harmony and public prosperity. The rich and poor had a mutual interest in cooperation. Montaigne himself claimed that private interests, even greed, contributes to public welfare. Self-interest can lead people to work hard and to work together, producing a general wealth. Montaigne went so far as to mock those who claimed that their occupations were chiefly motivated by public service and not private gain.[36]

The question before us is this: Could the unfair contract eventually engender a minimally decent, comfortable society, due to the contract's potential to secure an environment in which the interests of selfish humans produce public well-being? This question required a response from Rousseau, and that response was unequivocal: "For any two whose interest accord with one another, a hundred thousand perhaps are opposed to them, and there is no way to succeed except to deceive or ruin all those others. Here is the disastrous source of violence, treacheries, perfidies, and all horrors that are necessarily required by a state of things in which each feigns to work for the fortune or the reputation of others, but in fact seeks only to elevate his own interests above those of others, and at their expense."[37] Rousseau's response, in short, is that the contract exchanged one type of mutual warfare for another. In the second war of all against all, strife remained constant. Instead of mobs of poor bandits uniting against the rich, each individual became a solitary warrior, forming alliances only as long as they were useful, pretending to care for others, when in fact all endeavors were affixed to the private objects of *amour-propre*. In this new "liberal" war, in which violence was more subtle and battles tended to rage in the courts instead of the open streets, the rich were like commanding officers who prosper even when their troops suffer defeat. In this new war, in which the endless legal, commercial conflicts between individuals were understood as the achievement of justice, private interest directly opposed the public good: "What can we say of exchanges in which the reason of each private person dictates to him maxims directly contrary to those that public reason preaches to the body of society, and in which each finds his profit in the misfortune of others?"[38]

Rousseau maintained, then, that a society founded on a private contract, and not on a truly social one, promotes a way of life in which all relationships are reduced to contractual ones dedicated to the advancement of private interest.[39] This narrow pursuit, moreover, leads not to a harmony of interest but to endless battles that tend to favor the powerful. Here Rousseau anticipated a future French social theorist who would challenge the prevailing classical liberalism of his day. When Emile Durkheim, the French social philosopher who was greatly influenced by Rousseau, challenged Herbert Spencer, he stood by Rousseau as he claimed, "If mutual interest draws men closer, it is never more than for a few moments. . . . Indeed, if we look to the heart of the matter we shall see that every harmony of interests conceals a latent conflict, or one that is simply deferred. For where interest alone reigns . . . each self finds itself in relation to the other on a war footing, and any truce in this perpetual antagonism cannot be of long duration. Today it is useful for me to unite with you; tomorrow the same reason will make me your enemy."[40] Durkheim, moreover, went on to claim that legal contracts are often unjust, for the power of employers to set the terms of the contract frequently outstrips any bargaining power on the side of the employees. Rousseau had anticipated this as well when he described, in his highly rhetorical fashion, the terms of contracts offered by the powerful: *"You have need of me, because I am rich and you are poor. We will therefore make an agreement between us. I will permit you to have the honor of serving me, on the condition that you give me the little you have left, in return for the trouble I will take to command you."*[41]

Were things that bad? Are things that bad? Rousseau and occasionally Durkheim exaggerated the extent of conflict in modern European societies. But their normative criticism is valid. When the public life of a society is founded chiefly on private interests, that society is not protected by a natural harmony of economic interests, but is threatened by their frequent conflict, a conflict that occasions both public and private sorrow. Even if Hobbes's remedy to the war of all against all—the establishment of a Leviathan for the sake of law and order—could provide enough calm so that most of the people most of the time could ensure their survival, perpetual strife would persist as individuals constantly sought to surpass each other.[42]

Rousseau directly linked this "progress of inequality" to the loss of independence. The self-sufficing Solitaires existed prior to the evolution of the rich and poor, the powerful and weak, and the master and slave. Without property, none was rich or poor; without public authorities, none was powerful or weak; without tyrants, none was master or slave. These, we might say, are basic sociological conditions of inequality—private property under unjust social and political conditions—and within them occurs the loss of freedom because all become entangled in the prevailing structures of dependency.[43] Yet the psychological conditions of fallen freedom are as important as the sociological ones. Rousseau noted that individuals, motivated by *amour-propre*, were willing to serve some authorities in order that they be allowed to reign over others. "Looking rather below than above them, [individuals] come to love domination more than independence, and submit to slavery, that they may in turn enslave others."[44]

We have seen the lines of this argument elsewhere. What is noteworthy here is that, by linking loss of freedom to love of domination, and love of domination to *amour-*

propre, Rousseau has suggested that adjusting structural inequalities alone will not restore human self-determination. Insofar as we want to command, we will persist in submitting to those who, for better or worse, grant us authority to rule relative to our social standing, however lofty or lowly. This is a deeply pessimistic point of view. In spite of its overstatement, it is one of Rousseau's more successful replies not only to sanguine liberalism, but also to the somber liberalism of Mr. Hobbes. Even under an almighty Sovereign, there would exist a multitude of masters, other than Leviathan, to whom humans would find themselves enslaved. Some, Rousseau noted, may be tempted to call this miserable servitude a state of peace.[45] Rousseau's response, in contrast, was to juxtapose our "miserable servitude" to that "state of peace" defined by the Garden's Solitaires—by those who were neither enslaved to the prompting of *amour-propre* nor to the oppressive dependency that accompanies the division of labor and private property in the context of the political state.

The Age of Slavery

Slavery could be construed as the epitome of dependency, especially if, as in Rousseau's account, masters come to rely on slaves for their services and, perhaps as important, for their envy. It is not surprising that *stage seven*, the final stage of the Fall, can appropriately be called the age of slavery.[46] In the end, the once-free Solitaires become slaves dependent on two masters: the external master who commands with wealth and power, and the internal master, *amour-propre*, which commands with the desire for wealth and power. As the culmination of a long epic, this final stage, one might have thought, would present a dramatic ending. The conclusion, however, is rather anticlimactic. The narrative of the Fall ends with a familiar society, one in which citizens suffer from the state's excessive precautions against foreign nations, from heavy taxes to pay for professional armies even during times of peace, and from laws written by, or else ignored by, the powerful and wealthy.[47] Perhaps this anticlimactic ending should not surprise us. After all, at the outset of the second *Discours* Rousseau announced, "Listen, this is your history."[48] The last chapter of our history should sound disappointingly familiar. How could one expect the commonplace to startle us? Rousseau, however, wanted even this familiar ending to sound strange—unacceptably foreign. Was this not the sharp point of his narrative? His aim was that this drama of decline would shock us and cause great alarm over the current state of affairs. Toss a frog in boiling water and it will leap for safety; place the same frog in a kettle of cool water, bring to a slow boil, and you have frog legs. Starting as a slow simmer, history has brought us to a boil. The stages are meant to reveal this process—to warn us—so that we might be able to do something about it.

If the process is a frightening one, then the stark contrast between the beginning and the end is most alarming. It is precisely this contrast between the Garden and the lowest point of the Fall—to return to my original metaphor—that Rousseau employed to bring his narrative to a close. Of this seventh stage, Rousseau wrote that it is "the extreme point that closes the circle and touches the point from which it began. . . . There is here a total restoration . . . of a new state of nature."[49] This is the surprise designed to startle us when we learn of the disturbing similarities and even more distressing differences between the original and new state of nature.

As in the beginning, all are once again solitaires—isolated from each other due to the absence of community—except for a bitter dependency that results in painful conflicts, rivalries, and expressions of domination. As in the beginning, "here all private persons become again equal," only this time it is "because they are all nothing," because each is equally enslaved to masters, possessions, and passions, and because each is equally subjected to pain and tumult.[50] As in the beginning, there is "a return to the law of the strongest," only this time, in the absence of *pitié* and with the substitution of rapacious *amour-propre* for benign *amour de soi*, the conflict between the strong and weak is not infrequent, ephemeral, and innocuous, but is habitual, enduring, and virulent. As in the beginning, there is the absence of government, not because no government exists, but because it has become so despotic that it confronts the individual as a typhoon or a ferocious animal—chaotic, willful, dangerous. Finally, as in the beginning, here "all notions of good and all principles of equity again vanish," but this time the lack of virtue is not accompanied by the ignorance of vice. Vice is perfected as human development is now complete.

The seventh stage, then, relative to our stage in history, is pedestrian; relative to the Garden, however, it is astounding. Perhaps Rousseau did manage to bring his narrative to a climactic close, even if it merely leaves us at the threshold of our own home, our own status quo. He wanted us, he said, "to be struck by the vast distance which separates the two states."[51] The surprise is how far we have fallen, and how closely our own situation resembles what Rousseau and Hobbes alike deplored—the Hobbesian state of nature. Compare the mutual war at the end of the fifth stage with the one here in the seventh, and you will be struck by the similarity. Remember, the institution of political society and law was meant to bring an end to that earlier "horrible state of war." The revelation, then, is that even after the institution of government the war continues. The violence is perhaps less explicit, but the confrontation is still odious, and frequently deadly. We have traveled far from the peace and liberty of the Solitaires, and we have, in Rousseau's view, done little to recover what we have lost. Rousseau's final lesson, the end point of his second *Discours*, is to display the "total restoration . . . of a new state of nature, different from the one from which we began in that the first was a state of nature in its first purity, while this last one is the fruit of excessive corruption."[52]

Excessive hyperbole was a flaw Rousseau never eluded. I do not fault him for depicting the Garden. We have already seen that, in his own imaginary account, it was no Paradise. Yet here, at this final stage, I believe restraint of prose would have served him more admirably than his talent for embellishment. He did not, and we do not, live in a state of mutual war or in a despotic society. No doubt aspects of despotism, that is, arbitrary powers not subject adequately to the laws or not subject to adequate laws, pervaded Rousseau's Europe and still harm North Atlantic democracies. And the tyranny of *amour-propre* is undeniably ubiquitous. There were and are sizeable segments of contemporary, modern, and early modern societies that would, for good reason, see little in the way of exaggeration in Rousseau's account of modern corruption, hostility, and misery. Still, I believe that his narrative of the human Fall—or as he once described it to Voltaire, "the sketch of my melancholy reveries"—would have ended even more powerfully if the final stage looked more mundanely woeful.[53] This would have rendered the last stage even more recognizably our own, and hence its problems our problems.

No climax should cap this narrative, because there is no closure to this history. The story continues, and Rousseau's hope was that if we were more circumspect about our history, we might learn how to proceed toward a somewhat brighter future: "It is in following this slow succession of events that we see the solution to an infinite number of moral and political problems which the philosophers cannot solve."[54] These solutions, or avenues to restoration, would in any case have to be tentative and imperfect. Rousseau understood this. He also understood that it was unacceptable to accept our ousted condition without making an effort to save ourselves, even if incompletely. However, before we can turn to Rousseau's solutions in part II of our study, we need to become more cognizant of the obstacles to be overcome. In the next two chapters, then, we will conduct an inquiry, more systematic than Rousseau's study, into the nature of our ousted condition.

We will examine, among other things, a peculiar tension between the necessity and contingency of the Fall. This tension enabled Rousseau to portray us as suspended between fatalism and moral freedom, as well as between physical and moral evil. We will arrive at the surprising conclusion that the Fall into the social cannot be described either as unnatural or as unmitigated evil. This conclusion challenges the generally held belief that, in Rousseau's view, all things natural are good, all things social are corrupt. We will discover, however, that if we categorically identify the natural with the good and the social with evil, we fail to do justice to Rousseau's provocative account of the passage from the amoral Garden to the ambiguous moral progress and precarious human joy of the City. To escape the Fall into sociability is to dodge our humanity; yet to yield to the Fall is to court public injustice and personal pain. These are the broad strokes of the tragic vision that guided Rousseau's thought, and this vision will guide much of our investigation in the following two chapters.

5

The City

Life in the Ousted Condition

After centuries of flights and crashes—discoveries and mishaps, adaptations and devia-
tions, ingenuity and obtuseness—civilization, that is, Europe, had managed to create for
itself the antithesis of the Garden, namely, the City.[1] The City is a public home for the
crowd, a mass of disparate individuals that shifts and turns in near unison, as mole-
cules in a reaction, subject to the same social and psychological forces. All claim to be
free; all make the same bad choices. Communication in the City is like deciphering
codes in the military; to say what you mean, you must not mean what you say. Those
lacking this ability, this "linguistic capital," to use Pierre Bourdieu's term, are misunderstood, mishandled, and, in any case, mistreated by the crowd. Economic and social
inequality are as present as fairness and goodwill are absent. Luxury and want, the brick
and mortar of the City, are held together by envy and contempt. All are stuck together,
since all need each other, even if some are more needy than others. This is not to collapse the difference between the poor's hunger for bread and the affluent's craving for
regard. It is only to underscore a nexus between the two classes of desires: if the poor
properly speak the language of humility, and the rich the language of beneficence, charity will coat, though not fill, the stomachs of the poor.

Paris stood for the City, the ousted condition. That may be an understatement. Paris,
in Rousseau's eyes, was the incarnation of the City—an ideal type fully embodied. While
it is true that, except for Geneva, Rousseau rarely had a kind word for any city, Paris
was the model of things gone awry—a "city of noise, smoke and mud, where the women
have ceased to believe in honour and the men in virtue." In the labyrinth called Paris,
one becomes bewitched and forgetful of one's good, true self. "We search for love,
happiness and innocence; we can therefore never be far enough away from [Paris]."[2]
Rousseau wrote these lines when he was, ironically, rather unhappy in solitude in
Montmorency. Where, then, is one to search for love, happiness, and goodness? Are
these three basic human pursuits mutually exclusive? The second *Discours*—"On the Origin
of Inequality"—implicitly raised these questions and supplied some provisional answers.
Of this, however, Rousseau was sure: the City is no place for love, happiness, or goodness. And it was to the inhabitants of the City—whether they actually dwelled there or,
like Voltaire, carried it in their hearts—for whom Rousseau wrote. Like many reformers,

79

Rousseau claimed that he was "not interested in reforming people, but simply telling them the truth." He crafted the truth to disturb us, to make us—citizens of the City— aware of our frenzied, anxious existence, in the hope that with such awareness we might be able to evade aspects of our fallen, ousted condition.

Without forsaking the narrative I presented in the first four chapters, I now want to explore more systematically, in the next two chapters, several issues that the narrative has presented: the very idea of the state of nature, the inevitability of the Fall, the nature and origin of evil, and the prospect of restoration. In part II we will investigate Rousseau's proposed public and private remedies and the tension between them. Before we discuss any cure, we need to investigate more thoroughly the diseased condition from which we seek deliverance.

The State of Nature: Fact or Fiction

If an advantage of narrative is that it naturally situates ideas and claims in a concrete yet dynamic context, then it stands to reason that interpreting beginnings—that threshold between nothing and something—is as important as it is difficult. It is important because openings set the stage for the ensuing drama and thereby shape our expectations; "difficult" because they appear almost ex nihilo, as is so well expressed by the familiar, "Once upon a time. . . ." This is one reason commentators have strenuously struggled with Rousseau's "In the beginning"—that is, with Nature's Garden, the state of nature. What is the purpose of Rousseau's state of nature? A scientific, historical account of human prehistory? An eternally valid account of human psychology and sociology? A measuring rod in the hands of a social critic? A fantasy for the nostalgic? A metaphor of solitude? An argument against Hobbes? Rather than having to decide between these, we can explore each and see whether Rousseau didn't put the state of nature to many uses. Clarity on this will help us eventually reach its end—the paths that lead out of the City. We need, however, to proceed with caution. As I already noted, Anton Chekhov once said that it is in the beginnings and endings of stories that we are most tempted to lie. In part II we will examine Rousseau's deceptive endings; our aim now is to see what Rousseau's artful opening can teach us.

We start with the obvious. If we can assume that Rousseau knew his narrative would lead to the City, then he needed a starting point far from the maddening crowd. As Paris was becoming for him a tangible paradigm of human corruption, Nature's Garden would serve as his concrete model of pristine goodness, or at least gentle innocence. This expression, "concrete model," preserves the ambiguity of Rousseau's starting point that has baffled his interpreters. The ambiguity can be expressed as the question, does the state of nature function as an abstract *model* or as an actual, *concrete* historical reality? I would prefer, however, to drop that question, at least for the moment, and again note the obvious. Rousseau, desiring to provide a genetic account of humans' limited perfections and immense miseries, attempted to justify, document, and illustrate his arguments with as much historical and ethnographic material as possible.[3] Of course, unlike the historical stages of human development, the state of nature is by definition prehistorical. Yet with the help of missionary and travel reports, Buffon's *Natural History*, and the "province of philosophy when history is silent," Rousseau attempted to forward a decent guess about life in a state of nature. He never denied that it was conjecture, and he never claimed that it was logically necessary even if empirically insupportable.[4] He acknowledged that with the same evidence others could imagine differently the state of nature and the details of human development.[5] Nonetheless, Rousseau thought himself justified to consider his conjecture—extrapolation from empirical research—a fine specimen of sound inquiry.

Rousseau's scientific theodicy, then, begins with what most eighteenth-century scientific studies required—an account of origins. What is surprising about Rousseau's version—and what threatened to weaken its scientific credibility—is its level of detail. Accounts of origins were to be marked by necessary simplicity and simple necessity. Yet Rousseau held that "simple necessity"—logic dictating what must have been the case—placed too much confidence in reason. What of "necessary simplicity," that is, the art of succinct, sparse discourse? Could Rousseau not abide by it on this one occasion while describing the original state? Brevity would not serve him here, for he wanted to confront us with that which was both familiar and unfamiliar, that which was both ourselves and not ourselves, and for this he needed to have us encounter something tangible, substantial, and preferably real. He knew his state of nature was the result of conjecture, yet he also felt that his extensive research of distant places and customs had earned him the intellectual and moral right to challenge us with a rather thick description of the Solitaires in Nature's Garden. With enough detail, we might identify with the Solitaires while we wonder at the tremendous difference between them and us.

In creating this old world, then, Rousseau hoped that we might discover two worlds—the state of nature and our own world seen anew—and the vast distance between the two. He had learned, as have such anthropologists as Mary Douglas and Clifford Geertz, that studying "the other" culture is one of the best ways to fathom one's own. That is why in the second *Discours* Rousseau complained that most studies abroad focus on "stones and plants" rather than on "men and morals." If we were to expose ourselves to various peoples—and Rousseau here lists quite a few—"we would see a new world . . . , and we would thus learn to know our own."[6] Sadly, late in life, when Rousseau had learned too much about human deceit and callousness and not enough about human honesty and goodness, he felt compelled to retreat to the world of stones and, especially, plants. But that comes later. At this point he was more interested in reforming society than abandoning it. In confronting his society with the Solitaire—with that which is not human yet almost human—Rousseau extended to the limit the anthropological exercise of learning about oneself from the other. We have seen that Nature's Garden was no paradise for humans. Still, by exposing us to it Rousseau sought to stir within us a sense of longing or at least of loss. He was counting on some form of nostalgia here, an important even if limited form of social criticism.

Nonetheless, the status, nature, and character of the state of nature remains ambiguous; we are presented with a world before time, constructed from known worlds, in order to shed new light on our familiar world. Science aids the creative act but it accedes to moral imagination because moral truth, not scientific, was Rousseau's ultimate aim. For this reason he could write, "Let us begin by setting aside all the facts, as they do not affect the question."[7] Unfortunately, Rousseau never told us what exactly the question, or issue, was. And as it turns out, there was never only one, but several. Still, one statement stands out: "To disentangle what is original from what is artificial in the present nature of man, and to know well a state which no longer exists, which perhaps never did exist, and which probably never will exist; and of which it is nevertheless necessary to have correct notions, in order to judge well of our present state."[8] If this is the guiding principle, and I think it is, then the facts to be laid aside are those limited, ethnocentric judgments that we take to be eternal and universal.[9] This interpretation gains credence when we note that immediately before Rousseau suggested that the facts be laid aside, he had been complaining about "the philosophers" such as Grotius, Pufendorf, and Hobbes who ascribe their own cultural prejudices and productions to the state of nature.[10] They had, in other words, sullied the natural with the artificial, the original with the conventional. Their answers lacked fidelity to the question, What is original?

Yet what kind of question is that? Does it not ask for the absurd, along the line of—as Hegel might have put it—"What is not?" And how could Rousseau do better than the philosophers he criticized? He began by ignoring all "the facts," that is, by attempting to ignore his culture, his society. How else can we explain his claim to lay the facts aside while at the same time he marshaled an arsenal of facts, facts about *other* societies, to assist in the creation of the state of nature? Some have suggested that Rousseau's claim to lay the facts aside "is not to be taken too seriously; it was, in part at least, a sop to the religious authorities."[11] Yet Rousseau's claim is serious, even if troublesome. The external explanation—a subterfuge against the censor—is not convincing. It forgets that the censor was Rousseau's friend, Malesherbes. Rousseau's confidence in this friendship was so strong that he had not even sought an official license for the publication of the first *Discours*, "On the Arts and Sciences." Later, in 1762, when both *Emile* and *The Social Contract* were banned, we might want to say that Rousseau had been too trusting, but this only makes the external explanation seem all the less convincing.

If we fail to take seriously Rousseau's call to abandon the facts we risk overlooking one of his profoundest attempts and failures. Ignoring facts may seem easy, but in this case it is among the hardest tasks to accomplish. It is never easy to forget so much, to imagine so much, that we escape our world and discover another's. Rousseau's journey into cultural forgetfulness was not a mere exercise in reverie; he endeavored to climb out of his culture on the ladder of ethnographic research. Although the attempt is to be admired, he failed miserably. There is a simple epistemological account for his failure. Many accept by now, as do I, that the attempt to jump or wiggle out of our cultural skins is an impossible one. This simple epistemological account, however, is not the measure of failure that I have in mind. Rousseau's grand failure was not that he remained in his eighteenth-century skin, but that he remained so decidedly in Jean-Jacques's, and thus repeated the same error that he had identified in others. Grotius conveniently found in the state of nature a way to shore up justice on the high, international sea; Pufendorf discovered in the original state a way to secure the right to one's possessions; and Hobbes saw in it an authoritarian solution to the English problem of civil war. Now Rousseau, even while he denounced such self-deception, managed to add his own name to the list of those who project not only their culture's prejudices on to the distant silhouettes of the state of nature, but their own private fears and dreams.

With the aid of science and moral imagination, Rousseau fantasized about a place free from all that he abhorred about the City: a place immune to *amour-propre*, and where inequality doesn't hurt, where greed and envy have no footing, where self-loathing and hatred of others are replaced by gentle *amour de soi* and *pitié*. The Garden, his anti-type to the City, is not his ideal home—that would have been a Swiss mountain village peopled with good-natured, candid, independent folk (something very much like stage four of the Fall). Science demanded of him a far more primitive fantasy. Still, within the bounds of science, Rousseau succeeded to assemble from his own wistfulness and regret a private retreat far from the corruption and pain of the City. The Solitaire in Nature's Garden, then, was not only an admixture of moral inventiveness and scientific discovery, it was also the result of Rousseau's own self-exploration.

When I characterize Rousseau's failure here as "self-exploration," I am not being excessively charitable, I am changing the subject. I do not wish to belittle the error of mistaking one's own hopes and fears as humanity's. Yet it is tricky in this case simply to call this an error, since Rousseau never denied that he used self-examination as a means to generate universal knowledge. In order to write the second *Discours*, Rousseau spent days walking in solitude in the forest of Saint-Germain and later in the Bois de Boulogne. In his account to Malesherbes about how, on his way to Vincennes to call on the imprisoned Diderot, he had received the inspiration for the first and second *Discours* and *Emile* ("my three principal writings"), Rousseau depicted a rather mystical trance that he experienced as he sat under a tree.[12] The point is that Rousseau often portrayed himself as one who sought solitude in order to report on the universally relevant findings lodged within his breast. It was not so much his heart, he thought, that was unique, but his ability to inspect it.

This other source of knowledge—knowledge of and from the self—was not exactly opposed to science. Could one not probe the depths of the heart and discover clues to the riddle, What is original? Although my answer is no (in the depths of the heart lies not an original nature or universal knowledge, but buried private fears and longings, cultural biases and prejudgments), Rousseau's pursuit of knowledge through introspection was not unjustified. There are lengthy traditions—both religious and secular, both ancient and modern—that support introspection as a source of external knowledge. Moreover, Rousseau's anthropological research seemed to confirm that a shared humanity could be discovered, at least theoretically, in any heart. When Rousseau was confronted with otherness in his ethnographic material, he thought in that same material he had also identified sameness.[13] He recognized the distance separating him from the other as well as a common identity. This identity seemed to confirm the appropriateness of the inward method of research, the investigation of his own heart. He understood that it could be a useful technique only if his suspicion—which was to become a conviction—was correct, namely, that underneath the vast plethora of historical mutations, humans persist in sharing an eternal, common nature. Had he had followed the inward method alone, it would have taken him out of the emerging encyclopedic scientific tradition. Yet Rousseau usually employed both approaches, empirical investigation and inward exploration. Both were indispensable to him, and both, he thought, had revealed a common humanity.

This revelation is still another reason Rousseau felt that he could leave the facts—those of his own society—behind. Knowledge of others had relativized his society's claim to stand as *the* bearer of humanity, and had revealed the extent to which "education and habits" had disfigured the qualities of humanity. Yet since those qualities had not been "entirely destroyed," Rousseau searched his own heart for evidence of and for humanity.[14] In this search, "the facts"—again, those of his society—could mainly indicate only layers of sediment that had crusted over the original human form—that timeless pattern which was his principal destination. Having traveled through place and time—out of his own and into that of others—Rousseau ultimately sought to "forget time and place" in order to address "the whole human race." His message, even if it was informed in part by historicism, focused on the ahistorical—the eternal nature of humanity. For this reason Rousseau could criticize those philosophers like Pufendorf and Hobbes who never "doubted whether the state of nature ever existed."[15] Rousseau could entertain this doubt because he was chiefly documenting its eternal, not historical, existence.[16]

This emphasis on the eternal rescues Rousseau from one type of criticism and tosses him into the jaws of another. Those who have accused Rousseau of mistaking his conjecture for historical fact have not understood his project. Yet what of those who argue that Rousseau's very concept of a state of nature—whether it be real or theoretical—is as useless as it is incomprehensible? Useless because it purports to describe an ahistorical human nature; incomprehensible because it entails radically asocial humans.[17] The first problem is metaphysical: Is there such a thing as *the* nature of humans? The second one is epistemological: Can radically private nonlinguistic creatures tell us anything interesting about sociolinguistic humans? In Rousseau's view, the suspect ideas—that of an eternal human nature and of asocial humans—are interrelated. In order to reach the eternal and the natural, Rousseau thought he needed to get back behind history and convention. If he had begun with an account of humans in society, he never could have been sure, supposedly, whether he was depicting human nature or social artifice.

That was Rousseau's problem; ours is how to proceed now in light of his unfortunate though common eighteenth-century essentialism. I recommend, in short, that we drop both the metaphysical and the epistemological issue and see what moral, social, and psychological lessons, specifically regarding the relation between the public and private life, we can learn from Rousseau's narrative, including its imaginary Garden. While I am not particularly interested in the question of a universal human nature—even if there were such an entity, how could we verify our conception of it?—I am interested in Rousseau's critique of a society that shares a family resemblance with my own. Rousseau's normative judgments are expressed, in part, by means of the state of nature. The task, then, is to hear what Rousseau has to tell us about life alone and life together, and the relation between the two, without affirming his metaphysical claims. We will also want, however, to identify those aspects of his judgments that are distorted by unfortunate metaphysical claims.

As to the epistemological issue, I, too, hold with Naomi Bliven that "man is a social animal." But I am not prepared to say with her that the second *Discours* "relies on a concept as meaningless in political theory as it is in anthropology: man in himself—alone, or apart from society."[18] I wish to distinguish between an epistemological position that Bliven and I evidently share, namely, the irreducibly sociolinguistic nature of humans, and the normative positions that Rousseau managed to articulate by means of the Solitaire in Nature's Garden. Rousseau, no doubt, was interested in discerning the difference between the natural Solitaire and the artificial, social human. But our interest need not be bound to his. The task at hand, as I see it, is to demythologize Rousseau's "man in himself" by exploring those social conventions that irritated him and those

that he admired (yet often failed to understand as conventions). His customary designa-
tion for these two sets, the natural and the artificial, can be exchanged for others, such
as human traits and social practices that promote happiness and justice and those that
don't. Rousseau's Solitaire, then, has much to teach us in spite of its epistemological
and metaphysical oddities.

I should also mention that Rousseau's essentialism, unlike many of his contemporaries', is rather limited. Like Montaigne or Pascal, Rousseau was suspicious of those
who claimed to limn in detail the shape of the natural. Not only was such discernment
beyond human ability, but also, even barring that consideration, nature simply did not
fashion humans with an extensive constitution. Rousseau frequently criticized the pro-
liferation of Natural Law theorists who held in common only their subtlety and hubris
in affixing the name, "natural," to a collection of their own favorite principles. Rousseau
himself, we have seen, shaped the natural much in his own image. Yet that image was
notably simpler than most.[19] This is not to say that Rousseau did not provide a detailed
description of the state of nature. Indeed, it was thicker than most. But his elaborate
description entailed a rather simple, basic notion of human nature. Its simplicity, in
fact, is one of its salient features. Hence, for example, Rousseau criticized Diderot's concept
of an innate social instinct that naturally enticed early humans to form associations.
Diderot, in Rousseau's view, had ascribed too much social complexity to the early humans'
natural simplicity. Even Hobbes's original brutes, who were not endowed with innate
sociability, failed to qualify as Rousseau's unadorned "man in himself," for their inordinate greed rendered them too complicated.

As a skillful novelist, Rousseau developed a intricate, fertile story based on a few
simple tenets. Almost the whole of Rousseau's natural law was embodied in the Solitaire's
natural maxim, "Do good to yourself with as little harm as possible to others."[20] In
spite of my own historicist, anti-essentialist sensibilities, I must admit that *amour de
soi*—a profound regard for one's own preservation and freedom from pain—does strike
me as a not -unlikely candidate for a natural human disposition (though I also suspect,
with Freud, that hatred of self is almost as likely).[21] And should anthropologists declare
someday that *pitié*—a repugnance at seeing suffering in another sentient being—appears
to be a universal reaction, I would not be surprised (though I suspect that fascination
with suffering may be equally as universal). I of course have no interest in defending
Rousseau's essentialism; I only want to draw attention to its restricted scope as expressed
by the state of nature.

There is still another kind of limit to Rousseau's essentialism, his attraction to historicism. Rousseau maintained a deep conviction that humans are radically shaped—
often disagreeably—by their social histories. Even if he could have been certain that he
had identified the Solitaires' original human nature, he could not have been confident
that that nature had endured significantly. When we reach stage four of the Fall, where
there is the introduction of manners and customs, "everything now begins to change."[22]
Everything, including human nature itself? This question would haunt Rousseau, torn
as he was between a deep-seated historicism *and* essentialism. Curiously, the more he
became cognizant of human malleability in history, the more he looked to "the natural
heart" as a bright though distant beacon that faintly perforates the dreary fog of our
inescapable histories. This hardly resolves the tension between historicism and essentialism, but it did permit Rousseau to retain a bit of optimism; amid the winds and dust

of history, there is a compass (that original equipment of the Solitaires, *amour de soi* and *pitié*) with which we might find a somewhat better place. Without a guide, we wander from one city to the next, from misery to misery.

Many of us would have preferred a Rousseau who did not look to an innate human nature, however circumscribed, to help lead us out of the chaos of the City. Did he need the state of nature? Did he need the Solitaires? Could he not have been satisfied to investigate and champion the good qualities of those whom he respected—the Spartans, the Genevans, or the *montagnards* of Valais—without rooting that goodness in the distant Garden? Perhaps these societies could not have helped Rousseau battle Hobbes's contention that we stand in need of a brawny Leviathan to check a human nature that makes us naturally unruly and aggressive. If Rousseau had not traveled back behind human artifice to the original humans and identified their pacific nature and limited needs, he would have had no means, he thought, to explain why some peoples are happier than others. The folks of the high Valais, for example, were better off than the throngs in Paris because the social and natural environment of the Valais enabled its people to exist, relative to the Parisians, *naturally*. Likewise, the satisfaction of the citizens of Sparta sprang not from a repressed natural aggressiveness, but from a relatively *natural* lifestyle marked by limited needs (or put more ironically, from a socially engineered, mitigated *amour-propre*).

None of this is to say that the discovery of the state of nature was indispensable for Rousseau's appraisal of the ousted condition. He could have claimed to have identified, in the living humans and civilizations he knew, two loves, *amour de soi* and *amour-propre*, and then argued under what conditions the one love can be promoted and the other blunted. That is partly what I want to do. I use the state of nature as a counterfactual— a fictional comparison—to modern life, and see how it illuminates, among other things, the grief and joy of being alone and being with others. Rousseau's ambitions, of course, were grander and less pragmatic. He was determined to offer a radical diagnosis. By radical I mean that he aspired to expose the root of "the" human predicament, and in the eighteenth century that meant going back to origins, back to an original nature. Like many of us, he wanted to speak with authority, he wanted to convince people and help them; this required, he believed, that he discover and speak in the voice of nature. He was too skeptical of history to believe that alone it was capable of generating and sustaining normative judgments. He needed, or thought he needed, something external to history and yet not to humanity itself. Nature—which in theory is close to us, for it is lodged in our hearts, yet in practice is distant, for it has become veiled—met the requirement.

I have recommended that we drop Nature, this external apparatus—an artifice, if you will—meant to shore up Rousseau's social criticism and moral psychology. He can speak prophetically without it. Under this recommendation we do not ignore the state of nature, as Rousseau described it; we allow it, without its metaphysics, to reveal features of our social and private lives, or at least to remind us of some things once known but forgotten or ignored. This does not entail hoisting the state of nature up as an inspirational paradise. It was, we have seen, no utopia. Rather, between the Garden and the City—two ideal types, to be sure—we discover something of the hope and the tragedy of our actual existence. We are not asked by Rousseau to return to the Garden. We are invited, instead, to see our lives in light of the Garden, and are thereby encouraged to envision a future different from the arduous, often brutal present.

We are expected to long for aspects of the Garden life, but not that life itself. The Solitaires do not represent the good life; they depict profoundly—yet only—the utterly simple, painless life. They remind us of the needless complexity and suffering we face daily. Nostalgia is not the only form of social criticism that we should associate with the state of nature. It was, however, one of the chief tactics that Rousseau employed to arouse us. Longing for aspects of the past and dreaming of a brighter future, Rousseau understood, are closely related. His narrative, beginning with the state of nature, moves along the line between the actual and the possible. This line is parallel to the edge nostalgia cuts between dissatisfaction with the present and yearning for the past or future. Homesickness—*nostalgie*—is the desire for the future to resemble a happy past, not copy the dreary present. It can lead us to transform the present into the image of a distant past, however distorted or idealized. Hence nostalgia is not simply a motivating force, for it also contains a particular object—a particular state of affairs—that we long for. The idealized Garden life was designed to highlight the twisted conditions of modern European existence. Here, then, is one way to understand Rousseau's state of nature: By generating nostalgia for a carefully constructed past, the state of nature illuminates actual features of modern social life and reveals possible conditions for a happier future.

I agree with Ernst Cassirer that Rousseau utilized the state of nature as a tool to uncover our natural constitution. But that constitution, I have argued, is quite modest. The only morally "obligatory law" that emerges from the Garden is the natural maxim, and that simple maxim, Rousseau knew, is not adequate for a robust moral life. Thus while I concur with Cassirer that the state of nature does expose a high degree of "mere convention and caprice"—that is, unnecessary complexity and often cruel arbitrariness—it is surely too much to call it, as does Cassirer, the norm or standard by which we can measure our moral excellence.[23] Our situation is too different from that of the Solitaires. Marx once asserted that the Kingdom of God delivers a radical protest and critique of existing society because every aspect of society is found wanting when compared to it.[24] The Garden, in contrast, does not operate in this fashion; its critique is not total and complete. It is better viewed as a device that helps to illuminate aspects of our lives that cause unnecessary harm in our fallen condition, the only condition we truly know or can ever expect to know. But the Garden itself is not a moral alternative, and, as we will see in chapter 8, it does not provide a substantive plan for moral recovery.

The Garden can, however, cast considerable light on the human associations and on our temporary, partial breaks from them. We have seen, and we will continue to see, that the second *Discours* can be read as a history or fable about the development of and relation between the public and private life. *Amour de soi* and *amour propre*, for example, help us understand something about the independent private self and the dependent public self. In another example, the natural maxim illuminates the dangers of an ambitious morality that aims for the perfection and harmony of public and private lives—an ambitious morality that is willing to impose its arduous vision on those with a different and perhaps more modest vision.

My claim, then, is that we can reject Rousseau's essentialism and naturalism and still learn many helpful things from the Solitaires. I need, however, to caution that the

Solitaires are not always as innocent as they seem. The assumption that deep down inside we are like the Solitaires, namely, naturally innocent and perhaps even good, can lead to apathy and to the bad habit of blaming only forces outside ourselves. "The Devil made me do it" is not far from the pair of claims, "The individual is good; society is corrupt." While this unhappy consequence was never Rousseau's intention, too often he excused himself and sometimes others with, "Yet the heart is sincere." Rousseau's naturalism could also inspire a devotion to "the universal" and a suspicion of diversity—a suspicion that could make life miserable for those who do not have the wealth or power to claim that their way is an acceptable way.[25] Again, this was never Rousseau's design. His acceptance and celebration of diversity was impressive, especially when judged by eighteenth-century standards.[26] Nevertheless, his naturalism could—and has—inspired others to defend unwarranted repression in the name of "the universal." The French Revolution is only one, though surely the most impressive as well as ambiguous, instance of this.

On the title page of the second *Discours* Rousseau placed a line from Aristotle's *Politics*, "What is natural should not be considered in things that are deprived, but in those that are rightly ordered according to nature." This advice Rousseau took to heart. His chief concern, however, was the status—the presence, the potential help—of the natural in things that are depraved. Most of us live in the City, the point farthest from the state of nature. If Rousseau seemed preoccupied with the state of nature, it is because he hoped it could help him better understand and emancipate the City. By way of history, anthropology, speculation, and self-examination, Rousseau attempted to gain distance, that is, perspective, from which to gaze critically at our fallen, ousted condition—life in the City.

The Fall

Our distance from the state of nature could be said to be the measure of the depth of the Fall. However, we ought not to take the Fall, and hence social existence, as being synonymous with evil or even corruption. This is where even the most astute Rousseau commentators go wrong.[27] The tragedy of the Fall is missed precisely to the extent that it is declared an unmitigated evil. For humanity and virtue to develop, the Solitaires must leave the Garden. They must cease to be Solitaires.[28] The unfortunate truth is that the basic conditions of goodness and happiness—an assortment of social relations, commitments, goals, and loves—are also the conditions of inequality, hypocrisy, greed, and cruelty. The relation between the natural and the social cannot be described as a Manichaean battle between the Kingdom of Good and the Kingdom of Evil. Virtue and vice, joy and sorrow share too much social and psychological ground for them to be neatly relegated into such distinct camps. The pursuit of happiness and virtue leads to a sociability that is vulnerable to grief and depravity. The prized freedom of the Solitaires seems restrictive when one realizes that they are not free to love others because their primitive self-love (*amour de soi*) will not allow them to hazard heartache. Nor are they free to impose laws on themselves—the height of moral activity, according to Kant—for that would entail making commitments.

There is, then, too much good that Rousseau himself has associated with the social state for it to be simply spurned as evil. For this reason the Fall into the social may be described as what I earlier called a "blessed fall." Without the Fall, many human traits that we value most, such as loyalty to friends and country, would have no history. We never admired the Solitaires; we deplored the unnecessary obstacles blocking our joy. We never envied the Solitaires; we resented our busy schedules and chronic exhaustion. Our history, in Rousseau's drama, did not begin in Paradise with a pair whom we revere, but rather with childlike creatures whose simplicity and innocence, while alluring, are not suitable for adults. In order to grow up, the Solitaires *had* to leave the Garden. That much is clear. What is less clear is whether on balance the departure was worth the ensuing misery and harm.[29] Such hypothetical questioning is perhaps good only to remind us that all is not well and that tragedy haunts the passageways of even our greatest achievements. To escape the Fall is to dodge our humanity; to embrace the Fall is to court public injustice and personal pain.

I have said that the tragedy of the Fall is missed when it is considered entirely evil. The other contrary way to lose sight of the tragedy is to belittle the resulting pain and vice by claiming that these are merely necessary by-products of social and moral development.[30] It is simply the price to be paid, to change the metaphor, as recognized by any mature moral agent. Although I myself am about to argue that the Fall was indeed inevitable, its passage remains tragic in two senses. The series of misfortunes often seem all but necessary, as in a *fated* tragedy. Yet also, in another sense of the tragic, much of the misery appears *accidental* and *unnecessary*; things could have turned out better. Although there was no practical way to elude pain and corruption entirely, much could have been avoided. It is the elusive combination of these two kinds of misery, the inevitable and the unnecessary, that frames the tragic passage to ambiguous moral progress and precarious human joy.

Was the Fall inevitable? The question might sound merely quaint, an issue inherited from Christianity that once seemed pertinent but now appears unimportant and even meaningless. The question, however, is relevant, for it demands from Rousseau's philosophical anthropology an answer to another question, what can we hope for? This, in turn, is linked directly to Rousseau's soteriology, that is, the paths to moral recovery and joy. If we agree, for example, with Starobinski that the Fall, in Rousseau's view, was not necessary but was radically contingent, then we are likely to conclude with him that "there is no flaming sword that prevents our entering the lost paradise."[31] Yet if the Fall is held to be necessary, or at least inevitable, then Rousseau can only offer partial remedies, for the paths to recovery would not be able to skirt the ineluctable aspects of our fallen condition. I will argue that, in Rousseau's view, the Fall results neither from radical contingency nor from iron-clad necessity. Because I have described the Fall not as a single incident but a series of events, I need not confine myself to a monocausal account of it. This will help me feature Rousseau's textured portrait of our fallen condition, a condition that is suspended between helplessness and autonomy.

Rousseau, I have noted, has presented many faces for his commentators to quarrel over. Yet all seem to agree that Rousseau spurned any notion of original sin—of innate corruption—and that he, along with most *philosophes*, blamed corrupt, irrational social institutions for the majority of our miseries. This standard interpretation is supported by Rousseau's perhaps most famous line, "Man is naturally good."[32] I will argue, however, that Rousseau held that human wickedness springs not solely from social structures but from the human breast. Lodged within the human heart is a fallen condition that makes our failures empirically inevitable, yet not ontologically necessary. What, then, are we to make of Rousseau's claim that "man is naturally good"? As we will see, Rousseau tenaciously held both the belief that humans are not naturally corrupt and the belief that humans do inevitably corrupt themselves. He maintained both views, tensely. In chapter 6, I will explore these two apparently contradictory outlooks by locating Rousseau at the crossroads of Enlightenment optimism and Augustinian pessimism. For now it is enough to note that while it is clear that Rousseau rejected the Christian doctrine of original sin, at least in name, it is not patent that he rejected the inevitability of humans both finding themselves and putting themselves in a fallen condition. There is something remarkably natural about the Fall. What, after all, was the initial impetus to the human departure from the Garden? A severe winter, a lengthy drought. These are as natural as the human ability to cope with them. Freedom and perfectibility, remember, are part of the original equipment. When the Solitaires, in order to contend with an occasionally uncooperative Nature, developed primitive technologies and formed tentative alliances, they left the Garden.[33] Thus began the tumble from solitude, simplicity, and ignorance to sociability, complexity, and knowledge. In time, the natural environment and the Solitaire's innate features would create a social milieu that all but guaranteed the birth of *amour-propre*, that obsessive desire for public regard so endemic to modern society that one is tempted to call it *natural*. This, in turn, led to that litany of human sorrows that Rousseau would often rehearse: inequality, greed, envy, hypocrisy, callousness, and cruelty.

To address the question of whether the Fall was necessary in Rousseau's account, we can provisionally isolate three principal causes of the Fall: the natural environment, innate human faculties, and the social environment.

We call natural incidents such as floods and droughts "accidents of nature." Like other common accidents, such as those on our highways, to call them "necessary" seems too strong, while "avoidable" seems too weak. Theoretically they are not necessary, but practically they are inescapable or inevitable. I want to suggest that in Rousseau's narrative the Solitaires' first step out of the Garden was caused, in part, by inevitable accidents of nature. I add the qualifier, "in part," because alone such inevitable accidents as droughts or floods would have simply killed some Solitaires. In order for the natural environment to assist in transforming them, the Solitaires themselves had to have been predisposed to adjust to change. They must have been naturally mutable. Without the freedom to improve, the Solitaires never could have escaped the occasionally harsh and potentially fatal aspects of the natural Garden. Freedom and perfectibility, then, helped pave the way to a new fatality—life in the City. Of perfectibility, for example, Rousseau wrote that "this almost unlimited faculty is the source of all the misfortunes of man; it drags man, over the course of time, out of that original condition . . . it is this faculty—which cultivates through the ages his insights and his errors, his vices and his virtues—that makes him at length a tyrant over himself and over nature."[34] With the gift of perfectibility, then, Nature set up the Solitaires as creatures capable of escaping its Garden and becoming its master. This progress, however, eventually led the Solitaires to their own self-imposed slavery. Consequently, Rousseau managed to render ambiguous one of the Enlightenment's more crystalline tenets, faith in progress.

Some theologians claim that free will accounts for Adam and Eve's fall. Free will alone, however, cannot sufficiently explain why the first couple chose evil. If their wills were good and if they were surrounded only by the good, free will would yield only good choices. Hence the need for the serpent: evil must present itself as an option—as a good option in disguise. In Rousseau's Garden, however, there is no serpent—no moral evil. Yet the Fall occurs, and Rousseau must account for it. We have said that the faculty of freedom alone is not an adequate explanation, for in the absence of evil or a serpent, evil is not an option. We could say that severe winters and summers were a source of physical evil, and freedom's response to physical evil led the Solitaires out of the Garden. Presumably, at the end of such natural hardships as long winters and droughts, the early humans could have chosen to return to their Garden. With freedom alone, the Fall is neither inevitable nor fully comprehensible.

For a more adequate account, Rousseau would have us add to freedom the faculty of perfectibility. The very name of this faculty conveys all the irony and tragedy that Rousseau had in mind when he reflected on the human fallen condition. With this faculty humans are driven to perfect their virtue and vice, their art and war, their humanity and cruelty. We may well doubt the plausibility of such an innate faculty; do we not know people who appear not the least bit driven "to perfect" themselves? However, we cannot doubt that Rousseau had need of the concept when he rejected original sin. Civilization had marched forward and would continue in that direction—onward to greater heights and depths—until perhaps by some catastrophic event it would be reduced to some earlier primitive stage and begin anew its forward march.

It is seldom understood that Rousseau rendered the gift of freedom as ambiguous as that of perfectibility. The paradox of Rousseau, the champion of liberty, recommending that some be "forced to be free" seems less paradoxical when it is understood that, in his view, most spontaneously forge their own chains, and hence a wise republic may force the removal of painful shackles from the feet of benighted fellow citizens. Outside the Garden, then, most freely choose shackles. Yet if freedom brought only misery, there would be nothing ambiguous about it. Through freedom we can save ourselves from natural and social disasters, we can endeavor to be moral, and we can find joy in our spontaneity and choices. Its darker side, however, is not to be missed. In Rousseau's view, we choose to perfect our wickedness and misery more than our goodness and joy. In fact, our poor choices occur with such regularity that one might doubt whether in fact we are free to escape such a fate. Bad choices cannot be necessary, for that would suggest that humans are in a state analogous to original sin; Rousseau spurned that Christian dogma by declaring, if only twice, that "man is naturally good." Still, there can be no denying that humans, in Rousseau's own account, consistently choose to fall. They choose to leave the Garden and, eventually, to migrate to the City. This journey may be slow for some civilizations, fast for others, but all seem destined to reach the City.

The Solitaires' first step out of the Garden, then, was inevitable, given the likelihood of natural calamities and the Solitaires' own innate ability to cope with them. More-over, the Solitaires became social rather gracefully in the first four tumbles of the Fall, moving from nature's careless shove to the joint deer hunts, and then from the gentle familial associations to the Second Garden's cautious neighborhoods. Although these early tumbles into the social are in the direction of the City, Rousseau was torn between his infatuation with the Solitaire and his fantasy for simple, relatively harmless human community. He explicitly called stage four of the Fall "the happiest epoch," "the best for humans."[35] Apparently change, history, and the social are not pure evil, for between the first and the Second Garden (stage four) the distance is vast. By the time we reached the Second Garden, the Solitaires were unrecognizable. They had become sociolinguistic humans living in community. Much had happened since the days of the Garden, and yet each change appeared natural, inevitable, and even salutary.

I am not suggesting that, in Rousseau's account, the human race experienced unambiguous progress as it advanced through the first four stages. Much was lost: with each stage, human cares multiplied. Increasingly there was more anxiety and labor, less tranquility and simplicity. These losses Rousseau never belittled. Nonetheless, the early stages of the Fall cannot be characterized as an unswerving downward path. As we move in Rousseau's narrative from an ideal (in the Weberian sense) private life to an idealized associational life, good things come from the changes. The neighborhood of the Second Garden exemplifies a cautious sociability that, theoretically, combines the invulnerability of independent family life with the joy of community life. It is here, at a middle stage of the Fall, in the middle of history, that we discover Rousseau attempting to dodge tension between the private and public by portraying an ideal family life delicately situated in a setting that is neither intensely private, like the Garden, nor fiercely public, like the City.

The precariousness of this balancing act, however, is a measure of Rousseau's grasp of the difficulties of such a dodge. The hope of reconciling the public and private life that the Second Garden might have offered dims considerably in the shadow of the next stage—the plunge down the chute of *amour-propre*. In the short run, the fragile neighborhood of the Second Garden could have fallen either toward the private, breaking into disparate pieces, or toward the public, tightening gradually into an economically, socially, and psychologically entwined knot. In the long run, however, it must progress toward the public, toward the City. Perfectibility would not permit the families to continue with subsistence farming when an increased division of labor offered the chance of economic growth and material betterment. More important, *amour-propre*, once kindled, is almost impossible to extinguish. It ensured that humans inhabit ever-larger public arenas in which to distinguish themselves. The chute of *amour-propre* secured the procession to the City.

I have claimed that, all things considered, the first tumbles of the Fall appear quite natural; can this be said of the chute as well? Recall the circumstances of that fatal plunge. As they sang and danced, people noticed each other: "Whoever sang or danced best . . . came to be the most highly regarded; and this was the first step toward inequality and at the same time toward vice."[36] I have identified this as the saddest episode of Rousseau's bleak narrative. From social festivity came the misery that springs from making comparisons—inequality, envy, contempt, and cruelty. The innocent origins of the plunge, a public fête, serves to underscore the tragedy of the event. The trip off the narrow ledge may seem accidental, but as long as there is singing and dancing, such falls are inescapable. The tragedy lies not in a contingent but an ineluctable aspect of human existence: social interaction opens avenues to both joy and grief. How, after all, were the inhabitants of the Second Garden to avoid their fate? By forbidding singing and dancing? by prohibiting making comparisons, or at least potentially destructive ones, such as the recognition that she can count better than I, or that his hair is fairer than mine? The prospect of policing such thoughts sounds absurd, because making comparisons is a natural human activity.[37] Rousseau highlighted its naturalness, even its innocence, by tracing its source and its fatal consequences to a simple outdoor public festivity, the very kind that he himself would soon espouse in his *Letter to M. d'Alembert*.

Surprisingly, it seems that the plunge down the chute of *amour-propre* is as natural and inevitable as are the initial tumbles of the Fall. There are still no serpents to blame for the fall into tumultuous sociability, only natural occurrences like droughts, innate human features like freedom, and predictable developments like making comparisons and acquiring an imagination. *Amour-propre* itself appears natural insofar as it is endemic in humans who gather together, and such gathering now seems all but inescapable.[38] Insofar as a serpent does arise in Rousseau's narrative, its name is *amour-propre*. Although *amour-propre* is the result of innocent changes—an innocuous history—it is the cause of colossal misfortune. Above, on the ledge of the Second Garden, the serpent is not recognized as a serpent, and that, in part, confers its credentials: it seemed so innocent. Below, at the bottom of the chute, where human frames are broken and disfigured, the serpent sheds its disguise, and we see it for what it is: our own heart, rendered avaricious and violent by our neglect of the gentle ways of *amour de soi* and *pitié*. The calm passions of the Solitaires are replaced by chaotic ones as the advanced human renders homage to its new god—a self within that no longer offers equanimity and guilelessness but demands public esteem and the opportunity to exhibit derisive contempt. The old self marked by *amour de soi* is sacrificed to the new self driven by *amour-propre*.

As we move from the plunge to the ruse to the age of slavery, stages five through seven of the Fall, *amour-propre* becomes increasingly powerful, pestilent, and dictatorial. In its image society is increasingly shaped, and the chances of escaping its reach diminish accordingly. By the time we reach the bottom of the chute, the nature of the tragedy has changed. The slip off the ledge was inevitable, yet many choices on the way down were short-sighted, stupid, and avoidable. Much of the suffering, then, was self-inflicted, for even if it was impossible to avoid the initial effects of *amour-propre*, much could have been done to safeguard against its more damaging and damning sway. Not only was next to nothing done, but most freely traded the goods of *amour de soi* for those of *amour-propre* as fast as they could.

Before the plunge, we saw that the march in the direction of the City was all but necessary. All but necessary because while no feature like original sin made the tumbles ontologically necessary, the tumbles were highly predictable under the circumstances. It is logically possible to flip a coin for an hour and get only heads, for there is no necessity built into the universe that demands tails from any given toss. Yet inevitably, in practice, tails will turn up. So with the Solitaires. Their tumbles were not logically necessary, but empirically inevitable or highly predictable (and the predictable is often a standard of the natural). Nature, in Rousseau's account, grants freedom; that freedom, ironically, guarantees certain outcomes, including the initial turn toward the City. At no point, however, is human choice determined by an absolute internal or external necessity. Even when we are most tempted to say of a phenomenon such as the development of iron, "That was inescapable," Rousseau desperately adds some contingency—

in this case, the eruption of a volcano.[39] Unlike many of his peers, Rousseau resisted rigid determinism. This becomes increasingly clear as the narrative of the Fall unfolds. During the procession of the first four stages, all we saw appeared unstoppable; during the last three stages, Rousseau announced louder and louder, "It could have been otherwise."[40] The narrative moves from steady inevitability to wobbly autonomy. In spite of the odds stacked against us—weak wills in the face of *amour-propre*—we could have done better, and we are thus held responsible for what we have created: petty selves and corrupt societies. Some of the evil, no doubt, was inescapable. But much of it was not, and for that we are held culpable.

Before I explore in some detail issues pertaining to the nature of evil and the assignment of culpability, I want to exonerate what, in Rousseauean scholarship, have become the standard suspects as the perpetrators of evil, namely, change, history, and society. Starobinski, for example, puts his case quite bluntly when he claims that "Rousseau does not believe in hell, but he does believe that change is evil. . . . Rousseau needs history only in order to explain evil. It is the idea of evil that gives his system its historical dimension." Shklar claims that Rousseau believed "change was the proof of the imperfection of all human life. . . . [Change] was at all times a source of suffering."[41] These interpretations, while not without merit, do not do justice to Rousseau's nuanced account of the Fall. Our close reading has disclosed that it is not change per se, but particular changes that are lamentable. Starobinski and many others associate change and history with the artificial, and then they declare the artificial to be evil and the natural to be good. Yet we have seen that the case is not so categorical. When Rousseau ascribed perfectibility to humans as a natural faculty, he implicitly declared history a natural human milieu. For, what flows from perfectibility if not the creation of change, that is, history? Our exploration of the Fall has led us to conclude that Rousseau did not consider change in and of itself to be synonymous with evil. It is, rather, a natural product of a natural human feature. We have also seen that society per se is not evil, for Rousseau depicted social conditions in which humans were happy with themselves and with the world around them. I will develop this claim when I discuss the relation between the public and private life in part II. But for now, I need to explore the nature of evil and human culpability in the context of a fall that begins with practical inevitability and ends with limited autonomy.

Evil: Physical and Moral

The Fall proceeds from a Garden where evil is exclusively physical—pain and hunger, droughts and storms—to a City where the dominant evil is moral evil. If we take physical evil as *unavoidable harm*, and moral evil as *unnecessary harm*, then we again confront the tragedy of Rousseau's account of the Fall and our fallen condition. The inevitable suffering of the Garden was restricted, bounded by nature's limits; the avoidable suffering of the City, in contrast, is unlimited, fueled by boundless desires. As humans become social, their capacity for joy and morality increases in proportion to their chance of encountering evil, both moral and physical. Outside the Garden, not only is there a new form of evil, moral evil, but the forms of physical evil multiply. This is because social humans, unlike the Solitaires, can suffer from such natural—inevitable—human limits as imperfect communication and the resulting painful misunderstandings. (The Solitaires, in their simplicity, were more transparent than the inhabitants of the City, but in the absence of social relations, such transparency amounts to little.) As my argument unfolds, we will see that just as the line between the inevitable and the escapable is often fine, so is the distinction between physical and moral evil. In such cases, assigning moral culpability becomes difficult, as does finding remedies to ease our pain in the fallen condition. For the moment, however, our purposes are better served by starting with a less ambiguous case.

To illustrate moral evil, the earthquake of 1755 that killed twenty thousand people in Lisbon might not seem like an ideal, or an unambiguous, example. Typically earthquakes fall under the heading of "acts of God," that is, events outside human control. Surely the quake that shook Lisbon works best as an illustration of physical—unavoidable—evil. Yet it is precisely this example that Rousseau employed to depict moral evil. "Admit," Rousseau wrote to Voltaire, "that nature did not assemble there twenty thousand houses of six to seven stories high, and that if the inhabitants of that great city had been scattered more equally, and housed more modestly, the damage would have been a lot less, and perhaps none at all." To make matters still worse, the inhabitants, instead of fleeing at the first tremble, "insisted on staying by the wreckage, exposing themselves to after shocks, because what is left behind is valued more than what one can take away."[42] The loss at Lisbon, then, counts as an instance of moral evil because it was so unnecessary. It could have been otherwise; much harm was avoidable.

Insofar as harm is unnecessary, humans are culpable: "I do not see that one can look for the source of moral evil other than in man, free, perfected, yet corrupted." Again, Rousseau smuggled tragedy into his account. It is a free and improved humanity that finds itself uniquely capable of producing moral evil. Rousseau rarely spoke as the misanthrope who delights in displaying human folly and grief; more often he played the social critic who highlights the tragic for the sake of reform. Hence Rousseau insisted to Voltaire that his "goal in depicting human misery was excusable and even laudable . . . for [he] showed men how they themselves brought about their misfortunes, and consequently how they could evade them."[43]

Earlier I claimed that in Rousseau's view, suffering is the worst thing. I would now like to revise that to read, *unnecessary* suffering is the worst thing. With respect to physical evil, Rousseau's stance was always rather stoic: the happy and virtuous soul recognizes and accepts that life entails natural limits and misfortunes. Moral evil, in contrast, is to be despised and avoided in every circumstance. Recognizing the assorted ways that we cause gratuitous harm reveals how perverse we have become, but it also exposes some grounds for hope; while we cannot hope to evade physical evil, there is a chance we can, to some degree, mitigate moral evil. This news, however, is not particularly heartening when we recall the long genealogy of uniformly poor choices that paved the way to the City. We can take the natural maxim, "Do good to yourself with as little harm as possible to others," as a minimal test of those choices. We fail the test rather miserably, in Rousseau's view, for we injure others unnecessarily and in the process neglect to be good even to ourselves. As I mentioned in chapter 1, the elevated level of suffering in the City as compared to life in the Garden resulted not simply from a missing equilibrium between one's desires and powers, but from attempting to gratify the wrong kinds of needs—those which are prone to breed needless pain.

The fine line that we have seen between the inevitable and the accidental nature of the Fall marks the tension between moral fatalism and freedom. Within the tension between fate and freedom, much human conduct takes place. Rousseau never wavered in holding us responsible for the harm that we needlessly inflict. Yet his description of the Fall and our fallen condition portrayed the individual both as an oppressor and as oppressed. This does not excuse humanity for the harm it has spawned. Moreover, while all roam the continuum between inevitable and avoidable fallenness, some spend more or less time nearer one pole or the other. This describes the difference between victims, whose suffering comes principally from the hands of others and whose chance at happiness is denied by others, and oppressors, who willfully injure others and whose culpability is patent. Yet most of us, most of the time, find ourselves in both positions, as those who torment and who are tormented.

The pain we receive and inflict, then, is often on the boundary between the avoidable and the inescapable, on the threshold between moral and physical evil. We find ourselves both destined and free to commit evil, to cause injury. This aspect of the tragedy makes culpability difficult to determine, since we cannot be held blameworthy for that which is beyond our control. This is especially true of the *structural evil* that Rousseau frequently depicted—suffering at the "hands" of corrupt, callous institutions. Most of the time, however, Rousseau held us responsible either because we chose to make a bad situation worse or because we allowed ourselves to enter circumstances that placed severe limits on our freedom to avoid causing harm. Perhaps we are now trapped and unable to flee moral evil, but we have, to a large extent, fashioned the snare ourselves and, hence, have ourselves to blame.

This complex and uncomfortable position in which we find ourselves trapped— helpless, yet responsible—is tersely expressed by Rousseau's theological and anthropological declaration, placed in the mouth of God, "I made you too weak to leave the abyss, because I made you strong enough not to fall into it."[44] That we could have avoided the abyss can be supported empirically, in Rousseau's view, by looking at present alternatives to the corrupt City: Geneva, the temperate city; Valais, the home to simple mountain folk; solitude, the retreat from tumult. Rousseau presented these alternatives, ranging from the more public to the more private, both to condemn and to encourage us. For, they implicitly announce that it could have been otherwise and still can be. No one is absolutely fated to live in the City; it is exceedingly difficult but not impossible to break out. Of his own escape from Paris Rousseau was always rather proud.

No matter where we go, however, we cannot dodge physical evil. Although the inhabitants of Lisbon could have escaped much harm had they not zealously followed the path to the City, an earthquake can hurt even those who dwell modestly in the country. Rousseau's painful and humiliating urinary disorder accompanied him in and out of the City. The inevitable pain that nature brings to us is a natural condition of life; to refuse to accept this is bound to bring more, not less, suffering. The experimental and often painful practices of the medical profession became for Rousseau a symbol of Europeans' refusal to accept natural limits and of the distress that accompanies that denial, especially the denial of death.[45] Rousseau never doubted that nature is well-ordered. Yet nature, like God, operates independently of our personal wishes. When lightning strikes, when cancer spreads, when wind devastates, the particulars of our lives run up against a harmonious, indifferent nature. If such disasters are not exacerbated by human folly, we have unambiguous examples of physical evil.

Many painful events, however, appear to be an admixture of moral and physical evil. In these cases the line between inevitable and avoidable harm is a fine one. Earlier I referred to the natural aspects of the Fall as those incidents that seemed unavoidable, for example, when droughts and severe winters shoved the Solitaires out of the Garden. This is a clear-cut case of physical evil. Yet what of the Solitaires' decision not to return to the Garden and the pain that issued from that decision? This would seem to be an instance of moral evil, since human volition was involved. Yet Rousseau's account of the Fall suggests that the Solitaires, at this point, were in fact *driven* by the innate faculty of perfectibility to continue on the trail out of the Garden. Is this, then, a case of physical evil, since a *natural* faculty played a decisive role in rendering the departure irrevocable? It would seem that in both the earthquake of Lisbon and the departure from the Garden, we discover a commingling of moral and physical evil.

Evil, then, is frequently the result of a combination of poor choices and nature's decrees. When social humans confront natural limits, they are often inspired to beget unnecessary harm. When the Solitaires encountered such natural limits as disease or aging, only two forms of physical evil ensued, pain and hunger. All this changes for social humans. The manifestations of evil that now spring from a confrontation with nature's limits are myriad, because humans outside the Garden possess a multitude of needs subject to frustration. An incident from Rousseau's childhood illustrates how confronting a natural obstacle can yield a species of suffering that fuses the inevitable and the accidental. When Rousseau was twelve years old and living in Bossey (outside Geneva), he was accused by M. and Mlle Lambercier, his guardians, of breaking a comb that had been drying on a stove top. After Jean-Jacques "stubbornly maintained" his innocence, lying was added to the original charge, and he was punished for both offenses. Fifty years later Rousseau maintained his innocence ("I declare before Heaven that I was not guilty") and claimed that this event "ended the serenity" of his childhood ("from that moment I never again enjoyed pure happiness"). Immediately after the event, nothing about his situation at Bossey, in terms of appearances, had changed. In reality, however, everything was now different. Like Adam after the Fall, "still in the Garden yet ceasing to enjoy it," the young Jean-Jacques saw his old, idyllic world in a painful, new light.[46]

It is not surprising that Maurice Cranston describes this incident as the "result of an unjust accusation."[47] After all, Rousseau was innocent. Still, a close reading of the passage suggests that the accusation itself was warranted, and that Rousseau's suffering was largely the result of a natural misconception. It is remarkable that in this dramatic tale of paradise lost, Rousseau inserted no demonic or evil character. Rather than employing the archetypal motif of an innocent suffering at the hands of the wicked, as, for example, Charles Dickens's portrayal of the young David Copperfield in the grip of Mr. Murdstone, Rousseau went to great lengths to depict the legitimacy of the charges against him. At the outset of his account of the broken comb affair, Rousseau asked, "Who was to be blamed for this? I was the only person who had been in the room." The Lamberciers took the incident seriously—"as it deserved," Rousseau interjected. There is no suggestion that they had overreacted. Lying, after all, is a serious matter. I do not mean to blunt the image of the guileless Jean-Jacques "suffering a most grave injustice at the hands of the people he loves best and most deeply respects." I do want to suggest, however, that the "grave injustice" was not a case of unadulterated moral evil caused by the callousness of the Lamberciers. When Rousseau the adult pondered the event, he concluded that, as a twelve-year-old, "I had not yet sufficient reasoning power to realize the extent to which appearances were against me, to put myself in my elders' position." The evidence was against him, and there was no other theory to account for it. Even as an adult Rousseau was baffled by what had happened to the comb: "I have no idea, and I cannot understand it."[48]

This tragic episode, it would seem, was not a case of the young Jean-Jacques confronting a disordered, cruel world whose wicked social nature was radically antithetical to natural goodness, as some commentators imply.[49] Jean-Jacques ran up against a natural, human limit. We cannot read each other's minds, at least not perfectly. We have no surefire way to distinguish in every case between truth-telling and lying. This is the consequence of an epistemological limit that becomes manifest only in the context of autonomous agents who can choose to withhold, distort, or fabricate information. The Solitaires, by definition, could not have suffered from a natural limit that manifests itself principally in social circumstances. To imagine a radically private existence is to envision a self isolated, mute, and without needs that require truth or lies from the lips of others. Jean-Jacques, in contrast, as a social creature, suffered because he loved and was thereby susceptible to the disappointment and pain that is endemic to human finitude. He was misapprehended. His love for the Lamberciers was not the only aspect of the episode that accounts for his distress; it was, however, the one that Rousseau chose to highlight. That love was perhaps betrayed; the Lamberciers no doubt could have handled the incident more wisely, perhaps even more lovingly. Yet parents and guardians of goodwill often scold their children in the name of love to keep them from harm's way or for the sake of future moral development. And good parents make mistakes. That much is ineluctable, and that is what I am drawing to our attention; just as there is something quite natural—quite inevitable—about the events of the Fall, so here, too, in this dramatic turning point in the life of the young Jean-Jacques, natural inevitability plays a central role.

Immediately after his trial and punishment, Jean-Jacques "gave up tending [his] little gardens, the herbs and flowers." He left the Garden and entered a world divided into two distinct spheres—one public, the other private, with the bridge between them carefully guarded. Previously, his undivided world at Bossey had been marked by intimacy. There had been no monitored border between a public and a private domain because the two had yet to be defined or developed. In the comfortable world of a child, the division has no place: familiarity and candidness know no bounds (hence children's unique ability to embarrass their parents in public). When Jean-Jacques's world was shattered, "the ties of intimacy and confidence" were slashed. The Lamberciers were no longer as "gods who read" his heart. In turn, he closed his heart to them, became "secretive," and began "to lie." He thus joined an intricate world in which individuals hide much of themselves by donning a variety of masks, often misrepresenting themselves in order to manipulate the outward, public order. Once initiated to such complex practices, Jean-Jacques ceased to be at ease in the Garden; he "no longer went out to scratch gently the soil and shout with joy at discovering a sprout from one of the seeds he had sown."[50]

His departure from the Garden, however, was as inevitable as the germination of one of the countless seeds sown. Growth was bound to occur. It could have occurred less painfully; hence moral evil—unnecessary harm—is a feature of the broken-comb episode. Nonetheless, pain resulting from misunderstanding is inevitable, and hence physical evil—unavoidable suffering—is also present. If the line between them is fine, it is because there emerges from Rousseau's account of the Fall and fallenness an elusive yet incessant tension between the accidental and the necessary.

Perhaps nature could have ushered the Solitaires out of the Garden more gently, but the parting itself was inexorable. If nature plays such a salient role in turning us toward the social, can the gap between the natural and the social be as wide in Rousseau's thought as it is usually portrayed by his interpreters and, on occasion, even by Rousseau himself? Again we discover that if we identify categorically the natural with the good and the social with evil, we fail to do justice to Rousseau's nuanced account of our passage from the Garden to the City.

Even so, in Rousseau's saga, as humans continue on the path to the City, they exercise more and more autonomy and increasingly become the authors of their own pain. With each step toward the City, moral evil advances disproportionately compared to physical evil. Tension between the two, however, persists, and to account for this we now turn our attention to Rousseau's struggle with two sets of vocabularies, or two world views, that of Christian pessimism and Enlightenment optimism.

6

Overcoming Moral Evil

Rousseau at the Crossroads

Soteriology: Can We Save Ourselves?

Rousseau is often celebrated or cursed as an exemplar Enlightenment *philosophe* who declared that although humans are naturally good, society tampers with us and thereby corrupts us. Although Rousseau's complex and even contradictory writings engender disagreement among his interpreters, all seem to agree that Rousseau spurned any notion of original sin—of innate corruption—and that he blamed corrupt, irrational social institutions for the majority of our miseries.[1] I will argue, however, that this standard interpretation of Rousseau's account of evil is too facile. Rousseau positioned himself at the crossroads of Enlightenment and Augustinian thought, and this awkward position enabled him to produce a rich and complex view on the nature of evil and human culpability. We will see that, in Rousseau's view, humans *naturally* gather and court harm and that, in spite of this pessimism, Rousseau could also optimistically declare God's creation and human existence to be good.

    Ernst Cassirer claimed that "the concept of original sin is the common opponent against which all the different trends of the philosophy of the Enlightenment join forces. In this struggle Hume is on the side of English deism, and Rousseau on the side of Voltaire."[2] This statement would ring more true had Cassirer limited his claim to the name, not the concept, of original sin. For such *philosophes* as Rousseau in France and Immanuel Kant in Prussia retained aspects of the concept of original sin even as they denounced that doctrine by name.[3] Still, like all decent caricatures, the caricature of Enlightenment hope in progress exaggerates an authentic feature, a pervasive optimistic faith; this faith clearly clashed with the pessimistic Augustinian assessment of humans marked by original sin. Enlightenment hope had more to do with the sacred texts of Plato and the humanists than those of Saint Paul and Augustine.[4] The Platonic notion that virtue is knowledge and vice is ignorance seemed to sanction the *philosophes'* commitment to bring prosperity, well-being, and goodwill to European societies by means of enlightenment. Never mind that this portrait of Platonic good and evil conveniently overlooked the crooked, insolent dark horse that, according to Plato's *Phaedrus*, constitutes one-third of the human soul.[5] Such details were not to dampen the hope for the eradication of evil by the illumination of knowledge. This generation had seen Europe ravaged by war and cruelty at the hands of superstition, fanaticism, and tyranny. It would cling tightly to the belief that the light of Reason could guide Europe out of its darkness.

This belief carried with it a view of human nature that conflicted with Augustinian Christian anthropology. Augustine held that humans cannot cure themselves of sin or evil. The disposition to sin—an impaired will unable to order and pursue one's loves properly—is acquired at birth and remains until death, or longer if one is not fortunate enough to be among the elect. Original sin, simply put, is fatal. It is invasive and, in terms of human effort, irreversible. Baptism can wash away the guilt inherited from Adam, but the will remains disfigured. Only upon death can the will of the elect become perfectly restored and free, that is to say, unable to will anything but the good. The nuances of Augustine's doctrine of original sin need not delay us here. For our purposes, the central issue is the declaration that since Adam, humans are only free to sin, variously. This sums up the contest between Enlightenment optimism and Augustinian pessimism, for it insists that no measure of enlightenment can rid humans of a deep-seated proclivity to beget disordered lives that wound the individual and the community. Should society offer a better education, for example, this would simply enhance its citizens' ability to sin in a more erudite or sophisticated fashion; should society curtail poverty, this would simply permit more citizens to sin more affluently. Social engineering alters the range of possible sins, not the sinful condition itself.

If we were to characterize the contest between the Platonic and the Augustinian positions as answers to the question, "What can we do to save ourselves?" the Augustinian response would be "Not a thing"; the Platonic, "Quite a bit." The debate between these broad positions have played themselves out in history in various ways. Pelagius, a peer of Augustine, held that Adam's sin stayed with Adam, and that the human will is not fatally impaired. This denial of the transmission of original sin affirms the human ability to will the good and hence, in some measure, to save oneself—at the very least to be willing to avail oneself of God's grace. Since Augustine and Pelagius, cultures influenced by Christianity have never been entirely free from a debate that positions Plato at one end, Augustine at the other, and Pelagius somewhere in between. In the sixteenth century, the debate set at odds Renaissance humanists and Protestant reformers, especially Lutherans and Calvinists. Sides were firmly drawn after the famous contest between Erasmus of Rotterdam and Martin Luther. Erasmus had argued that the will is free and able to turn to God, prompting Luther to insist that the will is in bondage to sin and therefore unable to direct itself toward God. Erasmus, in other words, held that human nature, originally good, is intact to the degree that one can do something to save oneself. Luther, in contrast, maintained that human nature is utterly distorted by sin and thus deliverance is exclusively an act of God.

Although Renaissance humanism was by no means a monolithic tradition, it was generally Pelagian; hence, like Platonism it occupies a prominent place in that wide genealogy of optimism that sustained the Enlightenment hope that humans can do something to improve themselves. The Reformation, in contrast, reintroduced to Europe the full force of Augustinian pessimism, culminating in Calvin's doctrine of double predestination, a doctrine that declares humans to be perfectly powerless to save themselves. This emphasis on God's work, as opposed to humans', made its way into the

Roman Catholic Counter-Reformation of the sixteenth century. At the Council of Trent, for example, moderates sought to mollify evangelicals by supporting doctrines that subordinated human effort to God's grace. Since then, French intellectual traditions have received and expressed variously the stances of Augustinian pessimism and Pelagian, if not Platonic, optimism.

In the seventeenth century, Augustine was a central figure in French theological and moral thought.[6] His works were widely read, in part due to Montaigne's earlier interest in him, and also to the controversy that had erupted over views held by the Augustinian Jansenists at Port-Royal. The Dutch Roman Catholic theologian and bishop, Cornelius Jansenius, attempted to reform Roman Catholicism by using Augustine as his guide. His posthumous work, *Augustinius* (1640), had managed to offend both political and ecclesiastical authorities. Politically, the work appeared seditious because it condemned the opulence of the government and the wealthy, implicitly advocating a retreat from corrupt secular and political domains. Theologically, the work was suspect because it advanced an extreme form of predestination that was subsequently condemned in two papal bulls. This theological aspect of the work inspired Saint-Cyran, who, continuing the lines of Jansenius's Augustinian pessimism, argued that Adam's descendants inherit a corrupt will which is unable to choose the good.[7]

The Jansenists were not alone in espousing Augustinian pessimism. Neither Camus nor Sénault was a Jansenist, yet they argued that before the Fall, our love was in harmony with God's, but afterward the human soul was torn between two opposing loves, selfish *amour-propre* and selfless *charité*. Anticipating Kant and Freud, this French Augustinian tradition held that these loves cannot be reconciled: the self is destined, after Adam, to be a divided one, barring the mysterious grace of God. Human knowledge and volition are impotent in the face of deep-seated *amour-propre*. In seventeenth-century France, then, theologians and moral philosophers of various Augustinian stripes opposed humanist optimism and the classical notion that knowledge and reason can deliver us from evil.

Yet bleak Augustinianism was not the only mood of the period. Some celebrated a sovereign human will that could soar above instinct and passion and embrace the good. These more optimistic thinkers, such as Descartes, Guez de Balzac, and Le Moyne, rejected Augustinian claims that human goodness is dependent on irrational grace. The Neoplatonic Le Moyne described the will as a "natural monarch" and, rejecting the two-love theory, championed a Platonic neutral love that could be directed toward either higher or lower objects.[8] Such confidence in a free and good will had been nurtured by a robust French humanist tradition, rooted notably in François Rabelais. In contrast to strict Calvinist and austere Roman Catholic views, Rabelais's description in *Gargantua and Pantagruel* of the abbey of Thélème, for instance, acclaimed the goodness of human nature and the joyful spontaneity of *thelema*, the human will.[9] La Boétie, a peer of Rabelais, anticipated aspects of Rousseau's thought when he declared that we are naturally free and good but society has trained us to wear the yoke of slavery, and hence the title of his discourse, *On Voluntary Servitude*.[10] Custom has bent low our free and good human nature, although some, through education and recollection, can still escape much social tyranny.

We can, then, describe sixteenth- and especially seventeenth-century French thought as beset by two opposing traditions, Augustinian pessimism and humanist Enlightenment optimism. Not surprisingly, these traditions were occasionally woven together in the tensive thought of single individuals. Two, in particular, Montaigne and Pascal, who had a tremendous impact on subsequent French thought, particularly on Rousseau, grappled with both traditions and formulated a rich blend of optimism and pessimism concerning human nature and our ability to do something to save ourselves.[11] Montaigne, having been influenced by Augustine, rejected the notion that natural reason could reveal an intrinsic human goodness that promised to bring social prosperity and harmony. The humanists, he believed, had overestimated our ability to discover universal moral principles and had underestimated the depths of human pride and avarice. "The world is ill fitted to cure itself," he once lamented.[12] Following Augustine, Montaigne was convinced that the public realm was marked by conflict, utterly and entirely, and that a semblance of outward peace could be achieved only by an established—and not necessarily "rational"—muscular authority. He did not, however, escape the influence of the humanists, especially that of his dearest friend, La Boétie; rather, Montaigne directed and limited humanist optimism to the private realm. By means of honest introspection and moral effort, the inner kingdom—the domain of the self—can be understood, rationally controlled, and enjoyed. Peace, integrity, and knowledge—these three humanist goals could be achieved in the private life. We cannot cure the world, but as individuals we can do much to cure our own souls. We cannot love the world, but we can love such individuals as we claim as friends. The tension between duty to the public and duty to self—between politics and morals—that marks Montaigne's thought sprang from his standing at the intersection of the two contrary traditions.

Pascal, whom Voltaire referred to as that "sublime misanthrope," never tired of offering litanies of human depravity.[13] His conception of the public world was thoroughly Augustinian: an iniquitous and irrational domain in which force, not reason, supplies order. Human reason, having been vitiated by sin, is incapable of revealing or establishing a natural, harmonious social order. Nonetheless, Pascal's anthropology supports a tensive account of human nature as marked by both prelapsarian goodness and postlapsarian degeneracy. Although we may dwell in the realm of the flesh, we keep a foot, or in some cases a toe, in the empire of intellect and charity. And while salvation is a gift of God, Pascal concurred with the humanists that we can and must do something to receive it; the will secures our readiness to be rescued. A catalyst for such willingness is a recognition of our corruption and limitations. Fallen reason can document our plight and our need for God. Reason reveals reason's limits: "Know then, proud one, what a paradox you are to yourself. . . . Learn that man infinitely surpasses man."[14] The irony of Pascal's having achieved a reputation as a champion of the limits of reason, on the one hand, and of Cartesian, analytic thought on the other, springs from his attempt to navigate between French Augustinianism and humanism.

The Enlightenment, for good reason, is generally associated with humanist optimism. In his superb study on Kant, Gordon Michalson notes that "in many ways, Kant and his Enlightenment peers are devoted to the notion that knowledge is not only power, but virtue as well, and that most of what we call evil in the world can be attributed to the drag effect of a received tradition of priestcraft and illegitimate royal authority." Michalson, however, not satisfied with caricatures, goes on to show that Kant, perhaps unwittingly, was torn between the worlds of Augustinian pessimism and Enlightenment optimism. Yet note the role Rousseau plays in his argument: "For all the influence on

Kant of Rousseau, there is a very clear parting of the ways between the two thinkers on the question of evil. Kant flatly rejects Rousseau's notion that an originally good human nature is corrupted by society, as though culpability resides in something that overrides individual accountability. . . . In playing out the broadly Platonic tradition that associates evil with ignorance . . . Rousseau would turn our attention to our surroundings."[15] I can hardly fault Michalson, in his study on Kant, for not treating Rousseau with as much care as Kant. I can, however, endeavor to provide a portrait of Rousseau as nuanced and complex as Michalson's Kant, specifically on the problem of evil. We have observed in Rousseau's account of the Fall and fallenness a perplexing tension between the accidental and the necessary, between moral and physical evil, between avoidable and inescapable harm. This tension, I will now argue, is the result of Rousseau's efforts to work within the two opposing traditions, Augustinian pessimism and humanist optimism.

Rousseau at the Crossroads

To unravel the tangled knot that Rousseau made of the two traditions, we can begin by noting his affinity and enmity for each. It is commonly claimed, justifiably, that Rousseau rejected original sin. He emphatically stated his opposition to this aspect of the Augustinian tradition in his letter to the Archbishop of Paris, Christophe de Beaumont. "It seems to me that this doctrine of original sin, subject to such terrible difficulties, is not housed in the Scriptures so clearly or so cruelly as the Rhetorician Augustine and our theologians have been pleased to maintain." In contrast to Augustine's dour anthropology, Rousseau offered the Archbishop a happier view: "That man is a being naturally good, a lover of justice and order; that there is no original perversity in the human heart, and that the first movements of nature are always right." Rousseau went on to suggest that the doctrine of original sin is both fatalistic and antisocial, for it implies that God has determined that we be vicious and that we are therefore destined to work against human well-being, inflicting "cruel wounds to humanity." Although Rousseau's argument at this point is truncated at best and botched at worst, this much is clear: if we hold that "man is made for society, the religion most true must also be the most social and the most humane," the doctrine of original sin cannot belong to the truest religion, for it is neither social nor humane.[16]

Here we have a glimpse of Rousseau's affinity with a tenet of humanist and Enlightenment optimism. Humans are social creatures and any creed that insists that we are intrinsically wicked is a doctrine against humanity, against true religion. How, then, are we to account for Rousseau's own long list of indictments against humanity? This brings us to the best known of Rousseau's responses: "Man is good naturally, it is by institutions alone that men become wicked";[17] "Fools who continuously complain of nature, learn that all your trouble comes from yourselves!"[18] This is the message of his first *Discours*, and Rousseau repeated it variously throughout his life. With the declaration that human woe is not principally the result of divine or natural mandates, but of foolish, unjust, and superstitious human institutions, Rousseau joined *philosophes* as diverse as Diderot, d'Holbach, and d'Alembert. This shared creed encouraged many to take heart. If there is no such ontological necessity as original sin that accounts for human misery, that is, if we have contingently created our own grief, then we can do something to heal ourselves. In Rousseau's musings, however, this creed seldom inspired optimism. The discovery that we have freely wrecked ourselves gave him little cause for celebration, for in spite of knowledge or innovation, we remain subject to anomic desires, dashed hopes, impotence, and envy.

Referring to eighteenth-century France, Richard Rorty claims that "utopian politics sets aside questions about both the will of God and the nature of man and dreams of creating a hitherto unknown form of society."[19] As is often his practice, Rorty has skillfully sketched a large canvas with pronounced strokes. Yet the details are troubling. Did utopian politics set aside "questions about both the will of God and the nature of man," or were its dreams a result of some answers to these questions? No doubt by recognizing the contingency of our history and institutions, we may be more willing to entertain novel approaches to public and personal problems that would otherwise remain intractable. And many of Rousseau's peers would have accepted Rorty's tenet that there is a natural, logical connection between on the one hand, the recognition that we alone—without God—have authored our history, and on the other hand, a robust optimism that we will, therefore, create splendid, life-enhancing institutions in the future. Rousseau, however, gave a different response to the recognition that there is no such ontological necessity as original sin or God's will that accounts for human misery. He responded with singular pessimism: we freely injured ourselves in the past, and there is no reason to expect anything different from humans in the future.

Some of Rousseau's generation expressed optimism by maintaining not only that humans are not fundamentally corrupt, but that they are basically good. Rousseau himself, we have seen, on occasion said as much, though not as often as one might think. Moreover, when he did declare that humans are naturally good, he usually meant that humans are not naturally bad. In chapter 2 we discovered this in our study of the Solitaires, and we now find the same in Rousseau's letter to the Archbishop de Beaumont. In the very next sentence, after having asserted that "man is a being naturally good," Rousseau claimed that "the only innate human passion, self-love [*amour de soi*], is a passion indifferent in itself to either good or evil." We cannot be deemed good or bad, Rousseau explained, unless we have a conscience, and we cannot have a conscience until we have experienced relationships. The Solitaire, Rousseau noted to the Archbishop, has no conscience because he has no relationships, no loves: "he neither hates nor loves anything."[20] Humans are naturally good, because in the absence of *amour-propre*, they do no unnecessary harm. Yet once humans find themselves in social relations, their nature becomes more complex and capable of committing good and evil.

Rousseau's rather neutral portrayal of the natural, human moral condition is a departure from much Enlightenment thought. His implicit dismissal of a substantive view of natural human goodness kept him from sharing in many of the sanguine hopes and dreams of his generation. He questioned, moreover, not only his peers' trust in human goodness but in human reason. Ridiculing the idea that "human reason would progress always perfecting itself," as if "each century adds its insights to those of the preceding centuries," Rousseau placed himself at odds with a central dogma of Enlightenment hope.[21] In an important footnote to his *Letter to M. d'Alembert* Rousseau argued that social harmony is more likely to emerge when society is based not on so-called universal reason, but on the recognition that "human reason has no common measure well-defined."[22]

Acknowledging the limits of reason could make us more tolerant and peaceful citizens, for we would be less prone to call irrational those who disagree with our judgments. Rousseau was especially critical of those who applied the abstract flight of reason to bold ventures in social engineering. In a phrase reminiscent of Wittgenstein, Rousseau likened the *philosophes'* grandiose schemes for social reform to the attempt to "push the boat one is in without touching anything outside." Such plans are too theoretical, failing to address the actual conditions of society and its citizens. Should philosophers direct their attention to concrete social circumstances, they would find themselves confronted with "the inclinations of the human heart."[23]

It is here, in the vicinity of the heart, that we discover Rousseau's affinity for Augustinian pessimism. The philosopher's "system is very good for the people of Utopia; it is of no value for the children of Adam." The sons and daughters of Adam are like the prodigal who "*knows* perfectly well that he is ruining himself, yet does not alter at all his direction." After these gloomy biblical references, Rousseau cited Ovid, though it might as well have been Saint Paul or Augustine: "I see and I recognize the better things; I pursue the worse things."[24] Similarly, in *Emile* Rousseau wrote, "I see the good, I love it, and I do the bad."[25] Even if reason could escape its limits and enlighten us, we would still be inclined to harm ourselves and others. Within the breast of the social human, then, lies a *natural proclivity* for evil. The scale here between moral and physical evil is unsteady, for insofar we speak of a *proclivity*, and not a necessity, it tilts toward moral evil; yet insofar as we speak of a *natural* proclivity, it shifts toward physical evil. Alone, as Solitaires, there was no occasion for moral evil, yet as Solitaires we were not truly human. In the company of others, psychological and social complexities—a tangle of predictable personal and public actions and reactions—inevitably emerge and catch us in the latticework of moral and physical evil.

"The first tears of children," Rousseau noted, "are prayers. . . . They soon become orders. . . . Thus from their own weakness, the source of their first feeling of dependence, is born the idea of empire and domination." Thus Rousseau, here in *Emile*, echoed the author of original sin, St. Augustine, when in his *Confessions* he attempted to show that infants give evidence of original sin. Rousseau, however, is not Augustinian but is rather caught between Augustinian pessimism and Enlightenment optimism, and hence in the above passage he immediately added that if one can discern the "secret intention" of the infant, then one can thwart the "idea of empire and domination."[26] He has again, therefore, refused to assign an ontological necessity to evil. Yet to avert evil, here, requires a God-like ability to discern secret intentions—and those of infants no less. Guileless infants, then, are as likely as telepathic tutors.

Social and personal reformation no doubt may spare us some harm. Yet the snare of evil is fundamentally inescapable, and is therefore radical; it becomes rooted in us as we become social creatures. We cannot escape moral evil, then, unless we cast off our social nature. This, however, would entail forsaking our humanity as well.[27] We are again confronted with tragedy. Our misfortunes often seem inevitable, as in a *fated* tragedy, as well as tragically *accidental* and *unnecessary*; things could have turned out better, or we could have done better. Our errors spring from a location somewhere between the ontological necessity supported by Augustinian original sin, and the human autonomy supported by Enlightenment optimism. It is the elusive combination of the two kinds of misery, the inevitable and the unnecessary, that frames the tragic passage out of the amoral Garden to the ambiguous moral progress and precarious human joy of the City.

By alluding to the inscrutability of the heart of social beings, Rousseau placed limits on the aspirations of those who sought, by means of critical reason and knowledge, to save us from ourselves by ourselves. At the crossroads of Augustinian pessimism and Enlightenment optimism, Rousseau recast the biblical drama to tell of a Garden inhabited by content, simple creatures whose Fall was neither absolutely necessary nor entirely accidental. To become moral beings, the Garden's creatures had to eat of the tree of the knowledge of good and evil. Yet to leave the Garden is to embrace travail, moral struggle amid social complexity. In this trial, the hand of God is not available to guide us, though the limited voice of Nature, that is, of conscience, can assist us.[28] Unlike the biblical narrative, in Rousseau's account, history is not a linear path from the Garden through the abyss to God's final redemption. And, unlike what we usually identify as the Enlightenment view, history is not the shedding of error, the accumulation of knowledge, that promises progress and emancipation. More like Freud, Rousseau often thought the most we could hope for is the transformation of profound misery into common, everyday unhappiness. Yet also like Freud, Rousseau could not offer satisfactory explanations for the inevitable struggle lodged in the breast of moral beings. To describe what he observed, Freud eventually turned to mythology, conjuring the image of Bios and Thanatos in battle. Rousseau, in contrast, turned to a biblical narrative, reconstructing it for his own purposes.

Rousseau's explanations are not satisfactory, for he failed to give an account for why we inevitably harm ourselves and others. Yet perhaps, in this case, the explanation is the description. Perhaps Rousseau's nuanced depiction of the path from the Garden to the City is a useful account of much contemporary public and personal misery. From it we learn, among other things, that the more we advance toward the City, the more freedom we exercise and the more damage we cause. This aspect of the explanation of our present woe—namely, that it is self-incurred—belongs, ironically, perhaps more to the humanist than the Augustinian tradition. For in the Augustinian view, we are not free not to sin; we are fated to sin, albeit variously. In the humanist view, we are free to do something to save ourselves, and hence, by implication, when we freely harm ourselves, we exercise a robust, humanist free will. There is, then, a subtle shift in Rousseau's account as the tragic aspect of the narrative moves from the fated to the unnecessary, declaring, we could have done better. Rousseau seemed to think that by highlighting our responsibility for our own joy and sorrow we might seek to become more like the simple folk of the Valais or the disciplined citizens of Geneva who experience more joy than pain because their worlds are less complex, more transparent.

This brings us, however, to the other lesson set in Rousseau's depiction of the path from the Garden and to the City; utopia is not a human option. This is due to the empirical inevitability of moral and physical evil. In the *Confessions*, Rousseau noted that "we are so little made for happiness here below that of necessity either the soul or the body must suffer, if they do not both suffer, and the good state of the one almost always causes harm to the other."[29] Common, much less utopian happiness is not a likely human possibility. Rousseau has often been placed in the category of revolutionary utopians. This springs from an exclusive preoccupation with *The Social Contract*, and even that work, it could be argued, makes more sense as a condemnation of existing states than as a blueprint for new ones. The blueprint that Rousseau did provide us, *The Government of Poland*, reads like a pragmatic survival guide for endangered nations—hardly utopian.

On occasion *Emile* as well is read as a utopian tract for private transformation. But that interpretation disregards the sequel to *Emile*, namely, *Les Solitaires*. One might have thought that *Les Solitaires* would have gathered up and set before us abundant fruits of labor of Emile's extraordinary god-like tutor. Instead we find Emile taking Sophia, his wife, to "the City" (the first of many mistakes) and, becoming absorbed in his work, Emile neglects Sophie. In the end, Sophie becomes pregnant with another man's child, and Emile abandons his family and eventually is captured as a slave in Algeria. Although at this conclusion Emile declares himself free—free from the anomic desires of *amour-propre*—his glorious education has permitted him to be free only as a slave.

My reference here to *The Social Contract*, *Emile*, and *Les Solitaires* is meant to underscore what I am calling the second lesson found on the path from the Garden to the City: the inevitability of moral evil casts aside utopian aspirations. Along with Augustine and Pascal, Rousseau held that humans consistently fall short of replete human goodness and flourishing. Recognition of human limits is perhaps one of the highest accomplishments of our limited condition. In part II we take up the subject of Rousseau's remedies for our fallen condition and will discover that the cures are partial and provisional. For now it is enough to note that at the crossroads Rousseau, like Janus, gazed in two directions at the same time, or at least in rapid succession. In one direction, Rousseau beheld humans as naturally innocent and able to be content; in the other, he perceived humans as inevitably destructive and destined for immense suffering.

Sometimes Rousseau, perhaps aware of this awkward, cross-eyed vision, tried to straighten out his view by claiming that while the *individual* can experience a measure of purity and happiness, *society* remains corrupt. At such moments Rousseau, like Montaigne before him, hoped that individuals could cultivate a virtuous private life in spite of the detrimental influences of immoral society.[30] Yet Rousseau could not consistently hold this position, for he often thought he perceived an ineluctable penchant for wickedness and misery within the breast of the individual. It could be argued that the evolution of Rousseau's thought between the first and second *Discours* is similar to what happened to Reinhold Niebuhr's thought between his *Moral Man and Immoral Society* and the book he later said he should have written, "Immoral Man and Immoral Society."[31] Reflecting on Rousseau's famous line, "Man is naturally good," Starobinski asks, "Has that natural goodness been lost forever? Yes, if we are looking at man in society; no, if we are looking at individuals. Evil is not in human nature but in social structures."[32] Rousseau, however, never abandoned either his belief that humans are not naturally corrupt or his belief that humans do inevitably corrupt themselves. He held both views, tensely. Often the face Rousseau presented was determined by whom he faced. To the Archbishop Beaumont, Rousseau was a *philosophe* (as well as "a sincere Christian"!) attacking the doctrine of original sin. To the *philosophe* Mirabeau, he was a pessimistic Augustinian assailing the doctrine of progress.

We can account for Rousseau's double vision by locating him at the crossroads of Augustinian pessimism and Enlightenment optimism. His proximity to both traditions probably blocked his perception of his entanglement with them. I suspect, however, that greater awareness of his historical locality would not have significantly altered his tensive position; Rousseau would still seek to inhabit some juncture from which he could remind us of both our responsibility for ourselves and our powerlessness to radically transform ourselves.

Who Is to Blame?

This awkward position makes assigning culpability problematic. Too often Rousseau's commentators have simply reiterated his tensive stances rather than analytically probe them. Note how Grimsley, a superb Rousseauean scholar, presents Rousseau's position: "Evil is not a genuinely integral part of human nature, one of its original features. Man is naturally good, not wicked. No sane man . . . will do evil for its own sake, and the notion of 'original sin' is dismissed as quite untenable. The wicked man is the one whose natural goodness has been stifled by pride, passion, and selfish reflection; he is the unfortunate victim of a society which makes it very difficult for people to know and follow the inclination of their natural feelings. . . . 'Moral evil' is derived from man's misuse of his freedom."[33] Here Grimsley reliably assembles Rousseau's various stances, but fails to highlight the friction between them. How are we to account for naturally good humans misusing their freedom? If the wicked man's wickedness is the result of his having been victimized by society, then is he culpable for his evil? What does it mean to blame society? Can we pronounce the individuals in society innocent and the society itself corrupt?

Grimsley is not alone in restating Rousseau's views on evil without wrestling sufficiently with the tensions between them. Starobinski poses the salient question but fails to give an adequate reply: "If man is naturally good, how did he become wicked? He became wicked because he surrendered to history. . . . In some mysterious way something between man and his world becomes distorted." Yet is not history, at least in part, the product of human choices and activities? Are humans victims of history per se, or of individuals and groups in history? And what is this "something between man and his world" that mysteriously becomes distorted? Perceiving correctly that Rousseau wanted to keep humans responsible for their woes, Starobinski notes that "the development of [latent] faculties is not inevitable. For Rousseau, there is nothing *necessary* about the transformation of perfectibility into perfection. Man is free to accept or reject, to hasten progress or slow it down."[34] Yet if there is nothing necessary or even inevitable about the human upward march toward vice, why are we only free to hasten or slow it down, and not escape it all together?

I do not mean to imply that in this chapter I have solved the problem of interpreting Rousseau's tensive stances on the nature of evil and human moral accountability. It strikes me, in fact, not as a problem to be solved but a perplexity with which to wrestle. I have come to believe, in this case, that Rousseau's stance is found in the tension between his various positions and that to try to resolve that tension would attenuate a significant aspect of his thought. In the Garden, we are content and amoral. In history, we are moral beings who ineluctably suffer, gratuitously wounding ourselves. We are no more victims of history or society than we are of morality itself; history and society are the conditions of our moral development, for better for worse. The tense structure of our moral existence is indicative of our capacity for virtue and vice. While there is no ontological necessity for our poor choices, as social beings we do suffer from alienating inclinations that lead us to injure ourselves and those around us. This yields the troublesome conclusion that we are accountable for those lamentable choices and actions that were not necessary but that occur inevitably in that tangled web of moral and physical evil. This can be restated less vexatiously: We are culpable for making our fallen condition even worse than it need be. To put it this way, however, is to risk understating the many obstacles that prevent us from escaping circumstances that lead us to inflict unnecessary harm. A more faithful portrayal of Rousseau's account would keep us suspended, anxiously, between an Enlightenment tradition that reminds us of our responsibility for ourselves and ability to heal ourselves and an Augustinian tradition that reminds us of our limits and inability to save ourselves. Between these views, virtue is cast as a cultivation of our powers and an appreciation of our limits that struggles against, but can never conquer, moral evil.

One might well wonder if Rousseau ever offered some sympathy for the human race, in light of his depiction of the suffering endemic to the human fallen condition. Is there no solace for humans who find themselves subject to an amalgam of moral and physical evil, to limited powers and countless hopes, to tragic choices and the perpetual perfectibility of vice and virtue? Rousseau offered little in the way of commiseration, perhaps because he feared that it might prove contrary to human responsibility for social and personal reformation. Moreover he was, I have said, convinced that we make our inescapable difficulties worse than they need be. His attitude toward his own body can be seen as a metaphor of the human confrontation with pain. Jean-Jacques was fated to have a frail, ailing body. Early on he was convinced that he would die young, and this fear, along with physical suffering, led him to seek medical assistance. However, he later came to believe that the medical profession—the artificial tampering with natural, inevitable pain—tends to escalate, not diminish, our suffering. His claim that the Solitaires do not fear death reflects his belief that the fear of death leads to the loss of life, at least quality of life. Unlike the equanimity of the Solitaires, we fight against the ineluctable and thereby cause unnecessary pain.[35] To accept that physical evil and death are endemic to human existence is to turn toward the quietude of the Garden. Resigning ourselves to necessary pain in no way slackens our responsibility to counter unnecessary suffering, moral evil. Rather, acquiescence, in this case, is an aspect of that responsibility.

Reading Jean-Jacques's body as a metaphor of how suffering is intensified in society discloses a thin sympathetic thread in the tangle of Rousseau's thought. It is similar to that theme that Starobinski, Grimsley, and especially Cassirer have identified: Society harms individuals more than nature does. Thus, insofar as we are victims, we are ravaged principally by society, not nature. Indeed, Rousseau insisted that "a man who lives ten years without doctors, lives more for himself and for others, than one who lives thirty years as their victim."[36] Rousseau's sympathy, here, is expressed in the vocabulary of victimization. Having hoped, innocently enough, that we might escape some pains in the hands of the doctors—in the comforts of the City—our pains were inadvertently multiplied. Yet multiplied by whom or what? Cassirer and Grimsley, among others, hold that Rousseau laid blame at the feet of "society," which in fact he on occasion did. Yet society, generalized, cannot satisfactorily be deemed the culprit of our misadventures, and Rousseau himself understood this. Without doctors, he observed, one lives more fully "for oneself *and for others.*" The full life is not juxtaposed to society, to the company of others. It is contrasted to the medical profession, a particular social institution that epitomizes, in Rousseau's view, the quest to defeat that which cannot be defeated. To fail to recognize our impotence, to disregard the lessons of the Augustinian tradition, is to court excessive suffering. And although the medical profession encourages us to become forgetful of our limits, we ultimately have no one to blame but ourselves, for we have allowed ourselves to be bewitched by doctors and all others who would teach us to assert ourselves in those very circumstances when we need to yield. Again, then, we could have done better and spared ourselves much pain. Our quest for perfection, which includes a life free from suffering, leads us out of the tranquil Garden and into the tumultuous City.

The Journey to Lisbon

Voltaire thought that Rousseau failed to show the appropriate sympathy for the unfortunate inhabitants of Lisbon, the city that quaked and fell in 1755. Early on, after reading the first *Discours*—"On the Arts and Sciences"—Voltaire formed and maintained the opinion that Rousseau, like Pascal, was something of a misanthrope. Yet Rousseau claimed that his motive for holding humans culpable for the majority of their sorrows sprang not from a hatred of humanity, but from a wish that we might reform what we can, thereby avoiding some future suffering. Voltaire's response to the great quake, "Poem on the Disaster of Lisbon," did not assign blame as much as it attacked the moral and religious view that had recently come to be known as "optimism." This view, usually associated with Leibniz's *Theodicy* and Pope's *Essay on Man*, alleged that we live in the best of all possible worlds.[37] To those who would question the design of God's creation, Pope declared:

> All Nature is but art, unknown to thee
> All chance, direction, which thou canst not see;
> All discord, harmony not understood;
> All partial evil, universal good;
> And, spite of pride, in erring reason's spite,
> One truth is clear, Whatever is, is right.[38]

To which Voltaire responded, Whatever we know, this truth is clear, that "*all is right today, is illusion.*" Only "deceived philosophers cry out, *all is right*" [*tout est bien*]. Perhaps once optimistic in his youth, Voltaire now could only utter, "*someday all will be right, that is our hope.*"[39] From what we know of the social critic Rousseau, we might assume that he would be only too willing to support Voltaire's emphatic rejection of any optimistic doctrine that suggests "all is well."

Indeed, Rousseau had recently challenged the theological optimism of Charles Bonnet, a Genevan philosopher who had criticized Rousseau's second *Discours*, "On the Origins of Inequality," on the grounds that it severed an essential link in "the vast chain of being, which from God began"—to borrow a line from Pope.[40] If, as Bonnet held, humans are the good creation of God, and society is the creation of humans, then Rousseau erred by portraying society as fundamentally diseased. In Rousseau's reply, he disputed

Bonnet's interpretation of the statement, "All that is, is good." Failing to distinguish between general and particular evil, Bonnet wrongly applied Leibniz's and Pope's optimism to society itself.[41] This application, Rousseau claimed, would yield the regrettable conservative position that we ought not to tamper with society: "The most perfect quietism would be the only remaining human virtue."[42] Had Bonnet distinguished between general and particular evil, he would have understood that humans encounter unavoidable particular evils (like an earthquake or flood) and in turn generate a host of unnecessary moral evils (like hazardous buildings or exploiting victims of tragedy), thus compounding human suffering. The appropriate response to this entanglement is not inaction, but admitting our painful mistakes and endeavoring to avoid them in the future. Escapism, then, is not what Rousseau had in mind. On the contrary, in his reply to Bonnet, Rousseau insisted that rather than desiring "to live in the woods," "searching for happiness in the middle of nowhere," one ought to live in "one's homeland in order to love and serve it." Apparently, Rousseau was eager to make it known that his pessimistic account of society does not recommend a retreat from society, but a renewed effort to establish flourishing societies "where humanity, hospitality, and kindness reign . . . where the poor one finds friends, loving moral exemplars, and reasonable guides that enlighten."[43]

A year later, in 1756, when Rousseau read Voltaire's "Poem on the Disaster of Lisbon," he must have had a sense of déjà vu. Had he not just seen the same mistake made twice? Both Bonnet and Voltaire assumed that the optimism of Leibniz and Pope was meant to be applied to society; however, whereas Bonnet supported this optimism, Voltaire challenged it. Voltaire questioned how one could remain confident that God's providence provided "the best among things possible," if a single earthquake on All Saints' Day could kill twenty thousand people. While Bonnet had pressed Rousseau to defend his pessimism concerning society, Voltaire now roused him to justify his optimism in God's providence. Rousseau was determined to defend God, if for no other reason than to establish that humans, not God, are responsible for their spoiled lives.

"The optimist," Rousseau claimed, never denied the existence of particular evil, only general evil. The question is not "whether each of us suffers; but if it were good that the universe exists, and if our pains were inevitable given the constitution of the universe."[44] To deny that an individual encounters particular evils would be absurd. Yet equally absurd would be to take particular evils as proof of a general evil that pervades the universe. In order to safeguard against future misinterpretations of the doctrine of optimism, Rousseau suggested a modest revision that would render the optimist's maxim more precise: "In place of *All is good* [*Tout est bien*], it perhaps would be better to say, *The whole is good* [*Le tout est bien*], or *All is good for the whole.*"[45] Rousseau acknowledged that in order to justify such optimism satisfactorily, one would need to have a perfect knowledge of the constitution of the universe.[46]

The impossibility of such a justification is, in fact, one of the principal lessons Rousseau wished to convey to Voltaire: Since we cannot judge that which is beyond our grasp, humility is warranted when making claims about overall goodness or evil in the universe.[47] This is not only an epistemological comment but a moral one. Pride and an inordinate penchant to see the world from our own limited self-interest prevents us from locating our hopes and loves, our aches and pains, in a larger more inclusive context. We lack perspective, and perspective, in Rousseau's view, is one of God's chief advantages over humans. "The common good" is a contextual term. We can talk of the common good of the family, the local congregation, the town, the society, or, as Rousseau invites us to consider, of the world—indeed, the common good of the universe. From God's perspective, a natural disaster in Portugal might be necessary for the survival of "all the inhabitants of Saturn"![48] In any case, some private pains can be palliated in the context of ever-enlarging concentric circles of a common, or general, good. In chapter 10 we will explore the analogy between, on the one hand, private goods in relation to God's general good for the universe (*le bien général*) and, on the other hand, the citizen's private will in relation to a society's general will (*volonté générale*). For now, it is enough to note that Rousseau's theodicy suggests that God, perhaps as the ultimate utilitarian Governor, permits private goods, like an individual's life, to be sacrificed for the sake of overall goodness.[49] Such loss, however, is the result of what we might call a second-order, not a first-order, causality. That is to say, God does not explicitly will that this building fall and that individual die. Rather, God established the general springs and gears of the universe, and these, on occasion, strike and crush an individual here and there.[50]

Rousseau worried that between the superstitions of the priests and the whining of the philosophers, God had become an object of ridicule. The superstitious interpret events as the result of God's direct divine intervention, and thereby deny the autonomous operations of the universe. Whatever happens is right and fitting, for it is the will of God—a volition that the priests, luckily, can interpret better than others. Being less pious, the philosophers, in their turn, either blame God for their toothaches and lost luggage or else, in the face of profound suffering, mock the very idea of God's providential care.[51] Both the priests and the philosophers have failed to appreciate the epistemological and moral limits of their judgments; that is, both lack a universal point of view and habitually form judgments about God that reflect their own self-interest. Both have failed to see that by creating a universe designed for overall good, God limited God's own self. Creation is as much an act of surrender as it is an act of power, for by empowering creation, including humans, God relinquished God's position as the sole power. The universe is granted autonomy, at least in the form of its own necessity. Physical evil, then, is the human experience of the sovereignty of nature that causes us to suffer when necessity collides with human goals, hopes, and desires. To have our house swept away in a lava flow, to lose crops to a drought, to have a spouse die of cancer are some of the ways that necessity can foil our desires and cause suffering.

Rousseau's account of moral evil requires this image of a God who has limited himself by empowering a creation outside himself. In his letter to Voltaire, he attributed the source of moral evil to "man, free . . . yet corrupted." A few years later, in *Emile*, Rousseau would reflect on the relation between providence, human freedom, and moral evil. Desiring to empower humans and make them in his own image, God endowed them with the gift of freedom. When humans abuse their freedom they commit moral evil. Hence Rousseau could write, "It is the abuse of our faculties that makes us unhappy and wicked. Our sorrows, our cares, our sufferings come to us from ourselves. Moral evil is incontestably our own work. . . . Man, seek no longer for the author of evil; that author is you yourself."[52] God does not check this abuse, for that would demean human nature, depriving it of that which makes it like God. To strip freedom from humans, then, would be more lamentable than to permit the evil humans freely choose, for in the absence of freedom there can be no morality: "To murmur about God's not pre-venting man from doing evil is to complain . . . that God gave him the right to virtue." Morality and moral evil, then, require the same condition: freedom. Physical evil—colli-sions with nature—is allowed by God, for the beauty of nature consists in its autonomy; likewise, moral evil is permitted, for the beauty of humans consists in their moral autonomy. Hence, Rousseau insisted that God has made us in his image that we might be "free, good, and happy" like God himself![53]

Free, good, and happy? Can these three describe anyone besides God? These three, and all the friction between them, bring to mind the tragic journey that led us out of the Garden. Freedom is that gift from God that enables us to become moral creatures and to experience happiness in goodness. Yet freedom is also that curse that permits us to become wicked and profoundly unhappy. Outside the Garden, we are mangled by both the necessity of physical evil (rooted in nature's autonomy) and the inevitability of moral evil (rooted in human autonomy).[54] Rousseau noted, with characteristic exaggeration, that "physical evil would be nothing without our vices." This line of thought led him to reflect still again on the Solitaire. "How few evils exist for the one living in primitive simplicity!" Lacking foresight, passions, and the fear of death, the Solitaire does not seek, as do we, "an imaginary well-being" that actually brings "a thousand real ills." If only we could possess the equanimity of the Solitaires and experience the goodness of the world as they do: "Take away our fatal progress, take away our errors and our vices, take away the work of man, and *all is good [tout est bien]*."[55] This brings us, then, back to Pope, back to optimism, back to the Garden, yet with the provision that we turn back progress—that tragic outcome of freedom and perfectibility, those twin gifts of God.

We can now make some sense of a rather baffling association Kant made between Rousseau and Newton: "Newton was the first to see order and regularity combined with great simplicity, where hitherto disorder and multiplicity had reigned, and since then comets move in geometric paths. Rousseau first discovered beneath the diversity of human shapes the deeply hidden nature of man and the latent law according to which Provi-dence is justified by Rousseau's observations. . . . Since Newton and Rousseau, God has been justified and Pope's thesis has come true."[56] As Newton had discovered that nature, abiding by its own innate laws, is autonomous and intrinsically intelligible, free and apart from God, so Rousseau discovered that humanity, abiding by its own nature, is self-directing. Since both nature and humans experience autonomy, physical and moral evil ought not be attributed to God, for God has consented to permit freedom outside God's self, a freedom that accounts for the wonder of nature and the excellence of humanity. God is justified, Pope was right; without autonomy, the universe and human existence is simply unimaginable, whereas with freedom, although there is undeniable risk, there is the possibility of splendor, moral happiness, and love.

To Rousseau, more than to Kant, freedom appeared as an ambiguous gift. Whereas Kant was preoccupied with how to carve out a realm for moral freedom in a Newtonian, deterministic universe, Rousseau wrestled with the equivocal nature of freedom itself.[57] Increasingly, Rousseau came to see freedom as a necessary condition for goodness and happiness that inevitably brings us corruption and sorrow. It is this awkward view that gives me pause in the face of Cassirer's interpretation of Kant's remark about Rousseau and Newton. Cassirer understands it as referring to a novel solution proposed by Rousseau to the problem of evil, that the source of evil is neither God nor the individual, but society.[58] Cassirer maintains that this solution allowed Rousseau to escape his own dilemma, namely, emphasizing human corruption while adamantly rejecting any and all notions of original sin or an Augustinian fall. The difficulty, then, was to discover the source of human corruption, and Cassirer insists that Rousseau's solution entailed exonerating the naturally good individual and benevolent God by assigning blame to society. As we have seen, Rousseau did on occasion state as much. Yet there is another current running in Rousseau's thought: Humans have undergone an inevitable fall, and freedom, a natural faculty granted by God or nature, was one of the principal culprits, exposing humans to risk and harm, jeopardizing human innocence and happiness.

Once again we discover that the facile interpretation of Rousseau's position on evil—namely, that society has corrupted otherwise naturally good humans—slights too much of the bothersome yet provocative ambiguity that besets Rousseau's actual account. His pessimism is extensive and cannot be directed at society alone, for Rousseau held that corruption springs, in part, from the individual's breast—from the faculty of freedom and perfectibility, and from the resulting *amour-propre*. We should be cautious, however, not to speak dualistically of individual versus social determinants of evil. Evil arose naturally from individuals *in* society—a natural location for humans. By "natural" I refer to the ease that marked the human journey out of the Garden to the City. The path to Lisbon was fairly smooth. Ironically, it began with such natural disasters as earthquakes and floods, for these inspired the first humans to gather together, in fact, to *become* the first humans (amoral solitaires can hardly be deemed human). The innate faculty of freedom allowed this gathering, and the innate faculty of perfectibility encouraged it. To gather, then, is natural. Tragically, to gather is also to court harm.

We have already rehearsed the account of how increased needs and desires of early individuals in society led to a heightened interdependency, especially as people sought to satisfy the demands of *amour-propre*. Lisbon was the natural result of the tangled web of psychological, sociological, and economic interdependence. A glance at the *View of Lisbon*, a sixty-five-foot-long panoramic frieze of the city from the early eighteenth century, reveals the intricacy of such mutual dependence. Each lovely blue-and-white painted tile bears the lines that connect the heights and depths, the wealth and poverty, the generosity and greed, the public and private of Lisbon.[59] In the beginning, an earthquake—a manifestly natural act—broke off a segment of the continent and compelled the Solitaires to face each other and develop language—a manifestly social act.[60] From one earthquake, then, Lisbon arose, and from another it fell. The flights and crashes of humanity, I would argue, are as natural as those quakes and as social as the acquisition of language and the construction of tall buildings. If the first quake illustrates the natural procession to the City, the second quake illuminates the failures of the City. We naturally became social, and socially we—as individuals, and as communities—failed.

It would seem that once again Rousseau stood at the crossroads of optimism and pessimism, this time at the intersection of the heartening Leibniz and the cynical Voltaire. This site explains why Rousseau, the relentless social critic, could insist to Voltaire optimistically that all things considered, the universe is well crafted, a truly excellent creation designed to promote the general good and even, with respect to humans, "freedom, goodness, and happiness." He could further insist that, in spite of our prodigious suffering, to have lived is better than not to have lived at all because "the sweet feeling of existence" defies measurement by any utilitarian ledger of pleasure and pain, and that, though we necessarily encounter physical evil and inevitably meet and commit moral evil, we are free to accept the former patiently and to combat the latter vigorously. These are the broad and bold strokes of Rousseau's optimism.

Note, however, that this optimism does not hold that someday history will disclose that all that we call misfortune had actually complied with a marvelous, detailed plan of providence. This instrumental view, often associated with Leibniz and Pope, lacks the tragic cast of Rousseau's thought. Like Voltaire, he could not countenance attempts to rationalize the largest portion of our suffering. How could unnecessary harm be justified? Perhaps he came close to offering such a justification by maintaining that the social and psychological conditions of goodness and happiness are the same as those of vice and misery. However, he never went so far as to link, logically or ontologically, human happiness and suffering. We do not need to experience pain in order to comprehend happiness, and the freedom that permits goodness does not logically require evil. It is his perception of the gratuitous nature of our pain that curbs Rousseau's optimism and highlights the tragic visage of his pessimism.

Knowing that we could have done much better is the counterweight to "the sweet feeling of existence."[61] Rousseau lamented bitterly those needless human works that mutilate the goodness of creation—defacing beauty, corrupting innocence, shredding equality. Moreover, his pessimism outstripped the Enlightenment environmental view of evil, namely, that evil is the product of social prejudice, ignorance, and superstition. The depths of Rousseau's pessimism, we have seen, reached deep into the human soul. Although he would not assert, with Augustine, that sinfulness is a necessary condition of humanity, he nonetheless rejected the Enlightenment optimist's view that evil is as corrigible as the social structures and prejudices that produced it. If evil were solely the result of unfortunate social conventions, we could have unlimited hope in future designs, having learned from past mistakes. Rousseau, however, could not look sanguinely to the future because of the regularity of mistakes made in the past. On occasion, we have seen, he even depicted the Fall and, due to its ubiquity, the serpent—*amour-propre*—to be as natural as human goodness itself.

This is surely the nadir of Rousseau's pessimism. Starobinski has claimed that Rousseau's view is that "evil is produced by history and society without altering the essence of the individual." Evil, in this account, is "relegated to the periphery of being."[62] I have argued, however, that Rousseau's position is bleaker. The journey out of the Garden was more of an inevitable departure than an accidental aberration. Early on, in chapter 2, we discovered Rousseau's grim principle: Alone, in the Garden, we were neither happy nor good; together, in the City, we suffer and are wicked. Freedom, our gift and curse, shares the same natural status as "man's natural goodness." That is our predicament. Rousseau had little interest in the metaphysical problem, how are we to account for moral freedom, given Newtonian necessity? He wrestled instead with the moral and political difficulty, how are we—as individuals and as a society—to govern freedom, given that it leads to our grandeur and our depravity? The universe may be fair and existence per se may be sweet, yet City dwellers have consistently chosen to erect injustice and bury things lovely and beautiful.

Nonetheless, to Voltaire Rousseau concluded his letter as the optimist: "Hope makes everything beautiful." In contrast to the comfortable and successful Voltaire who can "find only evil on earth," Rousseau, in spite of his sundry griefs, finds that "all is good."[63] His abiding hope in providence, that is, in the goodness of the universal arrangement of things, survived his bitter pessimism. Ironically, this hope was nourished in part by his engagement with the pessimistic Augustinian tradition, for that tradition affirms both the considerable depravity of humanity and the unequivocal goodness of God's creation. This tradition, which began in opposition to the Manichaean dualism between good and evil, insists that evil does not exist alongside goodness as an independent principle or entity. Rather, evil is the absence of good, as darkness is the absence of light. Evil results from disordered loves, the outcome of the will placing lower goods above higher ones. Food and sex, for example, are goods worthy of love, yet they can lead to gluttony and licentiousness if loved excessively.

Pascal and Malebranche, among others, had introduced Rousseau to this peculiarity in the Augustinian tradition, namely, that it matches the pessimistic assessment of humanity with the optimistic view that evil, in its essence, is nothing. Still, practically speaking, such Augustinian optimism does not amount to much. Because of an impaired will, humans, surrounded by the good gifts of God, inevitably deform those gifts. It is this paradox in Augustinian thought that inspired Rousseau to claim, often within the same paragraph, that there is no general evil, only humans endlessly begetting particular evils as they go about disarranging an otherwise good, orderly universe.[64] Augustinian "optimism" thus pales in the face of Enlightenment optimism, for while the former holds that creation is essentially good (barring the certain pain and wickedness introduced by an invariably chaotic human will), the latter claims that the phrase "all is good" should be substituted with "all will be good, someday"—someday, when the human will itself shall be healed through education and other reformed social institutions. Such thoroughgoing redemption in the Augustinian view, in contrast, arrives only upon death. Even our best reforms are limited by human frailty and degeneracy. Radical liberation cannot be achieved in human history. Contrary to what many of his interpreters would claim, Rousseau maintained the same, both in *Emile* and to Voltaire: Order returns only upon death; at death, everything becomes truly beautiful, truly good.[65] From this hope, Rousseau secured much metaphysical comfort and with it he abandoned much— though not all, as we will see in part II—of his peers' confidence in future reforms.

At the Crossroads Once Again

Contrary to the standard interpretations of Rousseau, our investigation reveals that he depicted evil—as well as sociability and history—as an inevitable and eradicable feature of human moral existence. Nothing less than moral evil can be expected from creatures naturally endowed with the gift of freedom and perfectibility. This pessimism, we have seen, Rousseau appropriated from a French Augustinian tradition. We have also noted, however, that Rousseau refused to grant evil an independent status; evil is essentially a disruption of God's good and orderly creation by human free will. Predictably, theologians have meticulously surveyed, delineated, and cataloged the assorted ways that humans sin against the divine order. Typically, pride—exalting love of self above all other loves, especially love of God—is ranked as the principal sin. The French Augustinian tradition was no different, for there we find Pascal, among others, depicting pride (*amour-propre*) as that incorrigible disposition that opposes God's general will.[66] Yet this same tradition frequently maintained that humans originally possessed, like God himself, a wholesome self-love. This salutary love of self, however, toppled with the Fall, and thereby fell from the sight and comment of the theologians. Rousseau, in contrast to the theologians, never lost sight of the laudable love of self, *amour de soi*.

His distinctive contribution to both Augustinian and Enlightenment traditions springs from his preoccupation with the two loves, *amour de soi* and *amour-propre*. If I had us linger in the Garden in chapters 1 and 2, it was to better examine wholesome self-love. If we moved methodically through the stages of the Fall in chapters 3 and 4, it was to better understand the steady, yet not absolute, transformation of salutary self-love into injurious self-interest. The attention we gave to the two loves is relevant now as we conclude our investigation of the nature of the Fall and the ousted condition.

Our final question for Rousseau is what would count as unmitigated evil. In light of the narrative of the Fall—a narrative that we have both discovered in Rousseau's work and have constructed for the sake of understanding that work—it would seem that the fundamental perversion of the good results from the metamorphosis of *amour de soi* into *amour-propre*, and the concomitant transformation of *pitié* into callousness.

Put somewhat differently, insofar as we can identify something that would qualify as unmitigated evil—the principal source of all other evils—we could describe it as the unnecessary opposition to the Solitaires' natural maxim, "*Do good to yourself with as little harm as possible to others.*"[67] The corruption of *amour de soi*, gentle self-love, leads to the envy, contempt, and inequality that flow from *amour-propre*; the corruption of *pitié*, uncomplicated compassion, leads to the social negligence, personal parsimony, and ubiquitous cruelty that spring from indifference to grief and suffering. To abide by the natural maxim is to endure, in every situation, the goodness of creation; to work against the maxim is to obstruct or evade that goodness. If elemental evil is to oppose salutary self-love and compassion, then the prospect of reversing or curbing this epidemic is faint because, as we have seen, the march away from the Garden's maxim and toward the City's corruption, while not logically necessary, is in a practical sense inevitable. For this reason, all things considered, Rousseau's stance is profoundly pessimistic. Moreover, the departure from the Garden also led to the opportunity for human moral existence, and for this reason Rousseau's thought is profoundly tragic.

What, then, can we say of the dispute between Voltaire and Rousseau occasioned by the earthquake that leveled Lisbon? In most ways, their arguments missed rather than clashed with each other. They were fighting different battles. Voltaire attacked the optimistic theological doctrine that held that all things happen for a reason, for a good reason—God's. Rousseau, for his part, attacked those who would blame God or nature for the woes that humans had brought on themselves. There is much common ground between them, if they had cared to notice it (something that, with age, both would increasingly fail to practice). Both combated the belief that all painful events are in fact disguised blessings; both resisted the consolation that our past and current sorrows are stones paving the way to a more glorious future; both refused to justify, in the name of a divine plan, corrupt human deeds.

Still, differences separated them. Rousseau held that moral evil is an inescapable result of that providential gift, freedom, and that human moral existence, without freedom, is unimaginable. This is not to say that he excused moral evil as simply the price of freedom and of the moral life. His lifelong infatuation with the untroubled, mostly amoral Solitaires exemplifies his conviction that moral development cannot be deemed unambiguous progress. Nonetheless, he avowed that in spite of the chaos and sorrow caused by freedom, life is still worth living; our grief is trumped by that "sweet feeling of existence." This optimistic belief was, in part, theologically required of Rousseau. He was determined to defend God against Voltaire and others who seemed, at least implicitly, to mock God's good creation. Rousseau's main apologetic was to demonstrate that it was not God but humans who author the particular evils tormenting their lives. Yet he wanted his defense to go further, lest some should claim that God's creation of humans was an unequivocal botch and that God never should have enabled humans to hurt themselves so.[68] With this in mind, he asserted to Voltaire that, all things considered, "It is better for us to be than not to be . . . even if we would expect no compensation for the evils we have suffered."[69] This avowal was not a testimony to human tenacity but to the abiding goodness of God's creation. If Rousseau had been a poet, he could have written something like these lines of Gerard Manley Hopkins:

> All is seared with trade; bleared, smeared with toil;
> And wears man's smudge and shared man's smell . . .
> And for all this, nature is never spent.[70]

To assert, however, that creation and human existence per se remain preferable to nothingness is hardly the height of optimism. Unlike Voltaire, who was rather surprised by the message delivered by the Lisbon quake, "Life really *is* hard," Rousseau's response to the quake was along the lines of, "Well, what did you expect? Isn't this what has been happening all along? This is what humans do; they make their lives shaky and unsafe and then blame anyone but themselves when it all comes down." When not being rhetorical, Rousseau would not have questioned the genuine achievements of Lisbon. Nor, however, would he have been astonished that those achievements were accompanied by certain sorrow. Again, this is not to say that there is a necessary nexus between our accomplishments and sorrows. While freedom allows us to move both upward and downward, it never requires us to plunge. We do that voluntarily, and we do it predictably.

We have seen Rousseau at the crossroads more than once now. First, he stood at the intersection of Enlightenment optimism and Augustinian pessimism. From that position, he reminded us of our responsibility for ourselves as well as our impotence to save ourselves. Now we see him at a nearby intersection, located *within* the Augustinian tradition. It is a juncture from which Rousseau could declare "all is beautiful," "all is good," while also insisting that humans inevitably obstruct or evade beauty and goodness. He seems to have once again sought a position from which he could depict our powers and obligations as well as our fated helplessness. As creatures made in the image of God, we share in the abiding goodness of creation and have the capacity to be "good, free, and happy."[71] We are born with gentle *amour de soi* and *pitié*, with heavenly freedom and perfectibility, and with that enduring "sweet feeling of existence." From the same position, however, Rousseau could glance the other way and report on our prodigious penchant to sabotage our opportunities for goodness, freedom, and happiness. It is this predictable yet gratuitous nature of our failures that renders Rousseau's account of the Fall and the ousted condition both pessimistic and tragic.

This juncture, which underscores both the goodness of creation and the depravity of humans, pervades Christianity and was inherited by one of its proudest children, the culture of the Enlightenment. That heir affirmed the goodness of Nature as well as the corruption of past and present civilizations that have departed decisively from Nature. Yet, as we have seen, the Enlightenment escaped the strains of this juncture by issuing an assuring prophecy: From yesterday's darkness and superstition Europe is marching into light and knowledge. Saving *scientia*—scientific knowledge—is on the horizon. Some philosophers even held that past miseries and errors were necessary for future felicity and enlightenment. This cheery forecast, we noted, is one of the principal differences between Augustinian pessimism and Enlightenment optimism. The Augustinian tradition, to be sure, also promises a bright future for the saved, but that future arrives only after history. On this question, the question of redemption, we will discover that Rousseau once again positioned himself precariously between the two traditions.

Rousseau's engagement with the religious and Enlightenment vocabularies of his day taught him—and can teach us—something about the limits and promises of public philosophy. Rousseau, no doubt, easily fits into any genealogy of public philosophy conceived as a discipline dedicated to scrutinizing the public life in order to minimize suffering caused by structural inequality and injustice. This facet of Rousseau's work has been well documented. Less understood, however, is that Rousseau was increasingly compelled to accept that no revolution or any amount of tinkering with social structures can rid us of our prodigious capacity for hurting ourselves. To attend to this lesson is to conclude, among other things, that there are no final solutions. It may even lead us to become practitioners of what Michael Walzer has called "exodus politics," a politics of continual reform ("a long series of decisions, backslidings, and reforms") while successfully avoiding "messianic politics," a politics of absolutized revolutions and once-for-all solutions.[72]

In the previous chapters, we have discovered that *amour-propre*, the mark of the human soul under social conditions, injures both the public and private life, giving rise to anomic desires, greed, and inequality. We have also observed that conflict between the public and private will persist under any social arrangement that attempts to sustain both. In a life of radical solitude the tension can be erased, but at the cost of eliminating the public life and hence the prospect of humanity flourishing. The other extreme, the totalitarian society, is not a happy solution, for in that society there is simply no place for the goods we associate with the private life.[73] We find ourselves, then, in a difficult spot with no escape that leaves us unscathed. In Rousseau's view, then, no social policy or institution, and certainly no appeal to "nature" or to "the good," can rid us of the inevitable conflict between the public and private life. Hence once again Rousseau, the so-called utopian thinker, has confronted us with a political and human limit. Perhaps an acknowledgment of the limits of public philosophy can check our goals and any extreme means we might contemplate to achieve them, while a recognition of our freedom and responsibility might encourage us to persist in our struggle to cope with the heartache we encounter in our public and private lives. In any case, the tension between such acknowledgment and recognition marks the tragic passage from the Garden to the City.

Now that we have traveled with Rousseau to the end of a rather dismal journey, we are in a position to inquire, in part II, whether there is a way to reverse our steps or somehow improve our condition. The question of restoration dominated much of Rousseau's thought. He posed two different, even contrary, remedies: the public path to redemption found most notably in *The Social Contract*, and the private path found most notably in *Reveries of the Solitary Walker*. The public path prescribes redemption by means of the reformed society, the private path by means of an escape into solitude. These two divergent paths, we will see, emerge from Rousseau's account of the Fall—an account that is marked by that perplexing tension between unnecessary and necessary harm, between moral and physical evil. This tension, we have noted, is the result of Rousseau's effort to work within the two opposing traditions, Augustinian pessimism and Enlightenment optimism.

At the crossroads of these two traditions, Rousseau developed his public and private remedies. The public path reflects, even if dimly, the Enlightenment hope that human fallenness can be overcome by reforming society; the private path reflects the Augustinian conviction that humans, due to their inward fallen condition, cannot cure themselves of sin or evil.[74] The one advocates that individuals dwell within the enlightened, educative community, the other that individuals cultivate an interior life and remove themselves from commitments and other social entanglements that exacerbate the human propensity to inflict harm. At the crossroads, in one direction Rousseau beheld humans able to transform their societies humanely; in the other, he perceived humans destined for immense suffering unless they dodge social involvement. Rousseau never managed to rectify this vexing double vision. Ultimately he insisted on the necessity of both community and solitude, the public and private, even as he detailed the inevitable conflict between them. And all remedies, Rousseau came to realize, are partial. There are no absolute cures.

Did Voltaire ever reply to Rousseau's lengthy letter on the disaster of Lisbon? *Candide* was his response.[75] At the end of that book Voltaire, though ironically it could have been Rousseau, concluded with the advice, "We must cultivate our garden."[76] This, too, is Rousseau's counsel to those who left the Garden for the City. We have traced the path from the Garden to the City. It is time to explore the routes that lead back toward, if not to, the Garden.

PART II

PATHS TO REDEMPTION

7

Reforming the City

The Extreme Public Path

The Remedies

In part I, I charted the contours of a Fall that seriously wounded us. Now, in part II, I will investigate the means of redemption. I will explore the question, How can we be saved? We needed to understand Rousseau's account of the complexity and depth of the problems that confront humans outside the Garden before we could turn to his soteriology. Hence in part I, I traced the intricacies of the stages of the Fall and lingered on the issue of evil. We are now in a position to view Rousseau's attempts to mitigate the suffering and cruelty that flow from an evil that can be called radical—radical because its source is not only social institutions but the human heart.

I have mapped Rousseau's soteriological strategies on what I call the five paths to redemption. We can think of these paths as moral schemes designed to restore some aspects of our Garden-like existence as Solitaires. This is not to say that Rousseau thought he could reinstate us in the Garden. He understood that, due to the radical nature of the evil from which we suffer, returning is not an option. Moreover, due to the moral growth experienced since leaving the Garden, we should not want to return to such an amoral, though benign, existence. Still, aspects of the peace and freedom that mark life in the Garden need to be recovered if we are to feel at home in the world. Identifying the various forms of peace and freedom found on the different paths is one of my tasks, as well as identifying the potential conflict between them. For now, however, I want to sketch briefly the paths to redemption.

Earlier in part I, for the sake of simplicity, I referred to the two paths to redemption, the public and private. But as you may have guessed, these designations are too stark for texts as rich as Rousseau's. I have, therefore, distinguished five paths, ranging from the most public to the most private. On one end of this spectrum there is what I will call the extreme public path, best represented by Rousseau's *The Government of Poland*; on the other end is the extreme private path, best represented by *Reveries of the Solitary Walker*. Between these is what I will call the middle way, exemplified by *The Social Contract*. Between the extremes and the center point there are two intermediate tracks, "Political Economy" on the public side and *Julie* on the private side. The chart of Rousseau's paths to redemption, then, is represented in figure 1.

Extreme Public Path		The Middle Way		Extreme Private Path
•	•	•	•	•
Poland	Political Economy	Social Contract	Julie	Reveries

Figure 1. Chart of Rousseau's paths to redemption.

These paths, I want to make clear, are neither explicitly mentioned by Rousseau nor the product of my fancy. Informed by Rousseau's work, I have fashioned five constructs to bring to light salient aspects of his thought. My hope is that these philosophical reconstructions will enable us to inspect those features of Rousseau's insight and blindness that pertain to our study of the relation between the public and private. I have associated a particular text with each construct, not because each path is found exclusively in one text, but because the five texts I have identified are especially representative of the five paths. All of the paths can be found in a variety of works. The extreme public path, for example, although best exemplified by *Poland*, is also found in "Political Economy" and *Letter to M. d'Alembert*, among other places.

The Extreme Public Path: An Overview

In the *Letter to M. d'Alembert*, Rousseau claimed that "the only pure joy is public joy."[1] There is, in Rousseau's view, a unique joy and well-being that can only emerge by belonging to and participating in community. Without community, individuals cannot experience wholeness. However, Rousseau believed that the circumstances of a people—its history, institutions, customs, and geopolitical locality—suggest distinct types of community or what we might call forms of public life. Too often, Rousseau's different prescriptions for people in different circumstances is taken as inconsistency rather than as attentiveness to varying sociopolitical details. Although all of Rousseau's prescriptions flowed from a somewhat singular and coherent vision, that vision was adjusted according to whoever was in sight. In this chapter, we focus on Rousseau's remedy for the Poles.

On the extreme public path, the public and private life are one and the same. Actually, the private life is subsumed under the public. A form of extreme patriotism, this extreme path seeks to cast the individual's soul into the collective soul of *le corps politique*, the political body. The loves of the individual are directed solely at the *patrie*, the homeland, and thus to lose one's country is to lose one's life. Indeed, Rousseau claimed that such a loss is worse than death, for one would inhabit a body without soul, a life without purpose.[2] On this path there is no distinction between virtue and patriotism, between morality and politics, between society and the state. This is the path Rousseau prescribed for Poland, and hence I use Poland as a symbol of this path, not as a reference to an empirical country or people.

Poland, in Rousseau's view, required an extreme communitarian way of life due to its frail, precarious situation. Its vulnerability was not due to internal but external threats, namely, its bellicose neighbors, Prussia and especially Russia. Rousseau advised the Poles to concentrate their limited resources not on external ramparts but on an internal fortress, cultivating in each Pole a national identity that could defy all outside threats.[3] Rousseau credited this political-cultural model to Moses and the Jews. The genius of Moses, the great legislator, was his ability to shape the Jews' identity in distinct ways that set them apart from their neighbors. By erecting an impressive border between insider and outsider, Jews were protected from being spiritually and morally crushed by the outsider. The Poles, like the Jews, did not have the military means to shield themselves from foreign invaders. Rousseau's strategy, with Moses as his guide, was to fortify an inward kingdom that no threat could reach. Regardless of outward attacks, the Poles would remain Poles and hence their *patrie*, at least internally, would survive.

Rousseau argued that such an inward fortification would require virtually the same martial virtues as if preparing for an actual war. Successful military operations require that soldiers thoroughly identify with the values and goals of their nation. In the case of the Poles, as the external hazard threatened all, the defensive strategy required that all, even children, be enlisted as spiritual warriors dedicated to protecting the inward kingdom. For children, this entailed that their games kindled in them an ardent national spirit; for adults, this entailed creating and joining a nonprofessional people's army in which citizens routinely engaged in military exercises. Both the children's games and the military activities were directed at the participants' hearts, not external military aims. Rousseau's admiration of military virtues have led some to ascribe to him a love of war. This, however, is to fail to note Rousseau's invariable condemnation of war, which he viewed as a state in which the powerful and rich profit at the expense of the helpless and poor. Rousseau's praise for military discipline and love of country was dedicated not to the acquisition of land or the exhibition of power, but to the politics of capturing and sustaining the human heart.[4]

I said that the aim of Rousseau's paths to redemption is to secure some aspect of prelapsarian liberty and peace. On this extreme public path, liberty emerges out of fatalism. This claim will surely surprise some. What liberty is available if the individual is submerged in an utterly politicized public life? Yet liberty was precisely one of Rousseau's central goals for this extreme path, and a genuine form of liberty can be found on it. This type, of course, has nothing to do with that contemporary ideal of liberty that refers to an agent's freedom to pursue *any* (legal) end. But it does refer to an agent's freedom to pursue *all* of his or her ends, as long as we add the strong communitarian proviso that those ends have been shaped from birth by the educative community. Rousseau neither lamented the loss of ends unique to the individual on this path, nor did he insist that public ends be intrinsically normative. As long as citizens' loves and goals are shared and are focused on the public good, such ends—unless intrinsically vicious—are justified, because they serve to forge unity and to curb individual anomie.[5] To embrace and contribute to the public life is to exhibit virtue, and virtue is the surest protection against a divided self and society. Virtue, here, is the capacity to pursue public ends, those ends being at the center of one's life. Bondage, in contrast, is to be torn by conflicting ends. Education is to inculcate virtue—the love of public ends—and thereby ensure that internal conflict—within the self and society—be kept to a minimum. On the extreme public path, then, individuals are able to pursue freely their deepest desires, desires that have been informed by public institutions.

Here we have a perverse version of Kant's religious hope that someday duty and desire become one. If freedom is understood as undividedly doing what one wants to do, then Rousseau's extreme path provides the social and psychological conditions likely to bring it about. Such freedom looks, formally, very much like the freedom found in the Garden. In part I, I could easily generalize and list the Solitaires' goals because the Solitaires had no more opportunity for truly private ends than Rousseau's Poles. In the case of the Solitaires, food, sleep, and sex can hardly be considered private ends when they are exhaustive and universally shared. The Poles, like the Solitaires, are free to do as they wish—to pursue all their desires—unless, of course, some natural limit, like death, is encountered. But that, in Rousseau's view, is not considered a limit to freedom. It is just part of life. There is, then, as little occasion for frustration in Rousseau's Poland as there is in Rousseau's Garden. In both hypothetical states, the self is at one with itself and thus free in itself, because it freely pursues its ends and there is no occasion for division.

Such lack of division is the mark of peace on the extreme public path. Peace and freedom, in this context, are closely related. If freedom on the public path is to follow freely one's deepest loves and desires, then peace is to pursue those loves in the absence of conflict. On the extreme path in which the private is engulfed by the public, peace is certainly achieved, because social and political arrangements afford so little opportunity for conflict. When there is widespread agreement on public ends and when private and public ends significantly overlap, conflict all but disappears. And the absence of conflict, both internal and external, is a form of peace that Rousseau often employed. Externally, that is, *among* the Poles, there would be a sense of oneness and belonging. Part of Rousseau's strategy, after all, was to instill a communal identity based on shared goals and on an absolute boundary between insiders and outsiders.[6] As insiders, the Poles would form a family-state and thereby experience the peace of enjoying the settled identity of a clan. Internally, that is *within* each Pole, duty and desire coalesce, and hence his or her deepest loves are reaffirmed and met daily. In Rousseau's political psychology for Poland, each time Poles serve their country—through work, military training, child-rearing, or even play—they attend as well to their own duty to self. Such lack of conflict is truly a recognizable version of peace.

I am not suggesting that these accounts of freedom and peace are exhaustive of Rousseau's views, only that they are the principal forms found on his extreme public path.[7] To our sensibilities, much is frightening about such a path. Rousseau himself was not satisfied with it. He could, however, imagine worse scenarios. This is a telling difference between Rousseau and ourselves, and reflecting on it is instructive of who Rousseau was and who we are. For us, the horror of totalitarianism is one of our greatest fears; Rousseau's plans for the citizens of Poland may look totalitarian, especially if by that we mean a society in which there is no space for, or control over, a private life. In Rousseau's view, however, the absence of a private life—that is, the pursuit of unique or personal goals—is preferable to a fragmented society in which individuals are painfully divided both within and among themselves. Such fragmentation, moreover, would render the Poles defenseless in the face of aggressive neighbors. We, in contrast, as members of pluralistic democracies, have a high tolerance for social diversity, conflict, and even fragmentation. One might say that if Rousseau celebrated, here, a freedom that requires exacting social constraint, we celebrate a freedom from all constraint. Caricatures aside, it is fair to say that, in the case of the Poles, Rousseau was willing to sacrifice the private life—a realm dear to both ourselves and to Rousseau—for the sake of gaining a distinctively Polish, communitarian society.

The plan for the Poles was not, however, totalitarian. Rousseau consistently opposed a strong centralized government, a requirement of an effective totalitarian state. Moreover, he strongly opposed the antidemocratic hereditary monarchy. The telling difference between ourselves and Rousseau does not turn on totalitarianism, but on the value of social solidarity and the means of achieving it. Solidarity is not the first goal of contemporary North Atlantic democracies, and insofar as it is a goal, we tend to follow Montesquieu or the Federalists in their belief that out of diversity emerge common goals and achievements, especially in relation to checking despotic individuals and majorities. Rousseau, in contrast, put social solidarity first and held that for the Poles to achieve that goal, diversity would need to give way to homogeneity. The private life, in Rousseau's view, is the seat of diversity, and the Poles could not afford that luxury. By "private life" here, I refer to goals and beliefs and activities that are not necessarily directed at larger public or political concerns. While Rousseau's Poles may lack a private life, they by no means lack an autonomous will that asserts itself in the public sphere. Their public life is not the empty life of the prisoners that I will discuss below. The prisoners are denied autonomy and the means to shape their social and physical environment. The Poles, in contrast, are involved in and shape a robust public life; due to their educative training, however, they have little concern to develop a rich private life. Rousseau's plan for the Poles is frightening not because it raises the specter of totalitarianism or belittles the value of human life but because there is no allowance for the private life. This deeply offends our sensibilities, as it did some of Rousseau's. His strategy for the Poles did not fully express his whole hope for humanity.

Having presented the extreme public path in broad strokes, I now want to detail some of its features, especially those that pertain to the relation between the public and private. The chapter is divided into six sections. We begin with Rousseau's *Politics of Identity*. With the help of Moses, Rousseau attempted to create a persistent Polish identity by fusing the private, public, and political. *How to Reach Rousseau's Poland* examines the sociological and psychological significance of education and civil religion for the preservation of the Polish nation. *Virtue in Poland* explores Rousseau's definition of virtue and the threat private pursuits pose to it. We then turn to *The Cost of Poland's Freedom*, an investigation of the losses that are incurred on the extreme path. In particular, I argue that the radical subordination of the private to the public, which is intended to strengthen the public life, in fact renders it unworthy of love. In *Poland's Women*, I argued that women on the extreme public path are not relegated to an isolated, apolitical private space. Women are confined to the home, yet the domestic sphere in Poland is not a retreat from the political, but a classroom that trains male citizens and female domestic teachers of virtue. In the concluding section, *Poles and Solitaires, neither Torn nor Whole*, I show that Rousseau's extreme public path, like all his paths to redemption, is the result of his awkward historical and intellectual location at the crossroads of

Augustinian pessimism and Enlightenment optimism. Moreover, Rousseau's own personal flight from the public to the private corresponds, surprisingly, with his opposite prescription for the Poles. Ultimately, Rousseau's own self-defense became Poland's.

Politics of Identity

The most distinctive aspect of this path is the private life held captive by the public. A private existence, that is, the individual attached to personal goals and values, would threaten the self's inner harmony and the state's social solidarity. Poland's public institutions are to infuse the individual with meaning and purpose, lest the individual acquire time and inclination to ponder and pursue private commitments, concerns, and delights. When the goals of the self are those of society, there is no tension between the individual and the citizen. The absence of such friction could not result from a police state in which coercion compels conformity. Duress produces an external harmony only. In Rousseau's politics of the heart, public institutions transform the inner self—the soul, so to speak—in a way that the beliefs and will of the public and those of the individual become indistinguishable.

Unity of public and private was not, for Rousseau, merely a matter of political expediency. It was not simply a drastic measure justified by Poland's *raison d'etat*. The extreme public path, I have noted, is not only found in *Poland*, but in "Political Economy," *Letter to M. d'Alembert*, and elsewhere. In his "letter" to d'Alembert—the famous enlightenment philosopher and mathematician—Rousseau held that "the most wicked of men is he who isolates himself the most, who most concentrates his heart in himself."[8] That was written in 1758 when Rousseau was living in isolation in Montmorency. Although ill and convinced he would soon die, Rousseau was enjoying a peace and happiness that, he claimed, can only flow from solitude.[9] He would have liked to have remained in solitude, yet he believed that one is culpable "every time private considerations" cause one to fail to put country and humanity first.[10] Rousseau was called out of his private attachment to solitude by d'Alembert's (unintentional) public affront and moral attack on Rousseau's homeland, Geneva. Writing on the relation between politics and the arts, Rousseau implemented the full dramatic art of politics: he framed his response to D'Alembert as the familiar biblical image of a vulnerable David taking on a formidable, and highly credentialed, Goliath. The sick and ailing Jean-Jacques, who identifies himself simply as "Citizen of Geneva," comes out of retirement to defend the city against the philosophical subtlety of d'Alembert, identifying him as a member "of the French Academy, the Royal Academy of Sciences of Paris, the Prussian Academy, the Royal Society of London, the Royal Academy of Literature of Sweden, and the Institute of Bologna."[11] This most public letter—"I do not speak here to the few but to the public"—is composed for the sake of the public—"love of the public good is the only passion which causes me to speak to the public." Rousseau here was enacting what had become for him an important principle: in cases of conflict, public duties supercede private felicity.[12]

Thus far I have characterized this extreme path mostly as the absorption of the private by the public. I now need to add that on this path the public and the political appear to be folded into one. This claim is not supported explicitly by the texts, yet it can often be inferred. In any case, on the extreme path Rousseau said little to nothing about the limits of the political.

In the fragment titled, "Of Public Happiness," Rousseau claimed that we are made miserable by being divided between "*l'homme et le citoyen*"—between our desires as humans and our duties as citizens. "Make man one," he went on to note, "and you will make him as happy as he can be." Although leaving humans to themselves, divorced from social institutions, is one way to heal dividedness, the more dependable remedy is to shape them into citizens: "Being nothing except by [the republic], they will be nothing except for her."[13] A clear account of citizen formation is found in "Political Economy." Forming citizens is "not the work of a day." It is necessary to "educate them when they are children," and above all, teach them what to love.[14] While most governments are concerned with the citizen's external actions, Rousseau on the extreme path would have government penetrate the citizen's "innermost being." Rousseau was never satisfied with external constraints that secure a dutiful citizenry by coercion. He wanted nothing less than that citizens spontaneously—that is, voluntarily—embrace their public duties: "Shape men, therefore, if you want to command men: if you want them to obey the laws, make them love the laws."[15]

On the extreme public path, then, love cannot be left to individual preference. What and how one loves is a deeply political matter. Hence Rousseau noted that if potential citizens were "trained rather early to regard their individuality only in its relation to the body of the state, and to perceive, so to speak, their own existence merely as a part of the state, they could come eventually to identify themselves, as it were, with this greater whole . . . and to love it with that exquisite sentiment which no isolated person has except for himself."[16] In this extraordinary passage, the citizen's self-love becomes identified not only with public goals—collective hopes and aspirations—but with the state. This aspect of the extreme path—the fusion of the political and private—is even found in the usually moderate *Social Contract*, where we are told that legislation, when at its highest level of perfection, can "transform each individual, who is by himself a complete and solitary whole, into part of a greater whole from which he, as it were, receives his life and his being."[17]

It is common for liberal theorists to make a sharp distinction between politics, which pertains to the public sphere, and morality, which pertains, in this view, to the private. For example, my favorite liberal, Judith Shklar, worries when politics and morals connect. In her view, a common condition for vice is when "politics and morals, the public and the personal, meet."[18] Rousseau might have agreed that public institutions can turn vicious when driven by one's private vision of morality; it would all depends on the nature of the moral vision. After all, Rousseau's ideal society of *The Social Contract* is founded on the moral vision of that single individual, the Great Legislator. Moreover, Rousseau held that we have much to gain—morally and politically speaking—when our vision of morality is deeply informed by just public institutions. This, of course, is not to discount Shklar's concern. I will explore it shortly, if for no other reason than because Rousseau took versions of it seriously. On the extreme path, however, Rousseau condemned any cleft between public and private, between politics and morality. In his *Letter to M. d'Alembert*, for example, he claimed that "everything which is bad in morality is also bad in politics." However, Rousseau laments, "The preacher stops at personal evil, the magistrate sees only public consequences."[19] While we may well be pleased that Rousseau did not limit the moral scope of religion to address private vice alone, we should pause when no distinction at all is upheld between the public and private, between politics and morals. We should insist, for example, that our politicians be honest in all public statements, while only hoping that they be honest to their spouses or friends. More to the point, we should insist that our laws are not immoral, not that the complete moral vision of our legislators be codified by the law.

On the moderate public path there is a tension, often salutary, between duty to self and duty to the state; on the extreme path, there is no tension. The private becomes political because what we love is who we are, and identity, on the extreme path, is not left to private whim. The surest way to fashion and preserve a people is to ensconce it in distinctive traditions and customs that will determine its identity regardless of contingent circumstances. As we have seen, Rousseau celebrated Moses' ability "to make his people, among other humans, outsiders forever." Rousseau began his discussion by emphasizing the Jews as outsiders only to end by disclosing how every barrier to their neighbors was a bond among Jews. "Outsiders forever" are bound eternally together. The status of outsider is won by distinctive customs, dress, laws, periodic assemblies, and so on. This status carries a heavy price, however. To be an outsider, Rousseau noted, is to receive "hatred and persecution." Nonetheless, Moses—Rousseau's symbol for the wise legislator, and for Judaism more generally—ensured Jewish identity by forging within the hearts and minds of Jews a love for the people that transcended any private loves. Rousseau presented the Jews, then, as his example of a people who bring together the most inner self with the most enduring public entity—a nation without a territory that "will live on and endure until the end of the world itself."[20]

Bringing attention to Rousseau's example of the Jews helps me deflect a possible charge against Rousseau's extreme public path, namely that it is a Hobbesian view under a different name. The temptation is to characterize the extreme path as the erection of a Leviathan, only to dismiss this path as the result of either Rousseau's childish infatuation with ancient Sparta or his zeal to circumscribe human desire at any price. As we saw in chapter 2, Rousseau and Hobbes did share many goals; in particular, both placed a high premium on peace and freedom. The routes to achieving these goals, however, and their understanding of them, separate the two. For Hobbes, freedom is to pursue one's desires in the absence of constraint. Freedom understood as such, however, brings chaos and war—the opposite of peace. The way to achieve both freedom and peace, then, is to grant a Leviathan unlimited power to guarantee order; in the midst of that order, Leviathan, in turn, will grant some (limited) realms in which to freely pursue private interest. External order—peace—permits some room for individual pursuits. In this model, society is composed of disparate individuals who share little in common beside their willingness to relinquish their natural freedom to Leviathan for the sake of gaining back a limited freedom in the context of peace.

Rousseau, in contrast, understood differently the key terms of freedom, peace, and society. Freedom is not the opposite of constraint, peace is not the mere achievement of external order, and society is not a mere aggregate of individuals. In Rousseau's model, society is a sui generis collective being—a political body—and the members of that body enjoy the freedom of belonging and the peace that flows from a unity of duty and desire. Whereas for Hobbes peace is an external condition that provides disparate individuals with some protected private space for the sake of free pursuits, for Rousseau peace is an internal condition that provides a freedom from conflicting desires in order that the individual can pursue collective goals. Peace, in Hobbes's view, is ultimately for the sake of private happiness; for Rousseau on the extreme public path, it is for the sake of public—shared—happiness.

To find happiness, peace, and freedom in community is closer to Jewish covenantal theology than to Hobbes's Leviathan. Shortly we will explore some reasons Rousseau's extreme public path should give us pause. But just as we saw that the extreme public path is not occupied by the phantom of totalitarianism, neither is it shadowed by fear of a mighty Leviathan. The coercion on this path is not in the form of a threatening, external political figure or institution. The coercion, if we want call it that, is in the form of the implicit and explicit social training and education that takes place on every social level—the domestic, occupational, civil, and political. Some will object to labeling such training coercive; others will object to the objection. The former will insist that such socialization is permissible and perhaps even inevitable; the latter will claim that such socialization is illiberal, given the extent of its reach. Before we enter this debate, I want to investigate in some detail Rousseau's plan for how the Poles can remain Poles, that is, how they can create an enduring Polish nation.

How to Reach Rousseau's Poland

Rousseau's pragmatism and historicism are evident in *Poland*. Throughout the work he insisted that there can be no nation-building from scratch. All reform must take place within existing institutions; all proposals must be culturally specific—written for the Poles and ultimately by the Poles. No doubt including himself, Rousseau claimed that "an outsider can hardly give anything more than general observations, in order to cast light on, but not to guide, your institution-building."[21] Some have complained that Rousseau did not do all the homework that one might expect of a social scientist or a political anthropologist who is invited to make recommendations for a new constitution. Yet by Rousseau's own admission, he didn't need to. The particulars were to come from the Poles themselves. Still, he tailored general recommendations for a specific nation, and that specificity, no doubt, is largely what accounts for the difference between *Poland* and *The Social Contract*. *The Social Contract*, not written for a particular country, is more theoretical and provides us with the best example of Rousseau's pristine political vision. *Poland*, in contrast, is less idealized because it is more concrete. In particular, it was the vulnerability of Poland as a country that led Rousseau to offer his clearest statement of what I am calling the extreme public path, one of the chief characteristics of which is a ubiquitous social and political education. Such an education, Rousseau insisted, was necessary to open and maintain this path. Indeed, Rousseau said more about the nature and importance of education than of the constitution about which he was asked to give counsel.

Poland, I have said, was in need of defense; "The heart of citizens," Rousseau claimed, "is the state's best guard."[22] Poland could save itself only if it fashioned Poles who loved Poland above everything. Education, then, was a salient political mission: "It is education that you should count on to give the souls of citizens a national, moral strength and to direct their opinions, their likes, and dislikes so that they will be patriotic by inclination, by passion, by necessity."[23] With Plato, Rousseau understood that if the state seeks not merely to control citizens by force but to fashion them from within, education cannot rest in the hands of the family or local community. In "Political Economy," Rousseau argued that education is "the most important business of the state" and that government should concern itself with the education of infants: "as one does not leave to the reason of each man to be the sole arbiter of his duties, one ought all the less to abandon to the intelligence and prejudices of fathers the education of their children, as that education is of still greater importance to the state than to the fathers." Part of his argument for the education of infants was based on a psychological theory concerning the early development and significance of habits. Good habits need to be nurtured in childhood, lest egoism and other "dangerous dispositions" arise, take root, and work against the love of country and justice. Surrounding children by moral exemplars is the surest method of training, for in the absence of exemplars, instruction is fruitless.[24]

I have thus far described Rousseau's educative goal as fashioning a people's loves. Shaping a people's aversions is equally important. To the Poles, Rousseau maintained that the most effective interdictions are not achieved by the law but by ensuring that odious behavior is "hated and despised." His argument, anticipating Durkheim, was that "the law's condemnation is never efficacious except when it reinforces the citizens' own judgment. Whoever would meddle with instituting a people must learn to dominate their opinions."[25] At best, the law can only support the moral opinion and collective judgment that is already in place. Passing stricter laws—or, for that matter, building more prisons—is an ineffectual way to curb crime or elevate a country's moral character.[26] The surer way is to invest in education, inform likes and dislikes, enable the law to reflect the actual moral demeanor of the land, and reserve punishment for occasional aberrant conduct. In his *Letter to M. d'Alembert* Rousseau asked, "By what means can the government get a hold on morals?" "By public opinions," he answered.[27] For the sake of public morals government must concern itself with public opinion. To control public opinion is to control the tides of social currents, and to control social currents is to steer the direction of a country. Thus on the extreme path censorship—a gate to public opinion and hence a potent form of adult education—was entirely reasonable. To dwell in a land of freedom and peace required no less. And the larger the country, the more difficult the task. Hence a large country like Poland, divided up into smaller federated regions, required a truly national curriculum—taught by the Poles about the Poles—that would secure unity in morals, loves, and aversions, by training and controlling public opinion.

Civil religion, in Rousseau's view, is an especially useful means to social and political education. Although much of chapter 10 is dedicated to the subject of Rousseau and religion, this topic cannot be relegated to one chapter alone, for it is never far from Rousseau's considerations. In *Poland*, we learn that the three genius legislators—Moses, Lycurgus, and Numa—installed civil religions that were "exclusive and national," "binding the citizens to the homeland and to one another." Few of us, Rousseau claimed, have understood "the strength and influence" of the rites of civil religion. They are far superior to the lifeless rites of modern churches which have no "national purpose" and which fail to remind their participants "in any way of their homeland."[28] Rousseau's three admired legislators used civil religion effectively to fashion citizens. Numa, for example, "the real founder of Rome," transformed robbers into citizens not by laws, but by sacred, civil rites.[29] Although Rousseau always abhorred the violent temperament of religious fanaticism, civil religion on the extreme public path does not safeguard tolerance and religious diversity as it does, for example, on the moderate public path of *The Social Contract*. Indeed, as I will show in chapter 10, a salient feature of the civil religion advocated in *The Social Contract* is the doctrine of tolerance (one of the six dogmas). This liberal virtue is to be inculcated in society's members, and those not abiding by it are to be banned (liberal irony). On the extreme path, in contrast, civil religion is not evoked as a means to teach liberal virtues but solely as a means to promote moral solidarity. Rousseau, we have seen, thought of external coercion as a paltry and ignoble means to induce obedience among citizens. Civil religion, on the other hand, enables citizens to work voluntarily for the common good by inspiring citizens, through collective rites and symbols, to embrace their public duties.

Highlighting the role of religion on the extreme path may seem at odds with Willmoore Kendall's now classic introduction to *Poland*. He claimed that *Poland* "avoids the topic of religion as if it belonged to the category of the unmentionable."[30] However, the silence that Kendall has identified pertains not to religion per se, but to Roman Catholicism in a Roman Catholic Poland. Rousseau avoided the subject of his own former religion because it seeks to be catholic, that is, universal, whereas the religion Rousseau promoted on the extreme path is local, that is, national. In *The Social Contract* Rousseau had described Roman Catholicism as a religion "that gives humans two sets of legislation, two rulers, and two countries, subjects them to contradictory duties, and prevents them from being able to be at the same time faithful to religion and to citizenship." This religion is "so obviously bad" that it would be "a waste of time amusing oneself to prove it such."[31] Given such an uncharitable view of Roman Catholicism, and given that Rousseau's pragmatism prohibits building institutions from scratch, he elected to remain silent on the subject of Poland's Roman Catholic institutions except to note that they should not interfere with education.

This exception is quite significant. Rousseau grasped the similarity between the outcome of religion and education. Again anticipating Durkheim, Rousseau investigated the moral solidarity that is achieved by religion and education and suggested that if the form and structure of religion were preserved, then its contingent content could be changed and used for social ends. This was, in fact, his implicit recommendation for Poland. The form of religion—the presence of creeds, rites, and moral community—would be preserved in *Poland*, but its contents would not be that of Roman Catholicism or any other traditional religion. Its content would be comprised of the national heroes and narratives that have become sacred to the Poles. Rousseau, then, is not silent about religion in Poland. He championed a Polish civil religion and, knowing that he could not ban Roman Catholicism, chose instead to render it publicly mute. And on the extreme path, to be muffled in public is to be sentenced to a certain if slow death.

Emphasis on education and training, I have claimed, is a distinctive trait of Rousseau's extreme public path. This will surprise those who associate Rousseau with a romanticism that rejects any social arrangement that obstructs individuality and fosters uniformity. It will also surprise those who think of Rousseau as the champion of the "natural savage." Later I will suggest the ways Rousseau has, in fact, attempted to fashion an environment for the Poles that shares features with Nature's Garden. We will see how the natural limits that the Solitaires enjoyed are transferred to Poland. For the moment, I want to note that Rousseau's emphasis on civic education takes him out of the social-contract tradition of Hobbes and Locke, for whom enlightened self-interest or reason, not social education and civil religion, inspire voluntary consent. In Rousseau's view, humans are not, *pace* Hobbes, naturally selfish and hence willing to cooperate socially for the sake of advancing private interest; nor are they, *pace* Locke, naturally social and hence willing to cooperate once enlightened. If humans in society are to become co-operative and moral creatures, that is, good citizens, they need to be fashioned and trained. As we saw in chapter 2, our natural selves are, all things considered, neither immoral nor moral, but amoral. We enter society with the potential to be miserable or splendid citizens, and the direction we take has more to do with social training than with appeals to so-called natural reason or selfishness.

This is not to say that Rousseau spurned reason. In Rousseau's view, reason is not an innate faculty waiting to be elicited by educators; it is a capacity that requires instruction and practice.[32] When Rousseau seemed distrustful of reason, he was suspicious that bits of knowledge could motivate humans more than their loves and desires. "The error of most moralists," Rousseau once claimed, "was always to take man to be an essentially reasonable being."[33] He doubted that discursive reasoning alone could produce courageous, moral lives. French Augustinian moral traditions had nourished Rousseau's skepticism concerning reason's capacity to produce virtuous individuals. Augustinian pessimism, we have seen, places severe limits on what we can expect of reason and, more generally, of the human ability to save itself from self-incurred evil and suffering. Not even Hobbes's solution, a reasonable appeal to human selfishness, could save humans from harming themselves. Although some Augustinians had endorsed Hobbesianism, Rousseau went farther with Augustinian pessimism; there can be no appealing to *amour-propre*, for it arouses irrational, even self-destructive behavior. Reflecting this pessimistic tradition, Rousseau's extreme public path entailed a strict regimen of discipline and training, as if attempting to make straight crooked bodies and souls. He believed, as we will see in chapter 11, that all political bodies are subject to inevitable decay and death. With enough training, however, sickness could be delayed.

Rousseau did not leave uncertain the reach of public education. Love of the home-land—"the love of the laws and of liberty"—is to make up the citizen's "entire existence: he sees only the homeland, lives only for the homeland; the moment he is alone, he is nothing."[34] We should not doubt that such training would produce a citizen with a passionate inner self. A self would not be missing, but rather missing would be a private life with goals separate from those of the public. Also missing, according to Rousseau, would be the suffering that attends anomie and living in a land where freedom is understood principally as pursuing private as opposed to public goals. Everything we know about Rousseau would suggest that he did not, in principle, object to the enjoyment of a private life. Citizens, however, and especially Polish citizens, belong to a special category of humans, and on the extreme public path, they are taught the craft of renunciation. Public education, here, implicitly teaches citizens that the joy of private pursuits pales next to the freedom and peace of belonging to a vital republic. This is one of the goals of education; it is the moral duty of government to provide such an education. Again anticipating Durkheim, Rousseau insisted that the primary function of government is not economic but moral.

I have been exploring how to achieve Rousseau's vision of Poland, that is, the social form of life found on the extreme public path. Giving special attention to training and education, I have thus far provided a sociological account. I now wish to add a psychological description, for Rousseau's politics of the heart invariably includes both sociological and psychological components. This often amounts to focusing on different aspects of the same phenomenon. Sociologically speaking, Poland is created by education. Psychologically, it is created by redirecting the individual's *amour-propre*.

We have seen that in Rousseau's writings *amour-propre* is an anxious preoccupation with oneself and one's public appearance. It can be associated with such dismal qualities as excessive vanity, consuming self-interest, anomic desire, and covetousness (desiring something because others desire it). We have seen that *amour-propre* is as inevitable as humans are social, and that it accompanies the radical and tragic nature of the human fall into sociability. It is destructive of both the self and the group, rendering the self anomic and cutthroat and the group splintered and litigious. The object of *amour-propre* is the self; its goal, self-aggrandizement. Given its tremendous injurious sway over social humans, Rousseau believed that it is imperative that social groups develop strategies to manage it. On the extreme public path, the fervor of *amour-propre* is conducted away from the self and to the group.[35] The individual is no longer preoccupied with self, but with the group. Rousseau was the realist on the extreme path. The battle he laid before the Poles was not the utopian goal of defeating *amour-propre*. Rather, acknowledging that *amour-propre* is irradicable, he proposed the more modest challenge of providing individual *amour-propre* with another object—the homeland.

The task, as Rousseau stated in "Political Economy," is to produce a love of country that "joins the force of *amour-propre* to all the beauty of virtue."[36] This passage is worth exploring. Rousseau had been arguing that "the feeling of humanity evaporates and grows feeble in embracing the earth." He rejected most forms of cosmopolitanism or universalism, believing that our love wanes as the object of our love becomes nebulous and abstract. This he understood as a psychological limit that posed political difficulties. In order to care for and be committed to a group, we must limit that group. He illustrated this rather bluntly, noting that "we cannot be touched by the calamities of Tatary or Japan, as by those of a European nation."

Many of Rousseau's fellow *philosophes* would not have agreed that this psychological limit was an inevitable feature of humans, and most would not have approved of Rousseau's next move, namely, to base a political principle on such a pessimistic premise. The principle is this: "Humanity should concentrate itself among fellow-citizens." Pessimism, here, leads to parsimony; the spirit of cosmopolitan generosity is not abundant on the extreme public path.[37] Rousseau's argument, grounded in Augustinian psychological insight, is that our weak wills can voluntarily embrace a common will only when it is shared by those whom we love; in contrast, if our love is dissipated, strewn before all humanity, we cannot unite within a common will. I want to postpone discussion of the expression "the general will" until we reach the moderate path of *The Social Contract*. I need to note, however, that in the context of the above argument, Rousseau did employ the expression; with it he starkly defined virtue as "the particular will *in all things* conformable to the general will" (emphasis added). Virtue on the extreme path, then, is the complete identification of the private with the public. This total identification is made possible by the force of *amour-propre*. Individuals are united as citizens, and separated from humanity, as *amour-propre* chases its new object of devotion—the homeland.

Rousseau was not alone in his attempt to have *amour-propre* drive the public good. Most, however, sought not to transform private *amour-propre* into a genuinely public form, but rather to coordinate private *amour-propre* for the sake of public ends. As we have already seen, Augustinian theology had considerably informed eighteenth-century French moral thought. This is not to say that theology dominated France's moral traditions, but that the moral and political inferences of Augustinian theology, even if severed from their theological base, had become entrenched. It was becoming increasingly common to hold that fallen humans, although restless and anxious in their search for security and power, could be shown that they can advance their interests if they act in cooperation with others. The wise government, assisting in the orchestration of its citizens' private *amour-propre*, implicitly announces that although not angels, humans after the Fall can contribute to social harmony, if not quite social unity. Although such an approach is based on Augustinian pessimism, it ultimately is a species of optimism; from fallen, self-centered individuals come hard-working citizens.

Rousseau, however, rejected the principle of private vice, public benefit. On the extreme path his aim, unlike that of his contemporaries, was not to coordinate private *amour-propre* in order that it *indirectly* contribute to public goals, but to transform *amour-propre* into a collective passion that would *directly* contribute to the public good.[38] Rousseau held that a society based on so-called coordinated self-interests experiences civil war waged by other means. This is not to suggest that Rousseau denied what we might call the primacy of the self. Rousseau shared the commonly held Augustinian view that love of self is the foundation of all loves. Many French theologians, I noted in chapter 6, asserted that even love of God begins as love of self. The task, then, in Rousseau's view, was neither to defeat self-love nor to coordinate the agitated activities of individuals being driven by love of self. The task was to train the individual to see its own body as an intrinsic part of the political body, in order that love of self and love of country may become one. Augustinian pessimism runs deep here. It is understood, for example, that vanity cannot be vanquished; it can, however, be deflected from the private body to the public body that contains it. On the extreme path we find neither egoists pursuing private interests nor altruists sacrificing interests. When the corporate body is seen as the individual's own true body, altruism loses its meaning, for the difference between public and private aims collapses.

Rousseau's unique contribution here was to probe the psychological depths of *amour-propre* and conclude that, under the special conditions of the extreme path, love of self could be converted into a sui generis public force. Only on the extreme path does *amour-propre* not divide but join citizens. Where Hobbes sought to impose order on the disorder caused by private *amour-propre*, Rousseau attempted to disarm the destructive force of *amour-propre* by focusing it on one thing, the political body. Public games, ceremonies, festivals, and military exercises are all polished lenses that focus the emotional energy of private *amour-propre* to a dazzling, public point. Under these lenses, patriotism is kindled, and under them citizens live every detail of their lives. In *Poland* Rousseau argued that the "soundest, most efficacious" means to cultivate patriotism "consists in seeing to it that all citizens sense that the eyes of the public are on them every moment of the day . . . that everyone is so completely dependent on public esteem as to be unable to do anything, acquire anything, or achieve anything without it."[39] Here we have a public embodiment of, to use a character from *Julie*, Wolmar's penetrating eye: all are under surveillance so that even one's motives become transparent. This is not, however, an example of state eavesdropping along the lines of George Orwell's *1984*. It is more comparable to small-town gossip, everyone watching and knowing everything about everyone, or perhaps to Bentham's ideal prison, but only in this respect: everyone, bar none, is conscious of existing in a state of "permanent visibility," to use Foucault's expression. Such gazing is participatory, whereas in the Orwellian model individuals remain in isolation as they are probed by the hidden eye of the state.

Moreover, the point of such reciprocal gazing has more to do with creating community than with regulation or punishment: "Only from the effervescence produced by collective emulation [everyone watching everyone] . . . are humans raised above themselves."[40] As Durkheim might have put it, the point of such a collective regard is to make members aware of themselves as a group and hence to experience the solidarity that flows from such awareness. Given the depths of Augustinian pessimism, a strong remedy is needed to manage *amour-propre*—"to raise humans above themselves." That remedy is collective effervescence: that dazzlingly shared point in which the many become one. The extremity of the remedy consists in the demand for an enduring heightened sense of social solidarity. Unlike the moderate path where, we will see, the unity of the general and particular will is episodic, on the extreme path such unity is constant. Solitude, one symbol and example of the private life, is unthinkable because it entails separation from the group. Liberty on the extreme path consists precisely in the absence of separation: when all citizens belong all the time, each citizen is free from internal conflict; when every *amour-propre* is focused on a shared life, each citizen freely embraces that public life.

Rousseau's conception of freedom on the extreme path reflects what he considered a realistic assessment of human limits, and this assessment, in turn, reflects his Augustinian proclivities. Social humans are ineluctably ensnared in *amour-propre*. Freedom from its destructive forces comes not by knowledge, but by love. Augustinian pessimism defines self-love as the problem, and Rousseau's response was to look to transformed self-love as the solution. This radical remedy—magnifying and focusing on self-love to the blazing point of patriotism—matches the radical evil that, as we saw in part I, Rousseau detected in the social human: the abiding penchant to do unnecessary harm.

The radical remedy tackles some of the most formidable problems that Rousseau had been identifying throughout his career. He had linked loss of freedom to love of domination, and love of domination to *amour-propre*. In this view, inequality and domination cannot be addressed by adjusting structural inequalities alone; insofar as we are guided by private *amour-propre*, we will continue to attempt to outdo and dominate our fellows, even if this requires that we submit to some in order to gain power over others. Yet if the drive for glory is diverted from the self and to the state, then the social sting of *amour-propre* is extracted; citizens strive not against each other to secure individual reputations, but work together to secure national prestige. Moreover, when personal passion and the public good become one, conflict between diverse social arenas is mitigated. Secondary groups exist for the nation, not principally for their own ends. One's roles as citizen, professional, parent, and lover are directed at shared aims, not exclusive pleasures.

The patriotic transformation of *amour-propre* solved many sociopolitical problems, and this was for Rousseau its principal allure. We could say that during Rousseau's mature years when he wrote *Poland*, Tacitus claimed his allegiance more than Cicero. Although throughout his life Rousseau maintained a juvenile fascination with a Ciceronian glorification of the state, increasingly he followed the pragmatic way of Tacitus, turning to patriotism as a means of ridding the human soul of inner conflict and society of disorder. On the extreme path, Rousseau offered the social and psychological conditions that promised freedom from social and personal dividedness, and freedom to participate virtuously in a vigorous public life.

Virtue in Poland

Virtue on the extreme path is the capacity to identify the totality of one's life with public pursuits. Clinging to private pleasures or goals is not only unpatriotic, but immoral. The military life can serve here as a paradigm of virtue: One studies and trains in the group, for the group. Rousseau, remember, celebrated the discipline and social solidarity that the military life produces, which consists not of victory on the battlefield, but triumph over each citizen's heart. Analogously, virtue has more to do with promoting unity—both within and among citizens—than with securing fame for the state. Patriotic glory, for Rousseau, was chiefly a means to fellowship and liberty, not an end in itself. Without a strong sense of public purpose, humans suffer from anomie. There can be no liberty, on the extreme path, without the internal—spiritual, if you will—restraints that come from commitment to public goals. Rousseau mocked those who held that "to be free they have only to be mutinous." If they realized how stern liberty's laws were, they "would run away from her in terror as from a burden about to crush them." Liberty, then, is not easy. It requires the work and discipline that attends the virtuous life, but it is good: "Liberty is good, tasty food that is difficult to digest: to handle it, one needs a good, strong stomach."[41]

Some have claimed that Rousseau's notion of virtue is utterly devoid of normative content.[42] In this view, patriotic commitment to *any* regime will qualify as virtue. This argument relies on Rousseau's occasional indifference to the nature of public goals as long as they are not vicious and they contribute to social solidarity. It fails to note, however, Rousseau's belief that the good and the just are most likely to be discovered when private interests are cast aside. Patriotic commitment is a means to secure a social environment conducive to justice.[43] If individuals are granted much private space, they are likely to develop desires that conflict with the public good and the demands of justice. Virtue, the suppression of self-interest for the sake of the public good, facilitates the discovery and pursuit of justice. Rousseau was not alone in associating virtue with patriotism and juxtaposing it to self-interest. Montesquieu had defined republican virtue as "love of the homeland." "This love," he held, "demands a continual preference for public interest over one's own, and from this love springs all particular virtues; they are, indeed, nothing but this preference."[44] Yet whereas Rousseau was willing to encourage society, at least the society of Poles, to travel down the extreme path that supported virtue and justice, Montesquieu feared that such a path was too difficult for most, and hence was likely to veer toward despotism and injustice. The safer though more modest, lowly path, in Montesquieu's view, was the way of the enlightened monarch coordinating—not eradicating—its citizens' private interests for the sake of the public good. Montesquieu did not reject the way of virtue on the extreme path because it was normatively deficient, but, on the contrary, because it seemed beyond the moral reach of most modern Europeans. Although Rousseau largely shared this assessment, he believed the way of intense civic virtue was the Poles's only path to liberation.

What I am calling the extreme public path, remember, is not located in *Poland* alone. We learn, for example, much about virtue on the extreme path in Rousseau's treatise on public entertainment, *Letter to M. d'Alembert*. The citizen's character, on the extreme path, is the business of the state. Just as many today worry about the effect of violence depicted in television and film productions, so Rousseau worried about the poisonous influence of eighteenth-century drama. And just as many today identify government as the only social agent capable of supervising popular entertainment, so Rousseau looked to the public censor to protect the citizen's character from the moral assaults of the entertainment industry. Entertainment on the extreme path is not a private affair. If citizens are to love and perform their public duties, their character must be strengthened, not weakened, by public amusement. Rousseau, the pragmatist, recognized that the nature of this task will vary from people to people: "We shouldn't seek among us for what is good for humans in general, but what is good for them in this time or in that country." Concerning eighteenth-century dramatic productions, Rousseau feared that the spectator in the isolation of the French theater became forgetful of public responsibilities: "One thinks that in the theater people gather together, yet it is there that each is isolated."[45] In the darkness of the theater, as in a propagandist state, we do not experience open association with one another, but a packaged production sent from a single source—the stage—that manipulates our character, mocking virtue and celebrating vice.

Rousseau allowed no place for solitude on the extreme public path; based on this exclusion we might be tempted to think that Rousseau denounced the detachment felt in the theater. However, solitude is not experienced in the theater. One is isolated from others, but one is not alone with oneself, with nature, or with God—the characteristics of solitude. In solitude, one encounters the self; in Poland, ideally construed, one encounters community; in the theater, one is diverted from self and community and encounters only the artificiality of the stage—upon which we "put our heart as if it were ill at ease within us." In Poland, we possess our hearts, share them freely, and thereby penetrate and shape each other; in the society that gives rise to the French theater, we are alienated from our hearts and seek to live outside ourselves: "We forget ourselves and become occupied with alien objects."[46] Our eyes are turned away from ourselves and toward exemplars that sabotage the social mores necessary to sustain a genuinely public life. These are the broad strokes of Rousseau's critique of the theater.

In Rousseau's virtue theory, the eyes play a salient role. We learn by watching and by being watched. We experience moral growth by watching those whom we respect, as opposed to hearing abstract, moral lessons or fearing the cane of instruction. And by being watched we flourish morally in the dazzling light of the public eye that makes transparent our motives and actions.[47] The City, like the theater, shelters us from the penetrating sight of others: "Morals and honor are nothing because each, easily concealing his conduct from the eyes of the public, shows himself only by his credit and is esteemed only for his riches." In the City, private eyes like gossipy spies see all, but "everything is judged by superficial appearances." One's moral character is hidden, while that which can be easily scripted and quickly flaunted, namely wit and wealth, are paraded for display, eliciting collective envy. On the extreme path, in contrast, "individuals are always in the eyes of the public" and "are censors born of one another."[48] This participatory moral education requires light and sight; everyone is clearly seen in open-air recreation. "It is in the open air, it is under sky that you must assemble and give yourselves over to the sweet sentiment of your happiness. . . . Have the spectators entertain themselves; make them actors themselves; make it such that each sees and loves himself in the others, that all should be better united."[49] In the theater, we do not see ourselves but rather we lose ourselves in the glare of the stage; in the City, we watch to see how others envy us; in Poland, we see our own public hopes and ideals in the faces of those around us and we love ourselves in those faces.

Rousseau, the realist, once again placed love of self at the center of his moral philosophy and psychology. Self-love in the City leads to atomism, for an individual's loves are focused on advancing his or her own social position. Self-love in Poland, in contrast, leads to solidarity, for the individual's loves are centered on advancing the goals of the community. Recreation on the public path, then, sustains virtue, the love of public duty. Rousseau needed a transformed self-love that would lead us out of ourselves. As love of God begins with love of self, so love of community must begin with the self. It does not, however, end there. This is the difference between the isolation of the City, where one is alone with self-love, and community in Poland, where by loving oneself in others one is "all the better united." As we unite in public recreation—reinforcing public commitments—we penetrate each other and participate in mutually shaping our public life. But if self-love (redirected *amour-propre*) is the spring of a participatory, public life, then that life is frail. Like nitroglycerin, *amour-propre* is potentially explosive and requires tremendous care. Properly handled, it powers the virtuous citizenry; without adequate attention, it devastates.

All this is to say that the virtuous citizenry requires attention; its health cannot be taken for granted. It needs to be defended. While we tend to separate the political order from the moral or aesthetic order, Rousseau saw such a separation as a failure to protect citizens from fierce attacks on their character. In the initial pages of *Poland*, Rousseau warned that the only financially rewarding entertainments are those that offer "lessons in corruption."[50] In Rousseau's literary criticism of Molière, among others, we do not hear a fearful, prudish voice warning us against such private sins as drinking, adultery, or gambling. Rather, we hear a powerful social critic that warns us of the consequences of becoming a society of the minimally decent, a society in which "wisdom consists in a certain mean between vice and virtue," in which "to be a decent man it suffices not to be an out-and-out villain."[51] Although Rousseau will likely fail to convince us of the need for a public censor, we should not refuse to acknowledge the risk of mediocrity that he associated with an entertainment industry that encourages narrow self-interest over shared public goals.

In Rousseau's view, the promise of the Enlightenment, symbolized by the knowledge of Diderot's *Encyclopedia* and the entertainment of Voltaire's plays, failed to address the character of the people. Its progress failed to include virtue. On the extreme path, virtue joins the private and public by pledging the former to the latter, whereas progress in the City, in the arts and sciences, divides the private and public. This great divorce, Rousseau believed, was exemplified by Voltaire's personal fancy—the construction of a theater in Geneva—finding its way into the *Encyclopedia*. Cloaked as a bit of Enlightenment knowledge, Voltaire's private wish was injurious to Geneva's public happiness and moral health. The private, far from being scrutinized for the sake of the public, was allowed to obscure and then define the public issue at hand.

This case also illustrated the menace of *amour-propre*. For Rousseau, as for the Augustinian tradition that Rousseau inherited, if our loves are not carefully managed, they will lead to harm, personal and public. One way to check *amour-propre*, we have seen, is the way of Poland: redirect *amour-propre* to public ends. This path, however, exacts a heavy toll. Conflict between the public and private is eliminated by erasing the private life. What I earlier called Rousseau's method of evasion is in full force here. This time, however, Rousseau has not systematically avoided public commitments in order to avoid conflict between the public and private. This time evasion carried him in the other direction: he systematically eliminated the private life. Virtue in Poland entails much loss.

The Cost of Poland's Freedom

Rousseau's Poland could never brook the likes of Jean-Jacques. Jean-Jacques runs away from the great Swiss city-state, Geneva; he abandons the five children he has with his live-in servant; he refuses the King when asked to serve the State as public musician; he spends most of his time in solitude writing philosophical treatises, two of which are banned in the name of the public good. His record as citizen, father, and husband are marked and marred by his determination to go his own way rather than follow the designated public path. From everything we know about him, we can be sure of this: Rousseau would have spurned the all-encompassing public life that he himself prescribed for Poland. One could say in defense of Rousseau's record that he never found a country he deemed worthy of his allegiance and that, had he found such a land, he would have gladly taken on the commitments of citizen, husband, and father. Or one could argue that Rousseau was in fact a dedicated citizen. Like a prophet, he refused to be put on the state's payroll, electing instead to remain independent and condemn the injustice of the land. Indeed, his harsh social criticism for the sake of the people led to his persecution and exile. One could argue in this manner. Yet my aim, here, is not to appraise Rousseau's life choices, but to suggest, as his own life demonstrates, that Rousseau's Poland, like his Garden, is not a place for humans to dwell—at least not for twenty-first century members of liberal democratic nations or for eighteen-century philosopher-critics.

Rousseau's Poland is in many ways Garden-like. Its citizens, like the Solitaires, are protected from inner conflict and anomic desires. By their daily and certain encounter with necessity, the Poles, like the Solitaires, gain freedom from gratuitous anxiety. The natural limits of the Garden are exported to Poland in the form of absolute social contours that confront and shape each citizen. For this reason alone there can be no prophets in Poland. A voice in the wilderness requires critical distance, a distance that cannot be allowed if the highest premium is placed on everyone being formed and united in the same public mold. On the first page of his *Confessions*, Rousseau claimed that he was unique and stood apart from his fellows: "Nature broke the mold in which she formed me." In Poland, then, there would be no room for Rousseau.

My critique of the extreme public path largely reflects my own commitment to the goals and ideals of the relatively recent and historically unique form of state and political culture, liberal democracy. I do not find the intense process of socialization on the extreme path problematic. A society, it seems to me, should be permitted to engage in "conscious social reproduction," to use Amy Gutmann's phrase.[52] The cultivation of civil religion, children's games, and various public ceremonies for the sake of fostering a society's highest goals and ideals is entirely legitimate. Socialization per se is not illiberal. What gives me pause about Rousseau's extreme path is not, then, the intensity of the socialization, but the goals of socialization. Too often virtue is equated with patriotism, that is, with devotion to the homeland—right or wrong. Too often social sentiments are directed not to the highest ideals of the land, including those of justice, but to the mere survival of the people. I do not wish to be cavalier. Poland's survival in the midst of hostile neighbors was an end worthy of rigorous means, and every state is entitled to prudential means of self-defense. But all is not fair in love and war. If the Poles are asked to sacrifice justice within their own land, including the moral autonomy that is necessary to determine the means and goals of justice, then the legitimacy of their country becomes suspect. In relation to the extreme path Rousseau did on occasion evoke the name of justice, but rarely did he detail any actual safeguards or goals of justice.

Educating a people for justice and liberty requires, at the very least, some premium placed on moral autonomy. This need not be understood as a Kantian requirement that individuals step outside their social traditions to engage in moral deliberation. Moral autonomy and social training are not mutually exclusive. The authority of society's shared understanding can cultivate and promote critical thinking. Rousseau himself is one of our best and earliest champions of the autonomous individual as devoted citizen whose tutored heart inspires independent thought for the sake of the common good. On the extreme path, however, Rousseau was not willing to risk the inevitable conflict between individual autonomy and the public good. He held, correctly, that autonomy enables citizens not only to contribute constructively to the common good, but to harm society by acting out of ignorance or narrow self-interest. Having acknowledged this legitimate aspect of Rousseau's fear of the individual on the extreme public path, I want to address his overreaction to that fear.

By radically subordinating the individual to the public, the public good ceases to be worthy of love in at least two respects. First, commitment to the public is maintained more by manipulation than by respect. What might have been social training for the sake of the flourishing state becomes coercion for the sake of uniformity and order. Second, the critical independent thinking that contributes to the vital life of a republic is cut at the root. By "independent" I do not mean radically aloof. Rousseau understood that critical thinking cuts deepest across common ground, that is, in the context of shared traditions and perspectives. What is missing in *Poland* is what Rousseau required elsewhere, that individuals, having learned a common moral vocabulary, think and vote independently about what is good for the shared life. What is missing from *Poland* is Rousseau's most famous political innovation, the general will. On the extreme path, Rousseau would not permit the general will because it is too dialectical; it presupposes a dynamic relation between the individual and society. It insists that individuals consult their own hearts regarding the common good. The individual is to ask, "What, in *my opinion*, is good for the common good?" Moreover, as we will see in chapter 10, the general will is an interval in one's life. One does not reside in the general will, but enters it when some public matter requires deliberation. In *Poland*, then, where every Pole ceaselessly inhabits the public and where there is no independent opinion, there can be no general will.

This brings me to my next complaint. Benjamin Constant was one of the first to claim that the 1789 French revolutionaries followed Rousseau's lead when they sacrificed the private life on the public altar.[53] This familiar charge misses the mark if the target is the bulk of Rousseau's work. However, of all the five paths to redemption, the charge does apply to the extreme public path and hence it deserves our attention. Above I argued that the denial of space for autonomy harms the public good. This sacrifice on the public altar, in other words, does little for the public. Now I want to show how this sacrifice potentially thwarts the complex moral life of society's members. When Rousseau subsumed the private under the public, he neglected to allow a moral division of labor that operates within a variety of spheres of being.[54] In flourishing societies that realize a full, complex moral life, the moral ethos that governs the domestic sphere, for example, is different from that of the occupational sphere, and that of the occupational sphere is different from the civic sphere. Without denying overlapping concordance, each sphere can be said to exhibit its own moral reasoning and practices. Rousseau was aware of such provinces of ethics. For example, he once noted that "one can be a devout priest, or a courageous soldier, or a dutiful senator, and a bad citizen."[55] On the extreme path, however, he would not tolerate a plurality of morals. He understood that among the provinces of ethics, conflict was as likely as common projects and shared values. Moreover, he held that in such cases of conflict, humans naturally give their allegiance to the more private spheres, which involves personal interest, than to the more public spheres, which involves duty: "Unfortunately, personal interest is *always* found in inverse proportion to duty; personal interest grows in proportion to the association becoming more narrow and the commitment less sacred."[56]

Once again, Augustinian pessimism informs Rousseau's political prescriptions. Due to a seemingly innate human proclivity to neglect public duties in the face of the personal interests that adhere to the more private spheres, Rousseau closed off this passage to moral negligence by abolishing the private. Moreover, to the political domain he steered all the various spheres that constitute public life, from work to entertainment to civic participation. Not only, then, is the private sacrificed to the public, but the public to the political: children's games serve the homeland. On the extreme path, Rousseau directed all loves and commitments to the largest association, the political body, in order to curb the destructive force of personal interest. Given the external threat of Russia and Prussia, Rousseau would not risk the Poles being split internally by lesser associations and the private interest they inflame. If the sacred, for Rousseau, grows in proportion to the reach of the association ("the voice of the people is in fact the voice of God"), then the more encompassing the association, the more sacred; the more private, the more profane.[57] As long as Rousseau associated the private spheres with the profane, the private life was stripped of moral excellence. Its goals and commitments became identified with the personal, and the personal with corruption.

From Rousseau's other writings, we know that he valued the private life and recognized that solitude, friendship, and family, for example, entail complex moral activities and duties that cannot be reduced to the public goals of the state. We know that, like Montaigne, Rousseau often depicted the private life as a sphere of being that afforded unique opportunities to pursue moral excellence. He held, moreover, that the results of solitude could enhance the public moral life (think, for example, of the very enterprise of his *Confessions*), but that the goods internal to solitude need not be pursued for the sake of public life. What are we to say, then, of the extreme path that he recommended to the Poles? A case of amnesia or inconsistency? Rather than charge Rousseau with forgetfulness or intellectual capriciousness, we can see the congruity of his work by interpreting the paths to redemption as strategies designed to stem the harm that flows from *amour-propre*. The way to arrest the corrupting force of *amour-propre* on the extreme public path is to transform it perfectly into a political passion. That transformation is the decisive mark of the extreme public path, and it requires the loss of the private.

Women in Poland

Loss of the private life in Poland does not mean the eradication of the domestic sphere. Family life is not made illicit, rather it is dedicated to the public. Women make a singular, vital public contribution from their appointed place in the home. Rousseau's depictions of women, which are invariably problematic and often disparaging, are most egalitarian on the extreme public and extreme private paths. On the private path, by egalitarian I mean that women and men share indistinguishable roles and capacities; on the public path, in contrast, by egalitarian I mean that women and men have different but equally important roles and capacities. Women's unique and integral role is to raise robust, dedicated citizens. Women are comrades in Poland, but their service to the state is rendered entirely behind the closed doors of the home. Interpreting their domestic labor as public service, and not merely as private concern, is supported by Rousseau's claim that the unfaithful woman is "guilty not only of infidelity but treason."[58] To fail in the domestic sphere is a public crime.

Rousseau was one of the earliest and most important contributors to what some have called the classical liberal separation of the public and private, including the separation of state and family. On the extreme path, however, that separation does not exist. We can take the private to mean, among other things, that its goals and activities are not pursued explicitly for the sake of the public good. When the domestic sphere belongs to the private, the home is often seen as a retreat from harsh public life. In late eighteenth-century Europe, women were increasingly relegated to the private; protected from the fierce public, they cared for their men and children providing domestic sanctuary. Rousseau contributed to this paradigm. Indeed, he could qualify as one of its principal authors. It is not found, however, in Poland. The domestic sphere in Poland is not a retreat, but a classroom to train male citizens and domestic teachers of virtue, that is, future wives and mothers.

Whether woman's role is to provide a private retreat or a classroom in public virtue, she is required to do her work out of public view. The ancient Greek women, Rousseau held, were models to the world, for their way of life exhibited the mandates of nature and reason alike. When they were married, "one no longer saw them in public; enclosed within their homes, they limited all their cares to their households and families. Such is the form of life that nature and reason prescribe for women."[59] As I argued earlier, Rousseau's portrayal of human nature was usually rather lean. He claimed that those who purport to describe in detail the contours of human nature are merely inscribing the local features of their own society onto a universal human form. In spite of his thin essentialism on most matters, Rousseau consistently presented, as if cast by Nature in stone, a division of labor between the sexes. The natural, social woman remains confined in the domestic sphere, for "there are absolutely no good morals for women outside of a withdrawn and domestic life." It is an offense to nature to have women, for example, on the stage as "preceptors of the public, and to give them the same power over the audience that they have over their lovers."[60] The sexual division of labor, in Rousseau's eyes, maintains that women's and men's capacities are separate yet equal. Mocking those who would suggest that one sex is superior to the other, Rousseau claimed that "in the union of the sexes each works equally toward the common aim, but not in the same manner."[61] Superiority cannot be attributed to one sex, because their roles and skills are incommensurate. The perfection of each sex is to follow its natural, social condition. Nature has provided a social condition that, when realized, brings a sense of fulfillment to each sex and a harmony to their union. Once again, then, we find that the social is not, in Rousseau's view, an unnatural condition for humans; in other words, "natural sociability" is not a Rousseauean oxymoron.

To underestimate the weight that Rousseau placed on women to serve as the hidden, moral backbone of society is to miss the hidden key to the extreme public path. Rousseau could not permit private, lesser associations for fear that *amour-propre* cease to be focused exclusively on the political body. Nor, however, could he imagine abolishing the family; that would oppose what he understood as one of the sweetest gifts of nature, domestic harmony. The republic on the extreme path must include the family, and the family must serve the republic. Women, and women alone, could enable Rousseau to design a republican family that provides civic training, domestic felicity, and an arena that renders women innocuous. Women in the home contribute powerfully to Poland, yet if placed in public view, their presence is dangerous to themselves and to men. Remember from chapter 3, that when the shady tree is cut into a wooden hut, when sex becomes love, and when undifferentiated male and female become differentiated husband and wife, the natural plays a new, normative role. Women in the home, I noted earlier, formed Rousseau's first example of *social* creatures leading a *natural* existence. Women come to hold tremendous sway over men, and with it the power for good or evil. In the home, women retain their status as nature's gift to society; outside, no longer acting naturally, women upset the balanced dependency between men and women. Their sexual magnetism makes them public objects of desire and competition and renders men impotent in the face of their demands. On the extreme path, to be distracted from public goals is the principal source of all corruption and disorder; hence Rousseau cannot permit women outside the home. Outside, they cause deviation. The careful yet precarious operation of redirecting *amour-propre* to public ends—the work of a lifetime, beginning with children's games—could be made null in the flash of a glance.

Rousseau's sexual division of labor contributed to what some have called classical liberal individualism—roughly put, society as a collection of discrete families, with the wife at home as caretaker and the husband in public as provider. His contribution, however, is only of the most indirect kind. Rousseau himself was certainly not, as he has been called, "the liberal individualist par excellence."[62] Some have run together Rousseau's promotion of a sexual division of labor with (supposed) support of emerging eighteenth-century bourgeois, laissez-faire capitalism. The argument is that because Rousseau assigned women to the domestic sphere, he was therefore in favor of laissez-faire market economies in which men freely work and negotiate in public, while women provide men and their children with domestic care gratis. While I cannot here comment at length on Rousseau's critique of all things bourgeois, including such basic features as private property, trade, and currency, I do want to note that to claim that Rousseau supported market capitalism or "atomistic individualism" or "ignored human interconnectedness" is to draw caricatures.[63] On the extreme path in particular, neither atomistic individualism nor market capitalism is permitted. Rather, we have an immoderate communitarian society that will not tolerate individualism of any form. Women do not serve in the home to enable men to experience independence or to participate in free markets. Women in Poland, like the men, serve the public, and while women alone are locked out of sight, both men and women are locked out of independence and autonomy.

Conclusion: Poles and Solitaires, neither Torn nor Whole

The extreme public path is problematic not only for women, but for humanity. By "humanity" I refer (parochially) to humans who value vigorous democratic deliberation on the one hand, the right to privacy on the other, and the complicated moral life that accompanies negotiating between public and private goods. Rousseau would be the first to admit that the values and goals of patriotism and those of "humanity" frequently collide; indeed, he was one of the first to make such a distinction and claim. In his *Letters from the Mountain*, Rousseau maintained that "patriotism and humanity are two virtues incompatible. . . . The legislator who would want both will obtain neither. . . . People cannot give two objects the same love."[64] From the perspective of the extreme path, Judith Shklar's claim holds true: we must choose between being "men or citizens."[65] Although I will argue in chapter 10 that Rousseau's middle path to redemption allows us to be both humans with complex moral commitments *and* citizens dedicated to the public good, Rousseau's prescription for Poland, in contrast, permits us to be citizens alone. It entails a patriotism that levels the otherwise varied moral terrain of the provinces of ethics that range from the political to the intimate. Poland's deliverance was to be a Promised Land free of the friction of the provinces. All were to dwell within the same, fortified walls.

Rousseau's Poland, then, is not a land for humans to dwell, and perhaps not even one for citizens. His model for Polish citizens is in many ways impoverished. Autonomous civic deliberation and action are traded for a stifling insurance that guarantees freedom to belong and freedom from conflict. Such freedoms, however, should not trump all other public concerns, such as the freedom to engage in vigorous civic criticism. Rousseau maintained, correctly I believe, that despotic monarchies can afford to tolerate the productions and pursuits of the more private spheres because civic order is imposed from above; hence the virtues of self-rule are not required of its citizens. Republics, in contrast, require that citizens be inspired by a public morality that equips them for self-rule and that mitigates conflict within and between rulers, that is, the citizens. In the case of Poland, however, Rousseau lost sight of the end of vibrant political and moral training, namely the self-determination of a people, by the people, for the people. Placing the preservation of the Poles' identity above all else, Rousseau disregarded what should have been promoted as an enduring aspect of that identity—the capacity to engaged in autonomous, democratic deliberation. The distinction between patriotism and nationalism can be a fine one. Not wanting to draw that line here, I will note that on the extreme path Rousseau too often placed, for the sake of unity, patriotic passion above the goals and values worthy of such passion. If, as Maurizio Viroli has skillfully argued, the patriot loves the republic and hates tyranny and corruption, whereas the nationalist loves unity and hates impurity and diversity, we may conclude that Rousseau's extreme path approaches nationalism.[66]

Those who characterize Rousseau as a romantic solitaire look the other way when they encounter him on such a dangerous path. We, longer than most, have remained with him on that path, because it is precisely at those critical junctures, when authors depart from our expectations, that we stand to learn the most. The way to Poland departs from many of Rousseau's own most cherished beliefs. As I noted in chapter 3, Rousseau's vision of humanity's happiest state is not lodged in either radical solitude or fatalistic social assimilation. I went on to claim, however, that the chances of sustaining a delicate balance between the public and private are, in Rousseau's view, remote. If Rousseau was convinced that such a balance was an impossibility for the Poles, given their sociopolitical circumstances, then perhaps he was willing to abandon some of his vision so that a portion of it might be realized. Ultimately, however, I will argue that we interpret the extreme path not as an aberration in Rousseau's work but as a work consistent with his overall way of thought. We should view the extreme path as one among the other paths that lead to what Rousseau understood as our (partial) redemption from the inevitable harm that we inflict on ourselves. His moves on the extreme path, in other words, will be shown to support my larger argument; caught between Enlightenment optimism and Augustinian pessimism, Rousseau ventured to construct a carefully engineered society—an Enlightened City—that could cope with human fallenness. A complete reversal of the fallen condition was, according to Rousseau's pessimism, too much to aim for; hence life in Rousseau's Poland falls well short of replete human flourishing. There the measures to control the plight of *amour-propre* (pernicious self-preoccupation) devastate both *amour de soi* (commendable care for the self) and *fraternité* (human community that accepts some boundary, some edge, around each member).

Rousseau was old and exhausted when he wrote *Poland* in the fall of 1770 and spring of 1771. His work at this time was focused on himself. He wrote *Confessions, Dialogues: Rousseau Judge de Jean-Jacques*, and *Reveries of the Solitary Walker* to understand Jean-Jacques in light of sixty years of remarkable fortunes but especially misfortunes. He wrote to discover himself and then to offer that self to future generations (he was quite self-conscious about this dual aim). I suggest that we read *Poland*, his last political work, as a segment of this venture in self-exploration. In that venture, Rousseau needed to define himself over against such *philosophes* as Diderot, Grimm, d'Alembert, and Voltaire, for, in Rousseau's mind, they were all leading characters—in this case, double-crossers, betrayers, and conspirators—in the story of his misfortunes. I am not suggesting, however, that Rousseau's *Poland* was an exercise in narcissism or revenge. *Poland* was written above all for the Poles.[67] Composed at a complex time in the life of the author, however, it served many ends. Rousseau, who would shortly die, who had recently returned from a painful exile, and who felt deeply misunderstood and betrayed by fellow *philosophes* and more generally by the public, was beginning to escape the pain of disappointment by retreating to a private life bereft of associations. He dodged the moral and emotional entanglement of public commitments. In the vocabulary I have been employing, Rousseau evaded conflict between the public and private by retreating to the private, in this case, to virtual solitude. Life in public proved too painful.

I will explore these claims in chapter 8, "Evading the City: The Private Path." For the moment, I want to note that Rousseau's flight to the private is the mirror image of his prescription for Poland. As Rousseau was attempting to dodge the grief and pain that is hazarded by life in public, he imagined an all-encompassing public life for the Poles. Both maneuvers belong to what I have identified as his strategy for evading conflict: reduce friction between the public and private by dodging those situations that put the two in conflict. His remedy for the Poles entailed this protective move; let a people have one love alone, the love of country, and you save them from the disappointment and conflict that spring from diverse loyalties and commitments. A totally public existence, like an utterly private one, can control disillusionment and strife by focusing one's existence on well-defined aims with assured outcomes. An enduring Polish identity, not national security as we normally understand it, was the goal Rousseau championed, and thus even foreign invasion and defeat would not have inflicted a fatal injury on the Poles. Rousseau's politics of the heart would have established a kingdom that was not subject to loss. Late in life and injured by life, Rousseau sought to establish for himself boundaries that sheltered him from the unpredictable, chaotic social world. He refused to remain vulnerable, to slacken his own private border control. Ironically, these are the same steps found on the extreme path. The Poles were to erect formidable emotive barriers that would defeat any outsider. Rousseau's self-defense became Poland's. Poland is modeled after the emotionally safe and secure family life that Rousseau longed for. Poland is Rousseau's ideal, private domestic life, written into the political body.

How to preserve independence in society, or how to make dependency benign, is a theme, I have claimed, that dominated much of Rousseau's thought. In his view, there is always something problematic about our finding ourselves reliant on the maze of divisions of labor that pervade our economic, legal, and civic institutions. Equally troubling is our addiction to, and hence dependency on, public opinion—a craving driven by *amour-propre*. As Rousseau sought to unleash himself from the ties of public dependency, he prescribed the dependent life for the Poles. Rather than interpret this as evidence of Rousseau the inconsistent thinker, I have fashioned a broad interpretive framework that includes both maneuvers. Rousseau's concern was not usually over dependency per se, but over the public oppression and personal pain that attends dependency on institutions that perpetuate injustice and inequality. If he gave special attention to *amour-propre*, it is because its anomic quests bring inequality and tolerate injustice. Dependency, however, can be rendered benign when institutions thwart inequality and when *amour-propre* is made innocuous, in this case, by being directed to public goals.

On the extreme path, radical dependency is as harmless as it is necessary. Necessary, because the total public life requires that each citizen receive all moral and social sustenance and approval from the *patrie*, the homeland; there are no lesser associations that compete either among each other or with the *patrie*, and hence there are no social junctures where an individual might exercise independence. Harmless, because when all are equally dependent on a fair *patrie*, dependency does not contribute to painful inequalities; the citizen's dependency on the just *patrie* becomes analogous to the Solitaire's dependency on Nature's Garden. The Solitaire's relation to nature is marked above all by necessity. Minimal needs allow the Solitaire to be self-sufficient, and self-sufficiency, in Rousseau's view, is important insofar as it protects one from unjust associations. The Solitaire relies on nature alone, and nature presents itself to the Solitaire as an impersonal, superior force. Such a matchless force provides clear limits in the form of necessity, and the Solitaire respects these limits and is hence content. This, then, is Rousseau's lesson from the Garden to humans outside it living in social conditions: to preserve well-being, humans must live in relation to an impersonal, superior force that presents clear limits that are respected.

If the impersonal force of society is to be respected, however, it must not loom as a capricious force, but as a just one, producing an experience similar to that of the Solitaires: the experience of impersonal limits imposed upon all equally. This condition requires just social institutions, and hence it is not coincidental that Rousseau's most powerful provisions for social justice are found on the extreme path. In Poland, have "neither beggars nor millionaires"; cure people of the desire for riches, which produces poverty for most, and the Poles "will put their attention and ambition in the service of the *patrie*"; "open a door to freedom for the serfs," leading them to communal lands and citizenship; establish public boards that provide for "overburdened families, invalids, widows, and orphans."[68] On the public extreme path, Rousseau's central complaint against the celebrated "sage" of Molière's *Misanthrope* focused on his indifference to the hardships of others. He is "one of those decent people of high society . . . who, at a fine dinner, maintains that it is not true that the people are hungry; who, with a well-lined pocket, finds it terribly unpleasant that one would speak in favor of the poor."[69] And in "Political Economy," another text of the extreme path, Rousseau insisted that one of the three essential duties of government is "the provision for the public wants." Such provision included treating not the symptoms of poverty by, for example, "building hospitals for the poor," but by "guaranteeing that citizens do not become poor"; imposing steep luxury taxes, "which relieve the poor and charge the rich, thus preventing the continual increase of inequality of fortune"; ensuring that justice cannot be bought, because while typically the rich receive justice, the poor are denied it. "The more humanity owes him [the poor one], the more society denies him. Every door is shut against him, even when he has a right to its being opened."[70]

In many respects, then, the extreme public path is a good one for the poor and disenfranchised. When the private is subsumed by the public, and when the moral life, which includes a strong commitment to social justice, is conflated with the political life, the poor have much to gain. Indeed, all have much to gain, in Rousseau's view. Humans, like the Solitaires, experience well-being when their environment provides impersonal limits that are imposed justly. What the Solitaires confronted as necessity the Poles will receive as justice, and they will thereby be free from arbitrary inequality and the personal and interpersonal strife that is caused by anomic desires. Mutual dependency, on the extreme path, is not an obstacle to freedom, but one of freedom's conditions. When all are equally dependent on the just *patrie*, all are free from inequality, free from arbitrary justice, free from internal conflict, and free to belong to a commonwealth that liberates one from the confines of the self.

Some have claimed that Rousseau, in bad faith, championed independence for men, dependence for women.[71] This, however, is not a nuanced interpretation of Rousseau. He consistently held that in society men and women are interdependent.[72] Rousseau, in fact, was one of the earliest Western writers to emphasize the social power of women. While others claimed that women were inferior because of their close proximity to nature, Rousseau highlighted women's power and equality in relations due to their unique social capacity to promote harmony and to thwart narrow self-interest. Needless to say, confining women to such roles is deeply offensive. "Separate yet equal" in liberal democracies is convincing only under limited circumstances marked by informed consent, and never by gender stereotypes. Still, on all of Rousseau's public paths, men and women are mutually dependent. That dependency, however, is defined differently for women and men. Men are dependent on women in the home and on just, public institutions. Women, in contrast, are dependent on their men alone.

Wherever women live, they live in Poland. This is not to deny that the goal of forming citizens in the home is most intense on the extreme path. Yet even on the more moderate public paths, women's lives are relegated to the highly structured space of the home. Wherever they live—which ever path they are on—women possess the freedom to belong, the mark and boon of Poland. Such freedom is a terrible cage. It is, however, a similar cage, though more confining, to the one in which Rousseau was eager to place men. Moreover, it belongs to what I am identifying as a comprehensive framework from which to interpret Rousseau's thought. His prescriptions for Poles and for himself, for men and for women, for the solitaires and the sociable, do not form, ultimately, a mass of tangled contradictions. They flow from the same vision, the same fears, the same hopes. Outside the Garden, we suffer tremendously unless we can mitigate the harm produced by associations which place our loves, public and private, in conflict—conflict which is made especially destructive by the injurious effects of *amour-propre*. In Poland, as in Nature's Garden, we—women and men—are free from internal conflict and from the risk of disappointment. This is not to say, of course, that we would want to live in Rousseau's Poland or Garden or as his women. It is to say that Rousseau's remedies, in all their diversity, for men and women alike, are treating the same disease, the same fallen condition.

In the Garden, as Solitaires, there was no conflict between duty to self and duty to others, because there were no others. Outside the Garden, in contrast, the conflict is inescapable. Immediately after Rousseau produced his perhaps clearest expression of the human fallen condition ("I sense myself enslaved and free at the same time; I see the good, I love it, and I do the bad"), he wrote, "If to prefer oneself above all else is an inclination natural to man, and if, however, the first sentiment of justice is innate in the human heart, let those who say man is a simple being remove these contradictions."[73] A natural tension exists between the public and private. For Rousseau, as for Kant and Freud, there is an eternal struggle between our concern for ourselves and our obligation to others. This struggle is checked on the extreme path, where love of self becomes virtually synonymous with duty to the *patrie*. This remedy cannot erase the tension entirely, but it can efface most of the private side of the conflict, and that is what makes the remedy equally powerful and frightening. Its potency must match the resiliency of the principal disease: a fallen condition that seems inevitably to lead to unnecessary harm.

The tension in the notion of inevitable yet unnecessary harm, with all its contractions, sums up Rousseau's awkward spiritual location between the two opposing traditions that I earlier identified, Augustinian pessimism and Enlightenment optimism. Maintaining that we are caught between our responsibility for ourselves and our powerlessness to radically transform ourselves, Rousseau sought a sensible way for the Poles to experience a way of life free from debilitating conflict, although that way, we have seen, is not without great loss. Given the depth of human fallenness, Rousseau's wager was that sacrificing the private to the public would produce more good than harm in the lives of the Poles. Besides, all paths to redemption entail some loss; all are only partial. Humans, in Rousseau's view, are not capable of healing themselves completely. Hence the redeemed Pole, like the Solitaire, although content and not torn, lacks wholeness. And I have argued that this price of redemption, the absence of the private, is too great. This is not to pit socialization against individualism as if those are the fundamental polarities that define the conflict.[74] The basic conflict is between the genuine, yet contending, goods that we associate with the public and private life. This basic conflict is exacerbated by *amour-propre*, which transforms the individual's harmless love for herself (*amour de soi*) into vain, anomic occupations that corrupt both public and private goods.

For some time now, Rousseau has been celebrated or loathed as the Romantic libertarian. In the view of one social theorist, "All restraint upon man's natural impulses Rousseau believes is bad—goodness consists in being liberated from law, from discipline, from authority, from the obligations imposed by God and our fellow man."[75] I have argued, in contrast, that Rousseau held that our doing harm is empirically inevitable and hence essentially "natural" and that, in Rousseau's view, one way to save ourselves, at least partially, is to imposed on ourselves the full burden of law, discipline, authority, and obligation. This way, the way to Poland, minimizes both conflict and human disappointment, for its goals are few and obtainable. There is another way, however, to bring these same advantages. In the next chapter, we will explore that way, as we venture on the private path.

8

Evading the City

The Private Path

The Solitary Walker

Much of this chapter is a reflection on Rousseau's *Reveries of the Solitary Walker*, and I would like to use that image, the solitary walker, to characterize provisionally what I will call Rousseau's private path to redemption. Imagine that you are walking alone in the woods, either for pleasure or on a necessary journey. Your walk on the private path could be in the City. Rousseau's *Reveries*, after all, was composed while walking in and around Paris. Yet to note the private path's distinctive features, it is better to begin this journey on what Rousseau considered to be its most pristine segment. So, you are alone in the woods, and your mind is unencumbered yet attentive, your sight is roving yet keen, your heart light yet meditative.

You are free, at least temporarily, from daily worries and hectic schedules. As you focus on the changing path in front of you, you gain perspective from which to consider your life not in its crushing details, but as a whole. Although you may contemplate some vexing problems, the expanse of the woods eases your mind and lends hope, placing problems and fears in helpful perspective. On this private path you experience healing, although you have done nothing to heal yourself except perhaps to allow this occasion to lend its gifts of restoration. Will admits grace. It won't last, of course, and you know this. You are not troubled, however, by the ephemeral quality of this elevated well-being and this new perspective. The occasion would fade even more quickly, you know, should you cling to it. For the moment, you are thankful, alert, and at ease with the world as you find it.

This caricature, or Weberian ideal type, of the private path allows us to highlight its features. On it, you are free from such distractions as blaring televisions, ringing phones, addictive newspapers, unremitting e-mail, or clamoring billboards. There are no external claims on you to write a memo or take out the trash. No one is present to hurt you; there is no threat of intimidation or humiliation. And there is no one you need to perform for or impress. You are temporarily released from *amour-propre*, that anxious and anomic pride, so dependent on public opinion, and from all its destructive barbs. Like the Solitaire in the Garden, you are guided principally by gentle *amour de soi*—healthy, gentle love of self. There is little opening for *amour-propre* because you are radically alone and hence independent. Free from pain and vulnerability, you experience a deep calm and restored vision. And the beauty of nature—what role does it play? It diverts unhelpful self-regard. By painlessly dissolving the ego, by diverting your eyes from your (petty and narrow) self, beauty enables you to better see yourself. When this happens, you do not lose sight of yourself, rather you see yourself and your problems differently. Some problems disappear, like water vapor absorbed by a wide, dry sky. Other problems remain, but appear differently, somehow made more clear and manageable. And you are different, if only for a moment. Your burdens lighten as your soul, so to speak, allows mild *amour de soi* to replace anxious *amour-propre*.

To tread the private path, I have said, it is not essential that you be isolated in the woods. You could walk the private path in the city, only there it is more difficult to follow. In the city, there is more danger of encountering a person or incident, a gesture or conversation, a leaflet or driver that will trouble you and perhaps inflame *amour-propre*. A reminder of a task, a grudge, a fear, a contest, a debt—such hazards abound and appear with little warning. Still, although difficult, you can follow the private path in the city. You need not be alone on the private path. It can include sharing a peaceful morning with a life-long partner, a weekly luncheon with a good friend, an evening shared with good company. Like the woods, such occasions can put you at ease and grant perspective. Again, however, there are more obstacles to the private path in the company of others than in solitude. The private path, above all, is a safe one; receiving and inflicting harm is kept to an absolute minimum. With family and friends, however, we are most vulnerable. With our defenses down, our attachments, usually sweet, can wickedly wound us, for loved ones know the precise location of old injuries. Alone in the woods, in contrast, we are safe from the cuts and bruises of intimacy: the flight of a bird, the sound of a brook, the breeze of the wind, the warmth of the sun—these caress our senses; not only do they not hurt us, they seem to make us whole and, if need be, forgiven.

Alone, then, and in the woods—with this image we begin, for here the private path is most exposed. Many of us are attracted to the private path, at least occasionally. The solitary walker can be an inviting image. This is in part because we have inherited a romantic tradition, in no small part shaped by Rousseau, that celebrates the image of the solitaire. Also, we live in a world that is increasingly marked by instrumental reasoning and frantic lifestyles. As each minute of our day becomes scheduled, and each act calculated for maximum yield, life becomes weary and insipid. When exhausted and perhaps despondent, we often long for the calm of the private path.

Rousseau created the private path in response to what he was experiencing and anticipating, namely, the mounting strains of modern existence. In part I, especially chapter 4, we rehearsed Rousseau's genealogy of modern alienation and misery. From the division of labor come the multiplication of commodities and complex systems of exchange, from these come a heightened sense of private property and public justice, and from rules of justice come conventions of inequality and the attending humiliation. This genealogy of sorrow is driven by both psychological and sociological developments, chiefly the progression of *amour-propre* and the division of labor. As *amour-propre* fuels anomic desires and drives us to advance in a public life increasingly marked by the impersonal—contracts, specialization, and bureaucracy—we crush those below us, strive to surmount those above us, and for our efforts are rewarded with endless labor and grief. Rousseau's private path was his answer, or rebuttal, to what he perceived as an increasingly barren public existence fed by a mass of frantic, covetous, private selves. In such a world Rousseau suffered, and he tried to break out of it. I am calling his attempted escape the private path.

In this chapter we will explore the private path on its most "ideal" or exemplary segment: the path that permits only one traveler at a time. Although solitude is not a synonym for the private life, the solitaire—the one who is disengaged from others, even if in the midst of others—will allow us to inspect some of the more conspicuous features of the private life. After we investigate this extreme private path, we will turn in the next chapter to the way of Clarens, the moderate private path. Clarens, Rousseau's preferred path, is the way of friendship, intimacy, marriage, and local community.

The Extreme Private Path: "Farewell Hope, and with Hope Farewell Fear"

I can sketch the rough contours of the extreme private path, the way of *amour de soi*, by offering a series of contrasts to the extreme public path. Like the extreme public path, on the extreme private path there is no conflict between public and private because there is no public life with which to clash. There are few obstacles to one's goals because there are no relationships and little contact with interfering institutions. Again, like the extreme public path, there is little diversity on the private path; one is alone. The very problem of diversity—how to manage it harmoniously in society—disappears. Indeed, most obstacles to freedom and peace vanish, if by freedom we mean to pursue freely one's chosen ends, and if by peace we mean to enjoy the absence of conflict (as opposed to, say, freedom as the liberty to contribute creatively to community, and peace as the contentment of belonging). Unlike the public paths, where virtue is often a joint achievement, on the private path virtue is an individual feat.

Why take the private path? There are many reasons, some courageous, others cowardly, some a matter of psychological survival. Here are the reasons Rousseau offered: You are just and sincere and cannot endure the injustice and insincerity of society.[1] You find oppressive the frosty, calculating ethos that pervades the public life.[2] You realize that as long as you remain in the City, you will inevitably become ensnared in the tangled webs of unnecessary harm. Hence you flee Paris, the City, in order to secure some virtue— some integrity and sincerity—and to evade the structures of receiving and inflicting pain.

Rousseau's recurrent Augustinian pessimism led him to hold, with the Jansenists, that sometimes our evil can only be minimized by withdrawing from associations. Augustinian pessimism is not necessarily related to the act of retreating. One could remain in the City and brood, or perhaps one could endeavor to carve out a private space for individual salvation in the form of personal integrity, close friendships, or familial piety. The latter was Montaigne's moral strategy, and something like it has been recommended by many forms of liberalism: do not endeavor to transform the public realm by your own moral lights, but rather perfect your private existence—the only realm over which you have any right or ability to control. Yet in Rousseau's view, evil's net in the City— whether Diderot's Paris or Montaigne's Bordeaux—is too broad to be evaded successfully, especially if one is dedicated to truth and sincerity.[3] Even Rousseau's best pupil, Emile, who was raised by a godlike tutor, fell into evil shortly after moving to Paris.[4]

Radical evil requires radical remedies. You cannot be in the City and not be of it, you must flee it. Poland isn't an option, because you're not Polish—you're an outsider. What of the way of Clarens (as described in *Julie*) or Geneva (as described in *The Social Contract*)?[5] The prospects are not good. Clarens, after all, is a fictional fantasy; and Geneva, it had become clear, isn't in fact the republic of *The Social Contract*, for it persecutes loyal citizens. Rousseau had recently been banned from Geneva, his homeland, because his writings were deemed blasphemous and seditious.[6] Your only sure path is the extreme private one. That is the path over which you have the most control, because success there does not depend on finding a happy social situation—a rarity, indeed.[7] On the private path, you flee dependency on others. Your destiny, like that of the Garden's Solitaire, is determined by a commingling of free will and Nature's necessity. This yields the greatest freedom and peace of its kind: freedom from the claims of others, and peace in the absence of City clamor and chaos.

On Poland's extreme public path, peace was an internal condition that provided a freedom from conflicting desires in order that the individual could pursue collective goals. On the private path, in contrast, Rousseau moved closer to Hobbes's view that peace is ultimately for the sake of private happiness. Yet a Leviathan is not required to support private happiness, in Rousseau's account. Indeed, on the private path, happiness has little to do with external circumstances, except perhaps this: the farther from sociability, the better. Rousseau, *pace* Hobbes, held that humans could be peaceful without a Leviathan. This is because Rousseau held that it is not altogether impossible to conserve those "tender and gentle passions that spring from love of self" [*amour de soi*]. Although the chances of such conservation are slim, the private path is one of Rousseau's moral strategies for restoring such Garden-like qualities as gentleness, self-sufficiency, and sincerity.

In the *Reveries of the Solitary Walker*, Rousseau claimed that he began moving toward the private path in 1752 when he turned forty years old: "From this time I can date my total renunciation of the world and my intense craving for solitude which has never left me since then. The work I set myself could only be executed in absolute retreat; it called for long and tranquil meditations that the tumult of society makes impossible."[8] Although "total renunciation" and "absolute retreat" exaggerate Rousseau's departure from Paris (which wasn't, in fact, until 1756), these descriptions do accurately depict his life in 1776 when, back in Paris, he began to compose the *Reveries*. The radical solitude of his old age had been, in his view, imposed on him by his adversaries. Still, he claimed that "by isolating me to make me miserable, they did more for my happiness than I would have known to do myself."[9] This was not the first time Rousseau had been forced to be free in solitude. When living in exile near Neuchâtel, for example, his house was stoned by an angry mob that distrusted the eccentric Jean-Jacques who dressed in Armenian costume, complete with a caftan and fur cap.[10] He took refuge on the Island of Saint-Pierre, and, in the *Reveries*, described his two months of solitary confinement on the island as "the happiest time of [his] life."[11] The island, Rousseau noted, agreed with his "peaceful tastes and solitary temperament."[12] He maintained that "on the island [he] would be more removed from men, more sheltered from their outrages, more forgotten by them, in a word, more free . . . for the contemplative life." His profound love for his island existence led him to fantasize that the nations of Europe, which were one by one issuing warrants for his arrest, would consign him to spend the rest of his days on the island: "I would like to be constrained to stay here, so that I would not be made to leave."[13] Later we will consider how forced solitude can become crippling loneliness. At this point in Rousseau's life, however, he himself was crippled by public persecution, both real and imagined.

Rousseau contrasted variously the chaos and anxiety of the City—his symbol, we have said, of perfidious social existence—to the calm and tranquil life of solitude on the private path. In the *Reveries* he noted the tumult of the world and asked if there was not a place where one could rest. He lamented, "Everything on the earth is in continual flux. Nothing keeps the same, unchanging form, and our affections, being attached to things outside us, necessarily pass away and change with them."[14] After doubting whether happiness could be achieved in such turmoil, Rousseau described the private path, "where the soul can find a place stable enough for it to rest blissfully and to gather together there its entire being, with no need to remember the past or reach into the future." On the private path "we can call ourselves happy." What is the source of this happiness? Many things, but Rousseau highlighted this: the presence of *amour de soi* and the absence of *amour-propre*. On the private path one is free to love, if only oneself, without corruption and unnecessary pain.

In the City, in contrast, we are consumed by *amour-propre*. Rousseau noted that as long as he was "in the world," *amour-propre* had been "exacerbated" in him; yet once he "fell back on [his] soul, severing the external relations that make it [*amour-propre*] so demanding, and renouncing all comparisons or preferences, it was enough to be good in [his] own eyes. And so, becoming the proper self-love [*amour de soi*], it returned to the true natural order and freed [him] from the yoke of opinion."[15] Rousseau, we know, had more than once denounced "living outside oneself" in the opinions of others.[16] The self living outside itself for others becomes a slave to public opinion. Moreover, since opinion is always in flux, this public slave becomes exhausted, constantly calculating what words, deeds, and gestures at what time will make the greatest impression in the eyes of the public. The public slave, obsessed with self-advancement, has little time to contemplate his or her loss of felicity. In the clamor of *amour-propre*, the voice of *amour de soi*, the call to healthy love of self, is lost.

Rousseau summed up his view with this claim: "Whatever situation we find ourselves in, it is only [*amour-propre*] that can make us constantly unhappy."[17] This claim is truly remarkable, considering the numerous sources of unhappiness that the aged Rousseau might have identified—treachery of friends, public humiliation, or banishment, to name a few. Yet the various sources of unhappiness, he believed, ultimately spring from *amour-propre*. Living in the clutch of *amour-propre*, we are driven by envy; we are anxious for public acclaim and become dependent on it. Living for oneself alone, in contrast, without concern for others, whether for their welfare or harm, one becomes invulnerable to the deeds and opinions of others. On the private path, one is numb to the sting of betrayal, humiliation, or even exile. For this reason, Rousseau insisted that he could remain free—that is, live for and within himself—even in a dungeon. We should not be surprised, then, to discover that Rousseau's favorite literary creation, Emile, ultimately experiences freedom in imprisonment and slavery.[18]

The private path is not principally a physical location, a place deep in the woods far from the crowd. It is, above all, a psychological place—a distinctive disposition or state of being. This disposition is achieved when, to use Rousseau's words, "*amour de soi* alone is at work, and *amour-propre* is absent."[19] In this state, one performs one's duty to self, avoids doing harm to others, and remains unattached to others. This calm state of nonattachment could, in principle, be obtained even during the rush hour, as people steal what we call our right-of-way and give offense. We experience the rage of offense when we are in the clutch of *amour-propre*'s excessive concern for honor and esteem. The self-love of *amour de soi*, in contrast, would not suffer such needless concern. One can, then, remain self-possessed in the City. The private path of *amour de soi* can be achieved anywhere. Rousseau's own *Reveries*, I noted, are reflections that emerged during his ten walks in Paris.

Invulnerability is both the goal and the prize of the private path. Perhaps one cannot control such outward circumstances as government or employment or rude behavior in others. One's own character, however, is always within reach. It is the one thing that may be perfected, in spite of external circumstance. Freedom from circumstance requires limited desires or minimal attachments. "We are attached to everything," Rousseau once complained. "We cling to everything—times, places, men, things. . . . Is it surprising that our ills multiply by all the locations where we can be wounded?"[20] To extinguish one's desires is to achieve the invulnerability, and the freedom, of the private path. On this path, invulnerability and freedom are synonymous. To these synonyms we can add happiness; the smaller the difference between our powers and our desires, the greater our chance for happiness. Since increasing our powers is difficult and risky, the more reliable way to achieve happiness is to limit our desires. Our desires are especially inflamed when we become preoccupied with possibility as opposed to actuality. Rousseau understood, as did two of his very different successors, Kierkegaard and Durkheim, that to dwell in the realm of possibility is to court infinite sorrow. "The real world," Rousseau cautioned, "has its limits; the imaginary world is infinite. Unable to enlarge the one, let us restrict the other. For, it is from their difference alone that are born all the pains that make us truly unhappy."[21] As long as our loves and desires are scattered wide and beyond our control, we remain woundable. Hence Rousseau's advice, "Gather your existence within yourself, and you will no longer be miserable."[22]

Invulnerability on the private path extends even to death. The fear of death, and not death itself, distorts life and makes us miserable. By submitting to its necessity, however, death loses its sting. When we cling unnecessarily to life and to its accessories—loved ones, for example—death is resisted and accompanied by moaning and struggle. "The best means of learning how to die," Rousseau insisted, "is to live free and to be attached little to things human."[23] On the private path, then, freedom from disappointment and sorrow, including those brought by death, sets severe limits on all relationships.

By limiting attachments, one learns not only to accept calmly one's own death, but the death of a loved one, even a spouse. Rousseau described a happy man—"fresh, gay, vigorous, in good health"—who receives a letter in the mail. Upon reading the letter, "instantly his air changes. He turns pale . . . he weeps, convulses, groans, tears his hair." Rousseau's comment on this sudden change is, "Senseless one, what evil has this paper done to you? What limb has it removed from you? . . . In sum, what has it changed in you yourself to put you in the state which I see you?" Emile's tutor engineers the identical scenario. With a letter in hand and a serious face, the tutor asks the happy and in-love Emile, "What would you do if you were informed that Sophie is dead?"[24] Emile's response is not unlike the man above who received his letter of misery. The tutor concludes that Emile, like Achilles, is not entirely invulnerable. A letter can only bring news of that which is outside one; the genuine walker on the private path, the solitaire who is occupied with *amour de soi* alone, is unscathed by the external. Emile, in contrast, is vulnerable to Sophie. And that is as it should be, for Emile is not on the private path.

That path, I have said, can lead through the City. It is easier, however, to obtain the calm of *amour de soi* in physical isolation, on a desolate island such as Saint-Pierre, for example. Alone, one is less likely to slide back into the teeth of *amour-propre*. With no one to impress or to fear or to care for, one is more likely to live "within oneself," to be genuinely self-possessed. In Paris, Rousseau's solitary reveries were on occasion punctured by rude encounters that ignited his *amour-propre*. Sounding much like St. Paul, Rousseau described a condition not unlike the weak will associated with Augustinian original sin: "In spite of all my efforts, *amour-propre* comes into play. . . . The foolishness of *amour-propre* I can see all too clearly, but I am not able to suppress it."[25] The folly of *amour-propre* runs deep. Rousseau developed personal strategies to attempt to reduce the role of *amour-propre* in his life and strengthen that of *amour de soi*. He would, for example, intentionally place himself in the height of the rush and social hour as an exercise in achieving the psychological state of *amour de soi*'s nonattachment: "A hundred times I walked on the public boulevards and to the busiest public places with the sole purpose of training myself to cope with cruel blunders." His goal was to live for himself alone, neither inflicting nor receiving unnecessary pain, in the midst of others. Yet Rousseau confessed, "Not only was I unable to do so, I did not even make any progress, and all my painful but fruitless efforts left me just as vulnerable as before to being troubled, hurt, and indignant."[26]

The more expedient approach is to avoid "things human." Hence Rousseau wrote, "The precept of never hurting another carries with it that of being attached to human society as little as possible."[27] Nonattachment prevents harm to others, as well as to the self. To avoid suffering, attach oneself only to those things that do not disappoint. Rousseau poignantly asked, "Do you want, then, to live happily and wisely? Attach your heart only to beauty that does not perish . . . learn to lose what can be take away from you . . . detach your heart from events lest it be torn up by them."[28] This brings us back to what we earlier called Rousseau's strategy for evading conflict: reduce the friction between the public and private by dodging those situations that put the two in conflict. On the public path, the way to Poland, conflict is evaded by subsuming most aspects of life under the public. On the private path, conflict is evaded by divorcing oneself from all ties to the public—indeed, to anyone outside the self. It becomes impossible to enter most commitments, because, lacking omniscience, one could never know in advance if a commitment would lead to conflict between love of self (*amour de soi*) and love of others.

Suffering and love travel together, in Rousseau's view: "I have always passionately loved what must bring me misfortune."[29] In his retreat from Paris to Montmorency, Rousseau expressed this fear in a letter to his new friend, Mme. de Luxembourg: "Why disturb the peace of a solitaire who was renouncing the pleasures of life in order no longer to feel its troubles? . . . Friendship, Madame! Ah, *voila* my misfortune! . . . I have become attached to you, and fresh sorrows are being prepared for me at the end of the game."[30] If love and friendship bring trouble, their absence brings freedom. Referring to his move to Montmorency, Rousseau declared that "deprived of the charms of lively attachments, I also became free of their weighty chains." At Montmorency, Rousseau sought only those acquaintances who "subjected [him] to no obligations."[31]

On the private path, then, the only permissible relationship is the weightless one. The ethics of the private path, if one can call it that, can be summarized like this: "As the first step toward the good is not to do evil, the first step toward happiness is not to suffer at all."[32] Later we will ask whether Rousseau, ultimately, added other steps to these "first steps" to the good and to happiness. On the private path, however, these first steps are the first and last. Avoid doing and receiving unnecessary harm—this constricted yet profound imperative sums up a radical yet safe existence. Again, the surest way to execute the imperative is to avoid "things human." Humans necessarily introduce hope, and hope inevitably brings risk of disappointment. "So farewell Hope, and with Hope farewell Fear." This line, spoken by Milton's Satan, expresses well the psychology of Rousseau's cautious private path.[33] By relinquishing hope, the solitaire and Satan become invulnerable.

Nature and Mysticism on the Private Path

In Rousseau's view, human relations are as painful and likely to disappointment as nature is salutary and safe. Having fled human things, we are not entirely alone on the private path, for now we are in a position to experience the equanimity and delights of nature. Reeling from exile and persecution, Rousseau found refuge in nature. "Oh Nature! Oh my Mother! I am here under your sole protection. Here there is no clever and deceitful man who places himself between you and me."[34] In order to enjoy the gifts of nature, Rousseau found it necessary to evade not only human encounters, but even "the memory of company" and the residual "fumes of self-love [*amour-propre*] and of the tumult of the world." The way of nonattachment, then, leads not only to living within the self, but also to living with nature: "It was only after I had detached myself from social passions and their sad cortege that I once again found nature with all its charms."[35] Although nature may be intrinsically worthy of love and admiration, one's sight must be cultivated to see it and recognize its loveliness. Regarding our ability to behold beauty in nature, Emerson once said, "The eye is the best of artists." Rousseau would have agreed and added: "In one's heart lies the life of the sight of nature; to see it one must feel it."[36] Such sight and feeling require that one escape the turmoil, pettiness, and destructive ways of anxious social existence.

The close connection between nature and the private path is manifest in Rousseau's favorite occupation—botany. Indeed, botany for Rousseau became a symbol of the private path.[37] We can think of botany as Rousseau's return, especially toward the end of his life, to one of his first moral and literary themes, Nature's Garden.[38] Like the Solitaire's life in the Garden, botany admits few companions, except plants. To pursue botany, one's tranquility and attention cannot be disturbed by chaotic relationships and anxious self-love. "There is in this playful occupation [botany] a charm which can only be felt when the passions are entirely calm, but which alone suffices to render our lives happy and sweet."[39] With botany, one cultivates and enjoys the ability to be attentive to the simple yet diverse green life that presents itself.

Botany, however, can easily become corrupted. Rousseau described the fall of the botanist, though he may as well as have been writing about the professor or anyone else who loses sight of the internal goods of a profession and focuses instead on such external goods as salary, rank, or fame. "As soon as we mix up botany with motives of interest or vanity, that we may obtain positions or write books, as soon as we learn only so that we can instruct, and botanize only to become authors or professors, all this sweet charm vanishes, and we no longer see plants except as instruments of our passions." This fall, like the fall from the Garden, is inspired by the same internal demon—*amour-propre* and its insatiable drive for self-recognition. Once again, the private life is toppled by, and tumbles toward, the anxious life of the public stage. After this fall, "we find no real pleasure in the study of plants, we do not want to know except to show what we know, and the woods become for us a public stage on which we are preoccupied with how to make admirers."[40] When botany is pursued for its own sake, however, it is a model and symbol of the private path, for it weaves together solitude, equanimity, attentiveness, nature, and beauty.

Beauty, for Rousseau, always possesses a moral aspect.[41] Thus far, the principal moral quality of the private path has been negative, namely, avoid all unnecessary harm to self and to others. The beauty of nature now introduces a positive moral component. Beauty, in Rousseau's view, can morally elevate the self, granting it a broad perspective and allowing it, painlessly, to be caught up with something outside narrow self-interest (*amour-propre*). Beauty, however, posses no threat to *amour de soi*, the self-love that suits the private path. "The love of beauty," Rousseau insisted, "is a sentiment as natural to the human heart as the love of self, *amour de soi*."[42] When we are enveloped in beauty, we can perceive, at least temporarily, the goodness in self and in nature. Such recognition leads to gratitude, and gratitude leads to prayer.

Nature, beauty, and God are Rousseau's trinity. In his *Confessions* he wrote, "I find no more dignified homage to the divinity than the silent admiration that is inspired by the contemplation of his works." It is not surprising, in Rousseau's view, that City dwellers, those who "see only walls and streets and crimes," are irreligious. Having little beauty in their lives, gratitude and wonder are not called forth. But how could those who live in the country, Rousseau asked rhetorically, "especially the solitary, have no faith at all? How is it that their souls are not elevated a hundred times a day with ecstasy to the author of the wonders that strike them?" As for Rousseau himself, prayer in a room was nearly impossible. To pray, he needed to encounter the "ravishing spectacle of Nature"; then his prayer usually consisted in a thankful yet inarticulate, "Oh!" or "Oh Great Being."[43] His prayers, or sighs of gratitude, were an expression of redemption. On the private path, in nature, Rousseau could find himself at ease with the world and with himself, as he experienced fleeting wholeness. Robert Frost, in his poem, "Directive," spoke of a similar redemption. The poem begins by urging the reader to withdraw from the complexity of the modern world: "Back out of all this now too much for us / Back in a time made simple by the loss / of detail." And it concludes with a compelling description of redemption in nature:

And if you're lost enough [in nature] to find yourself
By now, pull in your ladder road behind you
And put a sign up CLOSED to all but me.
Then make yourself at home . . .

. . . .

Here are your waters and your watering place.
Drink and be whole again beyond confusion.[44]

As we have discussed it thus far, Rousseau's trinity, and the redemption that accompanies it, includes the self—an elevated self. On occasion, however, the trinity on the private path leads to the utter loss of self. Free *from* the anxiety that springs from human encounter, free *for* the joy that springs from nature, the self temporarily dissolves as worries and concerns are exchanged for nature's measureless bounty. This loss of self is not the same as the loss of individuality that occurs on the extreme public path. In Rousseau's Poland, the self, although lacking private goals, is in love with public things and hence possesses a well-defined, albeit not unique, identity. On the private path, in contrast, we encounter on occasion a loss of self that is closer to mysticism than patriotism. Take, for example, the episode of the Great Dane in the second walk of the *Reveries*. When Rousseau regained consciousness after having been knocked down in Paris by the large dog, he experienced the following:

Night was approaching. I saw the sky, some stars, and a few leaves. This first sensation was a delicious moment. I was conscious of nothing else. . . . Entirely caught up in the present, I could remember nothing; I had no distinct notion of my own individuality. . . . I felt neither pain, nor fear, nor anxiety. . . . I felt throughout my entire being such a delightful calm that each time I recall this feeling, I can find nothing to compare with it.[45]

On the private path, there is only a short distance between love of self (*amour de soi*) and loss of self as one embraces the universal. One might have thought, with Kant, that the universal stands closer to public ventures in the common good, not private journeys of the self. In Rousseau's view, however, there is always something parochial about the common good. His notion of the general will, unlike Diderot's, is not universal but group-specific. And commitment to the group, in Rousseau's view, is often at odds with commitment to the universal. On the private path, standing outside the group, one has an opportunity to step outside oneself and experience, if but for a moment, not only a universal moral order, but the universe in its entirety.

One need not be knocked unconscious as a prelude to such mysticism. In his seventh walk in the *Reveries*, Rousseau reflected on the private joy of contemplating the beauty of nature: "A profound and sweet reverie seizes one's senses, and one is lost in blissful self-abandonment, losing oneself in the immensity of this beautiful order with which one feels at one. So, all particular objects escape one; one sees and feels nothing but the whole."[46] Again, later in the same "walk," Rousseau declared: "My meditations and reveries are never more delightful than when I forget myself. I feel ecstasy, inexpressible raptures in melting, as it were, into the system of beings and identifying myself with the whole of nature."[47]

In these passages, the final step of the private path—the path of gentle self-love—is toward the loss of self in the beauty and enormity of nature. This step reflects Rousseau's proximity to French Augustinian and Jansenist moral theology. The traditional French model held that the subordination of the private for the sake of the general good was the truly moral act; the more general, the more moral, and the more particular, the more evil. In that tradition, the short and final step was from society's general good to God's (these were often deemed one and the same). On his more public paths to redemption, Rousseau utilized this prominent French moral and theological tradition, although he transformed it by eliminating its final step—the identification of society's general will with the will of God. On the private path, however, this tradition is not found. Rather, employing a logic more akin to the radical theological traditions of the Port-Royal Jansenists, Rousseau held that there is a higher moral order than society's general good, and that the way to discover it is to withdraw from society—first retreating into oneself, and then moving out of the self and to the universal. Here, we find in Rousseau something similar to the beatific vision: the loss of self in the face of absolute beauty. To place oneself on such a journey, however, is not contrary to love of self (*amour de soi*); it is perhaps the ultimate aim of such love. The private path leads not only out of the grief of society but, on occasion, to the joy of the universal.

"History of a Soul"

John Chapman is not alone when he claims that, in Rousseau's view, human "judgments and actions are not hopelessly warped by original sin. . . . Virtue cannot be a personal achievement. Either men attain goodness together or not at all."[48] This standard interpretation is a long way from what we have discovered on the private path. On that path, human goodness is perhaps possible only when individuals are alone and occupied with their own well-being, as dictated by *amour de soi*. Such human goodness, I admit, is constricted in form. Yet as we saw in chapter 2, the Solitaire's peaceful existence looks moral when compared to the stormy and violent existence of many social humans. If we accept the standard view, we miss the depths of Rousseau's Augustinian pessimism and consequently miss the point of the private path. We choose the private path precisely so that we can avoid the corruption and pain of public life. Away from society, one is less likely to do or receive harm. Some forms of society, such as liberalism, recognize this and attempt to foster peace and order by establishing societies that safeguard the citizen's private path, that is, a safe and private space to pursue happiness and salvation on one's own terms. St. Augustine himself was one of the first architects of a social order built on the premise that virtue is not a joint achievement, and hence the most government can do is allow citizens to attempt virtue, free from harassment, on their own.

Rousseau's private path suggests a pessimism perhaps even deeper than Augustine's. At its most extreme, it assumes that all social orders will inevitably become corrupt and hurt their members. The only remedy, then, is to escape the City and follow the gentle way of *amour de soi*, even if imperfectly. There is no way to absolutely escape *amour-propre* and its destructiveness. There is no complete remedy. But the private path, heading out of the City, leaves behind much depravity. Rousseau's Augustinian pessimism is most apparent in his descriptions of humans *in society*. To put it this way, however, is not just to repeat Ernst Cassier and others who insist that, for Rousseau, the problem is humans in society and hence the solution is to reform society. This Enlightenment interpretation of Rousseau fails to place Rousseau at the crossroads of Enlightenment optimism and Augustinian pessimism. At the crossroads, Rousseau perceived that humans, *in the company of one another*, are fated to receive and inflict unnecessary harm. The inevitable, and hence radical, nature of our fallenness is most apparent in our associations.

The deleterious consequences of our fallenness, I have said, can be minimized by electing the private path. And there is also this: like Jansenists who saw a public mission in their private retreat behind high walls, Rousseau, too, held that the public can be served while traveling the private path. Rousseau understood himself as "a solitary who, living little among men, has fewer occasions to become saturated with their prejudices."[49] Critical distance—the sagacity and vision of a social critic—is enhanced, according to Rousseau, by stepping back from the social fray. For this reason, he called the forest of Montmorency "his study" or "work room." Location and solitude endowed Rousseau's writing, and his pen was his bridge to the public. About the composition of his perhaps most influential book, he noted, "In that profound and delicious solitude, among the woods and the waters, in concert with birds of every kind and the perfume of orange blossoms, in a continuous ecstasy I composed the fifth book of *Emile*, the fresh coloring of which I owed, for the most part, to the lively impression of the locality in which I wrote it."[50] Even Rousseau's political writings, *The Social Contract*, for example, were conceived during "solitary walks."[51] And his most seemly private reflections, the *Reveries*, for instance, were composed for the sake of public edification. Examination and reflection on the particularities of his existence was deemed by Rousseau as a form of public service. In private, he cultivated his experiences and resources and offered the harvest to us, his public. The "history of his soul" was to serve as a lesson book—a moral primer—for humanity.[52]

Publicly exposing the "history of his soul," however, threatened to bring down the very walls between public and private that he himself had helped to erect. Having already told us that he enjoyed being spanked by his guardian, Mlle. Lambercier, Rousseau revealed himself further: "I went searching for dark alleys and lonely spots where I could expose myself, from afar, to women in the condition in which I should have liked to be in their company."[53] Here Rousseau exposes intimate details of his private life, not to mention his private parts, thereby confounding the public-private distinction.

Eerily similar to the path to Poland, Rousseau offered all aspects of his private life for public examination. In *Poland*, it was required that the citizen's private life, insofar as she had one, was in plain, public view. On the private path, Rousseau elected to do likewise. Although such election was voluntary, the outcome was the same as in *Poland*: the private life was to be submitted to public judgment. On both paths, transparency was a critical link between the individual and society. On the extreme public path, transparency ensured that every aspect of the citizen's life was directed at the public good. On the private path, transparency allowed this solitaire, Jean-Jacques, to assure the reading public that he had revealed even the deepest, darkest pages of "the history of his soul."[54] "I should like," he declared, "to make my soul transparent to the reader's eye."[55]

His *Confessions* was, in part, an apologia, a defense of his sincerity and goodness. He believed that if he told all, we would forgive his limits as we forgive our own and admire and learn from his attempt to live a life dedicated to simplicity and honesty.

Alone, exiled in England, unable to speak English, Rousseau spent a cold winter writing the first six books, the most revealing, of his *Confessions*. Jean-Jacques the solitaire sought to have full communion with the public. True, he was in control of this communion; he crafted the host and ensured that it would be delivered only posthumously (and he constantly worried that his detractors would doctor this text, his life's history, upon his death). Still, Rousseau treated his reading public as if they were gods, allowing them to peer deep into the hidden recesses of his heart. Given Rousseau's determination to be invulnerable on the private path, it may seem remarkable that he exposed so many old wounds. I suppose he understood, however, that once dead, no one could hurt him (except by falsifying the "history of his soul" which he was so determined to control).

While discussing the private path, we have moved quickly from gazing at the beatific vision to Rousseau's backside. I have tried to articulate the paths to redemption not only as Rousseau's life choices, but as general forms of life. Although Rousseau's authorship and life are intertwined and often clarify each other, they need not be reduced to each other. Nonetheless, even this seemingly idiosyncratic aspect of Rousseau's life, namely, his need to show all and still gain public approbation, is instructive of the private path. Rarely are we content to be alone, entirely, unless for brief retreats. Nature and beauty can enhance our lives, but they can also remind us of our loneliness if there is no one with which to enjoy them. Rousseau, on the private path, seemed desperate for intimacy. When alone and in exile, he wrote much about love, friendship, and disappointment. And he was determined to reveal to us, his future public, more about himself than many of us would care to know.

His desire to write and build a bridge of words to the public was not unambiguous. Almost as strong as his urge to write was his fear of the pain his authorship could bring him. Many times he had decided to renounce his "profession of author," and, if we do not count his posthumous publications, he did in fact write little after the publication of *Emile* and *The Social Contract*. In the company of nature, what need did a solitaire have of a public? "Of what importance were readers to me," Rousseau asked rhetorically, "or a public, or the whole world, while I was soaring in the sky?"[56] Still, he could not stop writing. On his self-chosen private path, Rousseau was divided. He oscillated between his longing for solitude and his yearning for human company.

The Private Path and Its Limits

Ultimately, the extreme private path is not a place for humans to dwell. That Rousseau spent much time on it says more about the painful inadequacies of his society and friends, and of his own character, than about the adequacy of the path itself. Its toll is heavy. It requires the loss of public joys, commitments, and loves. Austere French Augustinians recommended retreat from society as a means to cultivate charity. Behind monastic walls one could attempt, however imperfectly, to love the world as does God. Rousseau's position was no less ironic. He held that on the private path, in the absence of *amour-propre*, one is capable of compassion (*pitié*). Yet such compassion is as theoretical as meaningful human encounters are rare. On the private path, one commits no unnecessary harm, yet one also has little opportunity to do loving or just deeds, except for oneself. On the private path, as in the Garden, there is neither humanity nor virtue proper, only gentle, solitary walkers and the natural maxim, *"Do good to yourself with as little harm as possible to others."*[57]

On the private path, then, we cease to be vulnerable to the disappointment, humiliation, and cruelty that is potentially unleashed by any relationship. Yet in the absence of vulnerability, in the fortress of complete self-sufficiency, happiness and love become hollow. There is much to be said for the private path, but in the end it is not a fully human path; although we are protected from much pain, we can be neither truly happy nor moral. This path to redemption, like all of Rousseau's paths, is partial and incomplete.

On occasion, Rousseau himself was candid about its limits, even in the *Reveries*. "Here I am alone in the world, having no longer a brother, a neighbor, a friend—no company except myself. The most sociable and loving of humans has been banished by an unanimous accord."[58] With these lines, surprisingly, Rousseau began his book most dedicated to championing the private path, the way of gentle self-love. Even when Rousseau intentionally sought solitude, he frequently found himself wishing for company. In the midst of his solitary ecstasies, for example, he would "sigh with sadness to be enjoying it alone."[59] His self-imposed exile from human company, in the heart of Paris near the end of his life, was especially difficult to endure. Toward the end of the *Reveries*, in the ninth walk, Rousseau lamented, "Oh, if I could have again some moments of those tender exchanges that flow from the heart, even if only from a small child, if I could see again in someone's eyes the joy and satisfaction of being with me, of my giving joy, how these short but sweet outpourings of my heart would recompense me for my suffering and pain. Ah! I would not need to seek among animals kind looks that I am now refused among humans."[60]

At the outset of this chapter I posed the question, why take the private path? Rousseau's response was emphatic—you take the private path by default, only after having tried to live socially. Solitude, nature, animals, plants—when these constitute a way of life, as opposed to an aspect of life, they become substitutes for human company. Are these surrogates adequate? The elderly in nursing homes, we are told, fare better in the company of plants and the resident cat than without such living comforts. This intelligence brings its own comfort to those of us who live outside nursing homes and who worry about their elderly occupants. Yet should we not also be haunted by the suspicion that only as a last resort do plants and animals become substitutes for human company? When Rousseau investigated himself in *Dialogues: Rousseau Judge of Jean-Jacques*, he left little doubt about why he sought community with plants: "One sees that [Jean-Jacques's] heart was attracted to the contemplation of nature. He had found a substitute for the attachments that he needed; but he would have left the substitute for the thing itself, if he had had the choice, and if he had not been reduced to converse with plants after vain efforts to converse with humans. I would leave voluntarily the society of plants for the society of men, he has said to me, at the first hope of returning to them."[61]

Rousseau understood the limits of the private path. He understood that solitude approaches what we earlier called still life, that is, a living death: "Absolute silence brings sadness. It presents an image of death."[62] The private path offers, then, an extreme remedy. This remedy is usually voluntary; one chooses the private path often as the result of failed attempts to live happily in society. Yet the path can also be imposed.

Solitary confinement in prisons, for example, could be counted as "cruel and unusual punishment" because the joy of solitude becomes bitter grief when solitude becomes an enforced way of life. If it is cruel, it is because solitude is a place to visit voluntarily, not a condition to be compelled.

What we impose on prisoners Rousseau prescribed for women. This is not to say that Rousseau consigned women to solitude. But many aspects of the extreme private path which he voluntarily chose for himself, he would have legislated for women. Of himself, Rousseau claimed that solitude was a natural condition: "Made to meditate at leisure in solitude, I could never speak, act, and do business among men. Nature had given me the former capacities and had refused me the latter."[63] Although we now know that this self-description is flawed, since Rousseau often longed for human company, it is remarkably close to his prescription for women and how he viewed their role in society. Like Jean-Jacques, women are supposedly better off not speaking, acting, or doing business among men. And this is the case, both for Rousseau and for women, due to gifts nature has given and withheld. This is not to say that Rousseau placed women on the private path. Women, in Rousseau's view, cannot take the private path because they are too needy, especially of men. But aspects of the private path—its retreat from the public realm, especially from the City—is ordained for women. Shortly, we will see that on the path that goes between the extreme public and private routes, women's lives are not radically relegated to the private, because the very distinction between public and private is not rigid. In the introduction, I noted that Sophie must inhabit an acute domestic space as an antidote to the corrupting public space of the City. Julie, in contrast, whose home is in a mountain village, does not require a domestic fortress, for the outside is not threatening. For now, I merely note that features of the private path which Rousseau chose for himself, largely out of despair, are the same features he prescribed for the women of Paris.

"Hope Makes Everything Beautiful"

Rousseau began the *Reveries* by identifying the object of his inquiry: "Me, detached from the whole world, what am I?"[64] What are we divorced from our social ties and relations? What are we when we systematically shun the company of others? The *Reveries* is a profound investigation of the private path, the path of pure self-love. This path, we have seen, is a safe one, safe for loving the self and doing no harm to others. One experiences on this path little suffering, unless we count the pain of inevitably drifting across that barbed psychological boundary between solitude and loneliness. Yet it is not a fully human or happy path. Rousseau's investigations produced profound, mixed results. Immediately after stating the object of his inquiry—himself, alone—he expressed the hope that his journey on the private path was all a "bad dream" and that he would awake to "find himself once again with friends."

There is no final word or pronouncement about the private path, however; there remains much to be said on behalf of it. Certain of its properties—the goal and capacity to live entirely within oneself, to shape one's destiny, to be free from the emotional pain that flows from attachment to the vicissitudes of human relations—remain attractive to many of us, especially when we are racked with insomnia and despair, having made ourselves vulnerable, having cared, and then finding ourselves wounded precisely where we once loved the most and tried the hardest. Add to such sharp personal pain the subtle despondency that festers amid an increasingly cold, bureaucratic public life, and the private path looks attractive indeed. It represents our longing to be safe and whole, to be free from both private injury and modern alienation. Additionally, the private path is not only a negative retreat from injury and defeat; it is also a positive path with its own ethic. If the way to Poland resounds with all the vigor, glory, and public esteem that Machiavelli could wish for, the way of the solitaire, in contrast, contains all the introspection, beauty, and individuality that Montaigne could hope for. The private path promises a radical form of freedom. When we long to be left alone, to be allowed to be oneself, we long to be on the private path. If nothing else, the private path acknowledges the moral importance we give to the protection of privacy. If people can enter our private lives, we insist that we have some control over their entrance. Otherwise, it is as if someone broke into our home and rifled through our belongings. It is a violation.

Finally, the private path is a way to equanimity. Disengaged from the cares and worries that come with human relations and social commitments, in private we can experience peace, reflection, and even self-knowledge. "I have traveled a good deal in Concord," boasted Thoreau.[65] Staying close to home, Thoreau traveled far, observing his townsfolk, exploring the local landscape, and examining his own inner one. When he freed himself from public distraction, Thoreau could confront and consider himself. Self-knowledge is hard to come by, especially when we are immersed in busy, noisy, hectic lives. We need to escape the turmoil, at least momentarily, if we are to confront our lives with some measure of discernment and honesty. Life is not hectic or noisy in solitary confinement. Prisoners locked up in Special Housing Units (SHUs) spend twenty-three hours a day alone in their cell. For one hour they can walk about, alone, in a tiny, isolated exercise area. I have been told by prisoners whom I respect that such solitary confinement is sometimes the only way for an inmate to become circumspect and to experience transformation. Being opposed to SHUs, I do not want to hear this. Several times I have pressed them on this issue, eager to learn why they would be willing to say anything positive about a practice that they dread and consider immoral. In solitude, I was told, we have fewer distractions. We usually lie to ourselves, but in solitary confinement, the lies are exposed. Hard questions arise, and we are more likely to answer them truthfully when we are alone.[66]

Whether in or out of prison, the private path has much to offer. It is not, however, an adequately human path. Emile was Rousseau's ideal human being. When it came to Emile's education and upbringing, nothing that could be left to chance was left to chance. Emile incarnated Rousseau's philosophy of life. And Emile was not intended for the private path. He did end up on that path, by default, as we are told at the conclusion of Rousseau's *Emile and Sophie, or the Solitaires*. In that work, imprisonment and the private path, once again, intertwine. Self-possessed, causing no unnecessary injury to others, and immune to social opinion, Emile exemplifies aspects of the ethics of the private path. Still, Rousseau left no doubt that for Emile to be fully human, he requires some society. Having quoted Genesis 2:8, "It is not good for man to be alone," Rousseau then added, "Emile is a man."[67] It is not good for humans to live alone, and hence Rousseau's ideal human, Emile, is meant to marry, raise a family, become involved in community, and when necessary, serve the greater society. As the stage approached for Emile to be introduced to social life, Rousseau announced to his readers, "exclusive pleasures are the death of pleasure. True entertainments are those one shares; those pleasures one wants to have to oneself alone, one no longer has at all. If the walls I raise around my park make it a melancholy cloister for me, I have at great cost only managed to deprive myself of the pleasure of walking."[68]

According to his own standards, Rousseau himself was not the ideal human. Immediately after championing a central tenet of the private path—to remain "independent of all external circumstances"—Rousseau struggled, feebly, to account for delivering his five children, one by one, to the Foundling Hospital.[69] It seems highly plausible that Rousseau's commitment to "independence" rendered his own children as a brood of "external circumstances." Here we confront the potential demon of living "within oneself." Here we confront the fear, or cowardliness, of being unwilling to assume the risks and responsibilities of love and commitment to something beyond the self.[70] As to the happiness or contentment that belongs to the private path, Rousseau well understood its limits. Toward the end of his life he had reached a state of infinite resignation in which neither good nor evil could touch him: "Nothing remains for me to hope for or to fear in the world, and hence my tranquility at the bottom of the abyss, a poor unfortunate mortal, but as unmoved as God himself."[71] Here Rousseau expressed the ambiguous merit of the private path. Free from pain and fear, as self-possessed as God, Rousseau's peace is rooted in the depths of an abyss.

Earlier in his life, Rousseau had anticipated the equivocal happiness of the solitaire: "A truly happy being is a solitaire; God alone enjoys absolute happiness."[72] I quoted this passage in chapter 1 and noted Rousseau's immediate rejoinder to himself: How can we talk of a happy human solitaire? "If some imperfect creature could be self-sufficient, what would he have to enjoy? He would be alone, he would be miserable." The private path highlights the tragedy of Rousseau's life and also an aspect of what could be called the human condition. On the private path, we are exempt from unnecessary pain, yet we must also resign ourselves to live without hope or love. During a happier time in his life, Rousseau had written to the cynical Voltaire, "Hope makes everything beautiful."[73] Later in life, the only peace he could attain required hopelessness. As to love, the private path rejects the conditions for love of others by shunning dependency, and hence vulnerability. Hence the passage that began, "A truly happy being is a solitaire," ended with, "I do not understand how one who has need of nothing could love anything; I do not understand how he who loves nothing can be happy." This passage, again, will serve as our transition from the private path to a more social existence—the way of Clarens, life in the Mountain Village.

Just as "Emile is not made to remain always solitary" or a "savage relegated to the desert," but rather must move from solitude to society, so we, too, must now venture on a more social path.[74] Like Emile, we will endeavor not to forget the private path, but to learn from its lessons. In some cases, this will entail retaining its positive lessons, such as the importance of remaining self-possessed. In other cases, it will entail acknowledging its negative lessons, such as its fear of social commitments. And beyond its specific lessons, the private path will continue to illuminate the morphology and logic of a way of life, namely, life alone. The private path hangs, prominently, in Rousseau's gallery of remedies—a hall arrayed with depictions of incommensurate, frail forms of life that humans forge as they struggle with their ambiguous, fallen condition.

On the private path, we learn perhaps less about a way to redemption than about the fallen condition itself. Like the Solitaires, we are protected from much pain yet we can be neither genuinely happy nor moral; in the company of others, we can experience some moral progress and precarious human joy, yet we hurt each other. These, I have argued, are the twin horns of Rousseau's description of our fallenness and the fault lines that stress and even shatter attempts to navigate felicitously the public and private. Rousseau has probed one of the deepest themes of modern social theory. As we venture out into the social life, self-love (*amour-propre*) leads us to hurt ourselves and those around us; in retreat, gentle love of self (*amour de soi*) renders us innocent yet morally disengaged. The remedy of the private path, we have seen, is as extreme as Poland's remedy. The one calls for the complete loss of the private life, the other the loss of the public. Both are effective if the goal is to live undividedly. Both are inadequate if the goal is to live a full, flourishing human existence. The Flourishing City—the religious, middle way—is Rousseau's attempt to bring together the two paths. There is another option, however, the way of Clarens: the path of friendship, love, marriage, community, and agreeable work. This path runs between the private path and the middle way. It incarnates Rousseau's deepest fantasy and harkens back to the Second Garden, stage three of the Fall, that precarious balance between solitariness and sociability.

9

The Mountain Village

The Path to Family, Work, Community, and Love

Just as Rousseau's *Reveries of the Solitary Walker* served as our central text for the extreme private path, Rousseau's famous novel, *Julie; or, The New Eloise*, will be our principal book for the moderate private path, the way of Clarens. Like "Poland" and the private path, the way of Clarens is a construction I have fashioned to illuminate a significant feature of Rousseau's thought. Clarens is the way to the Mountain Village, with its warm, supportive families, strong friendships, agreeable work, and its alternating seasons of solitude, family, and outdoor public festivities. "Friendship, love, and virtue" are the themes Rousseau himself identified in *Julie*.[1] In fact, almost all of Rousseau's favorite subjects and ideals appear in this work, and most of them in Julie's character. Julie, like Rousseau, places common sense above philosophy, candidness and sincerity above tact and tactics, the useful and agreeable above frivolity and luxury, and character and virtue above wealth and social status. In addition, Julie, unlike her atheist husband, Wolmar, is religious in a Rousseauean sense. She discovers God in beauty and worships God by service to others.[2] Clarens is the name of Julie's household and the name of Rousseau's domestic fantasy. Rousseau's ideal home was never Nature's Garden inhabited by the Solitaires. Rather, it was the Second Garden, or the Mountain Village. The Village is inhabited by simple, good-natured, hard-working, independent folk who experience daily the demands and beauty of nature. Clarens is more than a home. It is a way of life.

Clarens is also a geography. Rousseau had drafted or outlined what he thought could become one of his most helpful works, "Moral Sensitivity, or the Materialism of the Wise."[3] In this project, Rousseau wanted to show that our character and morals come not only from our social climate but also our physical surroundings. It is no coincidence that Clarens is located high in the Swiss mountains. The mountains and the hardy way of life that they demand endow the residents with virtue and character. Rousseau was one of the first to associate rugged landscape with stalwart, estimable character. The "salutary and beneficial mountain air," according to Julie's tutor, St. Preux, "is one of the great remedies of medicine and morality."[4] The salutary aspects of Clarens are not, of course, due to geography alone. The Alpine geography works together with Clarens's mountain manners. Like Emile's tutor or *The Social Contract*'s Great Legislator, the mountain manners at Clarens nourish the self without prompting false needs and *amour-propre*. At the same time, the difficult Alpine geography constantly confronts the self with ironclad necessity imposed by the natural world and curbs excessive, dangerous sociability. Together, these form a context in which the individual is neither extinguished nor inflated, but is placed in harmony with itself, neighbors, work, and nature.

After Rousseau, others such as Thomas Mann or Martin Heidegger would place their utopias or places of healing in towering mountains inhabited by a race of simple but wise folk. This elevated, bucolic landscape and tranquil, hardy way of life support a modest community existence. It resembles *Gemeinschaft* (cooperative community) more than *Gesellschaft* (competitive society), to use Ferdinand Tönnies' terms;[5] or country life more than city life, to use Rousseau's vocabulary. In the warmer months, the mountain inhabitants enjoy fetes in the open air. In the colder months, families occasionally visit each other, and come together in social "circles"—groups of families who enjoy song, games, and wine.[6] The community life is modest because the social ties, while affectionate, are entirely voluntary and easily uncoupled. This is not the land of devoted citizens who put nation above family or self. Nor is this the land of urbanites who celebrate novelty more than tradition, diversity more than affinity, dynamic street life more than habitual family life. The way of Clarens exemplifies the simplicity of rural life, the beauty and ruggedness of mountains, and the character of those immersed in both—mountain manners and unmannered mountains.

The Garden-Fall-Restoration narrative that I recounted in part I of this study can illuminate *Julie* and Rousseau's depiction of tension between the public and private. *Julie* begins with the gentle, peaceful existence of the title character, one as innocent as a Solitaire. In her gardenlike existence, she is surrounded by natural beauty, loving parents, her dear friend Claire, and a devoted tutor St. Preux. Yet, like the Solitaire's, if Julie's innocence is to become complex virtue, she must leave the garden and attempt to recapture features of the garden, albeit transformed. Her fall from innocence is occasioned by love and its artificial obstacles. An initially innocent romance between her and St. Preux becomes tangled and emotionally debilitating when their love is consummated and then thwarted by Julie's father, the status-conscious Baron d'Étange. He forbids Julie to marry St. Preux, a man without a title. As Julie and St. Preux's relationship becomes increasingly concealed, their private lives hidden from public view, they resort to lies and deceit. In their idyllic garden, Julie notes to St. Preux, their relationship was "easy and charming," marked by an "elegant simplicity" and "purity." Now, after their fall into sex, lies, and social artifice, "That happy time is no longer. Alas! It cannot return, and as the first effect of so cruel a change, our hearts have already ceased to understand each other."[7]

As I noted in chapter 5, when Rousseau's own garden existence was shattered by the broken comb incident, the loss of transparency and mutual understanding were among the first effects of the fall. The same logic of fallenness stalks Julie and St. Preux. Cast out of their garden, they can no longer openly share their most private hopes and fears. They now suffer tremendously, equally unhappy whether together or separated.

How does this gentle tale, that begins in such innocence, turn bitter and cruel? Although Julie and St. Preux are exceptional humans, they are incomplete alone; they need love, and love is dangerous. Their love for each other is obstructed by social convention; since St. Preux lacks a title, his merits will never be enough to gain Julie's father's approval. In her innocence and youth, Julie never saw the serpent, *amour-propre*, in her garden. She didn't know her garden belonged to a world where concern for social appearance and status ruins love. Many eloquent and persuasive arguments against her father's social prejudices are offered. Of St. Preux, Lord Bomston (a family friend) says to Julie's father, "In spite of your prejudices he is of all men most worthy of her. . . . Nobility? Vain prerogative. . . . But he has nobility even so, do not doubt it, not written in ink on old parchment but engraved on the foundation of his heart in indelible characters. In a word, if you prefer reason to prejudice, and if you love your daughter better than your titles, it is him you will give her."[8] Still, her father will not relent. His attachment to social status runs deep. For her part, Julie loves her father, and more important, she has a duty to him. Julie's private love for St. Preux, then, is thwarted ultimately by her filial obligation to her father and her duty to uphold public appearances—to marry well, to marry properly. Lord Bomston, a man who wears his wealth and titles lightly, characterizes Julie's plight when he writes to her, "The tyranny of an intractable father will drive you into the abyss which you will recognize only after the fall. . . . You will be obliged to contract an alliance [with Wolmar] disavowed by your heart. Public approval will be refuted incessantly by the cry of your conscience."[9] Julie's abyss is characterized as a world in which private love and public duty are in conflict, causing deep strife within and among its inhabitants. As she writes to Claire, "Whom will I support, my lover or my father? . . . Sacrificing myself to duty, I cannot evade committing a crime, and whatever course I take, I must die both unhappy and culpable."[10] Like Antigone, Julie is torn between love and duty, between private happiness and public appearance.

Eventually, their mutual redemption is occasioned, in part, by Julie's marriage to the godlike atheist, Wolmar. Wolmar enables the fallen Julie to become a new, redeemed Julie, a virtuous yet no longer innocent woman who discovers happiness in her duty as wife and mother. Wolmar heals St. Preux as well by engineering his return to Clarens and his reconciliation with Julie. St. Preux becomes a trusted friend of the family and derives much joy from that friendship. Living with her two men under the same roof, Julie learns to place virtuous duty above romantic love while cultivating a seasoned, spousal love for Wolmar and a friendship love for St. Preux. Every aspect of the household, we will see, is arranged to reconcile the public and private harmoniously. Still, a lingering tension remains between Julie's passion for St. Preux and her duty to Wolmar. Only upon her death is that tension erased completely. After diving into icy waters to save one of her children, Julie contracts and eventually dies from pneumonia. By this death—in the line of duty, not a fit of romance—her virtue is entirely vindicated and her redemption is complete. St. Preux, too, can be saved by performing his duty. After Julie's death, he is to remain at Clarens and tutor Julie's children. The circle of his Garden-Fall-Restoration can be closed; as his garden-innocence and fall were tied up with instructing Julie, his reclamation is to be made complete by educating her children. At the close of the novel, however, it is not clear whether St. Preux will return to Clarens.

The tale found in *Julie* is the same one told in the second *Discours*, "On the Origin of Inequality," and in many of Rousseau's other works. As long as we dwell in a private universe we may live as innocents, doing little good or harm. When we enter the social universe, however, our innocence is sacrificed for the possibility of achieving complex virtue, but also vice. For this transition to be relatively successful, aspects of the gardenlike existence must be preserved. On the extreme public path the serpent, *amour-propre*, was deflected away from the self and redirected to the group. When all is public, one is not divided between public duty and private love. Moreover, as in the Garden, one is confronted with necessity—the intractability of a highly socialized society. On the extreme private path, in contrast, where one lives entirely within oneself, the opposite strategy saves one. When all is private, one does not suffer from dividedness. Also, as in the Garden, one is motivated principally by *amour de soi*, and is confronted with the necessity of nature.

In contrast to these two extreme paths, the way of Clarens is neither strictly public nor private. Its mountain manners and Alpine geography create a natural, social context—the Second Garden—that enables individuals to integrate the public and private. At Clarens, one enjoys many aspects of the Garden as well as a modest sociability that does not bring into play the destructiveness of *amour-propre*. Yet, as we will see, unlike the other two paths, the way of Clarens, like the Second Garden, is unstable. Eventually love and duty, the private and public, will come into conflict. Clarens, then, is as fleeting as it is precarious.

The way of Clarens includes such natural and social circumstances as stellar characters, strong friendships, good marriages, useful and agreeable work, community fellowship, moments of solitude, natural beauty, and the necessary discipline and hardship of living in the Alps. Nature and artifice, working harmoniously together, create this Second Garden, Clarens.[11]

Clarens, the Second Garden

Julie's transformation is concomitant with the transformation of the Clarens household—a physical embodiment of a way of life that permits the reconciliation of the public and private. The household transformation begins with the arrival of Wolmar.[12] The household, St. Preux notes, is now orderly and peaceful, "and without show, without ceremony, everything there is gathered and directed toward the true human destiny!" In the absence of injurious social conventions, humans can work and dwell at peace with each other, nature, and self.

The house itself is altered: "It is no longer a house made to be seen but to be inhabited." Inordinately large rooms are made into useful apartments; ornate antiques are replaced with simple, comfortable furniture; everything is pleasant and cheerful, and "nothing there smacks of riches and luxury." The grounds, too, have been transformed. In place of the old billiard room are now a wine press and a dairy room. "The vegetable garden was too small for the cooking; they had made a second one out of the flower bed, but one so well put together that the flower bed thus converted pleases the eye more than before." Vineyards are planted, and decorative trees are replaced by fruit, nut, and shade trees. All in all, "everywhere they have substituted the useful for the agreeable, and yet the useful has almost always become agreeable." St. Preux mentions the delightful "noises of the farmyard"—the crowing of the cocks, the lowing of the cattle, the harnessing of the horses. He also notes the simple, pleasant meals taken in the fields, the shared labor in cultivation, and many other rural aspects that make the new Clarens "more lively, more animated, more gay . . . than it had been in its dreary dignity." In sum, Clarens has become a place "of joy and well being."[13] St. Preux, once a world traveler, now wonders why anyone would leave Clarens, where one finds a way of life that is natural, productive, and happy.

Clarens, however, is more than a house and yard. It is also an open and frank social atmosphere in which people say what they mean and mean what they say. There is no need to be unduly cautious about one's speech. Whether eating, strolling, or working, whether "in private conversation, or before everyone, one speaks always the same language." The transparency that Julie lost in the fall, and that is absent in the City, is reestablished at Clarens; with its arrival, a barrier between public and private is removed. This is not to say, as St. Preux notes, that the household members "indiscreetly spill all their affairs."[14] Everything need not, and should not, be told to all. But that which is revealed or concealed is not based on advancing social status or other forms of narrow personal gain. Concealment at Clarens, such as it is, is an acknowledgment of privacy as a fundamental aspect of what it is to be human. Some knowledge is appropriately guarded and protected, or else revealed only at one's discretion. At Clarens, then, there remains some distinction between public and private, but that distinction is not based on baneful conventions and pursuits. The distinction fosters harmony, not injury.

The public and private are made harmonious not only by open communication, but by the "useful yet agreeable" way of life at Clarens. Work and home are not relegated to strictly public and private domains. Public and private are intertwined, as are work and pleasure. Sociability at Clarens mainly takes place while doing chores, as opposed to during scheduled formal occasions in which people dress and behave to make a public statement. As they work, family members, neighbors, and other community members enjoy interacting with one another. Useful and pleasant endeavors reconcile the public and private at Clarens. Without idleness and luxury, the individual's powers and desires are more easily matched, for there is little time or concern for imagining how to make others envious. Private thoughts about public manipulation disappear. This leads not only to personal but social well-being.

Labor rests at the heart of Clarens. Alienation from work was an abiding concern for Rousseau. He feared that as capital in international markets became more fluid, as profit dominated all other goals, and as the division of labor increased, workers increasingly found limited meaning and satisfaction in their work. Their jobs were more specialized and curtailed, and often they did not know for whom or for what they worked. Labor at Clarens, in Rousseau's imagination, challenges these unhappy trends. St. Preux sums up the Clarens alternative in a single sentence: "One sees nothing in this household which does not join together the agreeable and the useful, but the useful occupations are not confined to pursuits which yield profit."[15] At Clarens, the very idea of work is redefined. Not reduced to profit or efficiency, work is yoked to that which is purposeful and agreeable. Rousseau, like Marx, sought to remind us that we are sensuous, tactile creatures who find our natural vocation in congenial work.

I am crafting an image of Clarens from material in *Julie*. This fantastic Second Garden, however, is not limited to *Julie*. It is found in the second *Discourse* and in the *Confessions*, among other places. Rousseau, we know, often celebrated nature. Less well known is his high regard for farm life. There is a connection, he maintained, between one's character and activities, and he felt that the activities of farm life—meaningful work in alliance with nature—brought both strength of character and joy. In the *Confessions* he recounted how, on the verge of death, he quit his doctor's pharmaceutical prescriptions and instead immersed himself in life on the farm, with its chickens, pigeons, cows, vegetable gardens, grape harvests, fruit gathering, and above all, honey bees.[16] Rousseau's various descriptions of the happiest chapters in his life are invariably rooted in farm life, and they often read like chapters out of *Julie*. In his happiest recollections, he is in the country—not in solitude, but with some company—involved in useful yet not overly burdensome activities.

Why are these the settings in which Rousseau discovered tranquility and purpose? Why Clarens? As in the Garden, Clarens is largely free of hurtful artificiality and unjust social conventions. As in the Garden, one is not free of necessity but encounters a necessity rooted in the rhythm of nature and household activities rather than in the compulsion of convoluted and obsessive social artifice, competition, and greed. As in the Garden, one experiences an intimate relation with nature. Yet, unlike in the Garden at Clarens, one enjoys human company. With *amour-propre* curbed, one can delight in nature and humans, both. As St. Preux notes, without pomp and pretense, with everything arranged so as to unite the useful and the pleasant, Clarens is "directed toward the true human destiny!"

If here St. Preux's voice is Rousseau's, and I think it is, then Rousseau rooted Clarens in *human* nature. Rousseau usually had a generous sense of the malleability of human nature, and he often warned Europeans against sanctioning their cherished yet parochial ideals by attributing them to nature. And to many of us, Clarens must seem nothing but parochial. Rousseau, however, felt he was on firm ground when he identified Clarens with nature, including human nature. Clarens seemed to have it all: beauty, useful work, domesticity, friendship, community, solitude, and the absence of injurious social artificiality. It was, we have said, his fantasy of the good life.

Marriage and family are part of that life. Rousseau's celebrations of domesticity are not limited to those found in *Julie*. In the *Confessions*, for example, he noted his domestic happiness with Thérèse, the woman he lived with for over twenty years before marrying her. Reflecting on their simple meals and walks together, Rousseau wrote, "Friendship, confidence, intimacy, sweetness of soul, what delicious seasonings they are!" Similarly, recollecting his reunion with Thérèse after political banishment had briefly separated them, he exclaimed, "Oh friendship, union of hearts, habits, and intimacy!"[17] Such passages, I realize, may sound more like accounts of friendship than marriage. Friendship and companionship, however, defined marriage for Rousseau. We have already noted that he rejected the then pervasive view that marriage should principally advance one's economic and social position. This position is also found in *Emile*, when Sophie's father, in one example, denounces titles and wealth as the basis of marriage, and declares, "We live happily in poverty . . . Sophie is our common treasure. It is for the spouses to match themselves. Mutual inclination ought to be their first bond."[18] Intimacy and companionship, not wealth and station, characterize the Rousseauean marriage and family.

When Rousseau wrote *Julie*, he had already endured the pain of moral isolation. He understood how one can feel alone even among a crowd. Loneliness prevails when the only options are radical social disengagement, characterized by isolation, or engagement with an insipid social existence, characterized by emptiness. Clarens rescues the alienated by offering the warmth, joy, and purpose of a closely knit, productive family. Clarens anticipated the modern family, that center of moral and social life. Julie, as wife, is Wolmar's intimate companion and friend. They are also coworkers. Julie and Wolmar address together all matters that pertain to the household. Yet the Clarens household, unlike the households of today, is not a narrow domestic space, but an inclusive space that brings together work and pleasure, utility and aesthetics, public and private, men and women. In *Julie*, we noted, work is not confined to specialized labor outside the home. Julie and Wolmar, then, have much to discuss and much work to pursue together.

Clarens is the way of marriage and family, but also of friendship. Lord Bomston and St. Preux, St. Preux and Julie, Julie and Wolmar, St. Preux and Claire, and above all, Claire and Julie—there are many friendships at Clarens. These friendships, like Clarens's family life, provide generous portions of support, warmth, and intimacy. Yet whereas family members are yoked by both love and duty, the union of friends imposes no duty. Love for the friend, Rousseau held, flows as naturally as one's own *amour de soi*. "Self-love [*amour de soi*], like friendship which is but a part of it, has no other law except the sentiment which inspires it; one does everything for his friend as for himself, not out of duty, but delight."[19] Rousseau often dreamed of a society of friends, of a society "where neither duty nor interest would enter, where pleasure and friendship alone would make the law."[20] Friends acknowledge one another's equality and independence. Without these, the friendship denigrates into patronage on one side, slavish dependency on the other. These conditions of friendship do not lessen but enhance the emotional depth. Rousseau, for example, described the "tears of emotion" he would shed each time he walked the eighteen miles to see his good friend, George Keith.[21] This strong friendship was based on respect, equality, and independence.

The world of Clarens may be a fantasy, but it is also a social protest. Its family and friendships condemn the utilitarian character of the marriages and friendships of Rousseau's age. In the effort to accumulate public status and wealth, spouses and friends were deemed useful. Clarens challenges this utility of the private life for public attention and personal gain. Family and friends, in Rousseau's view, are to offer the gifts of affection and moral support, not wealth and status. The realms of intimacy at Clarens oppose the cold, calculating, public world of Hobbesian market relations and Parisian social-climbing. Once infected with *amour-propre*, players in such public spheres threaten to undermine even private friendships. In the *Confessions*, Rousseau claimed that his friendships were ruined the moment he became a public figure: "I was born for friendship. . . . So long as I lived unknown to the public I was loved by all who knew me. . . . But as soon as I had a name I no longer had any friends."[22] Fame can make one an object of utility or envy among friends, eroding the equality and independence necessary for friendships. Utilizing the Garden-Fall-Restoration narrative, Rousseau would often describe times in his life graced by strong, private friendships, that then, inevitably, would be sabotaged by something or someone from the outside. Restoration, however, seldom occurred. Clarens, in its own, fictional way, became Rousseau's chief compensation—an imaginary restoration. For some time—too much time, really—he dwelt in this fantasy and it thereby eased his pain. His use of Clarens as a private salve, however, should not cloak Rousseau's public service of envisioning Clarens as an alternative and challenge to a world increasingly engaged in the manipulative pursuit of wealth, status, and power.

Women, Community, and Solitude at Clarens

Of all the friendships at Clarens, the one between Julie and Claire is the most note-worthy. What Montaigne once said of his best friend, La Boétie, could be said as well of Julie and Claire: "Our souls mingle and blend with each other so completely that they efface the seam that joined them."[23] In fact, Julie and Claire's friendship resembles in most ways Montaigne's description of the ideal friendship. One wonders if Rousseau was inspired by Montaigne's essay, "On Friendship," and also challenged by Montaigne's claim that women do not have the capacity for the sacred bond of friendship.[24] *Julie* is perhaps the most effective eighteenth-century refutation of Montaigne's insulting claim, for Julie and Claire exhibit all the virtues of friendship. They freely share their hopes and fears, their joy and suffering. They sustain each other with moral and emotional support, encourage each other to do their best, and delight in each other's company. Often they seem to compensate each other for the inadequacies of their male friends—St. Preux's rashness, for example, or Wolmar's reserve.

Rousseau's portrait of this strong friendship between two women adds to the per-plexity of assessing Rousseau's depiction of women in *Julie* and elsewhere. On the one hand, Julie exemplifies Rousseau's ideal human: self-possessed, yet engaged in the com-pany of others. Julie "knows and follows rules other than public opinion, [her] princi-pal honor being what [her] conscience delivers [her]."[25] It is Julie, therefore, and not her father, who sees through the pretensions of a patriarchal society that places status and wealth above intelligence and character. On the other hand, in spite of her inde-pendence, Julie yields to patriarchal authority, first to her father, then to her husband.

Julie is a companion to Wolmar, but she is also a helper, much as Eve was to Adam, at least as that tale is traditionally understood.[26] Although all matters are discussed to-gether, Wolmar is the head of the household. It turns out that in the Second Garden, at Clarens, social conventions are in place, conventions that Rousseau supports. Men's authority remains supreme. Rousseau would have us believe that such conventions are rooted in nature. I have said that Julie is a strong, independent woman, unlike Emile's Sophie, and she is not consigned to live out her life in a narrow domestic cage. At Clarens, women's lives are not radically relegated to the private, because the very dis-tinction between public and private is not strict. Julie, unlike Sophie, need not sustain an insular private space as an antidote to the corrosive effects of the City. The City is far from Clarens, and hence Julie's home need not function as a mighty, defensive fortress. Julie, then, is not Sophie. Still, neither is she is a woman liberated from patriarchy. She speaks her mind openly, she challenges existing prejudices, and she is a working woman with many significant responsibilities. Ultimately, however, she yields to her men. She trades her father's overbearing dominance for Wolmar's unimposing patriarchy. In either case, Clarens remains entirely patriarchal.

Yet Clarens also implicitly advanced the cause and rights of women. By portraying a marriage based on friendship and compatibility, it challenged the notion that women were chattels subject to contract. By displaying the vivid and admirable interior life of Julie and Claire, it defied the idea that women were docile and unimaginative. And by highlighting a sphere of intimacy, fondness, and trust, Clarens contributed to an effec-tive history that would eventually give birth to the right to privacy, a right that has pro-tected and empowered women in democratic societies. With the publication of *Julie*,

Rousseau highlighted the significance of a privacy that allows people to share such intimacies as letters, emotions, and beliefs without fear of public exposure. The privacy portrayed in *Julie* has become for us a given, an essential aspect of what it is to be human. This realm of trust also stands in striking contrast to what we experience in our contractual and litigious public existence. At Clarens, however, while privacy is found, the harsh contrast between public and private is not. The public life is as supportive of human flourishing as is the private, in part because the distinction between the two is softened.

The public life surrounding Clarens is not the interesting, diverse, crowded streets of London or New York. Nor is it the Spartan arena where citizens gather to remember past victories and cultivate an intense patriotism. Public life at Clarens is more like the county fair. Like the fair, it is seasonal: it arrives with warm weather. This is not to say that during the cold months there is no public life. There are the social circles, the taverns, and other places or occasions where people informally gather to play cards, chat, and drink. But inclusive public events take place when travel is easy and when celebrations can occur outdoors, under the bright sun, where all are fully illuminated. Group dancing, in spite of the church's prohibition, is a favorite activity, because it integrates young and old, male and female, employee and employer. At such intergenerational public fetes, there are no professional entertainers, no stage for all to stare at. Rather, the people entertain themselves, with song, dance, games, and music. This, in Rousseau's view, is a truly *natural* public life.

The natural public existence of Clarens is far from the public life of Paris, that is, City life. In Paris, that "vast desert of a world," St. Preux finds himself "alone in the crowd."[27] If transparency characterizes Clarens, hiddenness and superficiality identify Paris: "The men to whom one speaks are not at all those with whom one converses. Their sentiments do not at all emerge from their hearts, their insight is not at all in their spirit, their discourse does not at all represent their thoughts. One sees of them only their appearance."[28] St. Preux admits that the "vast diversity" of Paris offers much entertainment. But the hectic entertainment of Paris requires, or compensates for, "an empty heart and frivolous spirit."[29] St. Preux speaks for Rousseau when he suggests that an insipid public existence produces amusing, yet mindless, distractions.

In his *Letter to M. d'Alembert*, Rousseau provided what can serve as a theoretical account, and justification, of the public life at Clarens. Rousseau wrote this treatise to oppose the installation of a professional theater in Geneva. Its main topic is the nature and function of entertainment. In a city like Paris, professional entertainment serves to distract individuals from their hollow lives, providing a temporary, if intense, escape. The theater is a favorite entertainment for city dwellers, because, like television, it suspends the viewer's actual life, providing an intermission in an otherwise chaotic, empty, or lonely existence. This form of recreation, in Rousseau's view, provides some benefits, but they are highly limited. His main critique of city recreation is that it ultimately fails to re-create the human spirit. That is, it fails to enable community members to engage meaningfully with each other, thus refreshing—re-creating—their lives and social relations.

We may be tempted to dismiss Rousseau's anti-urban sensibilities as quaint or prejudicial; I know I have. In this study, I have used "the City" as a Rousseauean metaphor for an impersonal, banal public existence that increasingly requires an intense, self-indulgent private life. For Rousseau, however, the City was more than a metaphor. He distrusted and disliked big cities, especially Paris, but also London and others. This narrow prejudice, however, should not diminish in our eyes his achievement, namely, his success in naming one of the great plights of the modern era—moral and social isolation. At the heart of his critique of the theater we find his concerns about alienation and isolation. "People think that they gather together at the theater with others," Rousseau wrote, "but really it is there that each is isolated. It is there that they go to forget their friends, neighbors, and relations."[30] Like Marx, who sympathetically acknowledged that religion brings comfort to the alienated yet claimed that it thereby distracts them from discovering the true cause of their oppression, Rousseau, too, sympathetically acknowledged the value and need of city entertainments. He understood that they ease a person's pain, and that the need for such entertainment reflects suffering: "It is discontent with one's self, it is the weight of idleness, it is forgetting simple, natural tastes, that makes outlandish amusement so necessary." If we experience the need to occupy ourselves constantly with the stage—or television and video games, we might add—it is because "inside of us we are ill at ease."[31] Rousseau's insights are not limited to urban existence. All of us in contemporary Western society—regardless of geographic location—dwell in the City.

Clarens was Rousseau's attempt to awake us to a different kind of existence, a way of life in which the private and public nourish, not ruin, each other.[32] If Parisian entertainment is antisocial (the act of sitting alone, watching a stage) and is based on appearances (actors wearing masks), then entertainment at Clarens is communal; in place of professional actors, everyone assumes the role of entertainer. "But," Rousseau asks, "what then will be the objects of these entertainments?" The community itself can provide all that is needed. "In the middle of some place plant a stake crowned with flowers; gather together there the people, and you will have a fete. Better still: let the spectators give entertainment to themselves; make them actors themselves; make it so that each sees and loves himself in the others, thus all being the better united."[33] In this community entertainment, participants are moved not by scripted lines, but by the spontaneous emotion that comes from palpable interaction—touching, moving, smiling, singing. At Clarens, love of self (*amour de soi*) is cultivated in private, yet it is also reflected, and nourished, in the face of others.

Community life is a season, a rhythm at Clarens. So is solitude. After identifying our true vocation as "this oscillation between labor and recreation," St. Preux describes Julie's "recreation in a secluded place where she takes her favorite walk and which she calls her Elysium."[34] Julie's Elysium is a secluded, hidden, private garden, "which is always carefully locked with a key." It is closed to the public. Upon entering the Elysium, whose door would have been impossible to find without Julie's assistance, St. Preux was struck by the dense foliage, the abundance of flowers, the sound of a running brook, and the singing of birds: "I thought I saw the wildest place, the most solitary in nature, and it seemed I was the first mortal who had ever penetrated this desert." With St. Preux, we are back in Nature's Garden, or at least it would seem that way. The Elysium knows nothing of the symmetry or artificiality of formal, eighteenth-century French gardens. It appears to St. Preux as "uncultivated and wild"—beautifully wild. When Julie intimates that the Elysium is entirely under her direction, St. Preux balks— "I do not see at all any evidence of human work"—and insists that "it only cost Julie neglect." As is her way, Julie is patient yet firm with St. Preux: "It is true that nature has done everything, but under my direction, and there is nothing here which I have not ordered."[35]

If this is Nature's Garden, it is not the original one that we explored in chapter 1. That garden was the work of nature alone. Julie's Elysium, in contrast, is a work of art, or a "*desert artificiel*," as St. Preux would later describe it.[36] Rousseau again seems to declare that there is no going back to the original garden. Gardens—places of solitude, places of redemption—now require human effort and imagination. Julie's Elysium is natural insofar as only nature, not Julie, can give birth to a flower or a bird; natural, also, insofar as Julie chooses not to import "exotic plants or fruits," but rather to utilize those that are "natural to the country." Still, it is Julie who planted and cultivated the raspberries, currants, lilac bushes, wild grapes, hops, jasmine, hazel trees, and so on. It is Julie who diverted the water and enticed the birds to reside in her private sanctuary. Julie's garden, like the rest of Clarens, is the result of nature's laws and human art working together, in harmony. Rousseau is famous for having said on a few occasions that society, not nature, is the source of the vast majority of human woes. In *Julie*, however, Rousseau did not contrast society to nature, but rather better societies to worse societies, in accordance with whether they encourage or impede human flourishing. Like Julie's garden, Clarens itself may look entirely natural, as if it emerged organically from its mountain soil. In fact, however, every aspect of Clarens is shaped by human hands and imagination, in cooperation with nature. This cooperation entails a way of life that recognizes such natural limits as human hardship, suffering, and death, and that rejects such unnatural burdens as excessive competition, luxury with its attending discrepancy between rich and poor, and living without meaning or purpose. Clarens is a society, assembled by humans, in agreement with nature.

Solitude and beauty belong to the social order at Clarens. Rousseau's lengthy, elaborate description of Julie's Elysium underscores the importance and necessity of privacy and solitude in this well-run household and society. St. Preux exclaims that in Julie's garden he is transported "entirely out of the world"—at least for an hour or so.[37] After his respite in the garden, his time for contemplation and refreshment, he returns to the world to resume his work and life. Use of the garden is one of Julie's greatest gifts to St. Preux. With little money, some effort, and much love, Julie fashioned for herself and her friends a place of restoration. Julie understands that in the rhythm of life, solitude has its season, as does work and community. "The repose which serves as relaxation from past labors and which encourages other labors is no less necessary to man than the labor itself."[38]

Solitude, love, family, friendship, community, work—these are the components of Clarens, Rousseau's fantasy and moral measuring rod. Clarens is also a possible home for Emile, Rousseau's favorite imaginary pupil. Emile does not belong in Rousseau's Poland, for Emile was not trained to place citizenship above all else; he did not receive a public education that would shape his heart and mind in the image of the state. On the other hand, Emile does not belong on the private path in the Solitaire's garden. He was not raised, his tutor tells us, to live alone. Of all the places in Rousseau's moral geography, Emile is perhaps best suited for Clarens. Emile is made for family, friendship, work, solitude, and a modest measure of community and civic participation. Like Montaigne, mayor of Bordeaux, Emile fulfills his civic duty, but that duty can never capture or satisfy the entirety of his heart and soul. Neither citizen nor solitaire, Emile walks Julie's path of gentle sociability. Given his affectionate personality and religious sensibility, it would seem that Emile, not Wolmar, is the ideal companion for Julie.

Redemption at Clarens

The redemptive logic of Clarens is similar to that of the extreme public and private paths. In all three cases, the destructive fallout of *amour-propre* is kept to a minimum. On the extreme public path, private *amour-propre* is redirected to public ends; on the extreme private path, *amour de soi* curbs *amour-propre*. Both maneuvers employ Rousseau's strategy for reducing friction between the public and private by dodging those situations that put the two in conflict. Whether one embraces an absolute public or private existence, disillusionment and strife abate as one pursues well-defined aims with predictable outcomes. At Clarens, *amour-propre* is forestalled by good marriages, strong friendships, private retreats, public celebrations, demanding yet agreeable work, and a difficult terrain and climate. Here, we have a multitude of miraculous balancing acts. Its mountain manners and Alpine geography manage to keep all in place, at least provisionally. The mountain manners provide moral sustenance while checking false needs. The severe Alpine geography brings natural necessity into the daily life at Clarens, and it discourages dangerous, excessive sociability. Together, these form Clarens, a place where the self is neither squelched nor puffed up, but lives in harmony with itself, others, work, and nature.

Listen to Rousseau's description, in his *Letter to M. d'Alembert*, of a mountain community he once visited in his youth:

> An entire mountain covered with homes, each at the center of the land on which it depends, arranged such that these houses . . . offer to the numerous inhabitants of this mountain both the meditation of a retreat and the sweetness of society. These happy farmers, all at ease—free of poll taxes, tariffs, commissioners, and assigned labor—cultivate the soil, with all possible care, the bounty and produce of which is theirs, and employ the leisure that this cultivation leaves them to make thousands of handmade goods. . . . In the winter especially, a time when the deep snows hinder easy communication, each family stays warm at home in a pretty and neat home of wood, which they themselves built, occupying themselves with numerous enjoyable labors that chase boredom from their refuge and add to their well-being. Never did a professional carpenter, locksmith, glass-maker, or lathe-operator enter this country; all do everything for themselves.[39]

Rousseau goes on to note their useful books, their living rooms that look more like "a mechanic's workshop" or a "laboratory in experimental physics," their skill in drawing, and their singing and dancing. This Swiss mountain community no doubt served as a model for Rousseau's Clarens. It carries the design of what in chapter 3 we called the Second Garden, a fragile balance between solitariness and sociability. Its emphasis on self-sufficiency stays slavish dependency, a source of misfortune that travels with *amour-propre*. With the specialization of labor comes the multiplication of commodities and complex systems of exchange, and from these come arenas of competition, injustice, and oppressive dependency. When we stand in need of each other for basic goods, or for luxuries that are deemed basic, the more powerful exploit the more vulnerable, and from such exploitation come the ills that Clarens is protected from—humiliation, envy, contempt, and injustice. Dependency is found, of course, in the domestic sphere of Rousseau's mountain community. But domesticity, for Rousseau, is by definition a safe place for intimacy and trust. To this belief he clung in spite of his own disappointing domestic experience with his father and later with Madame de Warens.

Clarens, and perhaps even the mountain community that Rousseau described to d'Alembert, is nothing less than an elaborate, fictional portrayal of Rousseau's vision of humanity's happiest state, lodged neither in radical solitude nor fatalistic social assimilation. Clarens is placed between the extreme public and private paths. Its location, high in the Swiss mountains, makes it difficult to reach. This geography is not incidental. Few can achieve it. Many wouldn't want to. There is no theater. There are no ethnic restaurants. There is little pluralism. There is little anonymity. And even if you desire to live in a place like Clarens, such sites are scarce, and their counterfeits can be oppressive, even cruel. "Misfits" or "imbeciles" in a small community are sometimes "eccentrics" or "geniuses" in the City. Or, if that is too romantic a notion, in the City they are perhaps just ignored, a condition that most would prefer to derision and scorn.

When I say places like Clarens are scarce, I mean, empirically speaking, there are few places like it. This is mostly because its pivotal, delicate components are subject to breakdown. Clarens can easily cease to be Clarens. The marriage could have turned sour, with both partners caught up in *amour-propre*, competing with each other to attract other suitors or somehow gain the upper hand. The friendships, too, could have become competitive and been destroyed by envy. The private retreats could have become occasions to scheme for personal revenge or public conquest. The work could have turned oppressive for the employees and obsessive for the employers, if Clarens strove to accumulate riches and status. Finally, the climate could have turned mild and the roads and heating systems improved, thus providing more occasions for social interaction, more opportunities for *amour-propre* to ignite. Much could have gone wrong.

When I say Clarens is a fantasy, I mean Rousseau imaginatively created and populated it out of deep longing and angry protest. It was a protest against those market economies that were encouraging anomie, acquisitiveness, a fierce division of labor, and alienation from self, work, and community. Clarens, then, was a powerful social complaint against developing modern economies and the destructive, self-centered individualism that flowed from them. Yet Clarens was also a personal sigh. It functioned, in Rousseau's heart, as an emotional surrogate for intimacy, friendship, and community.

Rousseau often reported on his frustrated desire for love and fellowship. In a letter to Jacob Vernes he wrote, "What I hunger for is a friend; I do not know of another need in which I am not self-sufficient."[40] It is precisely here, in the sphere of love, friendship, and community, that Rousseau failed most miserably. It would have required of him emotional dependency and vulnerability, and he would not enter such risks. In chapter 3 we noted Rousseau's longing for what looked like a psychological impossibility: a warm, supportive family, one that engenders "the finest feelings known to humanity," that is risk-free. Of all his paths to redemption, this is perhaps the most fantastic. This is not to deny that Clarens is deeply instructive. It teaches us, above all, about the symptoms and causes of modern alienation. The importance of its lessons cannot be exaggerated. Yet, ironically, Rousseau's escape into the fantasy of Clarens soothed his own alienation to such an extent that it retarded those personal corrective steps that he needed to take to rescue his life from his own loneliness and alienation—such steps as commitment to a community or to his life-long companion, Thérèse, whom he married belatedly.

For some, the way of Clarens is the most promising path to redemption. It reinstates many features of Nature's Garden, such as simplicity, natural necessity, curbed *amour-propre*, while also introducing a set of human goods and joys missing from that Garden, such as intimacy, family, friendship, and community. Yet its redemption, like that of the preceding paths, is provisional and incomplete. Clarens culminates in death and sorrow. Julie's romantic passion for St. Preux is never fully extinguished. Her heart is still torn by her love for St. Preux and her duty to Wolmar. We might be tempted to attribute her dividedness to a merely contingent mistake made in her past. Yet Julie seems caught in a quandary more fundamental and inevitable. As long as we are not alone, as long as we enter relationships, conflict between duty and love is bound to arise. Even at Clarens, love can surprise one. One might not see it coming until it is too late. At that point, the well-ordered household is subject to dividedness, deception, chaos, and pronounced suffering. As long as we are social creatures, and we are not on the extreme public path, there is no sure way to protect ourselves from ourselves—from diverse loves that can collide with each other and with personal and public duties, from loves that can lead to bitter grief. Only Solitaires—only those who lead a still life, a *nature morte*—are sheltered from such risks.

Julie ends in death and sorrow, though there is nothing lifeless about these. On the final page, Claire names the central features of Clarens and declares them demolished: "Confidence, friendship, virtues, pleasures, playful games—the earth has swallowed all." As for her relation to friends and community, Claire confesses, "I am alone in the midst of everyone." The only voice she hears is that of the dead, the ghost of her best friend, Julie, "Claire, oh my Claire, where are you? What are you doing far from your friend?"[41] Only in death, it would seem, can Claire again achieve the joys of Clarens. With this final sentence the novel ends: Julie's "coffin does not entirely contain her . . . it awaits the remainder of its prey . . . it will not wait for long." Freedom from the pain of loneliness, longing, and dividedness comes only at death. The redemption Clarens has to offer is not complete. Moreover, its redemptive powers are frail. Clarens probably cannot survive the death of Julie; too much at Clarens hangs together precariously. Clarens, it turns out, is indeed the Second Garden; it, too, is a fleeting moment in time that reminds us of how things could be if we maintained the fragile balance between solitude and sociability, independence and dependence, love and duty, desires and powers, public and private.

Is there a redemptive path that, if not as Arcadian as Clarens, is not as frail? And if human flourishing entails, among other things, reconciling the public and private, is there a path that includes a broader sense of the public than what we found in Clarens? At the outset I called the way of Clarens the *moderate private* path. "Moderate," because it does not revolve around the solitaire; "private," because at its center stands the household, not community or an inclusive common good. Clarens has no political life. Perhaps it would not be Emile's ideal home. At Clarens, we encounter stellar individuals with immense capacities for love, friendship, and good work. But could Julie or St. Preux ever become committed citizens? Could their intense relationships and their family- or self-sufficiency be incorporated in a city-state like Geneva? Is there a way to bring together the good things that we associate with the three paths we have explored: the way of the citizen, the solitaire, and the friend, family, and community? In the next chapter we seek a path that attempts to include enjoyment of intimacy and commitment to a common good; devotion to family and to global justice; acceptance of diversity and love of common goals; self-assertion and renunciation; private perfection and public compromise; personal insouciance and social seriousness. We are seeking a middle way that leads to the Flourishing City.

10

Reconciling Citizen and Solitaire

Religious Dimensions of the Middle Way

The Social Function of Religion and the Religious Function of Solitude

Rousseau associated the deepest aspects of the public and private life with religion. Paying attention to Rousseau's religious vocabulary exposes the heart of the middle way. Religion, in Rousseau's view, can enable us to cultivate both a rich public and private life, assisting us to achieve a host of capacities and joys that pertain to various spheres of being—the universal, the civic, the domestic, and the realm of friendship and solitude.

Rousseau never mentioned a middle way. He never explicitly asked how we are to capture the benefits of the public and private paths while circumventing their liabilities. The path to the Flourishing City, the destination of the middle way, is an imaginative construction, designed to illuminate what I have discovered in Rousseau's writings. Terms such as "community" and "the common good," "individual rights" and "privacy" are not just abstract textbook entries; they represent clusters of values and ways of life that we negotiate, daily. These polarities define much of our moral life and the conflict that we encounter as we navigate that life. The question of how to reconcile the public and private is a question for our time. Yet it is not anachronistic to pose the question to Rousseau. Even if he did not explicitly formulate our question, his two most important books, *The Social Contract* and *Emile*, suggest a response to it. They suggest a middle way. In this chapter, I chart this way and evaluate its problems and promises.

Some will be surprised that *The Social Contract* and *Emile*, together, could offer a middle way. A standard complaint against *The Social Contract* is that it allows no room for the private life and individuality. Conversely, a common complaint against *Emile* is that it neglects public life and community. Yet I will suggest that by paying close attention to the role of religion in Rousseau's thought, we can reconcile *The Social Contract* and *Emile*, rather than pose them as alternatives. My investigation of Rousseau's religious vocabulary—a vocabulary that highlights the social function of religion as well as the religious function of solitude—elucidates his attempt to reconcile harmoniously the public and private.

Later, we will want to evaluate the success of this reconciliation. It is not at all clear whether Rousseau himself was hopeful about its success or even if success was ever his goal. He did depict a society that supports public and private endeavors. However, perhaps he intended this depiction to serve more as a social critique that illuminates society's failure in supporting the public and protecting the private, than as a blueprint for achieving a society that unites the two, perfectly. In any event, on the middle path friction remains between public and private. Rousseau used a religious vocabulary not only to suggest a partial reconciliation between public and private, but also to articulate the abiding conflict: civil theology versus inward spiritual longing; mandatory, civic faith versus sincere, private conviction; citizenship versus humanity; the local versus the universal. Religion, for Rousseau, profoundly conveyed these contrasting sets of legitimate goods. Nonetheless, I will maintain that the middle way, in spite of its precariousness and potential friction, is the most promising of Rousseau's paths.

I can briefly sketch the middle way by comparing it to the extreme public and private paths.[1] The public path is marked by an intense patriotism in which there is no conflict between public and private because the private is subsumed under the public; the private path is marked by an intense solipsism in which there is no conflict because there is no public life with which to clash. The middle way, in contrast to these paths, is marked by a temperate republicanism that encourages a public life, protects the private life, and tolerates some conflict between them. On the public path, there is no distinction between virtue and patriotism, morality and politics, society and the state; on the private path, virtue and morality are achieved in the absence of patriotism, politics, and social life. On the middle way, virtue and morality pertain to, but are not limited by, patriotism and politics; society is not identical to the state because society is the larger, more inclusive category. On the extreme public path, individual interests are shaped from birth to match those of the state; on the private path, only a random relation exists between individual interests and those of the state. On the middle way, the state appeals to an individual's interests, which have been informed by various social institutions, to live peaceably in a just nation.

On the extreme public path, the self is unitary and is devoted to the good of the state; on the middle way, the self is multiple, and only the civic self is dedicated exclusively to the good of the state. On the public path, diversity is not allowed; on the private path, diversity is not encountered because one is alone. The problem of how to manage diversity harmoniously in society disappears on the two extreme paths. On the middle way, in contrast, diversity is encountered, permitted, and protected by law. Peace and freedom on the extreme paths are not complex notions. On the public path, peace is absence of conflict, and freedom is the sense of belonging; on the private path, peace is absence of conflict, and freedom is self-determination and the absence of attachments. Peace and freedom on the middle way, on the other hand, are complex notions. Peace is satisfaction with one's private life but also the experience of social belonging; freedom is the pursuit of one's chosen ends but also the capacity to contribute distinctively to the common good. Finally, on the extreme public path virtue is a joint achievement, yet on the private path an individual feat. On the middle way, virtue is both a private and a shared endeavor.

This chapter does not provide a map to the graceful reconciliation of the fullness of the public and private. Rousseau, I have said, is not at all sanguine about ever finding, or making, such a map. This chapter is not about some proverbial happy middle way. At best, the middle way depicted here can be understood as a worthy challenge: the challenge to maintain commitment to both public and private spheres, even in light of conflict.

Rousseau articulated this challenge in the idiom of religion. He had become convinced of two things. First, a civil religion of some sort is necessary to instill in citizens a love of and a commitment to the common good. The law, with only the force of the law, is not enough to sustain a just and flourishing society. Second, freedom of religion, and a robust civic protection of such freedom, is necessary for individuals to flourish as human beings. When individuals are stripped of their freedom to pursue religious or philosophical comprehensive views, they will wither inwardly, both morally and spiritually. As citizens they will be unable to bring to society the imaginative, autonomous reflection required for democratic, political deliberation. Rousseau's challenge was to formulate a social model that would incorporate the public and private roles of religion, even though he was fully aware of the (potentially dangerous) tension between them.

The middle way, then, attempts to engender a common faith and safeguard personal belief. I want now to explore both forms of religion—public and private—starting with civil religion. Unlike in Montesquieu's or Locke's social model, where coordinated self-interests provide the fundamental social cohesion, in Rousseau's view cohesion is cemented by coupling individuals directly to a public life. This public life entails, among other things, a shared understanding—a common faith—that unites individuals in common beliefs and goals. Such commonality need not be comprehensive. That is, the common good of the political community, in Rousseau's view, does not require broad agreement on every issue. But societies, including liberal ones, need some common faith lest they waste away as citizens battle against one another in chronic, low-grade civil wars with such weapons as callousness, business brutality, exploitation of the poor, and litigation.

Rousseau was one of the first to recognize what may seem like a contradiction or paradox; a democratic nation that supports individual rights requires some form of public religion, that is, some shared beliefs and practices that generate moral community. Individual rights and liberties, in this view, are understood as salient features of a socially entrenched common good. When Rousseau attempted to express the strength and nature of those beliefs and practices that unite otherwise disparate modern individuals, he was compelled to adopt a religious vocabulary. It was the strongest vocabulary available for articulating the level of commitment and attachment required to sustain democratic institutions.

Rousseau was also convinced that if individuals were not allowed to pursue personal religious belief, their well-being, virtue, and capacity for autonomous reflection would be impeded. Individuals who are allowed to exercise autonomous thought in their private lives are more likely to cultivate reflective powers that benefit public deliberation. Moreover, Rousseau held that freedom of personal religious belief would serve the social function of reducing religious strife, thereby promoting peace. The liberal premise here is that people are less likely to fight over religion if they are allowed to pursue their own religion freely. Safeguarding personal religious belief, however, brings not only public benefits. It also contributes to the achievement of private virtue and joy. One is most at home in the world when one can freely pursue private hopes and beliefs and strive for excellence.

Safeguarding personal religious belief, that is, religious tolerance, can be interpreted broadly here. It need not apply exclusively to religious belief proper, but to a variety of deeply held beliefs and practices. Rousseau's eighteenth-century arguments for religious tolerances pertain to the life of the mind, the pursuit of happiness, and the rights of the private life. In Rousseau's day, the standard view was "one people, one religion"; to permit religious diversity was to court anarchy. Rousseau, in contrast, promoted a more radical view—one people, one civil religion, and a variety of personal, spiritual religions. The one religion for the people—the civil religion—was to be highly limited, supporting the social contract and protecting personal religious belief. Advocating religious tolerance in the eighteenth century is equivalent, in our time, to championing the protection of all kinds of beliefs and practices that some would deem mistaken, offensive, and even immoral. Rousseau himself understood the close connection between religious and civil tolerance. "It is intolerance," he wrote, "which arms men against one another and makes them all enemies of humankind. The distinction between civil tolerance and theological tolerance is puerile and vain. These two tolerances are inseparable."[2]

There is much potential for conflict between the public and private aspect of religion. We will explore this potential more fully in the following chapter. Here I only wish to note that Rousseau well understood that religion was at one and the same time a great enslaver and a great liberator of humanity. It could render one bloodthirsty or peaceful, fanatical or gentle. It could unite or tear apart a nation. It could contribute simultaneously to private fulfillment and public chaos, or to public harmony and private agony. In spite of these dangers, or perhaps because of them, Rousseau's middle way sought to capture beneficial aspects of public and private dimensions of religion, namely, a common faith to unite a people and a protected spiritual arena for private pursuits.

Religion, then, broadly understood, will highlight for us Rousseau's attempt to imagine the Flourishing City even as he maintained his Augustinian pessimism. Religion provided Rousseau with a window through which to view humans as eternally torn by an inner conflict. This conflict is rooted in a human nature that is neither at one with nor radically opposed to social existence. Religion can unite individuals in common belief, yet it can also separate individuals as each seeks to live and believe sincerely by his or her own lights. For Rousseau, then, religion represented the problem of and the solution to the human propensity to both gather together and remain alone. If established properly, religion could allow humans to flourish as social and private beings. It could powerfully unite individuals, satisfying a condition for the social contract and a human desire for solidarity; it could also gratify the human urge to follow private pursuits. To achieve these goals, religion would need to respect human nature as well as alter it, rendering citizens fit for civil society while protecting their private lives. Durkheim once offered the following gloss on Rousseau's social and political writings: "To change man and at the same time respect his nature is indeed a task that may well exceed human powers."[3] Religion is the tool Rousseau employed when he attempted this task—a task likely beyond human powers.

In the next chapter, I will draw attention to the inevitable remaining strain between the public and private and will ask whether Rousseau was willing to permit it. In this chapter, I investigate Rousseau's efforts to envision a form of life that contains both a vital public and satisfying private life. Special attention is given to the religious dimensions of this middle way. After examining its explicit religious dimensions, I turn to the implicit religious aspects of such concepts as the general will and the wise legislator. This investigation of religion discloses, in the end, Rousseau's understanding of the promise and limits of the political.

Rousseau's Religious Idiom and the Middle Way

In the nineteenth century, Marx, Weber, and Durkheim all agreed on two things: that modern Western societies and politics could not be adequately described in the categories of economics and narrow self-interest, and that the Industrial Age was in need of shared beliefs and practices not securable by classical liberalism. Within this context we can make sense of their interest in Rousseau's attempt to capture the benefits of liberalism—individual rights and liberties—in a moral vocabulary featuring a common good that is more than the aggregate of private goods. Yet much of Rousseau's vision is missing from these social theorists. Inwardness, solitude, and private perfection—this half of Rousseau's view cannot be found in these classical social theorists, and we have inherited this lacuna from them.

Rousseau had surveyed the terrain of the public and private and concluded that "society must be studied in the individual and the individual in society."[4] It is not always understood that Rousseau struggled to give equal treatment to both sides of the conjunction. Some have taken him as a precursor to totalitarianism, others as an early proponent of autonomy and liberal rights.[5] In this study I have argued that Rousseau offered several distinctive paths along the public-private continuum; I will now argue that an investigation of his religious vocabulary highlights his efforts to forge still another path, the middle way. I will focus on the potential for rapprochement of the public and private on the middle way by looking at two of Rousseau's books that to many seem irreconcilable.

Linking *The Social Contract* and *Emile* (both published in 1762) has posed problems for students of Rousseau. The standard textbook interpretation of *The Social Contract* goes something like this: *The Social Contract* is a political program designed to denature individuals by shaping them in the image of society. In the state of nature, humans were content insofar as they recognized plain limits imposed impersonally by nature. In civilization, however, humans incessantly imagine new needs and resent all obstacles barring their satisfaction. The cure for this dis-ease is to circumscribe individuals within the *volonté générale*, the general will, thereby checking unhappy egoism, that is, the self enslaved by its *volonté particulière*. Force, however, is needed to detach individuals from their private wills so that they can be "free" in the general will.

Now here is a standard interpretation of *Emile*: This educational tract is devised to enable humans to pursue their natural goodness by protecting them from that cardinal source of corruption, society. Rousseau claimed that "all the first impulses of nature are good and right"; it follows, then, that education should focus on the preservation and refinement of innate, natural impulses. If children are to encounter limits, teachers should ensure that they are natural limits and not artificial social conventions. Genuine freedom springs from accepting nature's restrictions, not society's.

How can the two works be reconciled? Rousseau seems to offer two radically distinct solutions for the recovery of happiness and virtue. Is freedom found in society's general will or in the individual's innate goodness? Is our true tutor Society or Nature? Rather than juxtaposing *The Social Contract* and *Emile*—and the public and private ways that we associate with them—I will suggest that a close reading of the role of religion in Rousseau's work enables us to reconcile them and to discern a third way.

On this reading, Rousseau contended that the Flourishing City is composed of members who have undergone a conversion to what he described as the religion of the heart. This conversion enables individuals to trade private willfulness and egoism for social cooperation and genuine selfhood. It requires as much solitude as social support; one consults the heart as one participates in the general will. There is, then, no abandonment of self, but of selfishness; no abandonment of society, but of social fatalism—the absorption of individuals into a social mass.

Without inwardness and the concomitant discovery of one's social commitments, society thrusts itself upon the self, raising the specter of coercion. Moreover, social members might be compelled to adopt what Rousseau called "the religion of the citizen," an intolerant religious nationalism that breeds discord and death among nations. Yet, on the other hand, without social involvement, one's solitude can turn into unhappy confinement and religion into an otherworldly, asocial cage. Of this unhappy religion Rousseau wrote, "I know of nothing more contrary to the social spirit."[6] The religion of the heart, in contrast, avoids these extremes, bringing together personal inwardness and social interaction, private perfection and social obligations.

Rousseau depicted in detail the religion of the heart in *Emile*, though it also can be found in the "Letter to Voltaire on Optimism," "Letters to Sophie," *Julie*, and *The Social Contract*. *The Social Contract* culminates in its last chapter, "Civil Religion," a chapter too often ignored by political philosophers. In this chapter, Rousseau described and rejected two models of religion—one exclusively private, the other exclusively public—and went on to champion a third model that embraces religion in both its private and public aspects. The exclusively private religion, "the religion of man," is a spiritualized version of Christianity or deism. This religion, "without temples, altars, or rites, confined to the purely inward cult . . . is the religion of the Gospel pure and simple."[7] In contrast, the exclusively public religion, "the religion of the citizen," is a nationalistic religion, "engraved in a single country . . . it has its dogmas, its rites, its external cult prescribed by law; outside the single nation that follows it all are considered infidel, foreign, and barbarous."[8]

Rousseau criticized the private model of religion for attaching people to a universal, otherworldly kingdom rather than to a specific, earthbound society. He complained that in this private cult, "religion, one of the great bonds of society, fails to operate. Indeed, far from attaching the hearts of the citizens to the state, it removes them from all earthly things."[9] This private religion, however, has its merits. It is sincere, and it does not falsify true religion, that is, religion that seeks to link humans to the divine. Yet as a purely private, interior cult, this religion, Rousseau argued, leaves the law only with the force of the law.[10]

A society, in Rousseau's view, requires more social cohesion than what the force of the law can provide. If law is not supported by a shared, moral understanding, then the law becomes a purely external constraint. Law is an expression of moral solidarity more than it is an enforcer of order. "Civil association," Rousseau would like to think, "is the most voluntary act in the world."[11] And religion, in some form, enables citizens to make this voluntary act, encouraging them to love their public duties. Rousseau, then, emphasized the need for shared beliefs and practices. This emphasis takes him out of the social-contract tradition of Hobbes and Locke, for whom enlightened self-interest, not civic education and religion, inspire voluntary consent. Within Rousseau's argument against the purely private religion is the view that liberal society requires some form of shared belief—a common faith—to support liberal solidarity. Without it participation in political community is unlikely, because such participation is neither easy nor particularly natural for the individual—hence the need for a civic religion. Civic religion can nurture individuals to love things held in common and to commit to such common projects as economic justice and individual rights, to use two of Rousseau's examples.

It would seem, then, that the second model of religion—the religion of the citizen—would be Rousseau's ideal. After all, this public religion "reunites the divine cult with love of laws, and it makes the country the object of the citizens' adoration, teaching them that to serve the state is to serve its tutelary god."[12] Yet Rousseau rejected this model on two grounds. First, he offered a religious objection. The religion of the citizen, "founded on errors and lies, deceives men, makes them credulous, superstitious, and it drowns the true cult of divinity in vain ceremonial." Its foundation is the fraudulent belief that there is an identity between divinity and the state, and this makes any sincere private religious belief next to impossible. Next, Rousseau offered a liberal, political critique. This public religion, readily becoming "exclusive and tyrannous, makes people bloodthirsty and intolerant, so that it breathes death and massacre, and it considers as a sacred act the killing of anyone who does not believe in its gods."[13] Rousseau's complaint, then, is that the religion of the citizen lacks all genuine spirituality and it makes citizens intolerant, raising the specter of civil oppression and foreign war.

After rejecting the exclusively public and private models of religion, Rousseau championed a model that secured both public and private aspects of religion. Rousseau wanted a religion that would (1) bind people's hearts to this world, to a particular society, unlike the purely spiritual, private religion; (2) exclude the dogmatism and intolerance that breed civil strife and international war; and (3) remain authentically spiritual, so as not to falsify true religion and thereby place citizens in contradiction within themselves. His hope, then, rested in a civil religion that could provide the citizen with the benefits of public and private religion, yet without creating a fatal division within the citizen.

The civil religion of *The Social Contract* is an indispensable feature of Rousseau's Flourishing City, and yet—unlike John Calvin, for example—Rousseau restricted its reach. The civil religion encourages citizens to love their duties and uphold just laws, but beyond these, each "may have what opinions he pleases." It is in this context that Rousseau quoted Marquis d'Argenson: "In the republic, each is perfectly free in that which does not harm others."[14] This liberal precept became, in the hands of Rousseau, a religious doctrine. He made tolerance a salient, dogmatic feature in his rather minimalist civil profession of faith (tolerance is one of six dogmas; the others support standard deism and the "sanctity of the social contract and the laws"[15]). This liberal virtue, tolerance, is to be inculcated in society's members, and those not abiding by it are to be banned (a liberal irony). Tolerance is a serious matter for Rousseau. A republic of free citizens must accept the responsibilities of freedom, and tolerance is foremost among them.

Rousseau's civil religion, then, engages individuals in society by way of a common faith, yet an aspect of that faith is the safeguarding of diversity.[16] We can think of this as a communitarian defense of an important feature of liberalism. I call it communitarian because Rousseau wanted to cultivate tolerance as a virtue; he called tolerance, after all, a religious dogma. Locke, for the most part, hoped that the individual would realize the pragmatic value of tolerance, that is, realize that it is in one's best interest to be tolerant. Rousseau, in contrast, was less sanguine about the results of such instinctive, enlightened self-interest and therefore required that tolerance be taught and enforced as a civic dogma. He offered an apparently paradoxical vision: a civil religion that serves to unite a people, transforming them into good citizens, with a chief feature of this solidarity being respect for private belief and practice. By permitting religious diversity, Rousseau honored what he considered to be the liberty required by sincere religion. And by relegating religious diversity to the private sphere, Rousseau made religion safe for the republic.

Society building does not exhaust Rousseau's concern with religion in *The Social Contract*.[17] Rousseau, we have seen, was also concerned with safeguarding the piety of the sincere heart; this entailed rejecting any account of religion that, "being founded on lies and error," made humans superstitious and manipulated them for purely social ends. Religion, no doubt, plays an important social function in *The Social Contract*, but that function becomes vitiated if fidelity to authentic individual religiosity is not observed. Rousseau was convinced that the creation of the Flourishing City would require supporting both public and private aspects of religion; a belief he described when he wrote, "All that breaks social unity is worthless; all institutions that put man in contradiction to himself are worthless."[18] To betray genuine spirituality is to live in contradiction; it is to be a materialistic *philosophe* or a religious fanatic!

The atheistic philosophers promised to bring progress and redemption to a battle-fatigued Europe. Rousseau saw in their words an inflated view of human reason and in their deeds indifference toward the human suffering that springs from inequality and injustice. Rousseau associated eighteenth-century atheism with impassive elitism. When atheists forsook religion, they abandoned the downtrodden and simple folk, and thereby surrendered their hearts, their moral hearts.[19] The fiery religion of the fanatics, on the other hand, was as impoverished and dangerous as the chill of the atheists. It, too, smothered genuine spirituality, placing ritual and dogma above spontaneous devotion and graciousness. If the *philosophes* fostered apathy, the fanatics fostered hatred.[20] Protecting private religion, then, was not only for the sake of engineering social order via tolerance; such protection permitted the possibility of genuine religiosity and the moral wherewithal that flows from it. Protecting private religion allowed the individual to pursue deep-seated beliefs, longings, and hopes. It allowed the individual to be an individual.

The religion of the heart, I have said, is found in *The Social Contract* and elsewhere, but it is expressed most clearly in "The Profession of Faith of a Savoyard Priest" (in *Emile*, book four). It is commonly held that the religion described in *Emile* is private and radically different from the public, civil religion in *The Social Contract*. I want to suggest, however, that the two accounts of religion share much in common.

Undoubtedly, we hear more about inwardness in *Emile*. In that work we are invited to resist all authoritarian voices and to consult the heart, that spiritual center which unites reason, the emotions, and moral wisdom. Jesus embodied the religion of the heart. Rousseau portrayed him as kind, tolerant, honest, sincere, natural, and in the face of death, solitary. This is not the Jesus of traditional Christianity. No miracles, no messianic claims, and no death for the sins of the world. The Jesus of Rousseau is like the Jesus of the deists, only more romantic and less moralistic. If this Jesus produced wine at the wedding feast, it was not as a display of power, but a desire "to prolong the joy of the feast," for Jesus, above all, has a "sensitive heart"—he is tender and amiable, "un homme de bonne société."[21] Jesus, then, is the good, sincere individual, uncorrupted by society, who voluntarily dies for it, not for its sin, but for its potential goodness.

How, then, does the religion of *Emile* compare to the civil religion in *The Social Contract*? Five of the six dogmas of the civil religion are explicitly upheld in *Emile*. Both books support the standard claims of deism, and both promote tolerance. Yet what of the remaining dogma, "the sanctity of the social contract"? Can this be found in *Emile*? The social contract is the covenant that binds the people, as a people, to their civic lives. It requires that each member work toward a common good not by denying the aspirations of the self, but by seeing the public good as a integral component of one's own aspirations. If there is something sacred about the social contract, it is because it is held in common and it serves the whole, not the few. This sacred aspect of the social contract is upheld in "The Profession of Faith" in *Emile*. "The good man," wrote Rousseau in *Emile*, "orders himself in relation to the whole, and the wicked man orders the whole in relation to himself. The wicked man makes himself the center of everything. . . . The good one is ordered in relation to the common center, which is God, and to all the concentric circles, which are the creatures."[22] The culmination of *The Social Contract* and *Emile* is the moral—even spiritual—integration of the individual into "the common center." One learns that to truly love the self, the self works and cares for the common good. Hence the last sentence of "The Profession of Faith" reads, "It is by forgetting oneself that one works for oneself. My child, self-interest deceives us; it is only the hope of the just which does not deceive."[23] These passages are not peculiar in *Emile*, they are representative of it. They represent the heart of *The Social Contract* as well, which supports not the exhausting pursuit of narrow, private interest, but the satisfying venture of the common good; not disparate individualism, but a just, public membership.

The religion of *Emile*, then, is not in opposition to the religion of *The Social Contract*. The religion of the heart opposes narrow self-interest, the chief threat to Rousseau's social contract and its laws. Jesus, in *Emile*, exemplifies the abandonment of self-interest as well as the achievement of selfhood. Genuine inwardness is contrasted to willful pettiness; the autonomous spiritual human becomes the truly social member. The Jesus of *Emile* becomes a symbol of unity between *The Social Contract* and *Emile*.[24] The "Profession of Faith" in *Emile* depicts a religiosity that brings much private fulfillment to members of the Flourishing City. It also, however, depicts the social commitment that flows from such a religiosity.

In this book, we are exploring Rousseau's depictions of the public and private and how he wrestled with the tension between them. On the extreme public path, we saw the elimination of conflict, for all was made public; on the private path, we saw the same erasure, this time by making all private. Now we see Rousseau's attempt to harmoniously bring together the public and private with the help of religion. Rousseau understood the benefits public and private religion could bring to the Flourishing City. Private religion, "the religion of man," is a universal religion, that is, a religion of humanity. Over and against the parochial and the politically expedient, "the religion of man" unites humans in compassion, tolerance, and shared spiritual yearning. I call this religion "private" because it has no public rites, dogmas, or places of worship. It stands for our innermost hopes, beliefs, and longings; it stands for sincerity, morality, and universality. Public religion, on the other hand, represents the shared hopes, beliefs, and longings of a particular people. Its civil theology both expresses and generates social solidarity. The "religion of the citizen" ensures the stability and unity of the state. It satisfies our desire to escape loneliness and participate in a rich shared public existence. Rousseau understood and had personally experienced these laudable aspects of public and private religion. Yet he knew, too, the liabilities of public and private religion. Political apathy, self-indulgent mysticism, quixotic idealism—these follow private religion. Fierce nationalism, intolerance, war—these cleave to public religion.

Is there a way to reap the benefits and shed the liabilities of both the public and private? The religion of the heart, as expressed in *Emile* and *The Social Contract*, was Rousseau's best attempt. It is the way to the Flourishing City. The City flourishes because its religion enables citizens to achieve private and public—moral and political— aims. The City flourishes because its members do not have to choose between being "men or citizens."[25] The City flourishes because its members achieve what they desire: a rich public and private life. This is not to say that all conflict between public and private can be eradicated. The residual tension will be explored in the next chapter. For now it is enough to note that Rousseau, not unaware of this tension, sought to cope with it rather than eliminate it. Although Rousseau hated dividedness and conflict, he seemed to have been willing, in the early 1760s, to allow it for the sake of this promising, although tensive, middle way. The middle way held the hope of a people embracing both humanity and citizenship, morality and politics, individuality and social cooperation.

The role of religion in Rousseau's work is too often ignored. I have listened for it, hearing it as an interpretive key. I have not said much about Rousseau's own deeply held religious beliefs. He was religious, but that is not my argument for taking seriously the role of religion in his moral and political writings. Rather, it is because Rousseau associated the deepest aspects of the public and private life with religion. What does this emphasis on religion mean for us today? If Rousseau's religion of the heart were to amount to a requirement that citizens profess a deistic faith, then my interest in the religion of the heart would be purely antiquarian. It would have little or no relevance for us today. I want to suggest, however, that Rousseau's religion of the heart addresses our main consideration: the public and private in democratic society.

The religion of the heart, after all, addresses two central features of democracies: commitment to the public life, on the one hand, and to private life, on the other. The social dimensions of this religion address the need in liberal democracies for some set of vital, dynamic shared beliefs and practices. Such shared beliefs and practices can be understood as a common faith. This faith, which is mutable, is sacred, in a Durkheimian sense. It is sacred because it is shared and it contributes to liberal solidarity. Robust liberal democracies cannot subsist on law and order alone, no matter how wise the laws and constitution. A liberal democratic *culture* is required, one that is morally committed to such common projects as economic justice and the eradication of racism.

On the other hand, the private dimensions of the religion of the heart address the need in democratic societies for the protection of the private life. The freedom to cultivate a vital private life, as well as the legal provisions and cultural resolve to protect such freedom, are central features of both the religion of the heart and liberal democracies. "The private dimensions of religion," I have said, need not refer to personal religious devotion as traditionally understood. Rather, private religion can refer to any deep, abiding personal beliefs that help individuals make sense of the moral and natural universe in which they find themselves. This aspect of the religion of the heart acknowledges the significance of a nurtured, interior life. Such an interior life can bring personal renewal and can enable a person to become "self-possessed," that is, capable of autonomous deliberation in private and public domains.

Rousseau's religion of the heart is a window through which to view problems and promises in contemporary liberal democracies. When Rousseau sought to portray and reconcile the various dimensions of the public and private, he reached for a religious vocabulary. It was the most powerful language available to him for capturing the multifaceted nature of public and private existence. Today, when such a vocabulary is foreign to many, we need to listen carefully to hear the nuances of Rousseau's voice. We also need to develop our own vocabulary. To that end, we should keep in mind that we do not need to restrict Rousseau's religion of the heart only to traditional or organized religion. Rather, it can encompass something like a shared democratic culture—the kind of culture that responds with righteous indignation when someone's rights are trampled on, as if a sacrilege had been committed. Rousseau himself suggested that such a broad interpretation of public religion was appropriate. He insisted, for example, that the civil profession of faith should be understood "not precisely as religious dogmas, but as social sentiments."[26] The freedom that we associate with liberal democracies requires from citizens a social commitment to uphold such freedom, a commitment that is similar in form to religious commitment. Liberalism may entail much secularism, that is, the absence of explicitly religious beliefs. But liberalism, if it is to be viable, must retain the elementary forms of the religious life, that is, shared beliefs and practices that forge moral community.[27]

Given a broad definition of religion, Rousseau's Flourishing City can be said to be a religious one. The social force of religion is employed to direct the individual's gaze from narrow self-interest to common goods and goals. Yet the religion of the Flourishing City is not the same as the religion in Rousseau's *Poland*. The civil religion in Poland was designed to shape the individual's soul into the collective soul of the political body. The religion of the heart, in contrast, protects diversity, allowing the individual to cultivate a satisfying private life. The religion of the Flourishing City attempts to ensure a common—civic republican—faith, and a feature of that faith is protection of the private life.

The Implicit Religious Dimension of the Middle Way

In the above section I examined the explicit religious aspects of the middle way. I now want to turn to what we may call the implicit religious aspects of this middle way. Our principal text will be *The Social Contract*. I will listen for the religious pitch in such notions as the general will and the wise legislator. Like most eighteenth-century European authors, Rousseau's work was informed, perhaps inescapably, by a pervasive yet tacit theological background. I will bring that background a bit to the foreground. One need not, of course, explore the religious dimensions of such "secular" topics as the general will or the wise legislator. The religious dimensions are often ignored or else characterized as something other than religious. Yet we have much to gain by attending to the religious background and assumptions that are implicit in so-called secular discourse. We are likely to hear something new, in this case, something that places our questions about the public and private in a larger, helpful context. Besides, Rousseau was a religious thinker, and we will not hear his full voice if we cannot hear its religious tones.

The General Will: Diverse Members in One Body

Of Rousseau and the general will, Judith Shklar wrote, "It conveys everything he most wanted to say."[28] Above all, it conveys Rousseau's attempt to bring together the public and private as well as to respect the distinction between them. In voting on the general will, for example, the citizen is to consult his or her own individual moral conscience, with the object of the vote being the public good. Without moral autonomy, the individual cannot assist the public in its search for the general will. When we think of the general will, we can associate "will" with the moral autonomy of the individual, and "general" with the public object of that willing. The general will, I am about to argue, is Rousseau's most ardent philosophical bid to acknowledge and reconcile the rights of the individual and the requirements of the social.

The general will concerns all members of a state, but not all the time. It is best understood as an interval in people's lives. One does not always play the role of citizen, putting aside one's private will to support the general will. If that were the case, the social contract would be no different from the social uniformity of Sparta or Poland. In *The Social Contract*, there is room for a private life. The general will does not prohibit the private, but requires that diverse citizens come together, on occasion, and vote on what is good for the public body. On such occasions, citizens voluntarily give up their particular wills for the sake of the general will. In fact, however, the general will also represents the citizen's best long-term effort at self-love (*amour de soi*). Diversity as expressed through freedom of religion is a good that the community has agreed to safeguard. Tolerance is a feature—indeed, as we have seen, a doctrine—of the common good. Desiring to secure agreement in the public sphere and diversity in the private, Rousseau struggled to protect the political body from strife and its members from oppression. This challenge goes to the heart of democracy, which requires a balance between—or at least a premium on—agreement *and* diversity. In his political writings (for example, "Political Economy," *Poland*, and even *The Social Contract*) Rousseau generally gave too much weight to agreement and thereby upset any balance. If all his works are considered as a whole, however, balance is achieved, even if unsteadily.

At the start of *The Social Contract*, Rousseau revisited the Garden and noted that the life of isolation is no longer an option.[29] The Fall from the Garden calls for humans to gather and generate new, sustaining social forms of life. Yet even in these new forms of life, aspects of the Garden need to be preserved and transformed. Above all, liberty and "the care one owes to one's self" must be maintained, in some form. Hence Rousseau set himself the task of finding "a form of association which defends and protects, with the whole common force, the person and goods of each associate, and in which each, uniting himself with all, may still obey himself alone, and remain as free as before."[30] Here Rousseau summed up the problem, as well as the form of the solution, that the social contract is designed to solve: the establishment of a *social order* in which *love of self* is preserved. Rights and justice emerge, according to Rousseau, when individuals in association contemplate how to best love themselves. If one truly loved oneself, one would seek out a social order in which the individual could take on limited and mutual social obligations, obligations which in fact serve one's own true interest. Rousseau, here, appealed to the individual's *amour de soi* to support rights and justice. As long as one followed the prompting of love of self (*amour de soi*), one would resist damaging the common good by introducing destructive particularity. In this way, Rousseau attempted to bring together interest and justice by appealing to one's best love for oneself.

This strategy is accomplished by the general will. The general will dialectically unites the law and the voluntary, the civic and the individual, the political and the moral—the public and private. As we will see, the general will does not oppose the individual will per se. Rather, it checks the *particular* will (to employ Rousseau's technical vocabulary), that is, the will that places narrow, petty interests (*amour-propre*) above such common goods as law, justice, and equality.

The religious background of the general will can illuminate its significance for our study on the relation between the public and private. In 1 Corinthians 12, Paul addressed the topic of how to conceive of diverse, individual members in relation to their group. His argument was that diversity is not to be shunned, but embraced, for "to each is given [various] manifestations of the Spirit for the common good."[31] He employed powerfully the metaphor of the human body and its various parts. "The body does not consist of one member but of many. . . . As it is, God arranged the organs in the body, each one of them, as he chose. If all were a single organ, where would the body be? As it is, there are many parts, yet one body. . . . Now you are the body of Christ and individually members of it."[32] This theological model of unity embracing diversity, specifically Paul's metaphor of the body, was quite influential in French religious, moral, and even political thought, especially among the French Augustinians, in the seventeenth and eighteenth centuries.

When Pascal used the Pauline body metaphor, he stressed unity and subordination over diversity and autonomy, yet he still managed to note that God intentionally created diverse creatures to work together for the general good.[33] For Descartes, the Pauline metaphor highlighted the harmonious governance of a diverse, natural world by a few general laws. Of all the seventeenth-century thinkers, Nicholas Malebranche most thoroughly explored the logic of Paul and the moral and theological implications of God's general will for "the body." In Malebranche's view, God does not exercise a particular will that favors some and not others. Rather, God wills generality, that is, God acts through an impartial general will that establishes universal harmony and justice. To imagine that one is the beneficiary of a partial, divine will is to suffer from *amour-propre*.[34] God's will and laws are just because they are general, applied equally to all.

This theological concept, God impartially willing the general good, became an influential political concept, namely, citizens willing the general good, having set aside their particular interests.[35] In *Emile*, I noted, Rousseau defined moral humans as those who order their lives to serve the whole, whereas "the wicked" attempt to use the whole to further their own narrow interests. The wicked are always trying to place themselves at the center of everything; the good, in contrast, are "ordered in relationship to the common center, which is God, and to all the concentric circles, which are the creatures."[36] Here, in *Emile*, Rousseau combined both the theological and political model. One's theological commitment is to the "common center," that is, to God, while one's political and social commitments are ordered in relation to the various "concentric circles." The more central the concentric circle, the more general and hence the greater its claim on one's life. Compared to *Emile*, we hear less about God in *The Social Contract*—it is, after all, a political treatise. God does not drop out of *The Social Contract* altogether, but Rousseau's focus was not on the universal common center, God, but rather on the first "concentric circle," the political sphere, or to employ the Pauline metaphor, the political *body*. In *The Social Contract*, then, the relevant center is the political body, and the general will of the citizens is the way to discover the common good of that body.

This theological background of the general will underscores that the general will—whether God's or the political body's—operates in the context of diversity, of distinct, individual members seeking a genuinely shared, public good. Diversity is not sacrificed for the sake of the body. As Paul rhetorically asked, without diverse members "where would the body be?" Without diversity, we would be on the extreme public path marching to Rousseau's Poland. The middle way, in contrast, seeks to preserve the common good and diversity. Rousseau placed the doctrine of the general will at the heart of *The Social Contract* because it allowed him to maintain the autonomy and rights of the individual as well as the sovereignty and prerogatives of the political body.

An approach that can be called the traditional French political model sought to elevate the public over the individual rather than to relate them dialectically. In this view, the more public, the more moral; the more private, the more immoral. This model was supported by the Augustinian theory of the two loves, concupiscence and charity. Love of public things—things outside the self—sprang from *charité*, whereas love of private things flowed from concupiscence, that is, from *amour-propre*. Another moral, theological model, however, maintained that there was a third love—a gentle love of self, *amour de soi*. Within these models, these traditions, Rousseau worked. The general will depends on individuals who can distinguish between *amour-propre* and *amour de soi*, and pursue the latter—genuine love of self.

Rousseau began *The Social Contract* claiming that he wanted to bring together the right and the useful, that is, some version of deontology and utilitarianism. This endeavor can be seen in the logic of the general will; while individuals have a *duty* to pursue it, it is also in the *interest* of individuals to pursue it. This strategy hangs on the distinction between gentle *amour de soi* and fierce *amour-propre*. Individuals principally motivated by *amour-propre* make poor citizens, because they cannot suppress their special interests long enough to vote objectively for the sake of the common good. Citizens motivated by *amour de soi*, in contrast, recognize that love of self would have them think and act objectively, that is, in light of the general will, for that is in their best, long-term interest. Even if Rousseau's social contract strategy is, in part, highly individualistic, appealing to the individual's interest in well-being, it does not belong to that prevalent French moral tradition which held that the activity of greedy individuals driven by *amour-propre* can, if properly coordinated, usefully serve public purposes.

Rousseau retained the distinct theological meaning of *amour-propre* and *amour de soi*, and he declared that although the interests generated by *amour-propre* divide, the interests of *amour de soi* can unite humans in common endeavors—namely, the establishment and operation of a just state. Rousseau, then, on his third path of the middle way, neither shared the traditional view that the public always stands in opposition to the private nor the coordination view, "private vice, public benefit." Instead, Rousseau argued that the interests of *amour de soi* can be served by the just state, and that truly common interests, directed at the good of the political body, can emerge. Ultimately, citizens' love of self (*amour de soi*) and love of justice can converge. Citizens realize that it is in their best interest to commit to the just state, and also derive pleasure in doing the good. On the middle way, the public and private are not radically divided; neither, however, are they radically identified, for the totality of one's being is not identified with one's civic role. Even in that civic role, one exists as an autonomous moral agent who makes a distinctive contribution to the political community.

The theological traditions within which Rousseau worked allowed him to articulate a model that maintains commitment to the individual and the common good. The Pauline language of the harmonious body comprised of diverse members, and the language of God's general will intending and sustaining a diverse creation, enhanced Rousseau's own vision of individual citizens working together to achieve a common good. Additionally, the theological distinction between vicious *amour-propre* and clement *amour de soi* provided Rousseau with a way to distinguish between acceptable and unacceptable self-pursuits. Equipped with the notion of a salutary self-love, Rousseau could imagine a felicitous political body populated by citizens engaged not only in common projects but in diverse, private pursuits—hence the significance of religious tolerance. Theological concepts assisted Rousseau as he created a legitimate political space for the individual. Rousseau, and the theological tradition of the general will to which he belonged, was not opposed to the individual will (*volonté individuelle*), but to willful individuals (those motivated principally by *volonté particulière*).[37] Rousseau received and augmented a French tradition that made individual free will a condition of all moral activity. This dimension of Rousseau's thought would have a profound influence on Kant. And like Kant, Rousseau would wrestle with the divided moral agent.

"Taking Men Such as They Are": Connecting Private Interests to Common Endeavors

In much classical social theory we can find some version of the divided self in need of healing—an old theological notion. The famous Kantian moral struggle between public duty (justice) and private desire (self-interest) is found in, and was largely inspired by, Rousseau. *The Social Contract* presents a complicated moral psychology of human dividedness and also offers strategies to overcome division. Rousseau rejected the view that humans must choose between duty and all self-interests. Rather, the moral task is to pursue one's genuine interests as opposed to those false or apparent ones generated by *amour-propre*.

A good example of the public-private dialectic on the middle way is found in Rousseau's effort to reconcile (public) justice and (private) self-interest. In the first sentence of *The Social Contract*, Rousseau set a decidedly non-utopian tone, noting that in his political investigations he was "taking men such as they are." His subject is not lifeless, abstract humans, but real, self-interested individuals with a wide range of needs and desires. In the next sentence of *The Social Contract* Rousseau states, "In this study I will attempt always to bring together what right [*le droit*] allows and what interest prescribes, so that justice and utility may in no case be divided."[38] To unite justice and utility is to reconcile public duty and private yearning. Rousseau sought to show citizens that it is in their true interest, as individuals, to be committed to public justice and to the common good. Rousseau's design to unite justice and interest is not based on the coordination of narrow self-interests (*amour-propre*), but on the appeal to duty to self, that is, to one's best interests as defined by *amour de soi*.

In Rousseau's moral psychology, as found in *The Social Contract* and elsewhere, humans are principally moved by love—self-love. And no political, social, or moral scheme can be successful if it fails to address the deep-seated loves—desires, interests, aspirations—of the individual. Rousseau, like Durkheim after him, held that public duty and self-love need not be opposed. Indeed, in contrast to Kant, Rousseau and Durkheim asserted that one can fulfill one's duty only when one loves or desires it. The basic psychology behind this, in Rousseau's words, is that "when we act, we must have a motive for acting, and this motive cannot be foreign to ourselves." Rousseau applied this psychology to the moral life: "Is it not true that if one said to you that a body had been pushed without anything touching it, you would say that was not conceivable? It is the same thing in ethics, if one believes that one acts without any interest."[39] We do our duty, we pursue the good, because to do so satisfies our loves and interests. The moral self, then, need not be the Kantian self in conflict between duty and love, justice and interest.

The Social Contract is Rousseau's attempt to apply his moral psychology to the political life. It is all very well, Rousseau noted, for the theorist to ask the abstract, lifeless citizen—the rational, calm one who acts out of "pure understanding"—to embrace the general will.[40] But this abstract citizen is not a flesh-and-blood human: "Where is the one who can thus separate oneself from oneself? . . . Do we not still need to see how personal interest demands that one consent to the general will?" The corporeal human asks, "What interest have I in being just?" To address that question, Rousseau wrote *The Social Contract*. Citizens have tangible, personal interests for discovering and sustaining the general will, and the establishment of equality and justice are chief among them. Rousseau was explicit about this: "Equality of right and the concept of justice which such equality creates derives from the preference that each man gives to himself."[41]

In *The Social Contract*, we do not find the language of self-sacrifice, but rather self-pursuit. For example, immediately after discussing the limits of the sovereign power, noting that individuals owe to the community only those things which are truly important to it, Rousseau stressed that even as one fulfills these limited social obligations, "one cannot work for others without working for oneself."[42] To those who would deny this, Rousseau responded, as might have Montaigne, "Each pretends to sacrifice his interests to those of the public, and they all lie." Given that "no one desires the public good except when it agrees with his own good," Rousseau asserted that "the harmony of the public and private good is the object of true politics that seeks to make a people happy and good."[43]

To make a people "happy and good" they must be led "to prefer their genuine interests to their apparent interests" [*intérêt bien entendu* to *intérêt apparent*].[44] This is not an easy task. It required from Rousseau such schemes as the general will and the wise legislator. The task may well be impossible, by Rousseau's own estimation, given all that he has said about the destructive and persistent force of *amour-propre*. He seems to be sighing, if only humans could grasp how to truly love themselves, how to escape anomic *amour-propre* and follow those interests that are dictated by *amour de soi*. When Rousseau wrote about the private path, late in his life and emotionally exhausted, he was quite pessimistic about the possibility of a people—as opposed to an individual here and there—defeating the prompting of *amour-propre*. He was somewhat more optimistic, as a younger man in the mid-1750s, when he began to write what would become *The Social Contract* (1762). This is not to say he was sanguine, by any measure. He had, after all, written devastating critiques of European governments and societies, and of humanity more generally. Nonetheless, *amour de soi*—healthy, wholesome self-love—remained for him a feature of the human condition. This love of self, this duty to self, was a basic principle of life and the basis of the moral and spiritual life. If Rousseau was to discover a form of life that was neither radically private nor socially authoritarian, it would require an integration of public and private, which in turn would require that citizens discern common interests that arise from a true—a properly understood—love of self.

The very expression, "common interest," suggests some kind of integration of public (common) and private interest. Yet what exactly did Rousseau mean by "common interest"? Just as there are two kinds of self-love, *amour-propre* and *amour de soi*, there are two corresponding types of interest, apparent and genuine. Chasing apparent interests, in Rousseau's view, leads to unhappiness in a variety of spheres, public and private. Following genuine interests, in contrast, can lead to contentment in the public and private life. In the political sphere, *amour-propre* (with its attendant apparent interests) produces a combative atmosphere, something like a domestic war waged within the limits of the law. As citizens jockey for advantage over each other, a contingent and temporary convergence of private interests may on occasion be exploited for the benefit of some. Such convergence is not what Rousseau meant by the expression, common interest. Common interest is not a group of overlapping apparent interests produced by *amour-propre*. Rather, it is a set of genuine interests, produced by *amour de soi*, which has a common public object. In the political sphere, citizens motivated by *amour de soi* possess and pursue such common interests as achieving justice and equality. Interests are common, then, when they are shared, prompted by *amour de soi*, and are directed at common projects. To employ Rousseau's love vocabulary, one aspect of rightly loving oneself entails loving one's public duty, as discovered in the common good and as articulated by the general will.

Rousseau's distinction between contingent, overlapping private interest and enduring common interest is parallel to the distinction he made between the will of all and the general will: "The general will considers only the common interest, while the will of all considers private interest, and is nothing but a summation of particular wills."[45] Here and elsewhere Rousseau insisted that the general will is not merely a summation or coordination of private wills pursuing private interest.[46] The general will depends on citizens who possess genuinely common interests. Like the Augustinians, Rousseau had come to believe that *amour-propre* is all but natural to humans, or at the very least, inevitable. Yet unlike the Hobbesian Augustinians, Rousseau never sanctified *amour-propre*. He never, in other words, interpreted *amour-propre* as a socially useful aspect of human nature. Even on the extreme public path in which he re-directed *amour-propre* to shared public ends, *amour-propre* needed to be transformed in order to become socially useful, and this transformation was purchased at a high price—the loss of individuality. Still, from Augustinian moral traditions Rousseau had drawn the notion that the private and the public need not be in opposition.

Earlier, especially in France in the seventeenth century, many held that the public good stood in opposition to the interests of the individual. The flourishing state required that individual aspirations be forfeited for the sake of public goals. Yet by the beginning of the eighteenth century, a new model emerged: the state could harness private interests for the sake of the public good. Interests, then, were seen as a source of both division and harmony, depending on whether the state was equipped to coordinate them. Rousseau, I have said, drew deeply from this development, yet he rewrote it with his love vocabulary of *amour-propre* and *amour de soi*. He insisted that while the interests generated by *amour-propre* divide, the interests of *amour de soi* can potentially unite humans in genuinely common projects. So whereas many eighteenth-century thinkers saw the public good springing from individuals' motivated by *amour-propre*, Rousseau saw this good deriving only from *amour de soi*. Individual interests springing from *amour de soi* are served by the just state, and common interests are expressed as citizens search for the general will. The Rousseauean citizens, on the middle way, realize some of their deepest aspirations as members of the political body. This theological vision, which goes back to Paul and Augustine and which travels in French thought via Pascal and Fénelon, maintained that the self is completed, not lost, in community. As Paul had sought to preserve both commonality and diversity in the body of Christ, so Rousseau sought to do the same for the political body.

This discussion of common interests and commitment to the political community should not belittle the individualism found in Rousseau's social strategy. If he worked hard to unite the public and private, he did so by starting with the individual's deepest concern—the concern for personal health and happiness. In this Rousseau was a realist. He was convinced that our fundamental motivation is directed by a basic duty to self. Even on the extreme public path, Rousseau employed a strategy that promised to individuals a distinctive form of peace and freedom, as discussed in chapter 7. In *The Social Contract*, the general will begins with the individual's interest in the establishment and preservation of the just state. This, indeed, is the aspect of Rousseau's general will that separates it from Diderot's understanding of the general will. For Diderot, the general will was based on universal benevolence. For Rousseau, in contrast, it was based on love of self (*amour de soi*).

Of course, above and beyond this ardent individualism found in *The Social Contract*, we also find a vision of community and common interest that is based not merely on convergent private interests, but on a truly shared concern for the good of the whole. In addition to appealing to the individual's self-love, Rousseau hoped to generate in citizens a profound love for the political body and for a common good that was more than a mere aggregate of private goods. Rousseau's middle way, then, in spite of its individualism, ultimately retained a sui generis collective life in which individuals discover ample fulfillment, a fulfillment which they cannot experience alone. As Rousseau put it, from the act of association, which creates a "moral and collective body," individuals *as citizens* derive their "common identity, life, and will."[47]

The chances of success of this middle way, seeking as it does to dialectically relate the individual and community life, are slim. In the next chapter, I discuss the various difficulties in achieving this theologically inspired vision. Rousseau shared Montaigne's deep skepticism of individuals who profess to act out of a sense of public virtue. *Amour-propre* renders individuals myopic; unable to see broad, common interest, they pursue only narrow, private interest. If citizens are to consult the prompting of *amour de soi* and be committed to the common good, *amour-propre* needs to be subdued. Yet that cannot be done easily or naturally. Individuals must be transformed if they are to become citizens. Hence Rousseau found himself in need of something like preternatural political solutions. In order to shape and strengthen the weak, divided, Augustinian will of the individual, Rousseau offered the general will and the godlike legislator.

The General Will and the Wise Legislator: Redemption at the Crossroads

The general will and the legislator are the result of Rousseau working once again at the crossroads of Augustinian and Enlightenment traditions. We can usefully view Rousseau's notion of the general will as a solution to the Augustinian problem of the weak will— the individual knows the good, but fails to do it. Yet we can also view the general will as belonging to those Enlightenment traditions that feature the individual's ability to exercise and implement moral reasoning. Rousseau's concept of the legislator can also be viewed as being located between Augustinian and Enlightenment traditions. The legislator belongs to Enlightenment thought insofar as the concept depends on the belief that good, educative institutions produce good, moral citizens, thereby implicitly denying any inherent defect like original sin. Yet the legislator also belongs to Augustinian thought. The legislator's ability to transform humans depends on the legislator's divine credentials and supernatural powers, and such requirements implicitly negate the very possibility of such a legislator and hence of human transformation.

In previous chapters, I have noted Rousseau's affinity with the Pauline and Augustinian pessimistic notion that individuals consistently fail to do what they know they ought to do. Even if reason could escape its limits and enlighten us, we would still be inclined to harm ourselves and others. In the words of Paul, "I do not understand my own actions. For I do not do what I want, but I do the very thing I hate. . . . I can will what is right, but I cannot do it. For I do not do the good I want, but the evil I do not want is what I do."[48] Now listen to Rousseau, as he attempted to establish the need for the general will and the legislator, in light of human weakness: "Individuals see the good they reject; the public wills the good it does not see. . . . Individuals must be compelled to conform their wills to their reason; the public must be taught to know what it wills."[49] The ultimate aim of the general will and the legislator is to "bring together understanding and will in the social body." This challenge, to bring together understanding and the will, can be seen as Rousseau working with his two sets of vocabularies, with the Enlightenment stress on reason and the Augustinian stress on will. Given Rousseau's location between these traditions, he found convenient Paul's formulation of the problem as moral understanding wedded to a weak will. Rousseau's Enlightenment instinct was to offer a solution to the Pauline problem, while his Augustinian inclination was to suggest the problem is insolvable. How does the general will and the legislator confront the Augustinian problem of knowing the good but not being able to do it? We'll start with the general will.

Rousseau needed to establish political devises that mitigated human corruption. The problem at the individual level is not deficient understanding, but a weak will; the problem at the corporate level is not a deficient will, but lack of understanding. The general will is designed to address these related problems. Citizens, in private, can vote and register their knowledge of the good. The state, via executive institutions, can enact the collective understanding of the common good, that is, administer the general will. Individual citizens, as subjects, provide the *understanding*; the citizens collectively, as sovereign, provide the *will*. Thus the Augustinian problem is addressed in the voicing and enacting of the general will; individuals in private see and voice the good, the collective implements it. The power of the collective (the sovereign) and the will of the individual (the citizen) is transformed together into an active moral will, an executed general will.

Citizens, according to Rousseau, are most likely to be able to consult their consciences and deliberate on the common good if they temporarily withdraw to reflect in private. Voting, a crucial public act, requires a private retreat into the recesses of one's own thought and conscience. The premium Rousseau placed on private retreat is parallel to, and perhaps informed by, the Pascalian and Augustinian recommendation that one withdraw from centers of worldly corruption in order to reflect on the good, including the good community. Yet what, exactly, is the object of contemplation for Rousseau's citizens? Is the general will an independent, pre-existent cognitive reality which citizens are asked to *discover*? Or is the general will a contingent, compiled representation that citizens *create* by voting?

The former view suggests that when one enters the voting booth, he or she puts away one's particularity and attempts to discover an objective general will, a will that exists independently of human preferences. The device of voting, with the majority deciding, is not a way of constructing the general will. Rather, voting is a way to discover what in fact the general will is, prior to the vote. Support for this view of the general will is found in *The Social Contract* at the beginning of the chapter, "Whether the General Will Can Err." There Rousseau claimed that "the general will is always right and always tends to the public advantage; but it does not follow that the deliberations of the people always have the same rectitude."[50] Later in the same chapter, however, Rousseau described the general will as a representation of citizens' common interests that emerges contingently from a vote. In this view, the general will is the product of a specified voting process that is designed to represent social agreement on the common good. The general will does not, in this view, exist independently, waiting to be discovered, but is rather created in the very act of voting.[51]

It is not particularly helpful to ask which view is Rousseau's, for both are found in *The Social Contract*. A more profitable question is why Rousseau held both views, vacillating between them in the same chapter. It would seem to be still another case of Rousseau fluctuating between faith in human achievement and an acute sense of human limitation. On the one hand, Rousseau, confident in human capability, believed that political authority could and should ultimately reside imminently within the political body. On the other, skeptical of human capability, he wanted an authority that transcended the political community. We have seen Rousseau in this awkward position many times before. The former view exhibits the confidence of those Enlightenment traditions that championed human reasoning as the highest authority; the latter view, in contrast, reflects those European theological traditions that maintained God's transcendent will—God's general will—as the highest political authority.

In either case, however, there remains something transcendent about the general will. This should not surprise us. Religious and Enlightenment traditions often shared much in common, because religious traditions gave birth to the Enlightenment. Whether the general will is grounded in reason or in God, in a deliberative process or in an ontological reality independent of that process, the general will is transcendent to the individual citizen and, potentially, even to the political community. An individual citizen, Rousseau told us, can be mistaken about the general will, even under ideal deliberative conditions.[52] Moreover, the political community as a whole can fail to discover the general will, if, for example, there are special-interest groups that, when voting, register their opinions not on what is the public good, but on their own particular interests.[53]

On either interpretation the general will, while infallible and always upright, is not always available to the individual or the community. Indeed, even on the "immanent" interpretation, the general will can only manifest itself if citizens vote objectively, bracketing their own particular interest. Yet from everything we know about Rousseau, he held such an objective act to be nearly impossible. The transcendence of, and hence the difficulty of discovering, the general will becomes all the more apparent when we add that the general will relies on Rousseau's most mythic and implausible character, the great legislator.

We can think of the legislator as the wise educator and society-builder. The legislator ensures that the social customs and political institutions that shape the citizens are sound. With just and wise beliefs and practices in place, citizens are equipped to vote their consciences and arrive at the general will. Much training is required if *amour-propre* is to be moderated and if citizens are to pursue genuinely common projects. Rousseau was unabashed about the legislator's extraordinary challenge and mission: "He who dares to undertake to establish a people ought to feel himself capable, so to speak, of changing human nature, of transforming each individual, who by himself is a complete and solitary whole, into part of a greater whole from which the individual receives, in some ways, his life and being."[54] The legislator, in short, must create a new citizenship, a new society. In *Emile*, the tutor shaped one pupil. In *Julie*, Wolmar and Julie created one household. Now in *The Social Contract*, the legislator creates an entire people.

Like the general will, the legislator is also the product of Rousseau's standing at the crossroads between Augustinian and Enlightenment thought. The legislator belongs to the Enlightenment tradition insofar as it implies that, by means of appropriate education and institutions, individuals can be radically transformed. In other words, there is nothing in the human heart or constitution, like original sin, that would hinder enlightenment and moral progress. The tradition of the wise legislator need not, of course, be relegated exclusively to Enlightenment traditions. Indeed, Rousseau's list of legislators point to such ancient traditions as Moses and the Jews or Lycurgus and the Spartans. Still, even Rousseau's appropriation of these ancient legislators is written in the language of the Enlightenment. The legislator, for example, is "the engineer who invents the machine."[55] Once the well-assembled machine, the enlightened society, is up and running, the legislator is no longer essential. Like God for the Enlightenment Deist, the legislator is mainly required to build the machine, not keep it going (though as I will argue later, the machine, in Rousseau's view, will eventually deteriorate and fail). The legislator is Rousseau's answer to the Enlightenment chicken-egg problem; enlightened institutions produce an enlightened people, but how do you initially produce the enlightened people to erect the enlightened institutions? Rousseau's solution, for all its magic, is the legislator.

The wise Architect, another Enlightenment metaphor that Rousseau attached to the legislator, designs a society that enlightens the mind and strengthens the will. The legislator is needed for the sake of what Rousseau called "public enlightenment"—or "the union of will and understanding."[56] Individuals are not naturally committed to the common good, even if such commitment represents their true interests, that is, their best chance at achieving freedom, equality, and justice. Individuals must be assisted to love and attain these social goods. Rather than "forcing one to be free," at least as that expression is often understood, the legislator establishes the social conditions that creates a people who love the freedom, equality, and justice that is manifested in the enlightened social body. Rousseau, unlike Locke, held that the social contract could not be established by appealing to self-interest alone. Individuals needed to be taught to love the social contract. Love—that is, a tutored, other-oriented regard—is antecedent to the contract.

The legislator, then, is the indispensable building block of Rousseau's Flourishing City, his middle way. The citizens of the Flourishing City are neither on the private path, dodging the public in order to achieve a peaceful private life, nor are they on the extreme public path, renouncing the private in order to achieve an entirely public life. The citizens on the middle way exercise moral autonomy and political allegiance; they pursue private aspirations and public projects. And there is much that could go wrong. The public and private could easily conflict, and society could topple in one of two directions—into chaotic narcissism or oppressive despotism. What enables society to follow the narrow middle way is the legislator, for the legislator creates social institutions that train individuals to skillfully navigate the public and private without spawning debilitating conflict. Such "public enlightenment," then, requires the legislator, but the legislator's own requirements, his credentials, make him Rousseau's most improbable character— even more improbable than Emile's tutor or Clarens's Wolmar. It is the legislator's supernatural credentials that implicitly deny the very possibility of the human transformation that is the indispensable work of the legislator. Rousseau's underlying message is that, although we cannot save ourselves on our own and we need the work of the divine legislator, no such savior is available. This implicit denial places the legislator in the tradition of Augustinian pessimism. The higher the qualifications of the legislator, the greater the limits on what we can hope for.

What are the qualifications of the legislator? The legislator would need to "behold all human passions without feeling any of them," being "completely unrelated to human nature and also knowing it through and through."[57] This formula, to know human nature without participating in it, resembles Gnostic descriptions of Jesus Christ, the god who appeared human. Rousseau himself noted of the legislator, "It would be necessary that gods give men laws."[58] The legislator's job is to "transform human nature," and to do so without force or violence. Hence Rousseau concluded that the task of the legislator is "an enterprise beyond human powers."[59] Gods, and gods alone, can transform the person, creating a new will, character, and set of emotions. Yet just such a transformation is necessary to keep the citizens of the Flourishing City from inflicting harm on themselves and on those around them. The redemptive society that preserves the precarious balance between the public and private requires an authority and power from the outside. If human reason were sufficient, the divine legislator would not be necessary. But reason is not sufficient, the divine legislator is necessary, and yet he remains, tragically, unavailable. Rousseau, again, anxiously worked the junctures of Enlightenment and Augustinian traditions; institutions and education can radically transform humans, but securing the necessary divine author of such institutions is not a human prospect.

Religion and the Promise and Limits of Politics

Did Rousseau ask too much of politics, or not enough? Was it too much to ask political institutions to transform humans into dynamic, autonomous, civic-minded human beings? Or was Rousseau too skeptical of the promise of politics by his intimating that such transformation requires nothing less than a supernatural presence? I noted in part I of this study that most commentators agree with Ernst Cassirer's claim that "society has inflicted the deepest wounds on humanity; but society alone can and should heal these wounds. . . . That is Rousseau's solution to the problem of theodicy."[60] The human Fall, on this account, was caused by social institutions, and it can thereby be reversed by them. I have argued, in contrast, that Rousseau presented a more complicated view, suggesting that all strategies for human transformation and amelioration are ultimately provisional and partial. In this concluding section, I discuss the promise and limits of Rousseau's social and political strategy for the Flourishing City.

Throughout this study, I have noted that destructive self-love (*amour-propre*) is the spoiler that must somehow be managed. On the private path, one attempts to dodge it; in isolation, the individual strives to pursue *amour de soi*, benign self-love. On the extreme public path, *amour-propre* is redirected to patriotic, public goals. The middle way attempts the greatest challenge: to assist a people to follow the sensible ways of *amour de soi* while also pursuing public, shared goals. This challenge is great because in social contexts, the dangers of *amour-propre* are always present. Earlier we discussed the role of dependency. In social circumstances, humans grow dependent on each other, viewing the self through the eyes of others and developing a fetish for, and hence dependency on, public opinion. Such excessive self-regard in relation to the public would undermine the search for and establishment of the common good, the objective of *The Social Contract*. If narrow particular interests are to be traded for genuinely common ones, if *amour-propre* is to be constrained and *amour de soi* encouraged, then social and political institutions must be created that train individuals in the ways of public life, while at the same time "not placing citizens in contradiction to themselves."

Moral evil has also been a theme of this study. Moral evil, for Rousseau, is the result of individuals placing themselves at the center of all things, displacing generality, or else God's general will. The urge to place oneself at the center is the result of that serpent, *amour-propre*. To contend with this urge, Rousseau proposed the devices of the general will and the wise legislator. The legislator trains a people to discover and enact the general will; the general will, we have seen, is formulated so as not to oppose citizens' proper self-love (*amour de soi*). Thus the general will, the center of one's political existence, and *amour de soi*, the center of one's moral existence, are not placed in contradiction. Without such contradiction, *amour-propre* is kept at bay. Moreover, a feature of the Garden is preserved in social existence. In the Garden, there was only the Solitaire and the laws of nature, that is, necessity—the unyielding center. The self cared for itself without attempting to make itself the center of all things. The *Social Contract* attempts to imitate this design by surrounding humans with social laws of their own making. By transcribing human freedom into laws, one both recognizes oneself in the laws and also experiences something akin to the necessity found in the Garden. Freedom and necessity are brought together. As the Solitaire in the Garden pursued the prompting of *amour de soi* and encountered only the necessity of nature (and hence accepted it), the citizen on the middle way follows *amour de soi* and encounters the constraint of self-legislated laws. In contrast, the rebellious one yields to *amour-propre* and spurns the laws, thereby displacing the generality of the law with the particularity of the self.

With sufficient social education, one accepts the social contract, because one recognizes that living in a just state agrees with one's true self-love. The middle way relies on, and attempts to preserve, *amour de soi* in a social context. Law, a result of the general will, can be thought of as a collective or extended form of *amour de soi*, that is, the product of a citizenry's self-love. *Amour de soi* entails duty to self, an intense effort to care for the self. If this care includes, among other things, participation in the just state, then one's civic participation, in conjunction with that of others, becomes a form of extended *amour de soi*.[61] This is not the strategy that Rousseau designed for Poland. On the extreme public path, *amour-propre*—not *amour de soi*—is redirected to public ends. The individual's private vanity (*amour-propre*) is redirected and transformed into a form of collective *amour-propre*, national pride.[62] In contrast to this strategy, on the middle way *amour de soi* is extended, and the loss of individuality is not required. Indeed, autonomy and critical thought are prized, for they contribute to the search for the general will. Moreover, participation in the Flourishing City does not entail the same intense shared identity among citizens. It is understood, for example, that a particular citizen's self-love may entail worshipping a minority religion, and that such individuality is protected by law.

On the middle way, Rousseau insisted on acknowledging and safeguarding the needs and privileges of both the private and public life, for he understood that preserving *amour de soi*, in a social existence, required this. In chapter 3, I noted that Rousseau's vision of humanity's happiest state, the Golden Age as described in the second *Discours*, is not found in either radical solitude or fatalistic social assimilation, but rather on a narrow, frail path between the two. This is similar to the path we find in *The Social Contract*—a middle way that promises a palpable but tensive commitment to both the individual and the political body. On the one hand, Rousseau never lost sight of the primacy of the self, the duty to self as expressed by *amour de soi*. On the other hand, Rousseau understood that maintaining benign self-love in a social context required the construction of a carefully engineered political body. Moreover, he genuinely cherished the distinctive joy and meaningfulness that spring from a shared, public life. If Rousseau, in *The Social Contract*, did not in every chapter stress the prerogatives of the individual, this is because he also gave much attention to the conditions of a shared, public life—in fact, to the very institutions and social customs in which individual rights take root. His goal was to imagine a social framework, a form of life, that supports both public and private projects.

Rousseau's strategy may be called a communitarian approach to liberal rights because it highlights the social conditions that are necessary to create, sustain, and extend rights. In the work of Rousseau, this approach has confused many and may account for why commentators have offered radically contrasting interpretations of *The Social Contract*. Alfred Cobban, for example, claims that "dictatorship is both the logical and also the historical consequence of the democratic theory of the General Will." In contrast, Robert Derathé sees *The Social Contract* as an early defense of individual autonomy and political rights.[63] I do not need to defend Rousseau against the charge of totalitarianism. Many have already done that quite convincingly. I do want to note, however, that those who saw in Rousseau the specter of totalitarianism were responding, in part, to his belief that a particular kind of society needed to be fashioned if rights were to protect individuals and, at the same time, not weaken but strengthen the common good. In Rousseau's view, there was nothing neutral or impartial about what we would call the politics of rights. It would require "changing human nature," the creation of a "new person" and a "new society." It would require the creation of liberal habits and character among citizens, such that citizens could sustain a shared public life and nurture vital private lives. Yet Rousseau's emphasis on character, education, and society building is at odds with much liberal theory with its emphasis on rights, neutrality, and individuality. Due to this, Rousseau has given many pause and even alarm.

My interpretation of Rousseau in this chapter may give alarm as well. To highlight the religious aspects of the middle way may appear an illiberal gesture. Increasingly we associate the vocabulary of community, character, and religion with conservatism. But Rousseau would have us consider whether a robust, civic-minded liberalism may in some fashion depend on such so-called conservative notions. Rousseau's political liberalism, I have said, is not a politics centered on individual rights, but rather on a form of life that supports both the public and private dimensions of life. I have also argued that in order to express this political liberalism, Rousseau often employed a religious vocabulary. He understood that the secular vocabulary at his disposal—that of private self-interest on the one hand, and public duty on the other—did not adequately capture the nature of public and private life. Herein lies Rousseau's powerful and unique contribution to social theory and public philosophy. He held that a vital public life required something like a religious common faith, and that a rich private life required self-possession or something like inward spirituality. Too often contemporary debates in social theory neglect the categories of common faith, on the one hand, and inwardness, on the other. The result is the public life often appears as nothing but a competitive arena of private contracts and state agencies, and the private life appears as an insensible domain of abstract selves protected by rights. Rousseau's political philosophy, in contrast, with its language of civil religion and inward spirituality, attempted to express the fullness of life committed to public and private hopes and projects.

I began this chapter with a discussion of Rousseau's explicit religious concepts in *The Social Contract* and in *Emile*. Next I explored the implicit religious dimensions of such concepts as the general will and the legislator. Our interpretation of these concepts, I argued, becomes more nuanced when we attend to their theological background and religious dimensions. But there is more. Rousseau's overall vision—a society in which freedom and law, liberty and equality, the individual and community embrace—can plausibly be described as a religious one. Rousseau's social contract is more a religious covenant than a contractual agreement. None of this is to say that there is a tacit theocracy or a confessional religion at work in *The Social Contract*. Rather, it is to say that Rousseau recognized that some form of religion, however secularized, is necessary to enliven and sustain liberal democracies. Liberalism may have emerged out of conflict among traditional religions, yet it never entirely escapes the elementary forms of religious life. Rousseau knew well the long history of bloodshed and civil unrest caused by religion. He held that such conflict was not, as many believed, principally the result of scarcity in absolute terms, but of anomic desires on the one hand, and clashes over moral and religious claims on the other. Yet rather than reject religion, Rousseau enlisted it to promote identity for the public life and tolerance for the private. Rousseau knew that religion, of some form, would persist. It would be naive, and perhaps dangerous, to fail to attend to the religious aspects of life together and life alone. He held that if a society had any shared life at all, any shared understanding and ideals and practices, then it assumed some religious form of life, even if a secular, democratic one.

Rousseau suggested, then, implicitly and explicitly, that the modern project of establishing society on a purely secular basis is tenable only if some form of the sacred is acknowledged. This sacred may be entirely internal to the society, emerging not from gods above but from social institutions, customs, and traditions. Produced tacitly by society for society, the sacred emerges in the creative process of forging a common life. And this common life, in the Flourishing City, treasures the autonomous, self-possessed individual. In sum, Rousseau employed religion to assist the political to fulfill what he considered to be its promise: the establishment of a just society that sustains public life and autonomous members.

Yet Rousseau also employed religion to express the limits of the political. Religion in *The Social Contract* not only has an immanent, internal expression, but also an external one. The legislator, the one who completely understands human nature but does not participate in it, is an external force. The exteriority of the legislator matches the preternatural job description: to establish institutions and customs that shape the character and habits of individuals who can thereby both exercise autonomy and belong to the political body. Seeming to originate outside history, the legislator shapes history by establishing traditions—which, in turn, shape the present. Truly, as Rousseau claimed, "it would take gods" to perform the job of the legislator. It would seem that Rousseau imposed on the Flourishing City an impossible condition. For Kant, the language of religion is the language of hope. For Rousseau, it becomes, at least in the political realm, the language of hopelessness. In the end, Rousseau's religious vocabulary intimates the limits of building and sustaining the Flourishing City of *The Social Contract*.

I do not wish to overstate Rousseau's pessimism. In the private realm, for Rousseau as for Kant, religion is a source of hope. And even in the political realm, Rousseau had some hope in the beneficial effect of civil religion. Yet Rousseau also subtly undermined this political hope. He knowingly established the Flourishing City on an impossible cornerstone, the divine legislator. At best, Rousseau seems to say that civil and inward religion can moderate or postpone the inevitable: the unraveling of the just society as *amour-propre* erodes the self-possessed inward life and the shared public life.

Satisfying public and private lives thrive together—and die together—on Rousseau's middle way. Without a vital public life, the private life grows self-absorbed, lonely, and alienated. Without a nurturing private life, the public life grows either cold and bureaucratic, or else fiercely patriotic, stifling the private life. The middle way will fail, because in life together, petty private interest generated by *amour-propre* will eventually dominate genuine common interests. The extreme public and private paths, the way of Poland and the Solitaire, will then become options. Yet as we have seen, these paths have severe liabilities. Again, Cassirer's interpretation of Rousseau—society caused human woes, and therefore society can cure them—does not adequately express Rousseau's tensive, pessimistic belief that no social arrangement can ultimately cure the woes of the social human. According to our investigation of Rousseau and the religious aspects of his political thought, Rousseau struggled with, and ultimately conceded, the inadequacy of a political solution to a spiritual problem. By spiritual, I mean that what ails humans is not merely poor social arrangements, but a deep, moral blight that lies within the human breast. *Amour-propre*, unhappy self-love, simply cannot be eradicated. Perhaps a liberal, civil religion can help contain it, temporarily. But in time it will emerge, and it will bring down civil society.[64]

Even if *amour-propre* could be moderated sufficiently to allow citizens to think and act publicly when needed, there would still be the potential clash between legitimate public and private projects. Rousseau's strategy for avoiding conflict, namely to dodge those circumstances that potentially place the public and private in conflict, is probably impossible to follow in the Flourishing City. Voting on the general will, for example, could place one's legitimate private hopes in conflict with the common good. In the next chapter, I explore in more detail the spheres of public and private in the Flourishing City and then examine the tension between these spheres. In conclusion to this chapter, I note that Rousseau's strategy for redemption—that is, for some form of life transformed and recovered from the Garden—turns out again to be provisional and partial at best, and perhaps untenable altogether. Rousseau's religious vocabulary has highlighted the hope and promise of the political on the middle way. It has also revealed its limits.

11

Residual Conflict

Democracy and Ineluctable Friction

If the claim is that Rousseau successfully united the private and public, the individual and society, there is reason to doubt on two counts: whether he was indeed successful, and whether in fact such success was ever Rousseau's claim. After all, Jesus—the symbol in *Emile* of the inward yet social being—was put to death. One way to account for this is to suggest that Emile's ideal education takes place under the actual conditions of existence and not within the ideal, imaginary world of *The Social Contract*. Perhaps in the latter world Jesus (and Socrates) would not have fared so poorly at the hands of society. But in Emile's world, where private tutors are necessary because public institutions are corrupt, individuals of goodwill can come into fatal conflict with society. The social cruelty inflicted on Rousseau's symbol of unity, then, can be accounted for along these lines: the less just a society, the more tension between public and private for the pure in heart.

That addresses part of the doubt. Rousseau often portrayed himself as that authentic, sincere individual whose private life could augment his public usefulness, if only corrupt society would cease to persecute the innocent. Yet there is still reason to question whether Rousseau maintained that, even under ideal circumstances, the friction between genuine selfhood and social cooperation can be entirely effaced. Throughout his work, he portrayed variously aspects of this friction: private perfection versus public compromise, self-reliance versus social dependence, self-love versus love of the common good, private contentment versus public felicity, self-esteem versus public pride, fidelity to a universal deity versus loyalty to a provincial civil religion.

Rousseau recognized this friction yet refused to surrender either side of the conflict, preferring to keep them together, precariously, in spite of the tension. He went a long way, to be sure, to mitigate the polarization, which he often achieved through his religious vocabulary. Yet the tension never disappeared in his work.[1] In the end, his refusal to evade the tension may be his greatest contribution to modern social thought. For determination to wrestle with such tension, without denying or eliminating it, is a hallmark of modern, democratic societies. In this chapter we investigate this tension. In order to better understand it, we begin by looking more closely at the spheres of the public and private on the middle way, the way of the democratic society seeking to protect the private and sustain the public. This is the way, I believe, of enhanced democracy in the twenty-first century.

Public and Private on the Middle Way: "To Teach Us to Enter Our Own Private Hearts to Discover There the Seeds of Social Virtue"

In 1766, four years after the publication of *The Social Contract*, Rousseau was asked what he thought of a particular young man who placed public duty above all other duties. Rousseau responded with a series of rhetorical questions: "Why doesn't he permit himself any sentiment that is foreign to this [public] duty? . . . There may be sad situations in life, there may be cruel duties which force us sometimes to sacrifice one duty to the others . . . but can there ever be duties which force us to suffocate such legitimate sentiments as those of filial, conjugal, and parental love? And what man who makes an expressed rule of no longer being a son or husband or father can dare to usurp the name of citizen, dare to usurp the name of human? . . . Are these different duties so incompatible that one cannot serve the homeland without renouncing humanity?" Rousseau concluded that to forsake all but civic duties in one's life is something "no imaginable situation can authorize."[2] Frequently in his writings, Rousseau identified various legitimate spheres of being that humans inhabit. In the quote above, for example, the role of child, spouse, and parent are treated as worthy occupations that should not be usurped by the role of citizen. This identification of legitimate spheres of being takes place in *The Social Contract* as well. For example, when discussing war, Rousseau claimed that "individuals are enemies not as men or even as citizens but as soldiers."[3] In this account, one can imagine a brief intermission during a battle, and enemies, who minutes earlier were attempting to kill each other, socialize with each other as friends. The role of "solider" is one role among many, and it does not supercede all other roles. Even when reflecting on war and its heightened patriotism, then, the concept of various spheres of being and roles operated as a basic premise in Rousseau's thought. Harmonizing diverse roles was one of Rousseau's ideals, and such integration, he held, was fundamental to human happiness. Still, he recognized that frictionless integration was not a human possibility. The tension among the spheres—spheres occupying that broad continuum from thoroughly public to intensely private—could never be entirely erased. Humans, after the Fall, are complex creatures, and the middle way, more than Rousseau's other paths, acknowledges and permits that complexity.

On the middle way, even the category of "citizen" is a complex one, invoking different roles and capacities. In *The Social Contract*, Rousseau constructed the concept of "citizen" out of the seemingly oppositional concepts and roles of "obedience and liberty," "subject and sovereign."[4] The citizen on the middle way is not a mindless or servile subject who trades personal autonomy for public safety. Rather, the citizen cultivates various dimensions of the self and willingly offers one's resources to the state, when needed. The will of the citizen couples love of the common good with the judgment of self-legislation. Consulting the self—the interior, moral life—one contributes to the political body. Yet the citizen possesses multiple commitments and attachments. The citizen does not pursue public goals exclusively, but rather achieves a dialectical relation between public and private aspirations. Rousseau's middle way, as expressed in *The Social Contract* and *Emile*, maintains a healthy respect for individual needs and goals. Still, the political and social orders are not designed principally to satisfy such individual desires as security and opportunity. The principal aim is to support and foster individuals whose self-identity is forged in a transactional relation to the political body, an identity in which one's public and private life are neither radically identified nor divorced.

The middle way's attempt to incorporate both the autonomous individual and the united political body is risky and difficult, requiring discerning citizens and just institutions. Anything less would fracture the middle way. Corrupt institutions would ruin the citizens, just as corrupt citizens would ruin the institutions. The extreme public and private paths do not run so precariously. The former has no autonomous citizens to tamper with the institutions, and the latter has no institutions to tamper with individuals. Yet these paths, we have seen, fail to achieve Rousseau's full vision for the public and private dimensions of human existence. They fail to convey Rousseau's principal hope, as he put it, to "draw the path of true happiness, to teach [us] to enter our own private hearts to discover there the seeds of social virtue."[5]

Rousseau's support for the private life on the middle way is due to his belief that the private life can contribute to both individual joy and public edification. The individual, temporarily withdrawn from public associations, can acquire valuable perspectives for the shared civic life. An extreme statement of this is found in *Emile*. Rousseau proposed Robinson Crusoe's desert island to serve as an imaginary position from which to consider one's social circumstances. "The best means of raising oneself above prejudices and ordering one's judgments about the true relations of things is to put oneself in the place of an isolated human and to judge everything as this one would judge."[6] In private, we gain insight on the public. For the sake of private joy and public enlightenment, then, the private life is protected on the middle way. This protection entailed, among other provisions, limited private property rights. Rousseau, who greatly distrusted the convention of private property, supported private property only insofar as it could protect one from becoming dependent on unjust and oppressive socioeconomic webs, as discussed in chapters 3 and 4. Throughout his life, Rousseau critiqued and condemned the oppression caused by large accumulations of private property. In every case he held that if private property were to be permitted, it must "be contained within the narrowest limits . . . subjugated and always subordinated to the public good."[7] The public good, here, includes the protection of the poor and powerless from the rich and powerful. Even with the idea of private property, then, Rousseau had in mind an interrelated set of public and private goals and interests.

In *The Social Contract*, Rousseau articulated a dynamic and tensive relation between public and private. He acknowledged, on the one hand, that there may be occasions when the public good eclipses private aspirations; yet he was also eager to circumscribe the claims of the public good. For example, the sovereign, he insisted, "cannot exceed the limits of general convention," "the limits of public utility," or "load on its subjects any chains useless to the community."[8] Rousseau shared and quoted the position of Marquis d'Argenson, "In the republic, each is perfectly free in that which does not harm others."[9] To this quotation Rousseau immediately added the gloss, "This is the invariable limitation; one cannot formulate it more exactly." Rousseau was wrong to suggest that this "invariable limitation" cannot be defined more precisely—think of the Bill of Rights, for instance. Nonetheless, Rousseau's middle way did follow d'Argenson's liberal principle, upholding the prerogatives of the private life. Citizens are not citizens all the time. Citizenship is one role—albeit a significant one—among many on the middle way.

Ineluctable Tension between Public and Private

The diverse roles and activities of the middle way occupy a broad continuum that ranges from public to private. Such diversity contributes to a flourishing and dynamic life and society, yet conflict among these various roles and spheres of being is inevitable. Rousseau described three varieties of conflict: (1) conflict between corrupt, or at least callous, public institutions and the private lives of honest, sincere individuals; (2) conflict between private willfulness and admirable public institutions; and even (3) conflict between ethical private lives and admirable institutions. I will look at each of these in turn.

At the outset of this chapter I noted that Jesus, Rousseau's symbol of the sincere, transparent individual, is put to death by society. Here the moral individual is in conflict with the Realpolitik of public institutions. Political expediency, in Rousseau's view, often leads to public persecution of the innocent. Moreover, even under the best social circumstances, the private life is subject to misunderstanding and unjust condemnation by the public. After the fall into a social life, in Rousseau's account, open communication becomes difficult. When the young Jean-Jacques, for example, was mistakenly accused of breaking the comb, he was initiated into a world divided into public and private spheres, with no guaranteed communication between them. After the broken-comb incident, Rousseau joined a complex world in which individuals hide themselves behind a variety of public masks, and even, or perhaps especially, those who choose not to hide behind masks—the sincere—are misunderstood.[10] Such misunderstanding, and the suffering that springs from it, is principally but not exclusively the result of callous or corrupt public institutions incapable of making fair judgments. There is, in Rousseau's view, a pervading, fallen condition among social humans that distorts communication, clouds transparency, and causes friction between public perception and private consciousness.

The domestic sphere is somewhat protected from the chronic misunderstanding and false appearances that brand public existence. The domestic sphere is characterized by an abundance of intimacy, transparency, and above all, trust. One is safe in the domestic sphere to act and speak candidly, as oneself. Rousseau wrote often about the pain and humiliation that is inflicted on those who refuse to conform to public opinion. In the domestic realm, in contrast, one is liberated from the chains of opinion, and freely expresses one's character through such vehicles as dress, speech, diet, art, music, and so on. This is not to say that Rousseau envisioned the domestic sphere as a sanctuary specifically for characters like Nietzsche's or Rorty's romantic, self-creating geniuses. For Rousseau, the domestic sphere was primarily a safe place, not a creative one. Protected from hardships that society often needlessly imposes, and sheltered from the crowd that would strip one of virtue, in the domestic space one can keep one's character intact and exercise freedom.[11] Moreover, in the domestic sphere one is free to let down one's guard, to reveal one's innermost heart, to dwell in trust. Yet Rousseau also understood that one can be dealt especially painful emotional wounds in the domestic sphere, because betrayed trust always comes as a surprise and reaches to the depths of one's heart.

The second form of conflict Rousseau identified was a conflict between private willfulness and admirable public institutions. There are individuals who habitually put particular, narrow interest above general, shared interest. And all of us have some propensity to pursue immediate, gratifying self-interest. Hence it is important for society to remind individuals of their shared common life. Rousseau recommended various public rituals and communal gatherings as a means to forestall the domination of narrow, particular interest. If one becomes disconnected from public life, one risks losing the capacity to think and act as a public person. And the likelihood of losing this public capacity, or failing to acquire it, is strong. All things being equal, private willfulness, in Rousseau's view, usually eclipses public considerations. As Rousseau put it in his summary of *The Social Contract*, one cannot assume that "a particular will shall always agree with the general will. Indeed, one ought to assume rather that it will conflict, for private interest tends always to preferences, whereas public interest always tends to equality."[12] Constant vigilance on the part of society is required to encourage citizens to be mindful of the concerns of the whole rather than exclusively the benefits of the particular. Such vigilance, we have seen, can veer toward social oppression, as found, for example, on the extreme public path in *Poland*. And even in *The Social Contract*, Rousseau employed strong language when describing how to overcome conflict between the public and private.

"Whoever refuses to obey the general will shall be compelled to do so by the whole body. This means nothing other than that one will be forced to be free."[13] This celebrated passage is the culmination of a discussion concerning the conflict, within each individual, between public and private interests. Rousseau claimed that every individual, as a human, "may have a particular will contrary or dissimilar to the general will, which one has as a citizen." In such cases of conflict, the individual, qua human, may be tempted to put private over common interest, seeing commitment to the common good as gratuitous and desiring "to enjoy the rights of citizenship without being willing to fulfill its duties." An individual who habitually places the private over the public would need to be compelled to adopt his or her own general will and forgo private willfulness. "Forced to be free," then, refers to being liberated from the conflict between one's selfish, particular will and one's just, general will. The particular will per se is not problematic. It becomes problematic when it consistently shuns such public obligations as upholding the laws and thereby undermines the conditions of both personal and public freedom.

"Forced to be free," I noted, is strong language. Yet the concept and practice which it refers to is common and legitimate. Every state has the right to require its citizens to abide by the general will, that is, by the laws of the land, even if those laws conflict with the private interests of some individuals. This is assuming, of course, that the laws are just, and Rousseau made it clear, at every turn, that he was discussing the workings of a legitimate state. If the laws fail to be just, then the state is no longer legitimate, and the nature of the public-private conflict alters.

I do not wish to ignore or understate what may alarm some about Rousseau's phrase, "forced to be free." On occasion, Rousseau seemed to suggest that disagreement on public issues is caused exclusively by the illegitimate assertion of the particular will. Pluralism in the private life is acceptable. Pluralism in public life, that is, diverse views concerning the public good, is suspect and dangerous, in Rousseau's view. He held as an article of faith that individual freedom, in a well-run, legitimate state, would lead not only to commitment to the common good, but also to shared views on the content and nature of that common good. Only when freedom is exercised wantonly, distorted by *amour-propre*, dangerous self-love, does it threaten a state by eroding the solidarity of public judgment. Rousseau paid little attention, then, to the possibility—to the likelihood—that people of goodwill can disagree on issues of supreme public importance. He held, remember, that there was something natural or at least inevitable about the presence of *amour-propre* in social humans. In all his writings, he worried about how to contain *amour-propre*. In his political writings, this worry expressed itself as a pervading suspicion of the assertion of the private over the public. He did, as I have stressed, protect various dimensions of the private life. Yet in cases of conflict between public and private, he usually assigned the blame to private willfulness.

The third and final type of conflict that Rousseau acknowledged are clashes between ethical private lives and just public institutions. Rousseau offered a dramatic depiction of this form of conflict in a passage that praises both the Roman statesman, Cato, and the Athenian philosopher, Socrates.[14] For Rousseau, their lives represent admirable, yet conflicting, moral visions. Socrates pursued the private quest for universal truth, "instructing a few individuals" on the way. Cato, in contrast, pursued the public path of citizenship, "defending the state, its liberty, its laws." The virtue of Socrates "would bring him his own happiness"; the virtue of Cato "would seek his happiness in the happiness of all." This passage may seem to contrast the public path to the universal, not the private, path. We often think of the private-public continuum as something like a series of concentric circles; moving out from the center, from the individual, the circles include larger and larger realms of being, concluding with the last and largest circle, the universal. Yet, as we have seen, Rousseau held that commitment to a group or nation is often at odds with commitment to a universal moral order, an order which is most likely to be discovered along the private path.

In Rousseau's view, Socrates, that single individual who pursued truth, not citizenship, lived for the universal. His understanding of virtue and justice were not confined to the Athenians, but included all humanity. Cato, in contrast, understood virtue and justice to pertain to his particular state alone. For Socrates, virtue pertained to humanity; for Cato, it pertained to patriotism. In his discussion of Socrates and Cato, Rousseau celebrated and contrasted both men and the sets of goods that they represent. In the end, however, he championed Cato over Socrates, offering a pragmatic reason. Only a few are capable of becoming the self-possessed philosopher, yet many can become devoted, happy citizens: "No one has ever made a nation of philosophers, but it is not impossible to make a people happy." These two moral visions, the individual's quest for truth and personal happiness, and the citizen's quest for the common good and public happiness, are in tension with each other. A moral choice, and some moral loss, is inevitable. On the public path, in "Political Economy" and in *Poland*, Rousseau articulated the tension between these paths, and espoused the way of Cato. The same tension, yet opposite endorsement, is found on the private path, for example, in *The Reveries of the Solitary Walker*.

In other writings, however, the conflict is explored yet no endorsement offered. Judith Shklar has made famous the stark choice found in *Emile*: "One must choose between making a man or a citizen."[15] A similar choice is offered in *Letters Written from the Mountain*: "The legislator who would want both virtues [those of the private pursuit of the universal and of the public pursuit of citizenship] will obtain neither the one nor the other; such accord has never been seen and never will be, because . . . one cannot give two objects the same passion."[16] (Rousseau himself, in fact, gave the public and private path the same passion, but whether he successfully reconciled them is another matter.) In the preceding chapter, I explored how Rousseau offered a tentative reconciliation of public and private by means of a religious vocabulary. He also, however, employed religion to articulate the conflict between the two: the religion of humanity versus the religion of the citizen; inward spiritual longing versus civil theology; sincere, private conviction versus mandatory, civic faith; inner wholeness versus social solidarity; morality versus politics; humanity versus citizenship; the universal versus the local. These contrasting sets of goods, which are profoundly expressed by Rousseau's religious vocabulary, speak of conflict between the legitimate claims of the public and private domains. Conflict, here, is not caused by corruption in the public or private life, but by mutually exclusive life alternatives.

On the middle way, Rousseau argued that the good state does not monopolize its citizens' entire moral life and duties. Nonetheless, duty to self, to one's own moral vision, to family, to friends, and to secondary associations can often collide with one's public, civic duties. Friendship, Rousseau argued, "is a contract like others, but it is the most sacred of all."[17] Within the bonds of friendship and family, one acquires profound duties— legitimate duties which can clash with public obligations. In some of Rousseau's political writings, he expressed concern over secondary groups, fearing that citizens would become torn between the worthy goals of a local community and those of the larger political body. In such cases, "some deliberation may be advantageous to the small community, but pernicious to the large one."[18] All conflict, of course, is not limited to clashes between the political realm and some other realm. A variety of types of conflicts occur on what I have called the public-private continuum. In *Julie*, for example, we saw Julie torn between her (private and legitimate) romantic love for St. Preux and her (public and legitimate) duty to obey her father. The varieties of the public-private conflict are legion.

I wish to conclude this discussion of inevitable conflict between legitimate public and private pursuits and duties by contrasting Rousseau to Emile Durkheim, the French social philosopher who was greatly influenced by Rousseau. Rousseau and Durkheim both attempted to secure the good things that we associate with liberalism (the politics of rights) and communitarianism (the politics of the common good); both sought to protect liberalism from egoism and communitarianism from fatalism; both related the private to the public by employing a religious vocabulary. Yet between Rousseau and Durkheim stand salient differences. The creative, though sometimes tragic, friction between genuine selfhood and social cooperation that Rousseau ultimately allowed to remain, Durkheim sought to eradicate. Rousseau was committed to the development of both a lively public and rich private life—the very conditions of a robust democracy—even as he anticipated potential conflict between the two. His refusal to evade the tension between the public and private is precisely what makes his work useful for democratic reflection.

Durkheim, unlike Rousseau, neglected to explore the significance of the private life, except to argue that the sadness that cleaves to the private—loneliness, isolation, and despair—is the result of social forces. We might be tempted to say that Durkheim, the social theorist, should not be expected to give a fuller account of the private realm. In Rousseau's view, however, this realm has social consequences; private sorrow and joy is often translated into social woe and weal. Durkheim understood this only in the reverse. He profoundly limned the ways that public institutions—depending on whether they be commendable or corrupt—can lead to individual joy and moral fortitude or to suffering and decadence. Rousseau did the same, yet he also explored the ways that the private life can shape public institutions. He occasionally interpreted himself, for example, as embracing inwardness and thereby securing the role of an outsider, gaining the necessary distance to speak to society as both critic and separated lover.

In Rousseau's account, however, the value of the private life is not confined to serving the public good. Solitude, for example, a genuine possibility in Rousseau's view, is a refreshing and liberating personal feat, especially if the individual is surrounded by a dissolute society. Durkheim's individual, in contrast, is rejuvenated only by participation in the collective. The contours of the Rousseauean self are less permeable, more hardened, than the Durkheimian self. Even amid an unhappy society the Rousseauean individual can capture some felicity.

In sum, Rousseau, like Durkheim, recognized the conflict between egoism (petty self-interest) and just social loves (the legitimate common good). Yet unlike Durkheim, Rousseau also documented two other varieties of potential conflict: those between the good-natured individual and the destructive society, and that same individual and the wholesome society.

Think of the contrast between Rousseau and Durkheim like this. In Rousseau, we find two kinds of religious vocabularies—the religion of the heart, which addresses the inwardness of the private life, and civil religion, which addresses the public life of the citizen. In Durkheim, we find only the latter. Both Rousseau and Durkheim understood the promises and risks that accompany civil religion. It can promote freedom (inspiring just loves) or oppression (inculcating, for example, fatalism or fanaticism). Rousseau alone, however, spoke of the inward aspects of the religion of the heart. He recognized that, if perverted, it leads to unhappy asocialism, even egoism. If genuine, it enhances personal joy and rectitude. Civil religion, in Durkheim's view, determines individuals' joy or sorrow; yet the religion of the heart, in Rousseau's view, can assert itself over and against social circumstances (including the dominant civil religion). Although Rousseau did not treat the two vocabularies as being radically incommensurate, and even allowed for a partial reconciliation, he did highlight their potential conflict. With a brief comment on the nature of this conflict, I can bring this section, and my contrast between Rousseau and Durkheim, to a close.

We have seen that insofar as Durkheim described a conflict between the public and private, it is a conflict between morality and egoism. He did, however, champion what he called "moral individualism," a communitarian defense of liberalism that articulates and promotes the dignity and rights of the individual in the moral idiom of social justice and commitment to a common good. To some, the very idea of a communitarian defense of liberalism is a sociological impossibility. Those skeptical would offer an internal critique of Durkheim, claiming that "moral individualism" (an oxymoron, to be sure) would eventually self-destruct into unprincipled liberalism. The argument here is that as individuals pursue their liberal rights, they reside within an increasingly contracted private space, sharing less and less in common with one another. Hence the liberal common good becomes thin and unable to generate agreement on public goods, values, and ends. Moral individualism, then, would necessarily degenerate into egoism. This is the position, I take it, that social theorists like Alasdair MacIntyre and theologians like Stanley Hauerwas would hold.[19]

While I believe Durkheim could satisfactorily respond to the charge of liberal self-destruction, I want to note that such an internal critique could not even be directed at Rousseau. On his account, if individuals, as a result of liberal rights, should find themselves alone with themselves, this would not in and of itself pose a threat to the common good. In private, individuals may experience "the simplicity of the heart," that is, a respite, renewal, and sense of well-being that is the outcome not of social endeavors but solitary ventures.

Nonetheless, consulting the religion of the heart will on occasion lead to the assertion of the private over the public. This need not be the result of a battle between egoism and public morality, but as a contest between two categories of genuine goods—the private and public. That they are in fact actual goods is underscored by Rousseau's development of two (distinct yet overlapping) religious vocabularies—that of a civil religion and of a religion of the heart. With these vocabularies, Rousseau described both the partial reconciliation and residual conflict between public and private.

Community and Women Rendered Safe

The presence of conflict on the middle way should not come as a surprise. After all, the middle way is traveled by reflective, autonomous individuals—individuals who will inevitably interact, speak their minds, and engage in disputes. One way to reduce conflict is to curtail unnecessary, potentially discordant social interaction. Between indispensable public and private activities there is a wide range of everyday activities, often taking place in various community associations and secondary groups. Rousseau worried about such gatherings. He would have liked to have minimized them, for he saw them as sources of conflict. For example, in Rousseau's view there would not be, ideally, any need for political parties or organizations. In the well-ordered state, widespread agreement on political issues would make public debate or political parties obsolete: "The first who proposes new laws merely says what all have already felt."[20] Secondary groups and associations, in contrast, could encourage factions and civic tension. Still, however much Rousseau distrusted such groups, he acknowledged "the right to state opinions, make proposals, divide, and discuss."[21] More than his fear of conflict, Rousseau feared a civic unanimity or silence enforced by coercion: "This is when citizens, falling into servitude, have neither liberty nor will. . . . They no longer deliberate, they worship or curse."[22] In the Flourishing City, then, political debate is not illicit, but there would be little need for it. Rousseau dreamed of an unanimity that arose voluntarily, spontaneously, free of coercion.

The middle way contained much that Rousseau loved—law and freedom, justice and equality, political unity and private diversity. Rousseau's ideal community life, however, is not found there—namely, a warm, intimate, tightly knit community like Clarens. The reason is partly a matter of size: Clarens, being smaller than the Flourishing City, is more able to foster community life. But there is still another reason. Rousseau could not trust close community life for the Flourishing City. Too much could go wrong. With too much intimacy, when the political body is like a large family, the search for the general will is easily threatened. Individuals, for example, could be tempted to vote out of personal loyalty, love, or obligation, and this could lead to factions. The personal could become political. Since Clarens itself had no political life, Rousseau had no need to worry about political factions there. At Clarens, we encountered remarkable individuals with great capacities for love, friendship, and good work. We did not, however, encounter committed citizens such as those on the middle way. This is not to say that Rousseau abolished intimacy from the middle way. Rather, he relegated it cautiously to the private realm of family and friends. A more public sphere, such as an association, could gain political power and become factious. The individual in the Flourishing City experiences the diversity of neighbors, the warmth of family and friends, and a strong attachment to the civic, political body. But there is no Gemeinschaft, no tightly knit community, no Clarens. There is religion. The religion of the heart satisfies the private yearnings of the individual, and its civic aspect attaches the individual directly to the state and to the collective whole, but not directly to fellow members. Religion, on the middle way, does not forge either the close community of Clarens nor the intense patriotism of Poland. The former would threaten the political body, the latter the private life. Either form of intense community would be too dangerous for Rousseau's Flourishing City.

The citizens of the Flourishing City, then, are united directly to the state, not to each other as fellow members. "Each citizen," Rousseau wrote, "should be perfectly independent from all others, and completely dependent on the state."[23] This is not a particularly communitarian position. To exist "perfectly independent" from all fellow citizens sounds more like a liberal possibility than a communitarian ideal. In most communitarian models, citizens interact with each other as fellow members of a cherished group, and their fellowship entails dependency in the way of mutual attachments, obligations, and commitments. In contrast to the standard communitarian model, Rousseau's middle way, acknowledging the basic individualism of each citizen, maintains distance between citizens, except insofar as there is occasion to gather at the center, the political body. Like spokes on a wheel, citizens touch at the center only. Citizens on the middle way, then, do not experience daily, cozy civic fellowship. Rather, they exist either alone with themselves, families, and friends, or else in unity with the state. Between these extremes, they have few interactions with fellow citizens in the way of secondary groups, associations, and so on. Unlike on the other paths, on the middle way Rousseau attempted to preserve citizens' independence while maintaining a coherent social order. To that end, Rousseau felt he needed to weaken the chains of dependency, for dependency brings the threat of arbitrary will and power. On the middle way, that threat is dodged, or at least mitigated, by discouraging dependent relations among citizens.

This is not to say that dependency is entirely absent from the public life. The citizen is as dependent on the state and its laws as the Solitaire was on nature and its laws. Conversely, just as the Solitaire was not dependent on other Solitaires, but only on nature, so too the citizen is not dependent on other citizens, but only on the state. The citizen, as a discrete individual, participates in the fashioning of the laws and also stands discretely in relation to those laws. Nothing social or personal is entailed. The citizen experiences impersonal law, not personal relationships. In one's relation to the law, however, there is civic affection, and even a civil religion to cultivate such affection. And the political body is a protective frame—a safe, familiar place of refuge and belonging. We do have a working Pauline body with its diverse parts, talents, reflective powers, and perspectives. But, again, its ambience is not that of the homey community, the familial state. Rousseau's twin loves—love of independence and civic solidarity—carry with them his twin fears—dread of dependency and alienation. The middle way attempts to capture the loves while escaping the fears. Civic solidarity is placed within the confines of one's direct relation to the political body, thereby protecting one's independence, and guarding against the dependency, conflict, and alienation that potentially come with intimate community life.

The intimacy of community is not forsaken on the middle way, I have said, but is confined to the domestic sphere. In Rousseau's view, intimacy—with all its intense emotion, profound vulnerability, and deep commitments—is safest if kept at home. Home is also a safe place for dependency. In the domestic sphere, men and women are dependent on each other, even if in different ways. Rousseau, we know, greatly feared dependency, and considered it a source of personal and social woe. Yet he also recognized the basic human need for intimacy, and he held that dependency inevitably follows intimacy. Men and women are dependent on each other for affection, affirmation, and mutual trust. In the public realm, intimacy and dependency are likely to bring conflict—family-like political feuds, for example. If, on the other hand, intimacy and dependency are relegated to the domestic sphere, not only can they be rendered safe, but they can contribute to public harmony. This entails another of Rousseau's magic acts, this time not that of the godlike Legislator or omnipotent Tutor, but of the Loving Wife.

In most of Rousseau's writings, the wife is the principal provider of domestic affection and moral education. The wife tempers the prompting of *amour-propre* of those around her, and cultivates in her men not only domestic gentleness but political rectitude. The husband is able to think and act politically, that is, to pursue the general will impartially, because his wife supplies his private needs for warmth and security and saves him from petty selfishness. For all this, the wife's reward is the satisfaction of knowing that her husband has been transformed into a worthy domestic partner and political agent—an agency which she herself is denied. Rousseau, the egalitarian, recognized the asymmetry of this arrangement, but he did not deem it morally problematic. From her domestic empire, the woman contributes to the political sphere by means of her man, and by him alone. This is not to suggest that, in Rousseau's view, women have no power, agency, or freedom. Their power over their men is great, their agency within the home is immense, and their freedom to creatively employ their gifts and skills is secure. But women's power, agency, and freedom is narrowly restricted to a significant yet lone realm—the private realm of the home.

A central characteristic of the middle way is its commitment to the enjoyment of both public and private projects. The middle way, then, Rousseau's most profound path, was not offered to women, for they were not permitted to enjoy its public pursuits. Women were essential for its maintenance, but they themselves were not allowed to travel on it. As Joan Landes claims of Rousseau, "Woman's duty consists of subordinating her independent aims and interests to a higher goal, the ethical life of the community. But unlike her male companion, of whom Rousseau also demands the sublimation of particular interests on behalf of a desire for the public good, woman is barred completely from active participation in the very sphere that gives purpose to her actions."[24] Although Landes implies, incorrectly I think, that for Rousseau the sole purpose of the private sphere is to sustain the public, she perceptively notes that women are barred from half the offerings of the middle way—the public half. Moreover, even within their own domestic realm, wives are subject to their husbands. The Rousseauean marriage is marked by mutuality in emotional dependence, not in shared authority.

In sum, Rousseau attempted to render social warmth and intimacy safe by confining them to the household and to the discrete citizen's relation to the collective whole. In both cases, women are essential. By taming men's *amour-propre*, women nurture in their men the capacity for participation in the public sphere and intimacy in the domestic sphere. Still, Rousseau worried greatly about the sustainability of this arrangement. He feared women's power, and his strategy was to harness it. But he understood the risks of doing so. Recognizing their own power, women would not rest satisfied with their domestic roles, and they would seek a life that included public participation. That, in turn, would make women more like men—petty, greedy, more concerned with the regard of others than with their own sense of self, with appearing just more than with being just. When women become men, no one remains to establish the protective retreat of the domestic sphere or to transform self-absorbed individuals into thoughtful citizens. Conflict would erupt in both private and public spheres, and society would ultimately disintegrate. In Rousseau's scheme, then, much weight is placed on women. Yet Rousseau feared that the weight was too much, that women would resist, and that conflict, inevitably, would arise.

Society's Inevitable Decline and Death

Women, then, were an important prophylactic against the social disintegration that follows the assertion of private willfulness against the public good. Yet eventually such decay would occur, with or without the devoted wife and mother. The human will is weak, in Rousseau's estimation. A well-ordered society can help to fortify the will against undue self-preoccupation, but it cannot cure it of its innate willfulness, *amour-propre*. As citizens lose sight of common goods, and even their private lives bring less and less satisfaction, decay and death eventually visit society. Throughout this study, I have highlighted the tension in Rousseau's work between Augustinian pessimism and Enlightenment optimism. By Augustinian pessimism I mean the view that humans will inevitably commit moral harm and that humans are beset by radical—that is, invasive—evil. By Enlightenment optimism, in contrast, I mean the view that humans can significantly improve their situation, because evil is not located in fixed human nature but rather in social structures that are subject to amelioration; since evil flows from unfortunate social arrangements, one can have unlimited hope in future, enlightened social arrangements, assuming society can learn from past mistakes. Rousseau was torn between these perspectives, and the strain is found in the middle way. In *The Social Contract*, there are optimistic, grandiose designs for the engineered Flourishing City. Yet within that same book, there is also a deep-seated pessimism that foresees the inevitable decay and death of even the best designed society.

Writing about "the natural and inevitable decline of even the best constituted governments," Rousseau maintained that such social demise is not the result of external circumstances. Rather, "the body politic, like the human body, begins to die from the moment of its birth, and it carries within itself the causes of its own destruction."[25] As the Solitaire suffered and fell from something like innate original sin, so, too, society carries within its soul the seeds of its own destruction. In part I, we charted Rousseau's account of the fall of humanity, paying close attention to the first and second *Discours*. Now, in *The Social Contract*, we chart Rousseau's depiction of the ineluctable fall of the body politic—the very body and offspring that issued forth from the fall of humanity. With the same pen, Rousseau both designed the Flourishing City and outlined its certain death. The fatal flaw, which no political or social engineering can correct, is the weak will: "As the particular will acts continually against the general will, so the government continually works against the sovereignty. . . . This is the inherent and inevitable vice which, from the moment of birth of the body politic, tends ceaselessly to destroy it, just as age and death destroy the human body."[26] Rousseau's fear of government is linked to his fear of private willfulness. The decay of society often starts with the corruption of government officials whose weak wills lead them to act against the sovereign, that is, against the people. When this corruption reaches an advanced stage, and the corruption spreads from the government to the people, "the state, near its ruin, maintains only an illusory and vain form, for the social bond is broken in every heart, and the meanest interest brazenly adorns itself in the sacred name of the public good . . . and iniquitous decrees directed solely at particular interest are passed under the name of law."[27]

Politically destructive willfulness, then, usually begins with government officials and then infects the general citizenry. Given this genetic account of social decay, Rousseau was especially wary of government officials. There was great temptation for such officials to become corrupt, that is, to put private interest above public good *in their capacity as public servants*. Such abuse of power ranked high on Rousseau's list of public sins, and yet such abuse was highly predictable. Rousseau expressed his abundant distrust of government even while maintaining that government was necessary for the Flourishing City. This dilemma could not, ultimately, be solved. Magistrates are not a unique breed, born especially susceptible to corruption. Hence finding the proper public officials is not a viable solution, for all are subject to *amour-propre*'s placing the particular will above the general. Rousseau was not describing a special case, but a universal one. It is due to their office that magistrates are in a position to do great harm. Their abuse of power weakens the social bonds and unleashes the tendency of citizens to work chiefly for private, narrow advancement, not public, common benefit. This is a sign that death is near. "As soon as public service ceases to be the principle business of the citizens . . . the state is near its demise."[28] At this advanced stage of decay, one no longer asks, "is this to the advantage of the state," but rather, "is it to the advantage of this man or that party."[29] At this point, there is no longer a genuine body politic. Ironically, with the death of the political body comes the termination of conflict between the public and private; the tension disappears with the end of the public life.

Even the most enlightened society is not immune to decay. Augustinian pessimism imposes the limit to the middle way, the conclusion to Rousseau's account, the end of the Flourishing City. Yet Enlightenment perspectives, too, have their place on the middle way. The very aspiration to protect a well-ordered public life *and* an autonomous private life is an Enlightenment prospect. If we are not going to take the extreme public path yet still desire to live in associations while also maintaining the domains of the private life, our only hope, in Rousseau's view, is to discover a well-designed, enlightened state. However, this very goal—the establishment of the enlightened government and the liberty of citizens—has within it the seeds of social destruction. The enlightened society, at best, can delay the inevitable. This fatalistic account can be placed in the framework of my general narrative for this study: *The Social Contract* recapitulates the story of the Fall; this time, however, the story is not about the gradual yet certain fall of the Solitaire, but of the Flourishing City. In both stories, the serpent remains the same character—*amour-propre*, that deadly assertion of petty and destructive willfulness that eventually gets translated into corrupt and oppressive social structures.

When the tutor introduced to Emile the study of social order and politics, he issued this warning: "The multitude will always be sacrificed to the few, and public interest to particular interest. Those specious names, justice and subordination, will always serve as instruments of violence and as arms of iniquity. . . . This is now the study which is important to us. But to do it well we must begin by knowing the human heart."[30] To understand the social and political order, one must not neglect to look to the human heart. Politics of the heart requires that when pursuing justice and equality, one recognize that enlightened social structures alone cannot guarantee a flourishing society. The human heart, with its two loves, *amour de soi* and *amour-propre*, has its own logic with which one must contend. It is a power that needs to be addressed. Rousseau's politics of the heart is what separates him from Marx, Durkheim, Foucault, or from any other social theorist who would interpret human suffering and joy principally as a product of social institutions. Rousseau, of course, was not blind to the fundamental significance of social institutions. Much, if not most, of his writing addresses the inequality and injustice that can arise from such institutional arrangements as social hierarchy, division of labor, private property, taxation, and government. Yet he did not reduce the study of human sorrow and well-being to institutional analysis. He insisted, rather, that "society must be studied in the individual and the individual in society."[31]

The heart—the human spirit, as Rousseau understood it—longs for freedom, peace, security, inwardness, community, and happiness. It longs to be fully human, that is, it is driven by the faculty Rousseau called perfectibility. That longing, we saw in part I of this study, led the Solitaires out of the innocent Garden into the complex realms of human associations and history. This trajectory is very much the Enlightenment story of the development of human splendor, and it is found throughout Rousseau's writings. Yet alongside it is another trajectory. The Solitaires' journey toward human splendor is also the path from guilelessness and wholeness to corruption and dividedness. These two narratives, in Rousseau's work, express a profound ambivalence that is the result of his attraction to both Enlightenment optimism (hence the evolutionary story) and to Augustinian pessimism (hence the regressive story). This awkward position, I have said, can account for many of the conflicting interpretations of Rousseau and for many apparent inconsistencies in his thought. If he had gained consistency, however, one wonders if he would have left too much out of his account of our experience of hope and despair as we seek the fullness of life together and life alone. Perhaps the very ambivalence with which Rousseau wrestled—and which he ultimately refused to resolve—speaks powerfully to the situation in which we find ourselves today: fiercely individual, yet seeking community; committed to individual liberty, yet also to social justice; eager to work for beneficial change, yet fearful that, in spite of our efforts, our lives and society are becoming increasingly polarized between self-absorbed private pursuits and bureaucratic public routines.

Of the middle way, Rousseau's chief fear was that the private life would eventually erode that very form of public existence that protects and supports the private life. He also feared, however, the opposite scenario, namely that the public, civic realm would overextend its reach and destroy private domains. Under difficult social circumstances, during times of want or chaos or insecurity, "a bloodthirsty, intolerant" regime and culture could emerge. Such a society distrusts the diverse, self-possessed, autonomous thought and practices that spring from societies that safeguard the private realm. Of course, Rousseau himself, I have just said, distrusted the private realm. What separates him from the fearful regimes that he condemned? Unlike such intolerant regimes, Rousseau supported the private life even while he was wary of it. He knew that it could lead to corruption, but to suppress it would block those possibilities of joy and satisfaction that belong uniquely to it. Suppressing the private life would deny the Flourishing City its very soul—a religion of the heart that honors both life alone and life together. It would turn the Flourishing City into Rousseau's Poland. Hence Rousseau championed the middle way even as he identified grave, indeed mortal, risks that cling to it. In the conclusion, we will examine Rousseau's complex stance on the middle way, a stance that remains committed to public and private forms of existence while at the same time it acknowledges the vulnerability and risks of doing so. This precarious stance, I will suggest, holds many lessons for democracy in the twenty-first century. Twenty-first-century democracies, I hope, will endeavor to protect and extend the rights and autonomy of citizens, while also recognizing the need to cultivate shared understandings and commitment to common goals. If this is the case, they will find themselves on something like Rousseau's middle way.

Conclusion

A Way Forward: Rousseau and 21st-Century Democracy

The implicit question, "What can we hope for?" runs throughout Rousseau's work. To what extent can we live without alienation within us and division between us? Do good and avoid inflicting harm? Be both self-possessed and other-oriented? These and other issues converge, in this study, on this question: Can we achieve a common life and also support thriving private lives? Rousseau, I have suggested, offered different responses to this question, depending on the situation he was assessing and on his own personal circumstances. I have interpreted and presented these various responses as paths to partial redemption or healing: the extreme public path of "Poland"; the extreme private path of the solitaire; Clarens's way of work, family, and community; and the middle way of the Flourishing City. In this concluding chapter I will ask if Rousseau held a dominant, normative view that informed his various depictions of social and personal health and healing. What, ultimately, was Rousseau's stance? What did he hope for? I am not asking for us to identify a single hidden inner essence to his thought, but rather a pattern or proclivity—what one might call a grammar—that guided his moral imagination. Finally, I will ask what Rousseau has to offer to us, to practitioners of twenty-first-century democracy. I will ask, what can we hope for?

"Our True Self Is Not Entirely in Us": Rousseau's Fundamental Stance

A basic premise that runs throughout Rousseau's thought is the primacy of the self—its hopes and fears, its beliefs and ideals. This self, we have seen, is not the Hobbesian self, naturally in a perpetual state of war with those around it. Nor, however, is the Rousseauean self naturally social, as if fully developed social sentiments were present at birth. Along with his belief in the primacy of the self, he held that the self is not radically self-sufficient and that human joy entails, inter alia, communion with others. "Our sweetest existence is relative and collective, and our true *self* is not entirely in us."[1] In the end, Rousseau maintained both the centrality of the self and the necessity of human fellowship. Neither solitude nor social fatalism is the ideal setting of the Rousseauean self. Human flourishing entails the ability to be self-possessed (as Rousseau put it, "To be oneself, even in the middle of society") and also to maintain and enjoy a variety of

229

social commitments. Our "sweetest existence" acknowledges both the centrality and the inadequacy of the self. Rousseau's starting point is the needs of the self, but this leads to the company of others.

What follows this basic, tensive premise in Rousseau's moral psychology? A type of individual and society that would esteem, and negotiate among, such goods and traits as self-determination and public obligation, interior spirituality and civic-spiritedness, private hopes and shared projects, among other apparent polarities that I have discussed in these pages. It would amount to something like a social incarnation of Rousseau's vision in Emile. Half of that book champions—and provides instructions for—the development of the self-possessed, independent individual. The other half seeks to happily integrate this skillful, independent human into such social circumstances as marriage, community, and civic activities. Alone, Rousseau's solitaires are incomplete and suffer accordingly. Together, Rousseau's solitaires become citizens and suffer from a different set of wounds.[2] Yet they never forget the importance of independence, freedom, and equality. Nor do they fail to acknowledge human vulnerability to a variety of emotional and moral injuries; hence the Solitaire's maxim, "Do no unnecessary harm," becomes a shared creed. Although Emile does not contain Rousseau's fullest account of a robust social life, it does express his complex dual vision for human flourishing.

A question that has persisted throughout this study is whether the dual vision can be brought together harmoniously. Did Rousseau think it possible? I have no doubt that it was his hope, and that during the early 1760s he even deemed it a possibility, albeit a distant one and for some small states only. Later in life, he oscillated between thinking it possible and impossible. Yet regardless of his own sense of the possible, his complex, sociopsychological moral philosophy nourishes our thought and drives us to confront fundamental matters. It can cultivate in us the desire to achieve both public and private goods while highlighting the difficulties of such an achievement. How are we to honor the interests of the individual and the requirements of the common good? How are we to cope with the tension between such potentially contrary demands? These challenges lie at the heart of democracy, and they form the weaves and tangles of Rousseau's thought.

On the extreme public and private paths, he offered us a way to dissolve the tension. By eliminating either the private or public life, conflict between them vanishes—but so does much human satisfaction and purpose. It is remarkable that one and the same person could have offered two such divergent ways, yet he loved aspects of each. Moreover, the two contrary ways are brought together on his ideal, normative path—the precarious middle way. I am speaking conceptually here. Chronologically, I should put it the other way around; Rousseau began by offering something similar to the middle way in the early 1760s, and then, later in life, discouraged and despondent, he offered his two contrary paths—the private path of radical self-exploration and the public path of intense patriotism. Even late in life, however, Rousseau often reflected on the inadequacy of the extreme paths. He offered a tragic account of humans in need of both yet, torn between them, unable to achieve either. At best, he thought we might negotiate a delicate, unsteady, ever-adjusting balance between the demands and goods of public and private. Rousseau would not offer some golden middle way that promised easy and complete reconciliation. Had he been a more systematic thinker, he might have yielded to that temptation for the sake of tidiness of thought. Instead, Rousseau did what he did best; he explored without systematizing the tangled ways of public and private, limned their various goods and limits, and revealed the sundry tensions that seem to increase as the two ways are brought together.

Conflict, then, remains on the middle way. We learn from Rousseau that the public and private spheres have their own dignity and demands, that we need both in our lives, and that we ought to resist radically conflating or separating them. Acknowledging the various demands and goods of the public and private without absolutizing either is Rousseau's difficult lesson for twenty-first-century democracy. His failure, or refusal, to secure a complete reconciliation between public and private is especially significant. In spite of our best attempts to preserve the goods of the public and private, conflict will remain, and we need to cope with it rather than yield to the temptation to eradicate it. To erase the tension would be to find ourselves on the extreme public or private path. The former path risks tyranny and oppression, the latter narcissism and anomie. To seek total harmony, then, leads to the dangerous prospect of Rousseau's *Poland* or to the lonely prospect of Rousseau's Solitaire. When Rousseau elegantly depicts the goods of the public and private, we learn, sometimes despite his own intention, to cultivate within ourselves an intricate moral resolve to sustain the public and private, and to consent to conflict between them.

Such resolve requires that we recognize subtle differences and similarities between public and private. Commitment to the common good can inform our individual identity, just as support and protection of diversity can inform our understanding of the common good. And diversity must not be relegated to the private sphere alone. Although Rousseau seldom celebrated pluralism in public life, he usually acknowledged it as a feature of common life and public deliberation, and he even provided some safeguards to protect it. Although he feared people making the wrong choices, that is, forsaking freedom and justice, he feared more the subjugation of a people, even for the sake of achieving admirable public aims.

Rousseau recognized that there are difficult choices involved in the moral and political life. Although I disagree with Judith Shklar's stark account of what she considers to be the Rousseauean options—that we become either *homme* or *citoyen*, that is, moral individuals or dedicated citizens—Rousseau did understand that the moral, political path we choose will necessitate conflict with other paths, other options. He profoundly depicted the moral gain and loss of our chosen ways. In this study, I have focused on the conflict between the equally compelling demands of the public and private. Choices between the good of a friend and that of the state, for instance, will involve inevitable loss. When confronted with such choices, the middle way provides few guidelines. Particular circumstances must be considered, and if we were to systematically choose one way over the other, then we would no longer be on the tense middle way, but on one of the extreme paths. Mainly, the middle way relies on the daily character and practices of a citizenry informed by civic liberalism, by a common faith that nurtures public-mindedness and private aspiration.

Rousseau and Rorty on the Public and Private

Rousseau's middle way seems to share much in common with Richard Rorty's work, specifically with Rorty's insistence that we stop our search for a vocabulary or way of life that can harmoniously unite the public and private. In *Contingency, Irony, and Solidarity*, for example, Rorty makes "a firm distinction between the private and the public."[3] This distinction does not follow along metaphysical or epistemological lines. Rorty often characterizes the public-private distinction as the line between two camps, those dedicated to "self-creation" and "private autonomy," and those to "a more just and free human community."[4] Rorty has no desire to mend this division. Indeed, he warns against any theoretical attempt to bring them together: "The vocabulary of self-creation is necessarily private, unshared, unsuited to argument. The vocabulary of justice is necessarily public and shared, a medium for argumentative exchange."[5] Private perfection and self-creation should have nothing to do with the practical world of politics and public accommodation, lest private aesthetics interfere with public pragmatism, or vice versa. "Always strive to excel, but only on weekends," is one of Rorty's slogans for maintaining a strict public-private barrier.[6]

Why does Rorty insist that no single vision, vocabulary, or theory can unite the public and private? He is convinced, epistemologically, that there is no truth within the breast or in the heavens to fuse self-interests and common involvements. Moreover, he is convinced, sociopolitically, that private pursuits and social justice are two radically different undertakings that are jeopardized when placed in contact. However, Rorty himself brings the public and private close together, I believe, by ascribing an individualistic mission to the public life. He claims, for example, that "the aim of a just and free society" is to let "its citizens be as privatistic, 'irrationalist,' and aestheticist as they please so long as they do it on their own time."[7] Rorty espouses here a romantic liberal order dedicated to allowing individuals to occupy their own self-made world of unique wishes and feelings. Separating the political from nonpolitical realms, thereby accommodating a citizenry with diverse beliefs and practices, is characteristic of most versions of liberalism. Rorty's version, however, comes close to subsuming the public under the private by limiting public goals to the protection of private projects.

Rousseau maintained provisional distinctions between the public and private, but, unlike Rorty, he also acknowledged their entanglement. In order to compare Rousseau and Rorty, we could reframe Rorty's public-private narrative about his favorite authors by locating them on the Rousseauean paths. We would place Rorty's aesthetes who pursue private perfection, such as Proust and Nabokov, on the private path. Rorty's public philosophers who subordinate the private to the public, such as Habermas and Marx, would be placed on the public path. Finally, Rorty's liberal ironists, those who value both the public and private yet manage to keep them separate, would be located on something akin to the middle way. Yet this last comparison, the middle way to the way of liberal irony, is precisely what distinguishes Rousseau from Rorty. Rousseau's traveler on the middle way—unlike Rorty's hero, the liberal ironist—seeks to relate, though without identifying, the private and the public. Any radical separation of public and private would be considered by Rousseau to be a source of personal dividedness and social alienation.

Recollect, for example, Rousseau's work on religion. On the middle way, religion maintains a distinction between public and private. A central dogma of the common civic faith is the protection of private religious belief and practice, broadly construed. Yet Rousseau also understood that an essential aspect of one's identity pertains to the sociopolitical world. Hence the civil religion also contains provisions that seek to cultivate a limited yet shared public vision. Without this shared common faith, Rousseau feared that individuals would experience a debilitating division between palpable private interests and remote public commitments. The middle way, then, both separates and unites the public and private. It acknowledges that an individual's personal identity is manifested in public and also that one's identity is informed by the public world. This entanglement, in Rousseau's view, can be intellectually and politically pulled this way and that, but it cannot always be pulled apart, as Rorty would have it. Rorty's private aestheticism and public pragmatism contain a wide range of beliefs and activities that, in spite of Rorty's claims to the contrary, ineluctably connect the public and private. In the modern, everyday world that individuals actually encounter, the public and private, for better or worse, already crisscross this way and that. Buying coffee, employing inclusive language, teaching in a private university, choosing a financial portfolio, publishing a novel—these so-called private acts are thoroughly intertwined in the public world. To talk, as Rorty does, of a firm distinction between the public and the private, or to place the latter over the former, is to fail to grasp their extensive interrelation.

Moreover, Rousseau intentionally connected the public and private by his insistence that we cultivate what could be called liberal virtues. If liberalism is to accommodate diverse views, citizens must be trained to honor diversity. Likewise, if liberalism is to exist as a genuine social order, and not simply as a band of Rorty's disparate eccentrics, citizens need to share something like a common liberal faith or vision. Civic liberalism needs to be understood as a fragile social covenant that requires maintenance—it calls for commitment, work, and education. Rousseau's understanding of "individual freedom as a social commitment,"[8] to borrow Amartya Sen's phrase, is a more useful approach to the ambiguities and conflicts and achievements of liberal societies than is Rorty's idea that we make a firm distinction between public and the private. For Rorty, human solidarity is "not a matter of sharing a common truth or a common goal but of sharing a common selfish hope, the hope that one's world—the little things which one has woven into one's final vocabulary—will not be destroyed."[9] Rousseau, in contrast, held that liberal solidarity required more. The rights and dignity of the individual are no doubt salient features of our solidarity. Yet these are accompanied by various social commitments and obligations, and they need to be situated in a shared moral context lest they promote egoism, "a common selfish hope," instead of civic liberalism, a common set of liberal dispositions and virtues.

Self-creation, then, is one good among many. It is not, however, the primary aim of a liberal democracy. Privatism and aestheticism have a place within the spheres of a liberal society. Yet the spheres are not dedicated to them alone. Even Rorty's admirable commitment to "put cruelty first," that is, to above all prevent cruelty, is articulated in an individualistic and aesthetic language. Basic individual rights need to be situated in liberal traditions and social practices that feature the individual's involvement in and commitment to public life. This is not only for the sake of shoring up individual rights, but to cultivate a public commitment to social justice. There are domains, Rousseau understood, in which the public-private entanglement is deeply problematic and requires public attention and restriction. As he never tired of reminding us, the private interests of the wealthy usually determine the public policy of everyone else. Rhetoric aside, in the last few decades we have seen the distance grow between the rich and the poor, the homeowners and the homeless, the well-fed and the hungry. These distinctions bear on any discussion of the public-private distinction. Public policy, determined by the private interests of the few, can have dire consequences for the many—in their public and private lives. It is not, then, that the aim Rorty has set for a just and free society is without merit. The problem is that our society is not sufficiently just and free, and therefore Rorty's preoccupation with "letting its citizens be as privatistic, 'irrationalist,' and aestheticist as they please," even if they commit no cruelty, appears careless.

Is the "pursuit of happiness" a fundamental aim of a democratic society? And is such happiness public, as in Pascal's view, or private, as in Rorty's? On the extreme public path, Rousseau sought a genuine public happiness that was more than an aggregate of private well-being. In the citizen, he sought to create a new being, one whose joys and loves were truly communitarian. He shared this vision with Pascal, who insisted that happiness cannot be achieved in isolation, but only in community. On the middle way, however, Rousseau articulated a more liberal form of happiness, namely, an individual happiness that comes from living in agreement with one's personal values, hopes, and goals. According to Judith Shklar, happiness for Rousseau "is like religious belief in that it depends entirely on those aspects of a man's character and disposition which are uniquely his and which differ greatly from man to man."[10] Yet I would suggest that, in addition to private, liberal happiness, there is a second type of happiness that can be identified on the middle way—a moderate form of communitarian happiness. Rousseau understood, theoretically and personally, that these two forms of happiness were bound to conflict. Nonetheless, he insisted on the importance of a public happiness that is shared and achieved together as well as a private happiness that is personal and achieved in more intimate spheres of being. Rorty, in contrast, understands happiness as a private matter of the aesthete's heart. Public commitments, in his view, do not spring from shared happiness or affections, but from pragmatic considerations, namely coordinated strategies that advance such individual pursuits as private happiness. This position stands in contrast to Rousseau's middle way. For Rousseau, democracies certainly support the pursuit of private happiness. Yet they also depend on, and cultivate, the very public happiness and affections which in turn sustain democratic institutions and culture.

Highlighting the Challenge

Is Rousseau's vision that of a pragmatic reformer or a prophetic judge? Is *The Social Contract* the work of a reformer who offered a practical plan to achieve social progress? Or, is *The Social Contract* the work of a harsh prophet who presented an ideal society as a means of total critique—as a severe measuring rod revealing how far existing societies have fallen?

There is evidence for both portraits of Rousseau. We see Rousseau the reformer, for example, in the first sentence of *The Social Contract*. Here he underscored that his reflections on civil order were based on a realistic assessment of everyday humans and workable law, that is, "men being taken as they are and laws as they might be." He wrote for "sons of Adam," and he even claimed that *The Social Contract* "depicted an existing object," namely, Geneva.[11] Rousseau, here, appears to be the realistic reformer, offering a pragmatic plan for an ameliorated, enlightened society—at least for Adam's *sons*.

Yet there is also evidence of Rousseau the harsh prophet, who presented the image of an ideal society as an absolute critique of societies probably beyond reform. Rousseau's certainty of the decline and death of even the best-designed society suggests severe limits to social reformation. A consistent, Machiavellian theme in Rousseau's writing is the difficulty and unlikely prospect of ameliorating corrupt, fallen societies. This view is most strongly stated in the first and second *Discours*, although it is also present in most of his major works. Even his "utopian scenarios"—such as the perfect student, Emile, or the exemplary household, Clarens, or the Flourishing City of *The Social Contract*—all these require miraculous, preternatural agents: the all-knowing Tutor, the all-seeing Wolmar, and the wise and all-powerful Legislator. Such supernatural provisions, I have argued, suggest the implausibility of actual reform. In this view, Rousseau was not the Enlightenment designer of the reformed society, but the biblical, Augustinian prophet holding up to us a devastating mirror, reflecting back the image of an unjust, degenerate society. Rousseau's mirror judges us, condemns us, and perhaps stirs in us a desire for a profound change that is unlikely to occur. In part I of this study, we charted the empirically inevitable, yet logically unnecessary, fall of humans. Now, at the conclusion of part II, we are reminded of the same logic; although theoretically Rousseau seems to say, reform is possible, empirically it is highly implausible.

These two opposing portraits of Rousseau reflect the two contrary traditions in which I have located his work—Augustinian pessimism and Enlightenment optimism. I see little reason to wish that Rousseau had conformed invariably to one tradition or the other. His work in general, and *The Social Contract* in particular, served many purposes. As a moral philosopher, Rousseau's judgments were especially Augustinian—severe and bleak. As an Enlightenment political philosopher, Rousseau's judgments were more practical and hopeful. Rousseau himself claimed that he was neither a reformer nor a moralizer, but simply a truth-teller: "I am the botanist who describes the plant."[12] Although this self-portrait fails to present Rousseau in all his complexity, it does depict his greatest talent—his ability to describe and diagnose many of our deepest and most enduring social woes. I, for my part, believe that there is a relation between diagnosis and healing.

How might a Rousseauean perspective assist us in diagnosing challenges and problems facing twenty-first-century democracy? His middle way, which features meaningful public institutions and nourishing private domains, assists us in our own thinking about the public and private in North American liberal democracy. Rousseau's voice—which is both foreign, because it emerges from the past, and familiar, because it belongs to the chorus of traditions we have inherited—confronts us with a perspective that is novel yet recognizable. When he complained of public institutions growing impersonal, commercial, and bureaucratic, and private lives becoming self-absorbed, hollow, and desperate for intense distractions, we begin to think and wonder about the health of our own institutions and way of life. Rousseau's voice warns that as the warmth and meaningfulness of public institutions wane, the private life is called on to compensate by providing ever-increasing levels of moral comfort and purpose. This places great pressure on the family, the spouse or partner, and the new household entertainers, television and the Internet, to supply meaning, comfort, and moral wherewithal. This may be an impossible demand, especially as the private space becomes increasingly constricted.

With a limited sense of history, we assume that the current way is the only way, that our present understanding of the public and private is built into the natural order of things. Perhaps only when we encounter different modes of thought and existence, either in our own history or in foreign cultures, can we see alternatives. Rousseau has presented us with alternatives, and those alternatives help us reflect on our ways of life and on how to ameliorate them. Helpful alternatives, of course, do not mainly come from present or past philosophers.

As I mentioned in the preface, I once lived in Angoon, Alaska, a town of about five hundred Tlingit Indians. Life was shared in Angoon. If a house burned down, the entire community joined together to help rebuild it. Some would make curtains and clothes for the household; others would gather materials from the community and construct the new home, while those too old or young would sit on the sidelines offering encouragement and telling jokes. Death, too, was a shared feature of life in Angoon. If a member of the Raven Tribe died, the Eagle Tribe would take care of all the needs of the mourning tribe, including digging the grave, purchasing and fetching the coffin, and hosting an all-night wake. Forty days after the burial, the Ravens would hold a party in honor of the Eagle Tribe who had helped them. At this party, members from each tribe would spontaneously stand up, one at a time, and tell stories about the deceased. One would tell a joke, and the whole place would roar with laughter. The next one would stand, crying, and would speak sorrowfully of the deceased—all now would be quiet, except for gentle weeping. Then another would stand with a joke better than the last—all would be in laughter again, the tears gone. From night until dawn, back and forth, between tears and joy, these people would tell stories and renew a common life.

There was much to love about Angoon. Life and death were shared, and this strengthened, rather than smothered, the individual. There was abundant diversity of personality, stellar characters, many differing points of view. Such pluralism, however, was held within a shared framework—a common history, a mutual future, joint commitments to the health of the community. The fragmentation of public and private spheres that I had become accustomed to in the San Francisco Bay area, and that I had assumed was natural, was absent in Angoon. Rather, I experienced there an integration that wove together work, family, friends, recreation, community, and love of self. In Angoon I began to question liberal individualism and wonder about alternatives.

My critique of our liberal society may sound harsh, and my assessment of Tlingit culture idealistic. There were and are problems in Angoon, many similar to those in Rousseau's Clarens. And there are strengths in our society. When writing about Angoon, I was juxtaposing what one culture does well with the areas in which our own culture needs help. I have approached Rousseau in much the same way. I have mainly concentrated on how his thought can assist us. This is not to say that I have ignored his limits, blunders, and errors, for these, too, have taught us much. But this study has not been a comprehensive critique of Rousseau, but rather an employment of Rousseau to help us think about our own society. I fashioned Weberian ideal types out of Rousseau's Solitaires and his Poland, the extreme private and public paths, to help us identify pronounced aspects of the public and private and then recognize more subtle manifestations close to home. The lessons from the extreme paths, and also from the middle way, have formed something like a broad argument for the need to support both the public and private in spite of possible conflict. Yet the current trajectory in our society,

I fear, is toward a diminished public life with a corresponding impoverished private life. By reflecting now on the life of Rousseau's Solitaires in comparison to that of prisoners, I can illustrate how the public and private wax and wane, together.

Lessons from the Garden, Lessons from Prison

When Rousseau pushed to the limit the idea of human existence detached from a public life, that is, radically self-sufficient and isolated beings, he created the Solitaires, an instructive thought experiment. Rousseau's Solitaires can serve as a pristine construct from which to view the private life because, in their simplicity and extremity, they illustrate some of its most notable positive and negative aspects. The Solitaires are in a perpetual state of retreat from what we know as the anxieties of public life—its onerous responsibilities, commitments, and concerns regarding status and reputation, money and career, future goals and past promises—not to mention crushing bureaucracies and infernal wars. The calm the Solitaires enjoy is what many seek on vacations to the countryside or on visits to museums or parks, in the music of a concert or the serenity of a leisurely walk, in the brief respite of a coffee break or a short nap. More desperately, our society attempts to attain the tranquility of the Solitaires with the aid of self-help books, New Age videos, sensory deprivation tanks, gravity boots, or even a generous dose of gin or Valium at the end of a long day.

The Solitaires, then, dwelling in a perpetual state of retreat that keeps them from inflicting gratuitous harm on others, appear to us as rather alluring creatures. Yet the permanence of their withdrawal illuminates troubling aspects of the private life and some hazards connected with liberalism. The Solitaires are alone—radically and perpetually. True, they are not lonely, for they know no social life, and hence loneliness is as meaningless as gregariousness. Still, we can note what they lack, even if they are not aware of it. They have no experience of the joys and risks of association—laughing or crying with a friend who is dying, dining with a family which is struggling, enjoying a public fete or religious service that is controversial. The Solitaires lack the satisfaction and meaningfulness of such public commitments and responsibilities as participation in the PTA, the Kids 'n' Cancer program, shelters for battered women and the homeless, and a host of other community and civic activities. Moreover, the Solitaires are missing that which enlivens the young and sustains the old—dreams and memories. These, we have seen, can bring pain, but the hope of a future can also provide moral stamina, and memories of the past can enrich the present and help guide us into the future. The stories and memories that bring joy to the old, for example, are typically not those of private accomplishment, but of personal relationships and meaningful public activities. Such memories, here, are a measure of the fullness of one's life. By this measure, the existence of the Solitaires is hollow. This same emptiness would stalk a society of Solitaires—an oxymoron only in its extremity—for it would lack plans and hope for the future and a treasury of traditions and lessons from the past.

By virtue of their conceptual purity, the Solitaires highlight both the potential serenity and emptiness of the private life. That same purity, however, also imposes a limit on the efficacy of employing the Solitaires to illuminate the private life and its relation to the public. The limit is this: insofar as the Solitaires' private life cannot be contrasted to a public life, for they have none, it is unclear that they can have a genuine private life. Ironically, by confronting this limit we learn from the Solitaires their most valuable lesson, namely, that the public and private life mutually define each other. In the absence of a public life, there can be no private life. We cannot make sense of perpetual retreat. For example, without the pressing commitments of the public life, one of the chief goods of the private life, that of temporary escape, becomes meaningless. Without the events and associations of a public life, the private life is deprived of stimulus and material for personal reflection. And without social interaction, one of the chief pleasures of the private life, that of being alone, quickly turns into the pain of loneliness. Solitary confinement can be counted as "cruel and unusual punishment" because the joy of solitude becomes bitter grief when solitude ceases to be a retreat from public life, but becomes a way of life.[13]

Unexpectedly, the Solitaires have taught us about the necessity of a public life for the sake of the private. By looking at inmates in maximum-security prisons, we can learn about the necessity of a private life for the sake of the public. It is rather evident that the modern prison system works systematically against the development of the prisoners' private life. The essence of prison life is regimentation: when and where to wake, work, eat, walk, and recreate are determined by prison administrators and enforced by guards. A complex language and structure of lines and bells, orders and regulations, ensure that the prisoner's private life is absorbed effectively by the institutional, bureaucratic milieu of the prison. The prisoner's private identity is stripped away at the first introduction to prison life—the anus is probed during the initiating "strip search." Insofar as life in prison can be seen as a paradigm of institutional life, it may seem to exemplify public life, albeit an extreme form. Yet it does not; exactly insofar as the prisoner's private life is impeded, it falls short of this model. Because prison life is rigidly and entirely organized without any input from the prisoners, prisoners have little opportunity to fashion their daily lives. They make few decisions, deliberate on few issues, and shoulder no responsibilities because every aspect and consideration of their lives has been defined and furnished. In the absence of opportunities to shape their public life, the prisoner's internal resources are not exercised. Autonomy, the prize of the Solitaires, is utterly pared in prison. Rousseau's notion of inwardness—with all its similarities to Kant's notion of liberty, namely, to obey the reasonable law that one prescribes for oneself—has no place in prison. One cannot be "true to oneself" where there are no opportunities to be oneself. When enforced routine determines all, there is no autonomy, and hence no genuine private life.[14]

Likewise, solitary confinement cannot enhance the private life as long as such solitude is imposed externally. If it borders on being cruel, it is because each of us already knows that solitude is a place to visit voluntarily, not a condition to be enforced. The difference between voluntary and coerced sex is one of the most pleasant unions compared to one of the most violent crimes. The difference between voluntary and coerced solitude is one of the most restorative activities compared to one of the most painful punishments. It is often reported that a loss of self, that is, a loss of identity, is a common outcome of radical seclusion. Evidently, to know ourselves we need to know others. Without public engagement, the private life suffers. The converse, however, is equally true. Without opportunities to develop and exercise one's private life and internal resources, the public life suffers. Prisoners, like the Solitaires, illustrate the intricate and interdependent relation between public and private.

We used the Garden as an ideal type to highlight features of the private life, including features that we celebrate. Can we not use prisons to illuminate laudable aspects of the public life? Perhaps only in this one sense: prisons reveal our capacity to escape ourselves and our private worries and concerns—in the throes of public life. We have noted that in solitude we can temporarily elude the anxieties and worries of the public life. There are times, however, when we want to escape the affairs of the private life, to evade, for example, our preoccupation with a chronic illness, the death of a friend, or a marital problem. A routinized public life can facilitate such a retreat. On occasion, we wish to leave behind our private life as we venture into the public, and it is this abandonment that prisons effect methodically, with or without the consent of the prisoner. Pascal cautioned us against the temptation of averting attention from ourselves by dwelling in the distractions of the public world. I want to suggest, however, that his warning about *divertissement* applies only to those who regularly exist outside themselves. Achieving temporary relief from pressing personal concerns by immersing oneself in public activities should not be dogmatically shunned. We can describe such relief as a retreat into public life. Prisons can highlight for us this form of retreat, but they do not provide it, for retreats into the public, like those into the private, cease to be retreats once they become a way of life, especially a coerced way of life.

Like Rousseau's Garden of the past, today's security prison is no place to dwell. Prison life exemplifies the worst aspects of public life. At the minimum, it elucidates the specter of a bureaucratic society that subtly strips from its citizens their autonomy, their capacity for public involvement, and the satisfaction that attends such involvement. In the extreme, it incarnates Orwellian nightmares of a totalitarian state in which there is no privacy (not even at the toilet can one be alone) and no meaningful public life (stripped of voting rights, prisoners are helpless to alter an utterly intractable environment).[15] In either case, we find neither personal nor public fulfillment, but rather loneliness and alienation, even amid the company of others.

A Normative Stance for 21st-Century Democracy

These reflective exercises—excursions into solitary gardens and totalitarian prisons—have the merit of placing liberals and communitarians on some common ground. By exploring extreme cases, liberals (champions of the politics of rights) and communitarians (champions of the politics of the common good) can better appreciate each others' fears. Our study of the Garden presents to liberals the dangers of a society excessively dedicated to quests for private fulfillment. Our reflections on the prison, in contrast, present to communitarians the dangers of a totalized public existence that truncates citizens' private lives. Additionally, we learned from the Solitaires that individual rights lose much significance without a robust public life in which to exercise them. And from the prisoners we discovered that the public life loses its distinctive merits if citizens are denied opportunities to pursue that life according to conscience. We have seen, in fact, that the public and private mutually deepen each other. The one enriches, or conversely, threatens the other. The private life does not only provide negative goods vis-à-vis the public, such as temporary retreats from public anxieties; the private life also provides the public life with a sense of renewal, energy, and vision. Likewise, the public life provides not only distractions from our private concerns, but sustains the private life with a sense of purpose, identity, and animation.

In the last decade or so there has been profusion of liberal and communitarian debate in our society. This debate is not without precedent, however. It has taken different forms in the past. The birth of the United States could be said to spring from a liberal and republican parentage. We as a people often grapple with the conflicting values and practices associated with the public and private. It is tempting to lament the current polarization between communitarians and liberals. I have done my share of bewailing.[16] Yet perhaps the current debate is not a sign of a paralyzing impasse, but of our society's struggle to remain committed to both public projects and private fulfillment. If the debate seems intransigent, it is, in part, because there can be no victory here without some loss. No settlement can perfectly capture the merits of each. And perhaps this is one debate that ought not to cease, but should continue, albeit in various forms, as we strive in different circumstances to express our commitment to both liberal and communitarian goods. This struggle would entail, among other things, deciding when and how to compromise; in some cases it would favor the private, in others the public, but it would generally allow the creative, though sometimes tragic, friction between private fulfillment and social cooperation to remain.

Rousseau's middle way has taught us much, yet perhaps the more powerful lessons come from his extreme paths. The extreme public path, the way to his *Poland*, reminds us of the heavy and unacceptable cost of a perfectionist government that would seek to instill uniform virtue in its citizens. It reminds us why we celebrate those Enlightenment figures who sought to free Europe from an oppression and cruelty that flowed from dogmatism, superstition, and intolerance. There is much to be said for a minimally decent, mediocre, free citizenry in comparison to the horrors that can spring from enforced virtue and homogeneity. This is not to say that these are our only options. But if they were, the extreme public path teaches us, in a negative fashion, that an authoritarian public existence is to be feared more than a society of disparate, narcissistic, liberal characters.[17]

Unfortunately, there may be a connection—sociologically and psychologically—between radical individualism and the rise of authoritarian states. Without public associations, symbols, ideals, and clusters of meaning, the private life can become hollow and solipsistic, and from this lonely position the individual can become desperate for significance and purpose. This condition is dangerous insofar as individuals, unanchored to democratic social traditions and symbols, can be swept up by transient crazes and ideologies. When individuals and the state succumb to vacillating rages, little beneficial social change is likely to occur. Instead, morally vagrant individuals can unwittingly place absolute power in the hands of those not worthy of it. The extreme public and private paths, then, are not necessarily miles apart. The recent growth of various extremists, whether among the religious right, white supremacists, or middle-class high school students firing on fellow students, may be due in part to the collapse of vital public and private lives and a resulting crisis in meaning.

The middle way seeks to navigate between the way of methodological individualism and national mysticism. In this study we have seen in detail the difficulties of this navigational task. Recognizing the various conditions and benefits of the public and private without absolutizing either requires that we accept friction between them. Yet mutual enhancement is as likely as conflict. Private autonomy, we have seen, fosters public deliberation, just as public deliberation contributes to private autonomy. In some cases, however, the public and private should be maintained and should not intersect. There is something to be said for a private realm of intimacy and inwardness that is protected from public debate and scrutiny. In these cases, one should be able to move safely between private and public ventures. Intimacy and privacy, not diversity and pluralism, separate the private from the public. As we work for a shared understanding on common projects, diversity and pluralism are not obstacles to be overcome, but resources to be tapped. Diversity is not a feature of the private sphere alone. Conversely, shared moral understandings, especially as expressed by law, are not to be excluded from playing a role in the private sphere. Protected privacy, for example, must never safeguard neglect and abuse in the domestic realm. Protected privacy is to contribute to personal fulfillment, not to private torment. It is to defend us from unwarranted observers, not to keep out those who can help protect the innocent from criminal abuse.

I constructed the middle way out of Rousseau's writings as a useful normative stance to help us reflect on democratic society. Endeavoring to fashion a democratic republic in which the private life is nurtured and protected and the public life is inclusive, lively, and just is a worthy challenge. We will often fail. No perfect harmony will be achieved. Still, the endeavor is the way forward. It is the challenge of democracy in the twenty-first century.

Democratic cultures must work not only to protect privacy and political institutions, as the middle way would insist, but also to achieve spheres that are neither radically private nor public. Such in-between spheres integrate domestic space and work space, recreation and community action, friends and citizens. Protection of such private pursuits as working on salvation and such public pursuits as upholding the Constitution are essential to healthy democracies. Yet democracies also require social spheres where the lines between public and private are less stark, where individuals can gather, share, and cultivate the matter and manners of their different yet related lives. These intermediate spheres—championed by Durkheim, held suspect by Rousseau—supply much of the moral and social scaffolding that support public deliberation and private contemplation. Yet if society were marked exclusively by intermediate spheres that sought to integrate home, family, friends, associates, work, pleasure, and community, then it would resemble Clarens and it would not promote a workable democracy.[18] It could not tolerate, for example, the very tension and conflict that I have placed at the heart of the shared moral life of liberal, democratic society. In spite of my own longing for Clarens and my attempt to achieve something like it in my life and community, I fear anything resembling a national Clarens. The threat of coercion—implicit or explicit—that haunts Clarens's integration and harmony of public and private should worry us more than its pleasures and satisfactions appeal to us. Any all-encompassing, national communitarian aspirations should give us pause.

Nonetheless, the way of Clarens has much to offer to local attempts to achieve lively, just, and flourishing communities. It seems clear that since the European and American industrial revolutions, the work sphere and the domestic sphere have become increasingly segregated. This development coincided with sequestering women and children to the private domestic sphere. New research suggests that in many rural, pre-industrial communities, women's and men's roles were more fluid, as the domestic and work spheres were less divided.[19] Today, many are seeking ways to bring employment into the home, and home and children into employment. Rousseau, of course, is hardly a model for battling the seclusion and oppression of women. But his Clarens does offer a helpful vision in which work and home, children and adults are less divided, more integrated.

Yet what if a local community should not only seek to integrate work and home, but also to keep, say, women's vocations limited to traditional domestic roles? Clarens, I noted in chapter 9, has no political life. It has neither a government nor a culture to safeguard individual rights. Democracies require a strong, national government to enforce rights and prohibit discrimination. Yet they require more than that; they need cultural resources that support democratic laws and practices. In this study I have highlighted Rousseau's civic religion not because I believe religion, traditionally understood, is the cause of or the solution to our woes. Rather, it was because Rousseau understood that freedom, equality, and individual rights require support not only from law but from common shared traditions and commitments—from a type of common secular faith. I employ the concept of "faith" because it intimates notions like commitment, hope, virtue, and a shared history and future, and also because faith is partisan. There is nothing neutral or value-free about the virtues, beliefs, and practices of a liberal democracy. There is nothing neutral about supporting individual rights or supporting a culture, a way of life, that inculcates the character and habits of citizens engaged in democratic practices. Rousseau still has much to teach those of us dedicated to progressive, democratic liberalism about the importance of the language and practice of a common faith and public virtue.

What Can We Hope For?

In spite of the premium Rousseau placed on individual freedom and rights, and on the natural maxim, "do no harm," he wanted more than a liberalism satisfied with minimal decency and the protection of rights. He wanted a society that loved tolerance and did not merely enforce it. He wanted a citizenry that understood duty to self to mean more than self-actualization, and duty to others to mean more than doing no harm. Justice, for Rousseau, was not only a juridical procedure to be upheld, but a commitment and affection to be fostered. He understood that virtue and joy must risk vice and pain. To move from the simple maxim to the virtues, from the Solitaires to humanity, requires that one be committed to things outside the self, and such commitment necessarily entails some jeopardy and vulnerability. In the realms of intimacy, one can suffer from much disappointment and heartache. In the public realm, love of social justice could turn to the enforcement of (private) morality. These risks are undeniable, although there are safeguards to protect us from worst-case scenarios, at least in the public sphere. Still, perhaps we risk as much if we establish society exclusively on the protection of individual rights. Perhaps too much safety can be a dangerous thing. I already discussed how society marked by disparate individualism can turn authoritarian. But there is also the risk that, should we follow the way of the Solitaires too closely—should we put the individual and the protection of rights first in every case—we risk losing not only a vital public but a rich private existence. With Aristotle and Montaigne, Rousseau came to understand that to love oneself alone leads to being unable to love anything outside oneself and eventually unable to love even one's own self. The self that is sound is both self- and other-regarding and is willing to cope with this double vision. The democratic society that is sound is both rights- and community-oriented, and is willing to cope with this awkward stance.

In spite of his infatuation with the Solitaires, then, Rousseau was never satisfied with the life they represented. Too much was missing from their safe existence. Although they committed no cruelty, they failed to love and to be committed to things outside themselves. They failed as human beings. This failure is by no means an indictment of liberalism and its commitment to protect the individual. Liberalism has proved to be an impressive social order, establishing individual rights and curtailing brutality. If pushed too far, however, if divorced from its opposing communitarian counterpart, the goods of liberalism become threatened. Liberalism would no longer be genuinely viable if, like the Solitaires, the safety of the individual were to become not a fundamental but the sole goal. For liberalism to continue as a promising social order, it must hazard the risks of shared commitments, joint projects, public virtues—a common faith. Some might claim that given what John Rawls has called the "fact of pluralism," the language and practice of a common faith is neither possible nor desirable. Yet with Rousseau, I would argue that pluralistic societies are especially in need of shared perspectives and commitments. And *pace* Rousseau, I would not lament the potential debate, quarrel, and conflict that would accompany the public search for a dynamic, multifaceted common good. The pursuit itself, with all its struggle and diversity, would augment liberal, democratic society.

As a people, we seem more suspicious of the language and practice of seeking common perspectives and goals than of the mass media and global corporations shaping a homogenized culture. We are comfortable perhaps with what I earlier called the coordination model of society: individuals, pursuing their own narrow self-interests, serving the interests of others as they enter into exchanges and other mutual services. This model, however, can easily lead to economic inequity, ecological degradation, and such social conflict as excessive litigation and cutthroat competition. Simply calling for government regulation is not enough. Without citizen participation, government is unduly influenced by powerful corporations. A citizenry needs to be actively involved in the democratic practices that inform government. Hence the need for renewed public, civic spaces in which diverse points of views contribute to common projects. Such civic space promises the best of liberalism—individual rights and autonomous reflection—and the best of communitarianism—commitment to shared goals and a common good. Disparate liberalism in the age of economic globalization, in contrast, promises the worst of individualism—self-absorbed individuals committed to consumerism—and the worst of unity—a homogenized global culture that watches the same television programming, reads the same news, and eats, drinks and wears the same corporate products. Atomistic individualism and insipid homogeneity sabotage any prospect for a vibrant civic life. Authoritarian regimes need not appear mean or despotic. Individuals, preoccupied with self-interest alone, can abnegate political responsibility and be managed by professional politicians who vow to keep the state going and not to burden citizens with having to know anything.

If Rousseau seemed at times torn between his call for a lively public life and for a protected private life, it is, in part, because he posed them as separate remedies to what he perceived as an increasingly shallow, bureaucratic, commercial society. Rousseau's plan for Poland and the way of the Solitaire were drastic protests. He even offered his own private life, as depicted in the *Confessions* and elsewhere, not as an ideal model but as a complaint against a society which he thought was marked more and more by conformity, commercialism, and greed. Toward the end of his life, Rousseau turned to botany, a return to one of his original themes, Nature's Garden. Alone, with plants, he experienced equanimity. With plants, he did no harm and pursued no financial gain or social status. His immersion in botany, his return to the Garden, was a turn away from social attachments and commitments. It was a move toward invulnerability. Plants could neither disappoint nor hurt him. In the world of plants, Rousseau could master himself, because his heart was not torn by the endless desires and attachments that come with life and love in society. But this way was neither Rousseau's personal ideal nor his normative, public hope.

Ultimately, Rousseau, like Nietzsche, came to understand that the greatest obstacle to be overcome is one's own self. "My dear Emile," the tutor says, "however hard I tried to dip your soul in the Styx, I was not able to render it everywhere invulnerable. A new enemy is arising which you have not yet learned to overcome and from which I can no longer save you. This enemy, it is yourself." The tutor had taught Emile how to accept death and suffer physically, but not how to cope with the troubles and vicissitudes of daily life that arise from our affections. The tutor, wanting to help Emile save himself from himself, went on to offer this warning and advice: "The more one increases one's attachments, the more one multiplies one's pains. . . . Learn to become your own master. Command your heart, oh Emile, and you will be virtuous. . . . Learn to lose what can be taken away from you; learn to cede everything when virtue dictates it, to put yourself above events and detach your heart lest it be shredded by them."[20] Sound advice? Impossible psychology? These words of counsel come near the end of *Emile*, when Emile has fallen in love with Sophie but has yet to travel and develop a sense of place, government, and civic duty. The counsel may seem to recommend that Emile become invulnerable by refusing to form attachments. It may seem that the tutor has recommended the path of the Solitaire for his pupil.

That is not the case, however. The tutor is not advocating going it alone in isolation, divorced from friends, neighbors, community, nation, and nations. The counsel has more to do with Emerson's notion of self-reliance, the capacity to forge a life from one's own convictions, than with self-sufficiency, living without the help of, or commitment to, others. After the tutor and Emile return from their travels, having encountered different cultures and forms of government, Emile is encouraged to stay home, put down roots, and develop commitments to a variety of spheres of life—family, friends, community, nation. The place and society in which Emile is to settle is not intrinsically worthy or special. But it is distinctive because it is where Emile has a history and hence some affection, some attachment. The society is not marked by the principles of *The Social Contract*. It is not an especially admirable society. Indeed, "the public good, which serves only as a pretext to others, is a real motive for [Emile] alone. He learns to struggle with himself, to overcome himself. . . . Do not say, 'Why should I care where I am?' It is important for you to be where you can fulfill all your duties, and one of these duties is an attachment to the place of your birth."[21]

The final advice of the tutor amounts to this; bring your self-possession, the self-reliance of the Solitaire, into a social context for which you already have some affection. Be committed to such worthy things as family, community, and civic life. But do not cling to the outcomes of these commitments, because ultimately you cannot control such consequences. Do your duty without being attached to the results of your work. That is the tutor's—and Rousseau's—instruction. And this instruction brings together Rousseau's twin remedies—a self-possessed individual engaged in public life, but not defeated by it. The instruction, or moral stance, also suggests a solution of sorts to Rousseau's most abiding dilemma: alone, as Solitaires, we are sheltered from pain, yet we can be neither truly happy nor moral; together, in the company of others, we experience ambiguous moral progress and precarious human joy, yet we hurt ourselves and those around us. We encountered this dilemma in part I of this study, as we traveled from solitary invulnerability to vulnerable sociability. We need one other to mature as humans, and yet that very need makes us dependent, vulnerable, insecure, and likely to injure each other. How to minimize the harm while furthering human flourishing? The tutor's final and difficult words of instruction suggest a way. Enter public life and personal commitments as a reflective, autonomous individual who is willing to work toward public and private ends, but without over identifying with the outcome of one's commitments, thus escaping much debilitating disappointment, pain, and anger.

This is difficult counsel, a hard word, an implausible psychology—to care and remain immune to the pain caring brings. It probably is not a human possibility, at least not for most of us. It certainly was not achieved by Rousseau. Late in life, his writing alternated between personal literature aimed at self-exploration and political treatises aimed at public solidarity. These two types of authorship recommended the two extreme paths to invulnerability: protect the self in the removed life of the Solitaire, or else lose the self in an all-encompassing public life. The tutor's instruction to Emile—to be engaged in social relations yet without being attached to outcomes—was too difficult, too out of reach for the tired and discouraged Rousseau. In the end, in his own life, he never satisfactorily came to terms with the tension between duty to self and duty to others.

Rousseau had linked too closely the middle way, a social, political stance, to the tutor's instruction, a psychological, spiritual stance. He understood that citizens, in order to thrive, required both vital public and private lives, and he also understood—and had personally experienced—the conflict that commitment to both produces. The tutor's instruction, a spiritual stance that permeates Rousseau's work, promised to minimize the conflict. The stance was essential in Rousseau's view for the middle way, because he could not endure the prospect of conflict. Throughout this study we have seen him exercise, in a variety of ways, methods to minimize conflict. The extreme public and private paths *dodge* conflict. The middle way, precariously traveling between the extreme paths, requires the tutor's method—engagement without being overly attached, "to lose what can be taken from you." Yet who among us can achieve it? It is a possibility for some, perhaps an ideal for many. Regardless, I, unlike Rousseau, want to put a wedge between the middle way, a normative stance supporting the public and private life in democratic society, and the tutor's psychological counsel, a spiritual stance promising to reduce personal heartache and conflict. I want to separate these because I do not think they require each other and because I am urging democratic participants to consider pursuing something like the middle way, not the tutor's spiritual counsel.

This is not to say that I am indifferent to the tutor's—that is, Rousseau's—psychological advice. I attempt to achieve it, at least in some dimensions of my life. But that is a personal goal, not a hope for a republic. Moreover, unlike Rousseau, I have been arguing that conflict is not the worst thing. On the contrary, I have maintained that we, a people dedicated to the complex virtues and goals of democratic forms of life, pursue something like the middle way in spite of the likely tension and conflict that will come from it. No acceptable political solution or remedy can spare us this risk.

Although Rousseau offered what I have called paths to redemption, that is, remedies to our dividedness, he understood that these paths, these solutions, were far from complete or perfect. The extreme public and private paths, we have seen, excluded too much of what he most celebrated, private autonomy or else public participation. As for the middle way, the way that captured his twin loves, he recognized that, barring the miraculous, it would yield what he dreaded—public conflict and private dividedness. Rousseau recognized that no political solution or social strategy could perfectly reconcile private aspirations and public goals, self-interests and the common good. I cannot make the claim that Rousseau, ultimately and explicitly, was willing to have us cope and deal with such tension and conflict rather than attempt to eliminate it. Yet he powerfully explored the tension and offered alternative ways to handle it; the very nature of his proposed alternatives suggest that, at least implicitly, he was not willing to sacrifice either the public or the private life. In his struggle to discover ways of life that support human flourishing, he managed to address the most profound and enduring issues of his and our time. In the maze of connections and tensions between public and private, dependency and independence, unity and diversity, Rousseau confronts his readers with the drama of human aspirations and limits, complaint and acceptance, hope and despair.

Rousseau loved as much as he hated. He loved the free spirit, simple pleasures, independence, and those inclusive activities and delights that spring from community. He hated enforced conformity, decadence, debilitating economic and social dependency, and the anomic pursuit of narrow self-interest. He loved *amour de soi*, that love of self that seeks good things for the self without harming others. He hated *amour-propre*, that self-love that seeks advancement by outdoing, surpassing, and subjugating others. To employ William James's categories, Rousseau was among both the healthy-minded and the sick-souls.[22] Like the healthy-minded, Rousseau held that the universe is good and harmonious and that humans are members and participants in this goodness. Yet like the sick-soul, Rousseau also held that humans are ignorant, wicked, fallen creatures in need of assistance to heal self-inflicted wounds. Rousseau inhabited both of James's camps. These camps express not only stances toward the world, but also influences in James's life: the optimistic Enlightenment spirituality of Emanuel Swedenborg, which his father embraced, and the pessimistic Augustinian religion of his grandfather, William James, an Albany, New York, millionaire. I have argued for a similar account of Rousseau's twin-stance. Drawn to and torn between Enlightenment optimism and Augustinian pessimism, Rousseau produced morally intricate views of the promise and limits of our capacity to dwell alone and gather together.

A Worthy Endeavor

I began this study by suggesting that we think of Rousseau as a travel companion, not an authoritative guide, for our journey into the maze of footpaths that crisscross the uneven topography of our public and private lives. The journey has hardly been a tidy one. With each chapter we encountered perplexities and difficulties not susceptible to easy settlement. Although Rousseau has not been a guide to follow blindly, I have attempted to emulate his willingness to explore ambiguity without unduly simplifying it. There is an urge in us to order and systematize our experience, even if these attempts belie the very experience we would like to better understand. In the academy we want clear and distinct ideas; who can blame us? Yet often we trade relevance and honesty for clarity and precision. I have tried to illuminate dilemmas, conflicts, and inconsistencies without offering neat solutions that falsify the tangled moral universe we encounter in our daily lives.

Some might argue that my focus on public and private is itself a falsification of sorts. Given the ambiguities and difficulties associated with attempts to define the public and private, would it not be preferable to simply drop the terms, and offer instead morally nuanced descriptions of the circumstances under consideration? I am not altogether opposed to this suggestion. Often our investigations would be more sound and insightful if we shunned the abstract concept, which we usually ask to do too much work, and replace it with detailed description. But that move is not always practical or desirable. The concepts public and private are part of our moral, legal, and everyday cultural discourse. To pretend that the public-private vocabulary does not warrant scrutiny, or that it does not contribute in significant ways to our collective and personal moral reflection, risks intellectual honesty. And it may risk more. To neglect the distinction between public and private could contribute to the political engulfing the private, as in an Orwellian nightmare, or else to the private eclipsing the public, as in the case of atomistic individualism. The way forward is to grapple with the difficulties and ambiguities of the concepts of public and private, noting how these concepts mutually and provisionally define each other; how they powerfully contribute to our moral reflection; and how they obscure it, for example, by assuming gender-based roles or by failing to account adequately for the vast cultural terrain that lies between them.

For my part, I have studied the public and private in democratic society by wrestling with a most perplexing thinker. Characterizing this study as a journey or conversation with Rousseau does cloak the drama behind the scenes. Behind the written page, I wrangled, shouted, even fulminated at Rousseau. Yet it is precisely the chaos of his life and tangles of his thought that make him useful for exploring the irregular contours of the public and private. The tensions and complexities of life alone and life together branded, even seared, his work. Self-possession and civic participation, private safety and public belonging, personal aesthetics and shared pleasures—these goals, commitments, and ideals animated Rousseau as he sought to capture them, all of them, in his life and thought. His failures are evident enough. But the attempt remains worthwhile.

Notes

Preface

1. I reflect on these terms, *public* and *private*, on pp. 11–22. For now I will say that although I have no essentialist definition of either term, I do offer some pragmatic definitions. The activities and practices we associate with the public and private often straddle different sets of polarities. The meaning of the terms *public* and *private* usually is disclosed by the various contexts in which I use them.

2. In this study, *liberal* does not refer necessarily to progressive, as opposed to conservative, political parties or positions. Rather, it refers to social orders that safeguard individuals' political and civil rights. Among other things, this entails political authority based on consent and the protection of diverse beliefs and practices.

Introduction

1. See Mark S. Cladis, "On the Importance of Owning Chickens: Lessons in Nature, Community, and Transformation," *Journal of Interdisciplinary Studies in Literature and the Environment* 7 (2000): 199–211.

2. *Emile*, in *Œuvres complètes* (henceforth O. c.), ed. Bernard Gagnebin and Marcel Raymond (Paris: Pléiade, 1959–1969), pp. iv, 524; for an English translation, see *Emile*, trans. Allan Bloom (New York: Basic, 1979), p. 235. In the following citations, I provide reference to a translation whenever possible. When the French reference comes first, the translation is my own.

3. My placement of Rousseau at the crossroads of Enlightenment optimism and Augustinian (Jansenist) pessimism is a dominant theme in this study. In the *Confessions*, Rousseau claimed that his early reading, especially of the writings of Port-Royal and the Oratory, made him "half a Jansenist" (O. c., i, 241; *Confessions*, trans. J. M. Cohen [New York: Penguin, 1953], p. 230). My argument will be that Rousseau never entirely extricated himself from Augustinian pessimism or from Enlightenment optimism.

I should note that I employ "Enlightenment optimism" and "Augustinian pessimism" more as ideal types than as the historically rich and diverse traditions of thought that each in fact could include. By Enlightenment optimism, I generally refer to the belief that humans are naturally good and, if unfettered, can deliver themselves from evil and oppression. Augustinian pessimism, in contrast, refers to the belief that humans cannot cure themselves and that no measure of enlightenment can rid humans of a deep-seated proclivity to beget disordered lives that injure themselves and those around them.

4. O. c., i, 242; *Confessions*, p. 230.

5. Through out this study, I capitalize "Solitaire" when I refer to the imaginary human species that inhabited Rousseau's Natural Garden or state of nature.

249

6. O. c., iii, 156; *The Discourse on the Origin of Inequality* in *The Social Contract and Discourses*, trans. G. D. H. Cole, revised by J. H. Brumfitt and John C. Hall (London: Dent, Everyman's Library, 1988), p. 76.

7. O. c., iv, 584; *Emile*, p. 279.

8. Judith Shklar, *Men and Citizens* (Cambridge: Cambridge University Press, 1987), pp. 1–32.

9. Rousseau often claimed that he was not a *philosophe*, and by that he usually meant he was not a system builder. In *Emile*, for example, Rousseau professed, via the Savoyard priest, "I have no system to support" (O. c., iv, 582; *Emile*, p. 278; see also *Lettres écrites de la montagne*, O. c., iii, 810). A narrative approach, I suggest, is more fitting for interpreting "edifying" as opposed to "systematic" philosophers, to employ Richard Rorty's terms (Rorty, *Philosophy and the Mirror of Nature* [Princeton, N.J.: Princeton University Press, 1979], pp. 365–72).

10. "The City" is Rousseau's symbol of the chaotic, corrupt, commercial existence in the modern European world. In chapter 5, I discuss Rousseau's critique of Paris, his favorite example of the fallen city. In spite of Rousseau's anti-urban prejudices, we can learn much from his symbol of impersonal, banal public existence and its concomitant moral and social isolation. As for me, the immense, impersonal canyons of New York City have often served as much as a salve as have the woods along the Hudson River. Moreover, city neighborhoods often possess more sociability than their suburban counterparts.

11. See Robert Putnam, *Bowling Alone: The Collapse and Revival of American Community* (New York: Simon and Schuster, 2000); and Robert Wuthnow, *Loose Connections: Joining Together in America's Fragmented Communities* (Cambridge, Mass.: Harvard University Press, 1998). For an alternative view, that is, a more sanguine assessment of contemporary social involvement, see Wade Clark Roof, *Spiritual Market Place: Baby Boomers and the Remaking of American Religion* (Princeton, N.J.: Princeton University Press, 1999).

12. Depending on the context, *amour-propre* can be translated variously. In *Inequality*, Rousseau juxtaposed the gentle, natural ways of self-love (*amour de soi*) to the turbulent, rapacious ways of *amour-propre*, "a relative and factitious feeling, born in society, that drives each individual to make more of himself than all others." I discuss the various connotations of *amour-propre* in chapter 3.

13. My elucidation of the distinction between the public and private life has greatly profited from the following authors: Hannah Arendt, *The Human Condition* (Chicago: University of Chicago Press, 1958), pp. 23–69; S. I. Benn and G. F. Gaus, "The Public and the Private: Concepts and Action" and "The Liberal Conception of the Public and the Private," in *Public and Private in Social Life*, ed. Benn and Gaus (London: Croom Helm, 1983); José Casanova, *Public Religion in the Modern World* (Chicago: Chicago University Press, 1994), especially, "Private and Public Religions"; Jean Bethke Elshtain, *Public Man, Private Woman* (Princeton, N.J.: Princeton University Press, 1981); Carole Pateman, *The Disorder of Women: Democracy, Feminism and Political Theory* (Stanford, Calif.: Stanford University Press, 1994), especially "Feminist Critiques of the Public/Private Dichotomy"; and the following chapters in *Public and Private in Thought and Practice*, ed. Jeff Weintraub and Krishan Kumar (Chicago: University of Chicago Press, 1997): Jean L. Cohen, "Rethinking Privacy: Autonomy, Identity, and the Abortion Controversy"; Krishan Kumar, "Home: The Promise and Predicament of Private Life at the End of the Twentieth Century"; Alan Silver, "'Two Different Sorts of Commerce'—Friendship and Strangership in Civil Society"; Jeff Weintraub, "Theory and Politics of the Public/Private Distinction."

14. O. c., i, 1062–63; *Reveries of the Solitary Walker*, trans. Peter France (London: Penguin, 1979), p. 108.

15. Michel Eyquem de Montaigne, *The Complete Essays*, trans. Donald M. Frame (Stanford, Calif.: Stanford University Press, 1958), pp. 139–40.

16. An additional—and fundamental—aspect of interpreting Islamic veiling pertains to the subjugation of women.

17. Mark Cladis, *A Communitarian Defense of Liberalism* (Stanford, Calif.: Stanford University Press, 1992), pp. 1–10; and Mark Cladis, *Durkheim and Foucault: Perspectives on Education and Punishment* (Oxford: Durkheim, 1999), pp. 6–9.

18. My argument here on the dangers of identity politics has been informed by Jean Bethke Elshtain's "The Displacement of Politics," in *Public and Private in Thought and Practice*, ed. Jeff Weintraub and Krishan Kumar, pp. 175–78.

19. Carole Pateman, *The Disorder of Women*, p. 119.

20. I profited much from Barbara Corrado Pope, "The Influence of Rousseau's Ideology of Domesticity," in *Connecting Spheres: Women in the Western World*, ed. Marilyn J. Boxer and Jean H. Quataert (Oxford: Oxford University Press, 1987), pp. 136–45.

21. Joan Landes, *Women and the Public Sphere in the Age of the French Revolution* (Ithaca, N.Y.: Cornell University Press, 1988), p. 69.

22. *O. c.*, iv, 867; *Emile*, p. 479.

23. *O. c.*, iv, 693; *Emile*, p. 358.

24. *O. c.*, ii, 127 and 152; *Julie; or, The New Eloise*, trans. Judith H. McDowell, pp. 108, 128.

25. See, for example, *Julie*, p. 190; *O. c.*, ii, 223.

26. See, for example, *Emile*, p. 364; *O. c.*, iv, 702.

27. *O. c.*, iv, 687; *Emile*, p. 351.

28. Mary Seidman Trouille, *Sexual Politics in the Enlightenment: Women Writers Read Rousseau* (Albany: State University of New York Press, 1997), p. 3.

29. Here, as elsewhere, Rousseau championed his own form of identity politics. He understood the powerful political implications of the so-called personal life.

30. Michel Foucault, "Structuralism and Post-Structuralism: An Interview with Michel Foucault," by G. Raulet, *Telos* 55 (1983): 206.

31. There is an increase in volunteerism in the United States. But as it turns out, this increase is mainly due to volunteers who are over sixty years old. See Putnam, *Bowling Alone*, p. 129.

Chapter 1

1. Throughout this study, I follow the custom of referring to the "Discourse on the Arts and Sciences" and "Discourse on the Origin of Inequality" as the first and second *Discours*, respectively; in the notes, however, I designate them as "On the Arts and Sciences" and "Inequality." The English translation of the two discourses is found in the *Social Contract and Discourses*, trans. G. D. H. Cole and revised by J. H. Brumfitt and John C. Hall.

2. *Rousseau juge de Jean-Jacques*, *O. c.*, i, 728.

3. "Inequality"; p. 48; *O. c.*, iii, 127. Rousseau quoted Persius in the original Latin, "Quem te deus esse jussit, et humanâ quâ parte locatus es in re, disce" (*Satires*, iii, 71).

4. *O. c.*, iv, 245; *Emile*, p. 37.

5. Alone, we cannot be truly happy or moral; together, we suffer and become corrupt. These, I argue in chapter 2, are the twin horns of Rousseau's dilemma. Due to this dilemma, it may be more accurate to think of the Garden as a home to innocence rather than to goodness. There are ways to construe the Solitaires as moral creatures; however, all things considered, they are best described, in general, as amoral beings.

6. *O. c.*, iii, 134; "Inequality," p. 52. While Rousseau occasionally used the word *sauvage* to refer to these primitive humans, he never described them as brutal.

7. *O. c.*, iii, 135; "Inequality," p. 52.

8. *O. c.*, iii, 143; "Inequality," p. 61.

9. For as we have seen, Rousseau omits sex from his first description of the primitives, and when he does mention it, he places its importance below hunger. See "Inequality," p. 84; *O. c.*, iii, 164. Of course, outside the Garden Rousseau will highlight the tremendous role of sex, as for example in *Emile*.

10. *O. c.*, iii, 164; "Inequality," p. 84.

11. John Harsanyi, "Rational Choice Models of Behavior versus Functionalist and Conformist Theories," *World Politics* 22 (1969): 524.

12. See "Inequality," pp. 77–79; *O. c.*, iii, 157–60.

13. See "Inequality," pp. 61–62; *O. c.*, iii, 143–44.

14. *O. c.*, iii, 160; "Inequality," p. 79.

15. *O. c.*, iii, 203; "Inequality," p.120.

16. See "Inequality," p. 61; *O. c.*, iii, 143.

17. See David Gauthier's "The Politics of Redemption," *University of Ottawa Quarterly* 49 (1979): 333–35, for an excellent discussion on the role that an equilibrium between desires and powers plays inside and outside the state of nature. Although I agree with Gauthier on the importance of an equilibrium between needs and powers in Rousseau's conception of the state of nature, I think he overstates its role in society, insofar as Rousseau desired to expose not only the difficulty, perhaps impossibility, of satisfying anomic needs, but more importantly the injustice and misery that flow from attempting to gratify the wrong kinds of needs.

18. "La faculté de se perfectionner," "Inequality," p. 60; *O. c.*, iii, 142.

19. For Rousseau's discussion of freedom and perfectibility, see "Inequality," pp. 59–60; *O. c.*, iii, 141–42.

20. In *Emile*, for example, Rousseau has the Savoyard priest say, "Conscience is the voice of the soul. . . . The one who follows conscience obeys nature. . . . Conscience! Conscience! divine instinct, immortal and celestial voice . . . infallible judge of good and evil, which makes man like God" (*O. c.*, iv, 594–95, 600–601; *Emile*, pp. 286, 290).

21. *O. c.*, iii, 142; "Inequality," p. 60.

22. Immediately after the claim that perfectibility makes man "a tyrant over himself and over nature," Rousseau agreed with the eighteenth-century scientist, Pierre-Louis Moreau de Maupertuis, that when one compared the good and evil of human life, "the evil greatly surpassed the good, and that, all things considered, life for man was a rather lousy gift" (*O. c.*, iii, 202; "Inequality," p. 118). But this conclusion, he argued, pertains only to life outside the Garden, that is, in civilization. And I should add that a year later, in his letter to Voltaire about the doctrine of optimism, Rousseau claimed that we have yet to make life so burdensome that we would "prefer nothingness to our existence." See, *O. c.*, iv., 1062–63.

23. In the translations, "compassion" is a common rendering of *pitié*. In the following pages, however, it is important to pay close attention to how Rousseau applied the concept to the Solitaires, lest "com-passion" in the Garden imply more social connection than Rousseau intended.

24. *O. c.*, iii, 126; "Inequality," p. 47.

25. *Rousseau juge de Jean Jacques, O. c.*, i, 669.

26. *O. c*, iii, 154, 126; "Inequality," pp. 73, 47.

27. *O. c.*, iii, 126; "Inequality," p. 47.

28. *O. c.*, iv, 504; *Emile*, p. 222.

29. Usually, Rousseau described natural *pitié* negatively, that is, as directing us to avoid doing harm. I suppose, however, that an "innate repugnance at seeing a fellow creature suffer" could lead to acts of assistance. Rousseau cited an example of *pitié* from Bernard de Mandeville's *The Fable of the Bees* which described "a man confined who sees outside a ferocious beast tear a child from the breast of its mother." Rousseau asked rhetorically, "What anguish would he not

suffer at this sight, not being able to give any assistance to the fainting mother and the dying child?" (O. c., iii, 154; "Inequality," p. 74). This, however, is clearly a post-Garden example, and hence it cannot clearly illuminate the effects of natural compassion, that is, compassion before it is modified outside the Garden in society.

30. See "Inequality," p. 75; O. c., iii, 155–56. Lévi-Strauss has powerfully captured the moral thrust of Rousseau's position: "Never better than after the last four centuries of his history could a Western man understand that, while assuming the right to impose a radical separation of humanity and animality, while granting to one all that he denied the other, he initiated a vicious circle. The one boundary, constantly pushed back, would be used to separate men from other men and to claim–to the profit of ever smaller minorities–the privilege of a humanism, corrupted at birth by taking self-interest as its principle and its notion" (Claude Lévi-Strauss, "Jean-Jacques Rousseau, Founder of the Sciences of Man," Structural Anthropology, vol. 2 [Chicago: University of Chicago Press, 1976], p. 41).

31. See "Inequality," p. 47; O. c., iii, 126.

32. O. c., iii, 219; "Inequality," p. 73.

33. O. c., iii, 156; "Inequality," p. 76.

34. O. c., iv, 503; Emile, p. 221.

35. Clearly I am not speaking here as a theologian. In the Abrahamic traditions–Judaism, Christianity, and Islam–one can find arguments that God is neither invulnerable to pain nor radically alone, and perhaps not even self-sufficient. The Crucifixion is one of the more famous examples of a suffering God, and this example will play a role in chapter 10 where I discuss Jesus as Rousseau's symbol of the inward yet social being. But Rousseau's Jesus is not God–he is a man. For the present discussion, think of God as the place holder for radical invulnerability, self-sufficiency, and solitariness–for the truly sui generis.

Chapter 2

1. O. c., iii, 202; "Inequality," p. 118.

2. See Thomas Hobbes, Leviathan (New York: Penguin, 1984), ch. xiii, pp. 183–88.

3. O. c., iii, 136; "Inequality," p. 54.

4. In L'Etat de guerre (1756) Rousseau argued that war is rooted in social existence: "Man is naturally pacific and fearful; at the slightest danger his first reaction is to flee. . . . It is only after he makes society with someone that he is determined to attack another; and he becomes a solider only after he has been a citizen. . . . Therefore there is no general war of man against man. . . . Everything carries the natural man to rest. . . . He has been made a furious creature always swift to torment his fellows by passions which . . . arise in the bonds of society. . . . The error of Hobbes and the philosophers is to confound the natural man with men whom they see before them" (O. c., iii, 601–2, 605, 611).

5. See "Inequality," pp. 71–72; O. c., iii, 153–54.

6. O. c., iii, 153; "Inequality," p. 72.

7. In his "Lettre à Christophe de Beaumont," for example, Rousseau claimed that "the darkness of ignorance is worth more than the false light of error." O. c., iv, 1004.

8. O. c., iii, 153–54; "Inequality," pp. 71–72.

9. Richard Rorty, for example, celebrates the "liberal ironist" who "thinks that what unites her with the rest of the species is not a common language but just susceptibility to pain and in particular to that special sort of pain which the brutes do not share with the humans–humiliation. On her conception, human solidarity is not a matter of sharing a common truth or a common goal but of sharing a common selfish hope, the hope that one's world–the little things which one has woven into one's final vocabulary–will not be destroyed" (Contingency, Irony, and Solidarity [Cambridge: Cambridge University Press, 1989], p. 92).

10. O. c., iii, 355; *Social Contract*, p. 186.

11. See "Inequality," p. 72; O. c., iii, 153; and "On the Arts and Sciences," p. 29; O. c., iii, 30.

12. See "Inequality," p. 71; O. c., iii, 152, where Rousseau claims that insofar as "the pure impulses of nature" guide the Solitaire, "he would have to be accounted most virtuous."

13. Judith Shklar, *Men and Citizens* (Cambridge: Cambridge University Press, 1987), p. 48.

14. O. c., iii, 152; "Inequality," p. 71.

15. See "Inequality," pp. 71–72; O. c., iii, 153.

16. This is not to deny that the moral consequences of such a constricted vision could be preferable to the gratuitous suffering that flows from a corrupt, ambitious moral vision such as the judicial torture of the Spanish Inquisition or Stalin's nationalism.

17. Rousseau's own infatuation with the Solitaires is not merely an expression of liberal fear of unnecessary and painful coercion. The Solitaires also represent the individual who, out of self-love and fear of hurting others needlessly, seeks to escape social involvement insofar as that is possible. Hence even such "private" obligations as those that come with friendship, marriage, parenting, and religious and political associations are to be dodged.

18. O. c., iv, 340; *Emile*, p. 104–5.

19. O. c., iv, 849; *Emile*, p. 467.

20. This is captured by the French expression for still life paintings, *nature morte*.

21. Support for this claim is found in Rousseau's "Lettre a Christophe de Beaumont": "The conscience is nonexistent in the man who has made no comparisons and has seen no relationships. In this state the man knows only himself. . . . He neither hates nor loves anything; limited to physical instinct alone, he is no one, he is animal; it is this that I showed in my *Discourse on Inequality*." O. c., iv., 936.

22. O. c., iii, 153; "Inequality," p. 71.

23. O. c., iv, 444; *Emile*, p. 177.

24. O. c., iii, 282 and 283.

25. Nor, of course, could it ever really be attained. But that is a different issue to be addressed in chapter 8.

26. "I do not understand how one who has need of nothing could love anything; I do not understand how he who loves nothing can be happy." O. c., iv., 503; *Emile*, p. 221.

Chapter 3

1. For the first stage, see "Inequality," pp. 85–86; O. c., iii, 165–66.

2. O. c., iii, 166; "Inequality," p. 86.

3. I develop this argument in chapter 10.

4. This is a frequent theme in Rousseau's writings; in *Emile*, for example, he noted that "every particular society, when it is narrow and unified, is estranged from the larger society. Every patriot is harsh to foreigners. . . . This drawback is inevitable yet slight. The essential thing is to be good to the people with whom one lives" (O. c., iv, 248–49; *Emile*, p. 39).

5. The Bodin quotation is cited by Nannerl O. Keohane's in her excellent study, *Philosophy and the State in France* (Princeton, N.J.: Princeton University Press, 1980), p. 455.

6. For the second stage, see "Inequality," pp. 86–87; O. c., iii, 166–67.

7. O. c., iii, 166–67; "Inequality," p. 87.

8. O. c., iii, 151; "Inequality," p. 70.

9. See "Inequality," pp. 64–70, 87, and 89; O. c., iii, 146–52, 167, and 168–69. Rousseau claimed, for example, that "one can conceive that among men brought together and forced to live together [on islands cataclysmically torn from the mainland], a common idiom must have

arisen sooner than among those who wandered freely in the forest of the continent" (O. c., iii, 168–69; "Inequality," 89).

10. Although he makes more of the conventional as opposed to the utilitarian nature of developed languages, see Maurice Cranston's insightful account of Rousseau's *Essai sur l'origine des langues* in *Jean-Jacques: The Early Life and Work* (London: Norton, 1982), pp. 289–91.

11. *Essai sur l'origine des langues*, ed. Charles Porset (Bordeaux: Ducros, 1970), p. 43.

12. *Essai sur l'origine des langues*, p. 54.

13. *Essai sur l'origine des langues*, pp. 197–99.

14. See "Inequality," pp. 87–89; O. c., iii, 167–69.

15. In *Discourse on Political Economy*, for example, Rousseau claimed that "it is certain that the right of property is the most sacred of all the rights of citizens, and more important in some respects than liberty itself, because the preservation of life more nearly depends on it" (O. c., iii, 262–63; "Political Economy," in *The Social Contract and Discourses*, p. 151).

16. O. c., iii, 164; "Inequality," p. 84. Comments such as this led to an intense antagonism between the usually poor Rousseau and the wealthy Voltaire. (As I write this, I am about one hundred yards from the tombs of Rousseau and Voltaire, which the Revolutionaries, ironically, placed next to each other in the Pantheon.) In contrast to Voltaire, Diderot was more receptive to, and even encouraged, Rousseau's social criticism. I should also note that throughout his writings Rousseau was unequivocal about the poisonous effects of private property under conditions of social inequality.

17. Rousseau's method of avoidance is described, for example, in *The Confessions* as a "great maxim of morality": "avoid situations that place our duties in opposition to our interests and show us our good in the misfortunes of others" (O. c., i, 56; *Confessions*, pp. 61–62).

18. O. c., iii, 168; "Inequality," p. 88.

19. I am thinking of Rousseau's broken relation with his father who deserted him, and of Rousseau's difficult and—literally—painful sexual relationships with women, especially with Madame de Warens. It would be a mistake, however, to reduce these relationships to mere brokenness, especially with respect to his father, whom he once claimed to be "the best of fathers," and to Madame de Warens, whom he always loved.

20. In part I of *La Nouvelle Heloïse, or Julie*, St. Preux frequently criticizes the institution of marriage along these lines. Rousseau's domestic fantasy is fully incarnated in *Julie*.

21. Rousseau's mother died seven days after giving birth to him, and hence it was especially painful when his father, his only parent, went into exile to avoid jail time and fines for poaching; Rousseau was ten years old. Five years later, when Rousseau himself was in exile in Savoy, Madame de Warens became his spiritual teacher, then his dear "Mama," and finally his lover.

22. O. c., iii, 168; "Inequality," p. 88.

23. The claim that Rousseau believed in a natural, sexually determined division of labor can be supported by many, indeed, perhaps most of his accounts of the relation between women and men. The two most famous accounts are his depictions of the marriages of Julie and Wolmar and of Sophie and Emile. I develop this theme in greater detail in chapters 7 and 9.

24. O. c., iii, 119–20; "Inequality," p. 41–42.

25. O. c., iii, 21; "On the Arts and Sciences," p. 19.

26. See *Politics and the Arts: Letter to M. d'Alembert on the Theatre* (Ithaca, N.Y.: Cornell University Press, 1968), pp. 47–49; *Lettre à M. d'Alembert* (Paris: Garnier-Flammarion, 1967), pp. 113–16.

27. *Lettre à M. d'Alembert*, p. 115; *Politics and the Arts*, pp. 48–49.

28. O. c., iv., 685; *Emile*, p. 316. There is a potentially liberating interpretation of the phrase, "Be oneself at all times." It could mean, for example, do not be inhibited by conventional gender stereotypes. This lesson can be extrapolated from Rousseau's thought, although, unfortunately, this was not his explicit or primary message to women.

29. See "Inequality," pp. 89–92; O. c., iii, 169–71.

30. O. c., iii, 171; "Inequality," p. 91.

31. O. c., iii, 169–70; "Inequality," p. 90.

32. "That anxious awareness of oneself as a social object" is how Judith Shklar once referred to *amour-propre*; *Men and Citizens*, p. ix.

33. O. c., iii, 219; "Inequality," p. 73.

34. Jean Starobinski has placed this theme at the center of his exceptional book, *Jean-Jacques Rousseau: Transparency and Obstruction* (Chicago: University of Chicago Press, 1988).

35. *Rousseau juge de Jean-Jacques*, O. c., i, 936.

36. Keohane, *Philosophy and the State in France*, p. 269.

37. O. c., iv, 493; *Emile*, pp. 174–75.

38. O. c., iii, 154; "Inequality," p. 73.

39. O. c., iii, 30; "On the Arts and Sciences," p. 29.

40. For example J. H. Brumfitt and John C. Hall, in their edition of the G. D. H. Cole translation of *The Social Contract and Discourses*, claim that "the distinction [between *amour de soi* and *amour-propre*] is somewhat arbitrary, since 'amour-propre' did not, and does not, necessarily have any such pejorative meaning in general usage" (p. 346). Nannerl Keohane, in contrast, although not providing an explicit genealogy of the two distinct types of love, has furnished many invaluable details that would go into such a genealogy. I am especially indebted to the chapter, "A Variety of Loves and the Sovereignty of Will," in her *Philosophy and the State in France*, pp. 183–212.

41. Augustine, *City of God*, XIV, 28, in *St. Augustine: The Political Writings*, ed. Henry Paolucci (Washington, D.C.: Regnery Gateway, 1962), p. 8.

42. Jean-Pierre Camus, *La Défense du pur amour contre les attaques de l'amour propre* (Paris: Henault, 1640).

43. Rousseau would certainly agree that *amour-propre* usually works against what is our true best interest. For this reason "self-interest" can be a misleading translation of *amour-propre*. For a good discussion on Rousseau and varieties of self-interest, see Jim MacAdam, "Rousseau's Criticism of Hobbesian Egoism," *University of Ottawa Quarterly*, 49 (1979): 367–87.

44. See Keohane, *Philosophy and the State in France*, p. 196.

45. Malebranche, Nicolas de, *Traité de morale*, in *Oeuvres complètes de Malebranche*, ed. Michel Adam (Paris: Vrin, 1966), xi, 28–42.

46. Patrick Riley, in his compelling book *The General Will before Rousseau*, has documented the "transformation of a theological idea, the general will of God to save all men, into a political one, the general will of the citizen to place the common good of the city above his particular will as a private self, and thereby to 'save' the polity" (p. ix).

47. See "Inequality," p. 75; O. c., iii, 155.

Chapter 4

1. O. c., iii, 171; "Inequality," pp. 91–92.

2. O. c., iii, 171; "Inequality," p. 92. See pp. 92–97 (O. c., iii, 171–76) for what I am calling stage five of the Fall.

3. O. c., iii, 171; "Inequality," p. 91.

4. O. c., iii, 172; "Inequality," p. 93.

5. O. c., iii, 172, 173; "Inequality," p. 93.

6. For an account of John Locke's influence on Rousseau, see Jean Morel, "Récherches sur les sources du *Discours de l'inégalité*," *Annales de la société Jean-Jacques Rousseau* 5 (1909): 143–60, 179–98; and Shklar, *Men and Citizens*, pp. 33–74. Rousseau's empirical sensibilities, that

is, his recognition of the powerful sway of external circumstances, comes not only from the English Locke but also from the French Montesquieu, Condillac, and d'Alembert.

7. See "Inequality," pp. 94–95, 49; O. c., iii, 173–74, 131.

8. O. c., iii, 171; "Inequality," p. 92.

9. O. c., iii, 174; "Inequality," p. 95.

10. O. c., iii, 189; "Inequality," p. 112.

11. This tradition has its roots in the English Hobbes as much as in the French Jansenist, Pierre Nicole. The dire Augustinian assessment of humans in their fallen condition made such French pessimists as the Jansenists receptive to Hobbes's anthropology, if not his politics. Nicole, however, unlike most of his fellow Jansenists, held that in the properly organized society, the individual's pursuit of selfish *amour-propre* would lead to public harmony and prosperity; driven by the quest for private gain, individuals would attempt to serve and please each other in order to profit from each other. See Pierre Nicole, "De la grandeur," *Œuvres philosophiques et morales*, ed. Charles Jourdain (Paris: Hachette, 1845). For a helpful discussion on Nicole and other Jansenists in relation to this early utilitarian tradition, see Jacob Viner, "The Invisible Hand and Economic Man," in his book *The Role of Providence in the Social Order* (Princeton: Princeton University Press, 1972).

12. O. c., i, 1069–70; *Reveries*, trans. Peter France (London: Penguin, 1979), p. 116. I have taken some liberty here with the context, as Rousseau was referring to the degeneration of botany when it is transported to "the cities and academies." Later, however, I argue that botany becomes Rousseau's metaphor of the simple, happy life.

13. Rousseau was well aware of what I am here calling the classical notion of a public stage in which the good opinion of others is sought after. In *The Government of Poland*, for example, Rousseau advocated that "every citizen shall incessantly fell being under the eyes of the public; no one shall advance and succeed except by public favor; . . . from the least of the nobles, or even from the least of the peasants up to the king, if that were possible, everyone shall be so completely dependent on public esteem so as to be unable to do anything, acquire anything, or achieve anything without it" (O. c., iii, 1019; *The Government of Poland*, trans. Willmoore Kendall [Indianapolis, Ind.: Hackett, 1985], p. 87). I explore this line of thought in chapter 7 where I discuss the extreme—and frightening—public path to redemption.

14. Montaigne, *Complete Essays*, pp. 774, 177, 758.

15. O. c., iv., 307, 308, 310; *Emile*, pp. 83, 84.

16. Here we can think of Rousseau's unusual habit of wearing an Armenian peasant costume and the stoning that this strange dress (among other things) occasioned at Môtiers. For an excellent account of this event, see Harry Payne, "Deciphering the Stones of Môtiers," *Eighteenth Century Life* 11 (1987): 61–77.

17. For an account of Rousseau's concern for "Everyman," and not for "the unique personality crushed by mediocrity," see Shklar, *Men and Citizens*, pp. 54–56. For an alternative account that emphasizes Rousseau the existentialist, see Ronald Grimsley, *The Philosophy of Rousseau* (Oxford: Oxford University Press, 1973), pp. 20–22.

18. I write "tremendous social forces," and yet these operate in conjunction with the psychological disposition, *amour-propre*, a disposition which, as we will see, could be described as inescapable in social humans (and, in my view, there aren't any other kind).

19. O. c., iii, 193; "Inequality," p. 116.

20. Blaise Pascal, *Pensée*, ed. Léon Brunschvicg (Paris: Le Livre de Poche,1976), no. 147.

21. O. c., iii, 135–36; "Inequality," pp. 53–54. I have reversed the sequence of events of Rousseau's version to highlight the obstacles that face nakedness. Rousseau, in contrast, wanted to draw attention to the strength of the Solitaire in comparison to the feeble "civilized man."

22. O. c., iii, 175; "Inequality," pp. 96.

23. *O. c.*, iii, 188–89; "Inequality," pp. 110–11.

24. *O. c.*, iii, 189; "Inequality," p. 112.

25. *O. c.*, iii, 175; "Inequality," p. 96.

26. From early on, Rousseau had identified with the poor and protested against their lamentable social circumstances. For example, as a young man in 1737 visiting Montpelier, Rousseau had already acquired the sight of a social critic. In a letter to his friend, Charbonnel, he wrote, "These streets are lined alternately with superb hotels and miserable cottages full of mud and dung; half the inhabitants are very rich, and the other half extremely impoverished. . . . You know without doubt how the Huguenots are regarded in Italy or the Jews in Spain: that's how outsiders are treated here; they are seen exactly as a species of animals made expressly to be plundered, robbed, and beaten to death" ("Lettre à Charbonnel," *Correspondance complète de Jean-Jacques Rousseau*, ed. Ralph A. Leigh [Geneva: Institut et Musée Voltaire, 1965], vol. 1, 61–62). I should add that throughout his life Rousseau invariably rejected any opportunities for wealth—and he was offered many, even by Louis XV himself—in order to maintain his identification with the common people. Of course, there was nothing common about Rousseau's rather celebrated—and occasionally displayed—simple lifestyle.

27. See, for example, "Inequality," p. 124; *O. c.*, iii, 206. Others, such as the Baron de Montesquieu in *L'Esprit des lois* (in *Oeuvres complètes*, ed. Roger Caillois [Paris: Pléiade, 1951], ii), condemned luxury, but they, unlike Rousseau, could also see some social benefits derived from the pursuit of luxury.

28. See "Inequality," pp. 94–95; *O. c.*, iii, 173–75.

29. *O. c.*, iii, 176; "Inequality," p. 97.

30. For the sixth stage, see "Inequality," pp. 97–112; *O. c.*, iii, 176–89.

31. England, moreover, was the country Rousseau thought might appreciate the second *Discours*. He had urged his editor to advertise the book in England, "the only country where, in my opinion, the book, if it is any good, will be esteemed for what it is worth" (*Correspondance complète*, vol. 3, 284; cited in Cranston, *The Noble Savage*, p. 6).

32. *O. c.*, iii, 178; "Inequality," p. 99.

33. *O. c.*, iii, 176; "Inequality," pp. 97–98.

34. *O. c.*, iii, 177; "Inequality," p. 98.

35. In order to support this judgment, Rousseau broke his narrative and engaged in a more analytic analysis of "other explanations of the origin of political societies" (see "Inequality," pp. 100–112; *O. c.*, iii, 179–89). He rejected, for example, Sir Robert Filmer's patriarchal account ("Nothing on earth can be farther from the ferocious spirit of despotism than the mildness of paternal authority"), and he supported Locke's view that no one can sell one's liberty—much less one's children's—so as "to submit to an arbitrary power which may use him as it likes" (thereby directly challenging Pufendorf, and indirectly Hobbes, for if the alienation of liberty is not legitimate, than neither is Leviathan). Rousseau even offered his own normative view of a "genuine contract," as opposed to the deceitful one, in which the chosen magistrates are accountable to the people. He had more to say on this subject in the project he had been working on, "Political Institutions," a portion of which would later find its way into *The Social Contract*.

36. "As for that fine statement under which ambition and avarice take cover—that we are not born for our private selves, but for the public—let us boldly appeal to those who are in the midst of the dance. Let them cudgel their consciences and say whether, on the contrary, the titles, the offices, and the hustle and bustle of the world are not sought out to gain private profit from the public" (Montaigne, *Complete Essays*, p. 174).

37. "Preface," *Narcisse, O. c.*, ii, 968–69.

38. *O. c.*, iii, 202; "Inequality," p. 118.

39. In the "Preface" to *Narcisse*, Rousseau wrote, "I lament that philosophy loosens the bonds of society which were formed by good-will and mutual benevolence, and I lament that the sciences, the arts, and all the other objects of commerce are tightening the social bonds by self-interest. It is the case that one cannot tighten one of these bonds unless the other is loosened by the same amount. There is not in this a contradiction" (*Narcisse*, O. c., ii, 968).

40. Emile Durkheim, *The Division of Labor in Society*, trans. W. D. Halls (New York: Free Press, 1979), p. 152.

41. O. c., iii, 273; "Political Economy," in *The Social Contract and Discourses*, p. 162.

42. Rousseau also hinted in "Inequality" (as Durkheim had explicitly argued) that the extreme "communitarian" solution to the war against all, namely, rendering individual and national identity as one and the same, merely led to still a different type of war; in this case, one in which "the most fair [*honnêtes*] people learned to count among their duties cutting the throats of their fellow-creatures . . . men massacred by thousands without knowing why. . . . Such were the first effects which one can discern from the division of humankind into different societies" (O. c., iii, 179; "Inequality," p. 100). Here Rousseau sensed the communitarian dilemma: distinctive group identity often breeds conflict with those outside the group. We will discuss Rousseau's solution to this dilemma when we investigate civil religion in chapter 10.

43. See "Inequality," p. 109; O. c., iii, 187.

44. O. c., iii, 188; "Inequality," p. 110.

45. See "Inequality," p. 103; O. c., iii, 181.

46. For stage seven, see "Inequality," pp. 112–17; O. c., iii, 189–94.

47. See "Inequality," p. 112–13; O. c., iii, 190–91.

48. O. c., iii, 133; "Inequality," p. 51.

49. O. c., iii, 191; "Inequality," p. 114.

50. O. c., iii, 190; "Inequality," p. 114.

51. O. c., iii, 192; "Inequality," p. 114.

52. O. c., iii, 191; "Inequality," p. 114.

53. *Correspondance complète*, vol. 3, 319. Cited in Cranston, *The Noble Savage*, p. 9.

54. O. c., iii, 192; "Inequality," p. 114–15.

Chapter 5

1. While I am suspicious of attempts to compare the well-being and sorrow of one historical era to another, I should note that some contemporary anthropologists and historians have concluded, with Rousseau, that human happiness diminished as humankind "advanced." For example, the Cambridge anthropologist Alan Macfarlane has argued that since the age of hunters and gatherers, human sorrows have increasingly multiplied. Hunters and gatherers were, for the most part, spared war, had plenty of food, were free of urban diseases and plagues, had much leisure time, rarely endured unjust concentrations of political power and intellectual resources, and experienced little degradation and much contentment (Oxford Marett Memorial Lecture, "Illth and Wealth," Trinity Term, 1995).

2. O. c., iv., 691; *Emile*, p. 355. The second *Discours* is dedicated to the republic of Geneva, and for some time Geneva played a role in Rousseau's thought as the natural, virtuous city. His adoration for Geneva, however, waned when that city republic banned both *Emile* and *The Social Contract*, and as Rousseau learned of—or finally recognized—Geneva's antidemocratic practices.

3. The empirically rich character of the second *Discours*, seated principally in the footnotes, is not evident in most English editions, as the editors, justifiably, omit this rather copious yet dated material.

4. See "Inequality," pp. 44–45, 82–83; O. c., iii, 123–24, 162–63.

5. Jean Starobinski overstates Rousseau's confidence when he claims that "the origins of mankind were incontrovertibly thus and so, Rousseau declared, and primitive man must have been exactly as he believed" (*Jean-Jacques Rousseau: Transparency and Obstruction*, trans. Arthur Goldhammer [Chicago: University of Chicago Press, 1988], p. 15). Rousseau himself, with less aplomb, confesses, "Let my readers not imagine that I dare to flatter myself with seeing what appears to me so difficult to in fact see"; and, "Since the events that I have to describe could have happened in a variety of ways, I cannot chose among them except by conjecture" (*O. c.*, iii, 123,162; "Inequality," pp. 44, 82).

6. *O. c.*, iii, 213–14; this reference is to a footnote not found in Cole's English edition.

7. *O. c.*, iii, 132; "Inequality," p. 50.

8. *O. c.*, iii, 123; "Inequality," p. 44.

9. In a telling footnote to the second *Discours*, Rousseau complained that although Europeans have "inundated" the world," due to "ridiculous prejudices" that blind us, "the only men we know are Europeans" (*O. c.*, iii, 212).

10. See Hugo Grotius, "Prolegomena," in *On the Law of War and Peace*, trans. Francis Kelsey (Oxford: Oxford University Press, 1925); Samuel Pufendorf, "On Natural Law," in *On the Duty of Man and Citizen*, trans. Frank Moore (Oxford: Oxford University Press, 1927), ch. iii; Thomas Hobbes, *Leviathan* (New York: Penguin, 1984), ch. xiii.

11. J. H. Brumfitt and John C. Hall, "The Development of Rousseau's Political Philosophy," in *The Social Contract and the Discourses*, p. xlix.

12. "Lettre à Malesherbes" (12 January 1762), *Correspondance complète*, vol. 10, p. 26.

13. Thus in the second *Discours* Rousseau celebrated those ancient times when true philosophers such as Plato and Pythagoras, "grasped by an ardent desire to know, embarked upon the greatest journeys solely in order to learn, and traveled far to shake off the yoke of national prejudices, to learn to know men by their *conformities* and by their *differences*" (*O. c.*, iii, 213). Emphasis added.

14. See "Inequality," p. 51; *O. c.*, iii, 133.

15. *O. c.*, iii, 132; "Inequality," p. 50.

16. My position here is at odds with Cranston's claim that Rousseau "argued that men had once actually lived in this 'savage' and solitary state" (*The Early Life and Work of Jean-Jacques Rousseau* [New York: Norton, 1982], p. 299). That claim, however, slights Rousseau's own disclaimer that "perhaps [the state of nature] never did exist." See "Inequality," p. 50; *O. c.*, iii, 132.

17. Naomi Bliven, for example, claims that the second *Discours* "relies on a concept as meaningless in political theory as it is in anthropology: man in himself—alone, or apart from society. There is no such person either realistically or theoretically, any more than there is a round triangle: man is a social animal. . . . [Rousseau's] notion that naturally good man is corrupted by society . . . does not account for the diversity of human societies and variety of ethical assumptions" ("Jean-Jacques: The Early Life and Work of Jean-Jacques Rousseau, 1712–1754," *New Yorker*, 4 July 1983, 89–90).

18. Bliven, "Jean-Jacques," 89–90.

19. Indeed, it is commonplace among contemporary French philosophers to say that Rousseau's notion of human nature is that we do not have one. There is much truth in this overstatement.

20. *O. c.*, iii, 156; "Inequality," p. 76. I write "almost," because although the natural maxim does entail freedom, it does not necessarily involve perfectibility.

21. In *Culture and Human Nature* (Chicago: University of Chicago Press, 1989), Melford Piro has convincingly argued that, on the basis of anthropological evidence, personal care is a universal human feature.

22. *O. c.*, iii, 169; "Inequality," p. 89.

23. Ernst Cassirer, *The Philosophy of the Enlightenment*, trans. Fritz Koelln and James Pettegrove (Princeton, N.J.: Princeton University Press, 1968), p. 271.

24. The problem, of course, in Marx's view, is that the Kingdom of God also transfers our hopes and energy to a place and time that stands outside history.

25. Although J. L. Talmon exaggerates Rousseau's contribution to such oppression, he has highlighted the potential danger. See *The Origins of Totalitarian Democracy* (Boulder, Colo.: Westview, 1985), chap. 3.

26. As we will see in chapter 10, the mandatory civil profession of faith that Rousseau advanced in *The Social Contract* safeguarded tolerance, ironically.

27. Both Shklar and Starobinski, for example, interpret history, change, and "the social" as equivalent to evil. See Shklar, *Men and Citizens*, pp. 28–29; Starobinski, *Jean-Jacques Rousseau*, pp. 21, 295.

28. See, for example, "Inequality," p. 112; O. c., iii, 189. Also, recall that Rousseau called stage four of the fall the happiest human epoch.

29. In the second *Discours* Rousseau stated that he is not surprised by Maupertuis's pessimistic calculation that in human life "the evil greatly surpasses the good, and that, all things considered, life for man is a rather lousy gift" (O. c., iii, 202; "Inequality," p. 118). A year later, however, in his letter to Voltaire about the doctrine of optimism and the Lisbon earthquake, Rousseau claimed that in spite of our tremendous ability to make ourselves miserable, we have yet to make life so burdensome that we would "prefer nothingness to our existence." In comparing good and evil, useful calculations are rare because philosophers "always forget the sweet feeling of existence, which remains independent of every sensation." See, O. c., iv., 1062–63.

30. See Cole's introduction to *The Social Contract and Discourses*, p. xiv; and Ronald Grimsley, *The Philosophy of Rousseau* (Oxford: Oxford University Press, 1973), pp. 60–61, 160.

31. Starobinski, *Jean-Jacques Rousseau*, p. 12.

32. O. c., iii, 202; "Inequality," p. 118.

33. Starobinski claims that the Fall is the introduction of pride. In the account I am presenting, however, the first steps out of the Garden were more innocuous. The introduction of complexity, not pride, is a more accurate description of the Solitaires' initial departure from the Garden. This observation highlights what Rousseau admired about the life of the Solitaires, namely, simplicity.

34. O. c., iii, 142; "Inequality," p. 60.

35. O. c., iii., 171; "Inequality," p. 91.

36. O. c., iii, 169–70; "Inequality," p. 90.

37. Although this reference to a "natural human activity" is a benign instance of essentialism, I should reiterate that I am reading Rousseau's narrative as an interesting story about North Atlantic societies, not about humanity in general.

38. In *Emile*, Rousseau—like Augustine—went so far as to declare *amour-propre* a natural condition for children: "Children will always take . . . the choice of *amour-propre*, it is a very natural choice" (O. c., iv, 356; *Emile*, 115).

39. Another example is found at the end of part I of the second *Discours*: "Having shown that *perfectibility*, the social virtues, and the other faculties which natural man potentially possessed, could never develop of themselves, that they required the fortuitous concurrence of many foreign causes that might never have arisen . . . it remains for me to consider and assemble the different accidents that could have perfected human reason while worsening the species, rendering a being wicked while making it social" (O. c., iii, 162; "Inequality," p. 82).

40. Keohane claims that "Rousseau went to some trouble to show that *amour-propre* is not the necessary condition of 'fallen men,' but is produced by a human enterprise, the development of a complex society and all the false needs and vain philosophy that accompany it" (*Philosophy and the State in France*, p. 431). My argument, in contrast, is that *amour-propre* is

endemic to social humans, yet it could have been—and still can be—curtailed more or less, depending on the circumstances. Moreover, Keohane's juxtaposition of the "condition of fallen men" to "complex society," "false needs," and "vain philosophy" is like juxtaposing a term against its definition. The fallen condition *is* "complex society," "false needs," and so on. The issue is not how to avoid *amour-propre* or the fallen condition entirely, but how to cope with it and mitigate its more deleterious effects.

41. Starobinski, *Jean-Jacques Rousseau*, pp. 16, 21; Shklar, *Men and Citizens*, pp. 28, 29.

42. "Lettre à Voltaire," *O. c.*, iv, 1061.

43. "Lettre à Voltaire," *O. c.*, iv, 1061. As we will see in chapter 6, Voltaire, among others, maintained that Rousseau was a misanthrope. Rousseau, in turn, claimed that his social criticism was motivated by his love of humanity. In his *Letter to d'Alembert*, Rousseau was no doubt thinking of himself as he defended the character of Molière's misanthrope, Alceste: "Who, then, is the misanthrope of Molière? A good man who detests the morals [*les moeurs*] of his age and the maliciousness of his contemporaries; who, precisely because he loves his fellow creatures, hates in them the evils they do to one another and the vices of which these evils are the outcome. If he were less touched by the errors of humanity, less indignant regarding the iniquities he sees, would he be more humane himself?" (*Lettre à M. d'Alembert*, p. 97; *Politics and the Arts*, p. 37).

44. *O. c.*, i, 64; *Confessions*, p. 69. Immediately preceding this declaration Rousseau wrote, "Virtue is an effort to us only through our own fault. . . . Inclinations that are easily surmounted irresistibly ensnare us. . . . Insensibly we fall into perilous situations." These ironic statements express both our power and our powerlessness, and the ambiguous culpability that lies between the two.

45. See, for example, *Emile*, p. 54–55; *O. c.*, iv, 270.

46. See *O. c.*, i, 18–21; *Confessions*, pp. 28–31.

47. Cranston, *Jean-Jacques*, pp. 33–34.

48. See *Confessions*, pp. 29–30; *O. c.*, i, 18–19. It was once suggested to me that the drying process itself broke the comb.

49. See for example, "Notes to *Les confessions*," *O. c.*, i, 1244, by Bernard Gagnebin and Marcel Raymond.

50. *O. c.*, i, 21; *Confessions*, pp. 30–31.

Chapter 6

1. See, for example, Ernst Cassirer, *The Question of Jean-Jacques Rousseau*, trans. Peter Gay (New Haven, Conn.: Yale University Press, 1989), pp. 72–77; Jean Starobinski, *Jean-Jacques Rousseau*, p. 295; Frederick M. Barnard, *Self-Direction and Political Legitimacy* (Oxford: Clarendon, 1988), p. 23; John Hope Mason, "Individuals in Society: Rousseau's Republican Vision," *History of Political Thought* 10 (1989): 90.

2. Cassirer, *The Philosophy of the Enlightenment*, p. 141.

3. For a superb exposition of evil and original sin as they appear in Kant's work, see Gordon Michalson, *Fallen Freedom* (Cambridge: Cambridge University Press, 1990), chaps. 2, 3. Michalson's treatment of Kant and original sin has greatly informed my own approach to Rousseau and the same issue.

4. This is not to deny that there is a conceptual and material relation between the Christian, linear view of history and Western notions of progress. In fact, some Christian traditions subscribe to postmillennialism, that is, the view that the world will enjoy a thousand-year reign of peace and justice before the return of Christ. Moreover, there are Christian perfectionist lines of thought that stand at odds with Augustinian pessimism. The more dominant Christian position, however, ascribes a deeply fallen condition to a world that cannot experience redemption until the end of time.

5. See Plato, *Phaedrus*, trans. W. C. Helmbold and W. G. Rabinowitz (Indianapolis, Ind.: Bobbs-Merrill, 1977), p. 38.

6. I have found Keohane's *Philosophy and the State in France* most useful for tracing Augustine's impact on French thought. I have also benefited greatly from Keohane's account of the sixteenth-century French humanists. See especially pp. 183–237 and 83–116.

7. Saint-Cyran, *Oeuvres chrestiennes et spirituelles*, as noted by Alexander Sedgwick, *Jansenism in Seventeenth-Century France* (Charlottesville: University of Virginia Press, 1977).

8. See Keohane, *Philosophy and the State of France*, p.191.

9. François Rabelais, *Oeuvres complètes*, ed. Jacques Boulenger and Lucien Scheler (Paris: Gallimard, 1962), chs. LIII-LVII.

10. Etienne La Boétie, *Oeuvres complètes*, ed. Paul Bonnefon (Geneva: Slatkine Reprints, 1967), p. 29.

11. As early as 1738, in a poem written at Les Charmettes and titled "Le Verger de Madame la Baronne de Warens," Rousseau referred to how he would spend his days in the company of—that is reading—Montaigne and Pascal, among others. See *Correspondance générale de J. J. Rousseau*, ed. Théophile Dufour and Pierre-Paul Plan (Paris: Armand Colin, 1924), pp. 358, 363.

12. Montaigne, "Of Vanity," *Complete Essays*, p. 731.

13. Voltaire, "Sur les *Pensées de M. Pascal*," in *Lettres Philosophiques*, ed. F. A. Taylor (Oxford: Blackwell, 1958), p. 94.

14. Pascal, *Pensées*, pp. 198–99 (no. 434).

15. Michalson, *Fallen Freedom*, pp. 15 and 48.

16. "Lettre à Christophe de Beaumont," O. c., iv., 937–38, 935–36, 969–70.

17. "Lettres à Malesherbes," O. c., i, 1136. "Man being good, men become wicked" is how Rousseau expressed a similar idea to Beaumont (O. c., iv, 937).

18. O. c., i, 389; *Confessions*, p. 362. In *Emile* Rousseau lamented, "It is the abuse of our faculties that renders us unhappy and wicked. Our sorrows, our cares, our sufferings come from ourselves" (O. c., iv, 587; *Emile*, p. 244).

19. Richard Rorty, *Contingency, Irony, and Solidarity*, p. 3.

20. "Lettre à Christophe de Beaumont," O. c., iv., 936.

21. "Lettre à Victor Riquetti, marquis de Mirabeau," 26 July 1767, *Correspondance complète*, vol. 33, p. 239.

22. *Lettre à M. d'Alembert*, p. 58; *Politics and the Arts*, p. 11.

23. "Lettre à Deschamps," 8 May 1761," *Correspondance complète*, vol. 8, p. 320. "We have got on to slippery ice," Ludwig Wittgenstein wrote, "where there is no friction and so in a certain sense the conditions are ideal, but also, just because of that, we are unable to walk. We want to walk: so we need *friction*. Back to the rough ground!" (*Philosophical Investigations*, trans. G. E. M. Anscombe [New York: Macmillan, 1953], no. 107).

24. "Lettre à Victor Riquetti, marquis de Mirabeau," 26 July 1767, *Correspondance complète*, vol. 33, p. 239–40. Rousseau quoted Ovid in the original Latin, "Video meliora proboque, deteriora sequor" (*Metamorphoses*, VII, 20–21). Compare this with Saint Paul, "I do not understand my own actions. For I do not do what I want, but I do the very thing I hate. . . . I can will what is right, but I cannot do it. For I do not do the good I want, but the evil I do not want is what I do" (Romans 7:15, 18–19; Revised Standard Version [Philadelphia: Westminter, 1946]). Along similar lines, see Augustine, *On Nature and Grace*, in *Nicene and Post-Nicene Fathers*, ed. Philip Schaff (Grand Rapids, Mich.: Eerdmans, 1971), vol. 5, ch. 61 [LIII], p. 142.

25. O. c., iv, 584; *Emile*, p. 279.

26. O. c., iv, 287; *Emile*, p. 66. Augustine, *Confessions*, ed. R. S. Pine-Coffin (New York: Penguin, 1978), book 1, chap. 6, 7, pp. 24–28.

27. In chapter 2 we observed that the Solitaires cannot be considered fully human. In his "Lettre à Christophe de Beaumont," for example, immediately after stating that the Solitaire

"neither hates or loves anything," Rousseau went on to say, "he is limited to physical instincts alone, he is nothing, he is animal" (iv., O. c., 936).

28. Rousseau often referred to the limits of the voice of conscience as a moral guide; to Archbishop Beaumont, for example, he noted that "conscience, weaker than excited passions, is suffocated by them and is stuck in humans' mouths only as a word made for mutual deceit" ("Lettre à Christophe de Beaumont," O. c., iv., 937).

29. O. c., i, 247; Confessions, 235.

30. His other hope, which we will explore in part II, was that society itself be reformed and thereby produce relatively virtuous citizens.

31. Reinhold Niebuhr, a prominent twentieth-century American theologian and public philosopher, had claimed in Moral Man and Immoral Society that "in every human group there is less reason to guide and check impulse, less capacity for self-transcendence, less ability to comprehend the needs of others and therefore more unrestrained egoism than the individuals, who compose the group, reveal in their personal relationships" (New York: Scribner's, 1960), pp. xi–xii.

32. Starobinski, Jean-Jacques Rousseau, p. 295.

33. Ronald Grimsley, Rousseau's Religious Thought (Oxford: Oxford University Press, 1970), p. 64.

34. Starobinski, Jean-Jacques Rousseau, pp. 295, 294.

35. See Emile, p. 54–56; O. c., iv, 269–72.

36. O. c., iv, 272; Emile, p. 23.

37. Gottfried Wilhelm Leibniz, Theodicy, ed. A. Farrer (New Haven: Yale University Press, 1952); Alexander Pope, An Essay on Man, in The Poetry of Pope, ed. M. H. Abrams (Arlington Heights, Ill.: AMH, 1954).

38. Pope, An Essay on Man, p. 56, epistle I, lines 289–95.

39. Voltaire, "Poème sur le désastre de Lisbonne, ou examen de cet axiome, Tout est bien," in Œuvres complètes de Voltaire, vol. 1 Poésies (Paris: Delangle Frères, 1828), pp. 239, 246.

40. See Charles Bonnet, "Lettre de M. Philopolis," O. c., iii,1383–84. Bonnet published his letter to Rousseau under the pseudonym Philopolis in the Mercure de France in October 1755 (Alexander Pope, Essay on Man, Epistle I, line 237). See also Arthur Lovejoy, The Great Chain of Being (Cambridge, Mass.: Harvard University Press, 1936).

41. In "Rousseau at the Crossroads," earlier in this chapter, optimism referred to Enlightenment hope in knowledge and progress; in this section, optimism refers to the theological position, "All that is, is good."

42. "Letter à Philopolis," O. c., iii, 234.

43. "Letter à Philopolis," O. c., iii, 235.

44. "Lettre à Voltaire," O. c., iv, 1068. It is perhaps worth noting that in this passage "our pains" [maux] could be rendered as our particular "evils." It is more common in French than in English to speak of evil in the plural. In both languages there are, however, some similar usages, for example, "choose the least of two evils" [de deux maux il faut choisir le moindre], or "to dodge the evils of life" [éviter les maux de la vie].

45. "Lettre à Voltaire," O. c., iv, 1068. "Au lieu de Tout est bien, il vaudroit peut être mieux dire: Le tout est bien, ou Tout est bien pour le tout."

46. Rousseau spoke more confidently in Emile, where, sounding a lot like Hume's Cleanthes in the Dialogues on Natural Religion, ed. Richard H. Popkin (Indianapolis, Ind.: Hacket, 1985), Rousseau professed that "general evil can only be in disorder, and I see in the system of the world an unfailing order" (O. c., iv., p. 588; Emile, p. 282).

47. Rousseau was aware that if nothing definitive could be established about general evil, then the same holds true of general good. He claimed that "one does not prove the existence of God by the system of Pope, but the system of Pope by the existence of God," and moreover, that

the existence of God is "not something that can be demonstrated." Some try to coerce belief, saying, "You should believe this, because I believe it." Yet that approach is clearly irreligious. Others, like the philosophers, attempt to advance definitive arguments for or against belief in providence. Yet the "sentiments" that support religious belief cannot be verified by proofs. In chapter 10 we will have an opportunity to explore in detail Rousseau's religious philosophy, especially as it pertains to the relation between the public and private life. For now I will simply note that Rousseau was content to believe in the existence of a benevolent God, and he offered to Voltaire a rather pragmatic reason for his belief: "That optimism that you [Voltaire], find so cruel, consoles me yet in regard to the same miseries that you described to me as insufferable. The poem of Pope eases my pain and brings me patience" (*O. c.*, iv., 1060). Rousseau concluded his letter to Voltaire with an ardent apologetic: "I have suffered too much in this life not to look forward to another one. All the subtleties of metaphysics will not make me doubt for a moment the immortality of the soul and a benevolent Providence. I feel it, I believe it, I want it, I hope for it, I will defend it until my last breath" (*O. c.*, iv., 1075).

48. See, "Letter à Voltaire," *O. c.*, iv., 1067.

49. Jean-Pierre Dupuy has made a similar argument about the role of theodicy in the thought of Adam Smith: "In Smith's system it is not mankind that is utilitarian, there being someone else to assume this role on its behalf: God. Instead of simply enlightening men, reason works in devious ways and harnesses nature to its ends" (Jean-Pierre Dupuy, "A Reconsideration of *Das Adam Smith Problem*," *Stanford French Review* 17 [1993]: 55).

50. Here Rousseau followed Nicolas de Malebranche, who held that God permits "the ruins of a house to fall on a just person who is going to assist an unfortunate one, as well as on a rogue who is going to cut the throat of a person of means" (*Méditations chrétiennes et métaphysiques*, in *Oeuvres complètes de Malebranche*, vol. 10, p. 39). Lest someone question God's goodness in the face of such random tragedies, Rousseau immediately restated his belief in "the immortality of the soul." Presumably, God can compensate such unfortunate individuals. In Rousseau's view, then, Providence and the afterlife are deeply and conveniently related. In *Emile*, Rousseau wrote, "If the soul is immaterial . . . if it survives the body, Providence is justified. If I had no other proof of the immateriality of the soul than the triumph of the wicked and the oppression of the just in this world, that alone would prevent me from doubting it" (*O. c.*, iv., 589; *Emile*, p. 245). Kant was impressed by this argument. What of "eternal punishment"? "None thinking well of God would ever believe in that" ("Lettre à Voltaire," *O. c.*, iv., 1070).

51. See "Lettre à Voltaire," *O. c.*, iv., 1068–69.

52. *O. c.*, iv., 587 and 588; *Emile*, p. 244.

53. See *O. c.*, iv., 587; *Emile*, pp. 243–44.

54. In *Julie, or the New Eloise*, St. Preux tries to show "the origin of physical evil in the nature of matter, and of moral evil in the liberty of man" (*La Nouvelle Héloise*, *O. c.*, ii., 595).

55. *O. c.*, iv., 588; *Emile*, pp. 244 and 245. Emphasis added.

56. Kant, *Werke*, ed. Gustav Hartenstein (Leipzig, 1867–1868), vol. 8, p. 630; cited in Ernst Cassirer, *The Philosophy of the Enlightenment*, pp. 153–54.

57. Yet, see Gordon Michalson's excellent work, *Fallen Freedom*, pp. 53–69, for a more nuanced and novel view of Kant, freedom, and radical evil, as found in Kant's *Religion within the Limits of Reason Alone*.

58. See Cassirer, *The Philosophy of the Enlightenment*, pp. 154–57, or Cassirer, *The Question of Jean-Jacques Rousseau*, pp. 72–77.

59. *View of Lisbon*, tile frieze from the first quarter of the eighteenth century, Museu Nacional do Azulego, Lisbon.

60. See "Inequality," p. 89; *O. c.*, iii, 168–69.

61. See "Lettre à Voltaire," *O. c.*, iv, 1062–63.

62. Starobinski, *Jean-Jacques Rousseau*, pp. 20–21.

63. "Lettre à Voltaire," *O. c.*, iv, 1074.

64. See, for example, *O. c.*, iv, 588; *Emile*, p. 244.

65. See "Lettre à Voltaire," *O. c.*, iv, 1075, and *O. c.*, iv, 589–90; *Emile*, p. 283.

66. See, for example, Pascal, *Pensées*, pp. 216-17 (nos. 473-476).

67. "Inequality," p. 76; *O. c.*, iii, 156.

68. This is precisely the issue Voltaire would later raise in *Candide*, when Pangloss and Candide, reflecting on human misery, ask the best philosopher in Turkey "why such a strange animal as man had been formed" (*Œuvres complètes de Voltaire*, ed. Theodore Besterman [Oxford: Voltaire Foundation, 1980], vol. 48, p. 257); and *Candide*, trans. Robert M. Adams, in *The Norton Anthology of World Masterpieces* [New York: Norton, 1979], p. 299).

69. "Lettre à Voltaire," *O. c.*, iv, 1063. Yet for Rousseau's own belief in such compensation, see note 41.

70. Gerard Manley Hopkins, "God's Grandeur," in *The Norton Anthology of Poetry*, ed. Alexander Allison et al. (New York: Norton, 1975), p. 424. Compare to Rousseau, "Lettre à Voltaire," *O. c.*, iv, 1063, 1067-68.

71. *O. c.*, iv., 587; *Emile*, p. 244.

72. Michael Walzer, *Exodus and Revolution* (New York: Basic Books, 1985); see pp. 16, 135-41, 144-49.

73. Rousseau, however, occasionally found himself mildly attracted to the despotic solution. In his letter of 26 July 1767 to Mirabeau, for example, he confessed that because it is impossible to establish a rational government that puts "the law above man," "it is necessary to move to the other extreme and immediately put the man as high above the law as possible, thus establishing arbitrary despotism, and the most arbitrary possible: I would like that the despot could be God." Yet a few lines further Rousseau exclaimed, "But the Caligulas, the Neros, the Tiberiuses? My God! I wallow in the dirt, and lament being a man" ("Lettre à Victor Riquetti, marquis de Mirabeau," 26 July 1767, *Correspondance complète*, vol. 33, p. 240).

74. This general claim will be qualified in part II, where I will argue, for example, that even the public path exhibits aspects of Augustinian pessimism and, conversely, the private path exhibits aspects of Enlightenment optimism.

75. Rousseau told the Prince of Württemberg in 1764, "My letter gave birth to *Candide*; *Candide* was his answer to it. I wanted to philosophize with Voltaire; in return he made fun of me" (MS R285, f. 123, Bibliothèque Publique et Universitaire, Neuchâtel; cited in, and translated by, Cranston, *The Noble Savage*, p. 31). See also *Confessions*, p. 400; *O. c.*, i, 430.

76. "Il faut cultiver notre jardin," *Œuvres complètes de Voltaire*, vol. 48, p. 260; *Candide*, p. 301.

Chapter 7

1. *Lettre à M. d'Alembert*, p. 249; *Politics and the Arts*, p. 136. Even in *Emile*, Rousseau claimed that the "purest pleasures" are those enjoyed in common rather than appropriated solely for oneself. See *O. c.*, iv, 689–90; *Emile*, pp. 353-55.

2. See *O. c.*, iii, 966; *The Government of Poland* (henceforth referred to as *Poland*), p. 19.

3. See *O. c.*, iii, 959-60; *Poland*, pp. 10-11.

4. "You cannot defend yourselves from those who attack you. . . . Keep your liberty alive in its only and true sanctuary, which is the hearts of the Poles" (*O. c.*, iii, 1013; *Poland*, p. 80).

5. See, for example, *O. c.*, iv, 962; *Poland*, p. 14.

6. Although Rousseau wrote to d'Alembert that outsiders always "do more harm than good," he recognized the usefulness of outsiders; they contribute to the identity of the insiders. The "harm" of outsiders occurs when they infiltrate, or worst, when they emerge from within, and

hence Rousseau's abiding fear of secondary groups (*Lettre à M. d'Alembert*, p. 243; *Politics and the Arts*, p. 132).

7. We will encounter a variety of Rousseau's notions of peace and freedom in the following pages. I should mention now, however, a notion of peace that occurs early in *Poland* and elsewhere. When Rousseau wrote, "Peace and freedom are incompatible," peace refers to a preference for languid inactivity over the strenuous activity required to secure freedom (O. *c.*, iii, 955; *Poland*, p. 3).

8. *Lettre à M. d'Alembert*, p. 221; *Politics and the Arts*, p. 117.

9. *Lettre à M. d'Alembert*, p. 50; *Politics and the Arts*, p. 7.

10. *Lettre à M. d'Alembert*, p. 43; *Politics and the Arts*, p. 3.

11. See title page, *Politics and the Arts*.

12. I should note, however, that both the *Letter to M. d'Alembert* and "Political Economy" acknowledge the value of the private life, even if the public is elevated considerably above it. Although these two texts often recommend the extreme public path, they portray some relation between the public and private, as well as between a related dichotomy, that of country and humanity. *Poland* alone systematically silences the private life and places country above humanity.

13. "Du Bonheur public," O. *c.*, iii, 510–11.

14. O. *c.*, iii, 259; "Political Economy," p. 147.

15. O. *c.*, iii, 251–52; "Political Economy," p. 139.

16. O. *c.*, iii, 259; "Political Economy," p. 148.

17. O. *c.*, iii, 381; *The Social Contract*, p. 214.

18. Judith Shklar, *Ordinary Vices* (Cambridge, Mass.: Harvard University Press, 1984), p. 231.

19. *Lettre à M. d'Alembert*, p. 209; *Politics and the Arts*, p. 109.

20. O. *c.*, iii, 956–57; *Poland*, p. 6.

21. O. *c.*, iii, 953; *Poland*, p. 1. A similar pragmatic sensibility is found in his *Letter to M. d'Alembert*: "One must not search among us for what is good for men in general, but what is good for them in this time or that country" (*Lettre à M. d'Alembert*, p. 67; *Politics and the Arts*, p. 17).

22. "Fragments politiques," O. *c.*, iii, 486.

23. O. *c.*, iii, 966; *Poland*, p. 19.

24. O. *c.*, iii, 261, 260; "Political Economy," pp. 149, 148.

25. O. *c.*, iii, 965; *Poland*, p. 18.

26. See also *Letter to M. d'Alembert*, where Rousseau claimed that "morals and justice are not regulated . . . by edicts and laws; or, if sometimes the laws influence morals, it is when the laws take their force from them. In this case, they return to morals this same force by a sort of reaction" (*Lettre à M. d'Alembert*, 143; *Politics and the Arts*, p. 66).

27. *Lettre à M. d'Alembert*, p. 144; *Politics and the Arts*, p. 67. See also pp. 148 and 74 (pp. 22 and 69, English edition) for Rousseau's discussion of the power of the "empire of opinion" and the necessity of government learning how to control it.

28. O. *c.*, iii, 958; *Poland*, p. 8.

29. O. *c.*, iii, 957; *Poland*, p. 7.

30. *Poland*, p. xv.

31. O. *c.*, iii, 464; *Social Contract*, p. 303.

32. Of Locke, for example, Rousseau complained, "To reason with children was Locke's great maxim; it is the most in vogue today. It seems to me, however, that its success does not warrant its popularity. . . . Of all human faculties, reason, which is in fact a compound of all the others, develops last and with the most difficulty, and yet it is this that we want to use to develop

the first faculties. The greatest work of a good education is to form a reasonable human; and we pretend to educate a child by means of reason" (O. c., iv, 317; *Emile*, p. 89).

33. "Fragments politiques," *O. c.*, iii, 554.

34. *O. c.*, iii, 966; *Poland*, p. 19.

35. For a good discussion on redirected *amour-propre*, see Gauthier, "Politics of Redemption," pp. 341–42, and Shklar, *Men and Citizens*, p. 16. Unlike Gauthier and Shklar, I do not believe that redirected *amour-propre* is a feature of the moderate path, that is, of *The Social Contract*. I will argue in chapter 10 that while redirected *amour-propre* belongs on the extreme path, extended *amour de soi* characterizes the moderate path.

36. *O. c.*, iii, 255; "Political Economy," p. 142.

37. This sentiment, I should note, it not unique to the extreme public path of *Poland*. For example, in *Emile*, a book dedicated to the creation of, to use Kierkegaard's expression, "that single individual," Rousseau stated that "every particular society, when it is narrow and well unified, alienates itself from the larger society. Every patriot is harsh to foreigners. . . . This drawback is inevitable yet slight. The essential thing is to be good to the people with whom one lives" (O. c., iv, 248–49; *Emile*, p. 39).

38. Rousseau shared this aim with Henri d'Aguesseau, who, in his "L'Amour de la patrie," argued that "the love of country becomes a species of *amour-propre*. One loves oneself truly in loving the republic, and finally comes to love it more than oneself" (Henri d'Aguesseau, *Oeuvres complètes*, ed. M. Pardessus [Paris: Chez Lefèvre, 1819], i, 229).

39. *O. c.*, iii, 1019; *Poland*, p. 87.

40. *O. c.*, iii, 1019; *Poland*, p. 87.

41. *O. c.*, iii, 974; *Poland*, pp. 29–30.

42. See, for example, Kendall's introduction to *Poland*, p. xxxii.

43. I discuss social justice on the extreme public path at the conclusion of this chapter.

44. Montesquieu, *L'Esprit des lois*, in *Oeuvres complètes*, ii, 267.

45. *Lettre à M. d'Alembert*, pp. 67, 66; *Politics and the Arts*, pp. 17, 16.

46. *Lettre à M. d'Alembert*, pp. 66, 129; *Politics and the Arts*, pp. 16, 58.

47. See, for example, *O. c.*, iii, 254, 261; "Political Economy," pp. 142, 150.

48. See *Lettre à M. d'Alembert*, pp. 130–32 ; *Politics and the Arts*, pp. 58–59.

49. *Lettre à M. d'Alembert*, pp. 233–34; *Politics and the Arts*, pp. 125–26.

50. *O. c.*, iii, 958; *Poland*, p. 9.

51. *Lettre à M. d'Alembert*, p. 110; *Politics and the Arts*, p. 45.

52. Amy Gutmann, *Democratic Education* (Princeton: Princeton University Press, 1987), pp. 14–15, 257, 287.

53. See Benjamin Constant, *Political Writings*, ed. B. Fontana (Cambridge: Cambridge University Press, 1988), pp. 320–28.

54. For an example of such a moral division of labor, see Mark Cladis, "Provinces of Ethics," *Interpretation* 17 (1989–1990): 255–73.

55. *O. c.*, iii, 246; "Political Economy," p. 133.

56. *O. c.*, iii, 246; "Political Economy," p. 133; emphasis added.

57. See *O. c.*, iii, 246; "Political Economy," p. 133.

58. *O. c.*, iv, 698; *Emile*, p. 361.

59. *O. c.*, iv, 705; *Emile*, p. 366.

60. *Lettre à M. d'Alembert*, pp. 168, 113; *Politics and the Arts*, pp. 82, 47.

61. *O. c.*, iv, 693; *Emile*, p. 358.

62. Zillah Eisenstein, *The Radical Future of Liberal Feminism* (New York: Longman, 1981), p. 55ff. I have learned much from Eisenstein's good account of Rousseau's patriarchal vision of the dependent woman and independent man. My chief complaint, however, is that she focuses

exclusively on the individualistic aspects of Rousseau's thought, thereby ignoring its communitarian features.

63. Eisenstein, *The Radical Future of Liberal Feminism*, pp. 74, 77, and 82. Although I disagree with Eisenstein's assessment of Rousseau, I have gained much from her excellent discussion of the emergence of eighteenth-century market capitalism and its relation to women's oppressive confinement to the home.

64. *O. c.*, iii, 706.

65. See Shklar, *Men and Citizens*, p. 5.

66. Maurizio Viroli, *For Love of Country: An Essay on Patriotism and Nationalism* (Princeton: Princeton University Press, 1995).

67. *Pace* Shklar, *Men and Citizens*, p. 102.

68. *O. c.*, iii, 1009, 1024, 1025; *Poland*, pp. 74, 94, 95.

69. *Lettre à M. d'Alembert*, p. 100; *Politics and the Arts*, p. 39.

70. *O. c.*, iii, 262, 258, 276, 272; "Political Economy," p. 151, 146, 165, 161.

71. See, for example, Eisenstein, *The Radical Future of Liberal Feminism*, p. 80; and Barbara Corrado Pope, "The Influence of Rousseau's Ideology of Domesticity," p. 140.

72. See *O. c.*, iv, 693; *Emile*, p. 358.

73. *O. c.*, iv, 584; *Emile*, p. 279.

74. On occasion Rousseau wrote as if the fundamental conflict is between unnatural, artificial society and the natural, unadorned individual; I have argued, however, that this famous contrast is more of a caricature than a intricate portrait of his work. In any case, our interest lies chiefly in those genuine, yet often conflicting, goods that we identify with the public and private life.

75. John Hallowell, *Main Currents in Modern Political Thought* (New York: Holt, 1950), p. 173.

Chapter 8

1. Rousseau held as a dogma the belief that the just will suffer in society, for the sensibility of the just will inevitably offend society.

2. Conversely, in a state with a flourishing, just public life, the importance of the private life diminishes. Hence in *The Social Contract* Rousseau claimed that "the better the state is constituted, the more public affairs encroach on the private. . . . The sum of common happiness furnishes a greater proportion compared to the happiness of each individual alone, so that he has less need to seek happiness in private" (*O. c.*, iii, 429; *Social Contract*, p. 266).

3. Rousseau held the view that those who are sincere and candid, who are not manipulative and calculating, will inevitably be treated cruelly by the public. See, for example, *Confessions*, p. 214; *O. c.*, i, 223.

4. See *Emile and Sophie, or the Solitaires*, the sequel to *Emile* (*O. c.*, iv, 885).

5. I discuss these two paths in detail in the following two chapters.

6. Rousseau was banned from Geneva in 1762 due to the publication of *Emile* and *The Social Contract*.

7. For this reason Emile is raised to be self-possessed under any social conditions, for the assumption is that Emile will not find "a country where one is always permitted to be a honest man." Hence, Emile is prepared for the "inevitable unhappiness" of living in a corrupt society and is ready to submit himself to this "law of necessity." See *Emile*, pp. 457–58; *O. c.*, iv, 835–36.

8. *O. c.*, i, 1015; *Reveries*, p. 52.

9. *O. c.*, i, 1015; *Reveries*, p. 52.

10. See *Confessions*, pp. 555, 579, and 586; *O. c.*, i, 601, 627, 634–35.

11. *O. c.*, i, 1042; *Reveries*, p. 83.

12. *O. c.*, i, 638; *Confessions*, p. 589.

13. *O. c.*, i, 646; *Confessions*, p. 596.

14. *O. c.*, i, 1046; *Reveries*, p. 88.

15. *O. c.*, i, 1079; *Reveries*, p. 129.

16. *O. c.*, iv, 307, 308, 310; *Emile*, pp. 83, 84.

17. *O. c.*, i, 1080; *Reveries*, p. 130.

18. I am referring to the second "letter" of *Emile and Sophie, or the Solitaires* (*O. c.*, iv, 916–17). After abandoning Sophie in Paris, Emile heads to Naples. His ship is attacked by pirates, he is sold into slavery, and he discovers true freedom in having become a "slave to necessity."

19. *O. c.*, i, 1081; *Reveries*, p. 131.

20. *O. c.*, iv, 307; *Emile*, p. 83.

21. *O. c.*, iv, 305; *Emile*, p. 81.

22. *O. c.*, iv, 308; *Emile*, p. 83.

23. *O. c.*, iv, 488; *Emile*, p. 208.

24. *O. c.*, iv, 307–8, 814; *Emile*, pp. 83, 442.

25. *O. c.*, i, 1081–82; *Reveries*, p. 132.

26. *O. c.*, i, 1082; *Reveries*, p. 132.

27. *O. c.*, iv, 340; *Emile*, p. 105.

28. *O. c.*, iv, 820; *Emile*, p. 446.

29. *O. c.*, i, 587; *Confessions*, p. 542.

30. *O. c.*, i, 533; *Confessions*, p. 493.

31. *O. c.*, i, 503; *Confessions*, p. 466. His success at this attempt was mixed.

32. *Julie, O. c.*, ii, 531.

33. John Milton, *Paradise Lost*, in *John Milton: Complete Poems and Major Prose*, ed. Merritt Y. Hughes (Indianapolis: Bobbs-Merrill, 1957), p. 280.

34. *O. c.*, i, 644; *Confessions*, p. 594.

35. *O. c.*, i, 1083; *Reveries*, pp. 133, 134.

36. Ralph Waldo Emerson, *Nature and Other Writings*, ed. Peter Turner (Boston: Shambhala), p. 10; *O. c.*, iv, 431; *Emile*, p. 169.

37. "I know no study in the world which matches better my natural tastes than that of plants, and the life that I have been leading for the last ten years in the country has been hardly anything but one continual botanization" (*O. c.*, i, 180; *Confessions*, p. 175).

38. For a discussion of this theme, see chapter 1.

39. *O. c.*, i, 1069; *Reveries*, p. 116.

40. *O. c.*, i, 1069; *Reveries*, p. 116.

41. Rousseau had St. Preux put it like this: "I have always believed that the good is only beauty put in action, that the one is intimately attached to the other, and that both have a common source in nature well ordered" (*Julie, O. c.*, ii, 59).

42. *Lettre à M. d'Alembert*, p. 76; *Politics and the Arts*, p. 23.

43. *O. c.*, i, 642; *Confession*, p. 593. See also, *Lettres à Malesherbes, O. c.*, i, 1141.

44. Robert Frost, "Directive," *Steeple Bush* (New York: Holt, 1947).

45. *O. c.*, i, 1005; *Reveries*, p. 39.

46. *O. c.*, i, 1062–63; *Reveries*, p. 108.

47. *O. c.*, i, 1065–66; *Reveries*, p. 111. For another example of Rousseau losing his self in the immensity of nature, see *Lettres à Malesherbes, O. c.*, i, 1141.

48. John Chapman, *Rousseau—Totalitarian or Liberal?* (New York: AMS, 1968), p. 33.

49. *O. c.*, iv, 348; *Emile*, p. 110.

50. *O. c.*, i, 404, 521; *Confessions*, pp. 376, 483.

51. See, for example, O. c., i, 394; *Confessions*, p. 368.

52. O. c., i, 278; *Confessions*, p. 262.

53. O. c., i, 88–89; *Confessions*, p. 90.

54. Rousseau confessed not only embarrassing details but also revealed, for example, how an innocent person lost her job due to his bold-faced lie, and how he placed his five children in the Foundling Hospital.

55. O. c., i, 175; *Confessions*, p. 169.

56. O. c., i, 162; *Confessions*, p. 158.

57. O. c., iii, 156; *Inequality*, p. 76.

58. O. c., i, 995; *Reveries*, p. 27.

59. O. c., i, 169; *Confessions*, p. 164.

60. O. c., i, 1089; *Reveries*, pp. 141–42.

61. *Rousseau juge de Jean-Jacques*, O. c., i, 794.

62. O. c., i, 1047; *Reveries*, p. 90.

63. O. c., i, 650; *Confessions*, p. 600.

64. O. c., i, 995; *Reveries*, p. 27.

65. Henry Thoreau, *Walden* (Roslyn, N.Y.: Black, 1942), p. 28.

66. I would not want this argument to defend the practice of solitary confinement. Like the private path itself it is a last resort, and a drastic one. It is a tragedy that some are compelled to take it. In the case of prisoners, it strikes me as a crime by our affluent society that the only time and place in their lives they can experience the necessary calm for self-reflection is in SHUs.

67. O. c., iv, 692; *Emile*, p. 357.

68. O. c., iv, 690; *Emile*, p. 354.

69. See *Confessions*, pp. 332–34; O. c., i, 356–58.

70. I wish neither to slight the complexities of Rousseau's handing over his children, nor to obfuscate the terrible deed in details. It was a relatively common practice, and Rousseau did constantly refer to it, usually while gnashing his teeth. Still, Rousseau deserves condemnation. No doubt the reasons for, as he put it, "trampling underfoot the dearest of obligations" are complex; yet I suspect that his fear of dependency and vulnerability were probably the main ones. Among other things, children would have required that he get a job and make some money, and he didn't want to have to "sell himself"; also, children would have made emotional demands of him that he dreaded.

71. O. c., i, 999; *Reveries*, p. 31.

72. O. c., iv, 503; *Emile*, p. 221.

73. "Lettre à Voltaire," O. c., iv, 1074.

74. O. c., iv, 654, 483–84; *Emile*, pp. 327, 205.

Chapter 9

1. O. c., i, 545; *Confessions*, p. 504.

2. See *Julie*, O. c., ii, 590–91.

3. For Rousseau's description of "Moral sensitive, ou le matérialism du sage," see *Confessions*, pp. 380–81; O. c., i, 408–9.

4. O. c., ii, 78–79; *Julie*, p. 66.

5. Ferdinand Tönnies, *Community and Society*, trans. Charles Loomis (New York: Harper, 1963).

6. For Rousseau's description of these mountain, social circles, see *Politics and the Arts*, pp. 99–113; *Lettre à M. d'Alembert*, pp. 193–214. These circles are among the few secondary groups of which Rousseau ever wrote approvingly. Although they inhabit a space between the public and private, Rousseau noted that they were "decent" and not "dangerous" because they

"neither wish to, nor can, hide that which is public" (*Lettre à M. d'Alembert*, p. 207; *Politics and the Arts*, p. 108).

7. *O. c.*, ii, 102; *Julie*, p. 83.

8. *O. c.*, ii, 168–69; *Julie*, pp. 137–38.

9. *O. c.*, ii, 200 ; *Julie*, p. 168.

10. *O. c.*, ii, 201; *Julie*, p. 169.

11. For a helpful account of how artifice works with nature in *Julie*, see Gauthier, "The Politics of Redemption," 331–33.

12. St. Preux's letter to Lord Bomston contains the most complete description of the changes; see *O. c.*, ii, 440–70; *Julie*, pp. 301–4. (The English edition is greatly abridged.)

13. *O. c.*, ii, 441–42; *Julie*, pp. 301–2.

14. *O. c.*, ii, 468; *Julie*, p. 302.

15. *O. c.*, ii, 470; *Julie*, p. 304.

16. See, for example, *Confessions*, p. 220; *O. c.*, i, 231.

17. *O. c.*, i, 354, 582; *Confessions*, pp. 330, 538.

18. *O. c.*, iv, 756; *Emile*, p. 400. See also *Emile*, p. 479; *O. c.*, iv, 866, where Rousseau states that when the romance between Emile and Sophie wanes, they will be friends.

19. "Letter to Mme D'Houdetot," *Correspondance complète*, iv, p. 394.

20. *O. c.*, iv, 683; *Emile*, pp. 348–49.

21. See *Confessions*, p. 551; *O. c.*, i, 597.

22. *O. c.*, i, 362; *Confessions*, p. 338.

23. Montaigne, *Complete Essays*, p. 139.

24. See Montaigne, *Complete Essays*, p. 138.

25. *O. c.*, ii, 91; *Julie*, p. 73.

26. Some feminist accounts argue that as God was a helper to Israel, so Eve was a helper to Adam—that is, as a leader and not a subordinate. See Phyllis Trible, "Eve and Adam: Genesis 2–3 Reread," in *Womenspirit Rising*, ed. Carol Christ and Judith Plaskow (New York: Harper and Row, 1979), p. 75.

27. *O. c.*, ii, 231; *Julie*, p. 196.

28. *O. c.*, ii, 235; *Julie*, p. 196.

29. *O. c.*, ii, 245; *Julie*, p. 201.

30. *Lettre à M. d'Alembert*, p. 66; *Politics and the Arts*, pp. 16–17.

31. *Lettre à M. d'Alembert*, p. 66; *Politics and the Arts*, p. 16.

32. Ironically, Clarens was also Rousseau's own escapist fantasy.

33. *Lettre à M. d'Alembert*, pp. 233–34; *Politics and the Arts*, p. 126.

34. *O. c.*, ii, 470–71; *Julie*, p. 304. For the full description of Julie's Elysium, her private garden, see *O. c.*, ii, 470–88; *Julie*, pp. 304–15.

35. *O. c.*, ii, 71–72; *Julie*, p. 305.

36. *O. c.*, ii, p. 474.

37. *O. c.*, ii, 478; *Julie*, p. 310.

38. *O. c.*, ii, 470; *Julie*, p. 304.

39. *Lettre à M. d'Alembert*, pp. 133–34; *Politics and the Arts*, pp. 60–61.

40. Letter to Monsieur Vernes, *Correspondance complète*, v, p. 65.

41. *O. c.*, ii, 745; *Julie*, p. 409.

Chapter 10

1. The following sketches of the extreme public and private paths are developed in chapter 7 and 8.

2. *O. c.*, iv, 628; *Emile*, p. 309.

3. Emile Durkheim, *Montesquieu and Rousseau: Forerunners of Sociology*, trans. Ralph Manheim (Ann Arbor: University of Michigan Press, 1960), p. 121.

4. O. c., iv, 534; *Emile*, p. 235.

5. For an example of the totalitarian interpretation, see the introduction by Ernest Barker, in Rousseau, *The Social Contract* (New York: Oxford University Press, 1948), pp. vii–xliv. For an example of the liberal interpretation, see David A. J. Richards, "Rights and Autonomy," *Ethics* 92 (1981): 3–20. Older scholarship and still many textbook accounts commonly pose an either/or fallacy—Rousseau the solitaire versus Rousseau the totalitarian. Happily, more recent secondary literature shows greater sophistication. See, for example, Tzvetan Todorov, *Frêle bonheur: Essai sur Rousseau* (Paris: Hachette, 1985); Alex Philonenko, *Jean-Jacques Rousseau et la pensée du malheur* (Paris: Vrin, 1984); the fine essays in *Rousseau and Liberty*, ed. Robert Wokler (Manchester, U.K.: Manchester University Press, 1995); and James Miller, *Rousseau: Dreamer of Democracy* (New Haven, Conn.: Yale University Press, 1984).

6. O. c., iii, 465; *Social Contract*, p. 304.

7. O. c., iii, 464; *Social Contract*, p. 303.

8. O. c., iii, 464; *Social Contract*, p. 303.

9. O. c., iii, 465; *Social Contract*, p. 304.

10. O. c., iii, 465; *Social Contract*, p. 304.

11. O. c., iii, 440; *Social Contract*, p. 277.

12. O. c., iii, 464–65 *Social Contract*, p. 303.

13. O. c., iii, 465; *Social Contract*, pp. 303–4.

14. O. c., iii, 467; *Social Contract*, p. 306. D'Argenson held several government offices in France, including counsellor to the parliament of Paris and minister of foreign affairs. Rousseau quoted from his manuscript, "Jusques où la démocratie peut être admise dans le gouvernment monarchique."

15. See *Social Contract*, pp. 307–8; O. c., iii, 468–69.

16. There are, of course, limits to this religious diversity: atheism—a view on religion if not a religious view—and religious fanaticism are not permitted. Rousseau did not ban atheists and religious fanatics "for impiety, but for being anti-social."

17. This interpretation is in contrast to Theodore Koontz's and Robert Linder's otherwise excellent work on Rousseau. See, Theodore J. Koontz, "Religion and Political Cohesion: John Locke and Jean Jacques Rousseau," *Journal of Church and State* 23 (1981): 95–115; and Robert D. Linder, "Civil Religion in Historical Perspective: The Reality That Underlies the Concept," *Journal of Church and State* 17 (1975): 399–421.

18. O. c., iii, 464; *Social Contract*, p. 303.

19. Rousseau was not opposed to every form of atheism. Rousseau offered, in the character of Wolmar, the atheist in *Julie*, the strongest eighteenth-century argument that an atheist could be moral: "Virtue is possible without God." But the godlike hero Wolmar rejects religion not because he is impious, but because his strict moral disposition could not tolerate religious hypocrisy.

20. In the *Confessions*, Rousseau recounted how the atheists despised him because he had religious beliefs, while the Jesuits persecuted him because they disagreed with his religious beliefs. He concluded, "Fanatical atheism and fanatical devoutness, touching each other by their common intolerance, can even unite. . . . Whereas a reasonable and ethical religion, rejecting all human power over consciences, deprives wielders of power all their resources" (O. c., i, 567; *Confessions*, p. 524).

21. O. c., iii, 753–54, *Lettres écrites de la montagne*.

22. O. c., iv, 602; *Emile*, p. 292. Rousseau was not alone in asserting that the "common center" belongs to God or the general good. Pascal wrote, "If the members of the natural and civic communities ought to tend toward the good of the body, then the communities themselves

should tend to another body, still more general, of which they are the members" (*Pensées*, no. 477).

23. *O. c.*, iv, 635; *Emile*, p. 313.

24. I write "the Jesus of *Emile*," and not the Jesus of *The Social Contract*, because in *The Social Contract* Jesus is portrayed as an otherworldly figure, and hence Christianity is not deemed a suitable religion for *citizens*, that is, for "the body politic" (see Rousseau, *O. c.*, iii, 464–67; *Social Contract*, 300–306).

25. Shklar, *Men and Citizens*, p. 5.

26. *O. c.*, iii, 468; *Social Contract*, 307.

27. This is essentially Emile Durkheim's definition of religion as found in Mark Cladis, ed., *The Elementary Forms of Religious Life* (Oxford: Oxford University Press, 2001), p. 46.

28. Shklar, *Men and Citizens*, p. 184.

29. See *The Social Contract*, pp. 190–91; *O. c.*, iii, 360–61.

30. *O. c.*, iii, 360; *Social Contract*, p. 191.

31. I Corinthians 12:7 RSV.

32. See 1 Corinthians 12:14–27 RSV.

33. See Pascal, *Pensées*, no. 473–83.

34. Nicolas Malebranche, *Traité de morale*, 11:31–32, and *Méditations chrétiennes et métaphysiques*, in *Oeuvres complètes* (Paris: Vrin, 1966).

35. Patrick Riley interprets Rousseau's general will as a distinctively French product, and he traces the transformation of Malebranche's theological notion of God's will governing *le bien général* to Rousseau's political *volonté générale*. I have greatly benefited from Riley's excellent work, *The General Will before Rousseau*.

36. *O. c.*, iv, 602; *Emile*, p. 292.

37. See Riley, *The General Will before Rousseau*, p. 249.

38. *O. c.*, iii, 351; *Social Contract*, p. 181.

39. "Réponse à M. D'Offreville," *Lettres philosophiques*, ed. Henri Gouhier (Paris: Vrin, 1974), 4 October 1761, no. 18, p. 71.

40. *O. c.*, iii, 286. This is the first version, or "the Geneva manuscript," of *The Social Contract*.

41. *O. c.*, iii, 373; *Social Contract*, p. 205.

42. *O. c.*, iii, 373; *Social Contract*, p. 205.

43. *O. c.*, iv, 937, *Lettre à Christopher de Beaumont*.

44. *O. c.*, iii, 288, first version of *The Social Contract*.

45. *O. c.*, iii, 371; *Social Contract*, p. 203.

46. When Rousseau offered genetic accounts of how society got started, he sometimes would speak of the important role of overlapping private interests. In the genetic account, this is an initial stage. In order for a society to move beyond this initial stage and become stable and moral, it must elect to pursue the general will, which is based on common, not private, interest (see for example, *The Social Contract*, p. 200; *O. c.*, iii, 368). As we will see shortly, for society to make this transition, something like the wise legislator is required.

47. *O. c.*, iii, 361; *Social Contract*, p. 192.

48. Romans 7:15, 18–19 RSV.

49. *O. c.*, iii, 381; *Social Contract*, p. 213.

50. *O. c.*, iii, 371; *Social Contract*, p. 203.

51. In the secondary material, the general will is usually described as being one way or the other, that is, as being either contingent or as necessary. Nannerl Keohane, for example, describes the general will as contingent upon voting (*Philosophy and the State in France*, p. 447). In contrast, F. M. Barnard argues that Rousseau's view of the general will wavers between being a matter of procedural rightness and transcendent rightness (*Self-Direction and Political Legitimacy*, p. 68).

52. O. c., iii, 441; *Social Contract*, p. 278.

53. O. c., iii, 371–72; *Social Contract*, pp. 203–4.

54. O. c., iii, 381; *Social Contract*, p. 214.

55. O. c., iii, 381; *Social Contract*, p. 214.

56. O. c., iii, 380; *Social Contract*, p. 213.

57. O. c., iii, 381; *Social Contract*, p. 213.

58. O. c., iii, 381; *Social Contract*, p. 213.

59. O. c., iii, 383; *Social Contract*, p. 215.

60. Cassirer, *The Question of Jean-Jacques Rousseau*, p. 76.

61. Lucien Scubla has argued that "les concepts de volonté générale et d'amour de soi . . . sont foncièrement du même ordre et presque identiques, puisque la volonté générale doit rétablir dans la cité les conditions même de l'état de nature où l'amour de soi l'emporte sur l'amour-propre" ("the concepts of the general will and *amour de soi* . . . are basically of the same order and are almost identical, since it falls to the general will to re-establish in the city the very con-ditions of the state of nature in which *l'amour de soi* prevails over *l'amour propre*"). From Lucien Scubla, "Est-il possible de mettre la loi au-dessus de l'homme?" in *Introduction aux science sociales: logique des phénomènes collectifs*, ed. Jean-Pierre Dupuy (Paris: Ellipses, 192), p. 114.

62. Both Judith Shklar and David Gauthier maintain the importance, for Rousseau, of a transformed *amour-propre* that supports public existence; neither specify the type of public exis-tence for which redirected *amour-propre* is appropriate. In other words, they do not distinguish between such types of public existence as what I have called the extreme public path and the middle way. See Gauthier, "The Politics of Redemption," pp. 341–42; and Shklar, *Men and Citizens*, p. 16.

63. Alfred Cobban, *The Crisis of Civilization* (London: J. Cape, 1941), p. 67; Robert Derathé, *Le rationalisme de J.-J. Rousseau* (Paris: Presses Universitaires de France, 1948), p. 167.

64. The destructive operations of *amour-propre* are analyzed in detail in chapters 3 and 4.

Chapter 11

1. Moreover, Rousseau occasionally employs the vocabulary of religion to express this ten-sion. See, for example, *The Social Contract*, p. 303; O. c., iii, 464.

2. "Rousseau à Comtesse de Wartensleben," 27 September 1766, *Correspondance complete*, vol. 30, letter 5450, pp. 384–86.

3. O. c., iii, 357; *Social Contract*, p. 187.

4. O. c., iii, 427; *Social Contract*, p. 263.

5. *Rousseau juge de Jean Jacques: dialogues*, O. c., i, 687.

6. O. c., iv, 455; *Emile*, p. 185.

7. *Projet de constitution pour la Corse*, O. c., iii, 931.

8. O. c., iii, 375, 467, 373; *Social Contract*, pp. 207, 306, 205.

9. O. c., iii, 467; *Social Contract*, p. 306.

10. See chapter 5 for a fuller treatment of the broken-comb incident.

11. Regrettably, Rousseau understood the proper use of freedom by women to be funda-mentally—and often oppressively—different from that exercised by men.

12. O. c., iv, 843; *Emile*, 462–63. Rousseau's précis of *The Social Contract* begins on O. c., iv, 836; *Emile*, 458.

13. O. c., iii, 364; *Social Contract*, p. 195.

14. See O. c., iii, 255; "Political Economy," p. 143.

15. O. c., iv, 248; *Emile*, p. 39.

16. O. c., iii, 706, *Lettres écrites de la montagne*.

17. O. c., iv, 520–21; *Emile*, p. 233.

18. O. c., iii, 246; "Political Economy," p. 133. Rousseau also feared that associations could accrue too much power; hence he insisted that "if there must be partial societies, have as many as possible to prevent them from being unequal" (O. c., iii, 372; *Social Contract*, p. 204).

19. Alasdair MacIntyre, *After Virtue* (Notre Dame: University of Notre Dame Press, 1981); Stanley Hauerwas, "Freedom of Religion: A Subtle Temptation," *Soundings* 72 (1989): 317–39.

20. O. c., iii, 437; *Social Contract*, p. 274.

21. O. c., iii, 439; *Social Contract*, p. 275.

22. O. c., iii, 439; *Social Contract*, p. 276.

23. O. c., iii, 394; *Social Contract*, p. 227.

24. Landes, "Rousseau's Reply to Public Women," p. 67. This line of thought is ably explored in Paul Thomas, "Jean-Jacques Rousseau, Sexist?" *Feminist Studies* 17 (1991): 195–217.

25. O. c., iii, 424; *Social Contract*, p. 260.

26. O, c., iii, 421; *Social Contract*, p. 257.

27. O. c., iii, 438; *Social Contract*, p. 275.

28. O. c., iii, 428; *Social Contract*, p. 265.

29. O. c., iii, 438; *Social Contract*, p. 275.

30. O. c., iv, 524–25; *Emile*, p. 236.

31. O. c., iv, 524; *Emile*, p. 235.

Conclusion

1. *Rousseau juge de Jean-Jacques*, O. c., i, 813. This follows his claiming "to know that absolute solitude is an unhappy state."

2. By "solitaires," I am not here referring to Rousseau's Garden creature—that hypothetical individual divorced from all sociolinguistic ties. I am referring, rather, to that reclusive (yet nonetheless sociolinguistically formed) individual described in chapter 8, "Evading the City: The Private Path."

3. Richard Rorty, *Contingency, Irony, and Solidarity* (Cambridge: Cambridge University Press, 1989), p. 83.

4. Rorty, *Contingency, Irony, and Solidarity*, pp. xiii–xiv.

5. Rorty, *Contingency, Irony, and Solidarity*, p. xiv.

6. Quoted by L. S. Klepp, "Philosopher-King," *New York Times Magazine*, 2 December 1990, 118.

7. Rorty, *Contingency, Irony, and Solidarity*, p. xiv.

8. Amartya Sen, "Individual Freedom as a Social Commitment," *New York Review of Books*, 14 June 1990, 49. Sen does not use this phrase in reference to Rousseau's position but to his own. For a similar effort to relate autonomy to social obligation, see Joseph Raz, *The Morality of Freedom* (Oxford: Oxford University Press, 1986).

9. Rorty, *Contingency, Irony, and Solidarity*, p. 92

10. Shklar, *Men and Citizens*, p. 194.

11. O. c., iii, 351; *Social Contract*, p. 181; *Lettres écrites de la montagne*, O. c., iii, 810. On the discrepancy between Rousseau's portrait of Geneva and the actual Geneva of the mid-eighteenth century, see Maurice Cranston, "Jean-Jacques Rousseau and the Fusion of Democratic Sovereignty with Aristocratic Government," *History of European Ideas* 11 (1989): 419.

12. *Fragments autobiographiques: mon portrait*, O. c., i, 1120.

13. In general, we should think of solitude as one form of the private life, and not as synonymous with it. For the Solitaires, however, the two—solitude and the private life—are one and the same.

14. I write here of how maximum-security prisons are designed to affect prisoners, and not of what individual prisoners have managed to accomplish in prisons. Moreover, prison reform

in the United States, especially in the aftermath of the Attica riots in 1971, brought prisoners some opportunities to shape and enhance their public and private lives. New religious freedoms granted to Muslim inmates, for example, have allowed them to observe dietary "restrictions" and holy days, to enjoy places designated for public and private prayer, and to form links with religious communities outside the prison. Such opportunities, however, are not universal, and they are subject to abrupt curtailment. Indeed, curtailment has become widespread at the turn of the century.

15. Again, I want to draw a distinction between the functions of prisons and what individual prisoners have managed to accomplish. Some prisoners have managed against all odds to cultivate both a vital private life and an engaged public life. For some, for example, a deep spirituality goes hand in hand with efforts to ameliorate prison life and to assist the outside communities from which they come.

16. Mark Cladis, *A Communitarian Defense of Liberalism*, pp. 3–5.

17. This, I take it, is the chief lesson from Judith Shklar's powerful defense of liberalism found in *Ordinary Vices*.

18. See chapter 9, "The Mountain Village: The Path to Family, Work, Community, and Love," for my description of Clarens.

19. See, for example, Karen V. Hansen, "Rediscovering the Social: Visiting Practices in Antebellum New England and the Limits of the Public/Private Dichotomy," pp. 268–302. In a summary statement, Hansen claims that "the historical evidence presented in this essay demonstrates how misleading gendered preconceptions [of current scholars] are—we find [in Antebellum New England] men involved in allegedly "private" and feminine activities, such as caring for the sick, and women out and about in the social sphere, hardly confined to their domiciles" (p. 292).

20. O. c., iv, 815–16, 818, 820; *Emile*, pp. 443–46.

21. O. c., iv, 858; *Emile*, p. 473.

22. William James, *Varieties of Religious Experience* (New York: Penguin 1985), pp. 85–165.

Works Cited

Aguesseau, Henri d'. "L'Amour de la patrie." In *Oeuvres complètes*, edited by M. Pardessus. Paris: Chez Lefèvre, 1819.

Arendt, Hannah. *The Human Condition*. Chicago: University of Chicago Press, 1958.

Augustine. *City of God*. In *St. Augustine: The Political Writings*, edited by Henry Paolucci. Washington, D.C.: Regnery Gateway, 1962.

——. *Confessions*. Edited by R. S. Pine-Coffin. New York: Penguin, 1978.

——. *On Nature and Grace*. In *Nicene and Post-Nicene Fathers*, edited by Philip Schaff. Grand Rapids, Ill.: Eerdmans, 1971.

Barker, Ernest. Introduction to *The Social Contract*, by Jean-Jacques Rousseau. New York: Oxford University Press, 1948.

Barnard, Frederick M. *Self-Direction and Political Legitimacy*. Oxford: Clarendon, 1988.

Benn, S. I., and G. F. Gaus. "The Public and the Private: Concepts and Action" and "The Liberal Conception of the Public and the Private." In *Public and Private in Social Life*, edited by Benn and Gaus. London: Croom Helm, 1983.

Bliven, Naomi. "Jean-Jacques: The Early Life and Work of Jean-Jacques Rousseau, 1712-1754." *New Yorker*, 4 July 1983, 89-90.

Camus, Jean-Pierre. *La Défense du pur amour contre les attaques de l'amour propre*. Paris: Henault, 1640.

Casanova, José. *Public Religion in the Modern World*. Chicago: Chicago University Press, 1994.

Cassirer, Ernst. *The Philosophy of the Enlightenment*. Translated by Fritz Koelln and James Pettegrove. Princeton, N.J.: Princeton University Press, 1968.

——. *The Question of Jean-Jacques Rousseau*. Translated by Peter Gay. New Haven, Conn.: Yale University Press, 1989.

Chapman, John. *Rousseau–Totalitarian or Liberal?* New York: AMS, 1968.

Cladis, Mark S. *A Communitarian Defense of Liberalism*. Stanford, Calif.: Stanford University Press, 1992.

——. *Durkheim and Foucault: Perspectives on Education and Punishment*. Oxford: Durkheim, 1999.

——. "On the Importance of Owning Chickens: Lessons in Nature, Community, and Transformation." *Journal of Interdisciplinary Studies in Literature and the Environment* 7 (2000): 199-211.

——. "Provinces of Ethics." *Interpretation* 17 (1989-1990): 255-73.

——, ed. *The Elementary Forms of Religious Life*. Oxford: Oxford University Press, 2001.

Cobban, Alfred. *The Crisis of Civilization*. London: Cape, 1941.

279

Cohen, Jean L. "Rethinking Privacy: Autonomy, Identity, and the Abortion Controversy." In *Public and Private in Thought and Practice*, edited Jeff Weintraub and Krishan Kumar. Chicago: University of Chicago Press, 1997.

Constant, Benjamin. *Political Writings*. Edited by B. Fontana. Cambridge: Cambridge University Press, 1988.

Cranston, Maurice. *Jean-Jacques: The Early Life and Work*. London: Norton, 1982.

———. "Jean-Jacques Rousseau and the Fusion of Democratic Sovereignty with Aristocratic Government." *History of European Ideas* 11 (1989): 417-25.

———. *The Noble Savage*. Chicago: University of Chicago Press, 1991.

Derathé, Robert. *Le rationalisme de J.-J. Rousseau*. Paris: Presses Universitaires de France, 1948.

Dupuy, Jean-Pierre. "A Reconsideration of Das Adam Smith Problem." *Stanford French Review* 17 (1993): 45-57.

Durkheim, Emile. *The Division of Labor in Society*. Translated by W. D. Halls. New York: Free Press, 1979.

———. *The Elementary Forms of Religious Life*. Edited by Mark S. Cladis. Oxford: Oxford University Press, 2001.

———. *Montesquieu and Rousseau: Forerunners of Sociology*. Translated by Ralph Manheim. Ann Arbor: University of Michigan Press, 1960.

Eisenstein, Zillah. *The Radical Future of Liberal Feminism*. New York: Longman, 1981.

Elshtain, Jean Bethke. "The Displacement of Politics." In *Public and Private Thought and Practice*, edited by Jeff Weintraub and Krishan Kumar. Chicago: University of Chicago Press, 1997.

———. *Public Man, Private Woman*. Princeton, N.J.: Princeton University Press, 1981.

Emerson, Ralph Waldo. *Nature and Other Writings*. Edited by Peter Turner. Boston: Shambhala, 1994.

Foucault, Michel. "Structuralism and Post-Structuralism: An Interview with Michel Foucault." By G. Raulet. *Telos* 55 (1983): 202-12.

Frost, Robert. "Directive." In *Steeple Bush*. New York: Holt, 1947.

Gauthier, David. "The Politics of Redemption." *University of Ottawa Quarterly* 49 (1979): 329-56.

Gouhier, Henri, ed. *Lettres philosophiques*. Paris: Vrin, 1974.

Grimsley, Ronald. *The Philosophy of Rousseau*. Oxford: Oxford University Press, 1973.

———. *Rousseau's Religious Thought*. Oxford: Oxford University Press, 1970.

Grotius, Hugo. *On the Law of War and Peace*. Translated by Francis Kelsey. Oxford: Oxford University Press, 1925.

Gutmann, Amy. *Democratic Education*. Princeton, N.J.: Princeton University Press, 1987.

Hallowell, John. *Main Currents in Modern Political Thought*. New York: Holt, 1950.

Hansen, Karen V. "Rediscovering the Social: Visiting Practices in Antebellum New England and the Limits of the Public/Private Dichotomy." In *Public and Private Thought and Practice*, edited by Jeff Weintraub and Krishan Kumar. Chicago: University of Chicago Press, 1997.

Harsanyi, John. "Rational Choice Models of Behavior versus Functionalist and Conformist Theories." *World Politics* 22 (1969): 513-38.

Hobbes, Thomas. *Leviathan*. New York: Penguin, 1984.

Hopkins, Gerard Manley. "God's Grandeur." In *The Norton Anthology of Poetry*, edited by Alexander Allison et al. New York: Norton, 1975.

Hume, David. *Dialogues on Natural Religion*, edited by Richard H. Popkin. Indianapolis, Ind.: Hacket, 1985.

James, William. *Varieties of Religious Experience*. New York: Penguin, 1985.

Keohane, Nannerl. *Philosophy and the State in France*. Princeton, N.J.: Princeton University Press, 1980.

Koontz, Theodore J. "Religion and Political Cohesion: John Locke and Jean Jacques Rousseau." *Journal of Church and State* 23 (1981): 95–115.

Kumar, Krishan. "Home: The Promise and Predicament of Private Life at the End of the Twentieth Century." In *Public and Private in Thought and Practice*, edited by Jeff Weintraub and Krishan Kumar. Chicago: University of Chicago Press, 1997.

Landes, Joan. *Women and the Public Sphere in the Age of the French Revolution*. Ithaca, N.Y.: Cornell University Press, 1988.

Lévi-Strauss, Claude. *Structural Anthropology*. Vol. 2. Translated by Monique Layton. Chicago: University of Chicago Press, 1976.

Linder, Robert D. "Civil Religion in Historical Perspective: The Reality That Underlies the Concept." *Journal of Church and State* 17 (1975): 399–421.

Lovejoy, Arthur. *The Great Chain of Being*. Cambridge, Mass.: Harvard University Press, 1936.

MacAdam, Jim. "Rousseau's Criticism of Hobbesian Egoism." *University of Ottawa Quarterly*, 49 (1979): 377–89.

Malebranche, Nicolas de. *Méditations chrétiennes et métaphysiques* and *Traité de morale*. In *Oeuvres complètes de Malebranche*, edited by Michel Adam. Paris: Vrin, 1966.

Mason, John Hope. "Individuals in Society: Rousseau's Republican Vision." *History of Political Thought* 10 (1989): 88–112.

Michalson, Gordon. *Fallen Freedom: Kant on Radical Evil and Moral Regeneration*. Cambridge: Cambridge University Press, 1990.

Miller, James. *Rousseau: Dreamer of Democracy*. New Haven, Conn.: Yale University Press, 1984.

Milton, John. *Paradise Lost*. In *John Milton: Complete Poems and Major Prose*, edited by Merritt Y. Hughes. Indianapolis, Ind.: Bobbs-Merrill, 1957.

Montaigne, Michel Eyquem de. *The Complete Essays of Montaigne*. Translated by Donald Frame. Stanford, Calif.: Stanford University Press, 1958.

Montesquieu, Baron de. *Esprit des lois*. In *Oeuvres complètes*, edited by Roger Caillois. Paris: Pléiade, 1951.

Morel, Jean. "Récherches sur les sources du *Discours de l'inégalité*." *Annales de la société Jean-Jacques Rousseau* 5 (1909): 143–98.

Nicole, Pierre. "De la grandeur." In *Œuvres philosophiques et morales*, edited by Charles Jourdain. Paris: Hachette, 1845.

Niebuhr, Reinhold. *Moral Man and Immoral Society*. New York: Scribner's, 1960.

Pascal, Blaise. *Pensées*. Edited by Léon Brunschvicg. Paris: Le Livre de Poche, 1976.

Pateman, Carole. *The Disorder of Women: Democracy, Feminism and Political Theory*. Stanford, Calif.: Stanford University Press, 1994.

Payne, Harry. "Deciphering the Stones of Môtiers." *Eighteenth Century Life* 11 (1987): 61–77.

Philonenko, Alex. *Jean-Jacques Rousseau et la pensée du malheur*. Paris: Vrin, 1984.

Piro, Melford. *Culture and Human Nature*. Chicago: University of Chicago Press, 1989.

Plato. *Phaedrus*. Translated by W. C. Helmbold and W. G. Rabinowitz. Indianapolis, Ind.: Bobbs-Merrill, 1977.

Pope, Alexander. *An Essay on Man*. In *The Poetry of Pope*, edited by M. H. Abrams. Arlington Heights, Ill.: AMH, 1954.

Pope, Barbara Corrado. "The Influence of Rousseau's Ideology of Domesticity." In *Connecting Spheres: Women in the Western World*, edited by Marilyn J. Boxer and Jean H. Quataert. Oxford: Oxford University Press, 1987.

Pufendorf, Samuel. *On the Duty of Man and Citizen*, translated by Frank Moore. Oxford: Oxford University Press, 1927.

Putnam, Robert. *Bowling Alone: The Collapse and Revival of American Community*. New York: Simon and Schuster, 2000.

Rabelais, François. *Oeuvres complètes*, edited by Jacques Boulenger and Lucien Scheler. Paris: Gallimard, 1962.

Raz, Joseph. *The Morality of Freedom*. Oxford: Oxford University Press, 1986.

Richards, David A. J. "Rights and Autonomy." *Ethics* 92 (1981): 3–20.

Riley, Patrick. *The General Will before Rousseau*. Princeton, N.J.: Princeton University Press, 1986.

Roof, Wade Clark. *Spiritual Market Place: Baby Boomers and the Remaking of American Religion*. Princeton, N.J.: Princeton University Press, 1999.

Rorty, Richard. *Contingency, Irony, and Solidarity*. Cambridge: Cambridge University Press, 1989.

——. *Philosophy and the Mirror of Nature*. Princeton, N.J.: Princeton University Press, 1979.

Rousseau, Jean-Jacques. *Confessions*. Translated by J. M. Cohen. New York: Penguin, 1953.

——. *Correspondance complète de Jean-Jacques Rousseau*. Edited by Ralph A. Leigh. 51 vols. Geneva: Institut et Musée Voltaire, 1965–1995.

——. *Correspondance générale de J. J. Rousseau*. Edited by Théophile Dufour and Pierre-Paul Plan. Paris: Armand Colin, 1924.

——. *Emile*. Translated by Allan Bloom. New York: Basic, 1979.

——. *Essai sur l'origine des langues*. Edited by Charles Porset. Bordeaux: Ducros, 1970.

——. *The Government of Poland*. Translated and with an introduction by Willmoore Kendall. Indianapolis, Ind.: Hackett, 1985.

——. *Julie; or, The New Eloise*. Translated and abridged by Judith H. McDowell. University Park: Pennsylvania State University Press, 1968.

——. *Lettre à M. d'Alembert*. Edited by Michel Launay. Paris: Garnier-Frammarion, 1967.

——. *Œuvres complètes*. Edited by Bernard Gagnebin and Marcel Raymond. Vols. 1–4. Paris: Pléiade. 1959–1969.

——. *Politics and the Arts: Letter to M. d'Alembert*. Translated by Allan Bloom. Ithaca, N.Y.: Cornell University Press, 1989.

——. *Reveries of the Solitary Walker*. Translated by Peter France. London: Penguin, 1979.

——. *The Social Contract and Discourses*. Translation by G. D. H. Cole, revised by J. H. Brumfitt and John C. Hall. London: Dent, 1988.

Scubla, Lucien. "Est-il possible de mettre la loi au-dessus de l'homme?" In *Introduction aux science sociales: Logique des phénomènes collectifs*, by Jean-Pierre Dupuy. Paris: Ellipses, 1992.

Sedgwick, Alexander. *Jansenism in Seventeenth-Century France*. Charlottesville: University of Virginia Press, 1977.

Sen, Amartya. "Individual Freedom as a Social Commitment." *New York Review of Books*, 14 June 1990, 49.

Shklar, Judith. *Men and Citizens*. Cambridge: Cambridge University Press, 1987.

——. *Ordinary Vices*. Cambridge, Mass.: Harvard University Press, 1984.

Silver, Alan. "'Two Different Sorts of Commerce'—Friendship and Strangership in Civil Society." In *Public and Private in Thought and Practice*, edited Jeff Weintraub and Krishan Kumar. Chicago: University of Chicago Press, 1997.

Starobinski, Jean. *Jean-Jacques Rousseau: Transparency and Obstruction*. Translated by Arthur Goldhammer. Chicago: University of Chicago Press, 1988.

Talmon, J. L. *The Origins of Totalitarian Democracy*. Boulder, Colo.: Westview, 1985.

Thomas, Paul. "Jean-Jacques Rousseau, Sexist?" *Feminist Studies* 17 (1991): 195–217.

Thoreau, Henry. *Walden*. Roslyn, N.Y.: Black, 1942.

Todorov, Tzvetan. *Frêle bonheur: Essai sur Rousseau*. Paris: Hachette, 1985.

Tönnies, Ferdinand. *Community and Society*. Translated by Charles Loomis. New York: Harper, 1963.

Trible, Phyllis. "Eve and Adam: Genesis 2–3 Reread." In *Womenspirit Rising*, edited by Carol Christ and Judith Plaskow. New York: Harper and Row, 1979.

Trouille, Mary Seidman. *Sexual Politics in the Enlightenment: Women Writers Read Rousseau.* Albany: State University of New York Press, 1997.

Viner, Jacob. *The Role of Providence in the Social Order.* Princeton, N.J.: Princeton University Press, 1972.

Viroli, Maurizio. *For Love of Country: An Essay on Patriotism and Nationalism.* Princeton, N.J.: Princeton University Press, 1995.

Voltaire, François Marie Arouet de. *Candide.* In *The Norton Anthology of World Masterpieces,* translated by Robert M. Adams. New York: Norton, 1979.

———. *Œuvres complètes de Voltaire.* Edited by Theodore Besterman. Oxford: Voltaire Foundation, 1980.

———. "Poème sur le désastre de Lisbonne, ou examen de cet axiome, Tout est bien." In *Œuvres complètes de Voltaire.* Paris: Delangle Frères, 1828.

———. "Sur les *Pensées* de M. *Pascal*," in *Lettres Philosophiques.* Edited by F. A. Taylor. Oxford: Blackwell, 1958.

Walzer, Michael. *Exodus and Revolution.* New York: Basic, 1985.

Weintraub, Jeff. "Theory and Politics of the Public/Private Distinction." In *Public and Private in Thought and Practice,* edited Jeff Weintraub and Krishan Kumar. Chicago: University of Chicago Press, 1997.

Wittgenstein, Ludwig. *Philosophical Investigations.* Translated by G. E. M. Anscombe. New York: Macmillan, 1953.

Wokler, Robert, ed. *Rousseau and Liberty.* Manchester: Manchester University Press, 1995.

Wuthnow, Robert. *Loose Connections: Joining Together in America's Fragmented Communities.* Cambridge, Mass.: Harvard University Press, 1998.

Index